Bears' Guide to Earning Degrees Nontraditionally

I3TH EDITION

John Bear, Ph.D.
Mariah Bear, M.A.

Published by

DEGREE.NET BOOKS

Financial Times Management, Inc.
6921 Stockton Avenue
El Cerrito, CA 94530
(510) 528-3984

Library of Congress Catalog Number: 98-071045 • ISBN 0-9629312-4-1

Also by John Bear and Mariah Bear:
Finding Money for College (Ten Speed Press, 1998)
College Degrees by Mail and Modem (Ten Speed Press, 1998)

Some Other Books by John Bear:
(Ten Speed Press books can be purchased at most bookstores, or by calling 1-800-841-BOOK)
Send This Jerk the Bedbug Letter: How to Be a More Effective Complainer (Ten Speed Press, 1996)
The #1 New York Times Bestseller (Ten Speed Press, 1993)
Computer Wimp No More: The Intelligent Beginner's Guide to Computers (Ten Speed Press, 1992)
Morning Food: Breakfast Cooking at the Cafe Beaujolais (with Margaret Fox, Ten Speed Press, 1989)
How to Repair Food (with Marina Bear, Ten Speed Press, 1988)
Cafe Beaujolais Cookbook (with Margaret Fox, Ten Speed Press, 1984)
Computer Wimp: 166 Things I Wish I Had Known Before I Bought My First Computer (Ten Speed Press, 1983)
The Alternative Guide to Higher Education (Grosset & Dunlap, 1980)
Communication (Time-Life Books, 1976)
The United States of America: The Land and Its People (Time-Life Books, 1974)

Library of Congress Cataloging-in-Publication Data
(prepared by Quality Books, Inc.)

Bear, John, 1938–
     Bears' guide to earning degrees nontraditionally / John Bear, Mariah Bear. — 13th ed.
        p.   cm.
     Includes bibliographical references and indexes.
     Preassigned LCCN: 98-71045
     ISBN: 0-9629312-4-1
     1. Universities and colleges—United States—Directories. 2. Non-formal education—United States—Directories.
3. Correspondence schools and courses—United States—Directories. 4. Degrees, Academic—United States—
Directories. I. Bear, Mariah P. II. Title. III. Title: Guide to earning degrees nontraditionally

L901.B37 1998   378'.0025'73
                           QB198-553

Disclaimer
While the authors believe that the information in this book is correct as of the time of publication,
it is possible we may have made errors, which we will correct at the first available opportunity.
Neither we, the publisher, nor the distributor can be responsible for any problems that may
arise in readers' interactions with any schools described in the book.

Printed in the United States of America

10 9 8 7 6 5 4 3 2 1

CONTENTS

DEDICATIONS

Mariah's

To Joe,
the best darn husband commercially available.

John's

To Marina,
for the thirteenth consecutive time, with undiminished love,
thanks, and gratitude for all you have done.

ACKNOWLEDGMENTS

We do not have a staff. We do not have platoons of graduate students whom we can send to the library to do research for us. Like Blanche Dubois, we are dependent upon the kindness of strangers: those many hundreds of readers who regularly write, fax, and e-mail to tell us of errors, changes, new schools and new programs in old schools. There are far too many such kind people for us to list individually. We are especially grateful for the assistance, over the years, of Lal Balkaran in Canada, Jim Delmont in Nebraska, Allen Ezell in Florida, Lyndon Jones in England, Peter Proehl in California, Reg Sheldrick in Louisiana, William Sloane in Pennsylvania, Werner Stiewe in Germany, Josh Walston in Washington, and Sean Akbarian out west. Marina Bear and Gretchen Guidotti helped with the research. Thank you both.

For this 13th edition, we would like to thank Marc Polonsky for proofreading, Jeff Brandenburg for patiently correcting our design faux pas, Cale Burr for another glorious cover, and Leslie Bolick, Charlie Hall, and Clinton Marsh for support and levity in equal doses.

A MESSAGE ABOUT ADVERTISEMENTS

Regular readers will note that for the first time in 24 years, there are paid advertisements in this book. A brief explanation is in order. This 13th edition inaugurates our Degree.net book publishing business in which we have invited **accredited** schools to advertise their distance learning programs. Unlike some education guides that do not clearly distinguish paid advertisements from editorial copy, we have taken care to identify these paid advertisements and have separated the advertising and editorial sections.

As always, we welcome any comments or questions that will help us keep this the best guide to distance learning available.

The Publishers

ABOUT THE AUTHORS:
THEIR LIVES, THEIR BIASES, AND A REQUEST FOR HELP

This book was once called Bear's Guide. A few years ago, the apostrophe moved one notch to the right. No longer *Bear's Guide*, it is now *Bears' Guide*, signifying more than one Bear involved. Here is some of the background of the two Bears who produced this 13th edition.

John Bear attended school at a time when nontraditional education was virtually nonexistent in the United States. Still, he *was* able to create his own alternative program within the traditional framework. He started working full-time during his junior year at Reed College, and continued to hold a variety of demanding off-campus jobs while earning his Master's at Berkeley and Ph.D. from Michigan State University. He was generally able to integrate these jobs—which included working as a newspaper reporter, prison psychologist, advertising writer, and researcher at a school for the deaf—into his academic studies, but received little support or encouragement from faculty or administration.

Dr. Bear has taught at major universities (Iowa, Berkeley, Michigan State) and small schools (City College of San Francisco, College of the Redwoods), been a business executive (research director for Bell & Howell's educational division, director of communications for the Midas Muffler Shop chain), director of the Center for the Gifted Child in San Francisco, and consultant to a wide range of organizations, including General Motors, Xerox, *Encyclopaedia Britannica*, and the Grateful Dead. Since 1974, he has devoted much of his time to investigating and writing about nontraditional higher education.

In 1977, he established Degree Consulting Services, to offer detailed consulting to people seeking more personal advice than a book can provide. While he no longer counsels individual clients, the service is still available (see Appendix C for further information).

John's daughter Mariah can honestly claim a lifelong involvement with nontraditional education, beginning around the age of seven when she earned allowance money working in her father's office. She took six years to get her Bachelor's degree at Berkeley (Phi Beta Kappa), scheduling classes around a flex-time job with a major book publisher. (Well-intentioned admissions counselors discourage this sort of thing; they often seem to feel a challenging job is incompatible with academic success.) In graduate school, Mariah managed to schedule all but one of her required classes in the evenings, allowing her to freelance at *New York* magazine, the *Village Voice*, and other publications while earning a Master's in journalism from New York University.

She is now executive editor at a large publishing house, and has an increasingly large role in *Bears' Guide*.

The rest of the family pursued similarly nontraditional paths to higher education. Twenty years after completing her traditional B.A., Marina (wife of John, mother of Mariah) earned the nonresident M.A. in humanities at California State University, Dominguez Hills, followed by a Ph.D. at Vanderbilt University. The other two children, twin daughters, both left high school at age 15, midway through 10th grade, and passed the state high school equivalency exam. Susannah went on to college at that early age; Tanya worked for three years, then entered college at the "traditional" age of 18.

BIASES

As you read this book, you will note that it is biased. The authors have strong opinions about which schools and programs are good and which are not, and do not hesitate to say so. John has been sued three times for millions of dollars by people who operate what he called (and continues to call) illegal diploma mills. None has ever won a cent. While the research and experiences are largely John's, the opinions are shared by both authors.

Over the years, John has done consulting or advisory work for various schools in return for money, goods (generally the use of their mailing lists to help sell this book), and, in two cases, stock:

♦ In return for consulting work in the mid 1970s, Columbia Pacific University paid him with a small amount of its stock, which he sold more than fifteen years ago.

♦ Bear was one of four founders of Fairfax University, a not-for-profit nontraditional school. Once it was launched, he resigned, and had no further connection whatsoever.

♦ In 1987, eager to experience nontraditional education from the other side of the desk, as it were, he accepted the presidency of the International Institute for Advanced Studies, a small, older (in this field, being founded in 1972 makes one a true pioneer) nonprofit school. That school evolved into Greenwich University, where he served as full-time president in Hawaii for 18 months.

♦ In late 1991, John's company, IBE, Inc., was appointed the U.S. agents for the Heriot-Watt University Distance Learning M.B.A. Heriot-Watt is a large

Scottish university that was founded in 1821. They have opened an office in California for North Americans interested in this splendid program, the world's only accredited home-study MBA that does not require a Bachelor's degree. You will find it described on page 109. Several years later, IBE also took on a distributorship for the MS in Training and HRM by distance learning of Leicester University, England. And in March 1998, the assets of IBE were acquired by a subsidiary of Pearson plc, at the time the world's second largest publisher, for whom Mariah and John now work.

We are confident that these activities have had, and will continue to have, no bearing on the opinions expressed in this book. Hundreds of excellent schools have never even taken us to lunch, yet we recommend them highly. (We will probably accept if they ever do offer lunch.) On the other side of the ledger, there is no way in the world we can be persuaded to say good things about bad, or questionable, schools. While individual evaluations may change (schools do get better or worse, new information comes to light), the basic judgment criteria are not subject to outside influence. And contrary to what some operators of sleazy schools have claimed, no one has ever paid a cent to be listed in this book.

HELP

Over the years, readers have provided great amounts of immensely valuable feedback. If you are aware of schools or programs we have overlooked, please let us know. If your experience with a school is at odds with what we've written, please don't hesitate to tell us about it. This book may be biased, but the authors like to think they are open-minded, and many schools' evaluations have changed (both up and down) in the past 20 years.

Please communicate in writing, and if you'd like a reply (we can't guarantee it, but we'll do our best), please enclose a stamped self-addressed envelope or, outside the U.S., two international reply coupons, available at your post office. You can reach us at this address:

John and Mariah Bear
P. O. Box 7070
Berkeley, CA 94707 USA
Fax: (510) 528-3555
E-mail: john.bear@degree.net
          mariah.bear@degree.net

Thank you.

1

What Nontraditional Education Is All About

In times of great change, learners inherit the earth, while the learned find themselves beautifully equipped for a world that no longer exists.

MICHAEL PORTER

The man on the telephone was so distraught, he was almost in tears. For more than 20 years, he had been in charge of sawing off dead tree branches for a large midwestern city. But a new personnel policy in that city decreed that henceforth, all department heads would have to have Bachelor's degrees. If this man could not earn a degree within two years, he would no longer be permitted to continue in the job he had been performing satisfactorily for over two decades.

It is an unfortunate but very real aspect of life today that a college or university degree is often more important (or at least more useful) than a good education or substantial knowledge in your field, whether that field involves nuclear physics or sawing off branches. It doesn't matter if you've been reading, studying, and learning all your life. It doesn't matter how good you are at what you do. In many situations, if you don't have a piece of (usually imitation) parchment that certifies you as a Bachelor, Master, or Doctor, you are perceived as somehow less worthy, and are often denied the better jobs and higher salaries that go to degree-holders.

In fact, as more and more degree-holders, from space scientists to philosophers, are unable to find employment in their specific chosen fields and move elsewhere in the job market, degrees become more important than ever. Consider a job opening for a high-school English teacher. Five applicants with comparable skills apply, but one has a Doctorate while the other four have Bachelor's degrees. Who do you think would probably get the job?

Never mind that you don't need a Ph.D. to teach high-school English any more than you need a B.A. to chop down trees. The simple fact is that degrees are extremely valuable commodities in the job market.

Happily, as the need for degrees increases, availability has kept pace. Since the mid 1970s, there has been a virtual explosion in what is now commonly called "alternative" or "nontraditional" and "external" or "off-campus" education—ways and means of getting an education or a degree (or both, if you wish) without sitting in classrooms day after day, year after year.

The rallying cry was, in fact, sounded in 1973 by Ewald B. Nyquist, then president of the wonderfully innovative University of the State of New York (now called Regents College). He said:

> There are thousands of people . . . who contribute in important ways to the life of the communities in which they live, even though they do not have a college degree. Through native intelligence, hard work and sacrifice, many have gained in knowledge and understanding. And yet, the social and economic advancement of these people has been thwarted in part by the emphasis that is put on the possession of credentials . . . As long as we remain a strongly credentialed society . . . employers will not be disposed to hire people on the basis of what they know, rather than on what degrees and diplomas they hold. If attendance at a college is the only road to these credentials, those who cannot or have not availed themselves of this route but have acquired knowledge and skills through other sources will be denied the recognition and advancement to which they are entitled. Such inequity should not be tolerated.

Nontraditional education takes many forms, including the following:

♦ credit (and degrees) for life-experience learning, even if the learning took place before you entered school;

♦ credit (and degrees) for passing examinations;

♦ credit (and degrees) for independent study, even when not enrolled in a school at the time it was done;

♦ credit (and degrees) through intensive study (for instance, 10 hours a day for a month instead of one hour a day for a year);

- credit (and degrees) through guided private study at your own pace, from your own home or office, under the supervision of a faculty member with whom you communicate on a regular basis;

- credit (and degrees) for work done on your home or office computer, linked to your school's computer, wherever in the world it may be;

- credit (and degrees) from weekend schools, evening schools, and summer-only schools;

- credit (and degrees) entirely by correspondence;

- credit (and degrees) through the use of audio- and videotaped courses reviewed at your convenience.

This book endeavors to cover all these areas, and more, as completely as possible. Yet this is truly an impossible task. New programs are introduced literally every day. In recent years, an average of one new college or university has opened for business every week, while old, established universities are disappearing at the rate of two or three per month.

So, although this book is as current and correct as we can possibly make it, some recent changes probably won't be covered, and, inevitably, there will be errors and omissions. For all of these, we apologize now, and invite your suggestions and criticisms for the next edition. Thank you. Perhaps the best way to make clear, in a short space, the differences between the traditional (dare one say old-fashioned) approaches to education and degrees and the nontraditional (or modern) approach is to offer the following dozen comparisons:

Traditional education awards degrees on the basis of time served and credit earned.
Nontraditional education awards degrees on the basis of competencies and performance skills.

Traditional education bases degree requirements on a medieval formula that calls for some generalized education and some specialized education.
Nontraditional education bases degree requirements on an agreement between the student and the faculty, aimed at helping the student achieve his or her career, personal, or professional goals.

Traditional education awards the degree when the student has taken the required number of credits in the required order.
Nontraditional education awards the degree when the student's actual work and learning reach certain previously agreed-upon levels.

Traditional education considers the years from age 18 to age 22 the appropriate time to earn a first degree.
Nontraditional education assumes learning is desirable at any age, and that degrees should be available to people of all ages.

Traditional education considers the classroom to be the primary source of information and the campus the center of learning.
Nontraditional education believes that some sort of learning can and does occur in any part of the world.

Traditional education believes that printed texts should be the principal learning resource.
Nontraditional education believes the range of learning resources is limitless, from the daily newspaper to personal interviews; from videotapes to computers to world travel.

Traditional faculty must have appropriate credentials and degrees.
Nontraditional faculty are selected for competency and personal qualities in *addition* to credentials and degrees.

Traditional credits and degrees are based primarily on mastery of course content.
Nontraditional credits and degrees add a consideration of learning *how to learn*, and the integration of diverse fields of knowledge.

Traditional education cultivates dependence on authority through prescribed curricula, required campus residence, and required classes.
Nontraditional education cultivates self-direction and independence through planned independent study, both on and off campus.

Traditional curricula are generally oriented toward traditional disciplines and well-established professions.
Nontraditional curricula reflect a range of individual students' needs and goals, and are likely to be problem-oriented, issue-oriented, and world-oriented.

Traditional education aims at producing "finished products"—students who are done with their education and ready for the job market.
Nontraditional education aims at producing lifelong learners, capable of responding to their own evolving needs and those of society over an entire lifetime.

Traditional education, to adapt the old saying, gives you a fish and feeds you for a day.
Nontraditional education teaches you how to fish, and feeds you for life.

Traditional education had nothing to offer the dead-tree-limb expert.
Nontraditional education made it possible for him to complete a good Bachelor's degree in less than a year, entirely by correspondence and at a modest cost. His job is now secure.

2

What Are Colleges and Universities, and How Do They Work?

A college is a machine that transfers information from the notes of the professor to the notes of the student without it passing through the mind of either.

TRADITIONAL

The question posed by this chapter's title may sound trivial or inconsequential, but it turns out to be quite a complex issue; one for which there is no simple answer at all.

Many state legislatures have struggled with the problem of producing precise definitions of words like *college* and *university*. (One school even tried to sue its state's department of education to force them to define "educational process." The state managed to evade the suit.)

Some states have simply given up the problem as unsolvable, which is why they either have virtually no laws governing higher education, or laws that are incredibly restrictive. Needless to say, the former policy encourages the proliferation of degree mills and other bad schools, and the latter policy discourages the establishment of any creative new nontraditional schools or programs.

Other states have, from time to time, produced rather ingenious definitions, such as Ohio's (later repealed), stating that a "university" was anything that (a) said it was a university, and (b) had an endowment or facilities worth $1 million. The assumption, of course, was that no degree mill could be so well endowed. California once had a similar law under which the sum was only $50,000. In the 1980s, much tougher requirements were instituted and California soon lost its title as the state with the most unaccredited schools, first to Louisiana, and then to Hawaii.

Many people remember a famous CBS *60 Minutes* episode in 1978 (rerun many times since), in which the proprietor of a flagrant diploma mill was actually arrested while being interviewed by Mike Wallace. At the time, his school, California Pacifica University, was licensed by the state of California. The owner had bought some used books and office furniture, declared this property to be worth $50,000, and consequently received state authorization to grant degrees, up to and including Doctorates.

History repeated itself in 1990 when the proprietor of yet another degree mill, North American University, was enjoined from operating by the state of Utah on the very day that *Inside Edition*'s television crew arrived to film his nefarious operation.

The problem of definition is made even more complicated by the inconsistent way in which the words "college" and "university" are used.

In the United States, the two words are used almost interchangeably. Before long, they will probably mean exactly the same thing. Historically, a college has been a subdivision of a university. For instance, the University of California is divided into a College of Arts and Sciences, a College of Education, a College of Law, and so on. The University of Oxford is comprised of Balliol College, Exeter College, Magdalen College, and about three dozen others.

Today, however, many degree-granting colleges exist independent of any university, and many universities have no colleges. There is also an ever-growing trend for colleges to rename themselves as universities, either to reflect their growth or enhance their image, or both. In recent years, dozens of colleges, from Antioch in Ohio to San Francisco State in California, have turned themselves into universities. While many British traditionalists sneered at the U.S. for doing this, the same thing happened in the United Kingdom in the early and mid 1990s: dozens of technical schools, colleges, and institutes overnight became universities, at least in name.

The situation outside the United States makes all this even more complex. In most countries, the word "college" rarely refers to a degree-granting institution, and often is used for what Americans call a high school. American personnel managers and admissions officers have been fooled by this fact. An Englishman, for instance, who states on his job application, "Graduate of Eton College," means, simply, that he has completed the high school of that name.

3

Many readers have told us that they simply will not go to a "college," no matter how good it may be, because the word just doesn't sound *real* enough to them.

Finally, some degree-granting institutions choose a name other than "college" or "university." The most common are "school" (e.g., the New School for Social Research; California School of Professional Psychology, etc.) and "institute" (e.g., Fielding Institute, Union Institute, etc.).

HOW COLLEGES AND UNIVERSITIES WORK

The Calendar

In some countries, "calendar" refers to the school's catalogue or prospectus; in others, it refers to the scheduling of classes (which is the meaning we use here). There is no uniform pattern in calendars from one school to the next. However, most schools tend to follow one of four basic patterns:

1. **The semester plan.** A semester is 16 to 18 weeks long and there are usually two semesters per year, plus a shorter summer session. Many classes are one semester long, but some extend over two or more semesters (e.g., Algebra I in the fall semester and Algebra II in the spring).

   A class that meets three hours a week for one semester is likely to be worth three semester hours of credit. The *actual* amount of credit could be anywhere from two to six semester hours for such a class, depending on the amount of homework, additional reading, laboratory time, etc.

2. **The quarter plan.** Many universities divide the year into four quarters of equal length, usually 11 or 12 weeks each. Many courses require two or more quarters to complete. A course that meets three hours a week for a quarter will probably be worth three quarter hours, or quarter units, but can range from two to six. One semester unit is equal to one-and-a-half quarter units.

3. **The trimester plan.** A much smaller number of schools divide the year into three equal trimesters of 15 or 16 weeks each. A trimester unit is usually equal to one-and-a-quarter semester units.

4. **Weekend colleges.** This innovative and increasingly common system allows schools to make more efficient use of their facilities, and working students to earn a conventional degree. All courses are taught intensively on Friday nights, Saturdays, and/or Sundays. Hundreds of traditional residential schools in the U.S. offer some weekend programs, many of which are described in chapters 18 and 21. For additional programs in your area, check with nearby community colleges, colleges, and universities.

Other alternatives: National University, the University of Phoenix, and other relatively new schools have popularized a system in which students take one course per month, and can begin their degree program on the first day of any month. The school offers one or more complete, intensive course each month.

Many nonresident programs have no calendar at all. Students can begin their independent-study program as soon as they have been admitted.

How Credit Is Earned

In a traditional school, most credit is earned by taking classes. Nontraditional units may be earned in other ways. There are four common methods:

1. **Life experience learning.** Credit is given for what you have learned, regardless of how or where it was learned. For example, a given university might offer six courses in German worth four semester units each. If you can show them that you speak and write German just as well as someone who has taken and passed those six courses, they will award you 24 semester units of German, whether you learned the language from your grandmother, from living in Germany, or from Berlitz tapes. The same philosophy applies to business experience, learning to fly an airplane, military training, and dozens of other nonclassroom learning experiences.

2. **Equivalency examinations.** Many schools say that anyone who can pass an examination in a subject should get credit for knowing that subject, without having to sit in a classroom month after month to "learn" what they already know. More than 100 standard equivalency exams are offered, worth anywhere from two to 30 semester units each. In general, each hour of examination is worth from two to six semester units, but different schools may award significantly different amounts of credit for the same examinations. Some schools will design written or oral examinations in fields in which there are no standard exams.

3. **Correspondence courses.** Several hundred universities offer thousands of home-study courses, most of which can be taken by people living anywhere in the world. These courses are generally worth two to six semester units each and can take anywhere from a month or two to a year or more to complete.

4. **Learning contracts.** Quite a few schools negotiate learning contracts with their students. A learning contract is a formal, negotiated agreement between the student and the school, stating that if the student successfully completes certain tasks (for instance, reads these books, writes a paper of this length, does the

following laboratory experiments, etc.), the school will award an agreed-upon number of credits.

Learning contracts can be written for a few units, an entire degree program, or anything in between. Often the school will provide a faculty member to guide the course of study.

All four of these alternative ways to earn credit will be discussed in some detail in later chapters.

Grading and Evaluation Systems

Most schools, traditional and nontraditional, use one of four common grading systems. Grades are generally given for each separate course taken. Some schools assign grades to equivalency examinations, learning-contract work, and correspondence courses as well. Life-experience credit is rarely graded; schools usually assign it a certain number of units without further evaluation. The four common systems are:

1. **Letter grades.** An "A" is the highest grade, "B" means "good," "C" means "average," "D" stands for "barely passing" (or, in some cases, "failing"), and "F" is a failing grade. ("E" is rarely used.) Some schools add pluses and minuses—a B+ is better than a B, but not quite as good as an A-. Some schools use "AB" instead of B+ or A-. And some give an "A+" for superior work.

2. **Number grades.** Many schools grade on a scale of 0 (worst grade) to 4 (highest grade). The best students receive grades of 3.9 or 4.0; other outstanding students might get a 3.7 or 3.8. To pass, students usually must score at least 1.0 (or a 1.5). Just to make it even more confusing, some schools use a 0 to 3 or 0 to 5 scale, but 4 is the most common top grade. A small number of schools give the numerical equivalent of A+, a 4.5, which means that even on a four-point scale, it is possible to have a grade point average higher than four.

3. **Percentage grades.** A smaller number of schools follow the European system of grading each student in each class on a percentage score, from 0 to 100 percent. In most (but not all) schools, a grade of 90 to 100 percent is considered excellent, 80 to 90 is good, 70 to 80 is fair, 60 to 70 is either failure or barely passing, and below 60 percent is failing.

4. **Pass/fail.** Quite a few universities offer a pass/fail option, either for some classes or, more rarely, for all classes. In such a system, the teacher does not evaluate the student's performance beyond stating whether each student has passed or failed the course. At many schools students may choose the pass/fail option for one or two out of the four or five courses they are expected to take each semester or quarter. In some pass/fail situations, a numerical or letter grade is actually given, but not revealed to the student or used to calculate grade point average. And in a few schools, the actual grade will be revealed only if the student asks and, sometimes, pays an additional fee.

Grade Point Average

Most schools report a student's overall performance in terms of the G.P.A., or grade point average. This is the average of all grades received, weighted by the number of semester or quarter units each course is worth.

For example, if a student gets a 4.0 (or an A) in a course worth 3 semester units, and a 3.0 (or a B) in a course worth 2 semester units, his or her G.P.A. would be calculated like this: $3 \times 4.0 = 12$. And $2 \times 3.0 = 6$. So, $12 + 6 = 18$, divided by a total of 5 semester units, results in a G.P.A. of 3.6.

Pass/fail courses are generally not taken into account when calculating a grade point average.

One's G.P.A. can be very important. Often it is necessary to maintain a certain average in order to earn a degree—typically a 2.0 (in a four-point system) for a Bachelor's degree, and a 3.0 for a Master's degree or Doctorate. Honors degrees (*magna cum laude*, etc.), scholarships, and even permission to play on the football team are dependent on the G.P.A. (No, nonresident schools do not have football teams. Some of us are waiting for a chess-by-mail or computer-game league to spring up, however.)

3
Degrees, Degree Requirements, and Transcripts

It is not titles that honor men, but men that honor titles.

NICCOLÓ MACHIAVELLI

A degree is a title conferred by a school to show that a certain course of study has been successfully completed. A diploma is the actual document or certificate that is given to the student as evidence that the degree has been awarded.

Diplomas are also awarded for courses of study that do *not* result in a degree such as, for example, on completion of a program in real-estate management, air-conditioning repair, or military leadership. This can lead to confusion, often intentionally, as in the case of someone who says, "I earned my diploma at Harvard," meaning that he or she attended a weekend seminar there, and received some sort of diploma of completion.

The following six kinds of degrees are awarded by colleges and universities in the United States:

The Associate's Degree

The Associate's degree is a relatively recent development, reflecting the tremendous growth of two-year community colleges (which is the new and presumably more respectable name for what used to be known as junior colleges).

Since many of the students who attend these schools do not continue on to another school to complete a Bachelor's degree, a need was felt for a degree to be awarded at the end of these two years of full-time study (or their equivalent by nontraditional means). More than 2,000 two-year schools now award the Associate's degree, and a small but growing number of four-year schools also award it, to students who leave after two years.

The two most common Associate's degrees are the A.A. (Associate of Arts) and the A.S. (Associate of Science), but more than 100 other titles have been devised, ranging from the A.M.E. (Associate of Mechanical Engineering) to the A.D.T. (Associate of Dance Therapy).

An Associate's degree typically requires 60 to 64 semester hours of credit (or 90 to 96 quarter hours), which, in a traditional program, normally takes two academic years (four semesters, or six quarters) to complete.

The Bachelor's Degree

The Bachelor's degree has been around for hundreds of years. In virtually every nation worldwide, it is the first university degree earned. (The Associate's is little used outside the United States.) In America, the Bachelor's is traditionally considered to be a four-year degree (120 to 128 semester units, or 180 to 192 quarter units, of full-time study), although a rather surprising report in 1990 revealed that the average Bachelor's takes closer to six years. In most of the rest of the world, it is expected to take three years. Through nontraditional approaches, some people with a good deal of prior learning can earn their Bachelor's degrees in as little as two or three months.

The Bachelor's degree is supposed to signify that the holder has accumulated a "batch" of knowledge; that he or she has learned a considerable amount in a particular field of study (the "major"), and gained some broad general knowledge of the world as well (history, literature, art, social science, mathematics). This broad approach to the degree is peculiar to traditional American programs. In most other countries, and in nontraditional American programs, the Bachelor's degree involves much more intensive study in a given field. When someone educated in England says, "I read history at Oxford," it means that for the better part of three years he or she did, in fact, read history and not much else. This is one reason traditional American degrees take longer to acquire than most foreign ones.

More than 300 different Bachelor's degree titles have been used in the last hundred years, but the great majority of the million-plus Bachelor's degrees awarded in the United States each year are either the B.A. (Bachelor of Arts) or the B.S. (Bachelor of Science), sometimes with additional letters to indicate the field (B.S.E.E. for electrical engineering, B.A.B.A. for business administration, and so on). Other common Bachelor's degree titles include the B.B.A. (Bachelor of Business Administration), B.Mus. (Music), B.Ed. (Education), and B.Eng. (Engineering). Some nontraditional schools and programs award the B.G.S. (Bachelor of General Studies), B.I.S. (Independent Studies), or B.L.S. (Liberal Studies).

In the late 19th century, educators felt that the title of "Bachelor" was inappropriate for young ladies, so some schools awarded female graduates titles such as Mistress of Arts or Maid of Science.

The Master's Degree

Until the 20th century, the "Master's" and "Doctor's" titles were used somewhat interchangeably, and considered appropriate for anyone who had completed work of significance beyond the Bachelor's degree. Today, however, the Master's is almost always the first degree earned after the Bachelor's, and is always considered to be a lower degree than the Doctorate.

The traditional Master's degree requires from one to two years of on-campus work after the Bachelor's. Some nontraditional Master's degrees may be earned entirely through nonresident study, while others require anywhere from a few days to a few weeks on campus.

There are several philosophical approaches to the Master's degree. Some schools (or departments within schools) regard it as a sort of advanced Bachelor's, requiring only the completion of one to two years of advanced-level studies and courses. Others see it as more of a junior Doctorate, requiring at least *some* creative, original research, culminating in the writing of a thesis, or original research paper. Some programs let students choose their approach, requiring, for example, either 10 courses and a thesis or 13 courses with no thesis.

And in a few world-famous schools, including Oxford and Cambridge, the Master's degree is an almost meaningless award, given automatically to all holders of the school's Bachelor's degree who have managed, as the saying goes, to stay out of jail for four years, and can afford the small fee. (Most American schools had a similar practice at one time, but Harvard abolished it more than a century ago and the rest followed suit soon after. However, some ivy league schools—Harvard, Yale, etc.—do maintain the quaint practice of awarding a Master's degree to new professors who do not happen to have a degree from that school, even if they have a doctorate from one of equal renown. It is a sort of housewarming gift, so that all senior faculty will have at least one degree from the school at which they are teaching.)

Master's degree titles are very similar to Bachelors'—the M.A. (Master of Arts) and M.S. (Master of Science) are by far the most common, along with that staple of American business, the M.B.A. (Master of Business Administration). Other common Master's degrees include the M.Ed., M.Eng.,

M.L.S. (Library Science), and M.J. (either Journalism or Jurisprudence).

The Doctorate

The term "Doctor" has been a title of respect for a learned person since biblical times. Moses, in Deuteronomy 31:28 (Douay version), says, "Gather unto me all the ancients of your tribes and your doctors, and I will speak these words in their hearing."

About 800 years ago, in the mid 12th century, outstanding scholars at the University of Bologna and the University of Paris began to be called either "Doctor" or "Professor," the first recorded academic use of the term.

The first American use came in the late 17th century, under, as the story has it, rather amusing circumstances. There had long been a tradition (and, to a large extent, there still is) that "it takes a Doctor to make a Doctor." In other words, only a person with a Doctorate can confer a Doctorate on someone else.

But in all of America, no one had a Doctorate, least of all Harvard's president, Increase Mather, who, as a Dissenter, was ineligible for a Doctorate from any English university, all of which were controlled by the Church.

Still, Harvard was eager to get into the Doctorate business, so their entire faculty (that is to say, a Mr. Leverett and a Mr. Brattle) got together and unanimously agreed to award an honorary Doctorate to Mr. Mather, whereupon Mather was then able to confer Doctorates upon his faculty who, subsequently, were able to doctor their students.

This, in essence, was the start of graduate education in America, and there are those who say things have gone downhill ever since.

America's next Doctorate, incidentally, was also awarded under rather odd circumstances. In this case, a British physician named Daniel Turner was eager to get into the Royal Society of Physicians and Surgeons, but needed an M.D. to do so. In England, then as now, most doctors have a *Bachelor* of Medicine; the *Doctor* of Medicine is an advanced degree. No English university would give Turner a Doctorate because he did not belong to the Church of England. Scottish universities turned him down because he had published some unkind remarks about the quality of Scottish education. And of course no European university would give a degree to an Englishman. So Mr. Turner made a deal with Yale University.

Yale agreed to award Turner the Doctorate in absentia (he never set foot in America), and he, in turn, gave Yale a gift of 50 valuable medical books. Wags at the time remarked that the M.D. he got must stand for the Latin *multum donavit*, "he gave a lot."

Nowadays the academic title of "Doctor" (as distinguished from the professional and honorary titles, to be discussed shortly) has come to be awarded for completion of an advanced course of study, culminating in a piece of original research in one's field, known as the doctoral thesis or dissertation.

While traditional Doctorates used to require at least two years of on-campus study after the Master's degree, followed by a period of dissertation research and writing, the trend lately has been to require little more than the dissertation. More and more schools are letting people without a Master's into their doctoral programs, and awarding the Master's along the way, on completion of the coursework (and any qualifying exams). The total elapsed time can be anywhere from three years on up. Indeed, the trend in the 1980s and '90s has been for Doctorates to take longer and longer. In his splendid book, *Winning the Ph.D. Game,* Richard Moore offers evidence that a typical Ph.D. now takes six or seven years, with a range from three to 10 (not all of it necessarily spent in residence on campus, however).

Many nontraditional doctoral programs waive the on-campus study, on the assumption that a mature candidate already knows a great deal about his or her field. Such programs require little or no coursework, focusing instead on the dissertation, with the emphasis on demonstrating creativity.

Some nontraditional doctoral programs permit the use of work already done (books written, symphonies composed, business plans created, etc.) as partial (or, in a few cases, full) satisfaction of the dissertation requirement. But many schools insist on all, or almost all, new work.

The most frequently awarded (and, many people feel, the most prestigious) Doctorate is the Doctor of Philosophy (known as the Ph.D. in North America, and the D.Phil. in many other countries). The Doctor of Philosophy does not necessarily have anything to do with the study of philosophy. It is awarded for studies in dozens of fields, ranging from chemistry to communication, from agriculture to aviation management.

> Until well into the 20th century, the Ph.D. was also given as an honorary degree. But in the late 1930s, Gonzaga University in Spokane, Washington, spoiled the whole thing by handing out an honorary Ph.D. to one Harry Lillis "Bing" Crosby, to thank him for donating some equipment to the football team. Crosby made great sport about being a Doctor on his popular radio program that week. The academic world rose in distressed anger and that, effectively, was the end of the honorary Ph.D.

More than 500 other types of Doctorate have been identified in the English language alone. After the Ph.D., the most common include the Ed.D. (Education), D.B.A. (Business Administration), D.P.A. (Public Administration), D.A. (Art or Administration), Eng.D. (Engineering), Psy.D. (Psychology), D.Sc. (Science), and D.Hum. (Humanities). The latter two are often, but not always, awarded as honorary degrees in the U.S.; in the rest of the world, they are earned like any other Doctorate.

A Bachelor's degree is almost always required for admission to a Doctoral program, and many traditional schools require a Master's as well. However, more and more Doctoral programs are admitting otherwise qualified applicants without a Master's degree. Most nontraditional programs will accept equivalent career experience in lieu of a Master's, and, in rare instances, in lieu of a Bachelor's as well.

> In the late 1950s, someone submitted what was essentially Eleanor Roosevelt's resume (changing the name and disguising some of her more obvious remarkable achievements) as part of an application to various doctoral programs. Mrs. Roosevelt had never attended college. All 12 schools turned her down, most suggesting that she reapply after completing a Bachelor's and a Master's, presumably six to eight years later.

In Europe, but very rarely in America, a so-called "higher Doctorate" (typically the D.Litt., Doctor of Letters) is awarded solely on the basis of one's life work, with no further studies required. The great majority of those receiving a D.Litt. already have one Doctorate, but it is not essential. In most quarters, the D.Litt. is considered to be an earned, not an honorary degree, but there are those who disagree.

Finally, it should be mentioned that several American schools, concerned with what one called the "doctoral glut," are reported to be seriously considering instituting a new degree, *higher* than the Doctorate, presumably requiring more years of study and a more extensive dissertation. The name "Chancellorate" has been bandied about. Indeed, the prestigious *Chronicle of Higher Education* devoted a major article to this possibility a few years ago. It may well be that holders of a Chancellorate (Ph.C.?) would not appreciably affect the job market, since most of them would be drawing their old age pensions by the time they completed this degree.

Professional Degrees

Professional degrees are earned by people who intend to enter what are often called "the professions"—medicine, dentistry, law, the ministry, and so forth. In the United States, these degrees are almost always earned *after* completing a Bachelor's degree, and almost always carry the title of "Doctor" (e.g., Doctor of Medicine, Doctor of Divinity).

In many other countries, it is common to enter professional school directly from high school, in which case the first professional degree earned is a Bachelor's. (For instance, there is the British Bachelor of Medicine, whose holders are invariably called "Doctor," unless they have earned the more advanced Doctor of Medicine degree, in which case they insist on being called "Mister." No one ever said the British were easy to understand.)

One exception in the United States is the D.C. (Doctor of Chiropractic), a program that students used to be able to enter right from high school. It now requires two years of college, but still no Bachelor's degree. This may be one reason so many medical doctors look down their noses at chiropractors.

Another exception used to be the law degree which, until the mid 1960s, was an LL.B., or Bachelor of Laws. Many lawyers objected to working three or four years beyond their Bachelor's degree simply to end up with yet another Bachelor's degree, while optometrists, podiatrists, and others were becoming doctors in the same length of time.

Nowadays, virtually every American law school awards a Doctorate as the first law degree, usually the J.D., which stands for either Doctor of Jurisprudence or Juris Doctor.

Almost all law schools offered their graduates with Bachelor of Law degrees the option of turning in their old LL.B. diplomas and, in effect, being retroactively Doctored with a J.D. A fair number of lawyers accepted this unprecedented offer, although few actually call themselves "Doctor."

The LL.D., known as both Doctor of Law and Doctor of Laws, is now used almost exclusively as an honorary title in the U.S.; elsewhere in the world, it is an earned, advanced law degree.

The traditional law degree requires three years of study beyond the Bachelor's degree. Some nontraditional approaches will be discussed in chapter 25.

The only widely accepted medical degree in America is the M.D. (Doctor of Medicine), which requires four years of study beyond the Bachelor's degree, although some shorter approaches, and some alternative ones, will be discussed in chapter 26.

A number of other medical or health specialties have their own professional Doctorates. These include, for instance, D.O. (Osteopathy), D.P. (Podiatry), and O.D. (Optometry).

There are no accelerated approaches to the dental degree, and few of us would really want to go to a dentist who *had* taken shortcuts. The traditional dental degree for many years has been the D.D.S. (Doctor of Dental Surgery), although there has recently been a strong trend toward the D.M.D. (Doctor of Medical Dentistry). Both programs require four years of study beyond the Bachelor's degree.

More than 100 different professional degree titles have been awarded in the area of religion. None can be said to be *the* standard one. They include the S.T.D. (Sacred Theology), D.Min. (Ministry), Th.D. (Theology), D.D. (Divinity), D.Rel. (Religion), D.R.E. (Religious Education), D.S.R. (Science of Religion), and so forth, as well as the Ph.D. in religion.

> The Canadian mathematician and humorist Stephen Leacock writes that shortly after he received his Ph.D., he was on board a cruise ship. When a lovely young lady fainted, the call went out, "Is there a doctor on board?" Leacock says he rushed to the Captain's cabin, but he was too late. Two D.D.'s and an S.T.D. had gotten there before him.

Quite a few other degrees are deemed honest professional titles by those who hold them, but are regarded with vigorously raised eyebrows by many others. These include, for example, the N.D. (Naturopathy, Naprapathy, or Napropathy), D.Hyp. (Hypnotism), H.M.D. or M.D.(H.) (Homeopathic Medicine), D.M.S. (Military Science), Met.D. (Metaphysics), Graph.D. (Graphoanalysis), and so forth.

*For her ichthyology project, Leslie Bolick
lived with her trout for three weeks.*

Honorary Degrees

The honorary degree is truly the stepchild of the academic world, and a most curious one at that. In fact, it is a reflection of academic achievement to the same degree that former basketball star Doctor J's title reflected his medical skills. It is simply a title that some institutions (and some scoundrels) have chosen to bestow, from time to time, and for a wide variety of reasons, upon certain people. These reasons often have to do with the donation of money, or with attracting celebrities to a commencement ceremony.

The honorary Doctorate has no academic standing whatsoever, and yet, because it carries the same title, "Doctor," as the earned degree, it has become an extremely desirable commodity for those who covet titles and the prestige they bring. For respectable universities to award the title of "Doctor" via an honorary Doctorate is as peculiar as if the Army awarded civilians the honorary title of "General"—a title the civilians could then use in their everyday life.

More than 1,000 traditional colleges and universities award honorary Doctorates (anywhere from one to 50 per year each), and a great many Bible schools, spurious schools, and degree mills hand them out with wild abandon to almost anyone willing to pay the price. The situation is discussed in detail in chapter 27.

TRANSCRIPTS

A transcript is, quite simply, an official record of all the work one has done at a given university. While the diploma is the piece of paper (or parchment) that shows that a given degree has been earned, the transcript is the detailed description of all the work done to earn that degree.

The traditional transcript is a computer printout listing all the courses taken, when they were taken, and the grade received. The overall G.P.A. (grade point average) is calculated as of the end of each semester or quarter.

Nearly all nontraditional schools and programs issue transcripts as well. Sometimes they try to make the transcripts look as traditional as possible, listing, for instance, life-experience learning credit for aviation as "Aviation 100, 4 units," "Aviation 101, 3 units," etc. Other programs offer a *narrative transcript*, which describes the procedures used by the school to evaluate various types of experience.

The original copy of a transcript is always kept by the school. Official copies, bearing an official raised seal or, sometimes, printed on special paper that cannot easily be tampered with, can be made for the student, other schools, or employers, at the student's request.

Unfortunately, there is a great deal of traffic in forged transcripts. Students have been known to change a few grades to improve the G.P.A., or even add entire classes. Of course such changes would normally only affect the copy, which is why most schools and many employers will only accept transcripts that are sent directly from the office of the school's registrar. Beginning in the late 1980s, however, and continuing into the 1990s, there have been more than a few fake transcript scandals. Some involved creative use of color copiers and laser printers. Others involved tampering with a university's computer, either by hackers having fun or by dishonest employees selling their services. Such unfortunate behaviors raise questions about the validity of *any* university-produced document.

"I do enjoy studying at home. But why can't the school just mail me the damn books."

4

Is a Degree Worth the Effort?

*Question: I'm 38 years old, and thinking about pursuing a
Bachelor's degree, but I'm not sure I should, because
if I do, I'll be 42 years old when I'm done.
Answer: And how old will you be in four years if you don't do it?*

PARAPHRASED FROM THE DEAR ABBY COLUMN

The simple answer to the question in the chapter title is yes for nontraditional degrees; very likely no for traditional degrees. Let us first elaborate on why the nontraditional degree is worth the effort, and then offer arguments as to why the old-fashioned way may not be worth it.

WHY THE NONTRADITIONAL DEGREE MAKES SENSE

Much depends on the degree itself, and on the reasons for wanting it. If, for instance, you need to have a Bachelor's degree to get a job, promotion, or salary increase, then an accredited degree from Regents College, earned entirely by correspondence courses, is exactly as good as any Bachelor's degree earned by sitting in classrooms for four or five or six years at a state university, and it would be about 95 percent cheaper (not to mention that one can continue earning a living while pursuing the nontraditional degree).

As another example, a nonresident Doctorate, earned through a combination of life-experience credit and new work, from one of the better unaccredited state-licensed universities may be of minimal value in getting a faculty position at Harvard. But such degrees have proved useful in some cases for advancement in business, government, and industry, not to mention doing wonders for self-image and gaining the respect of others.

Finally, a Doctorate purchased for a hundred bucks from a no-questions-asked degree mill may ultimately bring shame, public embarrassment, loss of a job, and even a fine and imprisonment.

Many nontraditional degrees are good for most people in most situations. But there can be major exceptions, which is why it pays to check out any school that you are considering in advance (this book is a good place to start)

and to make as sure as you can that the degree you seek will satisfy any gatekeepers who may appear in your path.

> **A word of warning:** Please do not be misled by the results of a study on the acceptance of nontraditional degrees, sponsored by the National Institute of Education in the late 1970s. This study, by Sosdian and Sharp, has been misquoted and misinterpreted in the literature of dozens of nontraditional universities, in a most misleading effort to convince prospective students that their degrees will be accepted in the academic, professional, or business world.
>
> Sosdian and Sharp did indeed determine that there was a high level of acceptance—*but their research was based entirely on the acceptance level of Associate's and Bachelor's degrees that either were regionally accredited or, in a very few cases, state-run schools that were candidates for regional accreditation.* It is totally misleading to imply, as many have done, that results would be comparable for unaccredited degrees, much less Master's and Doctorates. It just isn't so, and those schools should be ashamed of themselves.

The important issue of choosing an accredited or an unaccredited school is discussed at length in chapter 9.

Now, let's look at the six main reasons why people choose to pursue nontraditional degrees, and the kinds of degrees that may be most appropriate.

1. **Job or salary advancement in business, industry, or civil service.** Many job descriptions specify that a certain degree is required, or that additional salary will be paid, if a certain degree is held. In a small number of these situations, a good unaccredited degree will suffice.

   It is crucial to find out in advance, whenever possible, if a given degree will be accepted. While some businesses, large and small, will recognize good unaccredited degrees, many will not. We have heard dozens of tragic stories from people who spent many thousands of dollars on degree programs, only to find that the degree they earned was not acceptable to their employer or potential employer.

2. **Job or salary advancement in education.** The academic world has been more reluctant to accept unaccredited degrees than has the world of business or government. Even some excellent accredited, nontraditional degrees have caused problems. However, the situation remains extremely variable. It is almost impossible to draw general rules or conclusions. Many universities refuse to consider hiring a faculty member with an unaccredited degree, or to admit people with such degrees into their graduate programs. The most enlightened schools will consider each case on its own merits.

Once again, the watchword is to check in advance before spending any money with any school.

3. **Job or salary advancement in the professions.** When a profession must be licensed by the state or a trade organization, that body often has certain degree requirements. Depending on the state, this may apply to psychologists, marriage counselors, engineers, accountants, real-estate brokers, social workers, hypnotists, massage practitioners, and others. Each state has its own policy, and so does each field of endeavor.

In one state, for example, a psychologist must have a traditionally accredited Doctorate while a civil engineer with sufficient career experience could have an unaccredited degree or no degree at all. In another state, it may be just the opposite. Many regulations are exceedingly unclear on this subject, so a judgment is made in each individual case. Once again, it is crucial to determine in advance if a given degree will meet a given need, and, to the extent possible, to consider future developments. Many people have discovered, when wishing to move from one state or country to another, that the degree or credentials that had served them well will not be honored in the new location.

4. **Admission to traditional graduate schools.** In an earlier edition, we suggested a trend toward increased acceptance of nontraditional degrees "including the better unaccredited degrees" for admission to Master's and doctoral programs at traditional universities. Extensive communications from readers over the past few years persuade us that if there is a trend, it is toward case-by-case determinations, rather than a blanket policy of any sort.

The key factor here is that while undergraduate admissions decisions are usually made by the admissions office of the school, at the Master's and Doctoral level, these decisions are made, or heavily influenced, by the academic department itself. It is generally accepted that if the department (or a key faculty member in the department) really wants a certain applicant, that person is likely to be accepted, regardless of the nature of his or her specific academic credentials.

5. **Self-satisfaction.** This is a perfectly good reason for wanting a degree, and no one should ever feel embarrassed about it. Many clients of the degree consulting service (see Appendix C) seek a degree (generally a Doctorate) for self-satisfaction, to gain respect from others, to feel more comfortable with colleagues, or to "validate" a long and worthwhile career. Such people are generally well satisfied with a degree from one of the more respectable unaccredited schools. One of the main criteria to consider here is avoidance of potential embarrassment. More than one holder of a degree from a legitimate, but not especially good, nontraditional school has suffered extreme discomfort or embarrassment when newspaper articles or television stories on the school made big local waves.

One of John's favorite consulting clients wrote to him that his doctoral dissertation had been rejected by Columbia University in 1910, and now he'd like to finish the degree. John wrote back offering suggestions, and mentioned what he thought was an amusing typographical error in the letter; he'd said 1910. No, the man wrote back, that's correct. He was now 96 years old, and these events had happened 70 years earlier. He was accepted by a good nontraditional external program, and completed his Ph.D. shortly before his 100th birthday.

6. **Fooling people.** An alarming number of people want fake degrees for all manner of devious purposes. After CBS broadcast its degree-mill report on *60 Minutes,* they received a huge number of telephone calls from people wanting to know the addresses and phone numbers of the fake schools they had just seen exposed.

Almost every week we hear from people who would like "a Doctorate from Harvard University, please, with no work required, and can it be backdated to 1983, and I need it by next Tuesday." The best one can do is warn these people that they are endangering their reputations (and possibly their freedom) by considering such a course. Then we usually suggest that if they must have a degree by return mail, they consider a degree from a far-less-dangerous, second-rate Bible college. Nothing to be especially proud of, but less hazardous to one's health.

WHY A TRADITIONAL DEGREE MAKES LESS SENSE

People attend traditional colleges for a great many different reasons, as Caroline Bird writes in her fascinating book, *The Case Against College*:

> A great majority of our nine million post-secondary students who are "in college" are there because it has become the thing to do, or because college is a pleasant place to be ... because it's the only way they can get parents or taxpayers to support them without working at a job they don't like; because Mother wanted them to go; or for some reasons utterly irrelevant to the course of studies for which the college is supposedly organized.

There seem to be two basic reasons people go to college: to get an education or to get a degree. The two can be quite independent. Some people only care about the training, others only want the degree, and some want or need both.

Sadly, there is a strong trend in America toward what David Hapgood calls "diplomaism" in his book of that title. He writes:

> We are well on our way to repealing the American dream of individual accomplishment and replacing it with a system in which the diploma is the measure of a man, a diploma which bears no relation to performance. The career market is closing its doors to those without degrees.... Diplomaism zones people into a set of categories that tends to eliminate the variety and surprise of human experience. In a system run by diplomas, all avenues to personal advancement are blocked except one: the school that gives the diploma.... When we leave the institution, like carcasses coming off a packing plant's assembly line, an anonymous hand affixes an indelible stamp ... which thereafter determines what we can do, and how we shall be rewarded. And that stamp, unlike the imprint on a side of beef, reflects neither our personal value to the society, nor the needs of the economic system.

There are, in fact, three major problems with traditional schools and traditional degree programs:

1. There is often little connection between degrees earned traditionally and on-the-job performance.

2. There is much evidence that vast numbers of students are spending huge amounts of time being trained for jobs that simply do not exist.

3. The cash investment in a traditional college education is frequently an extremely poor investment indeed.

Let us consider each of these three problems in greater depth.

Traditional College Training and On-the-Job Performance

Many studies have found little or no relationship between college coursework and "real life" performance, and in some cases that relationship was a negative one. One extensive study, by Ivar Berg of Columbia University, published under the delightful title, "Education and Jobs: The Great Training Robbery," looked at various jobs in which people with degrees and people without were doing identical work. In many situations, there was no difference in performance between the two groups, and in a few jobs (including air traffic controllers and pants makers), the people without the degrees were doing a better job.

Sadly, Berg also found that many bosses either ignored or refused to believe the evidence that had been collected in their own offices and factories. For instance, in one big chemical firm where the laboratory workers without degrees were outperforming those with degrees, the management steadfastly maintained its policy of promoting only those employees with degrees.

Hapgood believes that personnel practices at such firms are not likely to be changed in the foreseeable future, because "employers made it clear they were demanding diplomas for reasons that had little to do with job performance." The real reasons, he thinks, had to do with conformity to the dominant culture and with the "ability" to stay in school for four or more years. "It proves that he was docile enough (or good or patient or stupid enough; choose your own adjective) to stay out of trouble for 13 or 17 or 20 years in a series of institutions that demand a high degree of unthinking conformity."

John was given similar responses when he surveyed the personnel managers of major airlines. Almost all require pilots to have an accredited Bachelor's degree, but they don't care whether the degree is in aviation or Chinese history. The important thing, they say, is that an employee is disciplined enough to complete a degree program. You may have been flying for 10 years for the navy or the air force, but that doesn't count. And if the hypocrisy needs to be underlined, consider the fact that when pilot trainees are in short supply, the degree requirement mysteriously disappears.

Whatever the reasons, the system is a confused and disarrayed one, with the one strongly positive note being the increasing acceptance of nontraditional degrees, whose holders often have far more practical knowledge and experience through on-the-job training than those who learned about the subject in the college classroom.

There is an ever-growing number of employers who will say, for instance, that you learn more about practical journalism in your first two weeks working on a daily newspaper than in four years of journalism school. (The same goes for law, advertising, and dozens of other fields.) And the person who has both the experience and the nontraditional degree based, at least in part, on that experience may be in the best situation of all.

It used to be the case that many employers denied jobs to people without degrees, even if the degree had nothing to do with the ability to perform the job. But following a key Supreme Court decision (*Griggs v. Duke Power Company, 1971*), employers must now prove that a degree is required to do a certain job, or they cannot discriminate against those without them. This is equally true for high school diplomas, Doctorates, and everything in between.

Is a Traditional College Degree Useful in Today's Marketplace?

A certain large state prison used to take great pride in its vocational training program. It operated a large cotton mill, where the inmates learned how to run the equipment and, in fact, made their own prison uniforms. When they got out of prison, however, they learned that not only was the equipment they had learned to operate hopelessly out-of-date, but the nearest large cotton mill was 2,000 miles away. No wonder many of them returned to a life of crime.

Much the same sort of thing goes on in traditional colleges and universities. As an example, throughout the 1960s hundreds of thousands of students were told about the great teacher shortages that were coming, so they graduated with degrees in education. But, as Alexander Mood wrote in a report for the Carnegie Commission:

It has been evident for some time to professors of education that they were training far more teachers than would ever find jobs teaching school, but few of them bothered to mention that fact to their students. That is understandable, of course, since their incomes depend on having students.

Much the same thing happened with the study of space science and astrophysics in the 1970s, and again with computer science in the 1980s and '90s.

And so we find thousands of people with Doctorates teaching high school, people with Master's degrees teaching first grade, and an awful lot of people with Bachelor's degrees in education waiting on tables and doing clerical work.

In virtually any field you look at, from psychology to civil engineering, you find lots of well-trained and unemployed practitioners. In one recent year, for instance, there were over 100,000 graduates in the field of communications, and about 14,000 new jobs in the communications industries. Five thousand anthropology graduates are finding about 400 job openings in their field. And so it goes. Or doesn't go.

The field of business is a reminder that things are constantly changing, in one direction or another. One survey by the *Wall Street Journal* found copious numbers of highly disillusioned M.B.A. students and recent graduates. But only a few years later, M.B.A. graduates were in such demand, some of them were being offered ten or more high-paying jobs as their graduation day neared.

According to Bird, "Law schools are already graduating twice as many new lawyers every year as the Department of Labor thinks will be needed," and Mood says that

in the past, the investment in higher education did at least pay off for most students; that is, they did get access to higher-status jobs; now for the first time in history, a college degree is being judged by many parents and students as not worth the price. They see too many of last year's graduates unable to find work, or taking jobs ordinarily regarded as suitable for high school graduates. . . . Moreover, this is not a temporary phenomenon.

The Bureau of Labor Statistics says that about 25 percent of college graduates entering the labor market are getting jobs previously held by people without degrees. That doesn't mean the degrees are needed to perform those jobs, of course, but only that there are millions of job-seekers with degrees who cannot find jobs requiring their degrees.

So the outlook for the traditional degree is rather bleak. People will continue to pursue them for the wrong reasons, and industry will continue to require them for the wrong reasons. And enlightened people of all ages will, more and more, come to realize that a nontraditional degree can do just about anything a traditional one can—with a much smaller expenditure of time, effort, and money.

Is a Traditional Degree Worth the Cost?

Just what is the cost? Anything we write today will be out of date tomorrow, because traditional college costs are escalating so fast. In 1998 the average cost of attending a private college for one year in the United States was $21,424, including tuition, room and board, books, etc. Allowing a conservative growth rate of 6%, the cost of four years would be $93,719. At public colleges, the average cost for four years would be "only" $44,047.

Based on a highly conservative 6 percent rate of academic inflation (most schools do try to hold the line, but there are limits to how much they can do), here is how things may look in years to come with regard to college costs:

YEAR	4 YRS. PRIVATE COLLEGE	4 YRS. PUBLIC COLLEGE
1998	$93,719	$44,047
2003	$125,682	$58,944
2008	$168,191	$78,881

It seems more than likely that a child who was born in 1990, who will enter college in 2008, can expect to pay well over $100,000 for a traditional college education.

Even today, many people simply cannot afford to pursue a traditional degree. Yet a degree can almost always mean a higher salary, increased likelihood of getting better jobs, and personal satisfaction. For a while, the gap seemed to be narrowing. In the early 1980s, the average Bachelor's degree–holder was earning about 35 percent more than the average high-school graduate. In recent years, however, that trend has dramatically reversed. The most recent available census data (1996) show the average Bachelor's degree–holder earning 53 percent more than a high-school graduate.

Here, from those census data, are average lifetime earnings for males, based on levels of education. The amount shown is total lifetime earnings, from the year of entering the job market (at the age of 18 for high-school graduates, 22 for Bachelor's degree–holders, etc.) until age 65. The figures for women are roughly 40% lower. (Who says that the Equal Rights Amendment is unnecessary?)

EDUCATIONAL LEVEL	LIFETIME EARNINGS
Attended high school, did not graduate:	$962,000
High-school graduate, did not go to college:	$1,373,000
Attended college for 1 to 3 years:	$1,616,000
Bachelor's degree:	$2,113,000
Master's degree:	$2,613,000
Doctorate:	$3,007,000
Professional degree:	$3,580,000

EDUCATIONAL LEVEL	ANNUAL EARNINGS, MEN	ANNUAL EARNINGS, WOMEN
No high school diploma	$20,464	$10,881
High school diploma/GED	$29,218	$15,848
Some college	$35,923	$19,828
Bachelor's	$49,147	$28,926
Master's	$63,748	$36,711
Doctorate	$81,271	$51,751
Law or medicine	$102,309	$68,326

From the above numbers, it may look, to an 18-year-old on the brink of either college or a job, as if taking four years off to earn a Bachelor's degree is going to be worth more than $700,000 in the long run. However, Caroline Bird thinks that if the only reason people go to college is to make more money, then higher education may be a dumb financial investment.

She argues this way (we have adapted her 1976 figures to the reality of the different interest rates of the late 1990s): The average Princeton graduate will have spent about $200,000 to get a degree, including tuition, room and board, books, travel, etc. If such a person put that sum of money into certificates of deposit earning 6 percent interest, they would have over $2.5 million by the age of 65, without ever having done a day's work. That, needless to say, is about twenty percent more than the "the average Bachelor's degree–holder makes in a lifetime of work.

Of course, most people wouldn't have the $200,000 to invest at age 18. But Bird argues that if one enters the job market at 18, the earnings over the next four years, plus,

perhaps, some advance from parents on what they would otherwise have spent on college tuition, wisely invested, would produce a similar result.

A study by Drs. J. H. Hollomon of the Massachusetts Institute of Technology and Richard Freeman of Harvard University concludes that "in the brief span of about five years, the college job market has gone from a major boom to a major bust. Large numbers of young people, for the first time, are likely to obtain less schooling and potentially lower occupational status than their parents."

All very well and good, but none of these people takes nontraditional education and degrees into account. Bird and others have produced some powerful reasons not to pursue a traditional degree. But it is now possible, and will become increasingly easier, to earn degrees at a low cost while remaining fully employed, thereby having the best of both worlds.

Whether pursuing a degree for the learning, the diploma, or both, the alternative student seems far more likely:

♦ to be motivated to complete his or her program;

♦ to select courses and programs that are appropriate and relevant to his or her needs;

♦ to avoid cluttering up campuses and dormitories (which, in the words of former Columbia University president William McGill, are in danger of becoming "storage houses for bored young people");

♦ to save years over the time of traditional programs (or, alternatively, to pursue educational objectives without giving up job or family), and, perhaps most importantly for most people, to save a tremendous amount of time and money, compared with the demands and costs of a traditional degree program.

Many nontraditional programs, in fact, come very close to John Holt's ideal educational system, which he describes by analogy with a public library: you go whenever you want something it has to offer, no one checks your credentials at the door, you leave when you have gotten what you wanted, and it is you, not the librarian, who decides if it has been a worthwhile experience.

WHERE, THEN, ARE THINGS GOING?

One message of Charles Reich's fascinating book, *The Greening of America,* is that things are happening now that have never happened before; that for the first time, the standards and lessons of the past may have no relevance for the future.

Things are indeed changing almost amazingly fast in higher education. The direction in which they are changing is away from traditional education and degrees toward alternative higher education and nontraditional degrees.

It is always difficult—and challenging—to live in a time of great change. On one hand, we have universities that have refused (or were unable, by law) to invite people like Bill

Gates, Eleanor Roosevelt, Buckminster Fuller, Andrew Wyeth, or Eric Hoffer to lecture, because they never earned a college degree. On the other hand, we have people earning higher degrees entirely by correspondence, entering prestigious doctoral programs without even a high-school diploma, and earning law degrees without ever seeing the inside of a law school.

Thirty years ago, if you wanted to earn a degree without sitting in classrooms for three or four years, and wanted to remain in North America, you had exactly two legal alternatives: the University of London and the University of South Africa, both of which offered (and still offer) nonresident programs from the Bachelor's level through the Doctorate, as well as various professional degrees.

At the same time, predictably, many traditional universities and colleges are suffering the financial impact of decreased enrollments and rising costs. Unprecedented numbers of traditional schools are simply going out of business (an average of one accredited college or university in the United States every three weeks!), and many others are almost frantically implementing nontraditional programs as a last resort to stay afloat.

Alternative education and the nontraditional degree seem, indeed, to be the wave of the educational future.

5
Using Titles

*Question: What do you call the person who
finishes last in his or her medical school class?
Answer: Doctor.*

TRADITIONAL

One question that arose regularly in the degree consulting practice John used to operate was this: "If I earn a degree, especially an alternative or nontraditional degree, in what way am I entitled to use the degree, and the title that comes with it (in the case of Doctorates), in my life and career?"

There is no simple answer to this question, since rules and regulations vary from state to state, and from profession to profession. The basic philosophy behind these laws is, essentially, this: You can probably do almost anything you want in the way of titles, as long as you do not do it with the intent of deceiving anyone, and as long as it is not specifically forbidden by law. (Until recently, for instance, Florida had a law that prohibited people with unaccredited degrees, even from long-established, state-approved schools, from even mentioning those degrees in any way, in writing or orally, whether on a business card, letterhead, advertisement, etc. That law was found to be unconstitutional, so now Billy Graham does not have to worry about being nabbed upon crossing the Florida border.)

No one ever had Colonel Sanders arrested for pretending to be a military officer, nor is Doctor Demento or Doc Martens in danger of prosecution for impersonating a physician. However, when a man who has never earned a Doctorate gets a job as a meteorologist for a New York television station using the title of "Doctor," there *is* a major problem, because it can be reasonably assumed that the title helped him get the job—even if he was performing his duties satisfactorily without benefit of doctoral training. (That meteorologist lost his job after his lack of a degree was exposed.)

In general, as long as the degree comes from an unquestionably legal and legitimate school, there is usually no problem in using that degree in public life, as long as all local and licensing requirements are met.

In some states, a "quickie" Doctorate from a one-room Bible school is sufficient to set up practice as a marriage counselor and psychotherapist. In other states with stiffer licensing requirements, this same behavior could result in major legal problems.

The use of degree titles varies considerably from profession to profession, and from nation to nation. Most people in the United States do not append a Bachelor's degree notation to their letterhead or signature, while in most of the rest of the world, it is quite common to see, for instance, "Maxwell Zeryck, B.A." The name or abbreviation of the school is often appended as well: "Kata Galasi, B.A. (Oxon)" or "B.A. (Cantab)," indicating that the degree is from Oxford or Cambridge.

Master's degrees are more commonly used in print in the United States, especially the M.B.A. (e.g., "Joseph Judd, M.B.A.")

Holders of a Doctorate almost always use it in their public or professional lives—with the curious exception of politicians. (Most prominent politicians with earned Doctorates, from Woodrow Wilson to George McGovern, to Newt Gingrich, seem to have gone to great lengths to avoid public disclosure of the degree. Perhaps there is merit to columnist Herb Caen's belief that people will never vote for anyone they think is more intelligent than they are.)

There are, and probably always will be, educational conservatives who decry the use of nontraditional (and particularly unaccredited nontraditional) titles. A typical situation has occurred in the field of electrical engineering, where a gentleman in New York formed the "Committee of Concerned E.E.'s" for the purpose of carrying on a vigorous campaign against the right of electrical engineers with unaccredited Doctorates to use the title of "Doctor." The journals in this field often carry articles and letters from people on various aspects of this issue.

Thomas Carlyle's observation regarding the "peculiar ambition of Americans to hobble down to posterity on crutches of capital letters" notwithstanding, Americans are far less likely than Europeans and Asians to use all the letters at their command. Whereas a typical Englishman will list all his degrees, and perhaps a few fellowships besides (e.g., "Lowell James Hicks, B.A., M.A., Ph.D., F.R.S., L.C.P."), most Americans would only use their highest degree (e.g., "Heather Bourne, Ph.D."), unless they have more than one Doctorate, in which case both would be listed (e.g., "Howard Siegel, M.D., Ph.D.")

Not everyone agrees with this. The former president of a California religious school, for instance, regularly used all nine of his claimed Doctorates, with his civil-service rank (G.S.9) thrown in between Doctorates number four and five, for good measure. And then there was the chap who wrote to us from Massachusetts, using these letters after his name: L.R.A., M.N.G.S., B.S.A. When asked, he explained that the letters stood for Licensed Real Estate Agent, Member of the National Geographic Society, and Boy Scouts of America.

Holders of honorary Doctorates are treading on far more dangerous ground when they use their degrees in public, especially if such degrees were purchased "over the counter," no matter how legally. Still, public figures from Billy Graham to the late Edward Land, founder of Polaroid, regularly use (or used) the title "Doctor" based on honorary degrees from major universities.

Nonetheless, if an insurance agent makes a sale, if a clergyman makes a convert, or if a teacher makes a salary increase that can be attributed, even in part, to the prestige of being called "Doctor," and if that Doctorate is unearned, then the claim can always be made that that person is acting, at least in part, on false pretenses.

In 1994, the newly appointed secretary of education of a quite large western country proudly listed a doctorate from Harvard on his resume. Following an inquiry, his office later conceded that he had only a Master's degree from Harvard. A month later, his office announced that, actually, he did not even have a Bachelor's degree. In January of 1995, he resigned, admitting that, in fact, his academic career ended when he was expelled from the second grade for bad behavior.

There is also the matter of whether a Doctorate-holder chooses to call himself, for example, Roger Williams, Ph.D. or Dr. Roger Williams. Although either form would appear to be acceptable in many circumstances, a New York audiologist (someone who fits hearing aids) suffered legal repercussions for calling himself Dr. So-and-so rather than So-and-so, Ph.D. The prosecution's claim was that the use of the word "Doctor" in such a near-medical field was done to deceive clients into thinking he was a medical doctor. (Incidentally, it is incorrect to use the title at both ends of the name simultaneously. "Dr. Jeremy Dorosin, Ph.D." is a no-no.)

Another category of title abusers are those people who use degrees they never earned, and there are a surprising number of them. When the head of a major motion picture studio got into legal troubles a few years back, a sidelight of the case was that the degree he said he had from Yale University turned out to be nonexistent. At the same time, Yale revealed that they keep files on all cases of publicly claimed Yale degrees that were never actually awarded, and that to date they had logged more than 7,000 such fraudulent claims.

It seems reasonable to hypothesize that these 7,000 are just the tip of the iceberg. Untold thousands of others are going about free, only because so few people ever bother to check up on anyone's degrees. Most exposures happen in connection with other events, often when something good happens to a person. Let us give a number of examples, in the hopes of dissuading some readers from considering this course of action.

- The Arizona "Teacher of the Year" for 1987, after he entered the public eye, was discovered to have falsified his claim to a Doctorate. He forfeited the $10,000 prize that came with this honor, and his career was in jeopardy.

- Two of the 1988 presidential hopefuls, Biden and Robertson, got a lot of press coverage when it turned out their academic credentials were not as they had represented.

- The chairman of the board of a major university in the South resigned when it became known his Doctorate was from a "school" whose founder was in federal prison for selling degrees.

- The young woman whose 1981 Pulitzer Prize was taken away when it turned out she had falsified her story about a young drug addict also turned out to have two fake degrees listed on her *Washington Post* job application.

- A finalist for fire chief in a major Midwestern city in 1994 was found (by one of his opponents) to have a Bachelor's degree that he purchased for $45 from a Texas degree mill.

- The chief engineer of San Francisco's transit system lost his $81,000-a-year job when his employer discovered that he did not have the degree he claimed.

- The President-elect of Poland turned out not to have the Master's degree he listed on his official resume. This is a crime punishable by jail in Poland. "I passed all my exams," he said, "But never formally concluded my studies with a Master's degree."

- The superintendent of one of California's largest school districts lost his $98,000-a-year job and faced criminal charges when a reporter learned he did not have the Stanford doctorate he claimed.

♦ A prominent Florida university professor of surgery resigned when someone checked up and found he didn't have the Master's degree he had listed on his resume.

♦ A controversial member of the Canadian parliament got huge page one headlines in Toronto when it was learned that he was signing letters "LL.B." even though he did not have a law degree.

♦ During the 1996 elections, candidates in three states were discovered to be claiming degrees they did not earn. After the ensuing publicity, they all lost.

♦ The London *Daily Telegraph* revealed gleefully that Italian neo-fascist MP Alessandra Mussolini, granddaughter of Il Duce, had allegedly purchased her degree in history and moral philosophy from Rome's Sapienza University for about $500, utilizing professors' signatures forged by a porter. (The newspaper suggested that the porter might have been just as good a judge of moral philosophy as the professor.)

♦ A large midwestern county went to court to obtain a summary judgment to remove its health commissioner, after learning that the source of his graduate degree was less than reputable.

♦ The newly-hired president of an Idaho college got bad publicity (and perhaps worse) when trustees realized his doctorate was from the unaccredited "University of Berkley" and not the University of California, Berkeley.

♦ The very same man also got in trouble at his previous job for listing a doctorate from the University of Idaho when, in fact, he had only a Master's degree.

And so it goes. Do you know where your own doctor, lawyer, and accountant earned their degrees? Have you checked with the schools just to be sure? A diploma on the wall is not sufficient evidence. We know of three different places that have sold fake diplomas from any school, printed to order for a modest sum. John has two fake Harvard diplomas hanging on his wall, alongside his real ones. His medical degree cost $50 from a "lost diploma replacement service" in Oregon. What if your family doctor had their catalog? His Harvard law degree, purchased just before this edition of our book went to press, cost just over $50 from a "service" in Florida. (No, we are not going to give out names and addresses; these businesses do enough damage in the world as it is.)

This topic moves very rapidly from the abstract to the concrete when something happens nearby. It was clearly brought home some years ago when a locally prominent "certified public accountant" who lived just down the road from us hurriedly packed his shingle and left town. One of his clients had decided to check, and found out that he simply did not have the credentials he said he had.

So then, common sense should be sufficient to make your decision on how to use a degree in almost any situation that may arise. Where there is any doubt at all about using a given degree or title, it may be wise to seek legal advice, or at the very least to check with the relevant state agencies—generally the state education department (see chapter 6), or the appropriate licensing agencies.

And, in general, it isn't a bad idea to worry just a little about other people's degrees and titles. A lot of fakes and frauds are out there right now, practicing medicine, teaching classes, practicing law, counseling troubled families, building bridges, pulling teeth, and keeping books, without benefit of a degree, a license, or proper training. If more people would ask a few more questions about the title before the name, or the document on the wall, these dangerous phonies would be stopped before they do more harm to us all.

Big companies are often not nearly as thorough as one might wish. When some of the sleaziest schools put out lists of corporations who pay for their employees to get those degrees, they are often telling the truth. Either the companies confuse the sleazy school with another of similar or identical name, or they simply don't care.

Legitimate schools themselves, however, are getting better and better at detecting phonies. At the national registrars' conventions, for instance, there are always sessions on identifying fraud. Although some registrars grumble about having to become detectives, and lament the invention of the color laser copier and other tools of the scoundrels, they are doing good work on the front lines in the war against academic fraud.

Almost every school will confirm, either by mail or by telephone, whether or not a given person has indeed earned a degree from them. This is not an invasion of privacy, since the facts are known as "directory information," available to the public through printed directories or publicly accessible university information files.

(Glad you asked. John Bear's Ph.D. was awarded by Michigan State University, East Lansing, Michigan, on March 19, 1966, and you are most welcome to check it out with them.)

NONACADEMIC TITLES

There are two kinds of things people do, other than earning (or buying) degrees that result in letters after their names and/or titles before them. These "designations" and "titles" are not the main province of this book, but they are closely allied, which is why we address them briefly.

Designations

Designations are, typically, titles or credentials awarded by various professional and trade organizations and associations upon completion of a course of study and, often, examinations. Perhaps most common are the designations of C.P.A. (Certified Public Accountant) in the U.S. and C.A. (Chartered Accountant) in Canada. The designation is earned upon completing certain courses and passing examinations.

Other popular designations are those of C.L.U. (Certified Life Underwriter), C.F.P. (Certified Financial Planner), and Realtor. But there are many hundreds of others, some easy to gain, others requiring arduous examinations, and most permitting the holder to add letters following his or her name.

Some organizations, especially those in Europe, have several levels of designation, depending on which series of examinations one has passed. For instance, one can be an M.A.B.E. (Member of the Association of Business Executives) or, following additional exams, an F.A.B.E. (Fellow of the [etc.]).

Some designations are clearly academic, and are regarded as such by many institutions. For instance, an American C.P.A. will often not have to take either an accounting or a quantitative methods course if he or she enrolls in certain M.B.A. programs.

One thing the world has needed is a comprehensive guide to designations in all countries, making clear just what was done to earn them, and how each country regards other countries' designations. Happily, this information is now available in a series of books (including, for instance, A Guide to Over 400 Organizations and their Designations, from LBA Publications, at 12 Celeste Drive, Suite 3E, Scarborough, ON M1E 2V1 Canada).

Titles

People often ask, "Well, if I can't become a Doctor overnight, what about becoming a baron or a knight or something?" Indeed, it has been suggested that one reason honorary Doctorates are so popular in America is that we don't have titles of nobility. This topic is really not within the scope of the book, but if you have interest, there are plenty of books, articles, and Internet sites out there. Indeed, when we did an Internet search for the category "Titles of Nobility," a total of 19,177 sites were found, offering the opportunity to become a Baron of Bosnia, Knight of the Byzantine Empire, Knight of Malta (at least 19 competing organizations), Knight Templar, and Patriarch of Antioch.

According to some books, there are various European services that specialize in getting their clients either married into or adopted into the royal houses of Europe at fees ranging from $20,000 to more than $300,000. In this vein, *Parade Magazine* reported that Zsa Zsa Gabor's eighth husband, Prince Frederick von Anhalt, Duke of Saxony, Count of Ascania, is the son of a German policeman, who was adopted by an impoverished German princess, after which he sold 68 knighthoods at $50,000 each.

In earlier editions, we printed the addresses of some of these dispensers, but they seem to move often, sometimes without awarding the titles that had been ordered. So we'll pass on the details this time. Anyway, if truth be known, we worried that readers might be arrested for impersonating a baron, or be drafted into the Byzantine army.

If you simply must have a title, consider the Council of Westphalia, The Roman Forum, 13 Oakleigh Road, Stratford-upon-Avon, Warwickshire CV37 0DW, England, which is in the business of finding extinct British titles that are unlikely ever to be used again, and bestowing them on people who support their archaeological research.

"Don't want to work on my dissertation.
Want to ride my horsey."

6
How to Evaluate a School

Some people spend more time deciding which soda to buy from a soft drink machine than they do in choosing the school where they will earn their degree.

PROSECUTOR AT THE TRIAL OF A STATE PSYCHOLOGIST WITH A PHONY PH.D.

An investigative reporter for a large newspaper once told John that he could go into any building on the street, "that office, that hospital, that laundromat, that factory—and given enough time and money, I would find a story there that would probably make page one."

The same is very likely true of virtually every school in this book, from Harvard on down. Some simply have a lot more skeletons in a lot more closets than others.

It would be wonderful to have an army of trained investigators and detectives at our disposal. With our very limited resources and manpower, we cannot do a detailed and intensive investigation of every single school. Happily, we have received a great deal of assistance from readers of this book, who have followed our advice on checking out schools and have reported their findings to us.

Here, then, is the four-step procedure we recommend for investigating schools that are not covered in this book, or looking further into those that are. And please, if you do this, share your research with us at P. O. Box 7070, Berkeley, California 94707. (Thank you.)

Step One: Check It Out in This Book

If a school isn't here, it may be because it is very new, or because we didn't consider it sufficiently nontraditional for inclusion—or quite possibly because we simply missed it. And even if it *is* listed here, don't take our opinions as the gospel truth. Hardly a day passes that we don't get a letter challenging our opinions. Sometimes they begin, "You idiot, don't you know that . . ." and sometimes they begin, "I beg to differ with you in regard to . . ." Whatever the tone, we are always glad to have these opinions. There have been quite a few instances where such a letter spurred us to look more closely at a school, resulting in a revised opinion, either upward or downward.

Step Two: Check It Out with Friends, Colleagues, or Employers

If you need the degree for a new job, a salary increase, or a state license, be sure to find out specifically if this degree will suffice before investing any money in any school. Many schools will gladly enter into correspondence with employers, state agencies, or others you may designate, to explain their programs and establish their credentials.

All too often, we hear horror stories about people who have lost thousands of dollars and wasted incredible amounts of time completing a degree that was useless to them. "But the school said it was accredited," they lament.

Step Three: Check It Out with the Proper Government Agency

Every state and every nation has an agency that oversees higher education. Check the school out with the agency in your state or in the state or country in which the school is located. A list of these agencies is given at the end of the chapter. Some correspondence schools are well known (positively or negatively) to the Better Business Bureau as well, but do not rely on this; some of the worst diploma mills have also been members of the BBB. And all nations have a department, bureau, or ministry of education that may be able to supply information on a school. They also all have embassies in Washington, DC and all national capitals, as well as United Nations delegations in New York to which questions may be addressed. You may get bogged down in voice mail, but it is worth the effort.

Step Four: Check Out the School Itself

Visit the campus or the offices if at all possible, especially if you have any doubts. If the school's literature does not make clear its precise legal or accreditation status, or if you still have any questions, check with the appropriate accrediting agency. They are all listed in chapter 8. If the accreditor is not listed in chapter 8, be careful. There are a lot of phony accrediting agencies in operation as well as phony schools.

Here are some of the questions you may wish to ask. **Do not just make up a form letter and send it to 50 or more schools, as more than a few readers have done.** Being more selective, both about schools and questions, will save you and the schools time and money. Also, match the question to the school. If you are inquiring of an obscure unaccredited school, it may be appropriate to ask where the president earned his or her degrees, but there is no need to ask that of, say, a major state university.

♦ How many students are currently enrolled? (Curiously, quite a few schools seem reluctant to reveal these numbers. Sometimes it is because they are embarrassed about how large they are, as, for instance, in the case of one alternative school that at one time had more than 3,000 students and a faculty of five! Sometimes it is because they are embarrassed about how small they are, as is the case with one heavily advertised school that has impressive literature, extremely high tuition, and fewer than 50 students.)

♦ How many degrees have been awarded in the last year?

♦ What is the size of the faculty? How many of these are full-time and how many are part-time or adjunct faculty? If the catalog doesn't make it clear, from which schools did the faculty earn their degrees?

♦ From which school(s) did the president, the dean, and other administrators earn their own degrees? (There is nothing inherently wrong with staff members earning degrees from their own school, but when the number doing so is 25 percent or more, as is the case at some institutions, it starts sounding a little suspicious.)

♦ May I have the names and addresses of some recent graduates in my field of study, and/or in my geographical area?

♦ May I look at the work done by students? (Inspection of Master's theses and doctoral dissertations can often give a good idea of the quality of work expected, and the caliber of the students. But you may either have to visit the school [not a bad idea] or offer to pay for making and sending copies.)

♦ Will your degree be acceptable for my intended needs (state licensing, certification, graduate school admission, salary advance, new job, whatever)?

♦ What exactly is your legal status, with regard to state agencies and to accrediting associations? If accreditation (or candidacy for accreditation) is claimed, is it with an agency that is approved either by the U.S. Department of Education or the Council on Higher Education Accreditation? If not accredited, are there any plans to seek accreditation? Is the school listed in any of the three major reference sources used by registrars and admissions officers worldwide: the *International Handbook of Universities, Commonwealth Universities Yearbook,* or *AACRAO World Education Series?*

No legitimate school should refuse to answer questions like these. Remember, you are shopping for something that may cost you several thousand dollars or more. It is definitely a buyer's market, and the schools all know this. If they see that you are an informed customer, they will know that they must satisfy you or you will take your business elsewhere.

Remember too that alternative education does not require all the trappings of a traditional school. Don't expect to find a big campus with spacious lawns, an extensive library, or a football team. Some outstanding nontraditional schools are run from relatively small suites of rented offices.

You definitely cannot go by the catalog or other school literature alone. Some really bad schools and some outrageous degree mills have hired good writers and designers, and produced very attractive catalogs that are full of lies and misleading statements. A common trick, for instance, is to show a photograph of a large and impressive building, which may or may not be the building in which the school rents a room or two. Another common device is to list a large number of names of faculty and staff, sometimes with photographs of their smiling faces. Our files are full of certified, deliver-to-addressee-only letters sent to these people that have been returned as undeliverable.

Finally, be very suspicious of schools with no telephones, or, perhaps even more of a red flag, schools where you can't call them, they have to call you. For instance, in 1989, we attempted to check out a new and heavily advertised school called North American University. The people who answered their toll-free phone line were cheerful, but after many calls, we were never put through to anyone. It was always, "Dr. Peters will call you back." "Dr. Peters" turned out to be an alias for the school's owner, a convicted felon, who would return calls from his home in another state.

On the other side of the ledger, some good, sincere, legitimate schools have issued typewritten and photocopied catalogs, either to save money or to go along with their low-key images. One sincere, very low-budget school even operated without a telephone for a while.

AGENCIES FOR HIGHER EDUCATION

USA

There is at least one agency in each state, and one in the District of Columbia, that oversees higher education. If you have any concerns about the legality of an institution, or its right to award degrees, these are the places to ask.

(In earlier editions, we also listed the SPRE, or State Postsecondary Review Entity, an abortive attempt to bring some uniformity to the diverse systems, but Congress did away with these in 1996.)

Whom Do You Ask First?

No simple answer, so be prepared to spend a bit of time on the phone or writing letters if you wish to learn the exact status of a school in a given state. Starting with the main higher education agency makes sense, although in some states a second agency (as with California or Hawaii) may be the best place.

We call various state agencies fairly often. We have found that once we get through the voice mail, the basic answers are generally correct, but often incomplete. A lot depends on who happens to answer the phone. For instance, one time when we called Alabama to check on an unaccredited school operating there, we were told, "Oh, we've been trying to close them down for years. At least we got them to agree not to accept students from the state of Alabama." But on another call to the same office, we were told, "The state of Alabama has no official position with regard to this school."

In another example, we called the proper California agency to ask about a school which we had heard had just lost its state approval. The helpful person on the phone confirmed this, and gave us the exact date it had happened. But then we found out, a few days later, that the school had gone to court and secured a Writ, which prohibited the state from enforcing its decision until further hearings were held, and thus the school continued legitimately in business.

The inconsistency from state to state, the level of knowledge of state personnel, and the volatile situation with regard to many schools and many laws, makes our job a harder one, and yours as well.

The following agencies are those that license, regulate, or are otherwise concerned with higher education in their state, province, or country. The listings include the telephone, in most cases the fax, and, where known, an e-mail address and the name of the person in charge. This information changes on almost a daily basis. If you discover errors or changes, please let us know. Thank you.

Alabama
Commission on Higher Education
100 North Union St.
Montgomery 36104
(334) 242-2108
Fax (334) 242-0268
E-mail achnh01@asnmail.asc.edu
Dr. Henry J. Hector, Executive Director

Another relevant agency
Department of Postsecondary Education
401 Adams Ave.
Montgomery, AL 36130
(334) 242-2900
Fax (334) 242-2888
Dr. Elizabeth French, Chancellor

Alaska
Alaska Commission on Postsecondary Education
707 A Street, #201
Anchorage 99501
(907) 269-7972
Fax (907) 465-5316
www.state.ak.us/acpe
Diane Barrans, Executive Director

Arizona
Arizona Board of Regents
2020 North Central Ave., Suite 230
Phoenix 85004
(602) 229-2500
Fax (602) 229-2555
E-mail idfhb@asuvm.inre.asu.edu
Frank H. Besnette, Executive Director

Another relevant agency
Arizona Commission for Postsecondary Education
2020 N. Central Ave., Suite 275
Phoenix, AZ 85004
(602) 229-2591
Fax (602) 229-2599
E-mail iceaj@asuvm.inre.asu.edu
Dr. Edward Johnson, Executive Director

Arkansas
Arkansas Department of Higher Education
114 East Capitol Ave.
Little Rock 72201
(501) 32371-2000
Fax (501) 371-2003
E-mail dianeg@adhe.arknet.edu
Dr. Diane S. Gilleland, Director

California

California Postsecondary Education Commission
1303 J St.
Suite 500
Sacramento 95814
(916) 445-7933
Fax (916) 327-4417
Dr. Warren Fox, Executive Director

Another relevant agency
Bureau on Private, Postsecondary and
Vocational Education
1027 10th St., Fourth Floor
Sacramento 95814
(916) 445-3427
Fax (916) 323-6571
(This is the former Council on Private, Postsecondary
[etc.], which was moved from the Department of
Education to the Department of Consumer Affairs in
1997. They are charged with evaluating the state's unaccredited schools, to determine if they should be granted
State Approval.)

Colorado

Colorado Commission on Higher Education
1300 Broadway, 2nd floor
Denver 80203
(303) 866-2723
Fax (303) 860-9750
E-mail dwayne_nuzum@cche.state.co
Dr. Dwayne C. Nuzum, Executive Director

Connecticut

Board of Governors for Higher Education
61 Woodland St.
Hartford 06105
(860) 566-5766
Fax (860) 566-7865
E-mail derocco@commnet.edu
Dr. Andrew G. De Rocco, Commissioner of
Higher Education

Delaware

Delaware Higher Education Commission
820 North French St.
Wilmington 19801
(302) 577-3240

Another relevant agency
Commission on Higher Education
3465 Norman Bridge Road
Montgomery 36105
(334) 242-1998
Fax (302) 577-3862
Marilyn B. Quinn, Executive Director

District of Columbia

Office of Postsecondary Education Research
and Assistance
2100 Martin Luther King, Jr. Ave. S.E., Suite 401
Washington 20020
(202) 727-3685
Fax (202) 727-2739
Dr. Ulysses S. Glee, Acting Chief

Florida

Postsecondary Education Planning Commission
Florida Education Center
Tallahassee 32399
(904) 488-7894
Fax (904) 922-5388
E-mail proctob@firnvx.firn.edu
William B. Proctor, Executive Director

Georgia

Board of Regents
244 Washington St. S.W.
Atlanta 30334
(404) 656-2202
Fax (404) 657-6979
E-mail chancellor@mail.regents.peachnet.edu
Dr. Stephen R. Portch, Chancellor

Hawaii

State Postsecondary Education Commission
2444 Dole St., Room 209
Honolulu 96822
(808) 956-8207
Fax (808) 956-5286
Dr. Kenneth P. Mortimer, Executive Officer

Another relevant agency
Department of Consumer Protection
(808) 587-3222
(If Hawaii ever decides to enforce the unaccredited
school registration law passed by the legislature in
1990, it would probably be administered through this
office.)

Idaho

Board of Education
P. O. Box 83720
Boise 83720
(208) 334-2270
Fax (208) 334-2632
E-mail board@osbe.state.id
Dr. Rayburn Barton, Executive Director

Illinois

Board of Higher Education
4 West Old Capitol Plaza, Room 500
Springfield 62701
(217) 782-2551
Fax (217) 782-8548
E-mail wagner@uis.edu
Dr. Richard D. Wagner, Executive Director

Indiana

Commission for Higher Education
101 West Ohio St.
Suite 550
Indianapolis 46204
(317) 464-4400
Fax (317) 464-4410
E-mail sjones@chevay.che.state.in
Stanley G. Jones, Commissioner

Iowa

State Board of Regents
Old Historical Building
East 12th St. and Grand Ave.
Des Moines 50319
(515) 281-3934
Fax (515) 281-6420
R. Wayne Richey, Executive Director

Kansas

Kansas Board of Regents
700 Southwest Harrison, Suite 1410
Topeka 66603
(913) 296-3421
Fax (913) 296-0983
E-mail steve@kbor.state.ks
Dr. Stephen M. Jordan, Executive Director

Kentucky

Council on Higher Education
1024 Capital Center Drive
Suite 320
Frankfort 40601
(502) 573-1555
Fax (502) 573-1535
E-mail che@mail.state.ky
Dr. Gary S. Cox, Executive Director

Louisiana

Board of Regents
150 Third St.
Suite 129
Baton Rouge 70801
(504) 342-4253
Fax (504) 342-9318
Dr. E. Joseph Savoie, Interim Commissioner

Maine

Department of Education
Division of Higher Education Services
State House Station #23
Augusta 04333
(207) 287-8951
Fax (207) 287-5900
E-mail proulx@saturn.caps.maine.edu
Judith Malcolm, Director

Maryland

Higher Education Commission
16 Francis St.
Annapolis 21401
(410) 974-2971
Fax (410) 974-3513
E-mail pflores@mhec.state.md
Dr. Patricia S. Florestano, Secretary of Higher Education

Massachusetts

Board of Higher Education
One Ashburton Place
Room 1401
Boston 02108
(617) 727-7785
Fax (617) 727-6397
Dr. Stanley Z. Koplik, Chancellor

Michigan

Department of Education
P. O. Box 30008
Lansing 48909
(517) 373-3345
Fax (517) 373-4602
Dr. C. Danford Austin, Assistant Superintendent for Postsecondary Education

Minnesota

Higher Education Services Office
550 Cedar Street
Suite 400
St. Paul 55101
(612) 296-8012
(612) 297-8880
E-mail info@heso.state.mn
Dr. Robert K. Poch, Director

Mississippi

Board of Trustees of State Institutions of Higher Learning
3825 Ridgewood Road
Jackson 39211
(601) 982-6623
Fax (601) 987-4172
E-mail debbie@ihl.state.ms
Dr. Thomas D. Layzell, Commissioner of Higher Education

Missouri

Coordinating Board for Higher Education
3515 Amazonas Drive
Jefferson City 65109
(573) 751-2361
Fax (573) 751-6635
Dr. Kala M. Stroup, Commissioner

Montana

Montana University System
2500 Broadway
Helena 59620
(406) 444-6570
Fax (406) 444-1469
Jeffrey D. Baker, Commissioner of Higher Education

Nebraska

Coordinating Commission for Postsecondary
Education
P. O. Box 95005
Lincoln 68509
(402) 471-2847
Fax (402) 471-2886
E-mail dpowers@ccpe.state.ne
Dr. David R. Powers, Executive Director

Nevada

University and Community College System
2601 Enterprise Road
Reno 89512
(702) 784-4905
Fax (702) 784-1127
E-mail rjarvis@nevada.edu
Dr. Richard S. Jarvis, Chancellor

New Hampshire

Postsecondary Education Commission
2 Industrial Park Drive
Concord 03301
(603) 271-2555
Fax (603) 271-2696
E-mail j_knapp@tec.nh
Dr. James A. Busselle, Executive Director

New Jersey

Commission on Higher Education
20 West State St., CN542
Trenton 08625
(609) 292-4310
Fax (609) 292-7225
Dr. Martine Hammond-Paludan, Executive Director

New Mexico

Commission on Higher Education
1068 Cerrillos Road
Santa Fe 87501
(505) 827-7383
Fax (505) 827-7392
E-mail bhamlett@che.state.nm
Dr. Bruce D. Hamlett, Executive Director

New York

State Education Department
Cultural Education Center, Room 5B28
Albany 12230
(518) 474-5851
Fax (518) 486-2175
E-mail jgrinage@higher.nysed.gov
Jeanine L. Grinage, Acting Deputy Commissioner

North Carolina

Commission on Higher Education Facilities
UNC General Administration
910 Raleigh Rd., Box 2688
Chapel Hill 27515
(919) 962-4573
Fax (919) 962-0488
Dr. Roy Carroll, Senior Vice President

North Dakota

North Dakota University System
600 East Blvd., 10th Floor
Bismarck 58505
(701) 328-2960
Fax (701) 328-2961
E-mail lisaak@prairie.nodak.edu
Larry Isaak, Chancellor

Ohio

Board of Regents
30 E. Broad St., 36th floor
Columbus 43266
(614) 466-6000
Fax (614) 466-5866
E-mail chancell@summit.ohio.gov
Dr. Elaine H. Hairston, Chancellor

Oklahoma

State Regents for Higher Education
500 Education Building
Oklahoma City 73105
(405) 524-9120
Fax (405) 524-9235
E-mail hbrisch@osrhe.edu
Dr. Hans Brisch, Chancellor

Oregon
Office of Degree Authorization
255 Capitol Street NE, Suite 126
Salem 97310
(503) 378-3921, ext 26
Fax (503) 371-0908
E-mail david.young@state.or.us
David A. Young, Administrator

Pennsylvania
Department of Education
333 Market St., 12th Floor
Harrisburg 17126
(717) 787-5041
Fax (717) 783-5420
Barbara Senier, Acting Commissioner, Postsecondary
and Higher Education

Rhode Island
Office of Higher Education
301 Promenade St.
Providence 02908
(401) 277-6561
Fax (401) 277-2545
Dr. Stephen T. Hulbert, Commissioner

South Carolina
Commission on Higher Education
1333 Main St., Suite 200
Columbia 29201
(803) 737-2260
Fax (803) 737-2297
Fred R. Sheheen, Commissioner

South Dakota
Board of Regents
207 E. Capitol Ave.
Pierre 57501
(605) 773-3455
Fax (605) 773-5320
tadp@bor.state.sd
Robert T. Perry, Executive Director

Tennessee
Higher Education Commission
404 James Robertson Parkway
Suite 1900
Nashville 37243
(615) 741-3605
Fax (615) 741-6230
Dr. Bryant Millsaps, Executive Director

Texas
Higher Education Coordinating Board
P. O. Box 12788, Capitol Station
Austin 78711
(512) 483-6101
Fax (512) 483-6127
E-mail hansen@thecb.state.texas
Kenneth H. Ashworth, Commissioner

Utah
Utah System of Higher Education
355 West North Temple, Suite 550
Salt Lake City 84180
(801) 321-7103
Fax (801) 321-7199
E-mail cfoxley@utahsbr.edu
Dr. Cecelia H. Foxley, Commissioner

Vermont
Department of Education
Career and Lifelong Learning
120 State St.
Montpelier 05620
(802) 2828-3101
Fax (802) 828-3146
Gerard Asselin, Manager

Virginia
State Council of Higher Education
101 North 14th St., 9th Floor
Richmond 23219
(804) 225-2137
Fax (804) 225-2604
E-mail mcdowell@schev.edu
Dr. Gordon K. Davies, Director

Washington
Higher Education Coordinating Board
917 Lakeridge Way
Olympia 98504
(360) 753-7810
Fax (360) 753-7808
Marcus S. Gaspard, Executive Director

West Virginia
State College System
1018 Kanawha Blvd. East , Suite 700
Charleston 25301
(304) 558-0699
Fax (304) 558-1011
E-mail trump@scucso.wvnet.edu
Dr. Clifford M. Trump, Chancellor

Wisconsin
Higher Education Board
131 W. Wilson St., Room 902
Room 1720
Madison 53703
(608) 262-2208
Fax (608) 267-2808
Valorie T. Olson, Executive Secretary

Wyoming
Postsecondary Education Planning and
Coordinating Council
Office of the Governor
Cheyenne 82002
(307) 777-7763
Fax (307) 777-6567
E-mail thenry@antelope.wcc.edu
Dr. Thomas Henry, Executive Director, Community
College Commission

American Samoa
Board of Higher Education
P. O. Box 2609
Pago Pago 96799
(684) 699-9155
Dr. Eneliko Sofai, Executive Officer

Guam
Pacific Post-Secondary Education Council
P. O. Box 23067
G M F Guam 96921
(617) 734-2962
William A. Kinder, Executive Director

Puerto Rico
Council on Higher Education
P. O. Box 19900
San Juan 00910
(787) 724-7100
Fax (787) 725-1275
Sandra Espada Santos, Executive Secretary

Canada

Alberta
Department of Advanced Education
7th Floor, Commerce Place
10155-102 Street
Edmonton T5J 1X4
(403) 427-2781
Fax (403) 427-4185

British Columbia
Ministry of Skills, Training and Labour
Parliament Buildings
Room 109
Victoria V8V 1X4
(250) 387-1986
Fax (250) 387-3200

Manitoba
Department of Education and Training
Postsecondary Adult & Continuing Education Division
Legislative Building, 400 Broadway
Winnipeg R3C 0V8
(204) 945-2211
Fax (204) 945-8692

New Brunswick
Department of Advanced Education and Labour
P. O. Box 6000
470 York St.
Fredericton E3B 5H1
(506) 453-2597
Fax (506) 453-3038

Newfoundland
Department of Education
Postsecondary Education Division
Confederation Building
P. O. Box 8700
St. John's A1B 4J6
(709) 729-5097
Fax (709) 729-5896

Nova Scotia
Department of Education
P. O. Box 578
Station "M"
Halifax B3J 3S9
(902) 424-5605
Fax (902) 424-0159

Ontario
Ministry of Education and Training
900 Bay St.
6th Floor
Mowat Block
Toronto M7A 1L2
(416) 325-2929
Fax (416) 325-2934

Prince Edward Island
Department of Higher Education, Training and Adult
Learning
P. O. Box 2000
Charlottetown C1A 7N8
(902) 368-5988
Fax (902) 368-6144

Quebec
Ministère de l'ènseignement supérior et de la science
Direction des communications
1035 rue de La Chevrotière
Edifice Marie-Guyart
19e étage
Québec G1R 5K9
(418) 643-7095
Fax (418) 646-6561

Saskatchewan
Ministry of Education, Training and Employment
Post-Secondary and Adult Education
2220 College Ave.
Regina S4P 3V7
(306) 787-6030
Fax (306) 787-7392

Agencies Outside the U.S. & Canada

Australia
Department of Education
MLC Tower, Keltie St.
Phillip, ACT 2606
(062) 891333
Minister for Education

Belgium
Ministry of National Education
Centre Arts Lux, 4th and 5th Floors
58 Ave. des Arts, BP5
1040 Brussels
(02) 512-66-60
Minister of Education

Brazil
Ministry of Education and Culture
Esplanada dos Ministerios, Bloco L
74.047 Brasilia, DF
(061) 214-8432
Minister of Education

Bulgaria
Ministry of Education
Blvd. A, Stamboliski 18
Sofia 1000
84-81
Minister of Education

Cuba
Ministry of Higher Education
Calle 23y F, Vedado
Havana
3-6655
Minister of Education

Denmark
Ministry of Education
Federiksholms Kanal 21-25
1220 Copenhagen K.
(01) 92-50-00
Minister of Education

Egypt
Ministry of Education
Sharia El Fellaky
Cairo
(02) 27363
Minister of National Education

Finland
Ministry of Education, Science & Culture
Meritullinkatu 10
P.O. Box 293
00170
(358-9) 134171
First Minister of Education for Veterans' Education
and Proprietary Schools

France
Ministry of National Education
110 Rue De Grenelle
75700 Paris
(1) 45-50-10-10

Germany
Ministry of Education and Science
Heinemannstr. 2
5300 Bonn 2
(0228) 571
Minister of Education

Greece
Ministry of Education and Religion
Odos Mihalakopoulou 80
Athens
(21) 3230461; telex 216059
Minister of Education and Religion

Hungary
Ministry of Culture and National Education
Szalay u. 10/14
1055 Budapest
530-600
Minister of Culture and National Education

India
Ministry of Education
Shastri Bhavan, New Delhi 110011
(11) 3012380
Minister of Education

Indonesia
Ministry of Education and Culture
Jalan Jenderal Sudirman
Senayan
Jakarta Pusat
(021) 581618
Minister of Education and Culture

Ireland
Ministry of Education
Marlborough St.
Dublin 1
(01) 717101; telex 31136
Minister of Education

Israel
Ministry of Education and Culture
Hakirya, 14 Klausner St.
Tel Aviv
414155
Minister of Education

Italy

Ministry of Education
Viale Trastevere 76A
00100 Rome
Telex 4759841
Minister of Education

Japan

Ministry of Education
3-2, Kasumigaseki
Chiyoda–Ku
Tokyo
(3) 581-4211
Minister of Education

Mexico

Secretariat of State for Public Education Republica de
Argentina y Gonzales
Obregon 28, 06029 Mexico, DF
5103029
Secretary of Public Education

Netherlands

Ministry of Education and Science
Europaweg 4, POB 25000
2700 LZ Zoetermeer
(079) 531911; telex 32636
Minister of Education and Science

New Zealand

Department of Education
Private Bag Wellington
(04) 735499
Minister of Education

Norway

Ministry of Church and Education
POB 8119, Dep., 0520 1
Oslo
(2) 11-90-90
Minister of Church and Education

Philippines

Department of Education, Culture, and Sports
University of Life Complex
Meralco Avenue, Pasig City
632-13-61
Secretary

Portugal

Ministry of Education
Av. 5 de Outubro 107
1000 Lisbon
731291
Minister of Education and Culture

Republic of Korea (South Korea)

Ministry of Education
77-6 Sejong–no
Chongno–Ku, Seoul
720-3315; telex 24758
Minister of Education

South Africa

Ministry of National Education
Civitas BLDG, Struben St, Private Bag X114
Pretoria
282551
Minister of National Education

Spain

Ministerios de Educacion y Ciencia
Alcala 34, Madrid 14
2321300
Minister of Education and Science

Sweden

Ministry of Education and Cultural Affairs
Mynttorget 1, 103 33 Stockholm
(8) 736-10-00; telex 13284
Minister of Education and Cultural Affairs

Turkey

Ministry of Education, Youth, and Sports
Milli Egitim, Genclik ve Spor
Bakanligi, Ankara
(41) 231160

United Kingdom

Department of Education and Science
Elizabeth House, York Rd.
London SE1 7PH
(171) 928-9222; telex 23171
Secretary of State for Education and Science

7

School Licensing Laws:
State, Provincial, National, and International

Morality cannot be legislated, but behavior can be regulated.

MARTIN LUTHER KING, JR.

This chapter, more than any other, could benefit from almost a daily update, as both the laws themselves and the way they are interpreted, are in constant flux. We start with the reminder that we are not lawyers (even if John did buy a $58 Harvard law degree by mail). If you have any question about whether a given school operates legally, whether its degree will meet your needs, or indeed how to start a school, you would be well advised to seek competent legal counsel.

Six Reasons Why This Chapter Is So Complicated

1. There are so many jurisdictions
Consider a university that uses a mailing address in a Caribbean country, actually operates from Europe, and has an office in the United States. And consider a potential student who seeks a degree in psychology, wishing to become a marriage counselor. Who's in charge here? The state or province where the student lives? (Each of the 50 U.S. states has its own school and licensing laws, as do the Canadian provinces and most other political subdivisions.) The psychology licensing board? (Again, each jurisdiction is different; some do not require any degree at all; others require a doctorate.) The accrediting agency? (But in the U.S. alone, there are a number of regional, national, and professional accreditors.) The national government? (But of which country? Or is it more than one?) Some international agency (or agencies)?

2. Laws change and interpretations change
What keeps many lawyers and judges in business is interpreting, reinterpreting, and challenging the law. And what keeps many politicians and bureaucrats occupied is writing, rewriting, and changing laws. Marijuana used to be legal. Birth control used to be illegal. In Florida, it was legal to use an unaccredited degree in public ways (as on a business card or in advertising). Then the court determined that it was illegal. Following a challenge, the state Supreme Court overturned the lower court ruling and made it legal. And now the legislature is considering new laws to make it illegal

3. Legality varies from one location to another
People are more mobile than ever before. A child therapist with an unaccredited California degree can probably take the state licensing exam in Colorado but not in Wyoming. A practicing lawyer with an unaccredited Virginia law degree may be able to take the Bar exam in New York, but not in Ohio. What about engineers from Kazakhstan who want to be licensed in Ontario? Accountants from Hong Kong who want to practice in Oregon? Linguists from Illinois who want to teach in Korea?

There are hundreds of states, provinces, and countries, and dozens of fields of study that are regulated in some, most, or all places. The regulation can come from any number of governmental, quasi-governmental, independent, or trade organizations, who do not always agree with one another.

4. It's not clear who has jurisdiction
When the school itself has a presence (or an apparent presence) in more than one location, the issue grows even more complex, for both acceptance of a credential, and for regulation of the school itself. The fraudulent Columbia State University, for instance, managed to exist for more than ten years because the attorney general of Louisiana was saying, in effect, "We know they're really in California, so it's not my business," while the California attorney general was saying, "They're using a Louisiana mailing address and telephone number, so it's not my business." Such operations fall

through the cracks, until finally some federal agency, which operates across state lines (typically the FBI, the Postal Service, the Federal Trade Commission, and/or the Internal Revenue Service) finally takes action.

5. It is not always easy to get information

In fact, sometimes it is downright impossible. It seems odd to us, still, that a reference book such as this one should have to say, "We aren't sure," or "We don't know." But when we have done all the library and Internet research we can, can't find certain information, and then dozens of letters and telephone calls and faxes to what may be the relevant agency go unanswered, short of staging a hunger strike in their lobby, what is one to do?

As one example out of many, we have been trying for more than seven years to get a copy of a U.S. Department of Education publication that lists all the schools that qualify for federal aid programs. We got a copy in 1991 when the person at a wrong number we reached in Washington took pity on us and sent us her personal copy. We write. We call. We fax. We spend hours in voice mail hell. We even attempted to enlist the aid of our congressperson, all to no avail.

6. People in power don't know, won't tell, or get it wrong

On more than a few occasions, we discover that the "right person" (or office) either doesn't know, won't tell us, or tells us something wrong. Again, if this sort of thing happened rarely, and only at obscure ministries in tiny or remote countries, it might be predicted and acceptable. But it happens over and over, in California, in London, and in Ottawa as well as in St. Kitts, in Costa Rica, and in Liberia. Sometimes they don't know (as in the case of a state Department of Education official who wrote to us that a 20-year-old state-approved university "is not known to the State of California. Perhaps they went out of business years ago"). Sometimes it is the people who, in earlier years, probably admired the Emperor's new clothes. It was an officer in the Department of Education and Science in Great Britain who wrote to us that "No unlicensed or unrecognised universities operate now from Britain." When we replied asking about Knightsbridge University, Somerset University, Greenwich University, Warnborough, Metropolitan, Trinity, Sussex, Brantridge, and half a dozen others, we received no answer, despite three requests.

There are, of course, many exceptions: caring, helpful, knowledgeable officials, who are helpful to us, and to members of the general public who call, write, fax, or e-mail for information.

• • • • •

Having said all that, here is the situation as best we can determine. Things used to be relatively stable. Some U.S. states militantly forbade any nontraditional schools or

programs, others allowed anyone to do anything, and most were somewhere in between. When there was a change in a state law or its interpretation, one could almost see the flow of schools from Place 1 to Place 2, and the arising of new schools in Place 2. From California to Arizona, then Arizona to Louisiana, then Louisiana to Hawaii and Iowa, with lesser ventures into Idaho, New Mexico, Wyoming, and South Dakota.

Obviously we cannot cover the situation with regard to every country, state, and province and with respect to all the various fields of study requiring licensing or certification. Here is the situation in the states with the greatest number of nontraditional schools, both good and bad, and in some of the countries where there exist other than 'official' state run or state funded institutions.

USA

Alabama

For many years, Alabama has had a school licensing law. It doesn't have much power. There is no evaluation; no visit by the state is required. The "campus" can be a post office box or secretarial service. Indeed, some Alabama universities are, in fact, run from Louisiana, Rhode Island, California, and other locations. The situation has been, for years, complicated by the fact that four universities operated by Dr. Lloyd Clayton from Birmingham (Chadwick, American Institute of Computer Science, and two health and nutrition schools) did not even have the most minimal state license, yet they clearly operated with the knowledge and, it seemed, permission of the state. They did not, however, accept students living in the state of Alabama. The schools' position was that this was simply their policy. It took us nearly five years of writing letters, sending faxes, and making telephone calls before we finally learned the truth. It seems that in the 1980s, the then-Attorney General of Alabama issued a ruling that schools that did not do business in the state of Alabama did not need to be licensed by the state.

In mid 1996, however, this all changed. In response to a request from the Department of Education, the current Attorney General ruled that all institutions based in the state *must* be licensed by the state, regardless of their policy for accepting instate students. Nearly two years later, Chadwick and the others finally got their license to operate.

California

Well, at least California is unfailingly interesting. For many years, until the late 1980s, California was the laughingstock of the nation (a mantle subsequently assumed by Louisiana, and then by the current holder, Hawaii). State authorization required little more than a short disclosure form, and evidence of $50,000 in assets. Shady operators were declaring that their homes were their universities, or buying a bundle of obsolete textbooks and declaring that they were worth $100 each. At the time diploma mill operator Ernest Sinclair went to federal prison for mail fraud (selling degrees), his California Pacifica University was still a state-authorized institution.

For a few years, the state had a three-tiered system: authorized (the $50,000 rule) for entire schools, state approved (for specific programs within schools), or accredited. The authorized category was dropped, and approval was extended to entire schools, resulting in the current two-tier system. At that time, dozens of schools closed down, and some of the big ones opened offices in other states: Kennedy-Western in Idaho (later Wyoming), Century in New Mexico, Pacific Western in Louisiana (later Hawaii), etc.

State approval used to be granted by the Department of Education, through the Council on Private Postsecondary and Vocational Education. Then things got really silly.

In 1992, California's Superintendent of Public Instruction was indicted, and in 1993 convicted of several counts of felony conflict of interest and removed from office. For three years, the state had no Superintendent, and things went somewhat adrift.

California has a "sunset" law, which decrees that state commissions automatically go out of business unless they are renewed by the legislature. Normally this is a routine rubber-stamp process. However in 1996, after the legislature had voted to continue the Council on Private Postsecondary and Vocational Education for another five years, Governor Wilson surprised many people, by vetoing the bill, declaring that the Council was not doing a good job, and should be replaced by something better. In the eight months between the veto and the expiration date, there was much bickering, but no solution. With a few days to go, it looked as if California would be without a school regulatory agency. The federal government suggested that such a situation could have a serious effect on student loans and other federal programs.

On the last possible day (June 30, 1997), the legislature extended the life of the Council for a generous eighteen days, and then the politicians got serious. On the 18th day, a compromise was reached: the Council on Private Postsecondary and Vocational Education would die on the last day of 1997, to be replaced by the Bureau of Private Postsecondary and Vocational Education, which would move from the Department of Education to the Department of Consumer Affairs. And thus it came to pass that California has become the only state in the country, perhaps the only government in the world, in which school licensing and regulation does not take place in the Department of Education.

It will probably take several years, at least, before it becomes clear how the Bureau will differ from the Council. One of the indicators will be the kinds of new schools that are approved, and the nature of that process. But at press time, we were told there was a backlog of more than 100 applicants, and the Bureau was both underfunded and understaffed. Another indicator will be how the process of renewal is handled. The Council had gotten unexpectedly tough on renewals in its final years, denying them to some major players in the state: Kensington, Pacific Western, and Columbia Pacific. (Kensington appealed but lost, and now uses a Hawaii address. Pacific Western also uses a Hawaii address for all but one of its programs. But both schools continue to be operated from California, a measure of how little power the state seems to have. Columbia Pacific also lost its appeal, but continues to operate from its California building. See their listing in this book for details.)

Another confusion in California is that the state senate decreed that holders of approved degrees should be permitted to take relevant state licensing exams, such as those in marriage, family, and child counseling. But the state board of professional licensing refused to go along with this automatic permission, saying that the standards for approval and the standards for certain exams were not at all the same. They now permit degree-holders from some schools, but not others, to take the exams. And almost no other state will accept California-approved degrees for state licensing purposes. Be sure to check on these matters if state licensing is part of your goal.

Florida

Florida is a classic case of what can happen when legislation gets out of hand. A 1988 Florida statute (Sections 817.566 and .567, Florida Statutes, 1988 Supplement) made it a crime to use an unaccredited degree in any way in that state, even if it is from a school approved or licensed in another state. It was a "misdemeanor of the first degree" [sic] for a person with, say, a California-approved or a Minnesota-approved degree, to reveal, within the boundaries of Florida, that he or she has that degree.

This rather extraordinary statute was challenged in court, and in July 1995, the State Supreme Court found it to be unconstitutional. However, the judge strongly suggested that if the legislature were to rewrite the law a bit more carefully, it could achieve the same intent and be within the bounds of the constitution. So at the present time, it would appear that holders of legitimate degrees from other states can use them in Florida, but it is clear the situation is far from over. Indeed the legislature is once again considering a strong school licensing law.

Hawaii

Until recently, Hawaii did not regulate any institutions of higher education at all. In 1990, a law was passed requiring the state Department of Consumer Affairs to register all unaccredited schools in the state. Eight years later, the department had not yet managed to produce the simple, but necessary, forms for schools to fill out, thus thwarting the will and intent of the legislature. Small wonder that Hawaii now has more unaccredited and highly questionable "universities" than the other forty-nine states combined. When Edward Reddeck, one of America's most notorious degree mill operators, moved his fake schools to the state of Hawaii, neither the state's attorney general nor the Department of Consumer Affairs showed any interest, nor did the education editor of Honolulu's major newspaper (who declined to run a story on this situation, stating, "Our job is to *report* news, not *make* news"). Fortunately, in this instance, federal authorities *did* care, and those phony schools were closed by the action of postal inspectors. *Then* the newspaper ran a big page-one story!

But that was just one phony. As other states grow tougher and tougher in their regulation of unaccredited schools, Hawaii increasingly has become the preferred destination. By 1998, more than fifty "universities" were operating with Hawaii addresses, the great majority of them from mailbox rental stores or secretarial services, while their owners run things from California, Texas, New York, Pennsylvania, Michigan, Ohio, and elsewhere.

Despite urgent warnings from some educators in the state that Hawaii was fast becoming known as the "state of last resort" for the unaccredited schools of America, authorities in the state have shown no interest in enforcing the existing legislation, with the lone exception of a modest consumer law, which requires unaccredited schools to state that fact in their literature in boldface type. Since the law doesn't specify the *size* of such type, you can imagine what some schools do.

In 1998, the state's Department of Consumer Affairs exercised a little muscle for the first time, with lawsuits for violation of the disclosure law, against American State University and Pacific Western University. And every year, the state legislature seems to get closer and closer to enacting a meaningful school licensing or regulating law. Some important politicians in the state have vowed that they will keep the pressure on until Hawaii has a meaningful school regulating law. It remains to be seen.

Iowa

Iowa is another state very much in transition. Until 1995, it not only had a somewhat misleading school licensing law, but it also seemed extremely lax in enforcing what little law they had. Registration with the state was virtually automatic, but only gave schools permission to offer classes in Iowa. It did not authorize them to award degrees or to claim they were an Iowa-licensed school. Nonetheless, at least half a dozen schools did just that.

In 1995, the legislature attempted to address this situation by requiring all unaccredited schools to be on an approved "accreditation track," or leave the state: the so called "up or out" provision. But three years later, nothing seemed to have changed, with some of Iowa's wonders still operating without benefit of accreditation or any motion toward it.

We finally learned, thanks to a persistent reader of this book, that the Department of Education felt that it was too much to expect a school to get on an accreditation track quickly, and so they quietly gave the Iowa unaccredited schools three years to get on track: an extension expiring in 1998. At least three of the Iowa schools have now applied for accreditation from the Distance Education and Training Council, thus presumably buying more time from the state, even more if the process is delayed or deferred. It remains to be seen how Iowa will ultimately enforce its legislation.

Louisiana

For many years, Louisiana has been the victim of what one highly-placed state regulator privately calls the "Woody Jenkins law." Jenkins is the prominent Republican politician who is so opposed to the state regulation of almost *any-thing* that even though he graduated from law school with highest honors, he has refused to take the Bar exam, believing that the state has no right to require such of lawyers.

Under Jenkins' influence, the legislature required that Louisiana's Board of Regents register any school that filled out a short form, with no evaluation whatsoever. This permitted some completely phony schools to advertise that they were "Appropriately registered with the Board of Regents," or even (improperly) that they were "Recognized by the Board of Regents."

In 1991, Louisiana passed a new law, which gave the Board of Regents power to regulate proprietary (privately owned) schools, although nonprofit schools were still exempt. In 1992, the Board of Regents decided that only proprietary schools with an actual physical presence in the state could be registered. Since dozens of "Louisiana" schools operate either from mail forwarding services or "executive suite" office-rental-by-the-hour establishments, quite a few schools using Louisiana addresses moved their addresses elsewhere, mostly to Iowa or Hawaii. More than 20 closed down.

Some people in Louisiana are saying that Woody Jenkins's power has significantly diminished following his loss in his run for the U.S. Senate, and that this means there may be a chance to get a law that will let the regents and the attorney general deal with those fraudulent not-for-profit schools that ostensibly operate from within Louisiana but, in fact, have nothing more than a convenience address and telephone answering service there. The fact that the biggest totally fake "university" in the United States, as of 1998, Columbia State University, operated as a not-for-profit Louisiana school (its actual office is in California) for ten years before the state finally acted, is a clear indication of the work still to be done.

There is one more loophole in Louisiana, one that would be amusing if it hadn't been used to take advantage of people. As in many states, religious schools are exempt from licensing as long as they only award religious degrees.

But there are Louisiana schools *all* of whose degrees, even their Ph.D.'s in physics or political science, are self-determined to be "religious" degrees, because, they argue, God created everything, including atoms and politicians, so no matter what you study, you are studying the work of God. The Louisiana courts agreed with this argument, and the religious schools in the state, including those that don't make clear they are church-run, or that they are run by churches established by the proprietors of the schools, continue to award "religious" degrees in chemistry, business administration, psychology, and the like. That the Federal government does not necessarily agree with this argument was made clear in the combined FBI-IRS-Postal Inspectors raid on La Salle University in 1996, and subsequent imprisonment of its president and founder. La Salle had been operated by a church established by said founder. (La Salle is now under new ownership, and no longer makes use of a religious exemption.)

The Rest of the United States

Often, legislation arises in response to behavior. If legislators don't like the behavior, they pass laws against it. Commonly, it is only after unaccredited schools (good, bad, or in between) become so numerous or so visible they cannot be ignored that states consider and even pass legislation to restrict or regulate them. Sometimes legislators are jarred into action by a responsibly-behaving press. At a time when Arizona was the U.S. center for sleazy schools, the Arizona *Republic* newspaper ran a four-day page-one series headlined, "Diploma Mills: A Festering Sore on the State of Arizona." Within weeks, legislation was introduced to deal with these "schools."

For some years, New Mexico had only one visible unaccredited school, Century University. But after the number reached two, then three, then four, with other schools looking in that direction and writing to the state agency in Santa Fe for information, New Mexico's Commission on Higher Education issued "Rule 730," a 21-page set of rules and guidelines for proprietary schools which either operate within the state, or recruit citizens of New Mexico from outside the state. This rule took effect on July 1, 1994, and makes it harder to operate an unaccredited school in that state.

Clearly the operators of unaccredited schools are shopping around, perhaps against the day when Hawaii changes. At least once a month, we hear from the proprietor of one school or another, looking for advice on where he might move. One by one, the sparsely-populated western states are being tried, with varying degrees of acceptance. Idaho

was not thrilled about the California school that moved there. Wyoming, which seems not to worry too much about what schools are like as long as they have an actual physical presence in the state, has attracted half a dozen. South Dakota recently got its first. And so it goes. We should mention here that we also hear from the education departments of various states, who want us to be sure not to encourage any schools to move in on their territory.

Unless and until there is more international cooperation, it may be that schools will be run like puppets: operators in one country pulling the strings that make the school work in another country. As an example, two of the apparently-large "Louisiana" universities (Fairfax and Somerset) are actually operated by men living in England who apparently do not often come to the U.S. Even the mail goes to England. But England apparently looks on them as "American" schools and doesn't try to regulate them. And the U.S. may consider them to be British schools, since they have neither offices nor personnel, only convenience addresses, in the U.S.

The Rest of the World

This is an evolving section, which may, one day, include both the laws and the actual practices of school licensing, in countries worldwide. This is no simple matter, in part because of the difficulty of getting information, and in part because some smaller countries are just not prepared to deal with the matter of newly appearing universities in their territory. A few years ago, no one would have predicted, for instance, that the tiny island nation of St. Kitts and Nevis, with no degree-granting institutions of its own, would be home to four international universities (which happen to be run from the U.S., England, and Australia). Surely not the Minister of Youth, Education, and Community Affairs, who issues Certificates of Accreditation with, it seems, no semblance of an evaluation process (and has never responded to our letters and faxes).

Thankfully, the United Nations has addressed this issue, and makes the process of determining the legitimacy of schools relatively straightforward, at least as far as many registrars, admissions officers, and other evaluators are concerned. The International Handbook of Universities, published annually by UNESCO, is the generally accepted arbiter in most places. If a university in Singapore or St. Kitts, Barbados or Bangladesh, appears in that book, then it is safe to assume that it has the appropriate licensing in its home location. If it is not in the book, it still might be OK, but more due diligence is suggested.

8

Accreditation

The comfortable world of accreditation seems to be unraveling.

OPENING SENTENCE, CHRONICLE OF HIGHER EDUCATION ARTICLE ON
THE STATE OF ACCREDITATION, 1993

The accreditation community is in the early stages of addressing [the] challenge . . . of distance learning.

COUNCIL ON HIGHER EDUCATION ACCREDITATION
QUALITY ASSURANCE AND DISTANCE EDUCATION CONFERENCE, 1998

ACCREDITATION "LITE"

*(This is a complex chapter. If you read
nothing else, read this small section.)*

1. Generally, you can't go wrong by choosing a school accredited by a recognized accrediting agency.

2. There are some legitimate and useful unaccredited schools.

3. There are a very few legitimate but unrecognized accrediting agencies.

4. There are a great many phony accrediting agencies.

5. The world of accreditation is slowly changing, generally in the direction of dealing more with outcomes: how schools teach or train their students and how well the students perform.

ACCREDITATION "REGULAR"

Accreditation is perhaps the most complex, confusing, and important issue in higher education. It is surely the most misunderstood and the most misused concept—both intentionally and unintentionally.

In selecting a school, there are four important things to know about accreditation:

1. What it is;

2. Why it is important in certain situations;

3. What are the many kinds of accreditors, and

4. What's all the fuss and bother that led to those two quotations at the top of this chapter?

We will address these matters more or less in this order.

WHAT IS ACCREDITATION?

Quite simply, it is a validation—a statement by a group of persons who are, theoretically, impartial experts in higher education, that a given school, or department within a school, has been thoroughly investigated and found worthy of approval.

Accreditation is a peculiarly American concept. In every other country in the world, all colleges and universities either are operated by the government, or gain the full right to grant degrees directly from the government, so there is no need for a separate, independent agency to say that a given school is OK.

In the United States, accreditation is an *entirely voluntary process*, done by private, nongovernmental agencies. As a result of this lack of central control or authority, there have evolved good accrediting agencies and bad ones, recognized ones and unrecognized ones, legitimate ones and phony ones.

So when a school says, "we are accredited," that statement alone means nothing. You must always ask, "Accredited by whom?" Unfortunately, many consumer-oriented articles and bulletins simply say that one is much safer dealing only with accredited schools, but they do not attempt to unravel the complex situation. We hear regularly from distressed people who say, about the degrees they have just learned are worthless, "But the school was accredited; I even checked with the accrediting agency." The agency, needless to say, turned out to be as phony as the school. The wrong kind of accreditation can be worse than none at all.

Normally, a school wishing to be accredited will make application to the appropriate accrediting agency. After a substantial preliminary investigation to determine that the school is probably operating legally and run legitimately, it may be granted correspondent or provisional status. Typically this step will take anywhere from several months to several years or more, and when completed does not imply any kind of endorsement or recommendation, but is merely an indication that the first steps on a long path have been taken.

Next, teams from the accrediting agency, often composed of faculty of already accredited institutions, will visit the school. These "visitations," conducted at regular intervals throughout the year, are to observe the school in action, and to study the copious amounts of information that the school must prepare, relating to its legal and academic structure, educational philosophy, curriculum, financial status, planning, and so forth.

After these investigations and, normally, following at least two years of successful operation (sometimes a great deal more), the school may be advanced to the status of "candidate for accreditation." Being a candidate means, in effect, "Yes, you are probably worthy of accreditation, but we want to watch your operation for a while longer."

This "while" can range from a year or two to six years or more. The great majority of schools that reach candidacy status eventually achieve full accreditation. Some accreditors do not have a candidacy status; with them it is an all-or-nothing situation. (The terms "accredited" and "fully accredited" are used interchangeably. There is no such thing as "partly accredited.")

Once a school is accredited, it is visited by inspection teams at infrequent intervals (every five to ten years is common) to see if it is still worthy of its accreditation. The status is always subject to review at any time, should new programs be developed or should there be any significant new developments, positive or negative.

Note: Everything in the foregoing section applies to accreditation as done by recognized agencies. Many of the other agencies, even those that are not illegal, will typically accredit a new school within days, even minutes, of its coming into existence.

THE IMPORTANCE OF ACCREDITATION

Although accreditation is undeniably important to both schools and students (and would-be students), this importance is undermined and confused by these three factors:

1. There are no significant national standards for accreditation. What is accreditable in New York may not be accreditable in California, and vice versa. The demands and standards of the group that accredits schools of chemistry may be very different from the people who accredit schools of forestry. And so on.

2. Some decent schools (or departments within schools) are not accredited, either by their own choice (since accreditation is a totally voluntary and often very expensive procedure), or because they are too new (all schools were unaccredited at one time in their lives) or too experimental (some would say too innovative) for the generally conservative accreditors.

3. Many very bad schools claim to be accredited—but it is always by unrecognized, sometimes nonexistent accrediting associations, often of their own creation.

Still, accreditation is the only widespread system of school evaluation that we have. A school's accreditation status can be helpful to the potential student in this way: while some good schools are not accredited, it is very unlikely that any very bad or illegal school is authentically accredited. (There have been exceptions, but they are quite rare.)

In other words, *authentic* accreditation is a pretty good sign that a given school is legitimate. But it is important to remember that *lack of accreditation need not mean that a school is either inferior or illegal.* Authentic accreditation is based on performance, not proposed performance.

We stress the term *authentic* accreditation, since there are very few laws or regulations anywhere governing the establishment of an accrediting association. Anyone can start a degree mill, then turn around and open an accrediting agency next door, give his school its blessing, and begin advertising "fully accredited degrees." Indeed, this has happened many times.

The crucial question, then, is this: Who accredits the accreditors?

WHO ACCREDITS THE ACCREDITORS?

The situation is confusing , unsettled, and still undergoing change and redefinition for the third millennium. To get some sort of a handle on the situation, it will be helpful to have a bit of a historical perspective. In this instance, it makes some sense to begin in 1980, when the Republican party platform echoed Ronald Reagan's belief that the Department of Education should be closed down, since it was inappropriate for the federal government to meddle in matters better left to the states and to private enterprise.

At that time, there were two agencies, one private and one governmental, that had responsibility for evaluating and approving or recognizing accrediting agencies:

1. The U.S. Department of Education's Eligibility and Agency Evaluation Staff (EAES), which is required by law to "publish a list of nationally recognized accrediting agencies which [are determined] to be reliable ... as to the quality of training offered." This is done as one measure of eligibility for federal financial aid programs for students. EAES also had the job of deciding whether unaccredited schools could qualify for federal aid programs, or their students for veterans' benefits. This was done primarily by what was called the "four-by-three" rule: Proof that credits from at least four students were accepted by at least three accredited schools (12 total acceptances). If they were, then the unaccredited school was recognized by the Department of Education for that pur-

pose. Schools qualifying under the four-by-three rule had to submit evidence of continued acceptance of their credits by accredited schools in order to maintain their status.

2. COPA, the Council on Postsecondary Accreditation. COPA was a nationwide nonprofit corporation, formed in 1975 to evaluate accrediting associations and award recognition to those found worthy.

President Reagan was unable to dismantle the Department of Education during his administration, although key people in the department strongly suggested that they should get out of the business of recognizing accrediting agencies, and leave that to the states. "Education President" Bush apparently did not share this view; at least no significant changes were made during his administration.

One of the frequent complaints levied against the recognized accrediting agencies (and not just by Republicans) is that they have, in general, been slow to acknowledge the major trend toward alternative or nontraditional education.

Some years ago, the Carnegie Commission on Higher Education conducted research on the relationship between accreditation and nontraditional approaches. Their report, written by Alexander Mood, confirmed that a serious disadvantage of accreditation is "in the suppression of innovation. Schools cannot get far out of line without risking loss of their accreditation—a penalty which they cannot afford." "Also," the report continued, "loss of accreditation implies that the curriculum is somewhat inferior and hence that the degree is inferior. Such a large penalty . . . tends to prevent colleges from striking out in new directions. . . As we look toward the future, it appears likely that accrediting organizations will lose their usefulness and slowly disappear. Colleges will be judged not by what some educational bureaucracy declares but by what they can do for their students. Of much greater relevance would be statistics on student satisfaction, career advancement of graduates, and other such data."

Faced with high-powered criticism of this sort, some accrediting agencies sponsored (with a major grant from the Kellogg Foundation) a large-scale study of how the agencies should deal with nontraditional education.

The four-volume report of the findings of this investigation said very much what the Carnegie report had to say. The accreditors were advised, in effect, not to look at the easy quantitative factors (percentage of Doctorate-holders on the faculty, books in the library, student-faculty ratio, acres of campus, etc.), but rather to evaluate the far more elusive qualitative factors, of which student satisfaction and student performance are the most crucial.

In other words, if the students at a nontraditional, nonresident university regularly produce research and dissertations that are as good as those produced at traditional schools, or if graduates of nontraditional schools are as likely to gain admission to graduate school or high-level employment and perform satisfactorily there—then the nontra-

ditional school may be just as worthy of accreditation as the traditional school.

The response of the accrediting agencies was pretty much to say, "But we already are doing just those things. No changes are needed."

But, with the Carnegie and Kellogg reports, the handwriting was on the wall, if still in small and hard-to-read letters. Things would be changing, however.

In 1987, then Secretary of Education William Bennett (later to become "Drug Czar," and then a bestselling author-philosopher) voiced similar complaints about the failure of accrediting agencies to deal with matters such as student competency and satisfaction. "Historically," he said, "accrediting agencies have examined institutions in terms of the resources they have, such as the number of faculty with earned Doctorates and the number of books in the library. Now [we] are considering the ways agencies take account of student achievement and development."

In 1990, Bennett's successor, Lauro F. Cavazos, while splitting an infinitive or two, said almost exactly the same thing: "Despite increasing evidence that many of our schools are failing to adequately prepare our children, either for further study or for productive careers, the accreditation process still focuses on inputs, such as the number of volumes in libraries or percentage of faculty with appropriate training. It does not examine outcomes—how much students learn."

Around the same time, John W. Harris, chairman of the National Advisory Committee on Accreditation, echoed these concerns: "It is not enough to know that teachers have certain degrees and that students have spent so much time in the classroom. The question is, can institutions document the achievement of students for the degrees awarded?"

The accrediting agencies continued to assure us that they *do* deal with such matters.

In 1992, Secretary of Education Lamar Alexander went further still, issuing an open invitation for new accrediting agencies to come forward and seek his department's blessing, strongly implying that the existing ones were not doing a satisfactory job. And around the same time, high administrators at at least three major universities seriously questioned whether accreditation was necessary for their school. "Why should we spend upwards of $100,000 in staff time and real money to prepare a self-study for the accreditors?" said one administrator. "It is quite likely that the University of Wisconsin would still be taken seriously even if it did not have accreditation."

In 1992, Secretary Alexander flung down an unignorable gauntlet by denying the usual "automatic" reapproval of the powerful Middle States Accrediting Association, because he maintained that their standards for accreditation did not meet the department's. (Middle States had previously denied reaccreditation to a major school because it did not meet certain standards of diversity, including "appropriate" numbers of minority students and faculty. Alexander suggested that Middle States was paying attention to the wrong things. Middle States finally backed down, and made its diversity standards optional.)

When Bill Clinton took office in 1993, the accreditation situation was no less murky, and his choice for Secretary of Education, Richard Riley of South Carolina, seemed more interested in primary and secondary education than in postsecondary. Into this already murky area came two bombshells.

Bombshell #1: First, in 1993, the six regional accrediting associations, claiming that "the concept of self-regulation as embodied in regional accreditation is being seriously questioned and potentially threatened," announced that they planned to drop out of the Council on Postsecondary Accreditation, and start their own new group to represent them in Washington. The *Chronicle of Higher Education* reported that "some higher-education observers said they questioned the significance of the action [while] others called it disturbing." The president of the American Council on Education said that "Their pulling out is tantamount to the destruction of COPA."

Bombshell #2: He was right. In April 1993, at their annual meeting in San Francisco, COPA voted itself out of existence as of year-end, by a vote of 14 to two, one abstention. One board member, C. Peter Magrath, president of the National Association of State Universities and Land-Grant Colleges, said that he thought COPA "focused too much on the minutiae of accreditation and not enough on the big issues of improving the quality of undergraduate education."

And so, in April 1993, things were indeed unsettled. The six regional associations were apparently planning to start a new organization to govern themselves, without the participation of the dozens of professional accreditors who were part of COPA. COPA was going about its business, but planning to turn off the lights and shut the door by the end of 1993. And the Clinton Department of Education was busily drawing up proposals that would turn the world of accreditation and school licensing on its ear.

The early thrust of the Clinton/Riley thinking echoed much that had been discussed during the Bush/Bennett/Cavazos/Alexander era: giving increased power to the states to decide what can and cannot be done in the way of higher education within their borders. The big stick wielded by the federal folks, of course, was student aid: loans and grants. The prospect of each state having different standards by which a student could get a Pell Grant, for instance, was daunting.

Around this time, Ralph A. Wolff, an executive with one of the regional accrediting associations, wrote an important 'think piece' for the influential *Chronicle of Higher Education*: "Restoring the Credibility of Accreditation." (June 9, 1993, page B1) Wolff wrote that

> We have constructed a Potemkin Village in which there is less behind the façade of accreditation than we might like to acknowledge. . . . The accreditation process has

not held colleges and universities accountable for issues such as the writing ability of graduates or the effectiveness of general-education requirements... If accreditation is to regain some of its lost credibility, everyone involved in the process needs to refocus on standards and criteria for demonstrating educational effectiveness. Even the most prestigious institutions will need to address how much students are learning and the quality of student life at the institution.

Right around the time Wolff was writing, the Department of Education was sending out a limited number of "secret" (not for publication or circulation) drafts of its proposed new regulations. And the six regional accreditors apparently rose up as one to say, in effect, "Hey, wait a minute. You, the feds, are telling us how to run our agencies, and we don't like that."

For instance, the draft regulations would have required accreditors to look at the length of various programs, and their cost vis-a-vis the subject being taught.

A response by James T. Rogers, head of the college division of the Southern Association (a regional accreditor) was typical:

> If final regulations follow the pattern in this latest draft, the Department of Education will have co-opted, in very profound ways, members of the private, voluntary accrediting community to serve as enforcement for the department. . . . This is an extremely disturbing abdication of the department's responsibility to police its own operation.

The *Chronicle* reported (August 4, 1993) that "many of the accrediting groups have sent notices to their member colleges urging them to be prepared to battle the department if the draft is not significantly altered."

And David Longanecker, Assistant Secretary for postsecondary education, was quoted in the *Chronicle* as saying "Many people in higher education say 'You can't measure what it is that we do, It's too valuable.' I don't buy that, and I don't think most people in America buy that today, either."

The battle lines were drawn or, as the more polite *Chronicle* put it on August 11, 1993, "Accreditors and the Education Department [are] locked in a philosophical disagreement over the role of accreditation." At this point, the six regional accreditors announced they would be joining with seven higher-education groups to form an organization to represent their interests in Washington. This lobbying group was to be called the National Policy Board on Higher Education Institutional Accreditation, or NPB-HEIA. And various subsets of the by-now lame duck COPA were making plans to start as many as three replacement organizations to take over some or most or all of COPA's functions.

During the rest of 1993, the Department of Education was busily rewriting its accreditation guidelines, taking into account the unexpectedly fierce "leave us alone" response from the regional and professional accreditors. Meanwhile,

Congress, not wishing to be left out of the mix entirely, passed, on November 23, 1993, the Higher Education Technical Amendments of 1993, which, among much, much else, decreed that the Department of Education was to cause each of the 50 states to establish a new State post-secondary review "entity" (SPRE) to evaluate schools within each state, both for compliance with various federal aid programs and, unexpectedly, to evaluate those colleges and universities that have "been subject to a pattern of complaints from students, faculty, or others, including...misleading or inappropriate advertising and promotion of the institution's educational programs...." If that wasn't an invitation for the states to go into the accreditation business, it was certainly in that direction.

Good-bye COPA, Hello CORPA

And while this was going on, the COPA-ending clock was ticking away. Ten days before COPA was to disappear forever, the formation of a single new entity to replace it was announced. COPA was to be replaced with (small fanfare, please) CORPA, the Commission on Recognition of Postsecondary Accreditation. All members of COPA were automatically recognized by CORPA. All COPA provisions for recognition of schools were adopted by CORPA, with the understanding that they might be refined and modified over time. And CORPA's initial Committee on Recognition was composed of the members of COPA's Committee on Recognition. All of this appears to be the academic equivalent of saying that The Odyssey was not written by Homer, but by another Greek with the same name. The only apparent difference between COPA and CORPA is the addition of the "R" and the fact that the six regionals were no longer members.

The Department of Education's guidelines were finally published in the Federal Register on January 24, 1994: 24 small-type pages on accreditors, and 20 more on the establishing SPREs, the State Postsecondary Review Entities. Once the regulations were published, the public and the higher education establishment had 45 days in which to respond. And respond they did. The headline in the next week's *Chronicle of Higher Education* read: "Accreditors Fight Back."

It turned out that the six regional accreditors, the American Council on Education, and other groups had been meeting privately in Arizona to formulate a battle plan. They considered abandoning the regional approach entirely, in favor of a single national accreditor, but scrapped that in favor of four still-quite-radical ideas (among others):

1. Establishment of minimum uniform national standards for accreditation;

2. Setting of higher standards for schools, focusing on teaching and learning (what a novel concept!);

3. Making public their reports on individual colleges and schools; and

4. Moving toward ceasing to cooperate with the federal government in certifying the eligibility of colleges for federal financial aid.

During the 45-day response period following publishing of the draft guidelines, hundreds of long and serious responses were received from college and university presidents opposing some, most, or all of the regulations that had been proposed by the Department of Education.

The issue of diversity and political correctness in accreditation remained just as controversial as before. While the Western Association (a regional accreditor) for instance, believes that academic quality and ethnic diversity are "profoundly connected," many colleges, large and small, apparently agree with Stanford president Gerhard Casper, who said, "No institution should be required to demonstrate its commitment to diversity to the satisfaction of an external review panel. The [Western Association] is attempting to insert itself in an area in which it has no legitimate standing." Other schools, including the University of California at Berkeley, defended the diversity policy.

By early May, 1994, the Department of Education backed away from some of the more controversial rules, both in terms of telling the accreditors what to look for, and in the powers given to the SPREs. They did this by continuing to say what things an accrediting agency must evaluate, but only suggesting, not demanding, the ways and means by which they might do it. In addition, SPREs would now be limited to dealing with matters of fraud and abuse, and could not initiate an inquiry for other reasons.

Under the then-final guidelines, accrediting agencies were required to evaluate these twelve matters, but the way they do it can be individually determined:

1. Curricula

2. Faculty

3. Facilities, equipment, and supplies

4. Fiscal and administrative capacity

5. Student support services

6. Program length, tuition, and fees in relation to academic objectives

7. Program length, tuition, and fees in relation to credit received

8. Student achievement (job placement, state licensing exams, etc.)

9. Student loan repayments

10. Student complaints received by or available to the accreditor

11. Compliance with student aid rules and regulations

12. Everything else, including recruiting, admissions practices, calendars, catalogues and other publications, grading practices, advertising and publicity, and so on.

And that is where we had gotten to by 1996. Then, just when it seemed as things were calming down a bit, two more bombshells (shall we call them #3 and #4?) were dropped.

Bombshell #3:
Good-bye CORPA, Hello CHEA

In late 1996, CORPA announced that it was closing down, in favor of a new organization, CHEA, the Council on Higher Education Accreditation, same address, but a new telephone number. So The Odyssey wasn't written by Homer or the other guy named Homer, but by yet a third Homer, this one apparently with closer ties to the administrators of the various accredited schools.

Bombshell #4:
Good-bye AACSB, Hello Confusion

For years, the main guideline for determining the validity of an accrediting agency has been whether it is recognized by the U.S. Department of Education (with additional recognition by COPA, CORPA, or CHEA as an added niceness).

Then the U.S. Department of Education determined that the Higher Education Amendments to the laws required it only to recognize those accreditors who help to enable the schools or programs they accredit to establish eligibility to participate in certain federal aid and other federal programs. As a result of this determination, more than a dozen respectable, well regarded, and formerly recognized accrediting agencies lost their Department of Education recognition, including the very prestigious AACSB, the American Assembly of Collegiate Schools of Business, which accredits Harvard, Yale, Stanford, and suchlike.

Does this mean that the accreditation of those nine agencies is no longer as useful? It is too soon to know, but unlikely, since the various professional fields still support that accreditation. The foresters, the social workers, the veterinarians, and so on, still regard accreditation by their professional associations as valuable and so, clearly, do the hundreds of schools that have or seek this accreditation. Finally, it seems more than likely that these nine agencies will retain their recognition by CHEA.

In any event, after decades of minimal interest and attention, the always fascinating world of accreditation is clearly getting more than its fifteen minutes of fame.

THE APPROVED
ACCREDITING AGENCIES

Each of the six regional associations has responsibility for schools in one region of the United States and its territories. Each one has the authority to accredit an entire college or university. And there are also about 80 professional associations, each with authority to accredit either specialized schools or specific departments or programs within a school.

Thus, it may be the case, for instance, that the North Central Association (one of the six regional associations) will accredit Dolas University. When this happens, the entire school is accredited, and all its degrees may be called accredited degrees, or more accurately, degrees from an accredited institution.

Or it may be the case that just the art department of Dolas University has been accredited by the relevant professional association, in this case the National Association of Schools of Art. If this happens, then only the art majors at Dolas can claim to have accredited degrees.

So if an accredited degree is important for your needs, the first question to ask is, "Has the school been accredited by one of the six regional associations?" If the answer is no, then the next question is, "Has the department in which I am interested been accredited by its relevant professional association?"

There are those jobs (psychology and nursing are two examples) in which professional accreditation is often at least as important as regional accreditation, sometimes more so. In other words, even if a school is accredited by its regional association, unless its psychology department is also accredited by the American Psychology Association, its degree will be less useful for psychology majors.

One of the legends about accreditation has arisen because of these matters: the widespread belief that Harvard is not accredited. Harvard University *is* duly accredited by its regional agency, but its psychology department, and many others, are not accredited by the relevant professional agencies.

In Great Britain, however, the similar legend that Oxford and Cambridge Universities are not accredited turns out to be partially true. While all the other British universities are accredited through the granting of a Royal Charter or by a special act of Parliament, it turns out that the two oldest universities have no Royal Charter of their own, although their constituent colleges do.

Totally unrecognized accrediting agencies may still be quite legitimate, or they may be quite phony. Some of the unrecognized ones will be discussed after the following listing of the recognized ones. Each of the approved accreditors will gladly supply lists of all the schools (or departments within schools) they have accredited, and those that are candidates for accreditation and in correspondent status. They will also answer any questions pertaining to any school's status (or lack of status) with them.

The Agencies That Recognize Accrediting Agencies

Department of Education
Division of Eligibility and Agency Evaluation
Bureau of Postsecondary Education
Washington, DC 20202
Phone: (202) 245-9875

CHEA, the Council For Higher Education Accreditation
One Dupont Circle NW, Suite 510
Washington DC, 20036-1135.
Phone: 202-955-6126, fax 202-955-612
E-mail: chea@chea.org
Website: www.chea.org.

WHAT IS GAAP?

Any school can claim that it is accredited; the use of that word is not regulated in any way. This chapter distinguishes between those accrediting agencies that are recognized under GAAP, Generally Accepted Accrediting Principles, and those that are not. In the U.S., there is near-unanimous agreement on GAAP (although not everyone calls it this, the concept is the same) by the relevant key decision-makers: university registrars and admissions officers, corporate human resources officers, and government agencies.

Note that in some countries, the word *accredited* is not used, although that country's evaluation process (e.g., the British Royal Charter) is accepted as "accredited" under GAAP. Note too that accreditors that do not meet the standards of GAAP are not necessarily bad, illegal, or fake. They simply would not be generally accepted as recognized accreditors.

GAAP Criteria

To offer recognized accreditation under GAAP, and accrediting agency must meet at least one of the following four criteria:

◆ Recognized by the Council on Higher Education Accreditation in Washington, DC

◆ Recognized by the U.S. Department of Education

◆ Recognized by (or more commonly, a part of) their relevant national education agency (as listed in chapter 6)

◆ Schools they accredit are routinely listed in one or more of the following publications: the International Handbook of Universities (a UNESCO publication), the Commonwealth Universities Yearbook, the World Education Series, published by PIER, or the Countries Series, published by NOOSR in Australia.

ACCREDITING AGENCIES RECOGNIZED UNDER GAAP

Regional Accrediting Agencies

Middle States Association of Colleges and Schools
Commission on Higher Education
3624 Market Street
Philadelphia, PA 19104
Phone: (215) 662-5606 Fax: (215) 662-5950
www.css-msa.org
Delaware, District of Columbia, Maryland, New Jersey, New York, Pennsylvania, Puerto Rico, Virgin Islands

New England Association of Schools and Colleges
209 Burlington Road
Bedford, MA 01730
Phone: (617) 271-0022 Fax: (617) 271-0950
www.neasc.org
Connecticut, Maine, Massachusetts, New Hampshire, Rhode Island, Vermont

North Central Association of Colleges and Schools
30 North LaSalle Street, Suite 2400
Chicago, IL 60602
Phone: (800) 621-7440 Fax: (312) 263-7462
info@ncacihe.org , www.ncacihe.org

Arizona, Arkansas, Colorado, Illinois, Indiana, Iowa, Kansas, Michigan, Minnesota, Missouri, Nebraska, New Mexico, North Dakota, Ohio, Oklahoma, South Dakota, West Virginia, Wisconsin, Wyoming

Northwest Association of Schools and Colleges
11300 NE 33rd Place, Suite 120
Bellevue, WA 98004
Phone: (206) 543-0195 Fax: (206) 827-3395
Alaska, Idaho, Montana, Nevada, Oregon, Utah, Washington

Southern Association of Colleges and Schools
1866 Southern Lane
Decatur, GA 30033
Phone: (800) 248-7701 Fax: (404) 679-4558
www.sacs.org
Alabama, Florida, Georgia, Kentucky, Louisiana, Mississippi, North Carolina, South Carolina, Tennessee, Texas, Virginia

Western Association of Schools and Colleges
Box 9990
Mills College
Oakland, CA 94613
Phone: (510) 632-5000 Fax: (510) 632-8361
wasc.mills.edu
California, Hawaii, Guam, Trust Territory of the Pacific

Professional Accrediting Agencies

The Arts

Architecture

National Architectural Accrediting Board
1735 New York Ave. NW
Washington, DC 20006
(202) 783-2007 • Fax: (202) 783-2822
(Recognized by CHEA but not by US Department of Education)

Art

National Association of Schools of Art and Design
Commission on Accreditation
11250 Roger Bacon Drive, Suite 21
Reston, VA 22090
(703) 437-0700 • Fax: (703) 437-6312

Dance

National Association of Schools of Dance
11250 Roger Bacon Drive, Suite 21
Reston, VA 22090
(703) 437-0700 • Fax: (703) 437-6312

Landscape Architecture

American Society of Landscape Architects
4401 Connecticut Ave. NW, 5th Floor
Washington, DC 20008
(202) 686-2752 • Fax: (202) 686-1001
www.asla.org/asla/
(Recognized by CHEA but not by US Department of Education)

Music

National Association of Schools of Music
11250 Roger Bacon Drive, Suite 21
Reston, VA 22090
(703) 437-0700 • Fax: (703) 437-6312

Theater

National Association of Schools of Theater
11250 Roger Bacon Drive, Suite 21
Reston, VA 22090
(703) 437-0700 • Fax: (703) 437-6312

Business

Accrediting Council for Independent
Colleges and Schools
750 First Street NE, Suite 980
Washington, DC 20002
(202) 336-6780 • Fax: (202) 482-2593

International Association for Management Education
600 Emerson Road, Suite 300
St. Louis, MO 63141
(314) 872-8481 • Fax: (314) 872-8495
(Recognized by CHEA but not by US Department of Education)

Association of Collegiate Business Schools and Programs
7007 College Blvd., Suite 420
Overland Park, KS 66211
(913) 339-9356 • Fax: (913) 339-6226
(Recognized by CHEA but not by US Department of Education)

Education

Blind and Visually Handicapped Education

National Accreditation Council for Agencies Serving the
Blind and Visually Handicapped
15 East 40th Street, Suite 1004
New York, NY 10016
(212) 683-5068 • Fax: (212) 683-4475
(Recognized by CHEA but not by US Department of Education)

Continuing Education

Accrediting Council for Continuing Education and
Training
600 East Main Street
Suite 1425
Richmond, VA 23219
(804) 648-6742

Distance Education and Training

Distance Education and Training Council
1601 18th Street NW
Washington, DC 20009
(202) 234-5100 • Fax: (202) 332-1386
www.detc.org

Liberal Education

American Academy for Liberal Education
1015 18th Street NW, Suite 204
Washington, DC 20036
(202) 452-8611 • Fax: (202) 452-8620

Montessori Education

American Montessori Society Review Committee
P.O. Box 278
Oxford, MD 21654
(410) 226-5527 • Fax: (410) 226-0177

Occupational, Trade, and Technical Education

Council on Occupational Education
41 Perimeter Center East, NE, Suite 640
Atlanta, GA 30346
(800) 917-2081 • Fax: (770) 396-3790

Accrediting Commission of Career Schools and
Colleges of Technology
2101 Wilson Blvd., Suite 302
Arlington, VA 22201
(703) 247-4212 • Fax: (703) 247-4533

Teacher Education

National Council for Accreditation of Teacher Education
  2010 Massachusetts Ave. NW
  Suite 200
  Washington, DC 20036
  (202) 466-7496 • Fax: (202) 296-6620
  www.ncate.org

Law

American Bar Association
  Indiana University
  550 West North Street
  Indianapolis, IN 46202
  (317) 264-8340 • Fax: (317) 264-8355

Medicine and Health

Acupuncture and Oriental Medicine

Accreditation Commission for Schools and Colleges of Acupuncture and Oriental Medicine
  1010 Wayne Avenue
  Suite 1270
  Silver Spring, MD 20910
  (301) 608-9680 • Fax: (301) 608-9576

Allied Health

Accrediting Bureau of Health Education Schools
  2700 South Quincy Street
  Suite 210
  Arlington, VA 22206
  (703) 998-1200 • Fax: (703) 998-2550
Accredits programs for Medical Laboratory Technician and Medical Assistant

Commission on Accreditation of Allied Health Programs
  35 East Wacker Drive
  Suite 1970
  Chicago, IL 60610
  (312) 553-9355 • Fax: (312) 553-9616
Serves as a coordinating agency for the accreditation of programs in Blood Bank Technology, Cytotechnology, Diagnostic Medical Sonography, Electroneurodiagnostic Technology, Emergency Medical Services, Medical Record Education, Opthalmic Medical Technician, Perfusion, Physican Assistant Education, Respiratory Therapy, and Surgical Technology

Chiropractic

The Council on Chiropractic Education
  7975 North Hayden Road
  Suite A-210
  Scottsdale, AZ 85258
  (602) 443-8877 • Fax: (602) 483-7333

Dentistry

American Dental Association
  211 East Chicago Ave.
  18th Floor
  Chicago, IL 60611
  (312) 440-2500 • Fax: (312) 440-2915

Dietetics

American Dietetic Association
  216 West Jackson Blvd.
  Suite 800
  Chicago, IL 60606
  (312) 899-4870 • Fax: (312) 899-1658
  www.eatright.com

Health Services Administration

Accrediting Commission on Education for Health Services Administration
  1911 North Fort Myer Drive
  Suite 503
  Arlington, VA 22209
  (703) 524-0511 • Fax: (703) 525-4791

National Accrediting Agency for Clinical Laboratory Sciences
  8410 West Bryn Mawr Ave., Suite 670
  Chicago, IL 60631
  (312) 714-8880 • Fax: (312) 714-8886
Accredits programs for Histologic Technician, Medical Laboratory Technician, Medical Technology, and Pathologists's Assistant

Medical Schools

American Medical Association
  515 North State Street
  Chicago, IL 60610
  (312) 464-4657 • Fax: (312) 464-5830
  www.ama-assn.org
The accreditor for medical schools in odd-numbered years, beginning on July 1.

Association of American Medical Colleges
  2450 N Street NW
  Washington, DC 20037
  (202) 828-0596 • Fax: (202) 828-1125
  www.aamc.org
The accreditor for medical schools in even-numbered years, beginning on July 1.

Naturopathy

Council on Naturopathic Medical Education
  P.O. Box 11426
  Eugene, OR 97440
  (503) 484-6028

Nuclear Medicine Technology

Joint Review Committee on Educational Programs in
Nuclear Medicine Technology
1144 West 3300 South
Salt Lake City, UT 84119
(801) 364-4310 • Fax: (801) 364-9234

Nursing

American Association of Nurse Anesthetists
222 Prospect Ave., Suite 304
Park Ridge, IL 60068
(708) 692-7050 • Fax: (708) 692-7137

American College of Nurse-Midwives
818 Connecticut Ave. NW
Suite 900
Washington, DC 20006
(202) 728-9877 • Fax: (202) 728-9897

National Association of Nurse Practitioners
in Reproductive Health
1090 Vermont Avenue, NW
Suite 800
Washington, DC 20006
(202) 728-9877 • Fax: (202) 728-9897

National League for Nursing, Inc.
350 Hudson Street
New York, NY 10014
(800) 669-1656 • Fax: (212) 989-3710

Optometry and Opticianry

American Optometric Association
243 North Lindbergh Blvd.
St. Louis, MO 63141
(314) 991-4100 • Fax: (314) 991-4101

Commission on Opticianry Accreditation
10111 Martin Luther King Jr. Hwy., Suite 100
Bowie, MD 20720
(301) 459-8075 • Fax: (301) 577-3880

Osteopathy

American Osteopathic Association
142 East Ontario Street
Chicago, IL 60611
(312) 280-5800 • Fax: (312) 280-3860

Pharmacy

American Council on Pharmaceutical Education
311 West Superior
Chicago, IL 60610
(312) 664-3575 • Fax: (312) 664-4652

Physical Therapy

American Physical Therapy Association
1111 North Fairfax Street
Alexandria, VA 22314

(703) 684-3245 • Fax: (703) 684-7344

Podiatry

American Podiatric Medical Association
9312 Old Georgetown Road
Bethesda, MD 20814
(301) 571-9200 • Fax: (301) 530-2752

Public Health

Council on Education for Public Health
1015 15th Street NW, Suite 403
Washington, DC 20005
(202) 789-1050 • Fax: (202) 789-1895

Radiologic Technology

Joint Review Committee on Education in Radiologic
Technology
20 North Wacker Drive, Suite 900
Chicago, IL 60606
(312) 704-5300 • Fax: (312) 704-5304
hudson.idt.net/~jrcert

Veterinary Medicine

American Veterinary Medical Association
1931 North Meacham Road
Suite 100
Schaumburg, IL 60173
(800) 248-2862 • Fax: (847) 925-1329

Religion
Bible College Education

Accrediting Association of Bible Colleges
P.O. Box 1523
Fayetteville, AR 72702
(501) 521-8164 • Fax: (501) 521-9202

Christian Studies Education

Transnational Association of Christian Colleges
P.O. Box 328, Forest Square
Forest, VA 24551
(804) 525-9539 • Fax: (804) 525-9538

Clinical Pastoral Education

Association for Clinical Pastoral Education
1549 Clairmont Road, Suite 103
Decatur, GA 30033-4611
(404) 320-1472 • Fax: (404) 320-0849

Commission on Certification and Accreditation United
States Catholic Conference
3501 South Lake Drive, P.O. Box 07058
Milwaukee, WI 53207
(414) 486-0138 • Fax: (414) 489-0006
(Recognized by CHEA but not by US Department of Education)

Rabbinical and Talmudic Education

Association of Advanced Rabbinical and
Talmudic Schools
   175 Fifth Avenue, Room 711
   New York, NY 10010
   (212) 477-0950 • Fax: (212) 533-5335

Theology

Association of Theological Schools in the United States
and Canada
   10 Summit Park Drive
   Pittsburgh, PA 15275
   (412) 788-6505 • Fax: (412) 788-6510

Science and Engineering

Computer Science

Computing Science Accreditation Board, Inc.
   2 Landmark Square, Suite 209
   Stamford, CT 06901
   (203) 975-1117 • Fax: (203) 975-1222
   csab.org/~csab
   (Recognized by CHEA but not by US Department of Education)

Engineering

Accrediting Board for Engineering & Technology
   111 Market Place, Suite 1050
   Baltimore, MD 21202
   (410) 347-7700 • Fax: (410) 625-2238

Environment

National Environmental Health Science & Protection
   Accreditation Council
   6307 Huntover Lane
   Rockville, MD 20852
   (301) 231-5205

Forestry

Society of American Foresters
   5400 Grosvenor Lane
   Bethesda, MD 20814
   (301) 897-8720 • Fax: (301) 897-3690
   (Recognized by CHEA but not by US Department of Education)

Industrial Technology

National Association of Industrial Technology
   3300 Washtenaw Ave., Suite 220
   Ann Arbor, MI 48104
   (313) 677-0720 • Fax: (313) 677-2407
   (Recognized by CHEA but not by US Department of Education)

Microbiology

American Academy of Microbiology
   1325 Massachusetts Ave. NW
   Washington, DC 20005
   (202) 942-9225 • Fax: (202) 942-6932
   (Recognized by CHEA but not by US Department of Education)

Social Sciences

Marriage and Family Therapy

American Assoc. for Marriage and Family Therapy
   1133 15th Street NW
   Suite 300
   Washington, DC 20005
   (202) 452-0109 • Fax: (202) 223-2329
   (Recognized by CHEA but not by US Department of Education)

Occupational Therapy

American Occupational Therapy Association
   4720 Montgomery Lane
   P.O. Box 31220
   Bethesda, MD 20824
   (301) 652-2682 • Fax: (301) 652-7711

Psychology

American Psychological Association
   750 1st Street NE
   Washington, DC 20002
   (202) 336-5979 • Fax: (202) 336-5978
   www.apa.org/ed/accred.html

Social Work

Council on Social Work Education
   1600 Duke Street
   Alexandria, VA 22314
   (703) 683-8080 • Fax: (703) 683-8099
   www.cswe.org
   (Recognized by CHEA but not by US Department of Education)

Speech-Language Pathology and Audiology

American Speech-Language-Hearing Association
   10801 Rockville Place
   Rockville, MD 20852
   (301) 897-5700 • Fax: (301) 571-0457
   www.asha.org

Vocational and Practical Fields

Construction Education

American Council for Construction Education
   1300 Hudson Lane, Suite 3
   Monroe, LA 71201
   (318) 323-2413 • Fax: (318) 323-2413
   (Recognized by CHEA but not by US Department of Education)

Cosmetology

National Accrediting Commission of Cosmetology
   Arts and Sciences
   901 North Stuart Street
   Suite 900
   Arlington, VA 22203
   (703) 527-7600

Culinary Arts

American Culinary Federation Education Institute
   959 Melvin Road
   Annapolis, MD 21403
   (410) 268-8375 • Fax: (410) 263-3110
(Recognized by CHEA but not by US Department of Education)

Funeral Service Education

American Board of Funeral Service Education
   13 Gurnet Road, #316
   Brunswick, ME 04011
   (207) 798-5801 • Fax: (207) 798-5988

Interior Design

Foundation for Interior Design Education Research
   60 Monroe Center NW
   Suite 300
   Grand Rapids, MI 49503
   (616) 458-0400 • Fax: (616) 458-0460
Recognized by CHEA but not by US Department of Education)

Journalism and Mass Communications

Accrediting Council on Education in Journalism and
Mass Communications
   University of Kansas School of Journalism
   Stauffer-Flint Hall
   Lawrence, KS 66045
   (913) 864-3986 • Fax: (913) 864-5225
   www.ukans.edu/~acejmc

Librarianship

American Library Association
   50 East Huron Street
   Chicago, IL 60611
   (312) 944-6780 • Fax (312) 280-2433
   www.ala.org
   ala@ala.org
Recognized by CHEA but not by US Department of Education)

Recognized State-Run Accrediting Agencies

New York State Board of Regents
   State Department of Education
   University of the State of New York
   Albany, NY 12224
   (518) 474-5844
   www.nysed.gov/regents/

ACCREDITING AGENCIES NOT RECOGNIZED UNDER GAAP

There are quite a few accrediting agencies that are not recognized under GAAP, the Generally Accepted Accreditation Principles, as described earlier in this chapter. These agencies are not recognized by either the Council on Higher Education Accreditation in Washington or the U.S.

Department of Education, nor by UNESCO or by the education departments or ministries of major countries. They range from a few sincere efforts which are working for recognition to many associations started by less-than-wonderful schools in order to accredit themselves. Following is a listing of many such accreditors that we have noticed over the years. New ones seem to be started every few weeks, so not every name you see will be listed here. If accreditation is important in a given situation, see the GAAP standards on page 42.

Accreditation Association of Ametrican [sic] College [sic] and Universities

Unrecognized agency from which the American University of Hawaii has claimed accreditation.

Accrediting Commission for Specialized Colleges

Gas City, Indiana. Established by "Bishop" Gordon Da Costa and associates (one of whom was Dr. George Reuter, who left to help establish the International Accrediting Commission, described in this section), from the address of Da Costa's Indiana Northern Graduate School (a dairy farm in Gas City). According to their literature, the accrediting procedures of ACSC seem superficial at best. The only requirement for becoming a candidate for accreditation was to mail in a check for $110.

Accrediting Commission International for Schools, Colleges and Theological Seminaries

Beebe, Arkansas. See also: "International Accrediting Commission for Schools, Colleges and Theological Seminaries" in this section. After the IAC was fined and closed down by authorities in Missouri in 1989, Dr. Reuter retired. A short time later, ACI opened in the adjoining state, and wrote a letter to the IAC schools offering them automatic accreditation by the ACI. I am not aware of any that turned it down. ACI refuses to make public a list of schools they have accredited. We have noted more than 130 schools that claim ACI accreditation, most of them apparently evangelical Bible schools, but more than a few nonreligious schools as well, including Century University, Columbia Southern University, Wisconsin International University, and Western States University.

Akademie fuer Internationale Kultur und Wissenschaftsfoerderung

See Association for Promotion of International Cultural and Scientific Exchange, below.

Alternative Institution Accrediting Association

Allegedly in Washington, DC, and the accreditor of several phony schools.

American Association of Accredited Colleges and Universities

Another unlocatable agency, the claimed accreditor of Ben Franklin Academy.

American Association of Independent Collegiate Schools of Business.

Unlocatable accreditor mentioned by Rushmore University.

American Association of Nontraditional Collegiate Business Schools

Another plausible-sounding but unlocatable accreditor mentioned by Rushmore University.

American Education Association for the Accreditation of Schools, Colleges and Universities

The accreditor claimed at one time by the University of America. Could not be located.

American Psycotherapy [sic] Association

Board of Psycotherapy [sic] Examiners, Katy, Texas, originally chartered in Florida, they say, while apologizing for but not correcting the misspellings.

Arizona Commission of Non-Traditional Private Postsecondary Education

Established in the late 1970s by the proprietors of Southland University, which claimed to be a candidate for their accreditation. The name was changed after a complaint by the real state agency, the Arizona Commission on Postsecondary Education (see Western Council, below).

Association for Promotion of International Cultural and Scientific Exchange (APICS)

With offices in Canada and Switzerland, this organization's secretary general is Dr. Denis K. Muhilly, who hasn't always been happy with things we've said about him in the past. All we know about this organization right now is that they've approached quite a few schools to discuss European accreditation. Also known by the German name Akademie fuer Internationale Kultur und Wissen-schaftsfoerderung.

Association of Accredited Private Schools

No listed telephone in Federal Way, Washington for this accredition who wrote to many schools in 1997, inviting them to send a $1000 application fee. No listed phone.

Association of Career Training Schools

A slick booklet sent to schools says, "Have your school accredited with the Association. Why? The Association Seal…could be worth many $ $ $ to you! It lowers sales resistance, sales costs, [and] improves image." Nuff said.

Commission for the Accreditation of European Non-Traditional Universities

The University de la Romande, in England, used to claim accreditation from this agency, which we could never locate.

Council for National Academic Accreditation

In 1998, they wrote to schools from Cheyenne, Wyoming offering the opportunity to be accredited on payment of a fee up to $1,850. No listed phone.

Council for the Accreditation of Correspondence Colleges

Several curious schools claimed their accreditation; the agency is supposed to be in Louisiana.

Council on Postsecondary Alternative Accreditation

An accreditor claimed in the literature of Western States University. Western States never responded to requests for the address of their accreditor. The name seems to have been chosen to cause confusion with the reputable organization originally known as the Council on Postsecondary Accreditation.

Council on Postsecondary Christian Education

Established by the people who operated LaSalle University and Kent College in Louisiana.

Distance Education Council of America

Quite reminiscent in name and literature to the recognized Distance Education and Training Council, DECA arose in Deleware in 1998, offering schools the opportunity to pay $200 or more for accreditation and $150 more for an "Excellence" rating.

InterAmerican Association of Postsecondary Colleges and Schools

The agency from which the Universitas Sancti Martin claims accreditation. We have not been able to locate this agency.

International Accreditation Commission for Post Secondary Education Institutions.

The University of the United States and Nasson University claim accreditation from this agency which, according to the schools' apparently shared website, has "not sought specific recognition from any single nation."

International Accreditation Association

The literature of the University of North America claims that they are accredited by this association. No address is provided, nor could one be located.

International Accrediting Association

The address in Modesto, California is the same as that of the Universal Life Church, an organization that awards Doctorates of all kinds, including the Ph.D., to anyone making a "donation" of $5 to $100.

International Accrediting Commission for Postsecondary Educational Institutions

Unrecognized agency from which Adam Smith University has, in the past, claimed accreditation.

International Accrediting Commission for Schools, Colleges and Theological Seminaries

Holden, Missouri. More than 150 schools, many of them Bible schools, were accredited by this organization. In 1989, the attorney general of Missouri conducted a clever "sting" operation, in which he created a fictitious school, the "East Missouri Business College," which rented a one-room office in St. Louis, and issued a typewritten catalog with such school executives as "Peelsburi Doughboy" and "Wonarmmd Mann." The Three Stooges were all on the faculty. Their marine biology text was The Little Golden Book of Fishes. Nonetheless, Dr. George Reuter, Director of the IAC, visited the school, accepted their money, and duly accredited them. Soon after, the IAC was enjoined from operating, slapped with a substantial fine, and the good Dr. Reuter decided to retire. (But the almost identical "Accrediting Commission International" immediately arose in Arkansas, offering instant accreditation to all IACSCTS members. See above.) Before he was apprehended, when someone wrote to Dr. Reuter to ask why this book had less-than-good things to say about his Association, Dr. Reuter replied, "Some of us do not rate Dr. John Bear very high. We think he is really a traditionalist and really favors those colleges and universities, and, at the same time, strives to plant dissent with others." Oh dear, oh dear.

International Association of Non-Traditional Schools

The claimed accreditor of several British degree mills; allegedly located in England.

International Commission for the Accreditation of Colleges and Universities

Established in Gaithersburg, Maryland, by a diploma mill called the United States University of America (now defunct) primarily for the purpose of accrediting themselves.

International Commission for Excellence in Higher Education, Inc.

According to Monticello University's on-line catalog, this commission "was formed by the Board of Trustees of Monticello University to ensure the highest possible standards of academic excellence in curriculum design and operational policies for member universities. Monticello University is the first distance learning institution to be accredited by this agency." We do not know of any other member institutions.

Middle States Accrediting Board

A nonexistent accreditor, made up by Thomas University and other degree mills, for the purpose of self-accreditation. The name was chosen, of course, to cause confusion with the Middle States Association of Colleges and Schools, in Philadelphia, one of the six regional associations.

National Accreditation Association

Established in Riverdale, Maryland, by Dr. Glenn Larsen, whose Doctorate is from a diploma mill called the Sussex College of Technology. His associate is Dr. Clarence Franklin, former president and chancellor of American International University (described in the chapter on diploma mills). In a mailing to presidents of unaccredited schools, the NAA offered full accreditation by mail, with no on-site inspection required.

National Association for Private Post-Secondary Education

Washington, DC. Mentioned, in 1990, in the literature of Kennedy-Western University. They say they are not an accrediting agency but a private association of schools, however Kennedy-Western claimed accreditation from them.

National Association of Alternative Schools and Colleges

Western States University claimed in their literature that they had been accredited by this organization, which we have never been able to locate.

National Association of Open Campus Colleges

Southwestern University of Arizona and Utah (which closed after its proprietor was sent to prison as a result of the FBI's diploma mill investigations) claimed accreditation from this agency. The address in Springfield, Missouri, was the same as that of Disciples of Truth, an organization that has in the past operated a chain of diploma mills.

The National Association for Private Nontraditional Schools and Colleges (formerly the National Association for Schools and Colleges) is a serious effort to establish an accrediting agency specifically concerned with alternative schools and programs. It was established in Grand Junction, Colorado in the 1970s by a group of educators associated with Western Colorado University, a nontraditional school that has since gone out of business. Although NAPNSC's standards for accreditation have grown more rigorous over the years, their application for recognition has been turned down many times by the US Department of Education, but they plan to keep trying.

National Council for the Accreditation of Private Universities and Schools of Law

Unrecognized agency from which Monticello University has claimed accreditation.

National Council of Schools and Colleges

Accreditation by this agency was claimed by International University, formerly of New Orleans, later of Pasadena, California, and now out of existence. Despite many inquiries, the proprietors of the school never provided information on their accreditor.

Pacific Association of Schools and Colleges

Established in 1993, this organization is operated by a man who had previously been a senior official in the California Department of Education (and who has a doctorate from an unaccredited school). PASC appears to be a serious attempt to create an accreditor that would be better able to deal with nontraditional schools.

West European Accrediting Society

Established from a mail-forwarding service in Liederbach, Germany by the proprietors of a chain of diploma mills such as Loyola, Roosevelt, Lafayette, Southern California, and Oliver Cromwell universities, for the purpose of accrediting themselves.

Western Association of Private Alternative Schools

One of several accrediting agencies claimed in the literature of Western States University. No address or phone number has ever been provided, despite many requests.

Western Association of Schools and Colleges

This is the name of the legitimate regional accreditor for California and points west. However it is also the name used by the aforementioned proprietors of Loyola, Roosevelt, etc., from a Los Angeles address, to give accreditation to their own diploma mills.

Western Council on Non-Traditional Private Post Secondary Education

An accrediting agency started by the founders of Southland University, presumably for the purpose of accrediting themselves and others (see Arizona Commission, above).

World Association of Universities and Colleges

Established in 1992 by Drs. Maxine Asher and Franklin T. Burroughs, and run from a business and secretarial service in Las Vegas, Nevada. The World Association declines to supply us with a list of schools they have accredited. It is safe to assume the list includes American World University (operated by Drs. Asher and Burroughs), and schools owned by Dr. Lloyd Clayton (Chadwick University, the American Institute of Computer Science, etc.), who has had an active role in the operation of WAUC. In February 1995, the national investigative publication *Spy Magazine* ran quite an unflattering article on WAUC. Dr. Asher also operates the Ancient Mediterranean Research Association which has produced a film that "clearly demonstrates the existence of Atlantis off the coast of Spain." When asked about the coauthor of this book, Dr. Asher has written to people that "Almost no one in higher education takes John Bear seriously."

Worldwide Accrediting Commission

Operated from a mail-forwarding service in Cannes, France, for the purpose of accrediting the fake Loyola University (Paris), Lafayette University, and other American-run degree mills.

BIBLE SCHOOL ACCREDITING AGENCIES

There are six recognized accreditors of religious schools, listed above, which cover everything from evangelical Christian schools to rabbinical seminaries. Religious schools often claim they have not sought accreditation since there are no relevant accreditors. They are not exactly accurate. There are also a great many unrecognized accreditors. Since many Bible schools readily acknowledge that their degrees are not academic in nature, accreditation of them has quite a different meaning. Some of these associations may well be quite legitimate, but their accreditation has no academic relevance. Some accreditors are apparently concerned primarily with doctrinal soundness; others may have other motivations. Among the Bible school accreditors are:

Accreditation Association of Christian Colleges and Seminaries, Morgantown, KY

Accrediting Association of Christian Colleges and Seminaries, Sarasota, FL

AF Sep (we don't know what this means, but Beta International University claims it is the name of their accrediting association), address unknown.

American Association of Accredited Colleges and Universities, address unknown

American Association of Theological Institutions, address unknown

American Educational Accrediting Association of Christian Schools, address unknown

American Federation of Christian Colleges and Schools

Association of Christian Schools and Colleges, address unknown.

Association of Fundamental Institutes of Religious Education (AFIRE), address unknown

International Accrediting Commission, Kenosha, WI

International Accrediting Association of Church Colleges, address unknown

National Educational Accrediting Association,
Columbus, OH

**Southeast Accrediting Association of Christian
Schools,** Colleges and Seminaries, Milton, FL

**World-Wide Accreditation Commission of Christian
Educational Instituations**

WORDS THAT DO NOT MEAN "ACCREDITED"

Some unaccredited schools use terminology in their catalogs or advertising that might have the effect of misleading unknowledgeable readers. Here are six common phrases:

1. **Pursuing accreditation.** A school may state that it is "pursuing accreditation," or that it "intends to pursue accreditation." But that says nothing whatever about its chances for achieving same. It's like saying that you are practicing your tennis game, with the intention of playing in the finals at Wimbledon. Don't hold your breath.

2. **Chartered.** In some places, a charter is the necessary document that a school needs to grant degrees. A common ploy by diploma mill operators is to form a corporation, and state in the articles of incorporation that one of the purposes of the corporation is to grant degrees. This is like forming a corporation whose charter says that it has the right to appoint the Pope. You can *say* it, but that doesn't make it so.

3. **Licensed or registered.** This usually refers to nothing more than a business license, granted by the city or county in which the school is located, but which has nothing to do with the legality of the school, or the usefulness of its degrees.

4. **Recognized.** This can have many possible meanings, ranging from some level of genuine official recognition at the state level, to having been listed in some directory often unrelated to education, perhaps published by the school itself. Two ambitious degree mills (Columbia State University and American International University) have published entire books that look at first glance like this one, solely for the purpose of being able to devote lengthy sections in them to describing their phony schools as "the best in America."

5. **Authorized.** In California, this has had a specific meaning (see chapter 7). Elsewhere, the term can be used to mean almost anything the school wants it to— sometimes legitimate, sometimes not. A Canadian degree mill once claimed to be "authorized to grant degrees." It turned out that the owner had authorized his wife to go ahead and print the diplomas.

6. **Approved.** In California, this has a specific meaning (see chapter 7). In other locations, it is important to know who is doing the approving. Some not-for-profit schools call themselves "approved by the U.S. Government," which means only that the Internal Revenue Service has approved their nonprofit status for income taxes—and nothing more. At one time, some British schools called themselves "Government Approved," when the approval related only to the school-lunch program.

THE SECOND-TO-LAST WORD ON ACCREDITATION

There have been quite an extraordinary number of new accrediting associations started in the last few years, and they are getting harder and harder to check out, either because they seem to exist only on the Internet, or because they exist in so many places: an address in Hawaii, another in Switzerland, a third in Germany, a fourth in Hong Kong, and so on. Some new ones have adopted the clever idea of bestowing their accreditation on some major universities, quite possibly unbeknownst to those schools. Then they can say truthfully, but misleadingly, that they accredit such well-known schools. This is the accreditation equivalent of those degree mills that send their diplomas to some famous people, and then list those people as graduates.

THE LAST WORD ON ACCREDITATION

Don't believe everything anyone says. It seems extraordinary that any school would lie about something so easily checked as accreditation, but it is done. Degree mills have unabashedly claimed accreditation by a recognized agency. Such claims are totally untrue. They are counting on the fact that many people won't check up on these claims.

Salespeople trying to recruit students sometimes make accreditation claims that are patently false. Quite a few schools ballyhoo their "fully accredited" status but never mention that the accrediting agency is unrecognized, and so the accreditation is of little or (in most cases) no value.

One accrediting agency (the aforementioned International Accrediting Commission for Schools, Colleges and Theological Seminaries) boasted that two copies of every accreditation report they issue are "deposited in the Library of Congress." That sounds impressive, until you learn that for $20, anyone can copyright anything and be able to make the identical claim.

9

Accredited versus Unaccredited: How Does One Decide?

LORD BROUGHAM: *Pray, Mr. Bickersteth, what is to prevent London University from awarding degrees now?*

MR. BICKERSTETH: *The universal scorn and contempt of mankind.*

1834 CONVERSATION, REPORTED IN THE GRENVILLE DIARIES

There are hundreds of colleges and universities in the world that do not have recognized accreditation. They range from totally fraudulent degree mills run by ex-convicts who sell worthless degrees to anyone willing to pay, to major new academic endeavors, well-funded and run by experienced educators of good reputation, and extremely likely to become properly accredited before too long.

In almost every instance, the unaccredited schools cost less, and offer a faster path to a degree, often with more flexibility. It is a tempting consideration, and a common dilemma for many people in search of a school. As a result, it is probably the most common question we get: should I pursue an unaccredited degree? Since we cannot know each questioner's situation and needs, we typically reply by saying, "If you are absolutely confident that an unaccredited degree will meet your current and your predictable future needs, then it might well be appropriate to pursue such a degree."

Note: for the purpose of the following discussion, we include schools with accreditation claimed from an unrecognized accreditor as equivalent to unaccredited, for that is how such schools are almost certain to be treated by evaluators and decision makers.

There is no simple answer

There truly is no simple answer to the accredited vs. unaccredited issue, other than to say that one can rarely go wrong with a properly accredited degree. We hear from a moderate number of people who have made good use of an unaccredited (but totally legitimate) degree, but we hear from many more who have had significant problems with such degrees, in terms of acceptance by employers, admission to other schools, or simply bad publicity.

Acceptance of unaccredited degrees

Acceptance is very low in the academic world and the government world, somewhat higher in the business world.

One large and decent unaccredited school, in operation for a quarter century, can only point to a dozen instances in which their degrees were accepted by other schools, most of those on a case by case basis. Some companies have no clear policy with regard to accreditation, and indeed may not even understand the concept, as was the case with the head of human resources for one of the ten largest companies on the planet, who got a copy of this book and then told us of her astonishment at learning that there were unaccredited schools and fake accrediting agencies.

Who can benefit from unaccredited degrees

The largest group are those people who really don't *need* a degree, but they want one, either for self satisfaction ("validating my life's work" is a phrase we hear often), or to give themselves a marketing edge. One large subset of satisfied unaccredited degree-users, for instance, are therapists, who typically need only a Master's degree for their state license. But they feel that if they have a Ph.D., and use that title in their advertising, yellow pages, etc., they will have an edge over competitors without the doctorate. The same is the case with owners or executives of small businesses. A real estate agent with an MBA or a business planner with a doctorate in finance, may get more clients because of the higher degree, and indeed may have additional useful knowledge.

What problems can arise?

We get a lot of mail from people who were having major problems with a previously-satisfactory unaccredited degree. This situation occurs after one of two events. One is a change in employer policy. A company that may have accepted or tolerated or unwittingly gone along with unaccredited degrees may have a change, either due to new personnel policies or new ownership, and previously-acceptable degrees no longer are. Similarly, when an employee seeks work at a new company, he or she may learn that the degree held is no longer useful. The other is when there is bad publicity, and the light of public scrutiny is focused on the school or the degrees. In recent years, the media have devoted more and more attention to these matters. *60 Minutes, American Journal, Inside Edition, Extra,* and dozens of local television consumer reporters have addressed the matter of bad schools and degrees. When American Journal devoted a long segment to a popular unaccredited school, and when a large daily newspaper gave an 8-column page-one headline to the state's lawsuit against another large and popular unaccredited school, many students and alumni of those schools had some highly uncomfortable moments.

Does the level of the degree make a difference?

We think it does. We can find very few reasons why it would ever make sense to pursue an unaccredited Associate's or Bachelor's degree. There are two reasons for this. One is that there are so very many distance Bachelor's programs with recognized accreditation, and those degrees can actually be faster and less expensive than some of the unaccredited ones. The other is that a person with at least one accredited degree, as the foundation, is seen to be someone clearly capable of doing university level work, and if they chose to pursue an unaccredited Master's or Doctorate, after earning the accredited Bachelor's, they must have had a good reason. Alternatively, a person with only an unaccredited degree, or series of degrees, will often be under a cloud of suspicion, especially in a world where it is possible to get a not-illegal Bachelor's degree in three months or less.

Will degrees with recognized accreditation always be accepted?

Most annoyingly, no. In the sometimes-snobbish world of higher education, schools without regional accreditation are sometimes seen to be inferior. As one simple but telling example, Regents College, one of the largest and best-respected distance learning schools in the US, itself with regional accreditation, will not accept degrees or credits from schools accredited by the Distance Education and Training Council, a recognized accreditor. Quite a few regionally-accredited schools *will* accept DETC accreditation, in our experience, but by no means all. This depressing fact is just one more reason to 'shop around' to be sure any given degree will meet your needs.

Another factor in acceptance is regional accreditation versus professional accreditation. In some fields, such as psychology, architecture, and engineering, accreditation from the relevant professional association can be especially important. For example, there are job descriptions for therapists that require degrees accredited by the American Psychological Association, a professional accreditor, which accredits fewer than half the psychology programs in America.

What happens if my school becomes accredited after I earn my degree?

Theoretically one only has an accredited degree if it was earned after accreditation. For many practical purposes, however, it is unlikely that an employer will say, for instance, "Did you earn your degree from the Graduate School of America before or after November 17, 1997?" Once a school has been accredited, it is likely (but not certain) that all its degrees will be regarded as accredited, whenever earned. Some schools offer the option of going back and doing a modest amount of additional work, and earning a "replacement" degree after the accreditation is gained.

What happens if the accreditor is recognized after I earn my degree?

In this scenario, the student earns a degree from a school that is accredited by an unrecognized agency, and later the agency is recognized by the Department of Education. This is such a rare situation, we really don't know if there is a precedent. Common sense suggests that if the school or degree was accredited all along, and if the only change is that the accreditor becomes recognized, then the student would have a degree with recognized accreditation. But common sense does not always prevail in the world of higher education.

Is unrecognized accreditation worse than none at all?

In many cases, we think so, because it adds one more layer of possible irregularity to attract the attention of investigators, regulators, decision makers, and others. When, for instance, a national magazine did an extremely unflattering article on the unrecognized World Association of Universities and Colleges (*Spy,* February 1995), the caustic comments and the various revelations led readers to think less favorably of the schools this association had accredited. On the other hand, some of the larger distance learning schools make no accreditation claims whatsoever (California Coast, California Pacific, Fairfax, Southwest, Greenwich, etc.), and still manage to attract students.

It is common for unrecognized accrediting agencies to talk or write about their intention to become recognized by the Department of Education. In our opinion, however, of the more-than-thirty active unrecognized accreditors described in the Accreditation chapter, only one has even a remote chance of recognition, and that one, the National Association, has been turned down many times over the past twenty years. Some of these accreditors suggest that it is their choice not to be recognized, by writing things like, "This association has not sought recognition ..." or "... does not choose to be listed by the Department of Education." And we have chosen not to be awarded the Nobel Prize for literature.

10

Scholarships and Other Financial Aid

If you think education is expensive, try ignorance.
DEREK BOK, FORMER PRESIDENT OF HARVARD UNIVERSITY

Financial assistance comes in four forms: **OUTSIDE SCHOLARSHIPS**. An outright gift of money paid to you or the school by an outside source (government, foundation, corporation, etc.).

INSIDE SCHOLARSHIPS. The school itself reduces your tuition and/or other expenses. No money changes hands.

FELLOWSHIPS. Money either from the school or an outside source, usually but not always in return for certain work or services to be performed at the school (generally teaching or research).

LOANS. From outside lenders, or from the school itself, to be paid back over a period of anywhere from one to 10 years, generally at interest lower than the current prime rate.

Sadly, as college costs continue to rise substantially, the amount of money available for financial aid is diminishing dramatically. Many loan and scholarship programs were either funded or guaranteed by the federal government, and much of this money was eliminated as part of the Reagan administration's cutbacks and has not been restored. After all, 300,000 canceled full-tuition scholarships can buy one nuclear-powered aircraft carrier. And already have. (This remark in previous editions has resulted in three stern letters from veterans asking, in effect, if we would rather be protected from a commie invasion by a nuclear battleship or by 300,000 scholars. We're still not sure.)

Still, billions of dollars are available to help pay the college costs of people who need help. The vast majority of it goes to full-time students under age 25, pursuing residential degrees at traditional schools.

Tapping into that particular fount is outside the scope of this book. There are several very useful books on this subject, which are described in the reference section, including our own book, *Finding Money for College,* published by Ten Speed Press, and thoroughly updated ever two years.

That book is the only one we know of that is specifically oriented to the nontraditional student, the older student, and the graduate student. It covers a wide range of nontraditional strategies, such as bartering skills (gardening, athletic coaching, etc.) for tuition, recruiting new students on a commission basis, and exploiting real estate and tax angles.

Some computerized services collect data on tens of thousands of individual scholarships, and can match their clients' needs and interests with donors for a modest fee. All but a few of these services are licensees, and tap into the same database, so there is no point in getting more than one report. If you'd like to see what they have to offer, you might wish to get the literature from the pioneer in this field, the National Scholarship Research Service, at 2280 Airport Road, Santa Rosa, CA 95403, (800) 432-3782 or (707) 546-6777, fax: (707) 546-6785, e-mail: nsrs@msn.com.

You can research a number of scholarship search services on-line at:
www.finaid.org/finaid/vendors/search-services.html

If you'd like to do your own research, this site is a great starting place. For folks who prefer to do their research off-line, Dan Cassidy, founder of National Scholarship Research Service, has made it easy for you. Their complete database of available scholarships has been published in a series of three books, for undergraduates, graduates, and people who wish to study abroad. Details are in the Bibliography section.

Some of the scholarships available are, admittedly, awfully peculiar: for rodeo riders with high grades, for Canadian petunia fanciers, for reformed prostitutes from Seattle, for people named Baxendale or Murphy, for people born on certain dates and/or in certain towns, and so on. And many are quite small and/or highly competitive. But many, too, are quite general, and a fair number do not depend on financial need or net worth.

Many colleges and universities subscribe to a service called CASHE (College Aid Sources for Higher Education), a data base of nearly 200,000 scholarships, grants, loans, fellowships, and work study programs. Some schools offer the service free to students or potential students; others make a nominal charge. Another very helpful resource is a website listing dozens of financial options.

Many students enrolled in nontraditional, even nonresidential programs have their expenses paid, all or in part, by their employer. Thousands of large corporations, including nearly all of the Fortune 500, have tuition plans for their employees, and so do a great many small ones. But *billions* of dollars in corporate funds go unclaimed each year, simply because people don't ask for them, or because neither employers nor employees realize that there are significant tax advantages to both in setting up an employee tuition-paying plan.

The tax laws governing such things are what drive the corporate funding. But the tax laws are not etched in stone. In parts of the years 1992-1994, for instance, companies were allowed to deduct up to $5,500 per employee per year for educational expenses, and the employees didn't have to pay tax on the employers' donations. This law expired, then was reenacted, and made retroactive to the expired time, but was then in jeopardy of expiring again. This is the sort of thing that keeps tax accountants solvent.

At times when the law is in place, it is quite a persuasive thing for an employee of any size company to go to his or her boss and say, in effect, "If you pay up to $5,500 of my school expenses, it is all tax deductible for you, and the benefit is not taxable to me."

Some, but not too many, corporations will pay for unaccredited programs. Some unaccredited schools list in their literature the names of hundreds of corporations as well as U.S. and foreign government agencies where their graduates are employed, but this does not necessarily mean the companies paid or reimbursed them.

Most nontraditional schools, accredited and unaccredited, offer inside scholarships to their students who need them. In other words, they will award a partial scholarship, in the form of tuition reduction (10 to 30 percent is the usual range), rather than lose a student altogether. Quite a few schools also offer an extended payment plan, in which the tuition can be paid in a series of smaller monthly installments, or even charged to a major credit card.

There are schools, traditional and nontraditional, that offer tuition reduction in the form of commissions, or finders' fees, for bringing in other students. This quite ethical procedure can result in a tuition reduction of from $50 to several hundred dollars for each referral, when the referred student enrolls.

But the biggest factors, by far, in financial aid for students at nontraditional schools are the speed of their education and the possibility of remaining fully employed while pursuing the degree. If even one year can be cut from a traditional four-year Bachelor's degree program, the savings (including revenue from a year of working for pay) are greater than 99 percent of all scholarship grants. And, as mentioned earlier, the average "four year" Bachelor's degree now takes six years, which should be taken into account in figuring time lost from jobs.

So, while it is nice to "win" money from another source, it is surely the case that to be able to complete an entire degree program for an out-of-pocket cost of from $3,000 to $7,000 (the typical range at nontraditional schools) is one of the great financial bargains of these ever-more-expensive times.

"I hereby take pen in hand to make application for the Marie Curie Scholarship in Nuclear Radionics. Alternatively, I wish also to be considered for the Babe Didrickson Zaharias Scholarship in shotputting."

11

Applying to Schools

*When any Scholar is able to read Tully or such like classical Latin Author ex tempore,
and to make and speak true Latin in verse and prose . . . and decline perfectly the paradigms
of nouns and verbs in the Greek tongue, then may he be admitted into the College, nor
shall any claim admission before such qualifications.*

ADMISSIONS STANDARDS, HARVARD COLLEGE, C. 1650

HOW MANY SCHOOLS SHOULD YOU APPLY TO?

No single answer to this question is right for everyone. Each person will have to determine his or her own best answer. The decision should be based on the following four factors:

Likelihood of Admission

Some schools are extremely competitive or popular and admit fewer than 10 percent of qualified applicants. Some have an "open admissions" policy and admit literally everyone who applies. Most are somewhere in between.

If your goal is to be admitted to one of the highly competitive schools (for instance, Harvard, Yale, Princeton, or Stanford), where your chances of being accepted are not high, then it is wise to apply to at least four or five schools that would be among your top choices, and to at least one "safety valve"—an easier one, in case all else fails.

If your interest is in one of the good, but not world-famous, nonresident programs, your chances for acceptance are probably better than nine in ten, so you might decide to apply only to one or two.

Cost

There is a tremendous range of possible costs for any given degree. For instance, a respectable M.B.A. could cost well under $10,000 at a good nonresident school, or more than $50,000 at a well-known university—not even taking into account the lost salary. In general, we think it makes sense to apply to no more than two or three schools in any given price category.

What They Offer You

Shopping around for a school is a little like shopping for a new car. Many schools either have money problems, or operate as profit-making businesses, and in either case, they are most eager to enroll new students. Thus it is not unreasonable to ask the schools what they can do for you. Let them know that you are a knowledgeable "shopper," and that you have read this book. Do they have courses or faculty advisors in your specific field? If not, will they get one for you? How much credit will they give for prior life-experience learning? How long will it take to earn the degree? Are there any scholarships or tuition reduction plans available? Does tuition have to be paid all at once, or can it be spread out over time? If factors like these are important for you, then it could pay to shop around for the best deal.

You might consider investigating at least two or three schools that appear somewhat similar, because there will surely be differences.

Caution: Remember that academic quality and reputation are probably the most important factors—so don't let a small financial saving be a reason to switch from a good school to a less-good school.

Your Own Time and Money

Applying to a school can be a time-consuming process—and it costs money, too. Many schools have application fees ranging from $25 to $100. Some people get so carried away with the process of applying to school after school that they never get around to enrolling in one, let alone earning their degree.

Of course once you have prepared a good detailed resume, curriculum vita, or life-experience portfolio, you can use it to apply to more than one school.

Another time factor is how much of a hurry you are in. If you apply to several schools at once, the chances are good that at least one will admit you, and you can begin work promptly. If you apply to only one, and it turns you down, or you get into long delays, then it can take a month or two to go through the admissions process elsewhere.

SPEEDING UP THE ADMISSIONS PROCESS

The admissions process at most traditional schools is very slow; most people apply nearly a year in advance and do not learn if their application has been accepted for four to six months. Nontraditional programs vary immensely in their policies in this regard. Some will grant conditional acceptance within a few weeks after receiving the application. ("Conditional" means that they must later verify the prior learning experiences you claim.) Others take just as long as traditional programs.

The following three factors can result in a much faster admissions process:

Selecting Schools by Policy

A school's admissions policy should be stated in its catalog. Since you will find a range among schools of a few weeks to six months for a decision, the simple solution is to ask, and then apply to schools with a fast procedure.

Asking for Speedy Decisions

Some schools have formal procedures whereby you can request an early decision on your acceptance. Others do the same thing informally, for those who ask. In effect, what this does is put you at the top of the pile in the admissions office, so you will have the decision in, perhaps, half the usual time. Other schools use what they call a "rolling admissions" procedure, which means, in effect, that each application is considered soon after it is received instead of being held several months and considered with a large batch of others.

Applying Pressure

As previously indicated, many schools are eager to have new students. If you make it clear to a school that you are in a hurry and that you may consider going elsewhere if you don't hear from them promptly, they will usually speed up the process. It is not unreasonable to specify a time frame. If, for instance, you are mailing in your application on September 1, you might enclose a note saying that you would like to have their decision mailed or phoned to you by October 1. (Some schools routinely telephone their acceptances, others do so if asked, some will only do so by collect call, and others will not, no matter what.)

HOW TO APPLY TO A SCHOOL

The basic procedure is essentially the same at all schools, traditional or nontraditional:

1. You write (or telephone) for the school's catalog, bulletin, or other literature, and admissions forms.

2. You complete the admissions forms and return them to the school, with application fee, if any.

3. You complete or provide any other requirements the school may have (exams, transcripts, letters of recommendation, etc.).

4. The school notifies you of its decision.

It is step three that can vary tremendously from school to school. At some schools all that is required is the admissions application. Others will require various entrance examinations to test your aptitude or knowledge level, transcripts, three or more letters of reference, a statement of financial condition, and possibly a personal interview, either on the campus or with a local representative in your area.

Happily, the majority of nontraditional schools have relatively simple entrance requirements. And all schools supply the materials that tell you exactly what they expect you to do in order to apply. If it is not clear, ask. If the school does not supply prompt, helpful answers, then you probably don't want to deal with them anyway. It's a buyer's market.

It is advisable, in general, *not* to send a whole bunch of stuff to a school the very first time you write to them. A short note asking for their catalog should suffice. You may wish to indicate your field and degree goal ("I am interested in a Master's and possibly a Doctorate in psychology . . .") in case they have different sets of literature for different programs. It probably can do no harm to mention that you are a reader of this book; it might get you slightly prompter or more personal responses. (On the other hand, more than a few grouchy readers have written saying, "I told them I was a personal friend of yours, and it still took six months for an answer." Oh dear. Well, if they hadn't said that, it might have been even longer. Or perhaps shorter. Who knows?)

ENTRANCE EXAMINATIONS

Many nonresident degree programs, even at the Master's and doctoral levels, do not require any entrance examinations. On the other hand, the majority of residential programs *do* require them. The main reason for this appears to be that nontraditional schools do not have to worry about overcrowding on the campus, so they can admit more students. A second reason is that they tend to deal with more mature students who have the ability to decide which program is best for them.

There are, needless to say, exceptions to both reasons. If you have particular feelings about examinations—positive or negative—you will be able to find schools that meet your requirements. Do not hesitate to ask any school about their exam requirements if it is not clear from the catalog.

Bachelor's Admission Examinations

Most residential universities require applicants to take part or all of the "ATP" or Admissions Testing Program, run by a private agency, the College Entrance Examination Board (888 7th Avenue, New York, NY 10019). The main component of the ATP is the SAT, or Scholastic Aptitude

Test, which measures verbal and mathematical abilities. There are also achievement tests, testing knowledge levels in specific subject areas such as biology, European history, Latin, etc. These examinations are given at centers all over North America several times each year for modest fees, and by special arrangement in many foreign locations.

A competing private organization, ACT (American College Testing Program, P.O. 2201 North Dodge Street, P.O. Box 168, Iowa City, IA 52243-0168) offers a similar range of entrance examinations.

The important point is that very few schools have their own exams; virtually all rely on either the ACT or the ATP.

Graduate Degrees

Again, many nonresidential schools do not require any entrance examinations. Many, but by no means all, residential Master's and Doctoral programs ask their applicants to take the GRE, or Graduate Record Examination, administered by the Educational Testing Service (Rosedale Road, Princeton, NJ 08541). The basic GRE consists of a three-and-a-half-hour aptitude test (of verbal, quantitative, and analytical abilities). Some schools also require GRE subject-area exams, which are available in a variety of specific fields (chemistry, computer science, music, etc.).

Professional Schools

Most law, business, and medical schools also require a standard examination, rather than having one of their own. The MCAT (Medical College Admission Test) is given several times a year by ACT while the LSAT (Law School Admission Test) and the GMAT (Graduate Management Admissions Test) are given five times a year by ETS.

There are many excellent books available at most libraries and larger bookstores on how to prepare for these various exams, complete with sample questions and answers. Some of these are listed in the bibliography of this book. Also, the testing agencies themselves sell literature on their tests as well as copies of previous years' examinations.

The testing agencies used to deny vigorously that either cramming or coaching could affect one's scores. In the face of overwhelming evidence to the contrary, they no longer make those claims. Some coaching services have documented score increases of 25 to 30 percent. Check the Yellow Pages or the bulletin boards on high school or college campuses for test-preparation workshops in your area.

Mrs. Ackerman-Gray dutifully follows along, as little Walkemar recites Marc Antony's funeral oration, the final lesson in his home study acting course from the Little Rascals Academy.

12

Equivalency Examinations

*In an examination, those who do not wish to know
ask questions of those who cannot tell.*

WALTER RALEIGH

The nontraditional approach to higher education says that if you have knowledge of an academic field, then you should get credit for that knowledge, regardless of how or where you acquired the knowledge. The simplest and fairest way of assessing that knowledge is through an examination.

About 3,000 colleges and universities in the United States and Canada, many of whom would deny vigorously that there is anything "nontraditional" about them, award students credit toward their Bachelor's degrees (and, in a few cases, Master's and Doctorates) solely on the basis of passing examinations.

Many of the exams are designed to be equivalent to the final exam in a typical college class, and the assumption is that if you score high enough, you get the same amount of credit you would have gotten by taking the class—or, in some cases, a good deal more.

While there are many sources of equivalency exams, including a trend toward schools developing their own, two independent national agencies are dominant in this field. They offer exams known as CLEP and PEP.

CLEP and PEP

CLEP (the College-Level Examination Program) and PEP (the Proficiency Examination Program) administer more than 75 exams. They are given at hundreds of testing centers all over North America and, by special arrangement, many of them can be administered almost anywhere in the world.

CLEP is offered by the College Entrance Examination Board, known as "the College Board" (45 Columbus Ave., New York, NY 10023; phone (212) 713-8064, fax (212) 713-8063, e-mail clep@collegeboard.org, web site www.collegeboard.org). Military personnel who want to take CLEP

should see their education officer or write DANTES, CN, Princeton, NJ 08541.

PEP is offered in the state of New York by the Regents College Proficiency Programs (7 Columbia Circle, Albany, NY 12203), and everywhere else by the American College Testing Program (P.O. Box 4014, Iowa City, IA 52243).

Many of the tests offered by CLEP are available in two versions: entirely multiple-choice questions, or multiple choice plus an essay. Some colleges require applicants to take both parts, others just the multiple choice. There are five general exams, each 90 minutes long, which are multiple choice, except English, which has the option of a 45-minute multiple choice and a 45-minute composition.

CLEP offers about 30 subject-area exams, each of them 90 minutes of multiple-choice questions. The cost is around $50 per test.

PEP offers 43 subject-area exams, most of them three hours long, but a few are four hours. The fees range from $40 to $125 per exam.

Each college or university sets its own standards for passing grades, and also decides for itself how much credit to give for each exam. Both of these factors can vary substantially from school to school. For instance, the PEP test in anatomy and physiology is a three-hour multiple-choice test. Hundreds of schools give credit for passing this exam. Here are examples:

- ◆ Central Virginia Community College requires a score of 45 (out of 80), and awards nine credit hours for passing.

- ◆ Edinboro University in Pennsylvania requires a score of 50 to pass, and awards six credit hours for the same exam.

- ◆ Concordia College in New York requires a score of 47, but awards only three credit hours.

Similar situations prevail on most of the exams. There is no predictability or consistency, even within a given school. For instance, at the University of South Florida, a three-hour multiple-choice test in maternal nursing is worth 18 units while a three-hour multiple-choice test in psychiatric nursing is worth only nine.

So, with dozens of standard exams available, and with about 3,000 schools offering credit, it pays to shop around a little and select both the school and the exams where you will get the most credit.

CLEP exams are offered in five general subject areas: social science and history, English composition (with or without an essay), humanities, mathematics, and natural science.

Specific subject-area exams are offered in the following fields. The fields, however, are subject to change, both through additions, deletions, or modifications.

Business
Information systems and computer applications
Principles of management
Principles of accounting
Introductory business law
Principles of marketing

Composition and Literature
American literature
Analyzing and interpreting literature
Freshman college composition
English literature

Languages Other than English
College-level French
College-level German
College-level Spanish

History and Social Sciences
American government
History of the US: early colonizations to 1877
History of the US: 1865 to the present
Human growth and development
Introduction to educational psychology
Principles of macroeconomics
Principles of microeconomics
Introductory psychology
Introductory sociology
Western civilization: ancient near east to 1648
Western civilization: 1648 to the present

Science and Mathematics
Calculus with elementary functions
College algebra
College algebra—trigonometry
General biology
General chemistry
Trigonometry
Calculus & elementary functions
College algebra

PEP exams are developed by Regents College. Exams have been offered directly by Regents in New York and outside the US, and through through the American College Testing Service elsewhere in the US. In late 1998, many of the exams became available on-line at the Sylvan Learning Centers nationwide. The address is: Regents College Test Administration Office, 7 Columbia Circle, Albany, NY 12203, phone (518) 464-8500, e-mail testadmn@regents.edu, www.regents.edu/100.htm.

The address for the American College Testing Program is: ACT, Inc., P. O. Box 4014, Iowa City, IA 52243, phone (319) 337-1363.

Exams have been offered in the following fields; as with all examination programs, the menu is adjusted from time to time.

Art and Science
Abnormal psychology
American dream
Anatomy & physiology
English composition
Ethics
Foundations of gerontology
History of Nazi Germany
Lifespan developmental psychology
Microbiology
Psychology of adulthood and aging
Religions of the world
Statistics
War in Vietnam

Education
Reading instruction, elementary

Business
Business policy and strategy
Human resources management
Labor relations
Organizational behavior
Productions and operation management

Nursing
17 specialized exams, ranging from professional strategies in nursing to maternity nursing.

How Exams Are Scored

CLEP exams are scored on a scale of either 20 to 80 or 200 to 800. This is done to maintain the fiction that no score can have any intrinsic meaning. It is not obvious, for example, whether a score of 514 is either good or bad. But any college-bound high-school senior in America can tell you that 400 is pretty bad, 500 is okay, 600 is good, and 700 is great. Still, each college sets its own minimum score for which it will give credit, and in many cases all that is necessary is to be in the upper half of those taking the test.

PEP gives standard numerical or letter grades for its tests.

Anywhere from one-and-two-thirds to six credits may be earned for each hour of testing. For example, the five basic CLEP tests (90 minutes of multiple-choice questions each) are worth anywhere from eight to 30 semester units, depending on the school. Thus it is possible to complete the equivalent of an entire year of college—30 semester units—in two days, by taking and passing these five tests.

CLEP tests are given over a two-day period at more than 1,300 centers, most of them on college or university campuses. Each center sets its own schedule for frequency of testing, so it may pay to "shop around" for convenient dates. PEP tests are given for two consecutive days on a variable schedule in about 100 locations, nationwide, including most of the Sylvan Learning Centers.

Persons living more than 150 miles from a test center may make special arrangements for the test to be given nearer home. There is a modest charge for this service.

There is no stigma attached to poor performance on these tests. In fact, if you wish, you may have the scores reported only to you, so that no one but you and the computer will know how you did. Then, if your scores are high enough, you can have them sent on to the schools of your choice. CLEP allows exams to be taken every six months; you can take the same PEP exam twice in any 12-month period.

How Hard Are These Exams?

This is, of course, an extremely subjective question. However, we have heard from a great many readers who have attempted CLEP and PEP exams, and the most common response is "Gee, that was a lot easier than I had expected." This is especially true with more mature students. The tests are designed for 18-to-20-year-olds, and there appears to be a certain amount of factual knowledge, as well as experience in dealing with testing situations, that people acquire in ordinary life situations as they grow older.

Preparing (and Cramming) for Exams

The testing agencies issue detailed syllabuses describing each test and the specific content area it covers. CLEP also sells a book that gives sample questions and answers from each examination.

At least four educational publishers have produced series of books on how to prepare for such exams, often with full-length sample tests. These can be found in the education or reference section of any good bookstore or library.

For years, the testing agencies vigorously fought the idea of letting test-takers take copies of the test home with them. But consumer legislation in New York has made at least some of the tests available, and a good thing, too. Every so often, someone discovers an incorrect answer or a poorly-phrased question that can have more than one correct answer, necessitating a recalculation and reissuance of scores to all the thousands of people who took that test.

In recent years, there has been much controversy over the value of cramming for examinations. Many counseling clients report having been able to pass four or five CLEP exams in a row by spending an intensive few days (or weeks) cramming for them. Although the various testing agencies used to deny that cramming can be of any value, in the last few years there have been some extremely persuasive research studies that demonstrate the short-term effectiveness of intensive studying. These data have vindicated the claims made by people and agencies that assist students in preparing for examinations. Such services are offered in a great many places, usually in the vicinity of college campuses, by graduate students and moonlighting faculty. The best place to find them is through the classified ads in campus newspapers, on bulletin boards around the campus, and through on-campus extension programs. Prices vary widely, so shop around.

The Princeton Review testing service claims that their preparation materials, in classes or through their book, increase scores by an average of 150 points. (Princeton Review, 2315 Broadway, New York, NY 10024, (800) 2-REVIEW.) Princeton has offices in all 50 states and worldwide. They help prepare for GRE, GMAT, GED, LSAT, MCAT, and TOEFL, but *not* for CLEP and PEP.

The Stanley H. Kaplan Educational Centers offer intensive preparation for dozens of different tests, from college admissions to national medical boards. Although the main method of preparation involves a good deal of classroom attendance at a center (from 20 to over 100 hours), most materials can be rented for home study. Residential tuition for most examination preparation courses is in the range of $150 to $300, but the cost goes as high as $850 for some medical exams. Rental of most sets of materials for home study costs from $100 to $200. Kaplan Centers operate in 40 states, the District of Columbia, Puerto Rico, and Canada. (Stanley H. Kaplan Educational Center, Ltd., 131 West 56th St., New York, NY 10019, (212) 977-8200; outside New York, (800) 223-1782.)

Often the best strategy is to take a self-scoring test from one of the guidebooks. If you do well, you may wish to take the real exam right away. If you do badly, you may conclude that credit by examination is not your cup of hemlock. And if you score in between, consider cramming on your own, or with the help of a paid tutor or tutoring service.

OTHER EXAMINATIONS

Here are some other examinations that can be used to earn substantial credit toward many nontraditional degree programs:

Graduate Record Examination

The GRE is administered by the Educational Testing Service (P.O. Box 6000, Princeton, NJ 08541, (212) 966-5853). There is a general test, which is more of an aptitude test, which is now given on demand at more than 600 computer centers throughout North America. On completing this exam by computer, the student is given the choice of either erasing the exam entirely and walking out (no harm, no foul), or pressing another button, and being given an instantaneous (but unofficial) score. That could be an interesting moment in testing. The paper version of the general GRE test will no longer be given after the spring of 1999.

The GRE Advanced Test is still given in written form, although this may change in the new millennium. It is a three-hour multiple-choice test, designed to test knowledge that would ordinarily be gained by a Bachelor's degree–holder in that given field. The exams are available in the fields of:

biology	history
chemistry	English literature
computer science	mathematics
economics	music
engineering	philosophy
French	physics
geography	psychology
geology	sociology
German	Spanish

Subjects change from time to time. For instance, education and political science were recently eliminated.

Few schools give credit for the general GRE. Schools vary widely in how much credit they will give for each subject-area GRE. The range is from none at all to 30 semester units (in the case of Regents College). Regents (and a few others, like Thomas Edison and Charter Oak) once gave 39 semester units for satisfactory performance on the GRE subject exams. Later that was reduced to 30 units, and, starting in 1997, semester units have been given based on performance: up to 30 for a high score, but less for a lower score.

A National Guard sergeant once crammed for, took, and passed three GRE exams in a row, thereby earning 90 semester units in ten and a half hours of testing. Then he took the five basic CLEP exams in two days, and earned 30 more units, which was enough to earn an accredited Bachelor's degree, start to finish, in 18 hours, starting absolutely from scratch with no college credit.

DANTES

The Defense Activity for Non-Traditional Education Support tests, or DANTES, were developed for the Department of Defense, but are available to civilians as well. The tests were developed by the Educational Testing Service, and are offered by hundreds of colleges and universities nationwide. While there is some overlap with PEP and CLEP, there are also many unique subjects. DANTES information is available from the DANTES Program, Mail Stop 3/X, Educational Testing Service, Princeton, NJ 08541. TPhone (850) 452-1089, fax (850) 452-1160, e-mail llipp@voled.doded.mil, www.voled.doded.mil/dantes.

Tests include, among others:

> Introductory College Algebra
> Principles of Statistics
> Art of the Western World
> Geography
> General Anthropology
> Criminal Justice
> Principles of Finance
> Principles of Financial Accounting
> Personnel/Human Resource Management
> Organizational Behavior
> Business Law II
> Basic Marketing
> Astronomy
> Principles of Physical Science I
> Physical Geology
> Beginning German I
> Beginning German II
> Beginning Spanish I
> Beginning Spanish II
> Beginning Italian I
> Technical Writing
> Ethics in America
> Introduction to World Religions

University End-of-Course Exams

Several schools offer the opportunity to earn credit for a correspondence course solely by taking (and passing) the final exam for that course. One need not be enrolled as a student in the school to do this. Two schools with especially large programs of this kind are Ohio University (Course Credit by Examination, Tupper Hall, Athens, OH 45701) and the University of North Carolina (Independent Study, Abernethy Hall 002A, Chapel Hill, NC 27514).

Advanced Placement Examinations

The College Board offers exams specifically for high school students who wish to earn college credit while still in high school. Exams in 13 subject areas are offered. (College Board Advanced Placement Program, 888 7th Ave., New York, NY 10106)

Special Assessments

For people whose knowledge is both extensive and in an obscure field (or at least one for which no exams have been developed), some schools are willing to develop special exams for a single student. Each school has its own policy in this regard, so once again it can pay to "shop around."

13

Correspondence Courses

*The postman is the agent of impolite surprises. Every week, we
ought to have an hour for receiving letters—
and then go and take a bath.*

FRIEDRICH NIETZSCHE

There are two kinds of correspondence study, or home-study, courses—vocational and academic. Vocational courses (meat-cutting, locksmithing, appliance repair, etc.) often offer useful training, but rarely lead to degrees, so they are not relevant for this book. The Distance Education and Training Council (1601 18th Street NW, Washington, DC 20009; www.detc.org) offers excellent free information on the sources of vocational home-study courses in many fields.

One hundred and thirty-five major universities and teaching institutions in the United States offer academic correspondence (or e-mail) courses—more than 13,000 courses in hundreds of subjects, from accounting to zoology. Virtually all of these courses can be counted toward a degree at almost any college or university. However, most schools have a limit on the amount of correspondence credit they will apply to a degree. This limit is typically around 50 percent, but the range is from zero to 100 percent.

That means that it is indeed possible to earn an accredited Bachelor's degree entirely through correspondence study. This may be done, for instance, through Regents College, Thomas Edison State College of New Jersey, and Western Illinois University. Courses taken at any of the 135 U.S. schools (and most of the foreign ones) can be applied to a degree at these schools.

Each of the institutions publishes a catalog or bulletin listing their available courses—some offer just a few, others have hundreds. All of the schools accept students living anywhere in the United States, although some charge more for out-of-state students. About 80 percent accept foreign students, but all courses are offered in English only.

A helpful directory called The Independent Study Catalog is, in effect, a master catalog, listing all course titles for each of the schools, with surprisingly informative one-line course descriptions: "Hist & phil of phys ed," "Fac career dev in schools," and 13,000 more. Popular subjects like psychology, business, and education will be offered at a number of schools, but some of the more esoteric topics may only be available at one or two, and the directory points you to them. It is revised approximately every three years by the publisher, Peterson's Guides (P.O. Box 3601, Princeton, NJ 08540, www.petersons.com). A second Peterson's Guide, The Electronic University, lists only those schools that offer courses by computer. Of course you can also write directly to the schools; nearly all of them send out free catalogs.

Correspondence courses range from 1 to 6 semester hours worth of credit, and can cost anywhere from less than $40 to more than $150 per semester hour. The average is just over $80, so that a typical three-unit course would cost about $250. Because of the wide range in costs, it pays to shop around.

A typical correspondence course will consist of from five to twenty lessons, each one requiring a short written paper, answers to questions, or an unsupervised test graded by the instructor. There is almost always a supervised final examination. These can usually be taken anywhere in the world that a suitable proctor can be found (usually a high school or college teacher).

People who cannot go to a testing center because, for instance, they are handicapped, live too far away, or are in prison, can usually arrange to have a test supervisor come to them. Schools can be extremely flexible. One correspondence program administrator told us he had two students—a husband and wife—working as missionaries on a remote island where they were the only people who could read and write. He allowed them to supervise each other.

Many schools set limits on how quickly and how slowly you can complete a correspondence course. The shortest time is generally three to six weeks, while the upper limit ranges from three months to two years. Some schools limit the number of courses you can take at one time, but most do not. Even those with limits are concerned only with courses taken from their own institution. There is no cross-checking, so in theory one could take simultaneous courses from all 135 institutions.

A sidelight: we would have thought that correspondence programs would remain quite stable, since so much time and effort is required to establish one. However, in the three years between editions of Peterson's Guides, it's not unusual for up to 10 percent of the list to change—five or six schools will drop their programs, and a similar number start new ones.

Students who want an even wider range of correspondence courses might consider taking one or more from a foreign university (see list below). While these courses are generally intended for citizens who cannot, for whatever reason, attend residential classes, Americans, Canadians, (and others) are often welcome to enroll. Although there's greater potential for problems (with the mails, deadlines, etc.), it's worth it for students who are interested in unusual fields or specific countries (studying Kiswahili with the University of Nairobi as part of an African-American Studies program, for instance). Unless otherwise specified, the programs are taught in the country's native language.

AMERICAN SCHOOLS

Coding is as follows:

★ = schools with the most undergraduate courses

♥ = schools that welcome students from outside the U.S.

✗ = schools that will not accept foreign students

In the past, we have made special note of schools offering electronic courses. Now, just about every program has at least some on-line component or option, with more being offered every day. To find out details, then, it's best to contact the school, check out their offerings on their website, or visit www.caso.com, where many schools' courses are listed.

We have noted those schools that offer a vast number of courses, which will be the resources of greatest interest to most readers, as well as those schools that only offer a few courses in specialized fields. We have also noted which offer graduate courses, a much less common thing. For more information, call the school in question, or check out their website.

Adams State College ♥
Division of Extended Studies
208 Edgemont
Alamosa, CO 81101
(719) 587-7671
www.adams.edu

Arizona State University ♥
Independent Learning
Ritter B-132, Box 874001
Tempe, AZ 85287-4001
(602) 965-6563 • (800) 533-4806
www.distlearn.pp.asu.edu/

Auburn University ♥
Distance Learning and Outreach Technology
204 Mell Hall
Auburn, AL 36849
(334) 844-3103
www.auburn.edu/outreach/dl

Ball State University ♥
Independent Study by Correspondence
School of Continuing Education
Carmichael Hall
Room 200
Muncie, IN 47306
(765) 285-1586 • (800) 872-0369
www.bsu.edu/distance/

Bastyr College ♥
Distance Learning Department
14500 Juantita Drive NE
Bothell, WA 98011
(425) 602-3154
www.bastyr.edu
All courses are in alternative health-related fields

Bethany College of the Assemblies of God ✗
External Degree Program
800 Bethany Drive
Scotts Valley, CA 95066
(408) 438-3800 • (800) 843-9410
www.bethany.edu

Brigham Young University ♥ ★
Independent Study
206 HCEB
Provo, UT 84602
(801) 378-2868 • (800) 914-8931
coned.byu.edu/is/
A large number of undergraduate and graduate courses

California State University, Dominguez Hills ♥
Coordinator, Humanities External Courses
1000 East Victoria Street
SAC 2-2126
Carson, CA 90747
(310) 243-3743
www.csudh.edu/hux
Graduate courses in the humanities only

California State University, Sacramento ♥
Office of Water Programs
6000 J Street
Sacramento, CA 95819-6025
(916) 278-6142
www.owp.csus.edu/
All courses deal with the fields of waste and wastewater management

Central Michigan University ♥
College of Extended Learning
Rowe Hall 128
Mt. Pleasant, MI 48859
(800) 950-1144, ext. 3865
www.cel.cmich.edu/dlonline.htm

Chadron State University ♥
Directed Independent Study
1000 Main Street
Chadron, NE 69337
(308) 432-6211
www.csc.edu/SCHOOLS/Regional/regional.HTML#DIS
In addition to a number of undergraduate courses, offers one graduate course, in education

Charter Oak State College ♥
Academic Affairs
66 Cedar Street
Newington, CT 06111-2646
(860) 666-4595
www.cosc.edu
Offers a number of undergraduate and graduate courses

Cincinnati Bible College and Seminary ♥
Academic Dean
2700 Glenway Ave.
P.O. Box 4320
Cincinnati, OH 45204
(513) 244-8160

College of West Virginia ♥
School of Academic Enrichment and Lifelong Learning
SAELL Program, P.O. Box AG
Beckley, WV 25802-2803
(304) 253-7351 • (800) 766-6067
www.cwu.net/

Colorado State University ♥
Division of Continuing and Distance Education
Spruce Hall
Fort Collins, CO 80523-1040
(970) 491-5288 • (800) 525-4951
www.colostate.edu/Depts/CE
A number of undergraduate and graduate courses

Columbia Union College ♥
External Degree Program
12501 Old Columbia Pike
Silver Spring, MD 20904
(301) 680-6570 • (800) 782-4769

Creighton University ♥
University College
2500 California Plaza
Omaha, NE 68178
(402) 280-2425
www.creighton.edu/UnivCol/isp.htm
Undergraduate courses in several fields; one graduate course, in synoptic meteorology

David N. Meyers College X
External Degree Director
112 Prospect Ave., Room 622
Cleveland, OH 44115
(216) 523-3848
www.dnmyers.edu

Eastern Kentucky University ♥
Correspondence Coordinator, Extended Programs
Coates Box 27A
Richmond, KY 40475
(606) 622-2001
www.eku.edu

Eastern Michigan University ♥
Distance Education Coordinator
Ypsilanti, MI 48197
(734) 487-1081 • (800) 777-3521
www.emich.edu/public/cont_ed/emucce.html
A number of undergraduate courses; one graduate course, in English

Eastern Oregon University X
Division of Extended Programs
1410 L Ave.
La Grande, OR 97850
(541) 962-3475
Offers both undergraduate and graduate courses (the latter in education, humanities, and psychology)

Eastern Washington University ♥
Director of Continuing Education
MS 162, 526 5th Street
Cheney, WA 99004-2431
(509) 359-2268
ewu69796.ewu.edu/dcesso

Embry-Riddle Aeronautical University ♥
Independent Studies
600 South Clyde Morris Blvd.
Daytona Beach, FL 32114
(904) 226-6397 • (800) 359-3728
www.db.erau.edu
Undergraduate and graduate courses, mainly in aeronautical fields

Emporia State University ♥
Office of Continuing Education
Campus Box 4052, 1200 Commercial Street
Emporia. KS 66801
(316) 341-5385
www.emporia.edu/www/conted/home.htm
Undergraduate and graduate courses

Governors State University ♥
Correspondence Course Coordinator
University Parkway
University Park, IL 60466
(708) 534-4089
www.govst.edu
Undergraduate and graduate courses

Home Study International/Griggs University ♥
Admissions/Records Office
P.O. Box 4437
Silver Spring, MD 20904-6600
(301) 680-6579 • (800) 782-4769

Indiana University ♥
Division of Extended Studies
Owen Hall, Room 001
Bloomington, IN 47405
(812) 855-2292 • (800) 334-1011
www.extend.indiana.edu/
Many undergraduate courses; one graduate course, in journalism

Johnson Bible College ♥
Distance Learning Department
7900 Johnson Drive
Knoxville, TN 37998
(423) 579-2254 • (800) 669-7889
ww2.jbc.edu/johnsonbiblecollege/frmain.htm
Undergraduate and graduate courses in religious fields

Kansas State University ✗
Division of Continuing Education
221 College Court
Manhattan, KS 66506
(785) 532-5687 • (800) 622-2KSU
Undergraduate and graduate courses

Life Bible College ♥
School of Correspondence Studies
1100 Covina Blvd.
San Dimas, CA 92833
(909) 599-5433 • (800) 356-0001
www.lifebible.edu

Louisiana State University and ♥ ★
Agricultural and Mechanical College
Office of Independent Study
E214 Pleasant Hall
Baton Rouge, LA 70803
(504) 388-3175 • (800) 234-5046
www.doce.lsu.edu/is/ishome.htm

Marywood University ♥
Office of Distance Education
2300 Adams Ave.
Scranton, PA 18509
(717) 348-6235 • (800) 836-6940
www.marywood.edu

Middle Tennessee State University ♥
Correspondence Course Coordinator
MTSU Box 22
1301 East Main Street
Murfreesboro, TN 37132
(615) 898-5332
www.mtsu.edu

Minot State University ♥
Continuing Education
500 University Ave. West
Minot, ND 58707
(701) 858-3822 • (800) 777-0750
www.misu.nodak.edu/conted/

Mississippi State University ♥
Independent Study
P. O. Box 5247
Mississippi State, MS 39762-5247
(601) 325-2652
www.msstate.edu/dept/ced

Moody Bible Institute ♥
Academic Affairs for External Studies
820 North LaSalle Blvd.
Chicago, IL 60610
(312) 329-4135 • (800) 955-1123
www.moody.edu
Undergraduate courses in Bible-related fields

Murray State University ✗
Center for Continuing Education
Academic Outreach
P.O. Box 9
Murray, KY 42071
(502) 762-4150

Northern Michigan University ♥
Continuing Education and Sponsored Programs
1401 Presque Isle
Marquette, MI 49855
(906) 227-1683
www.nmu.edu/ce

Northern State University ✗
Office of Continuing Education
1200 South Jay Street
P.O. Box 870
Aberdeen, SD 57401
(605) 626-2615
www.northern.edu

Norwood University ♥
University College
3225 Cook Road
Midland, MI 48640
(517) 837-4455 • (800) 445-5873
www.northwood.edu

Ohio University ♥ ★
Office of Independent Study
302 Tupper Hall
Athens, OH 45701
(740) 593-2910 • (800) 444-2910
www.cats.ohiou.edu/~indstu/index.htm

Oklahoma State University ♥
Independent and Correspondence Study
470 Student Union
Stillwater, OK 74078
(405) 744-6390
www.okstate.edu/education/inc.html

Oregon State University ♥
OSU Statewide
Office of Continuing Higher Education
338 Snell Hall
Corvallis, OR 97331
(541) 737-2676 • (800) 235-6559

Pennsylvania State University ♥ ★
Department of Distance Education
207 Mitchell Building
University Park, PA 16802
(814) 865-5403 • (800) 252-3592
www.cde.psu.edu/de/

Portland State University ♥
Independent Study
School of Extended Studies
P.O. Box 1491
Portland, OR 97207
(503) 725-4865 • (800) 547-8887
extended.portals.org/

Purdue University X
Continuing Education Administration
1586 Stewart Center, Room 116
West Lafayette, IN 47907-1586
(765) 494-2748 • (800) 359-2968
*Undergraduate courses in restaurant, hotel, and institutional
management only*

Regents College ♥
Learning Services
7 Columbia Circle
Albany, NY 12203
(518) 464-8577
www.regents.edu

Roger Williams University X
University College
Open Program
One Old Ferry Road
Bristol, RI 02809
(401) 254-3530 • (800) 458-7144
www.rwu.edu

Roosevelt University ♥
External Studies Program
430 South Michigan Ave.
Chicago, IL 60605
(312) 341-3866
www.roosevelt.edu/distance-learning

Saint Joseph's College ♥
Distance Education Admissions
278 Whites Bridge Road
Standish, ME 04084-5263
(207) 892-7841 • (800) 752-4723
*Undergraduate courses in many fields; graduate courses in
health-care administration*

Salve Regina University ♥
Extension Study
100 Ochre Point Ave.
Newport, RI 02841
(401) 847-6650 • (800) 637-0002
www.salve.edu
Undergraduate and graduate courses

Sam Houston State University X
Correspondence Course Division
P.O. Box 2536
1904 Avenue J
Huntsville, TX 77341
(409) 294-1003
www.shsu.edu/cor-www

San Jose State University ♥
Distance Education/University Continuing Education
One Washington Square
San Jose, CA 95192-1035
(408) 924-2619
conted.sjsu.edu/
*Several undergraduate courses; graduate courses in
education*

Savannah State University ♥
Coastal Georgia Center for Continuing Education
305 Martin Luther King Jr. Blvd.
Savannah, GA 31401
(912) 651-2849

Southern Illinois University ♥
Division of Continuing Education
MC-6705
Carbondale, IL 62901
(618) 453-5682
www.siu.edu/~conted/ilp.htm

Southern Utah University ♥
Office of Distance Learning
351 West Center Street
Cedar City, UT 84720
(435) 865-8084
www.suu.edu/WebPages/ContEdu/distance/inserv.htm
Offers both undergraduate and graduate courses

Southwest Texas State University ♥
Correspondence and Extension Studies
601 University Drive
San Marcos, TX 78666
(512) 245-2322
www.ideal.swt.edu/correspondence
Several undergraduate courses; one graduate course, in voc. ed.

SUNY, College of Environmental Science and Forestry X
Office of Continuing Education
1 Forestry Drive
Syracuse, NY 13210-2784
(315) 470-6891
www.esf.edu/
One course, in forest pathogens

SUNY, Empire State College ♥
Center for Distance Learning
2 Union Ave.
Saratoga Springs, NY 12866
(518) 587-2100 • (800) 847-3000
www.esc.edu

Stephens College ♥ ★
School of Graduate and Continuing Education
Campus Box 2083
Columbia, MO 65215
(573) 876-7125
www.stephens.edu
Undergraduate courses in a number of fields; graduate courses in business administration

Syracuse University ♥
Distance and Executive Education
700 University Ave.
Syracuse, NY 13244-6020
(315) 443-3480 • (800) 442-0501
www.syr.edu
Undergraduate and graduate courses in a number of fields

Taylor University ♥
Worldwide Campus
Institute of Extended Learning
1025 West Rudisill Blvd.
Fort Wayne, IN 46807
(219) 456-2111 • (800) 845-3149

Texas A & M University ♥
Department of Continuing Education
Correspondence/Binnion Hall
Commerce, TX 75429
(903) 886-5921
www.tamu-commerce.edu/academic/conted/index.html

Texas Tech University ♥
Division of Continuing Education
P. O. Box 42191
Lubbock, TX 79409-2191
(806) 742-2352 • (800) 692-6877
www.dce.ttu.edu
Undergraduate courses in a number of fields; graduate courses in education and psychology

Thomas Edison State College X
101 West State Street
Trenton, NJ 08608-11250
(609) 984-1150
www.tesc.edu

United States Sports Academy ♥
Continuing Education and Distance Learning
One Academy Drive
Daphne, AL 36526
(334) 626-3303 • (800) 223-2668
www.sport.ussa.edu
Graduate courses in sports-related fields

University of Alabama ♥
Distance Education
P. O. Box 870388
Tuscaloosa, AL 35487
(205) 348-9278 • (800) 452-5871
ualix.ua.edu/~disted

University of Alaska ♥
Center for Distance Education and Independent Learning
P.O. Box 756700
Fairbanks, AK 99775
(907) 474-5353
uafcde.uaflrb.alaska.edu
Undergraduate and graudate courses

University of Arizona ♥
Extended University/Independent Study
888 North Euclid Ave.
P.O. Box 210158
Tucson, AZ 85721-0158
(520) 622-4222 • (800) 772-7480
www.arizona.edu

University of Arkansas ♥
Department of Independent Study
2 East Center Street
Fayetteville, AR 72701
(501) 575-3648 • (800) 638-1217
www.uacted.uark.edu

University of California ♥
Student Services
Center for Media and Independent Learning
2000 Center St., Suite 400
Berkeley, CA 94704
(510) 642-4124
www-cmil.unex.berkeley.edu

University of Central Arkansas ♥
Independent Studies-UCA
201 Donaghey Ave.
Conway, AR 72035
(501) 450-5274
www.uca.edu/

University of Colorado, Boulder ♥
Division of Continuing Education
Boulder, CO 80309-0178
(303) 492-8756 • (800) 331-2801
www.colorado.edu/cewww
Undergraduate and graduate courses

University of Florida ♥
Independent Study
2209 NW 13th Street, Suite D
Gainesville, FL 32609
(352) 392-1711 • (800) 327-4218
www.doce.ufl.edu/indstudy

University of Georgia ♥
Center for Continuing Education
Independent Study
Athens, GA 30602-3603
(706) 542-3243 • (800) 877-3243
www.gactr.uga.edu/usgis/

University of Idaho ♥
Correspondence Study in Idaho
CEB 201
Moscow, ID 83844-3225
(208) 885-6641 • (800) 422-6013
www.uidaho.edu/indep-study
Undergraduate courses in many fields; graduate courses in adult education and counseling

University of Illinois ♥
Guided Individual Study
302 East John Street
Suite 1406
Champaign, IL 61820
(217) 333-1320
www.extramural.uiuc.edu/gis/index.html

University of Iowa ♥ ★
Guided Correspondence Study
116 International Center
Iowa City, IA 52242
(319) 353-2575 • (800) 272-6430
gcs.ccp.uiowa.edu
Undergraduate and graduate courses in many fields

University of Kansas ♥
Academic Outreach Programs
Continuing Education Building
Lawrence, KS 66045-2606
(785) 864-4792 • (800) 532-6772
www.cc.ukans.edu/cwis/units/IndStudy/MENU.html
Undergraduate and graduate courses

University of Kentucky ♥
Independent Study Program
Frazee Hall, Room 1
Lexington, KY 40506-0031
(606) 257-1100
www.uky.edu

University of Maryland University College♥
Distance Education, SFSC 3237
University Blvd. at Adelphi Road
College Park, MD 20742
(301) 985-7849 • (800) 283-6832
www.umuc.edu

University of Memphis X
University College
Johnson Hall G-1
Memphis, TN 38152
(901) 678-2754
www.memphis.edu

University of Michigan ♥
Extension Services
Office of Academic Outreach
837 Greene St.
Ann Arbor, MI 48109-3213
(313) 764-5300
www.outreach.umich.edu
Undergraduate and graduate courses

University of Minnesota ♥ ★
Independent Study
540 Rarig
Minneapolis, MN 55455
(612) 624-0000 • (800) 234-6564
www.cee.umn.edu/dis
Undergraduate courses in many fields; graduate courses in rhetoric

University of Mississippi ♥
Department of Independent Study
P.O. Box 629
University, MS 38677-0729
(601) 232-7313
www.olemiss.edu/indstudy

University of Missouri ♥ ★
Center for Independent Study
136 Clark Hall
Columbia, MO 65211-4200
(572) 882-6431 • (800) 609-3727
indepstudy.ext.missouri.edu
Undergraduate and graduate courses in many fields

University of Nebraska ♥
Distance Education
336 Nebraska Center
33rd and Holdrege
Lincoln, NE 68583-9800
(402) 472-4321
www.unl.edu/conted/disted/
Undergraduate courses in many fields; graduate courses in management

University of Nevada ♥
Independent Study by Correspondence
P.O. Box 14429
Reno, NV 89507
(702) 784-4652 • (800) 233-8928
www.dce.unr.edu/istudy
Undergraduate courses in many fields; graduate course in educational leadership

University of New Mexico ♥
Continuing Education
1634 University Blvd. NE
Albuquerque, NM 87131
(505) 277-1604
Approximately 52 undergraduate courses

University of North Carolina ♥
Division of Continuing Education
CB #1020
The Friday Center
Chapel Hill, NC 27599
(919) 962-1105 • (800) 862-5669
www.unc.edu/depts/fri_cntr

University of North Carolina at Greensboro ♥
Division of Continual Education
202 Forney Building
Greensboro, NC 27412
(910) 334-5414 • (800) 306-9033
www.uncg.edu

University of North Dakota ♥
Department of Outreach Programs
Division of Continuing Education
P.O. Box 9021
University Station
Grand Forks, ND 58201
(701) 777-4264 • (800) 342-8230
www.conted.und.edu/

University of Northern Colorado ♥
College of Continuing Education
Greeley, CO 80639
(970) 351-2926 • (800) 232-1749
Undergraduate and graduate courses

University of Northern Iowa ♥
Guided Correspondence Study
124 SHC
Cedar Falls, IA 50614-0223
(319) 273-2123 • (800) 772-1746
www.uni.edu/contined/gcs
Undergraduate and graduate courses

University of Oklahoma ♥
Independent Study Department
1600 South Jenkins Street
Room 101
Norman, OK 73072
(405) 325-1921 • (800) 942-5702
www.occe.ou.edu

University of South Carolina ♥
Independent Learning Coordinator
Correspondence Study
915 Gregg St.
Columbia, SC 29208
(803) 777-7210 • (800) 922-2577
www.sc.edu/deis/student.services

University of South Dakota ♥
Program Coordinator
Distributive Learning
SWES
Vermillion, SD 57069-2390
(605) 677-6110 • (800) 233-7937

University of Southern Colorado ♥
Continuing Education
2200 Bonforte Blvd.
Pueblo, CO 81001
(719) 549-2316 • (800) 388-6154
www.uscolo.edu/coned
Undergraduate courses in many fields; graduate courses in education

University of Southern Mississippi ♥
Office of Independent Study
P. O. Box 5056
Hattiesburg, MS 39406
(601) 266-4195
www-dept.usm.edu/~cice/ce/independent
Undergraduate courses in many fields; graduate courses in biology

University of Tennessee ♥
Distance Education and Independent Study
1536 White Ave., Room A119
Knoxville, TN 37996
(423) 974-5134 • (800) 670-8657
www.ce.utk.edu

University of Texas ♥
Independent and Distance Learning
P. O. Box 7700, 1.114 Lake Austin Center
3001 Lake Austin Blvd.
Austin, TX 78713-3461
(512) 471-7716 • (800) 252-3461
www.utexas.edu/dce/eimc/il/

University of Utah ♥
Continuing Education
2180 Annex Bldg.
Salt Lake City, UT 84112
www.dce.utah.edu/instudy

University of Washington ♥
Distance Learning Registration Services
5001 25th Ave. NE
Seattle, WA 98105
(206) 543-2350 • (800) 543-2320
weber.u.washington.edu/~distance

University of Wisconsin ♥ ★
Distributed Learning Services
Room 205 Extension Bldg.
432 North Lake St.
Madison, WI 53706
(608) 262-4727 • (800) 442-6460
www.uwex.edu/ilearn/

University of Wisconsn, Plattville X
Extension Program
Pioneer Tower 506
1 University Plaza
Plattville, WI 53818
(608) 342-1468 • (800) 362-5460
www.uwplatt.edu/edp
Mainly business and accounting

University of Wisconsin, Superior
Extension Program
1800 Grand Ave.
Superior, WI 54880
(715) 394-8494
www.uwsuper.edu

University of Wyoming ♥
School of Extended Studies
Off-Campus Credit Courses
P.O. Box 3294
Laramie, WY 82071
(307) 766-5631 • (800) 448-7801
scs.uwyo.edu/

Upper Iowa University ♥
External Program Office
P.O. Box 1861
Fayette, IA 52142
(319) 425-5283 • (888) 877-3742
www.uiu.edu

U.S. Department of Agriculture ♥
Correspondence School
STOP 9911, Room 112
1400 Independence Ave, SW
Washington, DC 20250-9911
(202) 720-7123
grad.usda.gov/corres/corpro.html
Undergraduate courses in a number of fields; graduate courses in library sciences and statistics

Utah State University ♥
Independent Study Division
1511 Independent Study
5000 University Blvd.
Logan, UT 84322-5000
(435) 797-2137 • (800) 233-2137
www.de.usu.edu/

Utah Valley State College ♥
Continuing Education
800 West 1200 South, Mail Stop 147
Orem, UT 84058
(801) 222-8004
www.uvsc.edu/

Washington Institute for Graduate Studies ♥
External Program, 2268 East Newcastle Drive
Sandy, UT 84093
(801) 943-2440
Graduate courses in tax law

Washington State University ♥
Extended Programs
Van Doren 204
P.O. Box 645220
Pullman, WA 99164-5220
(509) 335-3557 • (800) 222-4978
www.eus.wsu.edu/edp/

Weber State College ♥
Distance Learning
4005 University Circle
Ogden, UT 84408-4005
(801) 626-6785 • (800) 848-7770
www.weber.edu

Western Illinois University X
Extended Learning
401 Memorial Hall
Macomb, IL 61455
(309) 298-2496
www.wiu.edu/users/miebis
Undergraduate and graduate courses in a number of fields

Western Michigan University ♥
Department of Distance Education
Ellsworth B-102
Kalamazoo, MI 49001-5161
(616) 383-4195
www.wmich.edu

Western Oregon University X
Department of Extended and Summer Studies
345 North Monmouth Ave.
Monmouth, OR 97361
(503) 838-8483 • (800) 451-5767
www.wou.edu
Undergraduate courses in several fields; graduate courses in education and social science

Western Washington University ♥
Independent Learning
Bellingham, WA 98225-9042
(360) 650-3650
www.wwu.edu/~extended/ilearn.html

SOME FOREIGN SCHOOLS THAT OFFER CORRESPONDENCE COURSES

Australia

Adelaide College of TAFE
20 Light Squaare
Adelaide 5000 Australia
Over 300 external courses

Charles Sturt University
Albury Wodonga Campus
P.O. Box 789
Albury NSW 2640 Australia
Parks & rec, park management, and more

Curtin University
GPO Box U 1987
Perth WA 6001 Australia

Deakin University
Off-Campus Operations
Geelong 3217 Australia

Edith Cowan University
External Studies Dept.
P.O. Box 830
Claremont, Western Australia 6010
Library studies, justice administration, youth work

Engineering Education Australia
Eagle House
118 Alfred Street
Milsons Point NSW 2061 Australia
Continuing education for professional engineers

Flinders University
The Admissions Office
P.O. Box 2100
Adelaide SA 5001 Australia
Humanities, sciences, nursing

Hobart Technical College
School of External Studies
26 Bathurst Street
Hobart, Tasmania 7000 Australia
Administration, business, applied science

Ipswich College of TAFE
The Centre for Mineral Industries Studies
P.O. Box 138
Booval QLD Australia
Mining studies

James Cook University
The Admissions Officer
Townsville, Queensland 4811 Australia

Macquarie University
New South Wales 2109 Australia

Monash Distance Education Centre
Churchill, Victoria Australia 3842
Applied science, visual arts, engineering, health

Northern Territory University
NT External Studies Centre
Darwin NT 0811 Australia
Professional courses

Open Training and Education Network
199 Regent Street, Redfern
NSW 2016 Australia

Queensland University of Technology
Kelvin Grove Campus
Locked Bag 2
Red Hill, Queensland 4059 Australia
Education, computers, health fields

St. Johns College, External Studies
P.O. Box 817
Newcastle 2130 Australia
Anglican theology

University of Central Queensland
Distance Education Centre
Rockhampton M.C.
Queensland 4702 Australia
Continuing professional education

University of New South Wales
P.O. Box 1, Kensington NSW 2033 Australia
Sports medicine, business, and more

University of South Australia
Underdale Campus, External Studies
Holbrooks Road
Underdale, South Australia 5032

University of Western Sydney
The Registrar
Hawkesbury, Richmond
NSW 2753 Australia
Agricultural education, applied science

Victoria University of Technology
G.P.O. Box 2476V
Melbourne, Victoria 3001 Australia
Technical continuing education

Canada

Acadia University
Division of Continuing Education
Wolfville, NS B0P 1X0 Canada
Includes a graduate course in teacher education

Athabasca University
Office of the Registrar
1 University Drive
Athabasca, Alberta, Canada T95 3A3
www.athabascau.ca
Over 250 undergraduate courses

British Columbia Institute of Technology
Health Part-Time Studies
3700 Wilingdon Ave.
British Columbia, V5G 3H2 Canada
All levels of health-studies courses

Dalhousie University
The Registrar
Halifax, NS B3H 4HT, Canada
Business, marketing, law, and more

McGill University
Distance Education
3700 McTavish Street
Montreal, PQ H3A N2 Canada
www.mcgill.ca
Undergraduate courses in education and graduate courses in medical fields

Memorial University of Newfoundland
Centre for Distance Education Development
and Support
School of Continuing Education
St. John's, NF A1B 3X8
www.ce.mun.ca
Undergraduate courses in several fields; graduate courses in education and social work

Mount Saint Vincent University
EMF Room 121
166 Bedford Hwy.
Halifax, NS B3M 2J6 Canada
Courses in allied health, business, tourism and hospitality

University of Calgary
Distance Education
Off Campus Credit
2500 University Drive NW
Calgary, Alberta T2N 1N4 Canada
About 20 courses

University of Manitoba
Distance Education Area
188 Continuing Education Complex
Winnipeg, Manitoba R3T 2N2 Canada
(204) 474-8011
www.umanitoba.ca/
Undergraduate and graduate courses

University of New Brunswick
Extension and Summer Session
P.O. Box 4400
Fredericton, NB E3B 5A3 Canada
(506) 453-4646
www.unb.ca/coned/

University of Saskatchewan
Independent Studies Coordinator
Extension Division
Room 330 Kirk Hall
117 Science Place
Saskatoon, SK S7N 5C8 Canada
(306) 966-5562
www.usask.ca

University of Toronto
School of Continuing Studies
Distance Learning
158 St. George Street
Toronto, Ont M5S 2V8 Canada
Many courses

University of Waterloo
Teaching Resources and Continuing Education
Waterloo, Ont N2L 3G1 Canada
Many fields, including interdisciplinary studies

University of Windsor
Continuing Education
401 Sunset Ave.
Windsor, ON W9B 3P4 Canada
(519) 253-3000 • (800) 263-1242
www.uwindsor.ca

Wilfrid Laurier University
75 University Ave. West
Waterloo, Ont N2L 3C5 Canada
Music, arts, science, business

Chile

Universidad Austal de Chile
Programa de Educacion Continua
Independencia 641
Valdivia, Chile

Costa Rica

Universidad Estatal a Distancia
Apartado 474-2050 de Montes de Oca
San Jose, Costa Rica

Hungary

Euro-Contact
P.O. Box 433
H-1371 Budapest, Hungary
Management and business administration

Indonesia

Universitas Terbuka
P.O. Box 6666
Jakarta 10001 Indonesia
Programs for teachers

Jamaica

Eagle Foundation for Enterprise
30 Grenada Crescent
Kingston 5
Jamaica, West Indies
Business

Kenya

University of Nairobi
Institute of Adult and Distance Education
P.O. Box 30197, Nairobi, Kenya
Kenyan history, religious studies, and Kiswahil

Korea

Air & Correspondence University
169 Dongsung-Dong, Chongro-Ku
Seoul 110-791, Korea
Courses in languages, arts, law, agriculture

Norway

Jysk Aabent Universitet
Niels Juels Gade 84
DK-8200 Aarhus N, Denmark

NKI
P.O. Box 111
1341 Bekkestua, Norway
More than 250 courses

Norsk Fjernundervisning
P.O. Box 8197 Dep
0034 Oslo 1, Norway
Environmental education

Panama

Universidad Interamericana de Educacion a Distancia
Urbanizacion Obarrio
Calle 57 y Abe Bravo
Edificio Tolima, Panama
Many lifelong learning courses

Portugal

Universidade Aberta
Palacio Ceia, Rua da Escola Politecnica 147
1200 Lisbon, Portugal
Teacher training, languages, and literature

Pakistan

Allama Iqbal Open University
Sector H-8, Islamabad, Pakistan
Mainly education

South Africa

Damelin Correspondence College
Damelin Center
Corner Plein & Hoekl Sts.
Johannesburg 2001 South Africa
A wide range of high-school-level and professional courses

Promat Correspondence College
P.O. Box 95775
Waterkloof 0145
Weavind Park 0184
Pretoria, South Africa

University of Cape Town
School of Education
Rondesboch 7700, South Africa
Primary education for working teachers

Sri Lanka

Open University of Sri Lanka
P.O. Box 21
Nawqala, Nugegoda Sri Lanka

Sweden

University of Umea
901-87 Umea, Sweden
More than 150 courses

Tanzania

University of Dar Es Salaam
Institute of Adult Education
P.O. Box 20679
Dar Es Salaam, Tanzania
African history, Kiswahili, national development

Thailand

Sukhothai Thammathirat Open University
Bangpod, Pakkredl
Nonthaburi 11120 Thailand
Many fields

Vietnam

Vietnam National Institute of Open Learning
Vien Dao Tao Mo Rong
Nha B-101
Phuong Bach Koa
Quan Hai Ba Trung Hanoi, Vietnam
Mainly vocational and language courses

Zimbabwe

Zimbabwe Distance Education College
Moffat Street/Albion Road
P.O. Box 316
Harare, Zimbabwe
Management, administration, agriculture courses

A GRADUATE SCHOOL FABLE

One sunny day a rabbit came out of her hole in the ground to enjoy the fine weather. The day was so nice that she became careless and a fox snuck up behind her and caught her.

"I am going to eat you for lunch!", said the fox.

"Wait!", replied the rabbit, "You should at least wait a few days."

"Oh yeah? Why should I wait?"

"Well, I am just finishing my thesis on *The Superiority of Rabbits over Foxes and Wolves*."

"Are you crazy? I should eat you right now! Everybody knows that a fox will always win over a rabbit."

"Not really, not according to my research. If you like, you can come into my hole and read it for yourself. If you are not convinced, you can go ahead and have me for lunch."

"You really are crazy!" But since the fox was curious and had nothing to lose, it went with the rabbit. The fox never came out.

A few days later the rabbit was again taking a break from writing and sure enough, a wolf came out of the bushes and was ready to set upon her.

"Wait!" yelled the rabbit, "you can't eat me right now."

"And why might that be, my furry appetizer?"

"I am almost finished writing my thesis on *The Superiority of Rabbits over Foxes and Wolves*."

The wolf laughed so hard that it almost lost its grip on the rabbit.

"Maybe I shouldn't eat you. You really are sick . . . in the head. You might have something contagious."

"Come and read it for yourself. You can eat me afterward if you disagree with my conclusions."

So the wolf went down into the rabbit's hole . . . and never came out.

The rabbit finished her thesis and was out celebrating in the local lettuce patch. Another rabbit came along and asked, "What's up? You seem very happy."

"Yup, I just finished my thesis."

"Congratulations. What's it about?"

"*The Superiority of Rabbits over Foxes and Wolves*."

"Are you sure? That doesn't sound right."

"Oh yes. Come and read it for yourself."

So together they went down into the rabbit's hole. As they entered, the friend saw the typical graduate student abode, albeit a rather messy one after writing a thesis. The computer with the controversial work was in one corner. To the right there was a pile of fox bones, to the left a pile of wolf bones. And in the middle was a very large, well-fed lion.

The moral of the story:

The title of your thesis doesn't matter.

The subject doesn't matter.

The research doesn't matter.

All that matters is who your advisor is.

—*one of those wonderful things that is circulated on the Internet, but without credit to the author. Thank you, whoever you are. (Let us know!)*

76

14
Credit for Life-Experience Learning

Experience is the name everyone gives to their mistakes.

OSCAR WILDE

The philosophy behind credit for life-experience learning can be expressed very simply: Academic credit is given for what you know, without regard for how, when, or where the learning was acquired.

Consider a simple example: Quite a few colleges and universities offer credit for courses in typewriting. For instance, at Western Illinois University, Business Education 261 is a basic typing class. Anyone who takes and passes that class is given three units of credit.

An advocate of credit for life-experience learning would say: "If you know how to type, regardless of how and where you learned, even if you taught yourself at the age of nine, you should still get those same three units of credit, once you demonstrate that you have the same skill level as a person who passes Business Education 261."

Of course not all learning can be converted into college credit. But many people are surprised to discover how much of what they already know is, in fact, creditworthy. With thousands of colleges offering hundreds of thousands of courses, it is a rare subject indeed that someone hasn't determined to be worthy of some credit. There is no guarantee that a given school will honor a given learning experience, or even accept another school's assessment for transfer purposes. Yale might not accept typing credit. But then again, the course title often sounds much more academic than the learning experience itself, as in "Business Education" for typing, "Cross-Cultural Communication" for a trip to China, or "Fundamentals of Applied Kinesiology" for golf lessons.

Here are eight major types of life experience that may be worth college credit, especially in nontraditional degree-granting programs:

1. **Work.** Many of the skills acquired in paid employment are also skills that are taught in colleges and universities. These include, for instance, typing, filing, shorthand, accounting, inventory control, financial management, map reading, military strategy, welding, computer programming or operating, editing, planning, sales, real estate appraisals, and literally thousands of other things.

2. **Homemaking.** Home maintenance, household planning and budgeting, child rearing, child psychology, education, interpersonal communication, meal planning and nutrition, gourmet cooking, and much more.

3. **Volunteer work.** Community activities, political campaigns, church activities, service organizations, volunteer work in social service agencies or hospitals, and so forth.

4. **Noncredit learning in formal settings.** Company training courses, in-service teacher training, workshops, clinics, conferences and conventions, lectures, courses on radio or television, noncredit correspondence courses, etc.

5. **Travel.** Study tours (organized or informal), significant vacation and business trips, living for periods in other countries or cultures, participating in activities related to other cultures or subcultures.

6. **Recreational activities and hobbies.** Musical skills, aviation training and skills, acting or other work in a community theater, sports, arts and crafts, fiction and nonfiction writing, public speaking, gardening, visiting museums, designing and making clothing, attending plays, concerts, and movies, and many other leisure-time activities.

7. **Reading, viewing, listening.** This may cover any field in which a person has done extensive or intensive reading and study, and for which college credit has not been granted. This category has, for instance, included viewing various series on public television.

8. Discussions with experts. A great deal of learning can come from talking to, listening to, and working with experts, whether in ancient history, carpentry, or theology. Significant, extensive, or intensive meetings with such people may also be worth credit.

THE MOST COMMON ERROR MOST PEOPLE MAKE

The most common error most people make when thinking about *getting credit for life experience* is confusing *time spent* with *learning*. Being a regular churchgoer for 30 years is not worth any college credit in and of itself. But the regular churchgoer who can document that he or she has prepared for and taught Sunday school classes, worked with youth groups, participated in leadership programs, organized fund-raising drives, studied Latin or Greek, taken tours to the Holy Land, or even engaged in lengthy philosophical discussions with a clergyman, is likely to get credit for those experiences. Selling insurance for 20 years is worth no credit—unless you describe and document the learning that took place in areas of marketing, banking, risk management, entrepreneurial studies, etc.

It is crucial that the experiences can be documented to a school's satisfaction. Two people could work side by side in the same laboratory for five years. One might do little more than follow instructions—running routine experiments, setting up and dismantling apparatus, and then heading home. The other, with the same job title, might do extensive reading in the background of the work being done, get into discussions with supervisors, make plans and recommendations for other ways of doing the work, propose or design new kinds of apparatus, or develop hypotheses on why the results were turning out the way they were.

It is not enough just to say what you did, or to submit a short resumé. The details and specifics must be documented. The two most common ways this is done are by preparing a life experience portfolio (essentially a long, well-documented, annotated resumé), or by taking an equivalency examination to demonstrate knowledge gained.

Presenting Your Learning

Most schools that give credit for life-experience learning require that the student make a formal presentation, usually in the form of a life experience portfolio. Each school has its own standards for the form and content of such a portfolio, and many, in fact, offer either guidelines or courses (some for credit, some not) to help the nontraditional student prepare a portfolio.

Several books on this subject have been published by the Council for Adult and Experiential Learning. For a list of current publications, contact them at CAEL, 243 Wabash Ave., Chicago, IL 60606, (312) 922-5909, or go to www.cael.org.

CAEL offers for sale a number of books designed to help people prepare life experience portfolios. These and some from other publishers are described in the Bibliography section. Sadly, CAEL no longer offers sample portfolios for sale; that was an excellent service, now discontinued.

The following list should help to get you thinking about the possibilities, by presenting a sampling of some 24 other means by which people have documented life-experience learning, sometimes as part of a portfolio, sometimes not:

- official commendations
- audiotapes
- slides
- course outlines
- bills of sale
- records or photographs of exhibitions
- programs of recitals and performances
- videotapes
- awards and honors
- mementos
- copies of speeches made
- licenses (pilot, real estate, etc.)
- certificates
- testimonials and endorsements
- interviews with others
- newspaper articles
- official job descriptions
- copies of exams taken
- military records
- samples of arts or crafts made
- samples of writing
- designs and blueprints
- works of art
- films and photographs

HOW LIFE EXPERIENCE LEARNING IS TURNED INTO ACADEMIC CREDIT

It isn't easy. In a perfect world, there would be universally accepted standards, and it would be as easy to measure the credit value in a seminar on refrigeration engineering as it is to measure the temperature inside a refrigerator. Some schools and national organizations *are* striving to create extensive "menus" of nontraditional experiences, to insure that anyone doing the same thing would get the same credit.

There continues to be progress in this direction. Many schools have come to agree, for instance, on aviation experience: a private pilot's license is worth four semester units, an instrument rating is worth six additional units, and so forth.

The American Council on Education, a private organization, regularly publishes a massive multivolume set of books, in two series: *The National Guide to Educational Credit for Training Programs* and *Guide to the Evaluation of Educational Experiences in the Armed Forces* (see Bibliography for details), which many schools use to assign credit directly; others use them as guidelines in doing their own evaluations. A few examples will demonstrate the sort of thing that is done:

A nine-day Red Cross training course called The Art of Helping is evaluated as worth two semester hours of social work.

The John Hancock Mutual Life Insurance Company's internal course in technical skills for managers is worth three semester hours of business administration.

Portland Cement Company's five-day training program in kiln optimization, whatever that may be, is worth one semester hour.

The Professional Insurance Agents' three-week course in basic insurance is worth six semester units: three in principles of insurance and three in property and liability contract analysis.

The U.S. Army's 27-week course in ground surveillance radar repair is worth 15 semester hours: 10 in electronics and five more in electrical laboratory.

The Army's legal-clerk training course can be worth 24 semester hours, including three in English, three in business law, three in management, etc.

There are hundreds of additional business and military courses that have been evaluated already, and thousands more that will be worth credit for those who have taken them, whether or not they appear in these A.C.E. volumes.

The Controversy Over Graduate Credit for Life-Experience Learning

As Norman Somers writes, "Powerful forces in graduate education have declared the granting of credit for prematriculation experiences anathema. Many professors and graduate deans have spoken out against the assessment of learning experiences which have occurred prior to a student's formal enrollment."

The policy of the Council of Graduate Schools is that "no graduate credit should be granted for experiential learning that occurs prior to the student's matriculation." It should, they insist, be given "only when a graduate faculty and dean of an accredited institution have had the opportunity to plan the experience, to establish its goals, and to

monitor the time, effort and the learning that has taken place."

In other words, if I enroll in a school and then study and master advanced statistical techniques, they should give me, say, nine units of credit. But if, say, I learned those techniques during 20 years on the job as chief statistician for the Bureau of the Census, no credit should be given.

Fortunately, many schools and organizations, including the influential American Council on Education, disagree with this policy. Their guidelines, described earlier, regularly include recommendations for graduate credit, based on "independent study, original research, critical analysis, and the scholarly and professional application of the specialized knowledge or discipline."

SOME INSPIRATION

There are always some people who say, "Oh, I haven't ever done anything worthy of college credit." We have yet to meet anyone with an IQ higher than room temperature who has not done at least some creditworthy things. Often it's just a matter of presenting them properly, in a portfolio. Here are two sources of inspiration.

First, a list of 100 things that *could* be worth credit for life-experience learning. And second, a detailed description by an expert in portfolio preparation, detailing how he earned more than 80% of the credit for his Bachelor's degree by creative portfolio management.

100 Things

This list could easily be 10 or 100 times as long. Please note the "could." Some reviewers in the past have made fun of this list, suggesting that we were saying you can earn a degree for buying Persian rugs. Not so. We *do* suggest, however, that a person who made a high-level study of Persian art and culture, preparatory to buying carpets, and who could document the reading, consultations, time spent, sources, etc., could probably earn some portfolio credit for this out-of-classroom endeavor. Here, then, is the list:

Playing tennis
Preparing for natural childbirth
Leading a church group
Taking a bodybuilding class
Speaking French
Selling real estate
Studying gourmet cooking
Reading *War and Peace*
Building model airplanes
Traveling through Belgium
Learning shorthand
Starting a small business
Navigating a small boat
Writing a book
Buying a Persian carpet
Watching public television

Decorating a home or office
Attending a convention
Being a summer-camp counselor
Studying Spanish
Bicycling across Greece
Interviewing senior citizens
Living in another culture
Writing advertisements
Throwing a pot
Repairing a car
Performing magic
Attending art films
Welding and soldering
Designing and weaving a rug
Negotiating a contract
Editing a manuscript
Planning a trip
Steering a ship
Appraising an antique
Writing a speech
Studying first aid or CPR
Organizing a Canadian union
Researching international laws
Listening to Shakespeare's plays on tape
Designing a playground
Planning a garden
Devising a marketing strategy
Reading the newspaper
Designing a home
Attending a seminar
Playing the piano
Studying a new religion
Reading about the Civil War
Taking ballet lessons
Helping a dyslexic child
Riding a horse
Pressing flowers
Keeping tropical fish
Writing press releases
Writing for the local newspaper
Running the PTA
Acting in little theater
Flying an airplane
Designing a quilt
Taking photographs
Building a table
Developing an inventory system
Programming a home computer
Helping in a political campaign
Playing a musical instrument
Painting a picture
Playing political board games
Serving on a jury
Volunteering at the hospital
Visiting a museum
Attending a great books group
Designing and sewing clothes

Playing golf
Having intensive talks with a doctor
Teaching the banjo
Reading the Bible
Leading a platoon
Learning Braille
Operating a printing press
Eating in an exotic restaurant
Running a store
Planning a balanced diet
Reading *All and Everything*
Learning sign language
Teaching Sunday school
Training an apprentice
Being an apprentice
Weaving a rug
Learning yoga
Laying bricks
Making a speech
Being Dungeonmaster
Negotiating a merger
Developing film
Learning calligraphy
Applying statistics to gambling
Doing circle dancing
Taking care of sick animals
Reading this book

THE LEVICOFF PORTFOLIO

That sounds like a Robert Ludlum novel, but this is, rather, an essay by Steve Levicoff, Ph.D. (Union Institute) who earned his Bachelor's, Master's, and Ph.D. from accredited nontraditional schools. In his Bachelor's program, he made extensive use of the portfolio assessment approach. When we read this essay of his, explaining his approach to the process, we felt it would be of interest to our readers, and Dr. Levicoff kindly agreed to let us reproduce it here.

1. Choose a school that is flexible on portfolios (e.g., Edison is more flexible than Regents).

2. Go to a library that has a good selection of college catalogs—those from traditional colleges in general.

3. Leaf through the catalogs and make a photocopy of every course description (the course name plus the three- or four-line description of its content) that you feel you could challenge based on the description of the course. Make a note of the college, the year of the catalog, the department offering the course, and the catalog page number.

4. Next, go to your basement, closets, and any other place you store trivial papers, photographs, or other mementos that you thought would never do you any good and match whatever you find to the course description. Do the same for any significant papers in your filing cabinet(s).

5. Gather up any current documentation that you feel could be useful to challenging a course, especially work-related items if you are in a position that involves a lot of paperwork: memos, projects, etc. Match them up with the course descriptions.

6. Make a list of all relevant books you have read on the subjects you want to challenge. List any courses, professional workshops you have attended, and in-service training you have received. Start with your own bookshelf or any certificates you have in your file. Then relate them to the subjects you want to challenge.

7. Now just write up your rationale for earning credit for the courses you've chosen based on the "validating evidence" you can submit.

8. Seek out people with whom you work or have ever worked and ask them to write letters confirming your experience. Remember, these are not letters of recommendation, they are letters of validation. If your boss writes a letter saying "Bill Morrow is a nice guy," it won't get you anywhere. However, if he or she writes, "Bill Morrow coordinates administration, personnel, and purchasing for our firm and exhibits sound fiscal, legal, and negotiating skills," you've got enough to validate your submissions in three different courses: administrative management, personnel, and purchasing and negotiation. It also helps if you have written your company's administrative manual, employee handbook, and purchasing policies and procedures.

9. Make sure your course selection includes an adequate number of upper-level credits. At Edison, for instance, these are defined as any credits in a specific subject over six, which provides a tremendous amount of flexibility. For example, if you challenge three-credit courses in Trumpet I, French Horn I, and Piano I, one of them can be treated as upper level, even though they may all have lower-level course numbers in the college catalog from which you cut the descriptions. However, try to concentrate on four-year college catalogs, as some schools have a cap on the number of courses you can challenge from junior or community colleges.

10. Finally, learn how to "work the system." If, for example, you want to earn credit in "word processing," don't look for a four-year college that offers a course in word processing; look for a junior or community college that offers two or three courses in word processing and challenge them based on different levels (such as basic, advanced, and supervisory). Also, remember that when it comes to computer courses, a submission must have a significant math component in order to qualify for liberal arts; if it is practical in orientation, it does not qualify for liberal arts but can

still fit in as a free elective. (For example, BASIC, COBOL, or Intro. to Computer Science could qualify as liberal arts courses under the math/natural science header; RPG, word processing, and database management do not have significant math components, so they would fit into the free elective area.) Last but not least, be careful not to "double-dip" with similar course titles; in other words, don't try to challenge "19th Century American History" and "United States History 1801-1900." They're the same course.

Remember that the more culturally literate you already are, the more courses you will be able to challenge. If you have spent years watching PBS and reading nonfiction, you'll have a much easier time than someone who has spent years reading comic books and watching soap operas. Even then, chances are that, with a little research, you'll still find courses to meet your needs. (Even Berkeley offers a course titled "The Films of Keanu Reeves.") I once challenged a two-credit course in folk guitar (for the curious, I found that one in the catalog of Kent State U.), earning credit in about five minutes by playing two songs for the evaluator.

Also remember that, if you are culturally literate and can challenge a degree largely by portfolio, you won't learn a lot at the Bachelor's level (although you will certainly learn how to work the system). So start making plans to find a graduate program where you can actually learn something substantive and have some more fun.

Incidentally, if you don't have enough hard or written evidence for a portfolio challenge, don't let that stop you. Remember that you have the option of earning credit based on evidence alone, testing alone, or a combination of evidence and testing. If you opt for testing, try to do it in an oral exam format. Written exams tend to represent only the evaluator's perspective and do not allow the flexibility of the oral format. It's like dancing with your evaluator, with the difference being which party will lead and which will follow. Also remember that hard evidence can take many forms. It doesn't have to be a written work, but can be drawings or other art, musical compositions, playbills from acting experience, original recipes, sermons preached, talks given, *ad infinitum*. And the same evidence can be used for multiple submissions without being construed as "double dipping." For example, if you have written an employee handbook, it can be used as evidence in courses ranging from personnel administration to labor law to business writing.

Many schools, including Edison and Regents, have portfolio development manuals available; you should obtain copies of both so you have an idea of the language (or "jargon") they use.

For the curious, here's how I did my own B.A. in Humanities from Thomas Edison, earning 98 credits by portfolio, testing out of an additional 16 credits through TECEP and DANTES exams, and carrying in only six credits by previous coursework. Incidentally, even though I entered with only six credits, the whole ball of wax took me only a year and a half. With administrative and graduation paperwork included, I was in and out in one year and ten months, and have never been turned down by any graduate program to which I've applied.

The broad area headers below represent TESC's "distribution requirement" for a Bachelor's degree in a liberal arts area.

Written Expression (6)

Advanced Writing, Academic Forms, Portfolio, 3
Business English, Portfolio, 3

Humanities (12)

Solfeggio & Dictation I, Course, 2
Keyboard Harmony I, Course, 1
Performance Class, Course, 1
Chorus, Course, 2
Radio Production I, Portfolio, 3
Mass Media, Portfolio, 3

Social Sciences (13)

Alcohol Abuse—Fund. Facts, TECEP exam, 3
Substance Abuse—Fund. Facts, TECEP, 4
Society & Sexual Variations, Portfolio, 3
Arms Control & Disarmament, Portfolio, 3

Math/Natural Sciences (12)

BASIC, TECEP, 3
Intro. to Computers & Program Design Portfolio, 3
Human Reproductive Biology & Behavior, Portfolio, 3
Astronomy, DANTES, 3

Liberal Arts Electives (18)

A Comprehensive Analysis of Abortion, Portfolio, 3
Advanced Radio Production, Portfolio, 3
Public Speaking I, Portfolio, 3
Broadcast Journalism I, Portfolio, 3
Rudiments of Music, Portfolio, 3
Folk Music in the United States, Portfolio, 3

Concentration Area (33)

Public Speaking II, Portfolio, 3
Intro. to News Reporting, TECEP, 3
Publicity Methods in Organizations, Portfolio, 3
Recording Studio, Portfolio, 2
Harmony I, Portfolio, 3
Applied Piano, Portfolio, 3
Elementary Voice, Portfolio, 3
Folk Guitar Class, Portfolio, 2
Theology of the Cults, Portfolio, 3
Christian Social Ethics, Portfolio, 3
Toward a Theology of Peace, Portfolio, 3
Roman Catholic Theology, Portfolio, 2

Free Electives (26)

Administrative Management & Supervision, Portfolio, 3
Word Processing I, Portfolio, 3
Word Processing II, Portfolio, 3
Word Processing III, Portfolio, 3
Intro. to Publishing, Portfolio, 3
Piano Service Playing, Portfolio, 1
Cardiopulmonary Resuscitation, Portfolio, 1
Technical Writing, Portfolio, 3
Purchasing & Contracting, Portfolio, 3
Personnel Management, Portfolio, 3

Summary by subject area

Written expression, 9
Humanities, 64
Communications, 29
Music, 24
Theology, 11
Social Sciences, 16
Math/science, 13
Business, 18

Summary by source of credit

Courses transferred, 6
Testing (TECEP/DANTES), 16
Portfolio, 98

Summary by evaluation method

Accepted on evidence, 78
Testing, 6
Evidence plus testing, 6

15

Credit by Learning Contract

An oral agreement isn't worth the paper it's written on.

Samuel Goldwyn

A mainstay of many nontraditional degree programs is the learning contract, also known as a study plan, study contract, degree plan, etc. It is essentially a formal agreement between the student and the school, setting forth a plan of study the student intends to undertake, goals he or she wishes to reach, and the action to be taken by the school once the goals are reached—normally the granting either of a certain amount of credit or of a degree.

A well-written learning contract is good for both student and school, since it reduces greatly the chances of misunderstandings or problems after the student has done a great deal of work, and the inevitable distress that accompanies such an event.

We've heard from people who have been distressed to discover that some project on which they had been working for many months was really not what their faculty advisor or school had in mind, and so they would be getting little or no credit for it.

Indeed, one of the authors had a similar sort of experience. After John had worked for nearly two years on his Doctorate at Michigan State University, one key member of his faculty guidance committee suddenly died, and a second transferred to another school. No one else on the faculty seemed interested in working with him, and without a binding agreement of any sort, there was no way he could make things happen. He simply dropped out. (Three years later, a new department head invited him back to finish the degree, and he did so. But a lot of anguish could have been avoided if he had had a contract with the school.)

A learning contract can be legally binding for both the student and the school. If the student does the work called for, then the school must award the predetermined number of credits. In case of disputes arising from such a contract, there are usually clauses calling for mediation, and, if necessary, binding arbitration by an impartial third party.

Looking at examples of a simple, and then a somewhat more complex, learning contract should make clear how this concept works.

A SIMPLE LEARNING CONTRACT

The Background

In the course of discussing the work to be done for a Bachelor's degree, the student and her faculty advisor agree that it would be desirable for the student to learn to read in German. Rather than take formal courses, the student says that she prefers to study the language on her own, with the help of an uncle who speaks the language. If the student had taken four semesters of German at a traditional school, she would have earned 20 semester hours of credit. So the learning contract might consist of these eight simple clauses:

The Contract

1. Student intends to learn to read German at the level of a typical student who has completed four semesters of college-level German.

2. Student will demonstrate this knowledge by translating a 1000-word passage from one of the novels of Erich Maria Remarque.

3. The book and passage will be selected and the translation evaluated by a member of the German faculty of the college.

4. The student will have three hours to complete the translation, with the assistance of a standard German-English dictionary.

5. If the student achieves a score of 85% or higher in the evaluation, then the college will immediately award 20 semester hours of credit in German.

6. If the student scores below 85%, she may try again at 60-day intervals.

7. The fee for the first evaluation will be $200, and, if necessary, $100 for each additional evaluation.

8. If any dispute shall arise over the interpretation of this contract, an attempt will be made to resolve the dispute by mediation. If mediation fails, the dispute will be settled by binding arbitration. An arbitrator shall be chosen jointly by the student and the school. If they cannot agree in choosing an arbitrator, then each party will choose one. If the two arbitrators cannot agree, they shall jointly appoint a third, and the majority decision of this panel of three shall be final and binding. The costs of arbitration shall be shared equally by the two parties.

This contract has the four basic elements common to any learning contract:

1. The student's objectives or goals.

2. The methods by which these goals are to be reached.

3. The method of evaluation of the performance.

4. What to do in case of problems or disagreement.

The more precisely each of these items can be defined, the less likelihood of problems later. For instance, instead of simply saying, "The student will become proficient in German," the foregoing agreement defines clearly what "proficient" means.

A MORE COMPLEX LEARNING CONTRACT

What follows is an abridgement of a longer learning contract, freely adapted from some of the case histories provided in a catalog from the late, lamented Beacon College.

Goals

At the end of my Master's program, I plan to have the skills, experience, and theoretical knowledge to work with an organization in the role of director or consultant, and to help the organization set and reach its goals; to work with individuals or small groups as a counselor, providing a supportive or therapeutic environment in which to grow and learn.

I want to acquire a good understanding of and grounding in group dynamics, how children learn, and why people come together to grow, learn, and work.

I am especially interested in alternative organizations. I want to have the skills to help organizations analyze their financial needs, and to locate and best utilize appropriate funding.

Methods

Theory and Skill Development (40% of work)

I shall take the following three courses at Vista Community College [courses listed and described] = 20% of program.

After reading the following four books [list of books], and others that may be suggested by my faculty advisor, I shall prepare statements of my personal philosophy of education and growth, as a demonstration of my understanding of the needs of a self-directed, responsible, caring human = 10% of program.

I shall attend a six-lesson workshop on power dynamics and assertiveness, given by [details of the workshop] = 10% of program.

Leadership and Management Practicum (30% of work)

I shall work with the Cooperative Nursery School to attempt to put into practice the things I have learned in the first phase of my studies, in the following way: [much detail here]. Documentation shall be through a journal of my work, a log of all meetings, a self-assessment of my performance, and commentary supplied by an outside evaluator = 15% of program.

I shall donate eight hours a week for 20 weeks to the Women's Crisis Center, again endeavoring to put into practice the ideas which I have learned. [much detail here on expectations and kinds of anticipated activities] = 15% of program.

Organizational Development, Analysis, and Design (30% of work)

I shall study one of the above two groups (nursery school or crisis center) in great detail, and prepare an analysis and projection for the future of this organization, including recommendations for funding, management, and development = 20% of program.

Documentation will be in the form of a 40 to 50-page paper detailing my findings and recommendations and relating them to my philosophy of growth and organization development. This paper will be read and evaluated by [name of persons or committee] = 10% of program.

Outcome

Upon completion of all of the above, the college will award the degree of Master of Arts in organization development. [Arbitration clause comparable to Simple Contract]

Learning contracts are truly negotiable. There is no right or wrong, no black or white. Someone who is good at negotiating might well get more credit for the same amount of work, or the same degree for a lesser amount of work, than a less skillful negotiator.

Some schools will enter into a learning contract that covers the entire degree program, as in the second example. Others prefer to have separate contracts, each one covering a small portion of the program: one for the language requirement, one for science, one for humanities, one for the thesis, and so forth.

It is uncommon, but not unheard of, to seek legal advice when preparing or evaluating a learning contract, especially for a long or complex one covering an entire Master's or doctoral program. A lawyer will likely say, "It is better to invest a small amount of money in my time now, rather than get into an expensive and protracted battle later, because of an unclear agreement." Dozens of colleges and universities are sued every year by students who claim that credits or degrees were wrongfully withheld from them. Many of these suits could have been avoided by the use of well-drawn learning contracts.

In an earlier edition, we announced our first cartoon caption contest, inviting readers to submit an educationally-related caption to this picture. We offered a first (and only) prize: printing the winning entry in the next edition, with byline, plus an autographed copy, and a free lunch if we're ever in the same place. Congratulations to winner Carl Ludwigson from Texas.

"Why, with my doctorate from the Institute of Imagination Therapy and that Evelyn Woods Reading Dynamics course, I read the entire OED in 14 hours, Michener's Hawaii in seven minutes, and Pinocchio in four seconds."
—CARL LUDWIGSON

16

Credential and Transcript Evaluation Services

'Tis with our judgements as our watches, none
go just alike, yet each believes his own.

ALEXANDER POPE

There are many thousands of universities, colleges, technical schools, institutes, and vocational schools all over the world offering courses that are at least the equivalent of work at American universities. In principle, most universities are willing to give credit for work done at schools in other countries.

But can you imagine the task of an admissions officer faced with the student who presents an Advanced Diploma from the Wysza Szkola Inzynierska in Poland, or the degree of Gakushi from the Matsuyama Shoka Daigaku in Japan? Are these equivalent to a high-school diploma, a Doctorate, or something in between?

Until 1974, the U.S. Office of Education helped by evaluating educational credentials earned outside the United States and translating them into approximately comparable levels of U.S. achievement. This service is no longer available. There have arisen, to fill this gap, quite a few private independent credential and transcript evaluation services. Some deal exclusively with credentials and transcripts earned outside the United States and/or Canada, while others also consider experiential learning wherever it took place (such as military courses, aviation credentials, company training programs, and the like).

It is important to note that these organizations are neither endorsed, licensed, nor recommended by the U.S. government, nor is there any regulation of them. The various organizations would appear to have very different ways of going about their work, often yielding quite different results. We know this, because we conducted an informal but quite revealing survey, as follows.

We have a friend who has a quite unusual education background: initially educated on one continent, further schooled on a second continent, and now living on a third, accumulating along this long path a variety of earned academic degrees and designations.

We invited this person to submit applications to ten credential evaluation services. The results varied wildly, both in terms of the quality and level of their service (fees, for instance, ranged from $50 to over $600), and in the nature of their evaluations. For instance, the external Master's degree of a large old Royal Chartered British university was evaluated as the exact equivalent of a U.S. regionally accredited MBA by some of the agencies, the equivalent of an MA in business by several, and as not even at the level of an American Bachelor's degree by a another.

The message from this research, and from a considerable amount of communication from readers, is that it may well pay to shop around, especially if the evaluation from one agency doesn't meet your expectations.

We give this advice reluctantly, in part because it is annoying and expensive to have to do this sort of thing, and in part because of our concern that people with questionable credentials might still find validation. For instance, one traditional university shared with us an application from a student whose Bachelor's degree from a school we regard as so close to a diploma mill, we were quite uncertain whether to put them in that chapter or the chapter of "Others." But when this school challenged his degree, he shopped around and found one of these services (but only one) who evaluated his miserable degree as equivalent to an accredited American school. On that basis, the university provisionally admitted him, but he proved incapable of doing even the most basic of assignments.

Some of these organizations are used mostly by the schools themselves, to evaluate applicants from abroad or with foreign credentials, but individuals may deal with them directly, at relatively low cost. Many schools accept the recommendations of these services, but others will not. Some schools do their own foreign evaluations, while others have a short list of those credential evaluators they will accept.

It may be wise, therefore, to determine whether a school or schools in which you have interest will accept the recommendations of such services before you invest in them. We have also noted that schools who appear to require the evaluation from a certain agency or group of agencies are still, sometimes, willing to accept the evaluation from an agency not on their list.

Depending on the complexity of the evaluation, the cost runs from $50 to $200 or more. One agency, which we have deleted from our list, provided our experimental subject with a one-sentence response to his initial paid $50 application, and said that the full report would cost $800. Some of the services are willing to deal with non-school-based experiential learning as well. The services operate quickly. Less than two weeks for an evaluation is not unusual.

Typical evaluation reports give the exact U.S. equivalents of non-U.S. work, both in terms of semester units earned, and of any degrees or certificates earned. For instance, we would expect all of them to report that the Japanese degree of Gakushi is almost exactly equivalent to the American Bachelor's degree.

Given the significant differences in the opinions of these services, if one report seems inappropriate or incorrect, it might be wise to seek a second (and even third) opinion.

Some of the organizations performing these services include, in alphabetical order, first in the US, then Canada:

United States

AACRAO, (American Association of Collegiate Registrars and Admissions Officers)

Office of International Education Services
Credential Evaluation Service
Service offered only to schools; but they sell a wide variety of publications for people interested in doing evaluations

AACRAO

One Dupont Circle, Suite 520
Washington, DC 20036-1135
Phone: (202) 293-9161, Fax: (202) 872-8857
E-mail info@aacrao.com
Web site: www.aacrao.com

Educational Credential Evaluators, Inc.

P.O. Box 92970
Milwaukee, WI 53217
Phone (414) 289-3400, Fax (414) 289-3411
E-mail eval@ece.org
Web site: www.ece.org

Education Evaluators International, Inc.

P. O. Box 5397
Los Alamitos, CA 90721
Phone (562) 431-2187

Educational Records Evaluation Service

777 Campus Commons Road, #200
Sacramento, CA 95825
Phone (916) 565-7475, Fax (916) 565-7476
E-mail edu@eres.com
Web site: www.eres.com

Global Credential Evaluators, Inc.

P. O. Box 9203
College Station, TX 77842
Phone (409) 690-8912, Fax (409) 690-6342
E-mail jringer@mail.myriad.net

Global Education Group

1881 Washington Ave., #6C
Miami Beach, FL 33139
Phone (305) 534-8745, Fax (305) 534-3487
E-mail global@globaledu.com
Web site: www.globaledu.com

International Consultants of Delaware, Inc.

914 Pickett Lane
Newark, DE 19711
Phone (302) 737-8715

International Credentialing Associates, Inc.

150 2nd Avenue North
Suite 1600
St. Petersburg, FL 33707
Phone (813) 821-8852

International Education Research Foundation

P. O. Box 66940
Los Angeles, CA 90066
Phone (310) 390-6276, Fax (310) 397-7686
E-mail info@ierf.org
Web site: www.ierf.org

Joseph Silny & Associates, Inc.

P.O. Box 248233
Coral Gables, FL 33124
Phone (305) 666-0233, Fax (305) 666-4133
E-mail info@jsilny.com
Web site:: www.jsilny.com

World Education Services

P. O. Box 745
Old Chelsea Station
New York, NY 10011
Phone (212) 966-6311, Fax (212) 966-6395
E-mail nabdulla@wes.org
Web site: www.wes.org

Canada

International Qualifications Assessment Service
Alberta Labour
> 10011 109th Street
> 5th Floor
> Edmonton, AL T5J 3S8 Canada
> Phone (403) 427-2655

University of Toronto
> Comparative Education Service
> 315 Bloor Street West
> Toronto, ON M5S 1A3
> Phone (416) 978-2185

For those interested in educational equivalents for one particular country, there is the world education series of books or monographs published by AACRAO, the American Association of Collegiate Registrars and Admissions Officers (One Dupont Circle NW, Suite 330, Washington, DC 20036). Each publication in this series describes the higher education system in a given country, and offers advice and recommendations on how to deal with their credits.

The problem with these AACRAO reports is that they are issued with such low frequency that many of them are way out of date, and of minimal usefulness.

In the early 1990s, the Australians (whose higher education system is similar to that of the US and Canada) attempted to deal with this problem by commissioning the researching and writing of comparative monographs on the educational equivalency of 83 countries, all at the same time. The monographs are published by the Australian Government Publishing Service, GPO Box 84, Canberra ACT 2601, Australia. (John did the initial research and writing for 15 of these monographs.)

When the sports budget was cut at Oberon State, scholarship students were pressed into duty, serving as goalposts for the field hockey teams.

17

The Credit Bank Service

We give no credit to a liar, even when he speaks the truth.

CICERO

A lot of people have very complicated educational histories. They may have taken classes at several different universities and colleges, taken some evening or summer-school classes, perhaps some company-sponsored seminars, some military training classes, and possibly had a whole raft of other informal learning experiences. They may have credits or degrees from schools that have gone out of business, or whose records were destroyed by war or fire. When it comes time to present a cohesive educational past, it may mean assembling dozens of transcripts, certificates, diplomas, job descriptions, and the like, often into a rather large and unwieldy package.

There is, happily, an ideal solution to this problem: the Regents Credit Bank, operated by the enlightened Regents College in New York, and available to people anywhere in the world.

The Regents Credit Bank is an evaluation and transcript service for people who wish to consolidate their academic records, perhaps adding credit for nonacademic career and learning experiences (primarily through equivalency examinations). The Credit Bank issues a single widely accepted transcript on which all credit is listed in a simple, straightforward, and comprehensible form.

The Credit Bank works like a money bank, except that you deposit academic credits, as they are earned, whether through local courses, correspondence courses, equivalency exams, or other methods. There are six basic categories of learning experience that can qualify to be "deposited" in a Credit Bank account, and of course various elements of these seven can be combined as well:

1. College courses taken either in residence or by correspondence from regionally accredited schools in the U.S., or their equivalent in other countries.

2. Scores earned on a wide range of equivalency tests, both civilian and military.

3. Military service schools and military occupational specialties that have been evaluated for credit by the American Council on Education.

4. Workplace-based learning experiences, such as company courses, seminars, or in-house training from many large and smaller corporations, evaluated by the American Council on Education or the New York National Program on Noncollegiate Sponsored Instruction.

5. Pilot training licenses and certificates issued by the Federal Aviation Administration.

6. Approved nursing performance examinations.

7. Special assessment of knowledge gained from experience or independent study.

The first six categories have predetermined amounts of credit. The CLEP basic science exam will always be worth six semester units. Fluency in Spanish will always be worth 24 semester units. Xerox Corporation's course in repairing the 9400 copier will always be worth two semester units. The army course in becoming a bandleader will always be worth 12 semester units. And so forth, for thousands of already evaluated nonschool learning experiences.

While the Credit Bank offers an excellent option for many clients, there are others who have two kinds of learning experiences which may suggest the Credit Bank is not for them.

One is the matter of having extensive learning in a field for which there does not exist a standard test. One may be the world's leading expert in Persian military history, or be fluent in five Asian languages, but since there are no readily available tests of these areas, credit may not be given. Regents used to offer a special assessment service, in which people with such specialized knowledge could come to New York for an oral examination by two or more experts in the field, at the end of which credit was awarded, but this option is not listed in current literature.

The other consists of credits and degrees earned at schools accredited by certain recognized accrediting agencies other than regional agencies, such as the Distance Education and Training Council. If, for instance, a student earns a Bachelor's degree at American Military University or the California College for Health Sciences, those degrees are not acceptable to Regents. Such degrees and credits are accepted by many other regionally accredited schools, so this non-acceptance by Regents Credit bank seems unusual and unfortunate to us.

One more caution. The Regents Credit Bank literature states that foreign academic credentials must be evaluated by a company called ECE in Wisconsin, except for Israeli credentials, which are to be evaluated by a company called Josef Silny and Associates. As is made clear in chapter 17, which covers credential and transcript evaluation services, the various agencies that do this often differ widely in evaluating the same credentials. When one of these anomalies was pointed out to Regents, they agreed to accept the evaluation of an agency other than the two they list.

There is a $200 fee to set up a Credit Bank account ($75 if it is only to include PEP or Regents College examinations). There is a $25 fee each time a new "deposit" is made. (These rates are dramatically lower than those charged a few years ago.)

Work that is, for whatever reason, deemed not creditworthy may still be listed on the transcript as "noncredit work." Further, the Credit Bank will only list those traditional courses from other schools that the depositor wishes included. Thus any previous academic failures, low grades, or other embarrassments may be omitted from the Credit Bank report.

Students who enroll in Regents College automatically get Credit Bank service, and do not need to enroll separately.

The address is Regents Credit Bank, Regents College, 7 Columbia Circle, Albany, NY 12203, (518) 464-8500, e-mail: testadmn@regents.edu, web site: www.regents.edu/098.htm.

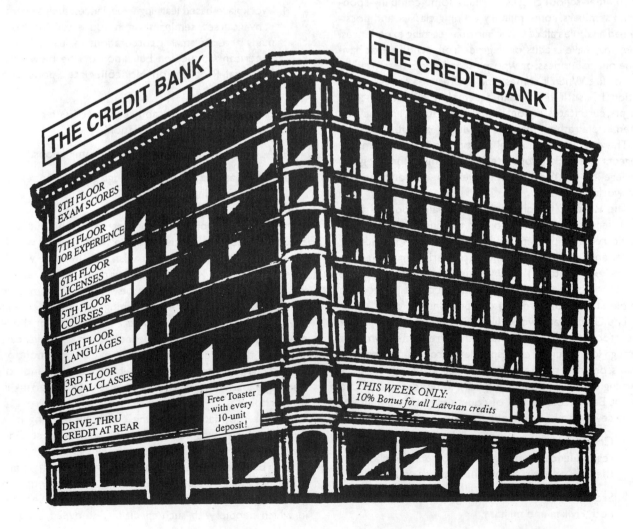

18

Accredited Schools
With Degrees Entirely by Distance Learning

Education is hanging around until you've caught on.

ROBERT FROST

Any school can claim that it is accredited; the use of that word is not regulated in any way. This chapter includes only those schools that are accepted as "Accredited" under GAAP, Generally Accepted Accreditation Principles. In the U.S., there is near-unanimous agreement on GAAP (although not everyone calls it this, the concept is the same) by the relevant key decision-makers: university registrars and admissions officers, corporate human resource officers, and government agencies.

Note that in some countries, the word "accredited" is not used, although the evaluation process in that country (e.g., the British Royal Charter), is accepted as "accredited" under GAAP.

Note, too, that schools that do not meet the standards of GAAP are not necessarily bad, illegal, or fake. They simply would not be generally accepted as accredited.

All schools in this chapter meet the standards of GAAP, which means that they meet any one of the following six criteria:

GAAP CRITERIA

◆ Accredited by an agency recognized by the Council on Higher Education Accreditation in Washington.

◆ Accredited by an agency recognized by the U.S. Department of Education.

◆ Listed in the International Handbook of Universities (a UNESCO publication).

◆ Listed in the Commonwealth Universities Yearbook.

◆ Listed in the World Education Series, published by PIER (Projects in International Education Research), a joint venture of AACRAO (the American Association of Collegiate Registrars and Admissions Officers) and NAFSA (the Association of International Educators) with the participation of the College Board.

◆ Listed in the Countries Series, published by NOOSR, the National Office for Overseas Skills Recognition, in Australia.

The basic format of each listing is as follows:

Name of School   **A**ssociate's, **B**achelor's, **M**aster's, **D**octorate, **L**aw, **D**iploma
Address
City, State Postal Code Country, if not U.S.
Fields of study offered
Year founded
Ownership (nonprofit or proprietary, state, private, or church-run)
Phone • Toll-free phone
Fax
E-mail address
Website URL

Note: We have in the past given cost information, but this changes so quickly and is so subjective that we have decided to discontinue the practice. If a program is extremely inexpensive, or disproportionately expensive, we've mentioned this in the listing. In most cases, the best way to find out about the cost of any particular program is to contact the school directly.

Allama Iqbal Open University   **B, M**
Sector H-8
Islamabad, Pakistan
Year founded: 1974
Phone: (92-51) 854-987
Fax: (92-51) 853-154
While this school does not yet admit distance-learning students from outside Pakistan, plans are underway to change this. Degrees are offered at the Bachelor's and Master's levels in a range of fields, ranging from the common (arts, com-

merce, education), to the unusual (Islamic studies, Iqbaliyat, Urdu, Pakistan studies) using text and broadcast media.

Allegheny University of the Health Sciences   B

1505 Race Street
M-S 629
Philadelphia, PA 19102
Fields offered: Emergency medical services
Year founded: 1848
Ownership: Nonprofit
Phone: (215) 762-6400
Fax: (215) 762-6909
E-mail: kelliher@allegheny.edu
Website: www.auhs.edu

B.S. in emergency medical services available only to students in Philadelphia and Pittsburgh, where courses can be delivered to home, office, or off-campus center in Pittsburgh. Interaction by videoconference, telephone, and e-mail.

American College of Prehospital Medicine   A, B

365 Canal St., #2300
New Orleans, LA 70130-1135
Fields offered: Emergency medical services
Year founded: 1991
Ownership: Proprietary
Phone: (504) 561-6543 • (800) 735-2276
Fax: (504) 561-6585
E-mail: admit@acpm.edu
Website: www.acpm.edu

Degrees in emergency medical services, open to any licensed EMT professional at or above the level of EMT/Ambulance. Credit given for prior training and experience. There is a small charge for information packet, call or e-mail for current details, or check their website. Foreign students are welcome as this is a wholly nonresident program, although they are warned that all course materials are in English. A Master's degree is expected to be up and running by the year 2000.

American Military University   M

9104-P Manassas Drive
Manassas, VA 20111
Fields offered: Military studies
Year founded: 1994
Phone: (703) 330-5398
Fax: (703) 330-5109
E-mail: amugen@amunet.edu
Website: www.amunet.edu

Offers a totally nonresident Bachelor's in military history (American or World), intelligence studies, or military management, and a Master of Arts in military science. A maximum of 15 (of the 36 required) credit hours can come from some combination of transfer credits, ACE-approved military training, and life experience learning. After enrolling in a course, the student contacts the instructor (4 phone contacts are a requirement) to ask about focus and expectations for the course of study. Most courses involve some small writing assignments, an "open book" mid-term exam, a research paper, and a proctored final exam (you nominate a proctor whom the university approves).

Anadolu Universitesi   B

Alkogretim Fakultesi
Yunus Emre Kampusu
26470 Eskisehir, Turkey
Fields offered: Economics, business administration
Year founded: 1982
Phone: (90-222) 335-0580
Fax: (90-222) 335-3616

This school provides a distance-learning B.A. in economics or business administration to students in Turkey, through printed materials, radio and TV programs, and video cassettes distributed to video education centers.

Andrew Jackson University   B, M

10 Old Montgomery Highway
Birmingham, AL 35209
Admissions Office
Fields offered: Communication, business, civil sciences, enviromental studies, religion, criminal justice
Year founded: 1994
Phone: (205) 871-9288 • (800) 429-9300
Fax: (800) 321-9694
E-mail: enroll@aju.edu
Website: www.aju.edu

Degrees are offered exclusively by distance learning and are, as follows: In the school of undergraduate studies, a B.A. in communication and a B.S. in business or criminal justice; in the school of business, an M.B.A. with a choice of concentration in general business, marketing, management, international business, or industrial management and safety; in the school of civil sciences, an M.P.A., an M.A. in international relations, and an M.S. in criminal justice; in the school of environmental studies, an M.S. in environmental studies; and in the school of religion, an M.A. in religion or an M.S. in Christian counseling.

Anglia Polytechnic University   B, M

School of Health Sciences
East Road
Cambridge, CB1 1PT U.K.
Fields offered: Radiography, medical imaging
Year founded: 1989
Phone: (44-1223) 363-271
Fax: (44-1223) 576-157
E-mail: jsvensson@bridge.anglia.ac.uk
Website: www.anglia.ac.uk/radiography/home.htm

Offers a B.S. in radiography, as well as an M.S. in either medical radiography and medical imaging (MRI and/or ultrasound), all geared to professionals working in these fields, and having access to a clinical setting. The course of study takes place entirely through distance learning, following a compulsory residential weekend induction course (required at the graduate level only). Available to overseas applicants.

Arizona State University   M

Distance Learning Technology
Tempe, AZ 85287
Fields offered: Engineering
Year founded: 1885
Ownership: Nonprofit, state
Phone: (602) 965-6738
Fax: (602) 965-1371
E-mail: idpbw.asuum.inre.asu.edu
Website: www.distlearn.pp.asu.edu

Arizona State's distance learning program offers a Master of Science in engineering that can be earned wholly through courses taken via cable, public television, and ITFS televised courses that can be viewed at 10 public sites and 24 corporate locations in the Tempe area, as well as a large number of courses in other subjects available via cable, public television, and/or ITFS nationwide, via the National Technological University. Courses are also available via CD-ROM, offered on the Internet, and also through more traditional correspondence study.

Arts and Sciences University

See: University of Distance Education

Aston University   M

Language Studies Unit
Birmingham, B4 7ET U.K.
Fields offered: English, business administration
Year founded: 1895
Phone: (44-021) 359-3611, ext. 4242
Fax: (44-021) 359 2725
E-mail: isu@aston.ac.uk
Website: www.aston.ac.uk/~abswww/home.html

The Master of Science in the teaching of English is a rigorous academic program for persons already teaching the English language—the school stresses that it is not a teacher training program. Assignments and the dissertation will relate directly to the student's own professional environment; topics studied include pedagogic principles, language learning theory, and production of original materials, among others. Applicants should hold an approved Bachelor's degree or equivalent, and have at least three years' professional experience.

Aston also offers a distance-learning M.B.A., but only within the United Kingdom. For information on that program, contact the Distance Learning M.B.A. Programme at telephone 21-359-3011, ext. 4928 or fax 21-333-4731.

Athabasca University   B, M

Box 10,000
Athabasca, AB T0G 2R0 Canada
Fields offered: Many fields
Year founded: 1970

Ownership: Nonprofit, independent
Phone: (403) 675-6100 • (800) 788-9041 (Canada only)
Fax: (403) 675-6145
E-mail: auinfo@admin.athabascau.ca
Website: www.athabascau.ca

An open distance-education institution serving more than 10,000 students across Canada. (Foreign nationals in the U.S. and Mexico can be admitted, but face various fees and restrictions. Contact the school for current details. Persons residing outside of North America are not normally eligible for enrollment unless there is "an inter-institutional agreement with a cooperating institution in their country of residence.") Bachelor's degrees in administration, arts, general studies, English, history, sociology/anthropology, psychology, Canadian studies, computing and information systems, and French. All distance-education courses are offered through sophisticated home-study packages. Students set up their own study schedules and work at their own pace. There are eight degree programs: Bachelor of Administration, Bachelor of Arts, Bachelor of Commerce, Bachelor of General Studies, Bachelor of Nursing, Bachelor of Science, an M.B.A. program, which requires several short visits to the campus, and a Master of Distance Education, in which much of the instruction and interaction occurs by modem. All students are assigned a telephone tutor to whom they have toll-free access from anywhere in Canada. (Students residing outside of Canada must pay their own long-distance charges.) Some courses are supplemented by radio and television programs, audio- and videocassettes, seminars, laboratories, or teleconference sessions.

Australian Catholic University   B

McAuley Campus
P.O. Box 247
Everton Park, 4053 Queensland 4053 Australia
Fields offered: Education
Year founded: 1991
Phone: (61-7) 855-7135
Fax: (61-7) 855-7249
Website: www.acu.edu.au

Offers a Bachelor of Education covering the basic professional training needed for teachers at the primary and/or secondary level, particularly those seeking a career in Catholic education, with a focus on the philosophy of Catholic education, the nature of Catholic school, and the teaching of religion.

Baker College   B, M

1050 West Bristol Road
Flint, MI 48507-5508
Fields offered: Business administration
Year founded: 1888
Ownership: Nonprofit, private
Phone: (810) 766-4390 • (800) 469-3165
Fax: (810) 766-4399

E-mail: on-line@baker.edu
Website: www.baker.edu

Baker College On-Line is part of Michigan's largest (nine-campus) private college system. It offers wholly nonresidential degrees (both a B.B.A. and an M.B.A.) via on-line services, following the same model as the well-known University of Phoenix-On-line. The Bachelor's degree requires an Associate's degree (or equivalent), and takes approximately two years to complete. The master's degree can be completed in 18 months. Interaction occurs via what is essentially an expanded e-mail system, allowing students to send and receive messages on-line and download assignments. Coursework can then be completed off-line. Each course takes place in a "virtual classroom," and students are provided 24-hour access to their "classes," as well as a private mailbox. Each course takes six weeks.

Ball State University   M

Muncie, IN 47306
Fields offered: Education, business administration
Year founded: 1918
Ownership: Nonprofit, state
Phone: (765) 289-1241 • (800) 872-0369
Fax: (765) 285-1461
E-mail: D000grad@bsuvc.bsu.edu
Website: www.bsu.edu/UP/cover.html

Master of Education program, including a special program in psychometrics, can be completed entirely through evening study. M.B.A. can be completed through satellite TV courses in cooperating workplaces. The phone number for the M.B.A. program is (317) 285-1931; the contact person is Tamara Estep.

Bangladesh Open University   B

House No. 16, Road No. 2
Dhanmondi Residential Area
Dhaka 1205, Bangladesh
Fields offered: Education
Phone: (880-2) 865-221
Fax: (880-2) 865-750

Offers a Bachelor of Education, with all instruction in the Bangla language, through printed materials, radio, television, and audio- and videocassettes.

Bellevue University   B, M

1000 Galvin Road
Bellevue, NE 68005
Fields offered: Business, criminal justice, management information systems
Year founded: 1965
Ownership: Nonprofit
Phone: (402) 291-8100 • (800) 756-7920
Fax: (402) 293-2020
E-mail: dij@scholars.bellevue.edu
Website: bruins.bellevue.edu

Bachelor's in business information systems, criminal justice, international business management, management information systems at baccalaureate level; Masters in management and business administration. One of the relatively few distance programs that can be completed 100% on-line.

Bemidji State University   B

Center for Extended Learning, Deputy Hall 335
Bemidji, MN 56601
Fields offered: History, social studies, criminal justice
Year founded: 1913
Ownership: Nonprofit, state
Phone: (218) 755-3924 • (800) 475-2001
Fax: (218) 755-4048
E-mail: admissions@vax1.bemidji.msus.edu
Website: www.bemidji.msus.edu

This program is available to U.S. citizens only. Some credit for life experience and prior learning may be applied toward the degree requirements. Credit is earned through on-campus classes, extension classes in other Minnesota cities, and independent guided home study. Learning packages (a syllabus, books, and sometimes audio- or videocassettes) are provided. Continued contact with B.S.U. is maintained in a variety of ways: by mail, telephone, e-mail, exchange of cassettes, and conferences with academic advisors. As the Coordinator of External Studies put it, "Unique solutions exist for unique situations."

Berean University of the
Assemblies of God   B, M

1445 Boonville
Springfield, MO 65802
Fields offered: Bible and theology studies
Year founded: 1985
Ownership: Nonprofit, independent
Phone: (417) 862-2781 • (800) 443-1083
Fax: (417) 862-5318
E-mail: berean@ag.org
Website: www.berean.edu

All courses can be completed by correspondence; credit can also be earned by examination and for life experience. Primarily for religious workers (clergy, missionaries). Offers a B.A. in theology, Christian counseling, Christian education, pastoral ministries, or missions & evangelism, and an M.A. in biblical studies, ministerial studies, or Christian counseling. Many courses available in Spanish.

Boise State University   M

1910 University Drive
Boise, ID 83725
Fields offered: Instructional and performance technology
Year founded: 1932
Ownership: Nonprofit, state
Phone: (208) 385-4457 • (800) 824-7017, ext. 4457
Fax: (208) 385-3647
E-mail: gradcoll@bsu.idbsu.edu
Website: www.idbsu.edu

Totally nonresident M.S. in instructional and performance technology (the study of human performance problems in various business and industry settings), offered via real-time computer conferencing courses. Applicants must have access to a compatible computer and modem for at least two hours a day, five days a week, and preferably a fax machine as well.

Bournemouth University   M
Talbot Campus
Fern Barrow, Poole
Dorset, BH12 5BB U.K.
Year founded: 1942
Phone: (44-0202) 524-111
Fax: (44-0202) 318-853
Website: www.usq.edu.au or www.bournemouth.ac.uk
A joint program with Australia's University of Southern Queensland offers a distance-learning M.B.A. in international tourism. Anyone with an undergraduate degree can enroll, from anywhere in the world. International students register through Queensland; see the website, above, for more information. The degree consists of 16 units, usually completed over four years. Each unit is a multimedia package including print, audio, video, computer-managed learning and electronic communications components.

British Columbia Open University
See: Open Learning Agency

Brock University   B
Faculty of Education
St. Catherines, ON L2S 3A1 Canada
Fields offered: Adult education
Year founded: 1964
Phone: (905) 688-5550, x. 3971
Fax: (905) 688-0544
E-mail: pstanley@dewey.ed.brocku.ca
Website: www.brocku.ca
Delivery via videotape; response by mail, phone, e-mail, or fax.

Brunel University   B, M
Uxbridge
Middlesex, UB8 3PH U.K.
Fields offered: Technology, science, social science, education
Year founded: 1966
Phone: (44-1895) 274-000
Fax: (44-1895) 812-556
E-mail: William.Callaway@brunel.ac.uk (undergraduate) or Mark.Judge@brunel.ac.uk (graduate)
Website: www1.brunel.ac.uk:8080/
This school offers a number of programs by distance learning; for full information, you should address inquiries to the program director for the relevant field and level (i.e. Program Director for B.A. in youth and community studies). Degrees include an M.S. in advanced manufacturing

systems, an M.S. in building services engineering, a B.A. or M.A. in youth and community studies, and M.S.'s in communication systems and packaging technology. Some courses may require some classroom attendance, contact the school for details.

Buckinghamshire College   M
Queen Alexandra Road
High Wycombe
Buckinghamshire, HP11 2JZ UK
Fields offered: Management, forest products technology
Year founded: 1893
Phone: (44-1494) 522-141
Fax: (44-1494) 524-392
Buckinghamshire offers a number of distance-learning degrees. Overseas enrollments are accepted in the forest products technology program, and students living in the U.K. and Western Europe may enroll in the European marketing program. Other programs, currently only open to those in the U.K., include an M.A. in strategic leisure management and an M.S. in timber engineering. The marketing degree is geared to Europeans currently employed in business, and the final project may well be centered on the student's actual workplace. While much of the study takes place at a distance, short residential sessions are required. The forest products technology program requires no residency, and can be completed from anywhere in the world. It consists of 8 modules, covering such topics as advanced wood science and global forest resources, and culminates in the writing of a major research dissertation of 15 to 20,000 words. The average student takes about 3 years to complete this degree at a distance.

Bukkyo University   B
Division of Education by Correspondence
96 Murasakinokita-Hananoboucyou
Kita-Ku, Kyouto-Shi
Kyoto, 603 Japan
Fields offered: Literature, sociology
Year founded: 1887
Phone: (81-75) 491-0239
Fax: (81-75) 493-9041
Website: www.bukkyo-u.ac.jp/ENGLISH/english.html
This school offers a B.A. in literature and a Bachelor of Sociology through courses delivered using a variety of distance-learning methods, including printed correspondence texts prepared for and/or by the institution, telephone counseling, and audiotapes.

California College for Health Sciences   A, B, M
222 West 24th Street
National City, CA 91950
Fields offered: Health services
Year founded: 1979
Phone: (619) 477-4800 • (800) 221-7374

Fax: (619) 477-2257
E-mail: cchsinfo@cchs.edu
Website: www.cchs.edu

Associate's in various health, education, and business subjects, Bachelor of Science in health services management, respiratory care, or advanced electroneurodiagnosis, and Master of Science in community health administration and wellness promotion, entirely through home-study courses. The Master's degree program program prepares health professionals to become health promotion specialists working in private industry or education.

California Institute of Asian Studies

See: California Institute of Integral Studies

California National University for Advanced Studies   B, M

16909 Parthenia Street, #303
North Hills, CA 91343
Fields offered: Business administration, engineering, health care management, computer science, human resource management, quality assurance
Phone: (818) 830-2411 • (800) 782-2422
Fax: (818) 830-2418
E-mail: cnuadms@mail.cnuas.edu
Website: www.cnuas.edu

CNU offers Bachelor of Science degrees in business administration and engineering, Bachelor of Computer Science, Bachelor of Quality Assurance Science and Master of Science in engineering, Master of Human Resource Management and Master of Business Administration. Study is through a combination of one-on-one contact with professors and computer- and text-based learning. CNU has an open enrollment policy, so admission can occur any time during the year. Courses are offered on a trimester basis. Applicants may opt to complete their entire program at CNU or choose to apply for transfer credit and challenge exams such as CLEP. International students are welcome.

California State University, Chico   B, M

Center for Regional and Continuing Education
Chico, CA 95929-0250
Fields offered: Computer science, liberal studies, political science, social science, sociology
Year founded: 1887
Ownership: Nonprofit, state
Phone: (916) 898-6105 • (800) 780-4837
Fax: (916) 898-4020
E-mail: Lwright@oavax.csuchico.edu
Website: www.rce.csuchico.edu

Chico State offers a variety of Bachelors degrees and other programs live via satellite to selected learning centers throughout the state of California. In addition, both a B.S. and an M.S. in computer science are offered to corporate subscribers across the nation, entirely through interactive satellite TV and videotape. To participate in the computer science program, individuals must work for a participating company.

California State University, Dominguez Hills   B, M

SAC 2, Room 2126
1000 East Victoria Street
Carson, CA 90747
Fields offered: Humanities, quality assurance, business, nursing
Year founded: 1960
Ownership: Nonprofit, state
Phone: (310) 243-3744
Fax: (310) 516-4399
E-mail: huxon-line@dhvx20.csudh.edu
Website: dolphin.csudh.edu/~hux/huxindex.html or orca.csudh.edu/~hux/index.html

The External Degree Program in Humanities offers a nonresidential M.A. in history, literature, philosophy, music, theater arts/film, and art. The program is offered by "parallel instruction." Nonresidential students do all the work that residential students do, in the same general time frame, but do not attend classes. Total of 30 semester hours for the degree. Eighty percent must be earned after enrolling, and applicants must have an accredited Bachelor's degree (in any field). Credit for independent study projects, correspondence courses, and a thesis or a creative project. Communication with faculty by mail and telephone. A full-time student can finish in one academic year. (This is a rare opportunity to earn an accredited Master's degree nonresidentially. We are biased. Marina Bear happily completed her M.A. here in 1985.) There is also a wholly online M.B.A. For information on this program, check out som.csudh.edu/internet.mba/

The M.S. in quality assurance requires 33 semester hours, with attendance at various business locations in southern California. Contact person for quality assurance: Eugene Watson. A B.A. in interdisciplinary studies, an M.B.A., and an M.A. in behavioral sciences (specialization in negotiation and conflict management) are offered through classes broadcast over Southern California TV station KLCS. For information on these programs, call (310) 516-4162. Finally, a B.S. and M.S. in nursing is available nationwide by satellite.

California State University, Fresno   B, M

2225 East San Ramon Ave.
Fresno, CA 93740-0121
Fields offered: Liberal studies, education administration
Year founded: 1911
Ownership: Nonprofit, state
Phone: 209-278-5766
Fax: 209-278-7026
E-mail: lydia_rodriquez@csufresno.edu (undergraduate)
shirlee_fulton@zimmer.csufresno.edu (graduate)
Website: www.csufresno.edu

Programs are available only to students in the area served by the local television and videoconference facilities. Bachelor's in liberal studies, M.S. in education administration and supervision.

California State University, Fullerton   B, M

P.O. Box 34080
Fullerton, CA 92834-9480
Fields offered: Nursing, electrical engineering
Year founded: 1957
Ownership: Nonprofit, state
Phone: (714) 773-2300
Fax: (714) 773-2341
E-mail: CSUComments@csumentor.edu
Website: www.fullerton.edu

Students with an AA in nursing may enter the B.S.N. program; an MSEE is also offered, both by television and video-conferencing.

California State University, Los Angeles   B

Department of Technology
5151 State University Drive
Los Angeles, CA 90032
Fields offered: Fire protection administration
Year founded: 1947
Ownership: Nonprofit, state
Phone: (213) 343-4550
Fax: (213) 343-2670
E-mail: jslanin@cslanet.calstatela.edu
Website: www.calstatela.edu

Bachelor of Science in fire protection administration and technology through a variety of nontraditional means, including interactive televised courses broadcast to workplaces or various public sites, teleconferencing, and video-cassette. Enrollment limited to the Los Angeles basin and surrounding counties.

California State University, Northridge   B, M

18111 Nordhoff Street
Northridge, CA 91330
Fields offered: Engineering, education
Year founded: 1958
Ownership: Nonprofit, state
Phone: (818) 677-2355 • (800) 882-0128
Fax: (818) 677-2316
E-mail: admissions.records@csu
Website: www.csun.edu

Bachelor's in special ed. and communicative disorders, as well as engineering management.

Capitol College   B

EE Department
11301 Springfield Road
Laurel, MD 20708

Fields offered: Electrical engineering
Year founded: 1964
Ownership: Nonprofit
Phone: (301) 953-3200
Fax: (301) 953-3876
E-mail: rweiler@capitol-college.edu
Website: www.capitol-college.edu

This degree is offered by distance learning, but only to students in the local area; courses and interaction occur through video conferencing.

Catholic Distance University   M

120 East Colonial Highway
Hamilton, VA 20158
Phone: (540)338-2700 • (888)254-4CDU
Fax: (540)338-4788
E-mail: cdu@cdu.edu
Website: www.cdu.edu

CDU's mission is to provide education in the Catholic faith. Undergraduate courses are offered, nonresidentially. They offer an accredited MRS degree (as a religious degree, it is not under Virginia jurisdiction); their Master's in Religious Studies degree is in the approval process. Virginia anticipates two years before approval will be granted.

Central Michigan University   B, M

Extended Degree Program
Rowe Hall 131
Mt. Pleasant, MI 48859
Fields offered: Administration, management, supervision, health sciences
Year founded: 1892
Ownership: Nonprofit, state
Phone: (517) 774-4456 • (800) 688-4268
Fax: (517) 774-3542
E-mail: celinfo@cmich.edu
Website: www.cel.cmich.edu/independent-learning.htm

The College of Extended Learning offers three distance-learning B.S. degrees, in administration, community development, and health sciences. (The latter is tailored to healthcare professionals.) The degree is awarded for a combination of previously earned college credit, credit for other prior learning, and distance education. No residency is required. Distance education is highly structured; students are provided with textbooks, study guides, student manuals and, where appropriate, audio- and videotapes. Instructors are available to answer questions and provide additional support if necessary.

The M.S. in administration program offers the graduate degree through intensive classes given at various locations nationwide (in Michigan, Washington, D.C., Hawaii, and locations throughout the Southeast and Midwest). One can earn a general administration and management degree, or specialize in public or health services administration. All programs are operated under the sponsorship of companies, military bases, or professional organizations. In most cases, anyone may enroll, whether or not they have an association with the sponsor. Twenty-one semester hours (of 36 required) must be completed through Central Michigan; up to 10 units can come from prior learning assessment. C.M.U. also offers programs in community college administration in Canada. For Michigan residents, there is also a program leading to a Bachelor of Individualized Studies, or a B.A. or B.S. in liberal studies. Thirty units towards each of these degrees must be earned from C.M.U.

Central Missouri State University   M

403 Humphreys
Warrensburg, MO 64093
Fields offered: Aviation safety, criminal justice, industrial safety management
Year founded: 1781
Ownership: Nonprofit, state
Phone: (816) 543-4984
Fax: (816) 543-8333
E-mail: criswell@cmsuvmb.cmsu.edu
Website: www.cmsu.edu

Courses leading to Master's degrees in aviation safety, criminal justice, and industrial safety management sent via television, videotape, videoconference, to workplaces or other local sites.

Central Queensland University   B, M, D

Distance Education Centre
Rockhampton M C
Queensland, 4702 Australia
Fields offered: Many fields
Year founded: 1967
Phone: (61-79) 30-9442
Fax: (61-79) 30-9772
Website: brampton.cqu.edu.au

Established to serve the people of central Queensland, this school offers a broad range of programs and, apparently, does admit some students from outside the area. Distance learning programs offer degrees at all levels through methods including written study materials, audiotapes, home laboratory kits, and computer-aided learning packages. Students also get support through teleconferencing, access to tutors, and regional study centers. Some courses have brief residential requirements. Programs include Bachelor's degrees in information sciences, business administration, accounting, applied science, arts, building surveying, business, computing, construction management, education, health science, information technology, information systems, mathematic science, teaching, and technology. Master's degrees are available in accounting, advanced health practice, applied science, education, education studies, business administration, health care management, financial management, information systems, letters, history, cultural studies, midwifery, primary health care, school management, and communication. There is also a Ph.D. in education and an Ed.D.

Centre Audiovisuel des Universités de Paris

See: Centre de Télé-Enseignement Universitaire

Centre de Télé-Enseignement Universitaire   B, M

6 Ave. H. Maringer, B.P. 33.97
Nancy, F-54015 France
Fields offered: Many fields
Ownership: Nonprofit, state
Phone: 33-40-02-45
E-mail: nussbaum@clsh.u-nancy.fr
Website: www.nancy2.u-nancy.fr/CTU/ctu.htm

The Centre is a confederation of seven universities (including the Centre National de Télé-Ensignment) offering degree studies by correspondence, based primarily on taped lectures (in French, of course), with supplementary written materials. The tapes are available by mail, and are also broadcast on the radio and available at various regional centers. Students must first enroll in one of the participating universities (Besançon, Dijon, Metz, Mulhouse, Nancy, Reims, or Strasbourg), and then in the Centre. Even though all coursework is done through the Centre, the degree is awarded by the university. Bachelor's studies are offered in many fields; the Master's in only a few.

Chadron State College   M

Dept. of Education
1000 Main Street
Chadron, NE 69337
Fields offered: Business administration, education
Year founded: 1911
Ownership: Nonprofit, state
Phone: (308) 432-6210 • (800) 600-3055
Fax: (308) 432-6473
E-mail: dsmith@csc1.csc,edu
Website: www.csc.edu

Distance learning M.B.A. and M.S. in education (the latter of which requires one summer sessions on campus) available to residents of 25 counties in western and central Nebraska, through on-campus courses televised to eight widely-dispersed sites. Computer conferencing, bulletin boards, e-mail, videocassette, and tele-videoconferencing are used to support the courses, and for advising. Open enrollment in courses means no prerequisites for enrollment, although certain deficiencies would need to be made prior to beginning the program. (Contact the school for details.)

Champlain College   B

163 South Willard Street
P.O. Box 670
Burlington, VT 05402-0670
Fields offered: Many fields
Year founded: 1878
Ownership: Nonprofit, independent
Phone: (802) 860-2777 • (888) 545-3459

Fax: (802) 860-2774
E-mail: CED@inet.champlain.edu
Website: www.champlain.edu

Champlain offers Bachelor's degrees in business, computer programming, executive administrative assistancy, hotel-restaurant management, legal administrative assistancy, liberal studies, marketing management, medical administrative assistancy, network and PC support specialist, office management, paralegal & legal studies, public relations & media communications, radiography, respiratory therapy, retailing & fashion merchandising, and sport management. In many cases essentially a degree-completion program, the SuccessNet on-line program allows students to transfer in either an A.A. or a certain number of credits, and then finish the degree on-line. Note that this is not correspondence, but on-line. Contact school for precise details of the program in which you are interested. Also offers Associate's degrees and professional certificates.

Charter Oak State College   A, B

66 Cedar Street
Newington, CT 06111-2646
Fields offered: Many fields
Year founded: 1973
Ownership: Nonprofit, state
Phone: (860) 666-4595
Fax: (860) 666-4852
E-mail: charter_oak@commnet.edu
Website: www.ctstateu.edu/~charteroak

The college is operated by the Connecticut Board for State Academic Awards, and offers the Associate and Bachelor's in Arts and Science. Each student is responsible for amassing 120 semester units, which may come from courses taken elsewhere, equivalency examinations, military study, correspondence courses, or portfolio reviews. As soon as the 120 units are earned, with at least half in the arts and sciences, and 36 in a single subject or major area, the degree is awarded. Only students resident in the U.S. may enroll. Original name: Connecticut Board for State Academic Awards. Also offers Associate's degrees.

Cheltenham Tutorial College   M

292 High Street
Gloucestershire, GL50 3HQ UK
Fields offered: Business administration
Phone: (44-1242) 241-279
Fax: (44-1242) 234-256
E-mail: tutor@chelt.win-uk.net

A distance-learning M.B.A. is offered through a variety of methods, including printed correspondence materials, audio- and videocassettes, and tutorial support. The school expects a high level of commitment from students, and in return promises a program that is well-written, logically structured, clearly presented, and reinforced with strong faculty support. Applicants should have practical experience in their field, and be able to support their application with strong references. In the third year of the program, students will be asked to undertake a research project examining in depth a topic of particular relevance to their interests and/or place of work.

Christopher Newport University   B

Newport News, VA 23606-2998
Fields offered: Government administration, philosophy & religious studies
Year founded: 1960
Ownership: Nonprofit, state
Phone: (804) 594-7000 • (800) 333-4CNU
Fax: (804) 594-7713
E-mail: on-line@cnu.edu
Website: cnuon-line.cnu.edu

This school offers on-line computer-managed distance-learning programs in addition to its complement of more traditional degrees. There is a B.A. in philosophy & religious studies, and a B.S. in government administration with concentrations in public management, criminal justice, and international studies. More programs are in the planning stages. Study is wholly on-line at a distance.

Chuo University   B

Correspondence Education Division
742-1 Higashinakano, Hachioji-Shi
Tokyo, 192-03 Japan
Fields offered: Law
Year founded: 1885
Phone: (81-426) 74-2341
Fax: (81-426) 74-2348
Website: www.chuo-u.ac.jp/index-j.html

A Bachelor of Law in Japanese law is offered through a variety of media and methods, including printed correspondence texts prepared by and/or for the institution, computer hardware and software, telephone, mail, or face-to-face counseling, and audiocassettes,

City University   B, M

335 116th Avenue SE
Bellevue, WA 98004
Fields offered: Business, education, human services
Year founded: 1973
Ownership: Nonprofit, independent
Phone: (425) 643-2000 • (800) 426-5596
Fax: (425) 637-9689
E-mail: info@cityu.edu
Website: www.cityu.edu

Distance learning degrees in business, health care administration, accounting, and finance are offered entirely by home computer (using e-mail), or by more traditional means. Their nonresident M.A. counseling program (choose Mental Health, Family/Couple/Child, or Vocational Rehab.) is one of the only regionally accredited ones. City University offers programs in a number of Washington cities, as well as Portland, Oregon; Santa Clara, California; several British Columbia locations; Zurich, Switzerland; and Frankfurt, Germany, leading to a Bachelor's in business administration, an M.B.A. or M.P.A. (public administration). The school is in the process of developing extensive on-line services; their plan is that students will be able to access university information and course syllabi, register, pay their tuition, communicate with faculty members and academic advisors via e-mail, and participate in real-time forum discussions. They expect to provide these services first to M.B.A. students, and shortly thereafter offer an on-line Bachelor of Science in computer information systems, with additional programs to follow. Check the web page for current status.

Clarkson College   B, M
101 South 42nd Street
Omaha, NE 68131-2739
Fields offered: Business administration, management, health service, nursing, medical imaging
Year founded: 1888
Ownership: Nonprofit, independent
Phone: (402) 552-3041 • (800) 647-5500
Fax: (402) 552-6057
E-mail: admiss@clrkcol.crhsnet.edu
Website: www.clarksoncollege.edu
Clarkson offers a B.S. in business administration and an M..S. in management (with a concentration in either health service management or business) entirely through distance-learning methods. The Bachelor's may be completed entirely through Clarkson, or by building on an Associate's in science, or courses taken for another B.S. Credit is available for life experience, through portfolio evaluation, military learning, and standardized tests. The B.S. in medical imaging can also be earned entirely though distance learning, and there are a number of graduate health-related programs in nursing and health service management that can be completed through distance learning, with the exception of several weeks on campus for clinical experience. A B.S. in nursing for registered R.N.s requires nine weeks on campus in Omaha, with the balance of the work done at a distance.

Cogswell College
See: FEMA National Fire Academy

College for Financial Planning   M
4695 South Monaco Street
Denver, CO 80237
Fields offered: Personal financial planning
Year founded: 1972
Ownership: Nonprofit
Phone: (303) 220-1200 • (800) 553-5343
Fax: (303) 220-5146
E-mail: ssc@fp.edu
Website: www.nefe.org
M.S. in personal financial planning, wholly through distance education, with emphasis in four fields: wealth management, or estate, tax, or retirement planning. The 12-course program is designed for applicants with some financial services background; students without such a background must

successfully complete a special noncredit "Foundations in Financial Planning" course before they will be admitted. Acquired from the National Endowment for Financial Planning in 1997 by the Apollo Group, the company that owns the University of Phoenix.

College of Estate Management   B
Student Services Division
Whiteknights
Berkshire
Reading RG6 6AW, UK
Fields offered: Estate management, construction, real estate
Year founded: 1919
Ownership: Independent
Phone: (44-1734) 9861-101
Fax: (44-1734) 9750-188
E-mail: k.p.wiggins@reading.ac.uk
Website: www.cem.ac.uk
Through an association with the University of Reading, this school offers three distance-learning degrees: a B.S. in estate management, an M.B.A. with a concentration in construction and real estate, and an M.S. in real estate, this last tailored to overseas students. Courses are taught through a combination of written instructional materials, audio- and videocassettes and, where feasible, face-to-face teaching sessions. While these latter are strongly recommended, special arrangements can be made for overseas students.

College of Great Falls   B
1301 20th Street South
Great Falls, MT 59405
Fields offered: Accounting, business administration, counseling psychology, criminal justice, human services, microcomputer management, paralegal studies, sociology
Year founded: 1932
Ownership: Nonprofit, church
Phone: (406) 761-8210 • (800) 342-9824
Fax: (406) 454-0113
E-mail: zgf1005@maia.oscs.montana.edu
Website: msucotgf.montana.edu/~msucotgf/general.html
B.A. and B.S. in the above fields for residents of Montana and Alberta, Canada, through distance-learning techniques including teleconferencing, telephone instruction, and audio- and videocassette. Open-admissions policy applies to the fields of counseling psychology, criminal justice, human services, paralegal studies, and sociology.

College of West Virginia   B
School of Academic Enrichment and Lifelong Learning
P.O. Box AG
Beckley, WV 25802-2830
Fields offered: Business, criminal justice, health care managment, nursing, interdisciplinary studies
Year founded: 1933

Ownership: Nonprofit, independent
Phone: (304) 253-7351
Fax: (304) 253-0789
E-mail: saell@cwv.edu
Website: www.cwv.edu/saell

Courses delivered to home, workplace, etc. by tapes, e-mail, and print. At least 18 credit hours must be earned after enrollment. These hours can be earned through on-campus classes, directed independent study, prior learning assessment, and either standardized or specially-developed challenge examinations. Prior learning assessment offers credit for college level knowledge acquired through work, independent reading, noncollegiate training, community activities, religious activities, and other experiences. Three options available for demonstrating prior experiential learning are newly-done portfolio assessment, portfolio assessment based on American Council on Education and other such standards, and competency assessment (exams).

Colorado State University   B, M, D

SURGE Program, Division of Continuing Education
Spruce Hall
Fort Collins, CO 80523-1040
Fields offered: Engineering, business administration, computer science, statistics, management, industrial hygiene
Year founded: 1870
Ownership: Nonprofit, state
Phone: (970) 491-5288 • (800) 525-4950
Fax: (970) 491-7885
E-mail: inquiries@lamar.colostate.edu
Website: www.colostate.edu/Depts/CE

The Colorado SURGE program is an innovative method of delivering graduate education (and, in certain cases, a second Bachelor's degree) to working professionals who cannot attend regular on-campus classes. Established in 1967, it was the first video-based graduate education program of its kind in America. An average of 80 courses are taught each semester via SURGE, from 17 departments in the colleges of agricultural sciences, applied human sciences, business, engineering (agricultural, chemical, civil, electrical, mechanical), natural sciences, and others. Regular Colorado State graduate courses are videotaped and sent, with other materials, to participating site coordinators. Site coordinators make these tapes and materials available to students, provide information about the program, supply registration forms, and proctor exams. Tapes may also be sent to individual students. There are plans to have an M.S. in industrial hygiene by video available by the fall of 1998.

One of the few distance M.B.A.s accredited by the AACSB. Contact Jamie Switzer, Director, at (491) 6471 or e-mail jswitzer@vines.colostate.edu. See also: National Universities Degree Consortium.

Columbia Union College   A, B

7600 Flower Avenue
Takoma Park, MD 20912-7796

Fields offered: Business administration, psychology, religion, respiratory care, theology, general studies
Year founded: 1904
Ownership: Nonprofit, church
Phone: (301) 891-4491 • (800) 782-4769
Fax: (301) 891-4022
Website: www.cuc.edu

The Associate and Bachelor of Arts (general studies, psychology, religion, theology) or Science (business administration, respiratory care), can be earned entirely through correspondence study. Credit available for standard equivalency examinations and/or work experience once the student has earned at least 24 semester hours in the program. At least 30 units (between eight and 12 courses) must be earned after enrolling. Students in the respiratory care program must complete some on-campus classes, held in two-week-long summer sessions. Every student must write a major paper, related to literature, religion, or arts, or pass a comprehensive examination, to qualify for graduation. The school is owned by the Seventh Day Adventist Church but non–church-members are welcome. Students may live anywhere in the world, but all work must be done in English.

Connecticut Board for State Academic Achievement Awards

See: Charter Oak State College

Consorzio per l'Universita a Distanza   B

Via G Marconi 32
I-87030 Renda CS, Italy
Fields offered: Many fields
Year founded: 1984
Phone: (39-984) 838-566
Fax: (39-984) 835-292
Website: www.cud.it

A consortium of universities, multinational companies, and government-related organizations, the CUD provides instruction leading to the equivalent of a Bachelor's degree, in a number of fields. All instruction is in Italian. Printed materials are supplemented by audio and videocassettes and computer software. Materials are provided to students at study centers (about 25 in Italy), where regular computer access is available, along with lectures, tutoring, and counseling. It is not clear whether students outside Italy can be admitted; at presstime we were still waiting for clarification.

Cornell University   M

169 Ives Hall
Ithaca, NY 14853
Fields offered: Industrial and labor relations
Year founded: 1865
Ownership: Nonprofit
Phone: (607) 255-3228
Fax: (607) 255 7774
E-mail: ale1@cornell.edu
Website: www.cornell.edu

Cornell offers videoconference and computer-based courses at the Master's-degree level in industrial and labor relations.

Curtin University of Technology   B, M

Careers & Prospective Students Service
GPO Box U1987
Perth, WA 6001 Australia
Fields offered: Many fields
Year founded: 1967
Ownership: Independent
Phone: (61-9) 351-2100
Fax: (61-9) 351-2777
E-mail: nworobecv@cc.curtin.edu.au
Website: puffin.curtin.edu.au/

A number of degrees are offered via distance learning. At the beginning of each semester, students are sent a package of study materials for each course in which they are enrolled—a typical package may include a course plan, a study guide, and a reader. They may also, if appropriate, have audio- or videocassettes, slides or photographs, maps or charts, and computer disks. Degrees offered include the following: Bachelor of Commerce in marketing, accounting, economics, finance, or banking, Bachelor of Applied Science in records management or library and information studies, Bachelor of Agriculture, Bachelor of Horticulture, B.S. in health and safety, B.A. in social sciences or education, Bachelor of Social Work, and Bachelor of Education. There are also two graduate degrees, a Master of Applied Science in information management and an M.S. in science education.

Darling Downs Institute of Advanced Education

See: University of Southern Queensland

David English House

See: University of Birmingham

David N. Myers College   B

112 Prospect Ave.
Cleveland, OH 44115
Fields offered: Business areas
Year founded: 1848
Ownership: Nonprofit, independent
Phone: (216) 696-9000
Fax: (216) 696-6430
E-mail: lhice@dnmyers.edu
Website: ellen.dnmyers.edu/

Adult students living within a 35-mile radius of the campus can complete a Bachelor of Science in management, marketing, accounting, health services management, and other business area at their own pace, with guidance from professional mentors. All work may be done nonresidentially, but on-campus meetings with mentors are required. Options for earning credit include home study (according to a learning contract), group study at various locations,

life/work experience and/or proficiency exams (both at 1/3 tuition), and/or previous credit transfer. Tuition can be greatly reduced by life/work experience credit and proficiency exams. The first such program approved by the Ohio Board of Regents, this is the oldest and largest external degree program in Ohio. Formerly Dyke College.

De Montfort University   M, D

Centre for Independent Study
The Gateway
Leicester, LE1 9BH England
Fields offered: Many fields
Year founded: 1897
Ownership: Nonprofit, state
Phone: (44-116) 255-1551
Fax: (44-116) 257-7625
E-mail: cork@dmu.ac.uk
Website: www.dmu.ac.uk/Leicester/index.html

The former Leicester Polytechnic, which became a university in 1992, offers a variety of graduate programs through distance learning, with minimal time required on the campus in England. Most programs are based on a learning contract or agreement negotiated between the student and the university. When a student is accepted into the program, he or she is assigned a mentor/supervisor, usually a member of the university staff, who will guide them through their program and assist in the formulation of a research or study proposal. Normally the mentor meets with the student once during each term; for foreign (non-U.K.) students, the school generally requires the student to have a local mentor as well as the university mentor. While meetings with the university mentor are generally done in person, it is possible that foreign students can meet the requirements by telephone, mail, or e-mail. In lieu of formal examinations, the university conducts "continuous assessments" through a variety of coursework assignments, plus a major project or thesis which will account for at least 40 percent of the total. An oral examination is held at the end of each program; in the U.K. Master's degrees by independent study are available in all departments. Applicants must normally have an undergraduate degree, although exceptions may be made. Successful applicants will demonstrate a capability to learn and research independently at the postgraduate level, in their chosen field of study.

Deakin University   B, M, D

Institute of Distance Education
Victoria, 3217 Australia
Off-Campus Operations
Fields offered: Many fields
Year founded: 1974
Ownership: Nonprofit
Phone: (61-52) 271-164
Fax: (61-52) 272-177
Website: www.deakin.edu.au

While established primarily for Australian students, Deakin does accept overseas enrollments; such students should apply directly to the Overseas Students Officer. Distance learning is facilitated through the use of readers and study guides, audio- and videocassettes, tutorial groups, video-conferencing and, where possible, weekend sessions. A number of degrees are offered, at all levels. These include: Bachelor of Arts in police studies or communication management, Bachelor of Applied Science in information management, Bachelor of Architecture, Bachelor of Commerce, Bachelor of Education, Bachelor of Engineering or Technology in comutronics, mechatronics, and environmental or manufacturing engineering, Bachelor of Laws, Bachelor of Letters, Bachelor of Nursing, B.S. in biological sciences, computer science and information systems, or mathematics and statistics, Bachelor of Social Work, , Ed.D., Ph.D. in art or education, and Doctor of Juridical Science. They also offer a Bachelor of Commerce by distance learning through Singapore's TMC Business School, and a fully on-line M.A. in science and technology.

Dublin City University

See: National Distance Education Centre (Ireland)

Dyke College

See: David N. Myers College

East Carolina University   M

School of Industry and Technology
Greenville, NC 27858
Fields offered: Digital communication technology
Year founded: 1907
Ownership: Nonprofit, state
Phone: (919) 328-6704 • (800) 398-9275
Fax: (919) 328-4250
E-mail: iteshelm@homer.sit.ecu.edu
Website: www.sit.ecu.edu/globalclassroom.htm
A wholly nonresident Master of Science in industrial technology with concentrations in digital communication technology and manufacturing. Students complete all coursework over the Internet. (The school recommends that applicants have a PC with, at minimum, a 486 processor, 8 megs of RAM, Windows 3.1, and a 14.4 modem. The school's software does not work well with the Macintosh platform.) Students with three or more years experience at a certain level in the field may take the Practitioner's Option, which excuses them from thesis, internship, and research project, but must take two additional advanced classes and submit a work portfolio.

Eastern Illinois University   B

Charleston, IL 61920
Fields offered: Many fields
Year founded: 1895
Ownership: Nonprofit, state
Phone: (217) 581-5000
Fax: (217) 581-2722
E-mail: bogba@eiu.edu
Website: www.eiu.edu/~adulted/

Bachelor of Arts, with a minimum of 15 units to be earned on campus or at sites approved by the director. This non-traditional program is designed to allow working adults who are 25 years of age or older the chance to complete most of their requirements off-campus, through independent study, equivalency examinations, and credit for life experience. A major is not required. Skills and knowledge acquired by nonacademic means can be evaluated for academic credit. See also: Board of Governors B.A. Degree Program

Eastern Oregon University   B, M

Division of Extended Programs
1410 L Avenue
La Grande, OR 97850-2899
Fields offered: Many fields
Year founded: 1929
Ownership: Nonprofit, state
Phone: (541) 962-3378 • (800) 544-2195
Fax: (541) 962-3627
E-mail: dep@eosc.osshe.edu
Website: www.eou.edu/dep
Eastern Oregon offers a number of wholly distance-learning degrees: a B.A. or B.S. in the following fields: liberal studies with a concentration in environmental studies, philosophy, politics, & economics (combined program), business economics, and fire services administration. Credit for independent study, cooperative work experience, assessment of prior learning, weekend college, and by examination. Coursework is accomplished via correspondence courses (with video/audio tapes), computer conferencing courses, web-based courses, and weekend colleges.. There is also an M.S. in social work available to Oregon residents through a combination of distance learning and small-group "cohort" sessions at five locations around the state. Master's in teacher education (M.T.E.) available largely through distance learning methods (locally televised courses, tele- and computer conferencing, satellite television), with one summer session on-campus. The contact for the M.T.E. is Jens Robinson, at (503) 962-3772. Eastern does not charge additional tuition for out-of-state students but does require that they have full Internet communication capabilities (e-mail and web browsing). To learn more about the degrees and the many courses available from Eastern, check out their web page. The school currently limits itself to working with English-speaking students in North America because they haven't completely figured out how to handle the postage costs and delays and test proctoring for students in other countries (although they do have a few experimental students in Brazil and Germany and are making plans to do further tests with other students). The school does accept applications for courses and degrees from students in prison, but recognizes that there are severe limits in working with prisoners and consequently has very few as students (e.g., most are not allowed to use computers in prison, so they cannot take on-line degree planning workshops or on-line courses).

Edith Cowan University B, M, D

External Studies
P.O. Box 830
Claremont, WA 6010 Australia
Fields offered: Many fields
Year founded: 1990
Phone: (61-9) 273-8500
Fax: (61-9) 442-1330
E-mail: extstudi@echidna.cowan.edu.au
Website: www.cowan.edu.au/homepage.html

This school offers a number of interesting programs entirely through distance education. Distance-learning methods employed may include workbooks and/or study guides, additional readings, audio-visual materials, and other instructional media. In addition, students may be directed to obtain and read various necessary texts and journal articles. The degrees offered are: Bachelor of Arts in aboriginal and intercultural studies, justice studies, religious studies, and accounting, management, and marketing (combined degree), Bachelor of Education, Bachelor of Health Science, Bachelor of Nursing, Bachelor of Science in computer science and security, Bachelor of Social Science in children's studies, youth work, and police studies, Master of Arts in applied linguistics, M.B.A., Master of Education, Master of Health Science in occupational health or occupation medicine, Master of Science in information science or development studies, and Ph.D.'s in interdisciplinary studies and education. Formerly Western Australian College of Advanced Education.

Electronic University Network B, M, D

1977 Colestin Road
Hornbrook, CA 96044
Fields offered: Business, liberal arts, psychology
Year founded: 1983
Ownership: Proprietary
Phone: (541) 482-5871 • (800) 22LEARN
Fax: (541) 482-7544
E-mail: DrEskow@aol.com
Website: www.wcc-eun.com/eun/

The Electronic University Network offers undergraduate courses for credit as well as Master's and doctoral programs from accredited institutions, using computer bulletin board services to connect students with instructors, other students, and support services such as a library and student union. A personal computer (IBM or Macintosh) with a modem is required. Study is self-paced and in most programs may begin at any time. Affiliated schools change from time to time. They include the on-line doctorate of the California Institute for Integral Studies, the M.B.A. of Heriot-Watt University, an M.S. in international relations from Salve Regina College, and several Associates and Bachelor's programs.

Embry-Riddle Aeronautical University B, M

Department of Independent Studies
600 South Clyde Morris Blvd.
Daytona Beach, FL 32119-3900
Fields offered: Aeronautics
Year founded: 1926
Ownership: Nonprofit, independent
Phone: (904) 226-6397 • (800) 359-3728 (undergrad)
(800) 866-6271 (grad)
Fax: (904) 226-7627
E-mail: indstudy@cts.db.erau.edu
Website: www.db.erau.edu

Bachelor of Science in professional aeronautics with no traditional classroom attendance. Applicants must have certified commercial or military training and professional experience in an approved aviation-related occupation (may include air traffic control, airways facilities, aviation weather, electronic operations, flight operations administration, navigation systems, certified flight instructor, etc.). B.S. in management of technical operations is designed for persons who already have competence in a technical specialty; applicants must have already competed 15 semester hours "in coherent topics which comprise a technical, mechanical, industrial, or scientific specialty that could be utilized in aviation." Credit is awarded for CLEP and DANTES, and credits may be transferred in from other accredited institutions. The Master of Aeronautical Science, with specialization in management or operation, is likewise tailored to civilian or military aviation personnel. A maximum of 12 aviation-related credits form a regionally accredited institution can be transferred into the graduate program.

Empire State College B, M

Center for Distance Learning
2 Union Ave.
Saratoga Springs, NY 12866-4390
Fields offered: Business, human services, interdisciplinary studies
Year founded: 1971
Ownership: Nonprofit, state
Phone: (518) 587-2100 • (800) 468-4390 (NY only)
Fax: (518) 587-5404
E-mail: cdl@sescva.esc.edu
Website: www.esc.edu

A part of the State University of New York, Empire State College provides programs in 40 locations across New York State. The primary mode of study is independent study guided by faculty mentors. Together, students and mentors develop a degree program within the college's 11 broad areas of undergraduate study. Credit is given for college-level learning gained from work and other life experience. The Bachelor's degree can be completed entirely by independent, faculty-guided study; classroom attendance generally not required. The Master of Arts requires four days on campus at the beginning and end of each semester, and is offered in business and policy studies, labor and policy studies, and culture and policy studies. They combine independent study with three three-or-four day weekends on campus each year. In addition, the Center for Distance Learning offers structured courses and degree programs in business administration, human services, and interdisciplinary studies for students seeking more structured learning without classroom attendance or travel; faculty guidance is by mail and telephone. See also: FEMA National Fire Academy

Emporia State University   B, M

    1200 Commercial
    Box 4052
    Emporia, KS 66801-5087
    Fields offered: business, education, library science, physical education
    Year founded: 1863
    Ownership: State
    Phone: (316) 341-5385
    E-mail: conted@esumail.emporia.edu
    Website: www.emporia.edu/www/conted/home.htm
Degree programs differ in residency requirements, so check their website for information on degree programs and more non-resident study opportunities. Currently, the only undergraduate degree is in business, and available only to people within range of the university. Graduate degrees are in either education-related areas or library science.

Engineering Education Australia   B, M

    13-21 Bedford Street, #202
    North Melbourne, Victoria 3051 Australia
    Fields offered: Engineering
    Year founded: 1991
    Phone: (61-3) 9326-9777
    Fax: (61-3) 9326-9888
    E-mail: frankm@deakin.edu.au or
    hartnell@deakin.edu.au
    Website: www.ieaust.org.au/eea/0001eea.htm
Not a school but a brokering institution, established to assist engineers in getting the education they need through distance means, drawing on the resources of a number of Australian colleges. May only be open to Australian nationals; as of presstime, our inquiry had not been answered.

Federation Interuniversitaire de l'Enseignement à Distance

    Teledix Bureau E217
    200 Avenue de la Republique
    F-92001 Nanterre, Cedex France
    Fields offered: Many fields
    Phone: (33-1) 4097-7551
    Fax: (33-1) 4729-1821
    E-mail: cguillard@magic.fr
    Website: www.formatel.com

A federation of 26 French universities with distance-learning departments or centers, the FIED offers over 2,000 different courses in fields including art, literature, philosophy, social sciences, education, history, law, mathematics, and various sciences. All courses offered in French, using a variety of methods, including printed correspondence texts, television, audio- and videocassettes, telephone tutoring and counseling, computer conferencing, supervised group work, and more. It is not entirely clear to us whether degrees are offered or just courses, nor whether students from outside France are accepted; as of presstime, our inquiry had not been answered.

FEMA National Fire Academy   B

    Degrees at a Distance Program
    16825 South Seton Ave.
    Emmitsburg, MD 21727-8998
    Fields offered: Fire administration, fire prevention technology
    Year founded: 1977
    Ownership: Federal government sponsored
    Phone: (301) 447-1127 • (800) 238-3358
    Fax: (301) 447-1178
    E-mail: ed.kaplan@fema.gov
    Website: www.usfa.fema.gov/tr_ddp.htm
Accredited Bachelor's degree in fire services areas, through independent study courses taken from any of seven universities and colleges. The program is offered through seven regional colleges (all accredited): Cogswell College (California), University of Cincinnati, University of Memphis, Western Oregon University, The University of Maryland University College, Western Illinois University, and Empire State College. All work is done by independent study. Students are sent a course guide, required textbooks, and their assignments. They communicate with instructors by mail and telephone. Supervised exams can be taken locally. Formerly called the Open Learning Fire Service Program.

FernUniversität   M, D

    Feithstrasse 140
    58097 Hagen, Germany
    Information Division
    Fields offered: Many fields
    Year founded: 1974
    Ownership: Nonprofit, state
    Phone: (49-2331) 987-2444
    Fax: (49-2331) 987-316
    E-mail: studentensekretariat@fernuni-hagen.de
    Website: www.fernuni-hagen.de
Germany's only distance teaching university offers about 1,700 distance courses, leading to the equivalent of Bachelor's, Master's and doctoral degrees, as well as post-doctoral theses. Fields of study span economics, humanities, and sciences, including computer science, education, history, modern German literature, political science, social behavioral sciences, electrical engineering, math, law, and more. Home-study materials are mainly printed lessons sent by

mail, although they may also include complementary materials delivered via Internet, CD-ROM, multimedia, audio and videotapes, etc. The university operates 64 study centers in Germany, Austria, Switzerland, and Hungary for the assistance and guidance of students. All instruction in German, although a nice color brochure is available in English. More than 3,100 of FernUniversität's over 55,000 students live outside of Germany.

Fitchburg State College   M
160 Pearl Street
Fitchburg, MA 01420
Fields offered: business, education
Year founded: 1894
Ownership: State
Phone: (508) 665-3181
Fax: (508) 665-3658
E-mail: dgce@fsc.edu
Website: www.fsc.edu

Master's degrees in business administration and in elementary education and secondary education for students living in Bermuda only.

Flinders University of South Australia   B, M, D
GPO Box 2100
Adelaide SA 5001, Australia
Fields offered: Special education, nursing, primary health care
Year founded: 1966
Phone: (61-8) 201-3074
Fax: (61-8) 201-3000
Website: adminwww.flinders.edu.au/Admissions/home.html

Offers many distance learning programs: a Bachelor of Special Education, Bachelor of Nursing, Master of Special Education, Master of Nursing (Research), Master of Nursing Studies, Master of Primary Health Care, M.S. in primary health care, and a Doctorate in Education. Courses are delivered using printed correspondence texts, supplemented by study guides, other readings, and sometimes audiocassettes and software. No residency required.

Florida Gulf Coast University   B, M
Distance Learning Program
10501 FGCU Boulevard
Fort Myers, FL 33908-4500
Fields offered: Many fields
Year founded: 1997
Phone: (941) 590-2315
E-mail: tdugas@fgcu.edu
Website: www.fgcu.edu

Candidate for regional accreditation. Bachelor's and Master's degrees are offered in a number of fields through a combination of traditional correspondence and on-line courses, and this new school is planning to add more programs in the next couple of years. Currently, there are Bachelor of

Science degrees in criminal justice, nursing, and health sciences, and Master's degrees in business administration, public administration, and health sciences. In 1998-99 they are adding a B.A. in liberal studies, a B.S. in clinical laboratory science, and an M.A. in educational technology. In 1999-2000, a Master's in physical therapy is planned. Exams are either waived in favor of additional projects, administered on-line, or proctored in the student's local area.

Fort Hayes State University   B
600 Park Street
Hays, KS 67601
Fields offered: Business, education, general studies
Year founded: 1902
Ownership: State
Phone: (913) 628-4291
Fax: (913) 628-4037
E-mail: adds@fhsu.edu
Website: www.fhsu.edu

Although offered via distance-learning methods, the Bachelor's degrees in business, education, and general studies are available to in-state students only.

General Motors Institute
See: Kettering University

George Washington University   M
2134 G Street NW
Washington , DC 20052
Fields offered: Educational technology leadership
Year founded: 1821
Ownership: Nonprofit, independent
Phone: (202) 994-1701
Fax: (202) 994-2145
E-mail: blynch@gwis2.circ.gwu.edu
Website: www.gwu.edu/~etl

Distance-learning M.A. in educational technology through a range of nontraditional teaching methods, including cable television, the Internet, computer conferencing and listserves, e-mail, and videocassettes. An M.S. in project management is under development—as of early 1998, only two of the 12 required classes were available by distance learning, but the plan was to expand this to include the entire program. For more information, visit the website (www.gwu.edu/~pmdl). This school also offers a number of interesting residential programs.

Georgia Institute of Technology   M
Continuing Education
Atlanta, GA 30332-0240
Fields offered: Engineering, computer science
Year founded: 1885
Ownership: Nonprofit, state
Phone: (404) 894-3378 • (800) 225-4656
Fax: (404) 894-5520
E-mail: mk2@prism.gatech.edu
Website: www.gatech.edu

This school's video-based instruction system allows working professionals to earn an M.S. entirely through videotaped classes and proctored exams from anywhere in the U.S. (and, in some cases, from other countries as well.). The available majors are electrical engineering (with options in computer engineering, digital signal processing, and power and telecommunications), environmental engineering, health physics/radiological engineering, industrial engineering, and nuclear engineering. While the degree is expensive, many companies have tuition-reimbursement plans for their employees.

Glasgow Caledonian University   M

> City Campus
> Cowcaddens Road
> Glasgow G4 0BA, Scotland
> **Fields offered:** Bulk solids handling technology
> **Year founded:** 1971
> **Phone:** (44-141) 331-3000
> **Fax:** (44-141) 331-3005
> **Website:** www.gcal.ac.uk

A Master of Science in bulk solids handling technology is offered through a series of comprehensive distance-learning packages. Offered by the school's Department of Physical Sciences, which in 1993 merged with the Centre for Industrial Bulk Solids Handling, the course of study consists of 12 modules and an industrially based project. While no residency is required, students are welcome to attend any of a number of short courses on the Glasgow campus. Applicants should have an undergraduate degree in an engineering and technological field; experience in bulk solids or a related field will be considered as part of the application.

GMI Engineering and Management Institute   M

> 1700 West Third Street
> Flint, MI 49504-4898
> **Fields offered:** engineering, manufacturing management
> **Year founded:** 1919
> **Ownership:** Nonprofit
> **Phone:** (810) 762-7494
> **Fax:** (810) 762-9935
> **E-mail:** bbedore@nove.gmi.edu
> **Website:** www.gmi.edu/official/acad/grad

Courses are delivered to workplaces and to other colleges via videotape.

Governors State University   B

> BOG Program
> University Park, IL 60466
> **Fields offered:** Many fields
> **Year founded:** 1969
> **Ownership:** Nonprofit, state
> **Phone:** (708) 534-4092 • (800) GSU-8-GSU
> **Fax:** (708) 534-8399

> **E-mail:** gsubog@govst.edu
> **Website:** www.govst.edu/bog

Bachelor of Arts may be earned through weekend, evening, and summer programs, as well as telecourses completed through the Board of Governors B.A. degree program. Fifteen credit hours must be completed through Governors State. These units may be earned through independent study, telecourses, classes offered on-line, and on- or off-campus courses, so it is possible to earn this degree without ever setting foot on campus. Credit is also awarded for nonacademic prior learning and CLEP proficiency exams.

Grand Canyon University   M

> College of Education
> Distance Learning Degree Program
> 3300 West Camelback Road
> Phoenix, AZ 85017-1097
> **Fields offered:** Education
> **Year founded:** 1949
> **Ownership:** Nonprofit, church
> **Phone:** (800) 600-5019 • (800) 604-6088
> **Fax:** (602) 589-2010
> **E-mail:** admiss@grand-canyon.
> **Website:** www.grand-canyon.edu

Offers a videocassette-based M.A. in teaching, geared to K-12 teachers.

Grand Valley State University   B. M

> Grandlink Satellite Programs
> 301 West Fulton
> Grand Valley, MI 49504
> **Fields offered:** Nursing
> **Year founded:** 1960
> **Ownership:** Nonprofit, state
> **Phone:** (616) 771-6618 • (800) 748-0258
> **Fax:** (616) 771-6520
> **E-mail:** go2gvsu@gvsu.edu
> **Website:** www.gvsu.edu

B.S. nursing degree completion program for holders of an R.N. or A.D.N., through courses beamed to six sites in Michigan (Alma, Benton Harbor, Harrison, Muskegon, Scottville, and Sidney). M.B.A. interactive TV-based program available at 50 sites within Michigan.

Grantham College of Engineering   A, B

> 34641 Grantham College Road, P.O. Box 5700
> Slidell, LA 70469-5700
> **Fields offered:** Computer science, engineering technology
> **Year founded:** 1951
> **Ownership:** Proprietary
> **Phone:** (504) 649-4191 • (800) 955-2527
> **Fax:** (504) 649-4183
> **E-mail:** gogce@aol.com
> 76771.1630@compuserve.com
> **Website:** www.collegeedge.com/details/college

Grantham offers nonresident A.S. and B.S. degrees in computer science, electronics engineering technology, and computer engineering technology. The first requires very minimal prior experience; the latter 2 are geared to students with practical and/or work experience. Students are given up to 15 months to complete each distance-learning semester (8 in all), but the average students takes more like 8 months each. Highly motivated students can finish even more quickly, and qualifying for advanced standing can reduce the required coursework significantly. Credit granted for prior college work, military and job training, approved exams (CLEP, etc.) and, in the engineering technology program, work experience and laboratory proficiency. All students must have access to an IBM-compatible computer. All lessons are delivered via traditional correspondence, but tests may be submitted by e-mail. Foreign students are welcome, but must be fluent in English. (An unofficial student website lists other schools that have accepted Grantham's degrees: www.blitz.de/~tedvera/gce.htm).

Greenwich School of Theology   B, M, D
29 Howbeck Lane
Clarborough, Notts. DN22 9LW UK
Fields offered: religion, theology
Phone: (44-1777) 703-058
Fax: (44-1777) 703-526
Offers degrees at all levels, in conjunction with the accredited South African Potchefstroom University for Christian Higher Education. Greenwich does the training, and Potchefstroom awards the degrees. Accredited in the UK by the Council for the Accreditation of Correspondence Colleges. Formerly, but no longer, affiliated with Greenwich University in Hawaii.

Griffith University   B, M
Griffith Flexible Learning Services
Nathan
Queensland, 4111 Australia
Fields offered: Adult education, justice administration, education, special education, technology management
Phone: (61-7) 3875 7771
Fax: (61-7) 3875 6585
E-mail: student_enquiry@gu.edu.au
Website: www.gu.edu.au
Bachelor of Adult and Vocational Teaching, Bachelor of Arts, Bachelor of Arts in justice administration, Bachelor of Education, Master of Special Education, Master of Technology Management, and various diploma and certificate programs, all through distance learning.

Griggs University   A, B
12501 Old Columbia Pike
Silver Spring, MD 20904
Fields offered: Religious fields
Year founded: 1909

Ownership: Nonprofit, church
Phone: (301) 680-6570 • (800) 782-4769
Fax: (301) 680-6577
E-mail: 74617,3325@CompuServe.com
Website: www.learnwell.org/~edu/griggs.shtml
The venerable Home Study International, which has offered correspondence courses for decades, now has a degree-granting university, offering a A.A. and B.A. in religion or theological studies, and a B.S. in religious education or church business management.

Hamline University   M, D
1536 Hewitt Avenue
Saint Paul, MN 55104
Fields offered: Public administration, liberal studies
Year founded: 1854
Ownership: Nonprofit, church
Phone: (612) 523-2900 • (800) 888-2182
Fax: (612) 523-2987
E-mail: gradprog@piper.hamline.edu
Website: www.hamline.edu/depts/mapa
Hamline is dedicated to serving the needs of working students, offering classes and entire programs through evening and weekend courses. Currently, they offer a Master's and a doctorate in public administration through an evening program for public administrators, corporate managers, and lawyers as well as M.A.'s in education and liberal studies and an M.F.A. in writing. Courses can be personalized with the use of independent study, directed reading (mentored by a faculty member) and internships. The school is also in the planning stages of a new doctorate in public administration, to be offered entirely through distance learning. For more information, contact John Vinton, Director, Public Administration at (612) 641-2858 or e-mail: jvinton@hamline.edu.

Hampton University   B
College of Continuing Education
Hampton, VA 23668
Fields offered: Business
Year founded: 1868
Ownership: Nonprofit
Phone: (757) 727-5000 • (800) 624-3328
Fax: (757) 727-5949
Website: www.hamptonu.edu
A Bachelor's in business management is offered nonresidentially through courses that are delivered to the student by video, audiotapes and print media.

Hebrew Union College   M
3101 Clifton Avenue
Cincinnati, OH 45220
Fields offered: Judaic studies
Phone: (513) 221-1875
Fax: (513) 221-2810
Website: www.huc.edu

The Hebrew Union is an institute furthering reform Judaism. With campuses in Cincinnati, New York, Los Angeles, and Jerusalem, and associations with a number of universities, they offer over 500 courses and over 20 advanced degree programs in rabbinic, cantorial, education, communal service, and graduate studies. Some programs are available via distance learning.

Henley Management College   M, D

Greenlands
Henley-on-Thames
Oxfordshire, RG9 3AU U.K.
Fields offered: Business, project management
Year founded: 1945
Phone: (44-1491) 571454
Fax: (44-1491) 410-184
E-mail: barbarab@henleymc.ac.uk
Website: www.henleymc.ac.uk

Henley bills itself as the oldest independent management college in Europe. They offer a D.B.A. in full-time, part-time, modular, distance learning, company and consortium modes. While much of the work can be completed by independent study, it is not a wholly distance degree—an annual residential study week is required, at one of the school's centers (in the U.K., France, or Singapore).

Henley also has about 7000 distance-learning M.B.A. students in some 80 countries. Applicants must have a Bachelor's degree from a recognized university and three years of relevant business/managerial experience. The average student age is 34, and the school stresses that this is not a program for the young and/or inexperienced. Henley itself has facilities in 23 countries to provide local support, tutoring, workshops, etc. Elsewhere (including the USA) participants use on-line access (via Lotus Notes) to conference, submit assignments, and so forth. They can also attend workshops in other countries if they wish. Also offered is an M.S. in project management.

Heriot-Watt University   M

U.S. agency: Financial Times Management, Inc.
6921 Stockton Avenue
El Cerrito, CA 94530
Fields offered: Business administration, technical fields
Year founded: 1821
Phone: (510) 528-3777 • (800) 622-9661
Fax: (510) 528-3555
E-mail: info@hwmba.net
Website: www.hwmba.edu

Heriot-Watt offers the only accredited M.B.A. program that does not require a Bachelor's degree or entrance examinations and that can be done entirely by home study. With more than 9,000 students in over 120 countries (including more than 2,000 in the U.S. and Canada), it is, by far, the largest M.B.A. program in the world. The only requirement for earning the degree is passing nine rigorous three-hour exams, one for each of the required nine courses (marketing, economics, accounting, finance, strategic plan-

ning, etc.). The exams are given twice a year on hundreds of college campuses. Students buy the courses one at a time, as they are ready for them. The courses consist of looseleaf textbooks (average: 500 pages) written by prominent professors specifically for this program. Courses are not interactive: there are no papers to write, quizzes, or other assignments, and no thesis. Each course averages about 160 hours of study time, so the entire M.B.A. can be completed in one year, but 18 to 36 months is more common. Hundreds of major corporations recognize and pay for the degree.

The M.B.A., an M.A. in TESOL (teaching of English as a second language), and several highly technical Master's degrees (acoustical science, vibration studies, construction management) are the only programs that can be done by distance learning. Financial Times Management, for whom Mariah and John Bear work, is the sole distributor of Heriot-Watt courses in North America; there are also agents and distributors in twenty other countries. For information on the M.B.A., contact the California office. For information on the technical or TESOL degrees, contact the main campus: Heriot-Watt University, Edinburgh EH14 4AS, Scotland, www.hw.ac.uk

Holborn College   B, Law

U.S. Agency: MRG Consultants, Inc.
c/o Garber & Co.
305 Broadway, #1400
New York, NY 10007
Fields offered: Law, business
Year founded: 1970
Ownership: Independent
Phone: (212) 923-0347
Fax: (212) 393-9335
E-mail: hlt@holborncollege.ac.uk
Website: www.holborncollege.ac.uk

The London-based Holborn College offers law degrees at the LL.B (Honours) and postgraduate LL.M levels, through an association with the University of Wolverhampton. The LL.B may qualify graduates to take the Bar in England. Both programs take a minimum of three years to complete, and were originally tutorials for the University of London's exams. Holborn's catalog notes that its degrees, legitimate in their own right, "can also be used by students as an access program" to the prestigious London degrees. The LL.B can be completed entirely by mail, with the exception of exams held yearly in London, Hong Kong, Kuala Lumpur, and elsewhere as well, by special arrangement.

Hong Kong Baptist University   B, M

School of Continuing Education
224 Waterloo Road
Au Shu Hung Garden Terrace
Kowloon, Hong Kong, PRC
Fields offered: Many fields
Year founded: 1990
Phone: (852) 2339-5487
Fax: (852) 2339-9987
E-mail: hkbu@hkbu.edu

Distance-learning Associate's and Bachelor's degrees in collaboration with Ohio University, M.B.A. in collaboration with the University of Strathclyde (Scotland), Bachelor of Specialized Studies with the University of Western Sydney, in addition to the school's own programs in business, international marketing, English, gemology, and other fields.

Hong Kong Tak Ming College   B

316-317 Lai Ho House
Lai Kok Estate
Cheung Sha Wan
Kowloon, Hong Kong.
Fields offered: Business administration, accountancy
Year founded: 1961
Ownership: Nonprofit, independent
Phone: (852) 2366-7880
Fax: (852) 2366-7282
Website: www.hktmc.edu

This school offers evening and weekend courses in Hong Kong and China, leading to a B.S. in accountancy and a B.B.A. In addition, and more useful to most of our readers, we've heard that the Dundee Institute of Technology has begun "franchising" its M.B.A. to several other schools. One of them, Hong Kong Tak Ming, has produced and is offering a distance-learning version thereof; interested parties should fax for more information.

Hosei University   B

2-23 Ichigaya Tamachi
Shinjuku-Ku
Tokyo 162, Japan
Division
Fields offered: Law, literature, economics
Year founded: 1880
Phone: (81-3) 5261-5150
Fax: (81-3) 3268-7021
Website: www.icdl.open.ac.uk/icdl/database/asia/japan/hoseiuni/inst/

Founded in 1880 as the Tokyo School of Law, Hosei offers correspondence programs leading to a Bachelor of Law, Bachelor of Economics, and B.A. in Literature. Coursework is delivered primarily by printed texts, and counseling occurs by phone or mail.

Illinois Institute of Technology   M

IITV
10 West 31st Street, 226 SB
Chicago, IL 60616
Fields offered: Engineering, chemistry
Year founded: 1890
Ownership: Nonprofit
Phone: 312-567-3167
Fax: 312-567-5913
E-mail: ia_pryor@vax1.ais.iit.edu
Website: www.dlt.iit.edu

Master's in chemistry is non-residential. Masters in chemical, mechanical, and aerospace engineering may require campus visits for examinations or presentations. Some courses available only to local area students. Check with school. Course information is exchanged through video-conferences, telephone, fax, and e-mail. Some courses use videotape.

Indiana University   B, M

Systemwide General Studies
Owen Hall 101
Bloomington, IN 47405
Fields offered: General studies, labor studies
Year founded: 1820
Ownership: Nonprofit, state
Phone: (812) 855-3693 • (800) 334-1011 outside IN
(800) 342-5410 in IN
Fax: (812) 855-8680
E-mail: bulletin@indiana.edu
Website: www.extend.indiana.edu

Bachelor of General Studies and Bachelor of Labor Studies available entirely through nonresidential study. The general studies degree can be done without a major, and there are many, many fields to choose from in picking courses. One hundred and twenty semester units are required, of which at least 30 must be earned from Indiana University. All 30 can be earned via independent study by correspondence. One quarter of the units must be upper division (junior or senior) level. The university also has evening courses, a weekend college, and a course to assist in developing a life experience portfolio. They also have many on-line graduate courses, although no degree programs as yet; still, these courses can be transferred to any school that accepts transfer credit. For course details, check out their distance-learning website.

Indiana University Southeast   B

School for Continuing Studies
4201 Grant Line Road
New Albany, IN 47150
Fields offered: General studies
Year founded: 1941
Ownership: Nonprofit, state
Phone: (812) 941-2315 • (800) 334-1011
Fax: (812) 941-2588
E-mail: bulletin@indiana.edu
Website: www.extend.indiana.edu

Bachelor's in general studies may be earned through a combination of weekend, evening, television, and correspondence study. Intensive summer courses are also available. Credit for independent study, self-acquired competencies, military training, and by examination. All coursework may be completed through the university's correspondence division. Students from outside the U.S. are welcome, and should direct their inquiries to: Indiana University, Owen Hall, Bloomington, IN 47405-5201. The telephone number is (812) 855-3693.

Indiana University System   B, M

School of Continuing Studies
Owen Hall
Room 205
Bloomington, IN 47405
Fields offered: General studies, labor studies, adult education, language & literacy education, nursing, therapeutic recreation
Year founded: 1912
Ownership: Nonprofit, state
Phone: (812) 855-8995
Fax: (812) 855-8997
E-mail: myoakam@indiana.edu
Website: www.indiana.edu/~scs/dl.html.

The Indiana University System has been offering distance learning courses since 1912. Bachelor's degrees are offered in general studies and in labor studies, Master's in adult education, language and literacy education, nursing (requires a prior B.S.N), and therapeutic recreation. Program employs the full spectrum of communications possibilities.

Indira Gandhi National Open University   B, M

Maidan Garhi
New Delhi 110 030, India
Fields offered: Many fields
Year founded: 1985
Phone: (91-11) 686-2598
Fax: (91-11) 686-0863
E-mail: igcomp@ren.nic.in
Website: www.indialog.com/ignou/acadprog.htm

Open to Indian citizens living anywhere in the world, and to foreigners residing in India, this school offers degrees in subject areas including social sciences, humanities, sciences, management, education, engineering & technology, health, and computer & information sciences. The degrees available through distance learning are: the Bachelor of Arts and Bachelor of Science in a number of fields, Bachelor of Commerce, Bachelor of Library & Information Science, Master of Arts in distance education, M.B.A., and Master of Library & Information Science. Coursework is accomplished via printed correspondence texts, audio- and videocassettes, satellite television and, for students living in India, study centers scattered all over the country.

Institute for Financial Management

See: University of Wales, Bangor

Institute of Transpersonal Psychology   M

744 San Antonio Road
Palo Alto, CA 94303
Fields offered: Transpersonal psychology
Phone: (650) 493-4430
Fax: (650) 493-6835
Year founded: 1975
E-mail: iitpinfo@best.com
Website: www.tmn.com/itp/

This school offers a Master's degree and several certificates in the field of transpersonal psychology, with concentrations in such fields as women's spirituality, wellness counseling, and creative development. Study begins with a seminar held somewhere near the student's home area, and continues through guided, mentored independent studies.

Institute of Public Administration   B, M

57-61 Landwdowne Road
Dublin 4, Ireland
Fields offered: Public management, business studies, health care management, economic policy
Year founded: 1957
Phone: (353-1) 668-6233
Fax: (353-1) 668-9135
E-mail: jarmstrong@ipa.ie
Website: www.ipa.ie/educ.htm

The Institute of Public Administration is a leading public sector management development agency, and it offers distance-learning degrees designed for Irish participants studying anywhere in Ireland. Degrees offered are a B.A. and an M.A. in public management, a B.A. in business studies, an M.A. in health care management, and an M.S. in economic policy. There are residential programs in Dublin, and opportunities to work as an intern in the European Parliament.

Instituto Politecnico Nacional   B

Avenida Instituto Politecnico Nacional
Mexico D.F., 14, Mexico
Fields offered: Economics, international trade
Year founded: 1936
Ownership: Nonprofit, state
Phone: (52-5)754-4706
E-mail: internet@ipn.mx
Website: www.ipn.mx

Mexico's open university system (sistema abierto de enseñanza) offers the Bachelor's degree in economics and international trade entirely through distance study, though study guides, slides, movies, records, and videocassettes, as well as group seminars held at various locations throughout Mexico. All work must be done in Spanish. The degree is awarded mainly on the basis of one's performance on final examinations.

International Correspondence Schools   A

Center for Degree Studies
925 Oak Street
Scranton, PA 18540-9887
Fields offered: Business and technological fields
Year founded: 1890
Ownership: Proprietary
Phone: (717) 961-4658 • (800) 275-4409
Fax: (717) 343-8462
E-mail: info@icslearn.com
Website: www.icslearn.com

The world's largest correspondence institution, which goes by the name ICS Learning Systems, offers a large number of vocationally targeted courses, as well as two Associate's degrees, with a number of specializations. The degrees are an Associate in Specialized Business, with concentrations in accounting, applied computer science, business management, management, finance, marketing, and hospitality management; also, an Associate in Specialized Technology, with concentrations in civil engineering technology, electrical engineering technology, electronics technology, industrial engineering technology, and mechanical engineering technology.

International University College

See: International University (Colorado)

International University (Colorado)   B, M

9137 East Mineral Circle
P.O. Box 6512
Englewood, CO 80155-6512
Fields offered: Business communication
Year founded: 1995
Phone: (303) 784-8045 • (800) 777-6463, ext. 3153
Fax: (303) 784-8547
E-mail: info@international.edu
Website: www.international.edu

I.U. began offering graduate courses leading to an M.A. in business communication in 1995; since then, a B.A. has been added, also in business communication. Courses are delivered over the Internet, and both degrees can be earned without any residency. In March of 1997, the school was accepted as an accreditation candidate by the North Central Association, and faculty members have degrees from an impressive range of schools (Northwestern, Purdue, Cornell, etc.) Formerly known as International University College.

Internet Distance Education Associates

2208 NW Market Street, #509
Seattle, WA 98107
Ray Levesque, Consultant
Phone: (206) 789-7326
Fax: (206) 783-2809
E-mail: rayl@idea-clc.com
Website: www.iclnet.org/robwes/robwes.html

This organization offers Internet-based degree programs through Roberts Wesleyan College in Rochester, New York. As the school's website was under construction at presstime, we are awaiting full information.

ISIM University   M

50 South Steele Street
Denver, CO 80047
Fields offered: Information resources management, business administration
Year founded: 1987
Ownership: Proprietary
Phone: (303) 333-4224 • (800) 441-ISIM
Fax: (303) 336-1144

E-mail: Admin@Isim.com
Website: www.isimu.edu

An M.S. in information resources management and an M.B.A. with a focus in information resources management are offered via "electronic campus," where instructor-guided learning takes place using the school's own telecommunications network and computer bulletin-board service. A thesis or major independent study project is required of every student. Formerly called International School of Information Management.

James Cook University   B, M, D

Townsville
Queensland 4811, Australia
Office of International Affairs
Fields offered: Social work/community welfare, education, interdisciplinary studies
Year founded: 1961
Ownership: Nonprofit, state
Phone: (61-7) 4781-4998
Fax: (61-7) 4781-5988
E-mail: InternationalAffairs@jcu.edu.au
Website: www.oia.jcu.edu.au

While mainly established for residents of Queensland, some of the school's distance-learning programs are available to persons elsewhere in Australia and overseas. Coursework is delivered largely via printed correspondence materials, with some audiovisual support. The distance-learning degrees are awarded at all levels, with specializations in adult education and training, education, interdisciplinary studies, and social work/community welfare. Full details can be found at the school's web site.

JEC College Connection   B, M

9697 East Mineral Ave.
P.O. Box 6612
Englewood, CO 80155-6612
Fields offered: Many fields
Ownership: Independent
Phone: (800) 777-MIND
E-mail: edcenter@jec.edu
Website: www.jec.edu

The cable education network called Mind Extension University, or ME/U, delivers live high school and college courses from more than 24 educational experts and regionally accredited colleges and universities. Through cable television, satellite, videotape, and other related transmission technologies, ME/U provides educational enrichment opportunities through basic viewing to people in over 19.5 million households, offices, schools and military bases. All students logistics, except for academic evaluation and transcript documentation, occur between the student and the ME/U Education Center reached through a toll-free number. The programs are prepared by each individual university and, just like on-campus education, range from lively and engaging to dry and tedious. The channel is on the air 24 hours a day.

Joseph Banks College   M
P.O. Box 52 Crafters
South Australia, 5152 Australia
Fields offered: Human resources
Ownership: Private
Phone: (61-8) 8212-3595
Fax: (61-8) 8339-3616
E-mail: joseph-banks@lynx.net.au
Website: lynx.net.au/~joseph-banks/
The graduate diploma in human resources offered by Banks is already accredited by the Australian government, and their Master's degree is currently undergoing the accreditation process. Credit is given for prior learning, including that which took place in the workplace. Studies take place through a combination of multimedia, mail, fax, phone, e-mail, and Internet.

Judson College   B
302 Bibb Street
Marion, AL 36756
Fields offered: Many fields
Year founded: 1838
Ownership: Nonprofit, church
Phone: (334) 683-5100 • (800) 447-9472
Fax: (334) 683-5147
E-mail: admissions@future.judson.edu
Website: home.judson.edu
Wholly nonresident Bachelor's degrees, for women over the age of 21 only, through an individualized study program based on a learning contract. The program awards credit for appropriate prior life-experience learning through portfolio assessment, standard equivalency exams, and proficiency tests prepared by Judson faculty. Students can major in art, business, chemistry, CIS, criminal justice, English, fashion merchandising, home economics, history, interior design, mathematics, psychology, religious studies, or sociology.

Kansas Newman College   B
Off-Campus Nursing Division
3100 McCormick
Wichita, KS 67213
Fields offered: Nursing
Year founded: 1933
Ownership: Nonprofit, church
Phone: (316) 942-4291 • (800) 736-7585
Fax: (316) 942-4483
E-mail: greent@ksnewman.edu
Website: www.ksnewman.edu
B.S. in nursing geared to allowing R.N.s in rural Kansas to obtain their degree by videocassette instruction.

Kansas State University   B, M
Non-Traditional Study Program
Division of Continuing Education
221 College Court
Manhattan, KS 66506
Fields offered: Interdisciplinary social science and agriculture, animal sciences & industry, engineering (several fields)
Year founded: 1863
Ownership: Nonprofit, state
Phone: (785) 532-5687 • (800) 622-2KSU
Fax: (785) 532-5637
E-mail: academic/services@dce.ksu.edu
Website: www.dce.ksu.edu
Kansas State offers two Bachelor's degree completion programs: the Bachelor of Science in interdisciplinary social science, and the Bachelor of Science in agriculture, animal sciences, & industry, with an animal products option. Applicants to either program must already have earned at least 60 semester college credits toward either the B.S. in social science (a 120-credit -hour program) or the B.S. in agriculture (127 credit hours). Students may transfer up to 90 credits to KSU, and assessment of prior learning is available after acceptance into the program. NTS students must earn at least 30 credits from KSU, which can be accomplished through video courses, guided studies, and classes offered over the Internet. Students will need a VCR and a computer with Internet access for some courses. See also: National Universities Degree Consortium.

Five Master's degrees are also offered, by videotape of compressed video broadcast—in electrical & computer engineering, civil engineering, chemical engineering, software engineering, or industrial & manufacturing systems engineering (with an engineering management specialty track). For more information on the Master's programs, contact Ellen Stauffer, Engineering Program Coordinator, by phone (785) 532-2562 or fax (785) 532-5637.

Keele University   M
Department of Academic Affairs
Staffordshire ST5 5BG, U.K.
Fields offered: Various management and education fields
Year founded: 1949
Phone: (44-1782) 621-111
Fax: (44-1782) 632-343
E-mail: aab01@admin.keele.ac.uk
Website: www.keele.ac.uk/
A number of Master's degrees tailored to working professionals seeking career development in their field. While courses are generally available only to persons resident in Great Britain, exceptions can be made; overseas applicants should contact the International Office in the Department of Academic Affairs for more information. Distance-learning degrees offered are: an M.A. in European industrial relations and human resource management, M.A. in human resources in health, designed for working public or private health resource people, M.A. in human resource management, and an M.A. in industrial relations.

Kettering University   M

1700 West Third Avenue
Flint, MI 48504
Fields offered: Engineering, manufacturing management
Year founded: 1919
Phone: (810) 762-7865 • (800) 955-4464
Fax: (810) 762-9837
E-mail: julseth@kettering.edu
Website: www.Kettering.edu

Formerly known as General Motors Institute, Kettering offers two graduate degrees (an M.S. in engineering, and an M.S. in manufacturing management) through programs offered at learning centers located at GM plants and other facilities around the country. The rigorous learning program is video-based. If enough people in a workplace are interested in the program, a learning center can be established there. If only a few people are interested, Kettering may be able to arrange for them to study at a nearby site.

Lakehead University   B, M

955 Oliver Road
Thunder Bay, ON P7B 5S1 Canada
Fields offered: General studies, nursing, forestry
Ownership: State
Phone: (807) 346-7730
Fax: (807) 343-8008
E-mail: leslie.malcolm@lakheadu.ca
Website: www.lakheadu.ca

B.A. and certificates in environmental assessment, tourism, and recreation resources management can be earned through distance learning. Each course package includes a manual, audio and/or video cassettes, and possibly supplementary reading and self-test materials. Students mail in up to six assignments per course, and take examinations on specified dates at about 30 locations in northern Ontario, and other Canadian locations by special arrangement. There is also a B.S.N. available (contact Dr. L. McDougall, School of Nursing, for information), and a Master of Forestry program (contact Dr. David Euler).

Laurentian University   B

Centre for Continuing Education
Ramsey Lake Road
Sudbury, Ontario P3E 2C6 Canada
Fields offered: Many fields
Phone: (705) 673-6569
Fax: (705) 673-6533
E-mail: dmayer@admin.laurentian.ca
Website: www.laurentian.ca

Offers a number of bachelor's degrees through a wide variety of bilingual methods, including printed course materials, teleconferencing, and the Internet. Degree programs offered in the English language are a B.A. in law & justice, native studies, psychology, women's studies, religious studies, and sociology, Bachelor of Social Work in native human services, Bachelor of Liberal Science, and B.S. in nursing. Courses offered in French are a B.A. in psychology or religious science, B.B.A., Bachelor of Liberal Science, and Bachelor of Social Work.

Lee College   B

External Studies
100 8th Street, NE
Cleveland, TN 37311
Fields offered: Religious studies
Year founded: 1918
Ownership: Church
Phone: (423) 614-8370 • (800) 533-9930
Fax: (423) 614-8625
E-mail: lee_ext1@chattanooga.net
Website: home.chattanooga.net/~lee_ext1/

Lee College offers an external studies program based almost entirely on independent study; its basic purpose is to prepare Christian workers in the area of biblical studies, theology, pastoral studies, music, missions, and evangelism.

Leeds Metropolitan University   M

U.S. agency: Financial Times Management, Inc.
6921 Stockton Avenue
El Cerrito, CA 94530
Fields offered: Information Management
Year founded: 1976
Phone: (510) 528-3777 • (800) 622-9661
Fax: (510) 528-3555
E-mail: lmu@degree.net
Website: www.lmu.ac.uk

The Master's of Science in Information Management consists of four full modules and four half modules. All materials are mailed to students, who submit coursework from each module for a final assessment. A dissertation is also required for the degree. Students are offered online support services.

Lehigh University   M

205 Johnson Hall
36 University Drive
Bethlehem, PA 18015
Fields offered: Chemistry, chemical engineering, molecular biology, quality engineering, business administration
Year founded: 1865
Ownership: Nonprofit, independent
Phone: (610) 758-5794
Fax: (610) 758-6269
E-mail: mak5@lehigh.edu
Website: www.lehigh.edu/~indis/indis.html

M.S. in chemistry chemical engineering, molecular biology, or quality engineering, as well as an M.B.A. through a highly innovative program that is, at present, available only to corporate-sponsored groups, allowing full-time working professionals to continue an education without ever visiting the campus. Classes are delivered nationwide via satellite television, and students can interact in real-time by 800 number, fax, or on-line message center/"electronic white-board."

Leicester University   M
See University of Leicester, this chapter

Lesley College   B, M
29 Everett Street
Cambridge, MA 02138 r
Fields offered: Many fields
Year founded: 1909
Ownership: Nonprofit, independent
Phone: (617) 349-8300 • (800) 999-1959
Fax: (617) 349-8313
E-mail: info@mail.lesley.edu
Website: www.lesley.edu

Lesley offers a range of nontraditional programs, including weekend Bachelor's degree programs, and an Intensive Residency Option, in which B.A. and B.S. students attend twice-yearly nine-day residencies in Massachusetts, then complete coursework on their own in between.

M.A. and M.Ed. degrees are offered worldwide through the Independent Study Degree program. Students work with a team of faculty advisors and are encouraged to concentrate on a specialized field that might not be available in a traditional program.

Liberty University   B, M
P.O. Box 11803
Lynchburg, VA 24506-9972
Fields offered: Religion, business, psychology
Year founded: 1971
Ownership: Nonprofit, church
Phone: (804) 582-2000 • (800) 424-9596
Fax: (804) 582-2304
E-mail: leonardwp@aol.com
Website: www.liberty.edu

Liberty's "School of LifeLong Learning" offers accredited degrees entirely through home study. Bachelor's degrees can be earned in church ministries, business administration, and psychology; Master's in counseling or religion. Faculty are regularly available, and a toll-free number is provided for all communications. The founder of Liberty is the Rev. Jerry Falwell.

Loma Linda University   M
School of Public Health
Office of Extended Programs
Nichol Hall, #1706
Loma Linda, CA 92350
Fields offered: Public health
Year founded: 1905
Ownership: Nonprofit, church
Phone: (909) 824-4595 • (800) 854-5661
Fax: (909) 824-4577
E-mail: mnewbold@sph.llu.edu
Website: www.llu.edu

The Extended Program at Loma Linda University's School of Public Health offers a unique and practical way for mid-career health professionals to obtain a Master of Public Health (M.P.H.) degree in either health promotion or health administration while maintaining their present employment. The format includes a combination of independent study (pre- and post-lecture assignments) and extensive student/instructor contact. The student is not required to spend time on campus at LLU. Instead, instructors travel to various sites in the United States to meet with students in intensive three-day class sessions, one per quarter at each site.

Loughborough University   M
Loughborough
Leicestershire LE11 3TU, U.K.
Year founded: 1909
Phone: (44-1509) 222-893
Fax: (44-1509) 212-535

It is our understanding that Loughborough has developed, or is in the process of developing, some unusual distance-learning Master's degrees, in fields such as packaging technology, advanced automotive engineering, and security management. We have written for more information.

Louisiana College   B
LC On-line, Box 606
1140 College Drive
Pineville, LA 71359
Fields offered: General studies
Year founded: 1906
Ownership: Nonprofit, church
Phone: (318) 487-7211
Fax: (318) 487-7310
E-mail: osborne@andria.lacollege.edu
Website: lcon-line.lacollege.edu

Southern Baptist affiliated college offers a computer-based program, using the Web, e-mail, Internet, and computer conferencing.

Loyola University (Louisiana)   M
6363 St. Charles Ave., Campus Box 14
New Orleans, LA 70118
Fields offered: Religious education, pastoral studies
Year founded: 1912
Ownership: Nonprofit, church
Phone: (504) 865-3250 • (800) 488-OCLP
Fax: (504) 865-3883
E-mail: LIM@beta.loyno.edu
Website: www.loyno.edu

Master of Religious Education or of Pastoral Studies, through off-campus programs administered through host sponsoring agencies, typically Roman Catholic dioceses. Students meet in their host site to view videotaped lectures, discuss assigned reading, and get assistance. Additional coursework is done as independent study; no visit to campus is required. Loyola also offers some off-campus programs for Louisiana residents only—a B.S. in nursing for licensed R.N.'s, and a Bachelor of Criminal Justice for Louisiana police officers.

Macquarie University   B, M, D, Law

Centre for Open Education
Sydney, NSW 2109 Australia
Fields offered: Many fields
Year founded: 1964
Ownership: State
Phone: (61-2) 850-7470
Fax: (61-2) 850-7480
E-mail: coe@ mq.edu.au
Website: www.coe.mq.edu.au/coe/centre/centre.htm
A number of degrees are offered through distance-learning methods that include specially prepared study guides, audiocassettes, assigned readings, and regular written assignments. While the programs were designed for Australian residents, applicants from abroad are considered if they have proper qualifications (contact school for details). Programs include Bachelor of Laws; Bachelor of Education; B.A. in majors including biology, geology, geophysics, education, Croatian, Macedonian, Polish, Russian, Serbian, Slovenian, and Ukrainian; B.S. in animal science, plant science, general biology, geology, and geophysics; Master of Education, Master of Early Childhood Education, and Master of Arts in Education; Master of Mining and Energy Economics, Master of Mineral Exploration Technologies, Master of Geoscience, and Ph. D. in Education.

Madurai-Kamaraj University   B, M

Institute of Continuing Education
Palkalai Nagar
Madurai, 625 021, Tamil Nadu India
Fields offered: Various fields
Year founded: 1966
Ownership: Nonprofit, state
Phone: (91-45) 331-712
Website: www-icdl.open.ac.uk/icdl/database/asia/india/maduraiu/prog/
Bachelor 's and Master's in a wide range of fields through a combination of correspondence study and examinations. (Indian universities generally award their degrees entirely by examination.) Madurai offers a wide range of correspondence courses designed to prepare students for its own examinations, which must generally be taken in India, but may be taken overseas by special permission. It is necessary to take the courses, or you will not be allowed to take the examinations. Degrees awarded are: Bachelor of Arts, Science, Commerce, General Law, and Education (this last available only to residents of Tamil Nadu and Pondicherry); Master of Arts in economics, English, history, political science, Tamil, and Gandhian thought, Master of Commerce, M.Ed. No course information was available on the web at presstime.

Maharishi University of Management   M

1000 North 4th Street
Fairfield, IA 52557
Fields offered: Business, computer science
Year founded: 1971
Fax: (515) 472-1179
E-mail: info@mum.edu
Website: www.mum.edu
M.S. in computer science and M.B.A. Formerly Maharishi International University.

Manchester Business School

See: University of Wales, Bangor

Manchester Metropolitan University   B

All Saints Building
Manchester, M15 6BH England
Fields offered: Fashion, geographic information systems, leadership
Year founded: 1970
Phone: (44-161) 247-2000
Fax: (44-161) 247-6390
E-mail: educational-services@mmu.ac.uk.
Website: www.mmu.ac.uk
A Bachelor's degree in the fields of fashion marketing and clothing manufacture, entirely through distance education. Applicants for the B.A. in clothing should hold the school's diplomas in Clothing and Footwear Institute, parts I & II; the program takes a year through distance learning, culminating in an honors dissertation. There is also a distance-learning M.S. in geographic information systems.

Manhattan College   B

School of General Studies
Bronx, NY 10471
Fields offered: General studies
Year founded: 1853
Ownership: Nonprofit, independent
Phone: (718) 862-8000
Fax: (718) 860-8019
E-mail: admit@manhattan.edu
Website: www.mancol.edu
Bachelor of Science in general studies may be earned through evening and summer programs. Cooperative nursing program with E. McConnell Clarke School of Nursing.

Mary Washington College   M

1301 College Ave.
Fredericksburg, VA 22401
Fields offered: Business administration, engineering
Ownership: Nonprofit, state
Phone: (540) 654-1000 • (888) 692-4968
Fax: (540) 654-1073
E-mail: admit@mwc.edu
Website: www.mwc.edu

Distance-learning M.B.A. and M.E. (engineering) through satellite television and telephone instruction. The M.B.A. is open to Virginia residents only, the M.E. to students world-wide. Also offers a Bachelor of Liberal Studies through evening and summer programs, with credit for independent study, exams, and nonacademic prior learning (by portfolio assessment).

McGill University   M

Distance Education
Faculty of Education
3700 McTavish Street
Montreal, Quebec H3A 1Y2 Canada
Fields offered: Occupational health sciences
Year founded: 1821
Phone: (514) 398-3457
Fax: (514) 398-2182
E-mail: inpb@musicb.mcgill.ca
Website: www.mcgill.ca
Master of Applied Science in Occupational Health Sciences in a program specifically for persons holing a degree in medicine or nursing. Study takes place via printed materials and videotapes, but students are required to attend six three-day practicums towards the beginning of study.

Memorial University of Newfoundland   B

Division of Continuing Studies
Room E2000, G.A. Hickman Building
St. John's, NF A1B 3X8 Canada
Fields offered: Commerce
Phone: (709) 737-8700
Fax: (709) 737-7941
E-mail: sturecru@morgan.ucs.mun.ca
Website: www.ce.mun.ca/dcs
This school offers a Bachelor's degree in commerce, as well as a number of certificate and diploma programs (business administration, public administration, Newfoundland studies, municipal administration, and criminology) through distance learning. Students study independently, completing correspondence assignments at home, supported by video- and/or audiotapes, as well as teleconferencing sessions. Assessment is by assignments and examination.

Michigan Virtual Auto College   B, M

3025 Boardwalk, Suite 220
Ann Arbor, MI 48108-3266
Fields offered: Courses and programs related to the automotive industry
Year founded: 1997
Ownership: private, non-profit
Phone: (734) 662-5725 • (888) 575-6822
Fax: (734) 662-7439
E-mail: mvac@mvac.org
Website: www.mvac.org
An effort to improve Michigan's economic productivity by linking the auto industry with the state's postsecondary educational resources. Many of Michigan's leading-edge

university research programs relate directly to the auto industry. By taking advantage of the world wide web, it can bring immediate access to Michigan's trend-setting schools, colleges, universities, and job training programs.

Mississippi University for Women   B

655 Eason Blvd.
Tupelo, MS 38834
Fields offered: Nursing
Year founded: 1884
Ownership: Nonprofit, state
Phone: (601) 844-0284
Fax: (601) 842-6883
E-mail: mfreeman@muw.edu
Website: www.muw.edu
Courses via computer software and conferencing delivered to student's home.

Monash University   B, M

Course Inquiry Section
Distance Education Centre
Gippsland Campus
Churchill, Victoria 3842 Australia
Fields offered: Many fields
Phone: (61-351) 226-244
Fax: (61-351) 226-578
E-mail: de.liason@dec.monash.edu.au
Website: www.dec.monash.edu.au
Monash offers an impressive range of Bachelor's degree programs wholly by distance education, and some Master's degrees as well. Coursework is accomplished through a range of methods, including audio- and videotape, written lessons, and independent study. Foreign students are welcome, although those for whom English is not a first language do need to prove fluency. Degrees offered with no campus visit are as follows: B.A. in humanities and social sciences, communication, journalism, double major in communication and computing, Bachelor of Business, Bachelor of Computing, double major Bachelor of Business and Computing, Bachelor of Education or Educational Studies, Bachelor of Nursing, M.A. in linguistics, and Master of Nursing. Many more programs are doable mainly by distance learning, with some attendance required for labs and the like (including psychology, engineering, applied sciences, and behavioral sciences). Also, a number of nondegree certificates and diplomas in the above subjects, at both the undergraduate and graduate levels, entirely through distance learning. According to a correspondent, Monash also offers a Bachelor of Business through Singapore's TMC Business School, but it doesn't appear to be listed in their current catalog.

Morehead State University   M

College of Business
Combs 215
Morehead, KY 40351
Fields offered: Business administration

Year founded: 1922
Ownership: Nonprofit, state
Phone: (606) 783-2183
Fax: (606) 783-5025
E-mail: msu-mba@morehead-st.edu
Website: www.morehead-st.edu

Morehead's M.B.A. program is designed for students who have completed an undergraduate degree in any field, although a person whose degree is in a business-related field may complete the M.B.A. in a minimum of 36 semester hours, as compared to 50 hours for those whose degrees are in other areas. The new nonresident "manager-friendly, schedule-friendly" program offers classes over the Internet as well as via two-way interactive audio/video offered at a variety of sites in the eastern Kentucky service area. The Internet courses can, of course, be accessed from anywhere. Courses are offered evenings, weekends, and Saturdays, on an 18-month rotation.

Mount Saint Vincent University   B, M

EMF Room 121, 166 Bedford Highway
Halifax, NS B3M 2J6 Canadar
Fields offered: Tourism and hospitality, many others
Year founded: 1925
Ownership: Nonprofit, church
Phone: (902) 457-6511
Fax: (902) 445-3960
E-mail: carolyn nobes@MSVU.Ca
Website: www.MSVU.com

Mount Saint Vincent's in primarily a women's college, although men are welcome as nonresident students. Bachelor degrees are offered in a number of fields, including arts, sciences, business administration, applied arts (child and youth study or information management), human ecology, public relations, and tourism and hospitality management; M.A. is offered in school psychology, and there is also a research M.A. program and an M.Ed. available. All programs are offered nonresidentially throughout Canada by teleconferencing, telephone instruction, and videocassette. Students are expected to make weekly contact with professors and/or group teleconferencing sessions. Assignments are delivered via post, fax, or e-mail (Internet classes are under development at this time), and proctored exams are arranged based on student's course requirements and location.

Murdoch University   B, M

External Studies Unit
South Street
Murdoch, WA 6150 Australia
Fields offered: Many fields
Year founded: 1973
Phone: (61-9) 360-2844
Fax: (61-9) 310-4929
E-mail: atkinson@csuvax1.murdoch.oz.au
Website: www.murdoch.edu.au

External study is open to anyone in Australia, and to Australians living abroad as well. Printed course materials are delivered by post, and counseling and other support takes place via both phone and e-mail. The degrees offered are: a B.A. or B.S. in general studies; Bachelor of Arts in Asian studies, Australian studies, British & European studies, communication studies, education studies, English and comparative literature, history, politics, combined degree in politics, philosophy & sociology, sociology, and women's studies; Bachelor of Economics; Bachelor of Education; Bachelor of Literature and Communication, Bachelor of Science in computer science, environmental science, mathematics, mineral science, physics, and population resources & technology; Master of Arts in city policy, development studies, ecologically sustainable development, literature & communication, public policy, and science & technology policy; and a Master of Veterinary Studies.

Napier University   M

219 Collington Road
Edinburgh, EH14 1DJ Scotland
Fields offered: Business administration, information systems
Year founded: 1964
Phone: (44-131) 455-6108
Fax: (44-131) 455-6191
Website: central.napier.ac.uk

Edinburgh's third-oldest university offers an "open learning" M.B.A., mainly geared to managers operating in Europe. This program is designed to allow students to gain an M.B.A. "after approximately two years hard work," according to the school's materials. Participants work full time, and study using specially prepared study materials, backed up with local study groups, and eight study weekends at the Edinburgh campus. Selection procedure is rigorous, designed to select only those applicants with sufficient business experience. There is also an M.S. in information systems, available largely through distance learning, with several one-day "surgery sessions." Learning takes place through printed correspondence texts, telephone and e-mail tutoring, and various Internet functions.

National American University   B

P.O. Box 9420
2577 North Chelton
Colorado Springs, CO 80909
Phone: (719) 471-4205
Fax: (719) 471-4751
Website: www.nationalcollege.edu/campussprings.html

Accreditation candidate, accreditation expected by late 1998. Degree programs will be offered online.

National Distance Education Centre (Ireland)   B

Dublin City University
Glasnevin
Dublin 9, Ireland

Fields offered: Humanities
Year founded: 1982
Ownership: Nonprofit, state
Phone: (353-1) 704-5813
Fax: (353-1) 704-5494
E-mail: mackeogk@ccmail.dcu.ie
foxs@dcu.ie
Website: www.dcu.ie/ndec/ndec.html

This program offers a humanities-centered B.A. in Arts, comprising at the moment studies in history, literature, philosophy, psychology, and sociology. They hope to add economics and politics as the program grows. Students register as a student at one of five Irish universities (Dublin City University, St. Patrick's College at Maynooth, University College Cork, University College Galway, or University of Limerick), but all study a common program administered by the National Distance Education Centre. Courses are presented in modules, allowing students to tailor the rate at which they progress through the program—it is possible to finish in three years, and 85 percent of students finish within six. Students who can demonstrate prior learning may be exempted from up to four modules; such exemptions will be considered on a case-by-case basis. Coursework is done entirely at a distance, although theoretically one is supposed to be a resident of Ireland. Students who move out of Ireland during their course of study are required to maintain an Irish address for correspondence. There is also a B.S. in information technology, a Bachelor of Nursing Studies, an M.S. in operations management and one in management and applications of information technology in the field of accounting.

National Extension College

18 Brook lands Avenue
Cambridge, CB2 2HN UK
Phone: (41-223) 450-200
Fax: (41-223) 313-586
E-mail: nec@dial.pipex.com
Website: www.nec.ac.uk

While this school does not offer any degree programs of its own, it does provide full tutoring and coursework for persons enrolled in the following University of London programs: B.A. in English, French, Geography, German, Italian, philosophy, Spanish & Latin American studies, and joint modern languages (French & German, German & Italian or Italian & French), B.S. in economics, management or management & law , Bachelor of Laws, and Bachelor of Divinity (BD). Students must first register with the University of London, then they can complete their studies with the extra guidance provided by NEC. The degree is awarded by London.

National Institute of Health Sciences   B

P.O. Box 3286
Mankuta, ACT 2603 Australia
Fields offered: Naturopathy
Year founded:
Ownership:
Phone: (61-2) 6282-8277
Fax: (61-2) 6282-8278

This school claims to be the only private education provider to offer a Bachelor's degree in naturopathy that is fully accredited by the Australian government. The course of study can be completed entirely by distance learning. The study plan covers a wide range of subjects, including philosophy, herbal medicine, homeopathy, nutrition, biochemistry, exercise physiology, and more. It is also possible to earn a diploma in naturopathy, or in some of its constituent parts (herbal medicine, homeopathy, or nutrition)

National Open University   B

172 Chung Cheung Road
Lu Chow Country
Tapei County
Taipei, Taiwan, 24702 R.O.C.
Fields offered: Many fields
Year founded: 1986
Ownership: Nonprofit
Phone: (886-2) 2282-9355
Fax: (886-2) 8282-3524
E-mail: yyc@hpdns.nou.edu.tw
Website: www.nou.edu.tw

Delivers courses through a variety of media, including television, radio, printed course materials and CD-ROM, along with correspondence and classroom instruction which is offered at the 14 learning centers. Specialized courses are offered in six academic areas: humanities, social sciences, business, living sciences, public administration, and management & information. Each area is further divided into several fields of study.

National Technological University   M

700 Centre Avenue
Fort Collins, CO 80526-1842
Fields offered: Technological fields
Year founded: 1984
Ownership: Nonprofit, independent
Phone: (970) 495-6400
Fax: (970) 484-0668
E-mail: Jeanne@MAIL.NTU.EDU
Website: www.ntu.edu

NTU offers a wide range of graduate courses and noncredit short courses in technological subjects. These are transmitted by satellite from 45 American campuses to corporate, government, and university worksites. Working professionals and technical managers take the classes, simultaneously, with telephone links to the classrooms. NTU offers the M.S. in computer engineering, computer science, electrical engineering, engineering management, hazardous waste management, health physics, management of technology, manufacturing systems engineering, materials science and engineering, software engineering, and special majors. Hundreds of additional short courses are broadcast on the NTU Network each year.

National Universities Degree Consortium   B

Colorado State University
Continuing Education
Spruce Hall
Fort Collins, CO 80523-1040
Fields offered: Many fields
Ownership: Nonprofit
Phone: (970) 491-5288 • (800) 525-4950
Fax: (970) 491-7885
E-mail: inquiries@lamar.colostate.edu
Website: www.colostate.edu/Depts/NUDC

The National Universities Degree Consortium was established to offer flexible, nontraditional degree completion programs to adult and part-time students nationwide. Thirteen universities are participating already: California State University–Long Beach, Colorado State, Kansas State, Oklahoma State, University of Alabama, University of Idaho, University of Maryland, University of New Orleans, University of Oklahoma, University of South Carolina, University of Wyoming, Utah State, and Washington State. Courses are delivered over local cable TV, with the assistance of ME/U: The Education Network (if a student cannot receive the cablecast, videotapes can be provided), interactive multimedia, computer networks, teleconferencing, live instruction, and correspondence courses.

NBCC Miramichi College   B

P.O. Box 1053
80 University Avenue
Miramichi, E1N 3W4, New Brunswick Canada
Fields offered: Many fields
Ownership: Nonprofit, state
Phone: (506) 778-6000
Fax: (506) 778-6001
Website: www.miramichi.nbcc.nb.ca/

New Jersey Institute of Technology   B, M

University Heights, NJ 07102
Fields offered: Information systems, engineering management, computer science
Year founded: 1881
Ownership: Nonprofit, state

Phone: (973) 596-3177 • (800) 624-9850
Fax: (973) 596-3203
E-mail: dl@njit.edu
Website: www.njit.edu

Bachelor of Arts in information systems offered entirely through distance learning, using videotaped courses, on-line conferencing, fax, and phone to stay in touch. Distance students study along with on-campus students, on the same schedule, and examinations can be administered in remote locations by an approved proctor. Students must have access to a PC and modem.

New Mexico State University   B, M

Box 3WEC
Las Cruces, NM 88003
Fields offered: Business, education, engineering
Year founded: 1888
Ownership: Nonprofit, state
Phone: (505) 646-5837
Fax: (505) 646-2044
E-mail: lames@nmsu.edu
Website: www.nmsu.edu/

A B.B.A. for students in the local area, and M.S. in education for in-state students, and an M.S. in engineering with no residency required are offered at this time.

New School for Social Research   B, M

Media Studies Admissions Office
66 West 12th Street, Room 401
New York, NY 10011
Fields offered: Media studies
Year founded: 1919
Ownership: Nonprofit, independent
Phone: (212) 229-5630
Fax: (212) 229-5357
E-mail: admissions@dialnsa.edu
Website: dialnsa.edu/95conf

Master of Arts in media studies which combines theoretical offerings with advanced production coursework. Offered through D.I.A.L. (Distance Instruction for Adult Learning) it is designed for both media professionals and students considering further graduate study. Evening and independent study. Students can take classes on-line through their personal computers.

Also offers a wholly nonresidential Bachelor's–degree completion program online.

New York Institute of Technology   B, M

Theobald Hall, Room 417
P.O. Box 8000
Old Westbury, NY 11568
Fields offered: Business administration, interdisciplinary studies, behavioral sciences, hotel administration
Year founded: 1955
Ownership: Nonprofit, independent
Phone: (516) 686-7516
Fax: (516) 626-6830

Website: www.nyit.edu

Through the On-Line Campus, this school offers the B.S. in business administration, in interdisciplinary studies, in behavioral sciences, and in hospitality management. Credit available for prior learning and work experiences, and for equivalency exams. All learning takes places over computer modem, by teleconferencing. The off-campus programs were formerly offered through American Open University. There is a graduate certificate in distance learning: For information on this program, contact Dr. Helen Greene, at hgreene@admin.nyit.edu. M.B.A. information: Call Dr. William Lawrence, Director, at (800) 222-NYIT.

North Central Bible College   B
Carlson Institute
910 Elliot Ave. S.
Minneapolis, MN 55404
Fields offered: Church ministries, Christian education
Year founded: 1930
Ownership: Nonprofit, church
Phone: (612) 332-3491 • (800) 446-1176
Fax: (612) 343-4778
Website: www.ncbc.edu

Wholly nonresident Bachelor of Arts or Sciences in church ministries or Christian education. Credit available for life-experience learning through portfolio assessment, and for equivalency exams. Twenty-seven of the 130 credits required must be earned from North Central.

Northern Territory University   B, M
NT Extended Studies Centre
Darwin, NT 0909 Australia
Fields offered: Education, nursing
Year founded: 1988
Phone: (61-89) 466-483
Fax: (61-89) 466-549
Website: www.ntu.edu.au

Degrees offered are a Bachelor of Education, Bachelor of Nursing, and Master of Educational Studies. Students receive both print and multimedia materials for each semester-long unit. Additional support is available via audioconferencing, residential periods, and workshops.

Nottingham Trent University   M
U.S. agency: Financial Times Management, Inc.
6921 Stockton Avenue
El Cerrito, CA 94530
Fields offered: Quality, customer service
Year founded: 1986
Phone: (510) 528-3777 • (800) 622-9661
Fax: (510) 528-3555
E-mail: ntu@degree.net
Website: www.ntu.ac.uk

The Quality Unit of Nottingham Trent was founded in 1986, and offers distance learners postgraduate diplomas and master's degrees in quality engineering, customer service management and total quality. Modules are mailed to students to study and pass by taking exams, which are held twice a year in a variety of locations. All Master's degrees require a dissertation. No qualifications are required for admission.

Nottingham Trent University   M
Law School
Burton Street
Belgrave Centre
Nottingham NG1 4BU, U.K.
Fields offered: Law
Year founded: 1945
Phone: (44-115) 948-6557
Fax: (44-115) 948-6884
E-mail: andrea.luff@ntu.ac.uk
Website: www.ntu.ac.uk

Nottingham Law School is the largest university law school in the U.K. It offers the LL.M. in advanced litigation, an M.B.A. in legal practice, and a postgraduate diploma in law largely via distance learning. The LL.M. requires six intensive study weekends, the M.B.A., eight. For the LL.M., applicants must be a qualified solicitor or barrister (or equivalent), and have at least two years' legal experience. The LL.M. is aimed at lawyers and senior management with functional management responsibilities, and applies the management principles and techniques already taught in business schools to address the particular needs of legal practice. LL.M. and M.B.A. Applicants should have at least five years' experience in a legal environment. All courses are open to applicants from the UK and overseas. Intensive residential weekends are available, but not required.

Oakland University   B
Wilson Hall
Rochester, MI 48309-4401
Fields offered: General studies
Year founded: 1957
Ownership: Nonprofit, state
Phone: (810) 370-2190
Fax: (810) 370-4475
E-mail: ccrum@oakland.edu

Courses delivered via television, videotape, computer software and print to your workplace, or two locations in Michigan.

Ohio University   B
External Student Program
301 Tupper Hall
Athens, OH 45701
Fields offered: Specialized studies
Year founded: 1804
Ownership: Nonprofit, state
Phone: (614) 593-2150 • (800) 444-2420
Fax: (614) 593-4229
E-mail: extdegprog@ouvaxa.cats.ohiou.edu
Website: www.cats.ohiou.edu/~adullear/esp.htm

The Bachelor of Specialized Studies (B.S.S.) degree can be earned entirely though nonresident study. The External Student Program provides a counseling and advising service, and also acts as a liaison in dealing with other university offices. Credit for the degree can come from assessment of prior learning experiences, correspondence courses, independent study projects, and courses on television. In many correspondence courses, one can take the examination only. If you pass, credit for the course is given. These exams can be administered anywhere in the world and must be supervised. Forty-eight quarter hours of credit must be completed after enrolling at Ohio. The university also has offered a college program for the incarcerated, at unusually low cost.

Oklahoma State University · M

512 Engineering North
Stillwater, OK 74078
Fields offered: Engineering, business administration, telecommunications management, agricultural education, computer science
Year founded: 1890
Ownership: Nonprofit, state
Phone: (405) 744-5146
Fax: (405) 744-5033
E-mail: laugann@okway.okstate.edu
Website: master.ceat.okstate.edu/grads/engext.html
pio.okstate.edu

M.S. in electrical, mechanical, or chemical engineering offered in the state of Oklahoma by two-way video, and in the U.S., Canada, and Mexico through the National Technical University's satellite programs (may soon be available nationwide directly from OSU via videotape; contact the school for latest details).

Also, an M.B.A. and an M.S. in telecommunications management via two-way video to participating corporate sites. Contact for the M.B.A. is Alexa Bargmann; for the M.S. it's Peter Rosen, both at (405) 744-5208.

See also: National Universities Degree Consortium.

Old Dominion University · B, M

5215 Hampton Blvd.
Norfolk, VA 23529
Fields offered: Engineering, nursing, business, professional communications, criminal justice, special education
Year founded: 1930
Ownership: Nonprofit, state
Phone: (757) 683-3000 • (800) YOUR-BSN (nursing only)
Fax: (757) 683-4505 engineering
(804) 683-5253 nursing
E-mail: admit@odu.ed
Website: www.odu.edu/college-info

B.S. in civil, mechanical, or electrical engineering technology and nursing, business, and professional communications; M.S. in nursing or a number of engineering fields (civil and environmental, electrical and computer, mechanical, and engineering management) through a variety of nontraditional means, including public and cable television, satellite and closed-circuit television courses delivered to remote sites, teleconferencing, videocassette and conferencing, and telephone instruction. Contact for engineering technology program is Dr. William D. Stanley, at (804) 683-3775. Nursing programs (R.N.-to-B.S.N. and R.N.-to-Family Nurse Practitioner) can be done wholly nonresidentially by televised courses for people within the range of their broadcast sites, with clinical practicums arranged in your area. Internet-based courses are in the planning stage.

Open Learning Agency

Communications and Corporate Relations
Open Learning Agency
PO Box 82080
Burnaby, BC V5C 6J8 Canada
Fields offered: Many fields
Phone: (604) 431-3000
Fax: (604) 431-3333
E-mail: studentserv@ola.bc.ca
Website: www.ola.bc.ca/

Open Learning Agency develops and acquires courses from other institutions for delivery using open learning methods. For residents of Canada. A complete course package is sent to the student on registration, including a course manual, course units, textbooks and assignment file. For some courses, additional support materials may be necessary, such as audio cassettes, slides, laboratory kits, videotapes, software, on-line learning, or television programs broadcast on the Knowledge Network. Support services are available including advisors to help with study skills and special needs support which may include adaptation of courses. Free round-the-clock library service for all students living in British Columbia and the Yukon. See also: Open University and Open College

Open Learning Institute of Hong Kong · B

30 Good Shepherd Street
Ho Man Tin
Kowloon, Hong Kong
Registry
Fields offered: Many fields
Year founded: 1989
Phone: (852) 2768-6000
Fax: (852) 2789-2725
E-mail: regwww@oliv1.oli.hk
Website: www.oli.hk

Applicants must be over 17 years old and have a Hong Kong ID number and a Hong Kong address. Distance-learning Bachelor's degrees are offered in arts, education, social sciences, international studies, business administration, science, technology, and general studies.

Open University and Open College   B

Open Learning Agency
P.O. Box 82080
Burnaby, BC V5C 6J8 Canada
Fields offered: Many fields
Year founded: 1978
Ownership: Nonprofit, state
Phone: (604) 431-3000 • (800) 663-9711 (BC only)
Fax: (604) 431-3381
E-mail: studentserv@ola.bc.ca
Website: www.ola.bc.ca

The Open University and Open College are services of Canada's Open Learning Agency; the university courses lead to Associates and Bachelor's degrees, the college's to certificates and diplomas. A wide variety of self-paced programs are available (contact the school for details). Coursework is delivered via on-line instruction, computer conferencing, videocassettes, televised classes, printed materials, telephone and video. Degrees offered are: Bachelor of Arts in a number of fields, Bachelor of Administrative Studies, Bachelor of General Studies, Bachelor of Health Science in physiotherapy or psychiatric nursing, Bachelor of Music in jazz studies, Bachelor of Music Therapy, Bachelor of Science in general sciences, and Bachelor of Technology in computer systems or technology management. Formerly the British Columbia Open University.

Open University (England)   B, M, D

Walton Hall
Milton Keynes, Buckinghamshire, MK7 6AA England
Fields offered: Arts, health and social welfare, social sciences, math, computers, technology, education, science, environment, management, languages, laws
Year founded: 1969
Ownership: Nonprofit, state
Phone: (44-1908) 274-066
Fax: (44-1908) 653-744
E-mail: CREL-GEN@open.ac.uk
Website: www.open.ac.uk

Established in 1969, the Open University is now the largest distance education institution in the world. Students study in their own homes and on their own schedules, using a combination of correspondence texts and audio- and videocassettes, software and e-mail, or, increasingly, the Internet. Study can lead to a degree, a certificate, or diploma. Some courses have week-long summer schools or weekend residential schools, and some require that the applicant be a resident of the U.K. or other European country. Single courses may be available for personal interest or professional updating. There are currently over 75,000 undergraduates and 20,000 associate students registered as well as some 7,000 higher degree students. Credit is earned through a combination of achieving a specified level of continuous assessment and passing the course examination. The M.A. in open and distance education involves heavy use of the World Wide Web. For more information on this program, contact Brenda Parish (Secretary, M.A. in Open and Distance Education Programme) at b.m.parish@open.ac.uk

The school is also actively involved in establishing a presence in the U.S., including seeking regional accreditation. More on this as it develops.

Open University of Hong Kong   B, M

30 Good Shepherd Street
Ho Man Tin
Kowloon, Hong Kong
Fields offered: Many fields
Year founded: 1989
Ownership: Private
Phone: (852) 2768-6000
Fax: (852) 2761-3935
E-mail: regwww@.ouhk.edu.hk
Website: www.ouhk.edu.hk

This school was originally created to serve Hong Kong students, but it is expanding into the rest of China, and eventually plans to enroll students from other parts of the world. Accredited by the Hong Kong Council for Academic Accreditation, this school offers a number of Bachelor's and Master's programs via distance learning, through a combination of transfer credits (up to 60 credits, or 80 in an honors program), comprehensive self-study packs, and supplementary audio-visual materials. In some cases tutorials are arranged, but they are not required, and may be subject to geographic limitations. Programs offered are a B.A. in Western arts and humanities, international studies, Chinese arts and humanities, social sciences, B.S. in applied computing, electronics, engineering, environmental studies, and mathematics, Bachelor of Nursing, Bachelor of Education, and Bachelor of Business Administration, as well as an M.Ed. and an M.B.A. While exams are generally administered at the Hong Kong campus, arrangements can be made to take them elsewhere. The school was modeled on the Open University U.K. and uses some of that school's course materials. The majority of the instruction is in English, although an increasing number of programs are available in Chinese. Formerly the Open Learning Institute of Hong Kong.

Open University of Israel   B

U.S. office: American Friends of the Open University
180 West 80th Street
New York, NY 10024
Fields offered: Many fields
Year founded: 1974
Ownership: Nonprofit, independent
Phone: USA: (212) 712-1800 Israel: (972-3) 646-0460
Fax: (972-3) 6460701
E-mail: infodesk@oumail.openu.ac.il
Website: www.openu.ac.il

Israel's first open university offers the Bachelor's degree on completion of 18 home study courses. Each course consists of a home study kit, which may include written materials (in Hebrew only), laboratory equipment, simulation games, videotapes, etc. Each course requires 16 to 18 weeks to complete, with a 15- to 18-hour-a-week time commitment. Courses are available in natural sciences, life sciences, social sciences, mathematics, computer science, education, international relations, Jewish studies, management, and humanities. Noncredit courses are also offered in management enrichment, computers, video production, and cultural enrichment. Study group formation is encouraged, and tutorial sessions are held in study centers throughout Israel.

Open University of Tanzania   B

P.O. Box 23409
Dar es Salaam, Tanzania
Fields offered: Many fields
Year founded: 1993
Ownership: Nonprofit, state
Phone: (255-51) 668-992
Fax: (255-51) 668-759

Tanzania's open university offers the B.A., B.S., LL.B., and B.Com. in a variety of concentrations, with a special focus on education. All courses are to be completed via distance-learning methods, supported by audiocassettes and other learning tools, although it is apparently expected that students be available in person for orientation and possibly counseling, tutoring, lab work, etc. Students may take up to eight years to complete any of the degrees.

Open University of the Netherlands   B, M, D

P. O. Box 2960
6401 DL Heerlen, Netherlands
Fields offered: Many fields
Year founded: 1984
Ownership: State
Phone: (31-45) 576-2222
Fax: (31-45) 576-2766
Website: www.ouh.nl

The Netherlands's first nontraditional university offers a wide range of self-study courses in seven general fields: law, economics, management and administration, technology, natural science, social sciences, and cultural studies. In this program, modeled on Britain's Open University, credit is earned solely by passing examinations, and tutoring is available in study centers around Holland, or by telephone anywhere in the world. However, as their catalog puts it, "the language of the great majority of courses is, naturally, Dutch." However, there is a new M.B.A. being offered in English, with an emphasis on European law (there's also a certificate in European law). For information on this program, check out their website, at www.ouh.nl/info-alg-english-programmes/european%20law.htm

Oral Roberts University   B

School of LifeLong Learning
7777 South Lewis Ave.
Tulsa, OK 74171
Fields offered: Church ministries, Christian care and counseling, business administration, elementary Christian school education
Ownership: Nonprofit, church
Phone: (918) 495-6236 • (800) 678-8876 (choose the SLLE option)
Fax: (918) 495-7965
E-mail: slle@oru.edu
Website: www.oru.edu/slle/index.html

The Bachelor of Science in church ministries, Christian care and counseling, business administration, elementary Christian school education, as well as degree-completion program in Christian school administration, Christian school curriculum, and Christian school teaching can be completed entirely through distance learning. There are also semi-residential and weekend college options; contact the school for more details. Credit is given for experiential learning, independent study, transfer courses, and equivalency exams. Applicants must sign a pledge stating they will abstain from tobacco, alcohol, lying, cheating, cursing, stealing, homosexual activity, and immorality. In addition, they must promise to participate in an aerobics program, attend church, and commit their lives to Jesus Christ.

Pennsylvania State University   A, B

Department of Distance Education
207 Mitchell Building
University Park, PA 16802-3601
Fields offered: Business administration, letters & sciences, dietetic management, liberal studies
Ownership: Nonprofit, state
Phone: (814) 865-5403 • (800) 252-3592
Fax: (814) 865-3290
E-mail: psude@cde.psu.edu
Website: www.outreach.psu.edu

Penn State's distance-learning division offers three Associate's degrees, as well as a Bachelor's degree in partnership with the University of Iowa. The Associate's degrees are in business administration, dietetic food systems management, or letters, arts, and sciences. This latter is a broad-based degree covering writing, mathematics, science, and more. In addition, students may use the degree's elective requirements to focus on a particular area of interest, such as business, psychology, health education, history, or math. The Bachelor of Liberal Studies is offered through the LionHawk joint studies program—the Associate's is awarded from Penn State, the Bachelor's from Iowa. For more details, see the school's website.

Portland State University   M

Statewide M.B.A. Program
P.O. Box 751
Portland, OR 97207-0751
Fields offered: Business administration, social work
Year founded: 1988
Ownership: Nonprofit, state
Phone: (503) 725-4822 • (800) 547-8887, ext. 4822
Fax: (503) 725-5525
E-mail: askadm@osa.pdx.edu
Website: extended.portals.pdx.edu/swmba.htm

P.S.U.'s School of Extended Studies offers the "Statewide M.B.A." at twelve colleges, community colleges, local businesses, and corporate sites throughout Oregon, and one site in Washington. A new site can be established in any Oregon or Southwestern Washington community where at least six students will enroll in the program. Classes meet two evenings a week, and students must also get involved in a study group with others at their site. One week after each lecture is delivered on campus, statewide M.B.A. students view that class on videotape. There is a toll-free phone number so students can communicate with faculty concerning coursework. The program takes three years to complete, and all students must go to the P.S.U. campus twice a year for a Saturday Program.

Potchefstroom University for Christian Higher Education   B, M, D

Faculty of Theology
Potchefstroomse Universiteit vir Christelike Hoër Onderwys
Privaatsak X6001
Potchefstroom 2520, South Africa
Fields offered: Theological fields, Greek, Semitic languages
Year founded: 1869
Phone: (27-18) 299-1840
Fax: (27-18) 299-1841
E-mail: ontjjjvr@puknet.puk.ac.za
Website: www.puk.ac.za

Offers distance-learning programs at all levels, in religious fields (ecclesiology, systematic theology, Bible education, etc.) as well as Greek and Semitic languages. Some programs offered in conjunction with the U.K.–based Greenwich School of Theology, listed earlier.

Prachathipok University

See: Sukhothai Thammathirat Open University

Queen's University of Belfast   M

97 Lisburn Road
Belfast BT9 7BL, North Ireland
Fields offered: Pharmacy
Year founded: 1845
Ownership:
Phone: (44-1232) 242-041

Fax: (44-1232) 247-794
E-mail: j.swanton@qub.ac.uk
Website: www.qub.ac.uk/pha/dl/slhome.htm

Master of Science in either clinical pharmacy or community pharmacy, through a program tailored specifically to the needs of working pharmacists. Applicants must have an undergraduate degree in pharmacy, and be working in the field. Coursework is done by correspondence, with tutorial support by telephone.

Queens University   B

Division of Continuing and Distance Studies
Kingston, ON K7L 2N6 Canada
Fields offered: German, history, political studies, psychology
Year founded: 1841
Ownership: Nonprofit, state
Phone: (613) 545-2471 • (888) 895-5558
Fax: (613) 545-6805
E-mail: ptsmail@post.queensu.ca
Website: www.queensu.ca/pts/

A Bachelor of Arts degree (15 courses in total) concentrating in German, history, political studies, or psychology can be completed entirely through correspondence. Study involves use of textbooks, tapes, course notes written by instructors and, in some courses, CD-ROM textbooks and use of the Internet. Students submit assignments for grading and write final examinations under supervision at various centers worldwide. Telephone contact with instructors is possible. Other concentrations can be fulfilled by taking a combination of correspondence courses through Queens and by transferring Queen's-approved courses from other universities to complete degree requirements.

Queensland University of Technology   B, M

Kelvin Grove Campus
Locked Bag 2
Red Hill
Queensland 4059, Australia
Fields offered: Law, education, justice studies
Year founded: 1989
Phone: (61-7) 3864-3218
Fax: (61-7) 3864-3995
E-mail: admissions.enq@qut.edu.au
qut.international@qut.edu.au
Website: www.qut.edu.au

The school's Open Learning Unit offers a Bachelor of Laws, a Bachelor of Education, a Bachelor of Arts in justice studies, a Bachelor of Teaching in early childhood education, and a Master of Education. Exact services provided to the student vary from course to course, but generally include printed written materials, and often teleconferencing, study sessions, audio- and videocassettes, and teletutorials. Preference in admissions is given to applicants living in Queensland.

Ramkhamhaeng University   B, M

Huamark
Bangkapi
Bangkok, 10240 Thailand
Fields offered: Law, business administration, humanities, political science, education, sciences, economics
Year founded: 1971
Ownership: Nonprofit, state
Phone: (66-2) 318-0867
Fax: (66-2) 319-0917
E-mail: admin@ram1.ru.ac.th
Website: www.ru.ac.th/

With over 300,000 students, Ramkhamhaeng, which operates on the open-admissions system, is one of the world's largest universities. They currently have over 76,000 distance-learning students, working on Bachelor's and Master's degrees in law, business administration, humanities, political science, education, sciences, and economics. Coursework is delivered via printed correspondence materials, satellite teleconferencing, audio- and videocassettes, the Internet, CD-ROM, and radio and TV broadcasts. The language of instruction is Thai. Cooperative arrangements with the University of Pittsburgh, Kansas State University, Northrop University, the University of Missouri–St. Louis, and Pittsburgh State University.

Regents College   A, B, M

7 Columbia Circle
Albany, NY 12203-5159
Fields offered: Business, liberal arts, liberal studies, nursing, and technology
Year founded: 1784
Ownership: Nonprofit, private
Phone: (518) 464-8500
Fax: (518) 464-8777
E-mail: rclearn@regents.edu
Website: www.regents.edu

A.A, A.S., B.A. and B.S. and M.L.S. (liberal studies) by nonresidential study. The largest and, along with Thomas Edison State College, the most popular nonresident degree program in the U.S. Until 1998, Regents was an integral part of the University of the State of New York, and the degrees were awarded by the University. In a controversial move in late 1997, Regents College purchased its independence in order to become an "independent member institution" within the University. The degrees now come from Regents College. This move seems to have distressed some students (who expected to earn their degree from the University, not the College) and some alumni, based on some concerned postings to educational newsgroups.

No one disputes, however, that this accredited and well-accepted school will remain both accredited and well accepted. Regents College evaluates work done elsewhere, and awards its own degrees to persons who have accumulated sufficient units, by a broad variety of means. Credit for nonduplicative college courses (both classroom and distance) and many noncollege learning experiences (company courses, military, etc., evaluated as college-level). Regents College recognizes many equivalency exams and offers its own as well, given nationwide and, by arrangement, at foreign locations, and recognizes portfolios as evaluated through partnerships with Ohio University, Charter Oak State College, and Empire State College. A new program delivers examinations by computer, making the examination process much simpler and more convenient. Each degree has its own faculty-established requirements with regards to areas of emphasis, but they are not restrictive. The program is described in brochures and catalogs, sent free to all who request them. If nonschool learning experiences cannot be assessed easily at a distance, or by exam, the student may go to Albany, New York, for an oral examination. Regents College makes available to enrolled students a service called DistanceLearn, which is a computer database of nearly 7,000 proficiency examinations and courses offered by other schools that can be completed through home study.

A Master's degree in liberal studies, incorporating many of the features of Regents' undergraduate programs was announced several years ago, but has been delayed several times, perhaps because of the change in status vis-a-vis the University. Interested parties should contact the school at (518) 464-8500 (press 1-3-2-3) or e-mail malibstu@regents.edu.

Regis University   B, M

School for Professional Studies
3333 Regis Blvd.
Denver, CO 80221-1099
Fields offered: Many fields
Year founded: 1877
Ownership: Nonprofit, church
Phone: (303) 458-4080
Undergraduate: (800) 967-3237
Graduate: (800) 677-9270
Fax: Undergraduate: (303) 964-5539
E-mail: Undergraduate: mualc@regis.edu
Graduate: admarg@regis.edu
M.B.A.: advise@mbaregis.edu
Website: www.regis.edu
www.mbaregis.edu

Regis's School for Professional Studies offers a variety of nontraditional adult programs at the graduate and undergraduate levels in a number of learning formats, including: classroom-based accelerated intensive evening and weekend courses offered at locations across Colorado and Wyoming, guided independent study (formerly known as the university without walls program), multimedia distance-learning programs, credit for prior learning (by portfolio evaluation), credit by exam, and on-site corporate education courses. They say their M.B.A. is one of America's largest accredited external programs. Check it out at www.mbaregis.com, or by calling (800) 622-7344.

The B.S. in business is "presented" entirely by distance (mostly televised) learning by Jones Education Company , for adults with a minimum of 30 semester hours (45 quarter hours) of credit from a regionally accredited college or university. Courses are offered in an 8-week format, so students can enter every two months.

Rensselaer Polytechnic Institute   M

RSVP Continuing and Distance Education
Troy, NY 12180-3590
Fields offered: Many technical fields
Year founded: 1824
Ownership: Nonprofit, independent
Phone: (518) 276-8351
Fax: (518) 276-8026
E-mail: katchc@rpi.edu
Website: www.rsvp.rpi.edu

Several M.S. degrees available by distance learning: in technical communication, engineering (materials, manufacturing systems, mechanical, management, or microelectronics manufacturing), and computer science, as well as certificate programs in a number of technical fields and a variety of related noncredit courses, workshops, and seminars. All program materials are delivered to participating corporate sites by satellite, videoconferencing, and videotape, enhanced by Internet sites and participation. More than 900 students enroll in Rensselaer's programs every semester.

Rhodec International   B

35 East Street
Brighton, BN1 1HL U.K.
Fields offered: General studies
Year founded: 1960
Phone: (44-1273) 327-476
Fax: (44-1273) 821-668
E-mail: rhodec@pavilion.co.uk
Website: www.pavilion.co.uk/rhodec

Rhodec offers degrees in interior design wholly through distance learning on a rolling admissions basis that allows students to begin study at any time. The course can be completed almost entirely over the Internet, or by more traditional correspondence methods.

Roberts Wesleyan College

See: Internet Distance Education Associates

Roger Williams University   B

University College Open Program
Bristol, RI 02809
Fields offered: Administration of justice, business management, industrial technology, public administration
Year founded: 1956
Ownership: Nonprofit, independent
Phone: (401) 254-3530 • (800) 458-7144
Fax: (401) 254-3560
E-mail: jws@alpha.rwu.edu

Website: www.rwu.edu
Through the "Open Program," students can earn a distance-learning B.S. in administration of justice, business management, industrial technology, or public administration. Credit given for prior-learning assessment, military training, CLEP and other exams, and prior college attendance. While enrolled, one may earn credit from external courses, independent studies, internships, and day, evening, summer, and special classroom courses. Some courses may also involve guided instruction via phone, fax, mail, or e-mail, or otherwise over the Internet. Each external course generally ends with a proctored exam, taken in the student's local area under an approved proctor. Preference is given to students who are able to enter with advanced standing, based on credits earned elsewhere, CLEP exams, military and/or job training. Does not accept students who are incarcerated.

Saint Patrick's College, Maynooth

See: National Distance Education Centre (Ireland)

Simon Fraser University   B

Centre for Distance Education
Continuing Studies
Burnaby, B.C. V5A 1S6 Canada
Fields offered: General studies, criminology
Year founded: 1964
Ownership: Nonprofit, state
Phone: (604) 291-3524 • (800) 663-1411 (B.C. only)
Fax: (604) 291-4964
E-mail: cde@sfu.ca
Website: www.sfu.ca

Offers a Bachelor of General Studies and a B.A. in criminology wholly through distance learning, as well as a number of diplomas, certificates, and additional correspondence courses in a wide range of subjects. Students receive a "complete learning package" for each course, which includes lecture notes as well as appropriate, audio- and videocassettes, slides, textbooks and supplementary reading guides. Some courses also integrate televised materials and/or Internet resources as well. The school assumes a high level of interactivity between students and faculty. Tuition is waived for Canadian citizens sixty years old and over. As distance students study along with classroom courses, there are, many close deadlines, and the school discourages persons outside Canada from enrolling, as mail and phone costs will be high.

Southern Cross University   B, M, D

P.O. Box 157
Lismore, NSW 2480 Australia
Publications Officer
Fields offered: Many fields
Year founded: 1989
Ownership: Nonprofit, state
Phone: (61-267) 732-999
Fax: (61-267) 733-269

E-mail: sservice@scu.edu.au
Website: www.scu.edu.au

Degrees at all levels are offered in a broad range of fields. Instruction is by the same faculty that teach on-campus courses, and is via various media, including printed lecture notes, interactive TV and radio, and video- and audiocassettes. Some subjects require students to attend a certain number of short residential vacation sessions on campus; voluntary weekend sessions are also available, the majority of them in Sydney. Enrollment in some programs is restricted to full-time residents of Australia, or Australians with resident status who are temporarily overseas. Degrees offered are: Bachelor of Business in tourism, Bachelor of Education, Bachelor of Health Science in nursing, Bachelor of Social Science, Master of Accounting Studies, M.A. and M.S. in many fields, M.B.A., Master of Business, Master of Education with an optional specialization in training and development, Master of Health Science, Master of International Tourism Management, Master of Laws, Master of Organizational Development and Training, and Doctor of Business Administration.

Southern Illinois University-Edwardsville   B, M

Campus Box 1047
Edwardsville, IL 62026-1047
Fields offered: Nursing, business
Year founded: 1957
Ownership: Nonprofit, state
Phone: (618) 692-2080
Fax: (618) 692-0281
E-mail: coxfprd@siue.edu
Website: www.siue.edu

Bachelor's in nursing; Master's in business administration.

Spertus College   M, D

618 South Michigan Avenue
Chicago, IL 60605
Fields offered: Jewish studies
Year founded: 1924
Ownership: Nonprofit, independent
Phone: (312) 322-1769 • (888) 322-1769
Fax: (312) 922-6406
E-mail: college@spertus.edu
Website: www.spertus.edu

Spertus currently offers two distance-learning programs: an M.S. in Jewish studies (M.S.J.S.) and a Doctor of Jewish studies (D.J.S.). The self-paced Master's degree is designed for students who hold an accredited undergraduate degree, and are interested in additional knowledge of Jewish subjects, or as a professional credential for work in Jewish education or communal service. Courses are delivered in a number of ways, including distance learning packages, intensive seminars, and independent study. Students are encouraged to spend at least 6 days a year at the Chicago campus for intensive seminars. The D.J.S. is designed for Jewish clergy, educators, and communal service workers. A "cut-

ting edge" program, it has highly selective admissions. Doctoral students take eighteen courses: seven reading, seven intensive seminars, and four geared towards the production of a dissertation, or other "project demonstrating excellence."

Stanford University   M

Center for Professional Development
496 Lomita Mall, Durand Building
Stanford, CA 94305-4036
Fields offered: Electrical engineering
Year founded: 1885
Ownership: Nonprofit, independent
Phone: (650) 725-3000
Fax: (650) 725-2368
E-mail: susan.low@stanford.edu
Website: scpd.staford.edu

In the fall of 1998, Stanford became the major U.S. research university to offer a Master's degree wholly on the Internet. The M.S. in telecommunications is offered, with a required concentration in one of three areas: wireless systems & networks, optical systems, or computer networking. Students take approximately 15 courses (of 30 available), to satisfy the 45-unit requirement for the degree. Part-time students have up to 5 years to complete the program. There are also 5 certificate programs in this field. Students study along with on-campus classes, viewing courses on-line either live or at their convenience, with full playback ability. Presentation visuals such as viewgraphs and computer images are displayed in a large window apart from the video. Students communicate with instructors via email or phone, and handouts are available from course web pages.

Stanford University   M

School of Engineering, SITN
401 Durand
Stanford, CA 94305-4036
Fields offered: Engineering, computer science
Year founded: 1885
Ownership: Nonprofit, independent
Phone: (650) 725-3000
Fax: (650) 725-2868
E-mail: amy.ewing@stanford.edu.
Website: www-scpd.stanford.edu/scpd

Stanford offers a distance-learning M.S. in engineering or computer science to corporate and government subscribers, through closed-circuit television, teleconferencing, Internet, and other nontraditional methods. It is recommended, though not required, that students outside the live broadcast area spend one quarter in residency. With the creation of Stanford Online, a project of the Stanford Center for Professional Development, the university is now capable of offering video courses with synchronous audio, text, and graphics on the Internet. Courses recorded by the Stanford Instructional Television Network are digitized and compressed, then stored on a video server. Students and instructors can then access them from a desktop computer. Supporting course materials are available through the Web and students can correspond with instructors or other classmates from their computers. For more information, contact Elaine Ray at (650) 723-7162.

Strathcylde Graduate Business School   M

Strathclyde University
130 Rottonrow
Glasgow, G1 Scotland
Fields offered: Business administration
Phone: (44-041) 553-6000
Fax: (44-141) 552-0775
E-mail: candace@sgbs.strath.ac.uk
Website: www.strath.ac.uk/Departments/SGBS/

This school reportedly offers an M.B.A. through distance learning methods; we have written for more information.

Sukhothai Thammathirat
Open University   B, M

Bangpood, Pakkred
Nonthaburi 11120, Thailand
Fields offered: Many fields
Year founded: 1978
Ownership: State
Phone: (66-2) 503-2121-4
Fax: (66-2) 503-3556
E-mail: stou@samsorn.stou.ac.th
Website: www.stou.ac.th

Distance-learning degrees at the Bachelor's and Master's levels from the schools of liberal arts, educational studies, management sciences, law, health sciences, economics, home economics, political science, agricultural extension & cooperatives, communication arts, and science & technology. STOU also offers a Master's degree program from the School of Educational Studies. Coursework is accomplished via a variety of methods, including face-to-face tutoring, where possible, printed materials, correspondence, audiocassettes, radio and television broadcasts, and other techniques. Also known as Prachathipok University, as both names are appellation of King Rama VII of Thailand. In the country, however, Sukhothai is the more commonly recognized name for this major school.

Technikon of Southern Africa   B, M, D

Private Bag X6
Florida, 1710 South Africa
Fields offered: Many fields
Phone: (27) 471-2000
Fax: (27) 471-2134
E-mail: info@tsamail.trsa.ac.za
Website: www.trsa.ac.za

South Africa's only distance-education technikon (technical university) offers a B.A. in theology and a B.Tech in nature conservation, real estate, financial management, human resources management, corporate law, and marketing, as well as an M.Tech in education, financial management, human resources management, and marketing, and a D.Tech in education, human resources management, and marketing. Study takes place through self-paced materials sent to students (85,000 currently) in the country and abroad. Students combine workplace experience with guided study, and take year-end examinations at approved examination centers (contact school for details). The school offers many support services to distance-learning students, including self-esteem courses, job-hunting assistance, assertiveness training, and more.

Teikyo Loretto Heights College   B

3001 South Federal Blvd.
Denver, CO 80236
Fields offered: Many fields
Year founded: 1918
Ownership: Nonprofit, independent
Phone: (303) 937-4202
Fax: (303) 937-4224
E-mail: lmoreno@tlhu.edu
Website: www.tlhu.edu

Loretto offers a university without walls program that allows enrollees to earn the Bachelor of Arts with little or no time spent on campus. The SAAD (Students at a Distance) program is available to students of all ages in the Rocky mountain area. The degree requires 128 semester units, of which at least the final 30 hours must be earned consecutively after enrolling. But these can be earned through a variety of nontraditional means as well as regular courses: independent reading and research, seminars in the field, independent field practicums, and assessment of prior learning experiences, CLEP and challenge exams, etc. Students are expected to meet periodically with faculty advisors, but those advisors are sometimes able to travel to a student's home location.

Tele-universite   B

Universite du Quebec
2600 boulevard Laurier
Tour de la Cite 7e etage
Case postale 10700
Sainte-Foy, QB G1V 4V9 Canada
Fields offered: Communications
Fax: (418) 657 2094
E-mail: info@teluq.uquebec.ca
Website: www.teluq.uquebec.ca

The Tele-universite is one of eleven institutions that together form the University of Quebec network. It also collaborates with Athabasca University in Alberta and the Open Learning Agency of British Columbia in the exchange of course materials. The only French-speaking university in North America that specializes in distance education.

Texas Wesleyan University   M

Graduate Studies in Education and Distance Learning
1201 Wesleyan
Fort Worth, TX 76105-1536
Fields offered: Education, law

Year founded: 1890
Ownership: Nonprofit, church
Phone: (817) 531-4941 • (800) 531-4954
Fax: (817) 531-4814
E-mail: info@txwesleyan.edu
Website: www.txwesleyan.edu

Texas Wesleyan offers an M.Ed. in distance learning targeted to the needs of educators, through a video-based program of instruction. Applicants must have an accredited undergraduate degree, with a GPA of at least 3.0, and be a full-time teacher with access to e-mail. The school puts distance-learning students in touch with others in their area for learning groups, guided by a faculty mentor. A maximum of 6 of the 36 semester hours required for the degree can be transfer credit from another accredited institution. Weekend programs are also available for a number of graduate and undergrad degrees.

Thomas Edison State College   A, B, M

101 West State Street
Trenton, NJ 08608-1176
Fields offered: Many fields
Year founded: 1972
Ownership: Nonprofit, state
Phone: (609) 984-1150
Fax: (609) 984-8447
E-mail: admissions@call.tesc.edu
Website: www.tesc.edu

Bachelor's and Associate's degrees in 118 areas of specialization. Unlimited credit can be earned through portfolio assessment (handbook available), Thomas Edison's own exams in dozens of subjects, guided study (independent-study courses using texts and videocassettes), the On-Line Computer Classroom™ (many courses available through the college's innovative CALL™ system: Computer Assisted Lifelong Learning), equivalency exams (over 400 available), military, business, and industry courses and training programs, credit for some courses taken at work, telecourses (centered on, for example, PBS's The Civil War, etc.), licenses and certificates (C.P.A.: up to 33 credits, FAA Mechanic certificate/Airframe and Power Plant rating: up to 55 credits; FAA Air Traffic Control Specialist: up to 60 credits, etc.), and transfer credit from accredited colleges. Unique academic advising available to enrolled students on an 800 number. Foreign students are welcome, with certain restrictions.

Also offers an M.S. in management through a program of study that requires three brief residential periods—one weekend and two one-week sessions.

TMC Business School

See: Deakin University

Troy State University   B

P. O. Drawer 4419
Montgomery , AL 36103-4419

Fields offered: Professional studies, international relations
Year founded: 1887
Ownership: Nonprofit, state
Phone: (334) 241-9553 • (800) 355-TSUM
Fax: (334) 240-7320
E-mail: edp@tsum.edu
Website: www.tsum.edu

Bachelor of Arts or Science in professional studies can be earned through a combination of learning contracts with Troy State University in Montgomery (TSUM), TSUM television courses, transfer credit from and transient credit at other regionally accredited colleges/universities, and prior learning assessment (credit by examination; evaluation of previous training in the military, business and/or industry; and portfolio assessment). Majors are available in resource management (business), English, history, political science, social science, and psychology. Students must complete a minimum of 50 quarter hours under TSUM sponsorship. A new program offers an M.S. in international learning, using video-based study.

Tulane University   M

University College
125 Gibson Hall
New Orleans, LA 70118
Fields offered: Health & safety management
Year founded: 1834
Ownership: Nonprofit, independent
Phone: (800) 862-2122
E-mail: murphree@mailhost.tcs.tulane.edu
Website: //caeph.tulane.edu/

A Master's degree program in health and safety management can be completed entirely over the Internet.

Universidad Austral de Chile   B, M

Programa de Educacion Continua
Independencia 641
Valdivia, Chile
Fields offered: Many fields
Year founded: 1955
Ownership: Proprietary
Phone: (56-63) 215-150
Fax: (56-63) 212-589
E-mail: flacam@uach.cl
Website: www.uach.cl/fac-for/flacam/indice.htm

Distance-learning degree programs at the undergraduate and graduate levels in the following fields: arts & humanities, communication & media studies, contemporary & cultural studies, philosophy, education & teaching, curriculum development, education psychology, and open & distance learning. Coursework is accomplished through printed correspondence materials, special readings, audio- and videocassettes, telephone tutoring, and practical fieldwork.

Universidad del Tolima   B

Instituto de Educacion a Distancia
Barrio Santa Helena A A 546
Ibague, Tolima, Colombia
Fields offered: Education, banking & finance, farming
Year founded: 1945
Phone: (57-82) 644-219
Fax: (57-82) 644-869
Website: calima.univalle.edu.co/scf/utolima.html
Distance-learning degrees available in the areas of education, banking & finance, and farming. Courses are delivered primarily via printed correspondence texts, supported by audio- and videocassettes, practical fieldwork, and counseling.

Universidad Estatal a Distancia   B, M

Apartado 474-2050 de Montes de Oca
San Jose, Costa Rica
Fields offered: Education, health fields, social services, business & financial fields, administration
Year founded: 1977
Ownership: Nonprofit, state
Phone: (506) 234-1909
Fax: (506) 234-1909
E-mail: vacademic@arenal.uned.ac.cr
Website: www.uned.ac.cr
Costa Rica's state university for distance learning offers correspondence study consisting of written units, audio- and videocassettes, computer-assisted instruction, telephone counseling, electronic classes, videoconferencing, and more. Degrees awarded are equivalent to the Bachelor's and Master's in the following fields: elementary teaching, educational administration, administration of child social services, civic education, administration of health services, rehabilitation, university studies, business administration, administration of cooperatives, agrarian administration, banking & financial administration, accountancy, and organization management. A Bachelor's can be earned in about two years of study.

Universidad Interamericana de Educacion a Distancia de Panama   B, M

Calle 57 y Abel Bravo
Edificio Tolima Panama
Fields offered: Education, administration, accounting
Phone: (50-7) 64-4633
Courses are delivered using printed correspondence texts prepared by/for the University, study guides, and a range of other media.

Universidad Mariana   B

Facultad de Educacion a Distancia
Calle 18, No. 34-104
Pasto, Narino, Colombia
Fields offered: Many fields
Year founded: 1967

Phone: (57-27) 230-873
Fax: (57-27) 230-874
Distance-learning programs via correspondence, supported by audio- and videocassettes, television courses, and telephone tutoring. Fields include: commercial and management studies, accountancy, administration, personnel and industrial relations, commercial, constitutional, labor & tax laws, education & teaching, curriculum development, educational policy & management, educational psychology, humanities, education (with a number of concentrations), social studies, career guidance and counseling, special work, sociology, and gerontology.

Universidad Mexicana del Noreste   B

5a Zona No. 409, Apartado Postal No. 2191J
Col. Caracol
Monterrey, N.L. Mexico
Fields offered: Banking, finance, leisure time management
Year founded: 1974
Phone: (52-40) 12-05
Fax: (52-40) 12-05
This open-university program offers the Bachelor's degree in banking and finance, and in management of leisure time, based on study by learning guide and audiocassettes. About four years are required to complete the degree.

Universidad Nacional Abierta   B

Av. Los Calvani No. 18—San Bernadino
Apartado Postal No. 2096
Caracas 1010, Venezuela
Fields offered: Many fields
Year founded: 1975
Ownership: Nonprofit, state
Phone: (58-2) 574-1322
Fax: (58-2) 574-3086
E-mail: gabriel.viloria@atei.es
Website: roble.pntic.mec.es/atei/texto/programa/ franja3/cursos/una.htm
Venezuela's open university offers the Bachelor's degree in social sciences, management, land and sea sciences, languages, history, education, engineering, mathematics, physics, and more. Students work at their own pace through teaching modules consisting of printed and audio-visual materials. Some courses are offered on radio or television. Laboratory work, where required, may be done at the university or at other institutions. While the programs are delivered entirely through distance learning, to begin them, one must be resident in Venezuela.

Universidad Nacional Autonoma de Honduras   B

Universitario de Educacion a Distancia
Tegucigalpa, DC, Honduras
Fields offered: Farm administration, teaching & education sciences, nursing
Year founded: 1845

Phone: (504) 322-208
Website: www.unah.hondunet.net
Courses are delivered using printed correspondence texts, audiovisual aids, and study centers, leading to Bachelor's-level degrees in farm administration, teaching & education sciences, and nursing.

Universidad Nacional de la Patagonia San Juan Bosco   B
25 de Mayo 427
9000 Comodoro Rivadavia
Chubut, Argentina
Fields offered: Mathematics, statistics, finance, genetics, chemistry
Year founded: 1980
Phone: (54-967) 242-48
Fax: (54-967) 344-42
E-mail: rcesar@unpori.edu.ar
Website: www.unp.edu.ar
Developed largely to aid in teacher education, this school offers degree-level courses in mathematics, statistics, finance, genetics, and chemistry. largely via correspondence.

Universidad NUR   B
Av Banzer No. 100
Casilla 3273
Santa Cruz, Bolivia
Fields offered: Business administration, commercial engineering
Year founded: 1994
Phone: (591-03) 363-939
Fax: (591-03) 331-850
E-mail: info@tabarsi.nur.edu
Website: www.nur.edu
Bolivia;s first distance-education program offers a Bachelor's-level degree in either business administration or commercial engineering, through printed correspondence texts, with video support materials.

Universidad Pedagogica Nacional   B
Sistema de Educacion a Distancia (SEAD)
Carretera Al Ajusco No 24
Col Heroes de Padierna
Delegacion Tlalpan
Mexico, DF 14200 Mexico
Fields offered: Education
Phone: (52-5) 652-3399, ext. 1146/1198
Fax: (52-5) 568-4394
For Mexican residents. Courses are delivered using printed correspondence texts prepared by/for the University; collections of readings compiled by the University; student manuals; formative evaluation; face-to-face and telephone tutoring and counseling; regional services; use of study centers; weekend schools.

Universidad Pontificia Bolivariana   B
Lic Gabriel Vlaencia Carrascal
Cir la, No. 70-01
Apartado Aereo 56006
Medellin, Colombia
Fields offered: Many fields
Year founded: 1936
Phone: (57-4) 411-8456
Fax: (57-4) 411-8456
Website: www.upb.edu.co
Courses are delivered using existing textbooks as a central teaching medium; collections of readings compiled by the University; audiovision; audio and video cassettes; face-to-face tutoring and counseling; weekend schools.

Universidad Virtual del Sistema Tecnologico de Monterrey   B, M
Virtual University Administration
Sucursal de Correos "J"
Av Eugenio Garza Sada 2501 Sur
Monterrey, NL 64849 MEXICO
Fields offered: Many fields
Year founded: 1989
Phone: (52-8) 358-2000 ext 6700
Fax: (52-8) 328-4017
E-mail: lalvarad@campus.ruv.itesm.mx
Website: www.ruv.itesm.mx
Telecommunications systems and electronic networks supported by teaching tools developed in multimedia, such as compact discs, the Internet, audiovisual and printed materials are used in the Virtual University. It comprises a telematic network, made up of libraries, electronic networks, and virtual laboratories interconnecting distant geographic areas.

Universidade Aberta
Rua da Escola Politecnica, 147
P–1250 Lisbon, Portugal
Phone: (351-1) 3973318
Fax: (351-1) 3973229
Website: www.univ-ab.pt/guiacurs/guiac_66.htm
Open to people over the age of 25 without a high school diploma who successfully pass an examination. Printed materials are supplemented by radio and television programmes, by telephone tutoring, and by facilities offered at study centres.

Universitas Terbuka
P.O. Box 6666
Jakarta, 10001 Indonesia
Fields offered: Education, economics and development study, management, social and political sciences, mathematics, natural sciences
Phone: (62-21) 749-0941
Fax: (62-21) 749-0147
Website: www.ut.ac.id/uter.htm

Open admission (except to school of education). Teaching methods include self-contained study packs (modules, audio cassettes, references, practical exercises, guidelines, textbooks, radio and television broadcasts, kits of equipment for practical experiments); study groups; student activities; and tutorials. At the end of each course, usually at the end of a semester, students sit for an examination.

University College Cork

See: National Distance Education Centre (Ireland)

University College Galway

See: National Distance Education Centre (Ireland)

University of Aberdeen   D

Centre for Continuing Education
Regent Building, Regent Walk
Aberdeen, AB24 3FX UK
Phone: (44-1224) 272-449
Fax: (44-1224) 272-478
E-mail: cce-aberdeen@abdn.ac.uk
Website: www.abdn.ac.uk/
Apparently offers a distance-learning or research doctorate; we have written for more information.

University of Abertay   M

Dundee Business School
Dudhope Castle
Dundee, DD3 6HF Scotland
Fields offered: Business administration
Phone: (44-1382) 322-260
Fax: (44-1382) 322-290
E-mail: L.Balfour@Abertay-Dundee.ac.uk
Website: www.dct.ac.uk
Abertay offers a part-time taught M.B.A. The course of study involves 10 core subjects and 2 electives, and generally takes 3 years. The program is tailored to meet the practical needs of businesspeople, and the school maintains close links with businesses.

University of Adelaide   B, M

Careers and Course Advice Centre
South Australia 5001, Australia
Fields offered: Education, labor studies, women's studies
Year founded: 1874
Ownership: State
Phone: (61-8) 303-5208
Website: www.adelaide.edu.au
Adelaide offers a Bachelor of Education, Bachelor of Labour Studies, Master of Arts in women's studies, and Master of Educational Administration via distance learning. Coursework is accomplished using a variety of methods, including printed correspondence texts, audiovisual aids, and tutorial support. Some programs have a required residency; we have written to find out the details, and which degrees can be earned entirely at a distance.

University of Alaska   B, M

706 C Gruening Building
Fairbanks, AK 99775
Fields offered: Education, rural development, social work
Year founded: 1917
Ownership: Nonprofit, state
Phone: (907) 474-7211
Fax: (907) 474-7225
E-mail: fyapply@aurora.alaska.edu
Website: www.uaf.edu
Programs for rural Alaska residents include a B.Ed. and an M.Ed., and B.A. in rural development or social work. Instruction is by a variety of nontraditional means, including audio- and videocassette, e-mail, and teleconferencing. Faculty and administrative support services are decentralized and located in various regional campuses and centers.

University of Arizona   M, D

School of Information Resources and Library Science
1515 East First Street
Tucson, AZ 85721
Fields offered: Information resources and library science
Year founded: 1885
Ownership: Nonprofit, state
Phone: (520) 621-3565
Fax: (520) 621-3279
E-mail: wilka@u.arizona.edu
Website: www.sir.arizona.edu
A Master's and a doctorate in library science are available through courses offered over the Internet, supplemented by cablecast lectures (students must have graphical web access, and provide an e-mail address upon registration). There is an optional thesis required for the Master's, and a required doctoral dissertation. A minimum of 12 units of coursework on campus at Tucson is required, but these may be done during the summer sessions. This program is new and evolving; check out their website for the latest information. The school stresses that this is a rigorous, substantive program.

University of Birmingham   B, M

School of Education
Edgbaston
Birmingham B15 2TT, United Kingdom
Fields offered: Education
Year founded: 1900
Ownership: State
Phone: (44-121) 414-4866
Fax: (44-121) 414-4865
E-mail: c.j.miller@bham.ac.uk
Website: www.bham.ac.uk
Bachelor's and Master's degrees are offered in special education with a wide range of specializations, including mul-

tisensory impairment, emotional and behavioral difficulties, teaching hearing impaired children, and more. Undergraduate study leads to a B.Phil; the graduate program, tailored to teachers already working with learning-impaired pupils, leads to an M.Ed. Students from outside the U.K. are occasionally admitted, with, the school tells us, "careful consideration of the support available to them for their study."

The university also offers a distance M.A. in the teaching of English as a foreign (or second) language in association with David English House in Hiroshima, Japan, through a two-year wholly nonresidential module program. Applicants should have "normal teaching experience," a "good first degree or equivalent," and, if English is not their first language, a score of 550 or better on the TOEFL. A dissertation is required, and it is hoped that students will be able to base this final project on practical classroom issues.

University of Bombay   B, M
Directorate of Distance Education
University Club House B Road
Churchgate
Bombay, 400 020 India
Phone: (91-22) 276272

Residents of India can study courses leading to Bachelor's and Master's degrees through correspondence.

University of Bradford   M
School of Health Studies
Unity Building
25 Trinity Road
West Yorkshire, BD5 0BB United Kingdom
Fields offered: Health and social care management
Year founded: 1957
Phone: (44-1274) 733-466
Fax: (44-1274) 386-327
Website: www.brad.ac.uk

A Master of Science degree in health or social care management for middle and senior management working in health or social care organizations. Coursework involves printed correspondence materials, supplemented by audio- and videocassettes, software, and tutorial support, culminating in a major work-based management project.

University of Bridgeport   B, M, D
Office of Admissions
126 Park Avenue
Bridgeport, CT 06601
Fields offered: Many fields
Year founded: 1927
Ownership: Nonprofit, independent
Phone: (203) 576-4552 • (800) EXCEL-UB
Fax: (203) 576-4941
E-mail: admit@cse.bridgeport.edu
Website: www.bridgeport.edu

Bridgeport offers a wholly on-line M.S. in human nutrition through courses posted on the Internet. Applicants should have an accredited Bachelor's degree and have taken certain prerequisites; contact the school for details. At the completion of the eight-course program, students must travel to the Connecticut campus for a single two-day exam. This is the only residency requirement. Up to 6 semester units of credit can be transferred in, with the Dean's approval. Financial aid is available.

University of British Columbia   B, M
2339 West Mall, Room 1170
Vancouver, BC V6T 1Z4 Canada
Distance Education & Technology
Fields offered: Many fields
Year founded: 1908
Ownership: State
Phone: (604) 822-6565
Fax: (604) 822-8636
E-mail: access@cstudies.ubc.ca
Website: det.cstudies.ubc.ca

Established as the Department of University Extensions at UBC in 1949, the Distance Education & Technology (DE&T) unit brings together resources from the faculties of a number of departments to provide distance-education programs in agricultural sciences, arts, education, forestry, nursing, computer science, civil; engineering, health sciences, applied science, and environmental studies. Courses are delivered using print-based materials, audio, video, CD-ROM, and the Internet. For a complete, up-to-date listing of the school's offerings, check out their website.

University of Colorado
Colorado Springs   M
Graduate School of Business
1420 Austin Bluffs Parkway
Colorado Springs, CO 80933
Fields offered: Business administration
Year founded: 1965
Ownership: Nonprofit, state
Phone: (719) 262-3408 • (800) 777-MIND
Fax: (719) 262-3494
E-mail: busadvsr@mail.uccs.edu
Website: www.meu.edu

Offers an M.B.A. via distance-learning methods, in cooperation with Jones Education Company. This individually tailored program uses a number of technologies, including video delivered over satellite and cable systems by the Learning Channel. The majority of the coursework, however, is accomplished over the Internet, as is student/faculty interaction. This is one of the few distance M.B.A.s that is accredited by the American Assembly of Collegiate Schools of Business.

University of Dallas   M
Graduate School of Management
1845 East Northgate Drive

Irving, TX 75062-4799
Fields offered: Health services management
Year founded: 1956
Ownership: Nonprofit, church
Phone: (972) 385-7696 • (800) 832-5622
Fax: (972) 721-5254
E-mail: undadmis@acad.udallas.edu
Website: acad.udallas.edu

M.B.A. in health services management available entirely by courses offered at health-care worksites (hospitals and other facilities). Only employees of facilities receiving either the HSTN Network or the Westcott network over their the cable service may enroll. The program takes between two and three years. Students who already have an M.B.A. earn the Master of Management instead.

University of Delhi   B, M

School of Correspondence Courses and Continuing Ed.
5 Cavalry Lines
Delhi, 110007, India
Fields offered: Many fields
Year founded: 1962
Ownership: Nonprofit, state
Phone: (91-11) 2517645 or 2517581 or 2522800
Website: www-icdl.open.ac.uk/icdl/database/asia/india/udelhi/inst/

The correspondence programs and degrees are only for residents of India, and for Indian citizens resident in other countries. A personal contact program is required in Delhi, or at other locations where a minimum of 200 students will attend.

University of Denver   M

University College
2211 South Josephine Street
Denver, CO 80208
Fields offered: Environmental policy & management, telecommunications
Year founded: 1864
Ownership: Nonprofit, independent
Phone: (303) 871-3155 • (800) 347-2042
Fax: (303) 871-3303
E-mail: ecolinfo@du.edu
Website: www.du.edu/ucol/

Both Master's degrees and certificates in the fields of environmental policy & management and telecommunications via distance learning. Delivery of course curriculum is primarily text-based with world wide web Internet links and graphics and may include occasional use of audio or video tapes. Students receive instruction, communicate with faculty and each other, and complete assignments using several communication channels including e-mail, voice mail, fax, U.S. mail, and the Internet. Distance learning students have access to the same resources as traditional ones, including financial aid, the career center, and more.

University of Derby   M

School of Health and Community Studies
Mickleover
Derby DE3 5GX, United Kingdom
Fields offered: General practice medicine, health services management, pharmacy
Phone: (44-1332) 622-222, ext 2143
Fax: (44-1332) 514-323
E-mail: d.gerrett@derby.ac.uk
Website: www.derby.ac.uk

A number of distance programs for persons already working in various medical fields. The M.S. in general practice medicine is for medical doctors, takes to two to five years, and is completed largely via computer. The M.S. in health services management is tailored to applicants with a relevant undergraduate degree and at last three years of experience in the field. It takes up to five years, and has a heavy multimedia component. Finally, there are two pharmacy M.S.'s, on in social and administrative pharmacy, the other in community pharmacy, for practicing pharmacists.

University of Distance Education   B

47A Inya Road
Yangon, Myanmar
Fields offered: Many fields
Year founded: 1992
Ownership: Nonprofit, state
Phone: (95-1) 525-138
Fax: (95-1) 532-555

More than 197,000 students are enrolled in this, Myanmar (formerly Burma)'s only nontraditional university. Bachelor of Arts, Economics, or Law can be earned entirely through independent study, with the help of texts, study guides, radio and TV lessons, optional face-to-face intensives, and passing necessary examinations. Sciences students must attend weekend lectures and practica. The course of study takes four years for arts, sciences, and economics, five for law. Formerly known as the Arts and Sciences University, it merged with the University of Yangon in 1992 to form this new institution.

University of Dundee   M

Centre for Medical Education
Tay Park House
484 Perth Road
Dundee, DD2 1LR Scotland
Fields offered: Medical fields
Year founded: 1981
Ownership: Nonprofit, state
Phone: (44-1382) 631-952
Fax: (44-1382) 645-748
E-mail: a.mason@dundee.ac.uk
Website: www.dundee.ac.uk/distlearning/welcome.htm

Dundee's Centre for Medical Education offers a Master of Medical Education through distance-learning methods, as well as courses in advanced nursing and palliative care, and both a certificate and a diploma in medical education. There is also a Bachelor of Nursing and a Bachelor of Midwifery, both of which require a minimum of five one-week sessions on campus (one per module; it can take up to three years to complete all modules). The M.S. in ortho-pedic and rehabilitation technology also requires a brief campus stay, although the school's materials do not make it clear exactly how long this stay needs to be. Students from around the world are accepted into this program.

University of Glasgow D

59 Oakfield Avenue
Glasgow, Scotland, G12 8LW UK
Ownership: State
Phone: (44-141) 330 4394
Fax: (44-141) 330 3525
E-mail: enquiry@ace.gla.ac.uk
Website: www.gla.ac.uk/
Offers research doctorates.

University of Hong Kong M

School of Professional and Continuing Education
Pokfulam Road
Hong Kong, China
Fields offered: Financial economics, construction management, property development & investment, pharmacy
Year founded: 1911
Phone: (852) 2859 2791
Fax: (852) 2559 7528
Website: www.hku.hk/
Text-based, with supplementary audio and video cassettes; weekend and evening seminars and lectures for some courses. Many classes follow the regular school terms.

University of Houston B, M

Distance Education
4242 South Mason Road
Katy, TX 77450
Fields offered: Many fields
Year founded: 1927
Ownership: Nonprofit, state
Phone: (281) 395-2810 • (800) 687-8488
Fax: (281) 395-2629
Website: www.uh.edu/academics/de/
Houston's distance-learning programs offer a number of degrees, through compressed video, microwave, and/or satellite courses beamed to remote locations, as well as through videotape, cable or public TV broadcast, and Internet courses. At the undergraduate level, students must transfer in the equivalent of two years of credits; distance courses then allow the student to complete the junior and senior years in fields including computer draft-ing design, computer engineering science, earth sciences, industrial supervision, hotel & restaurant management, English, and psychology. Master's degrees are available in education, engineering management, electrical engineering

(specialization in computers or electronics), computer sci-ence, hospitality management, and training & development. Most of these are 36-credit-hour, non-thesis options. Support for distance services include an on-line library, 24-hour phone information, e-mail account, software, and more. For specific program details, check out the pro-gram's website.

University of Huddersfield M

Queensgate
Huddersfield, HD1 3DH U.K.
Fields offered: Geographic information systems
Year founded: 1841
Phone: (44-1484) 472-219
Fax: (44-1484) 450-408
E-mail: international.office@hud.ac.uk
Website: www.hud.ac.uk
Huddersfield offers both a Master's degree and a post-graduate diploma in geographic information systems (GIS) through distance learning.

University of Idaho M

Engineering Outreach Program
40 Janssen Engineering Building
Moscow, ID 83844-1014
Fields offered: Engineering and related fields, computer science, psychology, education
Year founded: 1889
Ownership: Nonprofit, state
Phone: (208) 885-6373 • (800) 824-2889
Fax: (208) 885-6165
E-mail: outreach@uidaho.edu
Website: www.uidaho.edu/evo/
Master's degrees in agricultural, civil, computer, electrical, geological, mechanical, mining, and metallurgical engineer-ing, engineering management, computer science, and psy-chology (human factors), as well as a new M.A. in teaching (MAT) in mathematics are offered nonresidentially via the Engineering Outreach program. The school stresses that this is an intensive program that requires high levels of discipline and commitment from students. International students are accepted; those whose native language is other than English must present a minimum score of 525 on the TOEFL.

University of Illinois at Urbana-Champaign M

422 Engineering Hall, 1308 West Green Street
Urbana, IL 61801
Fields offered: Engineering, mechanics
Year founded: 1867
Ownership: Nonprofit, state
Phone: (217) 333-6634
Fax: (217) 333-0015
E-mail: L-Krute@uiuc.edu
Website: www.uiuc.edu

M.S. in mechanics, applied mechanics, and a number of engineering fields (mechanical, general, electrical, or theoretical), through telephone instruction and videocassette. On-campus courses are taped, and shown at off-campus locations around the state. Admission to this program is highly competitive.

University of Iowa   B, M, D

Division of Continuing Education
116 International Center
Iowa City, IA 52242-1802
Fields offered: Liberal studies, computer science
Year founded: 1847
Ownership: Nonprofit, state
Phone: (319) 335-2575 • (800) 272-6430
Fax: (319) 335-2740
E-mail: credit-programs@uiowa.edu
Website: www.uiowa.edu/~ccp

Nonresident Bachelor of Liberal Studies can be completed through guided correspondence study from anywhere in America, and through Iowa-based interactive and public television courses. Applicants must have completed 62 undergraduate credits elsewhere. B.S. in nursing, M.S. in computer science, and doctorate in pharmacology are offered through off-campus programs geared mainly to corporate subscribers in the Iowa City area, although others are admitted on a space-available basis. Instruction is through closed-circuit television, and one graduate-level seminar on campus is required. See also: Quad Cities Graduate Center

University of Kent

The Graduate Office
The Registry
Canterbury, Kent, CT2 7NZ UK
Phone: (44-1227) 764000
Fax: (44-1227) 452196
E-mail: graduate_office@ukc.ac.uk
Website: www.ukc.ac.uk/

Offers distance-learning research Doctorates.

University of Leicester   M

U.S. Agent: Financial Times Management, Inc.
6921 Stockton Avenue
El Cerrito, CA 94530
Fields offered: Training, human resource management
Year founded: 1921
Ownership: Nonprofit, public
Phone: (510) 528-3020 • (888) 534-2378
Fax: (510) 528-3555
E-mail: luhrm@degree.net

This venerable British University now offers a Master's degree in training entirely by distance learning, through an agreement with the author of this very book. To earn the degree, students do extensive reading in each of four five-month-long modules, writing a paper at the end of each module (four papers in all). Help is available by phone, fax, e-mail, and an optional residential weekend each year, and an interactive webboard is being developed on-line. There

are no examinations; grading is instead based on the four papers, plus a final thesis. Students who put in ten hours a week on the program complete the degree in under two years. The degree is designed not only for experienced trainers and human resource managers, but also for people interested in entering those fields. Applicants should have either a Bachelor's degree or an academic credential plus 3 years of related experience. Applicants without a Bachelor's degree can enter the Master's program by successfully completing one of Leicester's one-year diploma programs. Financial Times Management, Inc., for whom Mariah and John Bear work, is the North American agent for this program. People elsewhere in the world should contact the Centre for Labour Market Studies, at the U.K. address below.

University of Leicester   M

University Road
Leicester, LE1 7RH U.K.
Fields offered: Many fields
Year founded: 1921
Ownership: State
Phone: (44-116) 252-2298
Fax: (44-116) 252-2200
E-mail: eeglm@admin.leicester.ac.uk
Website: www.le.ac.uk/

In addition to the two programs offered through the North American office (immediately previous listing), Leicester offers a number of other degrees. There is an M.B.A. to students in the Far East. Study centers for students in this program have been established in Hong Kong, Singapore, Malaysia, Thailand, Indonesia, and Taiwan. There is also an M.B.A. with a concentration in educational management for qualified teachers, an M.A. in mass communications, and M.S. degrees in finance, marketing, risk, crisis, & disaster management, criminal justice, security management, and the sociology of sports and sports management.

University of Limerick

See: National Distance Education Centre (Ireland)

University of London   B, M, D, Law

Senate House, Malet Street
London, WC1E 7HU England
Fields offered: Many fields
Year founded: 1836
Ownership: Nonprofit, state
Phone: (44-171) 636-8000 ext. 3150
Fax: (44-171) 636-5894
E-mail: admissions@external.lon.ac.uk
Website: www.lon.ac.uk/external

London had the world's first external degree program and, after over a century and a half, it is still among the most popular. They have long had an annoying policy that only holders of their own Bachelor's degree can enroll in their research-based M.Phil or Ph.D. programs, but offer an increasing number of degrees specifically geared to correspondence students. In addition, we've heard from students currently enrolled in London's Master's programs that they will be allowed to enroll in the external Ph.D. program. (A side note: London does not consider these "external degrees." According to the school, the degrees are the same whether earned internally or externally. We're not quite sure why this is such a big deal, but it is duly noted.) The requirement of having a London Bachelor's only applies to the M.Phil. and Ph.D. programs. None of the others require a University of London degree although there are various entry requirements (e.g. for admission to the M.A. in Geography program you must have an undergraduate degree in Geography; for the M.S. in Occupational Psychology you must have an undergraduate degree in psychology although you can take exactly the same program and get an M.S. in organisational behaviour with an undergraduate degree in any field.) But for the external M.Phil. and Ph.D. a University of London degree is required and there is no provision for waivers. The Master's degrees recommended for distance-learning students are those in agricultural development, distance education, environmental management, health systems management, financial economics, financial management, teaching English to speakers of other languages, food industry management & marketing, infectious diseases, drug & alcohol policy & intervention, and organizational behavior/occupational psychology. There are also M.S.'s in dental radiology and community dental practice for working dentists. Courses are virtually non–time-limited (up to 8 years for undergraduate courses, and up to 5 years for postgraduate) and students work at their own pace to complete an individualized program. Assessment is by examination and (for some degrees) by thesis. We've heard from a student in Florida who tried to use the center in the Bahamas, which was closer, but they seemed to be in no hurry to respond to inquiries.

University of Luton   D
Park Square
Luton, LU1 3JU Bedfordshire England
Phone: (44-1582) 341-11
Fax: (44-1582) 486-260
E-mail: admissions@luton.ac.uk
Website: www.luton.ac.uk
A "Ph.D. by published work" is offered, based on "extensive research record and substantial publications." This is unusual; other programs require the research for the Ph.D. be completed after entry into a program. Luton is one of the former polytechnics, just north of London.

University of Manchester   M
Oxford Road
Manchester M13 9PL, United Kingdom
Fields offered: Education, pharmaceutical engineering
Year founded: 1851
Phone: (44-161) 275-2000
Fax: (44-161) 275-2407

Website: www.man.ac.uk
Manchester offers several Master's degrees through a variety of media and methods, including printed correspondence texts, tutorial support, videocassettes, e-mail, and the Internet. There is an M.A. in a variety of educational concentrations (educational technology, teaching of English to speakers of other languages, English language teaching) and an M.S. in pharmaceutical engineering, designed to give advanced training to engineers and scientists working in the pharmaceutical field. There are also two institutionally based M.Ed degrees, one in distance English-language teaching, the other in special education. In these programs, groups of teachers at an institution can take the courses, usually in conjunction with a center established for that purpose at a local university of another educational institution.

University of Manitoba   B
188 Continuing Education Complex
Winnipeg, Manitoba R3T 2N2 Canada
Fields offered: Political studies, history
Year founded: 1877
Phone: (204) 474-8013
Fax: (204) 275-5465
E-mail: admissions@umanitoba.ca
Website: www.umanitoba.ca
The University of Manitoba offers a Bachelor of Arts in political studies or history, with a number of minors available as well (Canadian studies, economics, geography, philosophy, psychology, and sociology). Instruction takes place in both English and French, and coursework is accomplished via special course manuals, sometimes supplemented with audiotapes.

University of Maryland   B, M
University College
University Blvd. at Adelphi Road
College Park, MD 20742
Fields offered: Many fields
Year founded: 1856
Ownership: Nonprofit, state
Phone: (301) 985-7000 • (800) 888-UMEC
Fax: (301) 454-0399
E-mail: UMUCinfo@nova.UMUC.edu or gradinfo@umuc.edu
Website: www.umuc.edu
University College, the continuing higher education campus of the University of Maryland system, offers on-line Bachelor's degrees in 13 academic areas (accounting, behavioral & social sciences, business & management, communication studies, computer & information science, computer studies, English, fire science, humanities, management, management studies, paralegal studies, and technology & management). Their website offers a wide range of distance-learning support services, including advice, downloadable software, and more. Four Master's degrees are currently offered on-line: an M.S. in computer systems

management, M.S. in technology management, an M.S. in Management, and a Master of International Management.

University of Massachusetts at Amherst M

Video Instructional Program (VIP)
College of Engineering
Marcus Hall, Box 35115
Amherst, MA 01003-5115
Fields offered: Mathematics and statistics, public health, management, and many engineering-related fields
Year founded: 1863
Ownership: Nonprofit, state
Phone: (413) 545-0063
Fax: (413) 545-1227
E-mail: levey@vip.ecs.umass.edu
Website: www.umass.edu

The Video Instructional Program (VIP) is an established distance-learning program providing graduate education to working engineers across the country. Using videotaped lectures and/or satellite broadcasts, professionals can enroll in the same classes offered to on-campus students, in both degree and nondegree formats. Master of Science degrees are offered (engineering management and electrical and computer engineering), as well as noncredit/training courses in a variety of engineering-related disciplines.

University of Melbourne B

Faculty of Education
Dept. of Early Childhood Studies
Parkville, VC 1052 Australia
Fields offered: Early childhood studies
Year founded: 1989
Phone: (61-3) 854-3333
Fax: (61-3) 854-3348
Website: www.unimelb.edu.au/

The School of Early Childhood Studies is a specialist provider. As such it is the only department within the University of Melbourne at present permitted to offer programs in the distance education mode. It offers the fourth year of the Bachelor of Education in external mode.

University of Memphis M

Department of Journalism
Memphis, TN 38152
Fields offered: Many fields
Year founded: 1912
Ownership: Nonprofit, state
Phone: (901) 678-2991
Fax: (901) 678-4287
E-mail: ewbordy@cc.memphis.edu
Website: umvirtual.memphis.edu

An on-line Master of Arts in journalism program is offered, wherein distance-learning students follow the same program as those on campus. Formerly Memphis State University. See also: FEMA National Fire Academy

University of Missouri—Rolla M

230 Engineering Management Dept.
Rolla, MO 65401
Fields offered: Engineering
Year founded: 1870
Ownership: Nonprofit, state
Phone: (573) 341-4571
Fax: (573) 341-6567
E-mail: daily@shuttle.ee.umr.edu
Website: www.umr.edu/~daily

Wholly nonresident M.S. in engineering management offered nationally through the National Technological University (call Gerry Johnson at (907) 495-6404 for more information). M.S. in engineering/computer science offered locally through televised courses sent to locations in the Kansas City area.

University of Montana M

School of Business Administration
Missoula, MT 59812
Fields offered: Business administration
Year founded: 1893
Ownership: Nonprofit, state
Phone: (406) 243-6195 • (800) 823-2416 (MT)
Fax: (406) 243-2797
E-mail: gradschl@selway.umt.edu
Website: www.umt.edu

M.B.A. offered by televised courses at sites in Billings, plus computer conferencing and instruction by telephone and fax. M.B.A. off-campus night programs in Billings, Butte, Kalispell, Helena, Great Falls, and Missoula. Please contact Dr. Clyde Neu, Ph.D., Director, Off-Campus MBA Programs (406) 657-2290. **E-mail:** mbaneu@wtp.net. Also, for students based in Montana only, an M.B.A. program from Missoula with live, interactive video.

University of Nairobi B

P.O. Box 30197
Nairobi, Kenya
Fields offered: Education
Ownership: Nonprofit, state
Phone: (25-4) 33-42-44
Fax: (25-4) 33-68-85
E-mail: IDIS@p430.f4.n731.z5.gnfido.fidonet
Website: www.diplomacy.edu/ITC97_IDIS/

A plan was announced in the early 1980s for a Kenyan external degree program, but it was delayed for some years, due to "unforeseen problems." Now, according to a newspaper clipping forwarded by a correspondent, the school is indeed offering an external B.A. in education, with a number of concentrations.

University of Nebraska—Lincoln M, D

Division of Continuing Studies
157 Nebraska Center
Lincoln, NE 68583-0900

Fields offered: Engineering, business administration, computer science, education, journalism, human resources, family sciences
Year founded: 1869
Ownership: Nonprofit, state
Phone: (402) 472-2175
Fax: (402) 472-1901
E-mail: atc@unlinfo.unl.edu
Website: www.unl.edu:80/conted/telecom/index.html
M.S. in several engineering fields (industrial and management systems, manufacturing systems, mechanical) and computer science, and an M.B.A. The teleconferencing, e-mail, and courses beamed to distance-learning sites around the state and regionally. Ed.D. in curriculum and instruction requires only two summer sessions on campus. Master's and Ed.D. in education delivered worldwide via Lotus Notes. Contact the school for residency requirements

University of Nevada—Reno   B

Division of Continuing Education
206 Midby Byron Bldg.
Reno, NV 89557
Fields offered: General studies
Year founded: 1874
Ownership: Nonprofit, state
Phone: (702) 784-4046 • (800) 233-8928
Fax: (702) 784-1300
E-mail: nealf@unr.edu
Website: www.unr.edu
Bachelor of General Studies program allows students who have already completed an Associate's degree elsewhere to earn a self-designed, wholly nonresident Bachelor's through a range of nontraditional methods, including correspondence courses and telecourses.

University of New Brunswick   B

Extension and Summer Session
P.O. Box 4400
Fredericton, NB E3B 5A3 Canada
Fields offered: Nursing
Year founded: 1785
Ownership: Nonprofit, state
Phone: (506) 453-4646
Fax: (506) 453-3572
E-mail: extension@unb.ca
Website: www.unb.ca/web/coned/
The Bachelor of Nursing degree is available wholly through distance education. In addition, undergraduate courses in arts, administration, education, and science are also available via distance education, as are selected courses at the Master's level in education and nursing. Various methods of course delivery are used, including audio and video conferencing, television, audiographics, and the Internet.

University of New England   B, M, D

Distance Education Center
Armidale NSW 2351, Australia

Fields offered: Many fields
Year founded: 1938
Phone: (61-67) 732-224
Fax: (61-67) 711-644
E-mail: rbrinkle@metz.une.edu.au
Website: www.une.edu.au
This school offers a truly vast number of Bachelor's and Master's degrees; some programs require a visit to Australia, but the information we have at the moment doesn't specify which; we have written for clarification. Learning takes place via printed correspondence texts, audio- and videotapes, radio and television broadcasts, and computer. UNE is Australia's oldest distance-education provider, and has over 10,000 students enrolled in external programs. Degrees offered are: Bachelor's in administrative leadership, agricultural economics, arts, laws, Asian studies, commerce, computing science, counseling, economics, education (several concentrations), financial administration, health management, health science, languages, nursing, professional studies, psychology, science, social science, and urban & regional planning. Master's degrees are offered in accountancy, arts, Asian studies, Australian studies, business administration, computing science, counseling, curriculum studies, defense studies, economics, education (several concentrations), engineering science, health management, health science, laws, letters, music, natural resources, nursing, professional studies, public health, public policy, resource science, rural science, science, scientific studies, social science, and urban & regional planning. Research doctorates are available in education, health services management, nursing, and philosophy.

University of Northern Colorado   M

College of Continuing Education
Greeley, CO 80639
Fields offered: Various fields
Year founded: 1889
Ownership: Nonprofit, state
Phone: (970) 351-1890
Fax: (970) 351-1880
E-mail: vhernand@admissions.univnorthco.edu
Website: www.univnorthco.edu
Wholly nonresidential Master's degrees for adult students with at least three years' experience in their field. (Although no credit is given for life-experience learning, it is awarded for equivalency exams.) Degrees include: Master of Arts in education (eight areas of concentration), agency counseling, or communication, and M.S. in statistics, operations research, or secondary science teaching. Instruction takes place through correspondence course, audio- and videotaped, televised courses, e-mail, telephone instruction, independent study, supervised fieldwork, and other innovative methods.

University of Northern Iowa   B

Center for Credit Programs
116 International Center

Iowa City, IA 52242-1802
Fields offered: Liberal studies
Year founded: 1847
Ownership: Nonprofit, state
Phone: (319) 335-2575 • (800) 272-6430
Fax: (319) 335-2740
E-mail: scott-wilcox@uiowa.edu
Website: www.uni.edu/

The Bachelor of Arts in liberal studies can be earned entirely by correspondence from the University of Northern Iowa. There are no majors in the program, but students must earn 12 credits in three of these five areas: humanities, communication and arts, science and math, social sciences, and professional fields (business, education, etc.). Credit is also earned through guided correspondence study courses. Students mail in assignments and take proctored exams. Credit can also be earned through on-campus evening and weekend courses, televised courses, off-campus course sites throughout Iowa, courses from other regionally accredited four-year colleges (both on-campus and correspondence), and telebridge courses. "Telebridge" is a statewide system of two-way audio conferencing which permits classes to be held at remote locations. To qualify for admission, a student must live in the United States and have completed 62 transferable units or have an Associate's degree. At least forty-five semester hours must be earned at the Iowa Regents Universities (University of Iowa, Iowa State University, University of Northern Iowa). See also: Quad Cities Graduate Center.

University of Northumbria M

Flexible Management Learning Centre
Newcastle Business School
Northumberland Building
Newcastle Upon Tyne, NE1 8ST U.K.
Fields offered: Business administration
Year founded: 1969
Ownership: Nonprofit, independent
Phone: (44-191) 227-4942
Fax: (44-191) 227 4684
E-mail: d.thompson@unn.ac.uk
Website: fmlc.unn.ac.uk

Some time ago, the Newcastle Business School established a performance-oriented flexible M.B.A. for working managers and professionals that allowed them to study and develop largely at home, and/or at work, with a few face-to-face meetings. Now, with the new Internet version of this program, all study is done at a distance. Creative solutions to formerly in-person portions of the program include exchanging photos and written "pen portraits," so that students can develop a sense of community. Challenge papers are posted on the web for discussion, and students are assigned to "buddy" groups. Students from around the world are accepted.

University of Otago B, M

Distance Learning
P.O. Box 913
Dunedin, New Zealand
Fields offered: Health sciences, humanities
Year founded: 1869
Phone: (64-3) 479-8237
Fax: (64-3) 479-8186
E-mail: rosemary.beresford@stonebow.otago.ac.nz
Website: www.otago.ac.nz/courseinfoenrol/distance/

New Zealand's oldest university offers individual papers and whole courses to people who are unable to come to the university. Distance learning program includes an undergraduate degree in theology as well as undergraduate certificates and diplomas and postgraduate certificates in a number of fields. The university also offers Master's degrees in consumer and applied sciences (community and family studies), clinical pharmacy, and general practice. Many of these are based on audioconference class sessions supplemented by written course materials supported by references, assignments, tapes, self-assessment exercises and, of course, regular contact with tutors by letter, phone, or electronic means. Web-based papers are gradually being developed with certain courses incorporating Internet accessed papers. Postgraduate certificates are equivalent to one semester (six months) full-time work, postgraduate diplomas are equivalent to 12 months' full-time work and Masters degrees are equivalent to two years of full-time work.

University of Paisley M

High Street
Paisley PA1 2BE, Scotland
Fields offered: Marketing, quality management, computer-aided engineering
Year founded: 1897
Phone: (44-141) 848-3000
Fax: (44-141) 848 3947
E-mail: dlu@paisley.ac.uk
Website: www.paisley.ac.uk/

An M.B.A. with a concentration in marketing or two M.S. degrees, one in quality management, the other in computer-aided engineering. All study materials are provided in printed and/or electronic form, and coursework is accomplished via written lessons, multimedia, and the Internet.

University of Phoenix M

Center for Distance Education
4625 East Elwood Street
P.O. Box 52076
Phoenix, AZ 85072
Fields offered: Business, technology management
Year founded: 1976
Ownership: Proprietary
Phone: (602) 921-8014 • 800) 366-9699
Fax: (602) 894-2152

E-mail: rrpaden@apollogrp.edu
Website: www.uophx.edu

In addition to its San Francisco–based on-line programs, discussed below, Phoenix also offers a text-based M.B.A., with an optional concentration in technology management. Study takes place by correspondence, with support given via phone, fax, and mail.

University of Phoenix Online   B, M, D

On-line Program Administrative Offices
100 Spear Street
San Francisco, CA 94105
Fields offered: Business, management, education, nursing
Year founded: 1976
Ownership: Proprietary
Phone: (415) 541-0141 • (800) 742-4742
Fax: (415) 541-0761
E-mail: on-line@apollo/uophx.edu
Website: www.uophx.edu/on-line2

In 1989, the Arizona-based University of Phoenix began offering degrees entirely via computer, through program headquarters in San Francisco. On-line students get their assignments, have group discussions, and ask questions of their professors over the Internet, without leaving their homes or offices. Each class meeting is spread out over an entire week, allowing busy students to complete their work at the most convenient time for them. Computer training and orientation is provided once a student enrolls. Degrees offered are a Bachelor of Science in business/administration, business/information systems, or business/management, an M.A. in education or organizational management, an M.S. in computer information systems, and an M.B.A., with optional concentrations in global management or technology management, as well as both a B.S. and an M.S. in nursing, for registered nurses. A short-residency Doctorate in management debuts in 1999.

University of Reading

See: College of Estate Management

University of Saskatchewan   B

Extension Credit Studies
Extension Division
330 KirkHall, 117 Science Place
Saskatoon, SK S7N 5C8 Canada
Fields offered: Many fields
Year founded: 1907
Ownership: Nonprofit, state
Phone: (306) 966-5562
Fax: (306) 373-5567
E-mail: grace.milashenko@usask.ca
Website: www.extension.usask.ca

A wide variety of undergraduate degree courses and certificate programs are offered via independent study. Coursework is accomplished largely through the mail, and courses rely primarily on printed materials, but may include audio or videocassettes, televised information, audio con-

ferences, computer-assisted delivery and occasional face-to-face sessions. Areas include: adult education, agriculture, anthropology, archaeology, biology, computer science, ecological education, English, French, geography, geology, history, horticulture, mathematics, microbiology, music, Native studies, philosophy, psychology, religious studies, sociology, and Teaching English as a Second Language. There is also a special B.S. in nursing for holders of nursing diplomas currently registered and working in Canada.

University of Sheffield   M

Centre for Psychoanalytic Studies
16 Claremont Crescent
Sheffield, S10 2TA U.K.
Fields offered: Psychiatry, philosophy, psychoanalytic studies, disability studies
Year founded: 1828
Phone: (44-114) 222-2961
Fax: (44-114) 270-0619
E-mail: j.m.taylor@sheffield.ac.uk
Website: www.shef.ac.uk/~psysc/

Sheffield offers an M.A. in disability studies through part-time distance learning; the degree is offered after two years and involves the writing of a 15 to 20 thousand word dissertation. The M.A. in psychiatry, philosophy, and society and that in psychoanalytic studies can be done by distance learning, but is expected that students will be able to attend short residential courses for about 3 weekends a year. This may be negotiable.

University of South Africa   B, M, D

P. O. Box 392, Muckleneuk Ridge
Pretoria, 0001 South Africa
Fields offered: Many fields
Year founded: 1960
Ownership: Nonprofit, state
Phone: (27-12) 429-2555
Fax: (27-12) 429-2565
E-mail: stidy-info@alpha.unisa.ac.za
Website: www.unisa.ac.za

UNISA offers Bachelor's, Master's, and Doctorates entirely by correspondence. Examinations are taken at South African embassies and consulates worldwide. Degrees at all levels are offered in arts, science, law, theology, education, and economic and management sciences through a technique called "tele-tuition," using course materials, tapes, slides, etc. A minimum of 10 courses is required for the Bachelor's degree, which takes at least three years to complete. The government-subsidized program is relatively inexpensive. Before registering, undergraduate students must obtain a Certificate of Full or Conditional Exemption from the South African Matriculation Examination, obtained from the Matriculation Board, P.O. Box 3854, Pretoria, South Africa 0001 (this is not necessary for students who already hold "a recognized or accredited" Bachelor's degree). People worldwide are admitted. Syllabi and course descriptions are available free of charge from the registrar. We used to make readers aware of a guide, by a graduate of the University, to negotiating their bureaucracy, and people still ask about it but, unfortunately, the student has decided to stop publishing it.

University of South Australia   B, M, D

International Programs
GPO Box 2471
Adelaide, SA 5001 Australia
Fields offered: Many fields
Year founded: 1991
Phone: (61-8) 8302 0731
Fax: (61-8) 8302 0733
E-mail: international.relations@unisa.edu.au
Website: www.unisa.edu.au

This school offers a wide range of programs through distance-learning methods, including some wholly nonresident research doctorates. Degree programs are: Bachelor of Accountancy, Bachelor of Arts in aboriginal affairs administration, aboriginal studies, Australian studies, Bachelor of Business in administrative management, human resource development, tourism & hospitality, Bachelor of Education in a wide range of specializations, from early childhood to geography to legal studies, and more, Bachelor of Social Science, Bachelor of Teaching, Master of Arts in aboriginal affairs administration, aboriginal studies, communication studies, religion studies, Master of Design, Master of Education, with several concentrations, Master of Gerontology, Master of Health Science in occupational therapy, and Master of Nursing. The research Ph.D., through the department of Education, is awarded in a number of specialist areas, including art education, curriculum leadership, early childhood education, religion education, distance education, women & education, and more. Interested students are invited to discuss other research areas of interest. The address and phone numbers above are for persons outside of Australia who are interested in these programs. Inside Australia, people should contact the school at:

Distance Education Centre
Underdale Campus, Holbrooks Road
Underdale SA 5032
Phone: (61-8) 302-6378
Fax: (61-8) 302-6580

University of Southern Colorado   B

2200 Bonforte Boulevard
Pueblo, CO 81001-4901
Fields offered: Sociology, psychology, history, political science, anthropology, economics
Year founded: 1933
Ownership: Nonprofit, state
Phone: (719) 549-2316 • (800) 388-6154
Fax: (719) 549-2938
E-mail: coned@uscolo.edu
Website: www.uscolo.edu/coned/

Bachelor of Science in social science through a combination of correspondence courses, transfer credits, and

exams. While this is primarily a degree-completion program, the school will help students to choose courses at local institutions (or correspondence courses from other schools) to meet their requirements. Degree-completion students must complete at least 32 credits with USC; a maximum of 96 credits can be transferred in, and 64 of those can be from junior colleges. Credits that are over 10 years old must gain special acceptance; unofficial evaluations are done for students as time permits. Degree requirements include 39 credits in general education (composition, speech, humanities, science), 44 credits in the major field (sociology, psychology, history, political science, anthropology, or economics), 20 credits in a supporting minor, and 33 elective credits.

University of Southern Queensland   B, M, D

Toowoomba
Queensland, 4350 Australia
Fields offered: Many fields
Year founded: 1967
Ownership: Nonprofit, state
Phone: (61-76) 31-2282
Fax: (61-76) 36-1049
E-mail: studadm@usq.edu.au
Website: www.usq.edu.au

The University of Southern Queensland evolved from the Darling Downs Institute of Advanced Education. They offer degrees at all levels, in engineering, education, humanities, nursing, psychology, management, economics, accounting, human resource management, marketing, computing, and journalism. Currently, students from 48 countries are enrolled in distance-learning programs. Bachelor's degrees usually require 6 to 8 years of study, while Masters degrees, including M.B.A.'s, and research doctorates require 4 to 6 years of part-time study. Distance study is accomplished through printed study materials, video- and audiotapes, Internet support, computer-assisted learning, computer-, video-, and teleconferencing, and optional (or, in some cases, compulsory) "vacation residencies." USQ is committed to providing a high level of support to distance students, whether by phone, Internet, or at regional centers across Australia. Credit may be given for previous relevant study, as well as for work and other life-experience learning. See also: Bournemouth University

University of St. Augustine for Health Sciences   B, M, D

170 Malaga Street,
St. Augustine, FL 32084
Fields offered: Physical therapy, occupational therapy, health care
Year founded: 1979
Phone: (904) 826-0084 • (800) 241-1027
Fax: (904) 826-0085
E-mail: info@usa.edu
Website: www.usa.edu

Combination distance study and resident courses leading to a post-professional Master of Science in Physical Therapy, Master of Occupational Therapy, and an M.S. in physical therapy. These programs are accredited by the Distance Education and Training Council. USA also offers an M.B.A. in health care in association with ISIM University, and Doctor of Physical Therapy either by distance learning (following a six-day residential colloquium) or with a clinical residency. Since our understanding has been that DETC cannot accredit schools that offer doctoral programs, we are a bit confused by this situation, and are hoping for clarification.

University of Stirling   M

Stirling, FK9 4LA UK
Fields offered: Retailing & wholesaling, public relations, entrepreneurial studies
Year founded: 1967
Phone: (44-1786) 473-171
Fax: (44-1786) 450-201
Website: www.stir.ac.uk

Stirling offers several largely distance-learning Master's degrees, geared to working professionals. The M.S. in entrepreneurial studies is designed for students in the U.K. and abroad; applicants who lack an undergraduate degree but have significant experience in the small-business sector may be admitted if they can prove ability to take on postgraduate-level study. Similarly, the M.S. in public relations may be open to professionals with significant P.R. experience even if they lack the normal academic qualifications. The M.B.A. in retailing & wholesaling is for persons with high levels of experience; the average student has at least 10 years work experience in the distributive trades. Students in all three programs are provided with specially designed materials, core textbooks, and audiocassettes. Face-to-face tutorials are expected in some programs.

University of Strathclyde   M

International Office
50 George Street
Glasgow, G1 1QE Scotland
Fields offered: Law
Year founded: 1796
Ownership: Nonprofit, public
Phone: (44-141) 548-3843
Fax: (44-141) 553-1546
E-mail: International@mis.strath.ac.uk
Website: www.strath.ac.uk

The Master of Law (LL.M) with a specialty in information technology is offered over the Internet; distance-learning options are available for the M.B.A. and M.S. in International Marketing as well, but only for students within traveling distance of a learning center; for locations of these centers, contact the school directly.

University of Sunderland   B, M

Edinburgh Building
Chester Road
Sunderland, SR1 3SD United Kingdom
Fields offered: Engineering, business studies, business information technology, business administration, computer information systems, education
Phone: (44-191) 515-2277
Fax: (44-191) 515-2279
E-mail: lds@sunderland.ac.uk
Website: www.sunderland.ac.uk

Sunderland offers a number of specialized distance-learning degrees, as well as a research doctorate option. The B.A. in business studies and business information technology can be earned through completion of 18 modules, using print study materials, with support by fax, e-mail, and Internet. Assessment is by examination, usually in the U.K., although arrangements can be made for students who do not wish to travel there. A B.Eng. is available through independent study; some attendance at approved learning centers is required, but the school is flexible. A B.A. in education usually requires some residency, but tutorial sessions may be able to be accomplished through videoconferencing.

At the graduate level, the is an M.B.A. offered via distance learning through centers in Saudi Arabia, Greece, and Malaysia. The M.S. in computer-based information systems is available by distance learning, with study centers in the U.K., Hong Kong, Bahrain, Saudi Arabia, Greece, Israel, and Malaysia.

University of Surrey   M

Guildford
Surrey, GU2 5XH U.K.
Information Office
Fields offered: Education, technological fields, business, management
Year founded: 1891
Ownership: State
Phone: (44-1483) 300-800
Fax: (44-1483) 300-803
E-mail: information @surrey.ac.uk
Website: www.surrey.ac.uk

The degree programs consist of modules based on printed materials, audio cassette, computer programs and Internet and workshops. It is possible to complete programs entirely through distance learning—some modules do not have the workshop requirements, and in those that do, it may be possible to fulfill them by meeting with approved staff in your area. Degrees offered are: an M.A. in linguistics with a concentration in the teaching of English as a second language, M.S. in English Language Teaching Management, M.S. degrees in interactive training systems, information technology training, applied professional studies (education and training), and management, an M.B.A., and an LL.M. for working lawyers. They do accept students from other countries. Non-native speakers are required to produce confirmation of English ability in form of Cambridge Proficiency IELTS band 6.0, TOEFL 550, or equivalent.

University of Tasmania   B

Distance Education Services
P. O. Box 1214
Launceston, Tasmania, 7250 Australia
Fields offered: Business, nursing
Phone: (61-03) 243-504
Fax: (61-03) 24 3-792
E-mail: International.Office@admin.utas.edu.au or Course.Info@admin.utas.edu.au (Australian residents only)
Website: info.utas.edu.au

Primarily for Tasmanians, although required tutorials may be conducted by telephone. Degrees offered are a B.A., Bachelor of Business with concentrations in accounting, business management, human resource management, or marketing and international business, and a Bachelor of Nursing. There is an M.B.A., but it requires a number of meetings in Tasmania.

University of the Philippines
Open University   M, D

Student Support Services
Alumni Center
College, Laguna, Philippines
Fields offered: Public health, social work, teacher education, agriculture, public management, research and development management
Year founded: 1995
Ownership: State
Phone: (63-49) 536-1605
Fax: (63-49) 536-1605
E-mail: upouoc@laguna.net
Website: www.uplb.edu.ph

Uses print, audio and video. In programs requiring practical work, summer residential schools may be required. Degrees currently offered are the Master of Public Health, Master of Social Work, Master of Hospital Administration, Master of Arts in nursing, Master of Public Management, and Ph.D. in education.

University of the South Pacific   B

University Extension
P.O. Box 1168
Suva, Fiji
Fields offered: Many fields
Year founded: 1970
Phone: (679) 313-900
Fax: (679) 300-482
E-mail: sarellite@usp.ac.fj
Website: www.tcol.co.uk/orgs/usp/usp.htm

Fiji's only accredited university offers programs via satellite link for tutorials and teleconferencing, text, audio and video cassettes used to connect students and faculty.

Bachelor of Arts/Science (many fields), Law, and Bachelor of Education.

University of the State of New York

See: Regents College

University of the West of England   M

Coldharbour Lane
Frenchay
Bristol, BS16 1QY UK
Fields offered: Business administration
Phone: (44-0272) 656-261
E-mail: prospectus@uwe.ac.uk
Website: www.uwe.ac.uk

This school offers an M.B.A. through distance learning methods.

University of Twente   M

Faculty of Educational Science and Technology
P.O. Box 217
7500 AE Enschede, Netherlands
Fields offered: Educational and training systems design
Year founded: 1993
Ownership: Nonprofit, state
Phone: (31-53) 489-3588
Fax: (31-53) 489-2895
E-mail: nelissen@edte.utwente.nl
Website: www.utwente.nl/masters/mscgen.htm

The M.S. in educational and training systems design can be completed through a resident year in Holland, or through distance learning to groups of students, usually a group of co-workers at a sponsoring workplace, through electronic and web-based technologies.

University of Victoria   B

Distance Education Services
P.O. Box 3030
Victoria, BC V8W 3N6 Canada
Fields offered: Child and youth care, social work, nursing
Ownership: State
Phone: (604) 721-8454
Fax: (604) 721-8774
E-mail: kates@uvcs.uvic.ca
Website: www.uvic.ca

Students at a distance receive instruction through print packages, audiotapes, computer-assisted learning, and videotapes. Instructors lead group discussions, using audio or computer conferencing, and tutors answer queries and discuss assignments by phone and/or electronic mail. Degrees currently offered via these methods are: a B.A. in child and youth care, a Bachelor of Social Work, and a B.S. in nursing.

University of Virginia   M

Televised Graduate Engineering
Thornton Hall

Charlottesville, VA 22903
Fields offered: Engineering
Year founded: 1819
Ownership: Nonprofit, state
Phone: (804) 982-2313
Fax: (804) 924-4086
E-mail: rfk2u@virginia.edu
Website: watt.seas.virginia.edu/~rfk2u/index.html

Master of Engineering in a number of fields, including chemical, civil, electrical, materials science, mechanical and aerospace, and systems engineering, available by satellite. Classes are televised live to numerous locations throughout the U.S. in the evening hours, four days a week.

University of Wales, Aberystwyth B, M, D

Old College, King Street
Aberystwyth
Ceredigion, Wales, SY23 4AT UK
Fields offered: Many fields
Year founded: 1872
Phone: (44-1970) 622-089
Fax: (44-1970) 622-921
E-mail: jdm@aber.ac.uk
Website: www.aber.ac.uk

The Aberystwyth campus of the University of Wales system offers a number of programs though distance learning. Some do require brief residency; contact the school for details. The distance-learning programs are: a B.S. in economics, with a specialization in library and information studies, M.S. in economic with a specialization in the management of library and information systems, or in health information management, and M.S.'s in environmental impact assessment, environmental auditing, environmental management, and protected landscape management. In addition, there are M.Phil and Ph.D. degrees that can be studies on a part-time basis, with students traveling to Wales for a couple of weeks a year, or handled full-time through a place of employment. This option is available in the following departments: accounting & finance, art, biological sciences, computer science, economics, education, English, European languages, geography & earth studies, history & Welsh history, information & library sciences, international politics, law, mathematics, physics, rural agriculture, and theater, film, & television studies, and Welsh (Celtic) studies.

University of Waterloo B

Distance Education Office
Waterloo, ON N2L 3G1 Canada
Fields offered: Arts, science, environmental studies
Year founded: 1957
Ownership: Nonprofit, state
Phone: (519) 888-4050
Fax: (519) 746-6393
E-mail: distance@corr1.uwaterloo.ca
Website: www.adm.uwaterloo.ca/infoded/de&ce.html

Bachelor's degrees can be earned entirely through distance education, including a non-major B.A. or B.S., a B.A. with a major in Canadian studies, classical studies, economics, English, French, geography, history, philosophy, psychology, religious studies, social development studies, or sociology, and a Bachelor of Environmental Studies in geography. Credit is considered for prior academic experience, but none for experiential learning. The programs are available to people residing in Canada and the United States, but U.S. citizens pay three to four times as much tuition. All courses are offered on a rigid time schedule, in which papers and exams must be done by very specific times. As a result, there have been postal delivery problems with some U.S. students. (Suggestion: there is a maximum of six assignments per course; it might well be worth the expense of sending them in via Federal Express or fax.)

University of Western Ontario B

Faculty of Part-Time and Continuing Education
University of Western Ontario
Stevenson-Lawson Building Room 23
London, ON Canada
Fields offered: Many fields
Phone: (519) 661-3631
Fax: (519) 661-3799
E-mail: questions@courier.ptce.uwo.ca
Website: www.ptce.uwo.ca

One of Canada's most prestigious schools offers Bachelor's degrees by correspondence, augmented by other media, such as lectures on audio- or videocassette, loaned lab kits, visual materials, and more. Students work towards a B.A. in one of a number of concentrations offered by the faculties of arts, science, social science, and kinesthesiology.

University of Westminster M

309 Regent Street
London, W1R 8AL United Kingdom
Fields offered: Management fields
Year founded: 1838
Phone: (44-171) 911-5000
Fax: (44-171) 911 5175
E-mail: international-office@wmin.ac.uk
Website: www.wmin.ac.uk

Westminster offers an M.B.A. with a concentration in design management and a Master of Arts in international business & management, both by distance learning. The M.B.A. is module-based, with a 4-day workshop at the end of each course of study; the M.A. has no required residency, although an optional residential week in July is offered.

University of Wisconsin—Madison M

Engineering Professional Development
432 North Lake Street, Room 313
Madison, WI 53706
Fields offered: Engineering
Year founded: 1849
Ownership: Nonprofit, state

Phone: (608) 262-0133
Fax: (608) 263-3160
E-mail: karena@engr.wisc.edu
Website: epdwww.engr.wisc.edu

This university offers two Master's-level programs, as well as a Professional Development Degree (PDD), which is a post-Bachelor's degree geared to helping engineers reach personal professional objectives. The two Master of Engineering degrees are as follows: the first, in professional practice, focuses on project management, international engineering strategies, statistics, problem-solving, and other "real world" fields. The degree is designed to be completed at a distance in two years. Applicants should be engineers with a B.S. in engineering from an ABET accredited school, and have four years work experience in the field. The second Master's is an M.E in technical Japanese, focusing on technical Japanese, the Japanese language, and current technological developments in Japan. It is open to students without an engineering degree, but such students must complete at least 16 undergraduate credits in science or engineering in order to be admitted. The degree can be completed in one year.

University of Wisconsin— Superior   B

Extended Degree Program
Erlanson 105
Superior, WI 54880
Fields offered: Many fields
Year founded: 1893
Ownership: Nonprofit, state
Phone: (715) 394-8487
Fax: (715) 394-8139
E-mail: extdegree@uwsuperior.edu
Website: www.uwsuper.edu

A Bachelor of Science can be completed entirely through off-campus independent faculty-guided study. However, some on-campus conferences with faculty members will be required. Each student designs an individualized major based on his or her personal or career goals. Self-paced courses developed by the university faculty in a wide variety of fields are the primary mode of learning, in addition to learning contracts. The student has the option of requesting credit for prior learning through the development of a portfolio. The program is open to Wisconsin residents and Minnesota residents who qualify for reciprocity.

University of Wisconsin—Whitewater   M

On-Line MBA
4033 Carlson Hall
College of Business and Economics
Whitewater, WI 53190
Fields offered: Business administration
Year founded: 1868
Ownership: Nonprofit, state
Phone: (414) 472-1945
Fax: (414) 472-1945
E-mail: zahnd@uwwvax.uww.edu

Website: www.uww.edu/business/gradprog

Offers an M.B.A. on-line with concentrations in finance, marketing, and management. (A number of other emphases, from health care to international business re offered through a combination of on-campus and on-line courses.) Students need a Pentium processor, modem, CD-ROM drive, and Windows operating system. Faculty contact is by phone, fax, and e-mail, and the university makes a point of its faculty being interested in a high level of student contact. Degrees in industrial hygeine, occupational safety and health management also offered.

University of Yangon

See: University of Distance Education

University on the Air   B

Taipei, Taiwan
Fields offered: Many fields
Year founded: 1986
Ownership: Nonprofit, state
Phone: (886) 282-9355

Degree courses are offered entirely by radio and television. Full-time students must be over 20 years old and hold a high-school diploma; anyone can study part-time. Sixty of the total 128 required credits must be in one fields of study. More than 30,000 students enrolled; all instruction is in Chinese.

Upper Iowa University   B

External Degree Program
P. O. Box 1861
Fayette, IA 52142
Fields offered: Accounting, business, human services, human resources management, management, marketing, social sciences, public administration
Year founded: 1857
Ownership: Nonprofit, independent
Phone: (319) 425-5283 • (888) 877-3742
Fax: (319) 425-5353
E-mail: extdegree@uiu.edu
Website: www.uiu.edu

Upper Iowa's External Degree Program offers the opportunity to earn a B.S. in accounting, business, human services, human resources management, management, marketing, social sciences, and public administration (this last with emphases in general, law enforcement, or fire science administration) entirely through self-paced directed independent study, with learning packets containing assignments and other course materials (also offers Associate's degrees in these fields). In many cases, lessons may be faxed or e-mailed. Frequent interaction with the faculty by phone, fax, e-mail, or regular post is encouraged. A two-week summer session is offered on the Fayette campus, allowing students to complete six semester hours of credit. Home-study courses are available in a wide variety of fields, from accounting to chemistry, history to fine arts.

Previous college work, job and military training, and other educational experience is evaluated for credit.

Victoria University　　　　　　　　M

Department of Communications Studies
P.O. Box 600
Wellington, New Zealand
Fields offered: Communication
Year founded: 1899
Phone: (64-04) 495-5266
Fax: (64-04) 495-5235
E-mail: lalita.rajasingham@vuw.ac.nz
Website: www.vuw.ac.nz/comms/courses/mcomms.htm

This New Zealand university is in the process of creating a Master's degree in communication to be offered entirely over the Internet, using audio, video, and interactive graphics.

Walden University　　　　　　　M, D

415 First Avenue North
Minneapolis, MN 55401
Fields offered: Administration/management, education, human services, health services
Year founded: 1970
Ownership: Nonprofit, independent
Phone: (612) 338-7224 • (800) WALDENU
Fax: (612) 338-5092
E-mail: help@waldenu.edu
Website: www.waldenu.edu

Walden offers graduate education geared to experienced professionals. It offers Ph.D.s in applied management and decision sciences, education, health services, human services, and psychology. The programs consist of self-guided curricula delivered through learning modules, known as knowledge area modules, or KAMs, plus a dissertation. Each KAM is broadly conceptualized, allowing students to tailor a written demonstration of knowledge to their unique areas of professional interest. Fulfillment of 32 residency units is required and can be completed through a variety of options, including intensive four-day weekend sessions held at locations throughout the country, and two- or three-week sessions on the campus of Indiana University. Master's programs are offered in education and psychology. Courses are delivered through electronic classrooms over the school's website. Students must have access to a personal computer, word-processing software, the Internet, and the World Wide Web.

Washington State University　　　　B

Extended Academic Programs
Van Doren 204
P.O. Box 645220
Pullman, WA 99164-5220
Fields offered: Social sciences
Year founded: 1890
Ownership: Nonprofit, state

Phone: (509) 335-3557 • (800) 222-4978
Fax: (509) 335-4850
E-mail: edp@wsu.edu
Website: www.eus.wsu.edu/edp

Washington State University's Bachelor of Arts in social sciences is a degree-completion program, designed primarily for students who have completed the equivalent of the first two years of a college degree program. It can be earned entirely nonresidentially through a variety of distance-learning telecommunication technologies, including correspondence and television courses, guided independent study, audio and videocassettes, and telephone instruction. See also: National Universities Degree Consortium.

Western Australian College of Advanced Education

See: Edith Cowan University

Western Illinois University　　　　　B

Non-Traditional Programs
5 Horrabin Hall
1 University Circle
Macomb, IL 61455
Fields offered: Many fields
Year founded: 1899
Ownership: Nonprofit, state
Phone: (309) 298-1929
Fax: (309) 298-2226
E-mail: np-bog@wiu.edu
Website: www.wiu.edu/users/mintp

The Board of Governors B.A. can be earned entirely by correspondence study. Fifteen of 120 semester hours must be earned through one or a combination of BGU Universities, and 40 must be upper division. The 15 units that must be earned through enrollment at a BGU University can be done by correspondence, on-campus in Macomb, or through extension courses at locations around the state. Students who did not graduate from an Illinois high school must pass an exam on the U.S. and Illinois state constitutions, or take an equivalent course in political science. All students must pass a university writing exam. Western Illinois provides a helpful guide to the preparation of a prior learning portfolio. Credit for learning experiences and many equivalency exams. The total cost of the program depends on the number and type of courses taken. The cost of assessing a life experience portfolio is only $30. Students from other countries are admitted, but they must have a U.S. address to which materials can be sent.

See also: Board of Governors B.A. Degree Program, Governors State University, FEMA National Fire Academy, Quad Cities Graduate Center.

Western Michigan University　　B, M, D

Campus III/Weekend College Program
Kalamazoo, MI 49008
Fields offered: Many fields

Year founded: 1903
Ownership: Nonprofit, state
Phone: (616) 387-1000
Fax: (616) 387-0958
E-mail: ask-wmu@wmich.edu
Website: www.wmich.edu

The following degrees are available entirely through off-campus regional centers: B.S. in general university studies and production technology, Master and Doctor of Public Administration, Master of Public Administration in health care administration, Master of Social Work, M.B.A., Master in Educational Leadership, Master in Early Childhood Education, Master in Elementary Education, Master in Reading, M.S. in vocational education, engineering management, industrial engineering, and mechanical engineering, and Master in Industrial Psychology. Residency requirements can be satisfied through work completed at an official Western Michigan University Regional Center.

Western Oregon University

See: FEMA National Fire Academy

Wilfrid Laurier University   B

Continuing Education
75 University Ave. West
Waterloo, Ont. N2L 3C5 Canada
Fields offered: Sociology, geography
Phone: (519) 884-4447
Fax: (519) 746-2472
E-mail: shughes@mach2.wlu.ca
Website: www.wlu.ca

Wholly nonresident B.A. in sociology through teleconferencing and videocassette, offered to students worldwide. Normal Ontario University admission requirements apply, according to the school's literature, although they don't elaborate on those for those of us less familiar with same.

Winthrop University   M

Distance Learning Center
Rock Hill, SC 29733
Fields offered: Business administration
Year founded: 1886
Ownership: Nonprofit, state
Phone: (803) 323-2696
Fax: (803) 328-2855
E-mail: larsenl@winthrop.edu
Website: www.winthrop.edu

Offers a "two-way, fully interactive" M.B.A. program via live video broadcast. We have written for more information.

Worcester Polytechnic Institute   M

Instructional Media Center
100 Institute Road
Worcester, MS 01609

Fields offered: fire protection engineering, business
Year founded: 1865
Ownership: Independent, nonprofit
Phone: (508) 831-5810
Fax: (508) 831-5881
E-mail: adln@wpi.edu
Website: www.wpi.edu/Academics/ADLN

Videotape and text -based programs. The M.B.A. focuses on management of technology. The M.S. in fire protection Engineering currently requires students to combine the limited number of FPE courses with other (non-FPE) ones to reach the 33-credit requirement.

World College   B

Lake Shores Plaza
5193 Shore Drive, #113
Virginia Beach, VA 23455-2500
Fields offered: Electronic engineering technology
Phone: (757) 464-4600 • (800) 696-7532
Fax: (757) 464-3687
E-mail: instruct@cie-wc.edu
Website: www.cie-wc.edu

World offers a Bachelor of Electronic Engineering Technology through independent study. All lab equipment, parts, and software are provided (student must have access to a computer), and the program's 300-plus experiments can be completed in the home.

Zentrum für Fernstudien
Universitaet Linz   B, M

Altenbergstrasse 74
Linz, 4040 Austria
Phone: (43-732) 2468/9550
Fax: (43-732) 759-666

ZFUL, the center for distance learning, is part of the University of Linz. The principal teaching medium is printed material. Complementary course materials are delivered via television, video, audiocassettes, computer and multimedia electronic communications. All coursework is completed in German.

INDEPENDENT STUDY

ROBERT NUNNALLY

Learning, like gifts, deserves a bit of fancy wrap
a ribbon of degrees, a bow of accreditation,
the sense that when you rip through all the fancy paper,
there's something different and solid inside,
perhaps a fruitcake or exotic nuts.

In his workaday world there was no room for school,
no student unions in the dark satanic mills,
whose forges burn, heedless of the liberal arts,
melding souls into more useful things,
like plyboard or plasticine.

His dreams were not bounded by paychecks or promotions,
he saw himself giving speeches in small museums,
brick meeting halls once owned by utopian communities,
but now filled with many people—mostly sane—
politely applauding his talks on local history, and where people lived
when they died.

So he headed to the bookstore with the computer terminals and clerks
whose faces are stamped, as if by a punch-press, with the expression that says
a major corporation may own this shop, but I still wear berets and drink cappucino,
as they add to the bottom line of corporations whose annual reports
speak in units sold rather than volumes read.

He found a pantheon of gods of correspondence study,
all the "doctor bear's" and "degree by mail" and "campus-free degree"
books one could imagine, promising secrets, perhaps mystic,
for entering into secret pacts with remote universities,
accredited ways to prove that one learned what one knows.

For in our curious world one is not entitled to profess to others
unless the letters on one's plaque say the right things;
"P's," "H's" and "D's" rather than "B's" or "A's;"
just as a surgeon wields no scalpel based on skill alone,
but based instead upon "M.D."

Now he labors, in his attic, his mouse upon his rolltop desk,
a scholar and postage-stamp purchaser,
sending mentors he's never met
manuscripts about obscure things,
so that someday these strangers will tell him he has knowledge.

19

Accredited Schools with
Short Residency Programs

I forget what I was taught. I only remember what I learned.

PATRICK WHITE

Any school can claim that it is accredited; the use of that word is not regulated in any way. This chapter includes only those schools that are accepted as "accredited" under GAAP, Generally Accepted Accreditation Principles. In the U.S., there is near-unanimous agreement on GAAP (although not everyone calls it this, the concept is widely accepted) by the relevant key decision-makers: university registrars and admissions officers, corporate human resource officers, and government agencies.

Note that in some countries, the word "accredited" is not used, although the evaluation process in that country (e.g., the British Royal Charter), is accepted as "accredited" under GAAP.

Note, too, that schools that do not meet the standards of GAAP are not necessarily bad, illegal, or fake. They simply would not be generally accepted as accredited.

All schools in this chapter meet the standards of GAAP, which means that they meet any one of the following six criteria:

GAAP CRITERIA

◆ Accredited by an agency recognized by the Council on Higher Education Accreditation in Washington.

◆ Accredited by an agency recognized by the U.S. Department of Education.

◆ Listed in the International Handbook of Universities (a UNESCO publication).

◆ Listed in the Commonwealth Universities Yearbook.

◆ Listed in the World Education Series, published by PIER (Projects in International Education Research), a joint venture of AACRAO (the American Association of Collegiate Registrars and Admissions Officers) and NAFSA (the Association of International Educators) with the participation of the College Board.

◆ Listed in the Countries Series, published by NOOSR, the National Office for Overseas Skills Recognition, in Australia.

The basic format of each listing is as follows:

Name of School   **A**ssociate's, **B**achelor's, **M**aster's, **D**octorate, **Law**, **D**iploma
Address
City, State Postal Code Country, if not U.S.
Fields of study offered
Year founded
Ownership (nonprofit or proprietary, state, private, or church-run)
Phone • Toll-free phone
Fax
E-mail address
Website URL

Note: We have in the past given cost information, but this changes so quickly and is so subjective that we have decided to discontinue the practice. If a program is extremely inexpensive, or disproportionately expensive, we've mentioned this in the listing. In most cases, the best way to find out about the cost of any particular program is to contact the school directly.

American College   M

270 Bryn Mawr Ave.
Bryn Mawr, PA 19010
Fields offered: Professional
Year founded: 1927
Ownership: Nonprofit, independent
Phone: (610) 526-1000
Fax: (610) 526-1310

E-mail: studentservices@amercoll.edu
Website: www.amercoll.edu
Offers an external Master of Science in financial services and a Master of Science in management, through a combination of distance courses and two one-week residency programs. Also offers the Chartered Life Underwriter (CLU), Chartered Financial Consultant (ChFC), Registered Health Underwriter (RHU), and Registered Employee Benefits Counselor (REBC) designation programs.

American Technological University
See: University of Central Texas

Andrews University   D
Berrien Springs, MI 49104
Fields offered: Education
Year founded: 1874
Ownership: Nonprofit, church
Phone: (616) 471-7771
Fax: (616) 471-6900
E-mail: enroll@andrews.edu
Website: www.cs.andrews.edu/index.html
The Ed.D. and Ph.D. can be earned entirely through summer residency over several summers.

Antioch University   M
Antioch International
Individualized Master of Arts Program
800 Livermore St.
Yellow Springs, OH 45387
Fields offered: Many fields
Year founded: 1852
Ownership: Nonprofit, independent
Phone: (937) 767-6325 • (800) ANTIOCH
Fax: (937) 767-6461
E-mail: admissions@antiochla.edu
Website: www.antiochla.edu
Antioch offers student-designed programs leading to the Master of Arts degree two five-day seminars must be attended on Antioch's Yellow Springs, Ohio campus. Each student develops an individualized curriculum under the direction of two degree committee members who are recruited by the student and approved by Antioch University, then completes the coursework in that student's own community. Coursework may include independent study, research, practicums, workshops, conferences, tutorials, and traditional courses at other institutions. Thesis is required. Popular fields include conflict resolution, peace studies, counseling, applied psychology, creative writing, environmental studies, women's studies, and education. Antioch also offers educational programs through campuses in Los Angeles, Santa Barbara, Seattle, Keene, New Hampshire, and other locations worldwide. Beginning in June 1997 the school has offered a short-residency M.F.A. writers program. This two-and-a-half-year program includes two ten-day residencies in Los Angeles, and ongoing communication with faculty mentors over the Internet. In addition, the school is working on a Ph.D. program in whole systems design, to be ready sometime in 1998. The school's L.A. campus is located at::
13274 Fiji Way
Marina del Rey, CA 90292
(310) 578-1090

Antioch University Seattle   B, M
2607 Second Avenue
Seattle, WA 98121-1211
Fields offered: Whole systems design, psychology, education, management
Phone: (206) 441-5352
Website: www.seattleantioch.edu
Has not responded to several requests for information about their nontraditional programs. Almost certainly affiliated with Antioch University in Ohio. A Ph.D. in whole systems design is supposed to debut by 1998.

Atlantic Union College   B
South Lancaster, MA 01561
Fields offered: Many fields
Year founded: 1882
Ownership: Nonprofit, church
Phone: (978) 368-2000 • (800) 282-2030
Fax: (978) 368-2015
Website: www.atlanticuc.edu
Students take one "unit" each semester. A "unit" is a six-month study project, requiring two weeks on campus, and the balance of the time in independent study. A minimum of at least the two final units must be taken within the Adult Degree Program; hence four weeks of residency is required to earn the Bachelor's degree. Bachelor's degrees are offered in art, behavioral science, communications, computer science, education, English, history, interior design, modern languages, personal ministries, physical education, psychology, regional studies, religion, theology, and women's studies. Experiential learning credit through portfolio appraisal.

Atlantic University   M
Building 3300, Suite 100
397 Little Neck Road
Virginia Beach, VA 23452
Fields offered: Transpersonal studies
Year founded: 1930
Ownership: Nonprofit
Phone: (757) 631-8101 • (800) 428-1512
Fax: (757) 631-8096
E-mail: admissions@atlanticuniv.edu or info@atlanticuniv.edu
Website: www.atlanticuniv.edu
Originally established in 1930 by the Edgar Cayce Foundation, but dormant from 1932 to 1985. The program is interdisciplinary, exposing learners to the transpersonal aspects of psychology, science, and various spiritual traditions. Concentrations are available in archetypal studies, holistic health and living, intuitive studies, transper-

sonal counseling, and visual arts from a transpersonal approach. The M.A. can be earned with ten correspondence courses, plus two courses taken in residence; these two can be taken in one intensive summer session.

Auburn University M

Graduate Outreach Program
202 Ramsay Hall
Auburn, AL 36849
Fields offered: Business, engineering
Year founded: 1856
Ownership: Nonprofit, state
Phone: (334) 844-4000 • (888) 844-5300
Fax: (334) 844-2519
E-mail: durrocl@eng.auburn.edu
Website: www.auburn.edu

Auburn offers an almost totally nonresident M.B.A. and Master of Engineering in a range of fields, including aerospace, chemical, civil/environmental, computer science, industrial, materials, and mechanical engineering. Graduate courses are taped in on-campus classrooms and mailed to distance students, who must keep the same pace as resident students. The M.B.A. requires three days on campus for a team case analysis; the engineering degrees require one day for oral exams. Homework and test dates are set during the quarter by each instructor. Auburn presently serves over 400 working professionals in 40 states through this graduate education program. One correspondent has told us he found the courses very pricy, and that some instructors don't allow enough time for mailing, meaning that video students are perpetually behind classroom students. Others have been very happy with the program; you might want to talk to each professor about how the transit time for videos and homework assignments is dealt with. The program is limited to U.S. residents; the only overseas students are U.S. military personnel with APO/FPO addresses.

Australian Graduate School of Business University of New South Wales

Sydney 2052
Australia
Fields offered: General management with an emphasis on strategy.
Year founded: 1977
Phone: (61-2) 9931-9412
Fax: (61-2) 9931-9205
E-mail: EMBA@agsm.unsw.edu.au
Website: www.agsm.unsw.edu.au

M.B.A. available through a combination of distance-learning, courses taken at sites around Australia, and four six-day residencies in Sydney during the final year. The program is only available to managers working in the six city network. Class attendance is mandatory.

Bard College B

Continuing Studies Program
Annandale-on-Hudson, NY 12504
Fields offered: Many fields
Year founded: 1860
Ownership: Nonprofit, independent
Phone: (914) 758-6822
Fax: (914) 758-4294
E-mail: admission@bard.edu
Website: www.bard.edu

Bachelor of Arts, Bachelor of Science, and Bachelor of Professional Studies, designed "to meet the special needs of adults who have left college without completing their studies." Credit for prior learning experiences and for achievement measured by standard proficiency tests. Students attend evening seminars and classes which meet two hours each week; they may also meet with tutors for advanced study twice a month over the course of a 15-week term, or enroll in the regular daytime undergraduate classes. Minimum time to complete the degree is one academic year (10 months), and 40 of the required 124 units must be earned from Bard.

Bishop Clarkson College B

333 S. 44th St.
Omaha, NE 68131
Fields offered: Nursing, health sciences, radiology
Year founded: 1888
Ownership: Nonprofit, independent
Phone: (402) 552-3100 • (800) 647-5500
Fax: (402) 552-2899
E-mail: admiss@clrkcol.crhsnet.edu
Website: www.clarksoncollege.edu

B.S. in nursing or radiology technology, M.S. in nursing or health sciences management through a combination of traditional courses, credit for exams, audio- and videotaped classes, independent study, instruction by phone, mail, or e-mail, supervised fieldwork, computer-assisted instruction, and externships. Students must attend one on-campus evaluation in Nebraska, and "geographically distant" RN undergrads meet with faculty three to four times each semester. Graduate courses meet three weekends out of every 12-week trimester.

Bluefield State College

See: West Virginia Board of Regents B.A. Program

Boricua College B

3755 Broadway
New York, NY 10032
Fields offered: Liberal arts, natural and social sciences, business, education
Year founded: 1974
Ownership: Nonprofit, independent
Phone: (212) 694-1000
Fax: (212) 694-1015

Website: www.greatcollegetown.com/boric.html
Bilingual (Spanish/English) college, offering a B.S. through individualized instruction, independent study, and field internships.

Brigham Young University B

305 Harman Building
P.O. Box 21515
Provo , UT 84602-1515
Fields offered: Independent studies
Year founded: 1875
Ownership: Nonprofit, private
Phone: (801) 378-4351
Fax: (801) 378-3949
E-mail: disoffice@byu.edu
Website: coned.byu.edu./dis/dis.htm

Brigham Young's Bachelor of Independent Studies Degree (DIS) program involves independent study and a short period of on-campus study. The degree requires attendance at a maximum of five two-week on-campus seminars—one for each of five areas of study—plus a one-week "closure seminar" prior to graduation. Prior college credits can be transferred into the program, where they will be applied towards DIS course requirements, as applicable.

Burlington College B

95 North Ave.
Burlington ,VT 05401
Fields offered: Cinema studies, transpersonal psychology, psychology, writing & literature
Year founded: 1972
Ownership: Nonprofit, independent
Phone: (802) 862-9616 • (800) 862-9616
Fax: (802) 658-0071
E-mail: admissions@burlcol.edu
Website: www.burlcol.edu

Bachelor of Arts through the primarily nonresident "Independent Degree Program" (IDP). IDP students must have completed 45 college credits and have "strong writing skills and a track record in independent study," and must be able to spend four days on the Vermont campus at the beginning of each semester. IDP students must complete a minimum of 30 credits through the program, regardless of prior experience. Although programs are highly individualized, the school specifically encourages applicants whose interests fall in the fields of fine arts, humanities, psychology, transpersonal psychology, or "almost any liberal arts area(s) of study." Formerly Vermont Institute of Community Involvement.

Caldwell College B

External Degree Program
9 Ryerson Ave.
Caldwell, NJ 07006
Fields offered: Many fields
Year founded: 1979
Ownership: Nonprofit, church

Phone: (973) 228-4424
Fax: (973) 228-2897
E-mail: CaldwellCE@aol.com
Website: www.caldwell.edu

Bachelor's degrees in the fields of accounting, business administration, communication arts, computer information systems, criminal justice, English, foreign languages, history, international business, management, marketing, political science, psychology, religious studies, and sociology. This is primarily an off-campus, independent study program that utilizes tutorial relationships with professors. Students spend one weekend per semester on campus. Credit is given for life experience assessment and by examination.

California Institute of Integral Studies B, M, D

9 Peter Yorke Way
San Francisco, CA 94109
Fields offered: Many fields
Year founded: 1968
Ownership: Nonprofit, independent
Phone: (415) 674-5500
Fax: (415) 674-5555
E-mail: info@ciis.edu
Website: www.ciis.edu

Master's degrees are offered in counseling psychology (with concentrations in drama therapy, expressive arts therapy, integral counseling psychology, and somatic psychology), East-West psychology, organizational development & transformation, social & cultural anthropology, and philosophy & religion (with concentrations in Asian & comparative studies, philosophy, cosmology & consciousness, and women's spirituality). The Ph.D. is available in East-West psychology, philosophy & religion, social & cultural anthropology, and transformative learning. Psy.D. is available in clinical psychology. Most programs involve a combination of intellectual study, on-line interaction, personal experience of psycho-spiritual growth processes, and practical fieldwork in counseling, community service, teaching, or creative independent study. Also offered is a B.A. completion program geared to working adults who need up to 45 credits to finish their degree (credit available for life-experience learning). Most programs involve a combination of intellectual study, "personal experience of psycho-spiritual growth," and practical fieldwork (counseling, community service, teaching, or creative independent study). Formerly California Institute of Asian Studies.

Calumet College B

2400 New York Ave.
Whiting, IN 46394
Fields offered: Many fields
Year founded: 1951
Ownership: Nonprofit, church
Phone: (219) 473-4215
Fax: (219) 473-4259
Website: www.ccsj.edu

Bachelor's degrees in general studies, social studies, humanities and arts, business administration, and other individualized programs. Up to 75 percent of the units required can come from an assessment of prior learning experience. A course is offered in the preparation of life experience portfolios. An off-campus degree-completion program was established in 1987. In this program, adult students who have already completed 60 credit hours can earn their B.S. in management in 54 weeks, attending class one evening per week.

Capital University   B

Adult Degree Program
330 Renner Hall
Columbus, OH 43209
Fields offered: Many fields
Year founded: 1976
Ownership: Nonprofit, church
Phone: (614) 236-6374
Fax: (614) 236-6374
E-mail: gsmith@capital.edu
Website: www.capital.edu

A University Without Walls program begun in 1976 by the Union for Experimenting Colleges and Universities and taken over in 1979 by the venerable Capital University. Beginning students must complete the equivalent of 124 semester credit hours, largely through guided independent study. Degrees that can be earned are: Bachelor of Arts, with various majors, Bachelor of General Studies with no major, Bachelor of Social Work, and Bachelor of Nursing. All students must complete a senior project, showing Bachelor's-level abilities and serving as a learning experience. The university maintains Adult Degree Program offices in Cleveland and Dayton as well. Evening and weekend courses and credit for experiential learning available through portfolio assessment/competency statement development.

Case Western Reserve University   M, D

University Circle
Cleveland, OH 44106
Fields offered: Nursing
Year founded: 1826
Ownership: Independent, nonprofit
Phone: (216) 368-2000 • (800) 825-2540
Fax: (216) 368-3988
E-mail: tfw@po.cwru.edu
Website: www.cwru.edu

According to a correspondent, the venerable Case Western has joined the ranks of the nontraditionalists, but hasn't advertised the programs, as they fill up on word of mouth alone. They offer an intensive M.S. in nursing for RNs who have a B.S. in nursing and have graduated from a nurse practitioner certificate program and hold certification as a nurse practitioner. Candidates who meet these criteria can be awarded as much as 22 semester hours of graduate credit. To complete the degree, Case offers four weeks

of intensive classes on campus, presented between semesters, and a final class completed independently. Nurse practitioners from across America—including Hawaii—are enrolled in the program. Students go to Cleveland for a week of intensive classes at a time, staying in dorm rooms for $10 per night. The program is a bit pricy, but leads to a degree from one of America's most prestigious nursing schools.

They also offer the Nursing Doctorate (N.D.) for M.S.N. students in the intensive format. The N.D. is a clinically (rather than research) focused degree.

CBN University

See: Regent University

Charles Sturt University   B, M, D

International Division
Locked Bag 676
Wagga Wagga, NSW 2678 Australia
Fields offered: Many fields
Year founded: 1989
Ownership: Nonprofit
Phone: (61-69) 22-2000
Fax: (61-69) 22-2639
Website: www.csu.edu.au

In 1989, Mitchell College of Advanced Education and Riverina-Murray Institute of Higher Education merged to form this school. According to their literature, about two-thirds of Charles Sturt's students study by distance education, and the school is active in developing correspondence courses for other universities. Degrees are offered in a range of fields, grouped into the basic fields: Bachelor of Applied Science, Arts, Business, Education, Health Science, Information Technology, Policing, Social Science, and Social Work, each with a range of concentration, including some unusual fields (i.e., viticulture, equine studies, food science, and more). Bachelors of Health Science in Pre Hospital Care grants advanced standing for previous paramedic training and can be done completely by correspondence. Master's degrees are available in accountancy, arts, and applied science, and there is a Ph.D. in commerce, arts, education, or science/agriculture, as well as an Ed.D. Students in the Americas may find it more convenient to contact the following agent:

Robert Millar
International Student Recruiting Services
2 Polo Court
Ancaster, ON L9K 1H8, Canada
Phone/fax: (905) 648-7130

Chicago State University   B

University Without Walls
95th Street at King Drive
Chicago, IL 60628
Fields offered: Many fields
Year founded: 1867
Ownership: Nonprofit, state

Phone: (773) 995-2455
Fax: (773) 995-2563
E-mail: bagolee@csu.edu
Website: www.csu.edu

Most University Without Walls students enter with some prior college experience, and are expected to be actively engaged in their proposed field of study and to commit 20 hours a week to the program. Students "identify their own educational needs and propose means to satisfy them," with the help of a faculty advisor and learning coordinators. All students must satisfy general ed requirements in English composition, humanities, mathematics, and natural and social sciences. Other work may include traditional classes, seminars, readings, research, reports and surveys, and so on. In the last term, every student must complete a final project demonstrating mastery in his or her field. See also: Board of Governors B.A. Degree Program

Columbia University   M, D

Teachers College, 525 West 121st St.
New York, NY 10027
Fields offered: Education
Year founded: 1887
Ownership: Nonprofit, independent
Phone: (212) 678-3000
Fax: (212) 678-4048
E-mail: jbf9@columbia.edu
Website: www.tc.columbia.edu

The Doctor of Education is offered through an innovative program called AEGIS: Adult Education Guided Independent Study. The program requires two years to complete, largely through guided independent study, with advisement by correspondence, telephone, or optional campus visits. Participants must attend a seminar on campus one Saturday each month, plus a three-week intensive summer session for both summers of enrollment. The program is designed for experienced, self-directed professionals with at least five years of experience in program development or administration of adult education or training. Admission is highly competitive; about twenty students are admitted every other year. The M.A. in technology & education is offered through independent study, with 2 or 3 summer sessions. There are concentrations in multimedia development in education, telecommunications & global issues, or teaching & learning with technology. The contact for this program is Howard Budin, phone (212) 678-3773, hb50@columbia.edu

Concordia University   B, M

School-Age Care Office
275 Syndicate Street North
St. Paul, MN 55104
Fields offered: School age child care
Year founded: 1893
Ownership: Nonprofit, church
Phone: (612) 641-8278 • (800) 211-3370
Fax: (612) 603-6144

E-mail: saccsp@aol.com • schoolage@luther.csp.edu
Website: www.csp.edu/sac.html

Bachelor's and Master's degrees in school-age care (a field involving the care of children before and after school) can be earned almost wholly through nontraditional methods, requiring only 5 days in residency for orientation. Coursework takes place through e-mail, on-line discussion groups, bulletin boards, phone conferences, and audio- and videotapes. This is the first program to address this field—focusing not just on daycare basics, but on child development, socialization, child-centered advocacy, and other factors.

Dalhousie University   M

Henson College
6100 University Avenue
Halifax, NS B3H 3J5 Canada
Fields offered: Business
Phone: (902) 494-1378 • (800) 205-7510
Fax: (902) 494-1107
E-mail: registration@hen.henson.dal.ca
Website: www.mgmt.dal.ca

Through its Henson College of Public Affairs and Continuing Education, Dalhousie University offers an impressive number of certificates in business-related and other fields (local government administration, fire service administration, police leadership, adult education, etc.) as well as an M.B.A. with a focus in financial services, in partnership with the Institute of Canadian Bankers. Designed for managers in the financial services industry, the courses are taught through a combination of distance and traditional methods, culminating in a week-long residential "capstone course."

Davis and Elkins College   B

Mentor-Assisted Program
100 Campus Drive
Elkins, WV 26241
Fields offered: Various fields
Year founded: 1904
Ownership: Nonprofit, church
Phone: (304) 637-1900 • (800) 624-3157
Fax: (304) 637-1419
E-mail: admiss@dne.wvnet.edu
Website: www.dne.wvnet.edu

The Bachelor of Arts or Science in business, management, and other fields can be completed by correspondence courses and independent study, with assistance and guidance by telephone, or with a total of two weeks on the campus, in a few short visits over the course of the program.

DePaul University   B, M

23 East Jackson Blvd.
Chicago , IL 60604
Fields offered: Liberal arts, nursing
Year founded: 1898
Ownership: Nonprofit, church

Phone: (312) 362-6300
Fax: (312) 363-6309
Website: www.depaul.edu
Bachelor's in general liberal arts, BSN and MSN offered via distance-learning methods, to local-area students only.

Duke University   M

The Fuqua School of Business
Box 90127
Durham, NC 27708-0127
Fields offered: Business
Year founded: 1838
Ownership: Nonprofit, independent
Phone: (919) 660-7705 • (800) 372-3932
Fax: (919) 681-7761
E-mail: fuqua-execed@mail.duke.edu
Website: www.fuqua.duke.edu
Duke's Global Executive MBA (GEMBA) program is a 19-month program designed for experienced managers who want to learn more about global management. It combines five 2-week residential sessions at sites in Europe, Asia, and North and South America with continuing distance education using a wide range of interactive communication tools. The majority of learning is done over the Internet using Lotus Notes or equivalent technology. In addition to using bulletin boards and e-mail for case discussion, students use multimedia lesson plans and Web pages, among other methods, to communicate, research, and learn. Prospective students in Europe can contact the following:

David Miller, Director of European Relations
The Fuqua School of Business
Duke University
IBM International Education Center
Chaussee de Bruxelles 135, Room 14245
B-13010 La Hulpe
Belgium
Phone: (32-2) 655-5857
Fax: (32-2) 655-5739
E-mail: 75677.2417@compuserve.com
The American contact for the program is Richard Staelin at the Fuqua School of Business.

East Carolina University   M

Industrial Technology
Flanagan Building
Room 126
Greenville, NC 27858
Fields offered: Industrial technology; education
Year founded: 1907
Ownership: Nonprofit, state
Phone: (919) 328-4249
Fax: (919) 328-1618
E-mail: itfreind@homer.sit.ecu.edu
Website: www.sit.ecu.edu/trp/masters/home.htm
An M.S. in industrial technology with three possible concentrations, safety, digital communication and manufacturing, is offered over the Internet. The program is career

oriented, and includes practical on-the job experience. The Master's may be completed without a thesis by taking two additional courses and submitting a portfolio of relevant work experience. M.Ed. for in-state students only.

Eastern New Mexico University   B, M

Station #9
Portales, NM 99130
Fields offered: Business, nursing
Year founded: 1934
Ownership: Nonprofit, state
Phone: (505) 562-2166
Fax: (505) 562-2168
E-mail: a.schreoder@enmu.edu
Website: www.enmu.edu/
Bachelor's and Master's degrees in business and nursing offered via distance learning to students in southeastern New Mexico only.

Elizabethtown College   B

Elizabethtown, PA 17022
Fields offered: Professional studies
Year founded: 1899
Ownership: Nonprofit, church
Phone: (717) 361-1411 • (800) 877-2694
Fax: (717) 361-1466
E-mail: admissions@acad.etown.edu
Website: www.etown.edu
Bachelor of Professional Studies offered through the EXCEL program. Majors offered in the B.P.S. degree program are: business administration, communications, criminal justice, early childhood education (non–teaching certification), human services, medical technology, and public administration. Applicants must have a minimum of seven year's work experience related to the major field of study and at least 50 semester hours of college study, grade C or better, at regionally accredited institutions, and reside within 400 miles of the college. Credit awarded for CLEP/DANTE exams, certain structured noncredit learning, and (up to 32 semester hours) for experiential learning in the major field of study.

Fielding Institute   M, D

2122 Santa Barbara Street
Santa Barbara, CA 93105
Fields offered: Psychology, human and organizational development, education leadership & change
Year founded: 1974
Ownership: Nonprofit, independent
Phone: (805) 687-1099 • (800) 340-1099
Fax: (805) 687-4590
E-mail: admissions@fielding.edu
Website: www.fielding.edu
Students must attend a five-day admissions workshop in Santa Barbara (held March, June, and September) before enrolling. This is the only required residency. Regional research sessions and academic seminars are offered at

various locations throughout the year. The human and organizational development program offers an Ed.D., a Ph.D. in human and organizational systems or human development, a D.H.S. (Doctor of Human Services), and a Master's degree. The psychology program offers a Ph.D. in clinical psychology. The degrees are neither fast nor easy, but are designed to enable mid-career professionals to attain advanced degrees. It typically takes three to six years to complete the requirements for a doctoral degree. The psychology program has a residency requirement that can be completed through attendance at local student meetings. All students and faculty must have access to an electronic network which offers electronic mail, bulletin board service, and academic seminars. A correspondent tells us that this is the only primarily distance program in clinical psychology recognized by the APA under its new "provisional accreditation" guidelines.

Florida Atlantic University   M

777 Glades Rd.
Boca Raton, FL 33431
Fields offered: Engineering, nursing, education, sciences
Year founded: 1961
Ownership: Nonprofit, state
Phone: (561) 297-3690
Fax: (561) 297-3668
E-mail: admisweb@acc.fau.edu
Website: www.fau.edu/

Degrees including M.S. and M.E. in engineering fields (civil, computer science, electrical, manufacturing systems, mechanical, and ocean engineering) through closed-circuit television and videocassette, offered statewide. Some on-campus residency required.

Framingham State College   B

100 State St., P.O. Box 2000
Framingham, MA 01701
Fields offered: Liberal studies
Year founded: 1839
Ownership: Nonprofit, state
Phone: (508) 620-1220
Fax: (508) 626-4017
Website: www.framingham.edu/

Bachelor of Arts in liberal studies in which units may be earned through equivalency exams, independent study, correspondence study, prior learning experiences, and "non-credit educational experiences." The remaining units must be earned by taking courses on campus, through a series of weekend or summer seminars, or by making other arrangements satisfactory to the advisory committee.

Friends University   B, M

College of Continuing Education
2100 University
Wichita, KS 67213

Fields offered: Management (business, human resources, total quality), computer information systems, criminal justice
Year founded: 1898
Ownership: Church
Phone: (316) 265-5300 • (800)794-6945
Fax: (316) 264-3269
E-mail: admit@friends.edu
Website: www.friends.edu

The Bachelor's degrees are done through the PACE model (one or two nights a week plus all day Saturday). The Master's degrees require one night a week for about 75 weeks total.

Goddard College   B, M

Plainfield, VT 05667
Fields offered: Many fields
Year founded: 1938
Ownership: Nonprofit, independent
Phone: (802) 454-8311 • (800) 468-4888
Fax: (802) 454-8017
E-mail: admissions@earth.goddard.edu
Website: sun.goddard.edu

Goddard has been a pioneer in nontraditional, progressive education for more than fifty years. They offer nontraditional options for studies in business and organizational leadership, education, psychology and counseling, natural and physical sciences, feminist studies, visual and performing arts, literature and writing, and social and cultural studies (history, philosophy, religious studies). The first eight days of each semester are spent in residency, where the work of the coming semester is planned. Students may choose to do the majority of their coursework off-campus while maintaining contact by mail every three weeks. Both Bachelor's and Master's programs require a minimum enrollment: two semesters for the Bachelor's, three for the Master's. Credit is available for prior learning, but life experience credit is given only at the Bachelor's level.

Goucher College   M

1021 Dulaney Valley Road
Baltimore, MD 21204
Fields offered: Creative nonfiction, historic preservation
Year founded: 1885
Ownership: Nonprofit
Phone: (410) 337-6200
Fax: (410) 337-6085
E-mail: center@goucher.edu

The Master's degree in creative nonfiction or historic preservation is available to US & Canadians only. Courses are delivered to the student's home, and three two-week summer sessions are required over the course of study.

Graceland College   B

Outreach Program, Division of Nursing
Lamoni, IA 50140

Fields offered: Nursing, liberal studies, addiction studies
Year founded: 1895
Ownership: Nonprofit, church
Phone: (515) 784-5000 • (800) 537-6276
Fax: (515) 784-5480
E-mail: admissions@graceland.edu
Website: www.graceland.edu/

B.S. in nursing designed for working R.N.s, and B.A. in liberal studies. Courses include projects, home study texts, learning guides (developed by Graceland faculty), videotapes, tests, and final proctored exam. Students are provided a toll-free number for contact with instructors. Up to 64 credit hours can come from evaluation of prior education and experience. B.S.N. program has clinical components; student can come to campus to fulfill these or find a college-approved preceptor to monitor their progress in their own community. There are mandatory two-week residency sessions twice a year.

(The) Graduate School of America   M, D

330 2nd Ave. South, #550
Minneapolis, MN 55401
Fields offered: Education, human services, business adminstration, organization and management
Year founded: 1993
Ownership: Proprietary
Phone: (612) 339-8650 • (800) 987-1133
Fax: (612) 339-8022
E-mail: tgsainfo@tgsa.edu
Website: www.tgsa.edu

The Graduate School of America is a major, well-funded relatively new institution created along the lines of Walden University and the Union Institute: long periods of guided independent study and research, with an intensive two-to-three-week summer residency. Currently, the school offers an M.S. in the following fields: education, human services (with optional emphases in counseling, health & human services, marriage & family services, and social & community services), health & human services, and organization & management (with optional emphases in communications technology, human resources, and training & development). The Ph.D. is offered in education (with a number of concentrations), human services, and organization & management (with an option concentration in communication technology). An M.B.A. is in the review stage; psychology degrees are in the offing, as are Bachelor's degrees. Certificates are also offered.

Henson College
See: Dalhousie University

Humanistic Psychology Institute
See: Saybrook Graduate School

Illinois Institute of Technology   M
IITV
10 West 31st St., 226 SB
Chicago, IL 60616

Fields offered: Engineering, chemistry
Year founded: 1890
Ownership: Nonprofit
Phone: 312-567-3167
Fax: 312-567-5913
E-mail: ia_pryor@vax1.ais.iit.edu
Website: www.dlt.iit.edu

Master's in chemistry is non-residential. Masters in chemical, mechanical, and aerospace engineering may require campus visits for examinations or presentations. Some courses available only to local area students. Check with school. Course information is exchanged through video-conferences, telephone, fax, and e-mail. Some courses use videotape.

Institute for European Business Administration   M

American office: 815B Rockville Pike, #155
Rockville, MD 20852
Fields offered: Business administration
Phone: (33) 1 60 72 40 00
Fax: (33) 1 60 74 55 00
E-mail: webmaster@insead.fr
Website: www.insead.fr/

This Belgian school offers American students an M.B.A. with an emphasis on European business through distance learning, with a five-week intensive residential program offered through the accredited George Mason University in Virginia.

Institute of Canadian Bankers
See: Dalhousie University

International Management Centres Inc.   B, M

Castle Street
Buckingham, England Mk18 1BP
Fields offered: Management, business administration, training and development
Year founded: 1964
Ownership: Nonprofit
Phone: (44-1280) 817-222
E-mail: imc@imc.org.uk
Website: www.imc.org.uk/imc/contact.htm

Offers the Bachelor's and Master's in management, business administration, and training and development. Credit for prior learning on Bachelor program except final credits. All programs are work-based action learning and must have a sponsorship of employers. Short residency requirements are at tutorial centers in one of 25 countries worldwide or in companies for groups of managers. Apparently the only doctorate-granting school accredited by the Distance Education and Training Council. Formerly associated with Northland Open University, and now with the Canadian School of Management.

Under their own headline of "GLOBAL PARTNERS' SELLING INTERNET BACHELOR & MBA" IMC's website announced a new company to promote on-line degrees.

They say "£300,000 has been subscribed by BSN and IMC (Europe and Africa) + IMC (Asia Pacific) Limited. This is to fund the initial design, Internet site, and marketing planning phases. The outcomes will be elegantly ready by December 5th."

Iowa State University B, M

100 Alumni Hall
Ames, IA 50011-2010
Fields offered: Many fields
Year founded: 1858
Ownership: Nonprofit, state
Phone: (515) 294-5836 • (800) 262-3810
Fax: (515) 294-0565
E-mail: admissions@iastate.edu
Website: www.iastate.edu/~adm_info/homepage.html

The university offers an external degree called the Bachelor of Liberal Studies, primarily for residents of Iowa who are able to attend one of the off-campus centers around the state or occasional courses on the Ames campus. Previous Iowa State students with sufficient credit may also be eligible for the program. In addition, evening and weekend courses are offered toward degrees in agriculture, business, design, education, engineering, family & consumer sciences, and liberal arts & sciences. Upper-division B.S. in agriculture (for students who have completed their first two years of study elsewhere) and Master of Agriculture (M.Ag) largely through locally available satellite and cable television programs, as well as videotaped programs. A Saturday M.B.A. program is also available. Many courses require one Saturday on campus per credit, plus one week during the summer. See also: Quad Cities Graduate Center.

Kings College B

Gateway Adult Program
Wilkes-Barre, PA 18711
Fields offered: Many fields
Year founded: 1946
Ownership: Nonprofit, independent
Phone: (717) 826-5865
Fax: (717) 825-9049
E-mail: admssns@leo.kings.edu
Website: www.kings.edu

For years, we've argued with Darlene A. Gavenonis, Office Coordinator for the school's Center for Lifelong Learning, over her desire that we not list Kings' innovative short-residency degree program. Okay Ms. Gavenonis, you win. We're not talking about it.

Korea National Open University B

Institute of Distance Education
169 Dongsung-Dong, Chongro-Ku
Seoul, 110-791 Korea
Fields offered: Arts, law, business, education, health, home economics, public administration, agriculture.

Study occurs via printed materials— correspondence textbooks, supplementary reading materials, and the university newspaper—radio and television broadcast lectures, audio and video cassettes. Attendance at a 5-day classroom session is required; computer mediated communication services supplement subjects.

Lindenwood College B, M

St. Charles, MO 63301
Fields offered: Many fields
Year founded: 1827
Ownership: Nonprofit, independent
Phone: (314) 949-2000
Fax: (314) 949-4910
E-mail: admissions@lindenwood.edu
Website: www.lindenwood.edu

B.A., B.S., M.A., and M.S. through the College for Individualized Education, in administration, psychology, health administration, gerontology, valuation sciences, communications, human and organizational development may be earned through evening and summer programs. The International Valuation Sciences degree program is primarily an off-campus degree program for experienced appraisers. There is a two-week on-campus session each year for at least two years. Credit for independent study, nonacademic prior learning, and by examination.

Liverpool John Moores University B

2 Rodney Street
Liverpool, L3 5UX England
Fields offered: Health care
Year founded: 1970
Phone: (44-151) 231-2121
Fax: (44-151) 709-0172
Website: www.livjm.ac.uk

The former Liverpool Polytechnic offers a B.A. in health care (specifically, quality assurance in nursing) through a combination of distance and residential learning. They also offer entirely nonresident diplomas in health care and community health care.

Liverpool Polytechnic

See: Liverpool John Moores University

Maine College of Art M

97 Spring St.
Portland, ME 04101
Fields offered: Art
Year founded: 1882
Ownership: Nonprofit, independent
Phone: (207) 775-3052 • (800) 639-4808
Fax: (207) 775-5069
E-mail: gsmith@meca.edu
Website: www.meca.edu

A 24-month Master of Fine Arts, combining intensive summer residencies (a total of about 500 hours each summer) with tutored independent study. The intent was to create a program that "meets or exceeds the rigors and vitality of the traditional model as the 'terminal' professional degree for studio art and design, that accommodates well-qualified and motivated individuals for whom a program of two nine-month residency periods of study is not feasible."

Maine Maritime Academy   M
Department of Graduate Studies
Castine, ME 04420
Fields offered: Maritime & port management
Year founded: 1941
Ownership: Nonprofit, state
Phone: (207) 326-2485 • (800) 227-8465
Fax: (207) 326-2411
E-mail: cjulrich@bell.mmu.edu
Website: bell.mmu.edu

Master of Science in maritime management or port management through modular graduate degree programs that can be completed "without career interruption." This is a business degree with emphasis on marine issues. Courses are scheduled in compact five-week modules that allow participants to remain fully employed while studying. A total of eight five-week modules are required for either Master's degree.

Marshall University
See: West Virginia Board of Regents B.A. Program

Mary Baldwin College   B
Adult Degree Program
Staunton, VA 24401
Fields offered: Many fields
Year founded: 1842
Ownership: Nonprofit, church
Phone: (540) 887-7003 • (800) 882-2460
Fax: (540) 887-7265
E-mail: adp@cit.mbc.edu
Website: www.mbc.edu

Bachelor of Arts program for residents of Virginia, in which work can be done independently, with very few visits required. Students need to come to the campus for a day of orientation, and to regional centers twice a year for conferences with advisors. Advanced standing may be given for work done at other schools, CLEP examinations, and the assessment of prior learning, by portfolio. The degree program has regional offices in Richmond, Charlottesville, Weyers Cave, and Roanoke, Virginia, in addition to the main office in Staunton.

Marywood University   B
Off-Campus Degree Program
2300 Adams Ave.
Scranton, PA 18509-1598
Fields offered: Business administration, accounting
Year founded: 1915
Ownership: Nonprofit, church
Phone: (717) 348-6235 • (800) 836-6940
Fax: (717) 961-4751
E-mail: pmunk@ac.marywood.edu

Website: www.marywood.edu/ww2/conted_adm/cted_de.htm

The Bachelor of Science degree in accounting or business administration (with concentrations in management, financial planning, or marketing) is earned through a combination of directed correspondence study (114 credits) and four weeks of residency (12 credits) held on the campus in one- and/or two-week increments each spring and summer. A minimum of sixty (60) of the required 126 credits must be earned after enrolling at Marywood. Transfer credit is available through the evaluation of prior learning. A deferred tuition payment plan is available as well as financial aid for those who qualify. Correspondence with faculty and administration is available via regular mail, phone, fax, voice mail, and e-mail.

Massachusetts Institute of Technology   M
Building 20B-040
77 Massachusetts Ave. Room 9-234
Cambridge, MA 02139
Fields offered: Engineering, management
Year founded: 1861
Ownership: Nonprofit, independent
Phone: (617) 253-3799
Fax: (617) 253-5229
E-mail: sdm@mit.edu
Website: www-caes.mit.edu

Students must have company sponsorship and be on campus for the first January of the program, and for one semester during the duration of the program.

Massey University   B, M
Centre for University Extramural Studies
Private Bag 11555
Palmerston North, New Zealand
Fields offered: Many fields
Year founded: 1960
Ownership: Nonprofit, state
Phone: (64-6) 350-5644
Fax: (64-6) 350-2268
E-mail: t.k.prebble@massey.ac.nz
Website: www.massey.ac.nz

Massey offers an external degree program, in which the majority of work can be completed by correspondence study, utilizing books, audio- and videocassettes, regional courses, and short on-campus courses, and supported increasingly by telecommunications and computer conferencing. Degrees are offered in humanities, social sciences, science, business studies, agricultural science education, information science, and technology. At present, enrollment in most courses is restricted to citizens of New Zealand.

Medical University of South Carolina   B
Office of Enrollment Services
171 Ashley Ave.
Charleston, SC 29425

Fields offered: Health science
Year founded: 1824
Ownership: State
Phone: (803) 792-5396
Fax: (803) 792-3764
Website: www.musc.edu/

Some courses are offered only in certain areas in the state; some meetings may be required at the Charleston campus. Otherwise, text, computer, and video communications are used to deliver courses.

Mercy College   B, M

555 Broadway
Dobbs Ferry, NY 10522
Fields offered: Many fields
Year founded: 1950
Ownership: Nonprofit, independent
Phone: (914) 693-7600 • (800) MERCY-NY
Fax: (914) 674-7382
E-mail: admissions@merlin.mercynet.edu
Website: merlin.mercynet.edu/programs

Bachelor's degrees through a wide variety of methods designed to accommodate the adult student, including evening classes held twice a week for eight weeks; once-a-week Friday or Saturday classes for 16 weeks; and a home-study program for students who prefer to work independently (on-campus orientation session, midterm, and final exam required). Also summer and January intersession programs. Parallel scheduling is designed to accommodate students who work rotating shifts, such as police and nurses, with the same class taught both day and evening, so that the student may attend either one. Credit is awarded for life achievement and by examination. In addition, the school offers a four-year bilingual program for Spanish-speaking students, and an extensive support program for the learning-disabled.

Metropolitan State University   B

700 E. 7th St.
St. Paul, MN 55101
Fields offered: Many fields
Year founded: 1971
Ownership: Nonprofit, state
Phone: (612) 772-7777
Fax: (612) 772-7738
E-mail: brookins@msus1.msus.edu
Website: www.metro.msus.edu

Metropolitan State University is a pioneer in nontraditional programs, offering flexible Bachelor's and Master's programs, including an individualized Bachelor of Arts, Bachelor of Arts in accounting, business administration, human services, information and computer systems, nursing, professional communications, and a Master of Management and Administration. Daytime, evening, and weekend classes are offered in facilities throughout the Twin Cities area.

Michigan Technological University   B, D

1400 Townsend Drive
Houghton, MI 49931
Fields offered: Engineering, surveying
Year founded: 1885
Ownership: State
Phone: (906) 487-3170
Fax: (906) 487-2463
E-mail: jschultz@mtu.edu
Website: www.damin.mtu.edu/eup

The engineering B.S. is considered a degree completion program. Students must be in proximity to laboratories. The B.S. in surveying can be fully distance learning. There is one doctoral program in mechanical engineering. Students must be sponsored by a corporation or business, and spend approximately 6 weeks on campus for examinations and dissertation defense.

Middlebury College   D

Modern Languages Department
Middlebury, VT 05753-6002
Year founded: 1800
Ownership: Nonprofit, independent
Phone: (802) 443-3000
Fax: (802) 443-2056
E-mail: admissions@middlebury.edu
Website: www.middlebury.edu

A DML, Doctor of Modern Languages, designed for teacher-scholars, is unique to Middlebury. Study is done in two foreign languages and can be completed in a series of summer sessions on the Vermont campus.

Montana State University   M

Intercollege Programs for Science Education
404 Linfield Hall
Montana State University
Bozeman, MT 59717
Fields offered: Science Education
Year founded: 1893
Ownership: Nonprofit, state
Phone: (406) 994-3580
Fax: (406) 994-3733
E-mail: smrc@montana.edu
Website: www.montana.edu/wwwxs

Designed specifically for middle school and high school science teachers, this M.S. in science education begins and ends with a 6-week on-campus summer session. The rest is done through distance learning, with asynchronous, computer-mediated communication. Students take core courses in mathematics and education (15 credits) as well as courses (15 credits) in science content areas including biology, chemistry, earth science, microbiology, and physics.

Murray State University   B, M

Bachelor of Independent Studies
P.O. Box 9
Murray, KY 42071-0009

Fields offered: Independent studies, nursing
Year founded: 1922
Ownership: Nonprofit, state
Phone: (502) 762-4159 • (800) 669-7654
Fax: (502) 762-3593
E-mail: phil.bryan@murraystate.edu
Website: www.mursuky.edu

Bachelor of Independent Studies through correspondence study, television, and contract learning courses. Some weekend and evening classes are available. Thirty-two of the 128 required semester hours must be taken with Murray State. Departmental challenge exams are available in some fields. If the exam is passed, credit is awarded. All students must attend a day-long seminar, held on Saturdays in April, August, and December. Admission to the program is based on satisfactory completion of the seminar. All students must earn credit in basic skills, humanities, science, social sciences, and electives, and complete a study project. Murray State charges a relatively low fee for portfolio assessment. Also, an M.S. for R.N.s who already have a B.S. in nursing, offered by remote television at three sites within a 100-mile radius of the campus. The contact for that program is Dr. Marcia Hobbs, at (502) 762-2193. Overseas applicants are not accepted, and the B.I.S. director tells us that this program seems to work best for students who live within commuting range of Murray State.

National University   M

11255 North Torrey Pines Road
La Jolla, CA 92037
Fields offered: Business administration
Year founded: 1971
Ownership: Nonprofit, independent
Phone: (619) 642-8212
Fax: (619) 642-8709
E-mail: pmontroy@nunir.nu.edu
Website: www.nu.edu

The GMBA requires students to be on campus for the final three courses of a 60 unit program.

New Mexico State University   B, M

Box 3WEC
Las Cruces, NM 88003
Fields offered: Business, education, engineering
Year founded: 1888
Ownership: Nonprofit, state
Phone: (505) 646-5837
Fax: (505) 646-2044
E-mail: lames@nmsu.edu
Website: www.nmsu.edu

B.B.A. for students in the local area, M.S. in education for in-state students, and M.S. in engineering with no residency required are offered at this time.

Northeastern Illinois University   B, M

5500 North St. Louis Ave.
Chicago, IL 60625

Fields offered: Liberal arts, education, business
Year founded: 1961
Ownership: Nonprofit, state
Phone: (773) 794-2600
Fax: (773) 794-6246
E-mail: webteam@neiu.edu
Website: www.neiu.edu

Bachelor of Arts with a minimum residency requirement of 15 semester hours, which can be completed in four months on campus. One of the five Illinois universities participating in the Board of Governors Bachelor of Arts program (see description under separate listing). Credit may be awarded for life experience and all prior learning experiences. New credit may be earned through regular courses at any of the five schools in the program, or by correspondence study and independent study. (The five Board of Governors schools started out with almost identical programs, but now two, Western Illinois and Governors State, offer totally nonresident programs).

Northern Arizona University   B, M

P.O. Box 6235
Yuma, AZ 85366
Fields offered: Education, liberal studies
Year founded: 1899
Ownership: Nonprofit, state
Phone: (520) 317-6432 • (800) 426-8315
Fax: (520) 317-6419
E-mail: undergraduate.admissions@nau.edu
Website: www.nau.edu

B.A. in liberal studies and Master of Education through course beamed in real-time two-way video from the main campus at Flagstaff to remote sites statewide. Remote students can ask questions and otherwise participate as though they were present in the classroom. Some on-campus residency required.

Northwood University   B

University College
3225 Cook Road
Midland, MI 48640-2398
Fields offered: Management
Year founded: 1959
Ownership: Nonprofit, independent
Phone: (517) 837-4411 • (800) 445-5873
Fax: (517) 837-4111
E-mail: uc@northwood.edu
Website: www.northwood.edu

Northwood offers A.A. and B.A. degrees in business for distance learners. The program is designed for students age 25 and older who are having trouble completing a traditional program, whatever the reason. Previous college work is transferred in, learning obtained in the work place is evaluated, and a degree plan is formulated for each student's needs. Depending on location, classes are available evenings, weekends or through home study. Residential campuses are located in Michigan, Texas and Florida, with outreach centers in these states, as well as Illinois, Indianapolis, Kentucky, Louisiana, and New Mexico. Independent study is completed through correspondence, with a residency requirement of two three-day seminars and an oral and written exam over all material. This can be combined with the second seminar.

Norwich University   B, M

Vermont College
College St.
Montpelier, VT 05602
Fields offered: Liberal studies, visual art, writing, art therapy
Year founded: 1834
Ownership: Nonprofit, independent
Phone: (802) 828-8500 • (800) 336-6794 (outside VT)
Fax: (802) 828-8855
E-mail: VCAdmis@norwich.edu
Website: www.norwich.edu

Vermont College of Norwich University offers several of the longest-running external degree programs in North America for adult learners. The programs are structured to allow students great latitude in designing their studies in conjunction with faculty mentors. The Adult Degree Program (B.A.), begun in 1963, features short residencies in Vermont (9 days every six months or one weekend a month) alternating with study at home. Faculty guide and support student work in the liberal arts, including psychology and counseling, literature and writing, management, and education The graduate program, started in 1969, offers self-designed studies in the humanities, arts, education, and social sciences including psychology and counseling. Regional meetings are held quarterly or monthly by program faculty. Students work with two advisors, a core faculty member who is responsible for a geographical region of the country and a field advisor, a local expert in the student's field of study. The M.A. in art therapy offers a 15-month program which includes summer residencies in Vermont. M.F.A. in writing or visual arts through off-campus programs with 9-day residencies twice a year in Vermont. The M.F.A. in music performance requires short, intensive summer and winter residency sessions alternating with six-month non-resident study projects.

A new program, the New College, is designed for "traditional age students." It combines brief on-campus stays with off-campus travel, internships, and relevant jobs. Each student is given a notebook computer, and they stay in touch with a faculty mentor and with other students via the Internet.

Nova Southeastern University   M, D

3301 College Ave.
Fort Lauderdale, FL 33314
Fields offered: Education, administration, business, computer systems, social and systemic studies, liberal studies, psychology, speech and language, law, teaching of English as a foreign language
Year founded: 1964
Ownership: Nonprofit, independent
Phone: (954) 262-7300 • (800) 541-6682
Fax: (954) 262-7621
Website: www.nova.edu

Nova University has one of the more nontraditional doctoral programs ever to achieve regional accreditation. The typical student attends one group meeting a month (generally two or three days), plus two one-week residential sessions, and from three to six practicums which emphasize direct application of research to the workplace. Total time: about three-and-a-half years. The university also offers a Doctor of Arts in information science in which students use interactive computers. A major part of instruction in this program is through teleconferencing, TELNET, and TYMENET. Residential work has been offered in 23 states. Nova will consider offering the program in the continental United States wherever a cluster of 20-25 students can be formed. Their latest program, a Master's and a doctorate in instructional technology and distance education, can be accomplished entirely on-line, with the exception of 2 extended weekends and an 8-day summer institute. The Master's takes 21 months, the doctorate 3 years. However, a person doing both programs with Nova can finish the doctorate in 2 years. Other degree programs available, most in the school of education (there are CYS, child and youth studies, programs for those working with children through age 18) and in computer science. Formerly Nova University; they merged with Southeastern Medical School, hence the name change.

Note: In 1998, Nova Southeastern's President Ferrero demanded that the school not be included in this book, and did not respond to our inquiries as to his reasons for the demand. We have written favorably about the school for 24 years, and will continue to do so.

Nova University

See: Nova Southeastern University

Ohio University   M

College of Business
Copeland Hall
Athens, OH 45701-2979
Fields offered: Business administration
Year founded: 1804
Ownership: State
Phone: (614) 593-2073
Fax: (614) 593-0319
E-mail: stinson@oak.cats.ohiou.edu
Website: oumba.cob.ohiou.edu/~oumba/

This largely distance-learning two-year program is designed for working professionals, allowing them to integrate on-the-job experiences into the learning process. There are three one-week residencies, one each at the beginning, middle, and end of the program. There are also three weekend residencies, spaced out between the longer stays.

Ohio University-Southern Campus   M

   1804 Liberty Ave.
   Ironton, OH 45638
   Fields offered: Business
   Year founded: 1956
   Ownership: State
   Phone: (614) 533-4608
   Fax: (614) 533-4632
   E-mail: cunningham@ouvaxa.cats.ohiou.edu
   Website: www.tcom.ohiou.edu/hems/

This MBA requires long weekends and two week-long sessions on the Ironton campus.

Oklahoma City University   B

   Competency-Based Degree Program
   NW 23rd at North Blackwelder
   Oklahoma City, OK 73106
   Fields offered: Many fields
   Year founded: 1901
   Ownership: Nonprofit, state
   Phone: (405) 521-5265 • (800) 633-7242 ext. 9
   Fax: (405) 521-5264
   E-mail: uadmissions@frodo.okcu.edu
   Website: frodo.okcu.edu

A Bachelor of Arts or Science degree can be earned by utilizing a combination of alternative methods: independent study, seminars, assessment of prior learning, and traditional courses. Each student must visit the campus to attend an orientation workshop, and additional campus visits may be necessary. The university has asked us to point out that the program may be suitable for some distance students; however, it may not meet the needs of others. An evaluation of each student's educational situation is necessary.

Open University of Sri Lanka   B, M, D

   Nawala
   Nugegoda, Sri Lanka
   Fields offered: Engineering technology, humanities & social sciences, natural sciences
   Year founded: 1980
   Phone: (94-1) 853-777
   Fax: (94-1) 436-858
   E-mail: postmast@mech.ou.ac.lk
   Website: www.ou.ac.lk

Incorporating the programs of the former Sri Lanka Institute of Distance Education, the Open University of Sri Lanka is essentially a distance-education university, offering some 30+ undergraduate academic programs in engineering technology, humanities & social sciences, and natural sciences. There are also opportunities for M.Phil and Ph.D. research degrees in a number of fields. Students must visit Sri Lanka occasionally for assessment tests and examinations.

Oxford Brookes University   M

   School of Business
   Wheatley Campus
   Oxford, OX33 1HX England
   Fields offered: Business administration, education
   Year founded: 1970
   Phone: (44-1865) 485-732
   Fax: (44-1865) 485-765
   E-mail: mba@brookes.ac.uk
   Website: www.brookes.ac.uk

A distance-learning M.B.A. offered using a variety of distance-learning methods, including printed text, audio- and videotapes, computer conferencing, and study groups. Some residency may be required on campus; we have written for details.

Panjab University   B, M

   Department of Correspondence Studies
   Chandigarh 160014, India
   Fields offered: Arts, commerce
   Year founded: 1947
   Phone: (91-11) 541-143
   Fax: (91-172) 541022

Admission is open to Indian citizens living in India and abroad, and foreign nationals working in missions in India. Courses are mainly delivered as printed text materials, sometimes supplemented by audio- and videocassettes and radio lectures. There are two "personal contact programs," of 8 days each. Degrees offered are the Bachelor of Arts, Bachelor of Commerce, and Master of Arts.

Pennsylvania State University   M

   256 Applied Sciences Bldg.
   University Park, PA 16802
   Fields offered: Acoustics, elementary education
   Year founded: 1855
   Ownership: Nonprofit, state
   Phone: (814) 863-4128
   E-mail: gadm@psu.edu
   Website: www.psu.edu

Master of Science in acoustics through a special program for employees of the U.S. Navy and its contractors nationwide. Learning takes place through compressed-video television courses; one two-week summer session required. M.S. in elementary education also available.

Prescott College   B

   Adult Degree Program
   220 Grove
   Prescott, AZ 86301
   Fields offered: Management, counseling, teacher education, human services, liberal arts
   Year founded: 1966
   Ownership: Nonprofit, independent
   Phone: (520) 776-7116 • (800) 628-6362
   Fax: (520) 776-5137

E-mail: applypc@aztec.asu.edu or adpmail@northlink.com

Website: www.prescott.edu

Prescott's Adult Degree Program offers a student-centered independent-study format, using instructors from a student's home community. Students normally take two courses every three months, meeting weekly with local instructors wherever they live. (Prescott helps locate them.) Students must come to the college for a weekend orientation at the beginning of their program, and for an additional liberal arts seminar, also held on a weekend. Degree programs can be individually designed to meet students' goals. Entering students normally have a minimum of 30 semester hours of prior college work. One year enrollment with Prescott is required to earn the degree. Credit for prior college-level learning can be awarded through the writing of a life-experience portfolio.

Purdue University   B, M, D

1080 Schleman Hall
West Lafayette, IN 47907
Fields offered: Education, engineering, technology, management, pharmacy, agriculture, veterinary medicine, science, liberal arts
Year founded: 1869
Ownership: Nonprofit, state
Phone: (765) 494-1776 • (800)494-5345 engineering only
Fax: (765) 494-0544
E-mail: admissions@adms.purdue.edu
Website: www.purdue.edu

B.S. in technology or pharmacy; M.S. in engineering for fully employed engineers (primarily through televised or live classes at the worksite) and in education (generally through summer classes) for persons already working in the field. M.S. in management is available entirely by home-computer classes (Macintosh only), plus a total of 12 weeks on campus. Master's in pharmacy and Pharm.D. available in part through videocassette. A few evening and weekend programs for adult students are offered in various Indiana cities.

Regent University   M, D, Law

Distance Education Program
Virginia Beach, VA 23464
Fields offered: Business, management
Year founded: 1977
Ownership: Nonprofit
Phone: (757) 579-4096 • (800) 477-3642
Fax: (757) 579-4369
E-mail: tomstan@regent.edu
Website: www.regent.edu/acad/

The M.B.A. and the M.A. in management can be earned through a combination of correspondence courses, guided independent study, audio- and videocassettes, and instruction by telephone and mail, plus a total of two one-week periods on campus. An accelerated program allows students

who have completed three years of undergraduate work (90 semester hours) and have five years' work experience to enroll in the Master's program without completing a Bachelor's. The university integrates traditional Judeo-Christian ethical principles in the teaching of each course. They have just added doctoral programs in communication studies and organizational leadership which require very short residency—a "pre-study workshop" in August, followed by independent study (most of it conducted over the Internet), with a doctoral seminar every summer following the coursework. These seminars can be as short as five days a summer. Founded as CBN University (named after Pat Robertson's Christian Broadcasting Network). Law school holds provisional accreditation by the American Bar Association. (The law school used to be located at Oral Roberts University, where it was called the O.W. Coburn School of Law.)

Rice University   M

School of Engineering, P.O. Box 1892
Houston, TX 77251
Fields offered: Electrical engineering, computer science
Year founded: 1891
Ownership: Nonprofit, independent
Phone: (713) 527-4955
Fax: (713) 285-5300
E-mail: elec@rice.edu or rhonda@cs.rice.edu
Website: www.rice.edu/

Master's in electrical engineering or computer science (M.E.E. or M.C.S.) offered to members of local industry, primarily through the Educational TV network. Some on-campus time is required for advising, seminars, and exams.

Rikkyo University   D

3-chome, Nishi-Ikebukuro, Toshima-ku
Tokyo, 171 Japan
Fields offered: Many fields
Year founded: 1874
Ownership: Nonprofit, independent
Phone: (03) 985-2204
Website: www.rikkyo.ac.jp

Doctoral degrees solely on the basis of a dissertation (which can be in English), plus a series of written examinations taken in Japanese in Tokyo. Rikkyo was established by an American bishop in 1874, and was taken over by the Japanese in 1920. Applicants are asked to request a copy of the regulations governing the awarding of degrees at Rikkyo before submitting any materials. Once a preliminary application (a 2,000-word summary of the dissertation and a curriculum vita) is accepted, then the full work is presented. The applicant then goes to Japan to take written exams in the topic of the dissertation, and in two languages other than his or her native one. If the applicant's level of academic achievement is commensurate with others who have eared the Doctorate at Rikkyo, then the degree is awarded. Also known as Saint Paul's University.

Robert Gordon University   B, M

Department of Nursing
Kepplestone Premises
Queen's Road
Aberdeen AB9 2PG, U.K.
Fields offered: Nursing, clinical pharmacy, electronic systems, human resource development
Year founded: 1750
Phone: (44-1224) 262-000
Fax: (44-1224) 263-363
E-mail: info-centre@rgu.ac.uk
or admissions@rgu.ac.uk
Website: www.rgu.ac.uk

While courses are largely completed via distance learning, most require a one- or two-week on-campus residency for a taught course held at the university. The degrees available are: a B.A. in community health nursing (concentrations in community psychiatric nursing, district nursing, health visiting, cancer nursing, or occupational health nursing), a B.A. in nursing or school nursing, and M.S.'s in clinical pharmacy, electronic systems, or human resource development.

Rochester Institute of Technology   B, M

72 Lomb Memorial Dr.
Rochester, NY 14623
Fields offered: Technical fields, art, design, graphic arts, photography
Year founded: 1829
Ownership: Nonprofit, independent
Phone: (716) 475-6768 • (800) CALL RIT
Fax: (716) 475-7164
E-mail: opes@rit.edu
Website: www.rit.edu

B.S. in many technical fields, including engineering and computer science, as well as photography and graphic arts; M.S. in engineering technology or business technology, all through a combination of evening study, independent study, and some fieldwork. B.S. in electrical/mechanical technology has no on-campus requirement for applicants who live outside New York state and have an Associate's degree (in-state students must complete two courses on campus). M.S. in mathematical statistics requires two short on-campus seminars, plus independent study and a thesis. M.S. in software technology can be earned nonresidentially through a variety of nontraditional methods, including videocassettes, e-mail, cable television courses, and courses on disk.

Royal Melbourne Institute of Technology   B

GPO Box 2476V
Melbourne, Victoria 3001 Australia
Fields offered: Transport & logistics
Phone: (61-3) 660-2260
Fax: (61-3) 660-3070
E-mail: ops@rmit.edu.au
Website: www.rmit.edu.au

A Bachelor of Business in transport & logistics is available largely through distance learning, although some attendance may be required at group and laboratory sessions or workshops in some subjects. Contact the school for details.

Sabana Open University

Fundacion Universidad de la Sabana
Facultad de Educacion
Instituto de Educacion a Distancia
INSE
Calle 70 No 11-79
AA 53753
Bogota, Columbia
Fields offered: Many fields
Phone: (57-1) 255 2455
Fax: (57-1) 215 98 88

Students are required to attend the University's headquarters in Bogota during June and December (school holidays) when group work, activities and workshops are undertaken. Between January and May, and July and November, they work in their own homes using printed self-study materials produced by/for the University and by other institutions, existing textbooks, collections of readings compiled by the University, audio and video cassettes, audiovision, and television. Tutoring and counseling by telephone or post is available, or face-to-face for those who can attend headquarters during the non-residential periods. Tutoring by audio and video teleconferencing is also available.

Saint Francis Xavier University   B

Continuing Education
Extension Department
Antigonish, NS B2G 2W5 Canada
Fields offered: Nursing
Year founded: 1853
Ownership: Nonprofit
Phone: (902) 867-5190
Fax: (902) 867-5154
E-mail: admit@stfx.ca
Website: www.stfx.ca

Bachelor's degree program for working nurses who have one year of clinical experience and a high-school diploma. Courses are built around correspondence materials (home-study readings and assignments, supplemented by audio- and videocassettes and telephone tutoring), but there is one annual visit to the campus required, for orientation and counseling. Hospital- and clinic-based resource centers provide a useful support system for this program.

Saint Joseph's College   B, M

External Degree Program, Department 840
Windham, ME 04069-1198
Fields offered: Health care administration, business, professional arts, long term care, radiologic technology
Year founded: 1912
Ownership: Nonprofit, church
Phone: (207) 892-7841 • (800) 752-4723
Fax: (207) 892-7480
E-mail: admissions@saintjoe.edu
Website: www.saintjoe.edu

Programs offered through faculty-directed independent study, with campus-based advising and instruction: Bachelor of Science in health care administration (with majors in general health care and long term care), business administration, professional arts (a degree-completion program for licensed health care professionals), and radiologic technology (a degree-completion program for rad techs); M.S. in health services administration. B.S. requires a three-week residency on-campus in Windham, Maine; M.S., two weeks.

Saint Joseph's College   B, M

Department 840
278 Whites Bridge Road
Standish, ME 04084-5263
Fields offered: business, health sciences and administration, professional arts
Year founded: 1912
Ownership: Church
Phone: (207) 892-7841 • (800) 752-4723
Fax: (207) 892-7480
E-mail: gcarro@sjcme.edu
Website: www.sjcme.edu

Most programs require one 2-week summer residency (except for the B.S. in nursing program which requires weekly clinicals in southern Maine). Video and audio tapes, computer software and e-mail delivery of course materials. A computer is a requirement for some courses.

Saint Mary's College (Minnesota)   M

2510 Park Ave.
Minneapolis, MN 55404
Fields offered: Human development, education
Year founded: 1912
Ownership: Nonprofit, church
Phone: (507) 874-9877
Fax: (507) 457-6967

E-mail: tpisciti@smumn.edu
Website: www.smumn.edu/

The Master of Arts in human development is for persons living within a 100-mile radius of Minneapolis, St. Paul, Winona, or Rochester, Minnesota. The Master of Arts in education program is for those living within the state of Wisconsin. All students must spend some time on the graduate campus in Minnesota or at a central location in Wisconsin. This residency may be as little as one weekend. Credit is given for completion of learning contracts negotiated between the student and the advisor. Most students complete the Master's in 24 to 30 months.

Saint Mary-of-the-Woods College   B, M

External Degree Program
Saint Mary-of-the-Woods, IN 47876
Fields offered: Many fields
Year founded: 1840
Ownership: Nonprofit, church
Phone: (812) 535-5106 • (800) 926-SMWC
Fax: (812) 535-4613
E-mail: PR-SMWC@smwc.edu
Website: www.smwc.edu/

Majors offered at the Bachelor's level include accounting, business administration, management, marketing, English, humanities, journalism, gerontology, paralegal studies, psychology, social science, theology, early childhood education, elementary education, kindergarten/primary education, and secondary education certification. Master's degrees available in pastoral theology. Life experience credit awarded to those with college-level knowledge acquired other than in a classroom environment. Students are guided by faculty via mail and phone in off-campus independent study, punctuated with brief on-campus residencies (an average of one day per semester). Only women are awarded the Bachelor's degrees, but both sexes can earn the Master's degree

Saint Paul's University

See: Rikkyo University

Salve Regina University   B, M

Extension Study
100 Ochre Point Avenue
Newport, RI 02840-4192
Fields offered: International relations, management, business, human development, liberal studies, nursing
Year founded: 1934
Ownership: Nonprofit, church
Phone: (401) 847-6650, ext. 2229 • (800) 637-0002
Fax: (401) 849-0702
E-mail: Mistol@salve.edu
Website: www.salve.edu

A B.A. in liberal studies and a B.S. in both business and nursing, available to adult students who have already completed at least 45 credit hours elsewhere (At least 60 of the 120 credits required for the degree must then be completed through Salve Regina within six years, with a GPA of

2.0 or higher.). Master's degrees are offered in management, international relations, and human development. These programs require 36 units to complete. The school says that "the usual number of transfer credit is 6," but that exceptions are made for graduates of U.S. military colleges, who may transfer in a maximum of 18 earned credits, as well as for CPCU's, who can transfer up to 12 units towards the management degree. In all programs, instruction is by correspondence courses and guided independent study, supported by regular mail, e-mail, and telephone contact with faculty. All programs require a brief residency, usually for two weeks in the summer.

Saybrook Graduate School   M, D

450 Pacific, 3rd Floor
San Francisco, CA 94133
Fields offered: Psychology, human science
Year founded: 1970
Ownership: Nonprofit, independent
Phone: (415) 433-9200 • (800) 825-4480
Fax: (415) 433-9271
E-mail: mmyers@igc.org
Website: www.saybrook.org

Courses are offered in a distance-learning format. A course guide is provided, specifying the required readings and including written lecture materials prepared by the faculty. Students may design their own courses as well. Student work focuses within nine areas of concentration: clinical inquiry, systems inquiry, health studies, peace & conflict resolution, creativity & art, organizational inquiry, social philosophy & political psychology, humanistic & transpersonal psychology, and consciousness studies. All students must attend a five-day planning seminar in San Francisco, and two one-week national meetings each year. Degrees can take from two to six years to complete. Many well-known psychologists have been associated with Saybrook (Rollo May, Stanley Krippner, Richard Farson, Nevitt Sanford, Clark Moustakas, etc.). Until 1982, Saybrook was called the Humanistic Psychology Institute; later, it was known as Saybrook Institute.

Sheffield Hallam University   M

School of Computing and Management Sciences
Hallamshire Business Park
100 Napier Street
Sheffield, S11 8HD U.K.
Fields offered: Statistics, enterprise network management, operations, total quality management
Year founded: 1969
Phone: (44-114) 253-3127
Fax: (44-114) 253-3161
E-mail: pgadof@shu.ac.uk
Website: www.shu.ac.uk

This school offers a number of Master of Science degrees in technical fields, with several short residency periods, for an annual study school, and for exams every six months. Coursework is done by correspondence, supported by tutorial assistance and audiotapes. Degrees offered are in the fields of applied statistics (including an optional concentration in statistical education), enterprise network management, operations management, operations research, and total quality management.

Skidmore College   B, M

University Without Walls
Saratoga Springs, NY 12866
Fields offered: Many fields
Year founded: 1911
Ownership: Nonprofit, independent
Phone: (518) 584-5000
Fax: (518) 584-3023
E-mail: admissions@skidmore.edu
Website: www.skidmore.edu/

Above address is the contact for the University Without Walls. For the external Master's degree program (also short residency), contact: Dr. Lawrence Ries, Director, Master of Arts in Liberal Studies, (518) 584-5000. Skidmore is one of the pioneers of the nontraditional movement, having offered a University Without Walls program since 1970. It is possible to earn a Bachelor of Arts or Bachelor of Science with a total of three days on campus: one for an admissions interview, a second for advising and planning, and the third to present a degree plan to a faculty committee. Skidmore makes it clear that they hold their graduates to "standards of knowledge, competence and intellectual attainment which are no less comprehensive and rigorous than those established by traditional . . . programs." In addition to fulfilling all other requirements in the degree plan each student completes a final project demonstrating competence in one's field. Students can major in any of the dozens of fields offered by Skidmore or, with the assistance of faculty advisors, devise a self-determined major. In 1992 Skidmore launched a Master's program in interdisciplinary studies, modeled on its highly successful undergraduate program.

Sonoma State University   B, M

1801 E. Cotati Ave.
Rohnert Park, CA 94928
Fields offered: Psychology
Year founded: 1960
Ownership: Nonprofit, state
Phone: (707) 664-2411
Fax: (707) 664-3113
E-mail: louis.naranjo@sonoma.edu
Website: www.sonoma.edu

The B.A. in psychology can be completed entirely through evening courses, and there is a one-year external Master's in psychology. Although there is no requirement to take any specific classes for the Master's, students must attend occasional meetings with a faculty advisor. The program is designed jointly by student and faculty, and can include coursework, fieldwork, research, and independent study. Applicants must have a Bachelor's degree, one year of graduate-level experience in humanistic psychology, and 9 unit of credit previously earned (in residence or by extension) from Sonoma State. A requirement of basic knowledge in psychology can be met through courses or by examination. About 40 new applicants are admitted each fall.

South Bank University   M, D

The Registry
103 Borough Road
London, SE1 0AA England
Fields offered: Many fields
Phone: (44-171) 928-8989
Fax: (44-171) 815-8155
E-mail: registry@sbu.ac.uk
Website: www.southbank-university.ac.uk

This school offers a research-based M.Phil and Ph.D. to candidates who have properly demonstrated their research of a topic, and defend a thesis through an oral examination, the satisfaction of a board of examiners. Supervised research at remote locations can be formally approved by the school, and it will consider non-U.K. students, provided they can demonstrate access to appropriate research facilities. Students are expected to spend some 6 weeks a year on the school's London campus, although some exceptions may be possible. While oral exams are generally held in the U.K., approval may be given in special cases for the examination to take place abroad. There is also an option under which a candidate may be awarded a Ph.D. on the basis of previously published work; such candidates are also expected to "have a significant connection with the University."

Southern California College   B

55 Fair Drive
Costa Mesa, CA 92626
Fields offered: organizational management, ministry & leadership
Year founded: 1920
Ownership: church
Phone: (714) 556-3610 • (800) 722-6279
Fax: (714) 668-6194
E-mail: dcp@sccu.edu
Website: www.sccu.edu

This is a degree completion program for adults with work experience and 40 or more units of college credit. Classes meet one night a week in various Southern California locations.

Southern Cross University   B, M, D

P.O. Box 157
Lismore, NSW 2480 Australia
Fields offered: Many fields
Year founded: 1989
Ownership: Nonprofit, state
Phone: (61-267) 732-999
Fax: (61-267) 733-269
E-mail: sservice@scu.edu.au
Website: www.scu.edu.au

Degrees at all levels are offered in a broad range of fields. Instruction is by the same faculty that teach on-campus courses, and is via various media, including printed lecture notes, interactive TV and radio, and video- and audiocassettes. Some subjects require students to attend a certain number of short residential vacation sessions on campus; voluntary weekend sessions are also available, the majority of them in Sydney. Enrollment in some programs is restricted to full-time residents of Australia, or Australians with resident status who are temporarily overseas. Degrees offered are: Bachelor of Business in tourism, Bachelor of Education, Bachelor of Health Science in nursing, Bachelor of Social Science, Master of Accounting Studies, M.A. and M.S. in many fields, M.B.A., Master of Business, Master of Education, with an optional specialization in training and development, Master of Health Science, Master of International Tourism Management, Master of Laws, Master of Organizational Development and Training, and Doctor of Business Administration.

Southern Methodist University   B, M

Evening and Summer Studies
Dallas, TX 75275-0382
Fields offered: Many fields
Year founded: 1911
Ownership: Nonprofit, church
Phone: (214) 768-5465
Fax: (214) 768-1001
E-mail: mclarke@mail.smu.edu
Website: www.smu.edu

Bachelor of Social Science, Bachelor of Humanities, and Master of Liberal Arts, all through evening study in the School of Continuing Education. In the North Texas area, students can earn an M.S. in engineering management, operations research, computer engineering or science, mechanical or electrical engineering largely through satellite television courses, visiting the campus only for exams. They have also added a video-based Master's degree in hazardous and waste materials through the Distance Learning School of Engineering and Applied Science.

Southern Oregon State College

See: Southern Oregon University

Southern Oregon University   B, M

1250 Siskiyou Blvd.
Ashland, OR 97520
Fields offered: Business & management, human services, nursing, criminology, education
Year founded: 1926
Ownership: Nonprofit, state
Phone: (541) 552-8106
Fax: (541) 552-6329
E-mail: admissions@sou.edu
Website: www.sou.edu

Off-campus Bachelor's degree-completion programs in business & management, human services, nursing, and criminology, and an M.S. in education is available to working teachers, mainly through courses viewed at distant sites, videocassette, computer conferencing, and telephone instruction. Most programs are offered evenings and weekends, or by "multiple technologies." Summer sessions and occasional campus visits are required in many programs. This program serves only the southern Oregon region. Formerly Southern Oregon State College.

Southern Polytechnic State University   B, M

1100 South Marietta Parkway
Marietta, GA 30060
Fields offered: Industrial distribution, computer science, quality assurance
Year founded: 1948
Ownership: State
Phone: (770) 528-5531
Fax: (770) 528-4990
E-mail: dramsey@spsu.edu
Website: www2.spsu.edu/ois/ois/html

The Bachelor's program is in industrial distribution; the Master's in computer science, electrical engineering technology and quality assurance. Some courses require access to a computer.

Southwestern Adventist College

See: Southwestern Adventist University

Southwestern Adventist University   B

Keene, TX 76059
Fields offered: Many fields
Year founded: 1893
Ownership: Nonprofit, church
Phone: (817) 645-3921, ext. 204 • (888) 732-7928
Fax: (817) 556-4742
E-mail: adpsec@swau.edu
Website: www.swau.edu

B.A., B.S., and Bachelor of Business Administration through the Adult Degree Program (ADP). Virtually all work can be completed at a distance, following a six-day admission seminar, held each March, June, and October. Credit is earned by transfer of credit, proficiency exams, credit for prior learning (portfolio), and independent study by mail, computer, and telephone. ADP students pay 80 percent of the tuition of on-campus students. Majors include business, communication, education, English, office administration, computer science, religion, social science, and history. Formerly Southwestern Adventist College.

Southwestern Assemblies of God University   B

1200 Sycamore
Waxahachie, TX 75165
Fields offered: Education
Year founded: 1927
Ownership: Nonprofit, church

Phone: (972) 937-4010 • (888) 937-7248
Fax: (972) 923-0488
E-mail: pbrooks@sagu.edu
Website: www.sagu.edu

Bachelor's in adult and continuing education through a largely nonresidential program open to anyone who makes a statement of Christian faith. Instruction is through audio- and videocassette, teleconferencing, and computer conferencing; students must spend two days on-campus at the beginning of each semester, for registration.

Sri Lanka Institute of Distance Education

See: Open University of Sri Lanka

State University College   B

Cooper Center
Brockport, NY 14420
Fields offered: Science, natural science, social science
Year founded: 1835
Ownership: Nonprofit, state
Phone: (716) 395-2211
Fax: (716) 395-2401
Website: www.brockport.edu

Bachelor of Liberal Studies, with a minimum of three weeks on campus for an annual seminar. The degree is offered in science, natural science, and social science. Students may design their own concentrations or majors. Credit is given for prior learning experiences, both formal and informal, as well as for equivalency exams, independent study, and correspondence courses. The minimum time of enrollment is one academic year (nine months).

Stephens College   B, M

School of Continuing Education
Campus Box 2083
Columbia, MO 65215
Fields offered: Many fields
Year founded: 1833
Ownership: Nonprofit, independent
Phone: (573) 876-7125 • (800) 388-7579
Fax: (573) 876-7248
E-mail: sce@wc.stephens.edu
Website: stephens.edu

Bachelor of Arts in business, psychology, English, health care, health science, philosophy, law, and rhetoric, as well as student-initiated majors combining two disciplines. A Bachelor of Science in health information management, and an M.B.A. are also offered. Degree requirements can be met through independent study and on-line courses. Students may also earn credits through short-term, intensive courses, CLEP exams, prior learning portfolios, approved courses taken locally, etc. Students attend a three-semester hour-long introductory liberal studies seminar at Stephens College prior to admission. The course is offered in seven-day or double-weekend formats several times throughout the year. A minimum of 36 semester hours must be completed with Stephens College faculty. Open to applicants 23 years of age and older.

Syracuse University   B, M

Independent Study Degree Programs
700 University Avenue
Syracuse , NY 13244-2530
Fields offered: Many fields
Year founded: 1870
Ownership: Nonprofit, independent
Phone: (315) 443-4590 • (800) 442-0501
Fax: (315) 443-4174
E-mail: suisdp@uc.syr.edu
Website: www.suce.syr.edu

A.A., B.A. in liberal studies, M.A. in advertising design or illustration, M.B.A., Master of Library Science, Master of Social Science, and M.S. in nursing, M.S. in communications, information resources, telecommunications & network, and engineering management, all with short residency on campus and independent study in between. All undergraduate degrees, the M.B.A., the communications and engineering degrees require three seven-day residencies per year. The Master of Social Science requires two 14-day sessions on campus in July; alternative sessions are offered in Washington D.C. and London. The M.A. degrees require three two-week summer sessions on campus and several shorter sessions offered in New York, San Francisco, Chicago, and other metropolitan areas. The M.L.S. and telecom degrees require three two-week summer sessions, and four additional weeks over a two-year period. The M.S. in nursing requires four short summer sessions.

Teikyo Loretto Heights College   B

3001 S. Federal Blvd.
Denver, CO 80236
Fields offered: Many fields
Year founded: 1918
Ownership: Nonprofit, independent
Phone: (303) 937-4202
Fax: (303) 937-4224
E-mail: lmoreno@tlhu.edu
Website: www.tlhu.edu

Loretto offers a University Without Walls program that allows enrollees to earn the Bachelor of Arts with little or no time spent on campus. The SAAD (Students at a Distance) program is available to students of all ages who live in the Rocky Mountain area. The degree requires 128 semester units, of which at least the final 30 hours must be earned consecutively after enrolling. These units can, however, be earned through a variety of nontraditional means as well as regular courses: independent reading and research, seminars in the field, independent field practicums, and assessment of prior learning experiences, CLEP and challenge exams, etc. Students are expected to meet periodically with faculty advisors, but those advisors are sometimes able to travel to a student's home location.

Texas A & M University   B, M

Family Nurse Practitioner Program
Corpus Christi , TX
Fields offered: Nursing
Year founded: 1974
Ownership: Nonprofit, state
Phone: (512) 994-5700 • (800) 293-0965
Fax: (512) 993-5853
E-mail: kolson@falcon.tamucc.edu
Website: tamucc.edu

B.S. and M.S. in nursing through a regional interactive television system, providing training towards practice as a family nurse practitioner. Some on-campus residency.

Thames Valley University   B

St. Mary's Road
Ealing
London, W5 5RF England
Fields offered: Business, information systems, human resources, health promotion
Year founded: 1881
Phone: (44-181) 579-5000
Fax: (44-181) 566-1353
E-mail: ravinder.bharaj@tvu.ac.uk
Website: www.tvu.ac.uk

This British school is in the process of developing distance learning programs, in which much of the study takes place at home, with occasional attendance at seminars or workshops. We would encourage foreign students to inquire about programs that interest them, and see if a way can be worked out to do them wholly at a distance, or to concentrate workshops into one visit. The school proudly announces that the number of programs offered by flexible and open learning grows each year; in addition to a number of certificate and diplomas, they are currently offering B.A.s in business studies and business administration, B.S.s in health promotion and information systems, an M.S. in human resource development, and an M.B.A.

Thomas Edison State College   M

101 West State St.
Trenton, NJ 08608-1176
Fields offered: Management
Year founded: 1972
Ownership: Nonprofit, state
Phone: (609) 984-1150
Fax: (609) 984-8447
E-mail: admissions@call.tesc.edu
Website: www.tesc.edu

Unique academic advising available to enrolled students on an 800 number. Foreign students are welcome, with certain restrictions. M.S. in management through a program of study that requires three brief residential periods—one weekend and two one-week sessions.

Trinity University   M

715 Stadium Drive
San Antonio, TX 78212
Fields offered: Health care administration
Year founded: 1869
Ownership: Nonprofit, independent
Phone: (210) 736-8424
Fax: (210) 736-7202
E-mail: roffice@trinity.edu
Website: www.trinity.edu

Master's in health care administration available almost entirely through home study. Each course begins with an intensive three-day on-campus program, followed by independent home study. Support is offered in the form of regular teleconferencing sessions with the instructor.

Union Institute   B, D

440 East McMillan Street
Cincinnati, OH 45206-1925
Fields offered: Many fields
Year founded: 1964
Ownership: Nonprofit, independent
Phone: (513) 861-6400 • (800) 486-3116
Fax: (513) 861-0779
E-mail: admission@tui.edu
Website: www.tui.edu

Union began in 1964 as the Union for Experimenting Colleges and Universities, a consortium including some large state universities, to be, in effect, their alternative program. When the consortium was dissolved, the Institute remained, and began grant degrees. At the undergraduate level, students can either study at one of the school five academic centers (in Cincinnati, Miami, Los Angeles, Sacramento, or San Diego), or work through the Center for Distant Learning, combining brief residencies with a variety of other learning methods, including the Internet. Students design their own program in the fields of arts and sciences, business, criminal justice studies, or psychology; credit is available for prior academic and experiential learning. 30 of the 128 units needed for the degree must be earned while enrolled at Union.

The graduate college offers independent study and research programs leading to a doctorate in interdisciplinary studies or professional psychology. No transfer or life-experience credit is accepted, and applicants must have a Master's degree. A total of thirty-five days of required residency can be accomplished through participation in university-sponsored activities held around the country. The program also requires an internship, and culminates in a dissertation-level work, the "project demonstrating excellence," which can be traditional or nontraditional. Length of time to complete the Doctorate varies, but a minimum of two years' enrollment is required; three to four years is typical.

United States Sports Academy   M

1 Academy Dr.
Daphne, AL 36526
Fields offered: Sports-related fields
Year founded: 1972
Ownership: Nonprofit, independent
Phone: (334) 626-3303 • (800) 223-2668
Fax: (334) 626-1149
E-mail: Academy@ussa-sport.ussa.edu
Website: www.sport.ussa.edu

The Master's degree is offered in sports management, sports medicine, sports coaching, sports fitness management, and sport research. This program involves two summers on the Academy's Daphne, Alabama campus and a "mentorship" in your home community. It is also offered via distance learning: students can begin at any time during the year and must travel to the campus only at the program's end for exam. Courses are delivered through a variety of media including printed media, mentorship, internships, video and audio tape, computer mediated instruction, interactive computer media, bulletin boards, data bases, fax, phone and various forms of directed study. For those students more comfortable in a group study environment, the Academy offers cluster study in various parts of the United States.

Universidad de Monterrey   M

Program de Investigacion y Desarrollo Educativo
Avenida Ignacio Morones Prieto No. 4500 PTE
San Pedro, Garza Garcia
Nuevo Leon, Mexico
Fields offered: Adult education
Year founded: 1969
Ownership: Private
Phone: (52-83) 384-270
Fax: (52-83) 385-619
Website: www.dsi.uanl.mx

A Master's in adult education for persons who have at least two years of experience in the field. Instruction takes place via directed reading, audio- and videocassettes, satellite video and television, telephone tutoring, teleconferencing, practical fieldwork, and some on-campus tutoring.

Universidad de San Jose · M, D

Regional Information office
7891 W. Flagler St., #123
Miami, FL 33144
Fields offered: Administrative sciences, education and humanities, psychology and behavioral science, social science, biological science, science.
Year founded: 1976
Ownership: Nonprofit, private
Phone: (305) 225-3500
Fax: (305) 382-0107
E-mail: Information@USJ.edu
Website: www.USJ.edu

The International Post-Graduate School offers nonresidential instruction in the English language, with a two-week on-campus residency requirement. Students are able to complete their studies for a post-graduate degree off-campus under the direct guidance of an academic advisor. The Master's program must be completed in less than three years, the Doctorate in less than five. Two study options are offered: a curriculum-based program for students who have the need to take traditional coursework in addition to the thesis/dissertation, and a research-based program for qualified students who already possess the necessary theoretical knowledge and experience in their area of expertise. While the government of Costa Rica confirms that the university is accredited, and it is listed in the International Handbook of Universities, documents provided by the government suggest that the doctoral programs are not included in the accreditation. We are still looking into this.

Universidad Nacional Abierta

Apartado No 2096
Caracas, 1010 Venezuela
Fields offered: Many fields
Phone: (58-2) 574-1322

For Venezuelan residents, courses are delivered using printed correspondence texts prepared by/for the institution; audiovisual media; face-to-face tutoring and counseling; use of study centers.

Universidad Nacional Autonoma de Mexico · B

Sistema Universidad Abierta
Circuito Exterior, Ciudad Universitaria
04510 Mexico City DF, Mexico
Fields offered: Many fields
Year founded: 1551
Ownership: Nonprofit, state
Phone: (52-5) 548-81-88
Fax: (52-5) 548-81-88
Website: serpiente.dgsca.unam.mx

Mexico's national open university has prepared substantial course texts, each created by a team that includes academics, audio-visual specialists, and a graphic designer. Each text consists of a work guide, written materials (in Spanish), boxes of laboratory or field experiments, self-evaluation materials, and perhaps movies, tapes, and other audiovisual aids. Student must visit the university in Mexico City to take examinations after completing each course. Courses are offered in accounting, business administration, dental surgery, economics, education, history, Hispanic literature, international relations, mass media, nursing, philosophy, poultry breeding, psychology, and sociology. The website has a brief section in English; otherwise, all material is in Spanish.

Universidad Nacional de Educacion a Distancia · B

Ciudad Universitaria
Baravo Murillo 38
Madrid 28015, Spain
Fields offered: Many fields
Year founded: 1972
Ownership: Nonprofit, state
Phone: (34-1) 398-6545
Fax: (34-1) 398-6037
Website: www.uned.es

Spain's national open university offers degrees in a wide range of academic subjects. Each group of 150 students has a professor-tutor responsible for guidance and personal contact. More than 40 centers around the country (including eleven within large business, government, and military offices) are available for seminars, conferences, and lectures. Most work is done at a distance by use of written and audio-visual materials.

Universidad Nacional de Educacion "Enrique Guzman Y Valle" · B

La Cantuta
Chosica, Peru
Fields offered: Literature, science, geography, mathematics, industrial technology
Year founded: 1905
Ownership: Nonprofit, state
Phone: (51) 91-00-52
Fax: (51) 91-00-52
Website: ekeko2.rcp.net.pe/UNE/

Peru's national open university pilot project is for working teachers. It offers them correspondence courses and short-residency study; most of the work is done at a distance.

Universiti Sains Malaysia · B

Minden
Penang, Malaysia
Fields offered: Many fields
Year founded: 1971
Ownership: Nonprofit, state
Phone: (60-4) 887812

Fax: (60-4) 6576000
Website: www.cs.usm.my
Open to all Malaysian citizens. B.A. and B.S. students work for a minimum of 5 and a maximum of 12 years toward the degree, mainly by correspondence and independent study using printed materials, tapes, and slides mailed to them. Tutorials are conducted by means of a two-way audiographic communication system linking the school with 10 regional centers. Students are required to come to campus once a year in November for a three-week residential program.

University of Alabama, New College   B
External Degree Program
P. O. Box 870182
Tuscaloosa, AL 35487-0182
Fields offered: Interdisciplinary studies
Year founded: 1831
Ownership: Nonprofit, state
Phone: (205) 348-6000
Fax: (205) 348-7022
E-mail: info@extdegree.nc.ua.edu
Website: ua1vm.ua.edu/~newcoll/exdhome.html
The Bachelor of Arts or Bachelor of Science may be earned entirely through nonresident independent study, with the exception of a three-day degree planning seminar on the campus at the start of the program. At least 32 semester hours of work must be completed after admission. This can be by out-of-class contract learning, correspondence courses, television courses, weekend college, prior learning evaluation, or on-campus courses at the university. Interdisciplinary degrees offered in human services, humanities, social sciences, natural sciences, applied sciences, administrative sciences, and communication. A 12-semester-hour senior project is required of all students. Academic advising and planning can be done by telephone.

University of Allahabad   B
Institute of Correspondence Courses and Continuing Education
Chatham Lines
Allahabad, 211 001 India
Fields offered: Commerce, arts
Year founded: 1887
Phone: (91-532) 50668
For Indian citizens. Text-based programs plus two weeks of compulsory contact programs, and radio and audio supplements for arts students.

University of Bath   M
Centre for Continuing Education
Bath, BA2 7AY U.K.
Fields offered: Construction management, integrated environmental management, electrical power systems, sports medicine, rheumatology
Year founded: 1894

Phone: (44-1225) 826-452
Fax: (44-1225) 826-849
E-mail: cce@bath.ac.uk
Website: www.bath.ac.uk.centre.cce
The University of Bath's Centre for Continuing Education offers three M.S. programs (construction management, integrated environmental management, and electrical power systems). Degree programs are offered in 6 to 8 modules, depending on the program, that are generally completed over a period of three to five years, by distance learning methods including correspondence, workbooks, audio- and videotapes, and regular contact with tutors. Distance students worldwide are offered a support network including newsletter, a website, counseling, and the like. The average program requires about 20 days residency—one ten-day session spent on the British campus in each of the first two years. Also offers two health-related postgraduate diploma courses for doctors: one in sports medicine, and one in primary care rheumatology. Both can be accomplished largely through distance learning, with some clinical weekends. Contact school for details.

University of Bradford   D
Management Centre
Emm Lane
Bradford
West Yorkshire, BD9 4JL United Kingdom
Fields offered: Management
Year founded: 1957
Phone: (44-1274) 234-393
Fax: (44-1274) 546-866
E-mail: 2clare@bradford.ac.uk
Website: www.brad.ac.uk
Bradford offers a research doctorate in management. in which part-time external students can complete the Ph.D. from overseas, visiting their dissertation supervisor once a year. Most part-time external students make their first visit coincide with doctoral induction week, which usually falls in late September.

University of Brighton   B, M
Mithras House
Lewes Road
Brighton BN2 2AT, United Kingdom
Fields offered: Podiatric studies, technology management, construction management, industrial pharmaceutical studies
Year founded: 1877
Phone: (44-1273) 600-900
Fax: (44-1273) 642825
E-mail: Admissions@brighton.ac.uk
Website: www.bton.ac.uk
Brighton offers a number of largely distance-learning courses; required residency varies by program. The B.S. in podiatric studies is for chiropodists who wish to become podiatrists. Study consists of one year of courses and one year of research, with seven two-day weekend meetings, and

a one-week summer school. The M.B.A. in technology management takes one to five years, and requires eleven 5-day residential modules, and a 2-day workshop. The M.S. in construction management takes a minimum of two years of part-time study, with eight 5-day residential modules. The M.S. in industrial pharmaceutical studies takes about two years, with three one-week residencies each year. Finally, the M.S. in technology management takes one to 5 years, with 10 five-day residential modules.

University of Calgary   B, M

Centre for Distance Learning
2500 University Drive, NW
Calgary, Alberta T2N 1N4 Canada
Fields offered: Nursing, education
Year founded: 1980
Ownership: Nonprofit, state
Phone: (403) 220-7346
Fax: (403) 777-1959
E-mail: ikirek@acs.ucalgary.ca
Website: www.ucalgary.ca

Degree-completion program for R.N.s leads to a B.S. in nursing, through teleconferencing and videocassette. M.Ed. in educational leadership and Master of Continuing Education also available largely through distance learning. The first requires one six-week summer session on campus, the latter a three-week orientation at the program's beginning. Courses are delivered via a range of media, including tele- and videoconferencing, computer networks, videocassette, and telephone, fax, and e-mail.

University of Calicut   B, M

School of Distance Education
University P.O. Box 673 635
Kerala, India
Fields offered: Business, arts, library & information sciences, humanities, social sciences
Year founded: 1981
Ownership: State
Phone: (91-493) 800-288
Fax: (91-493) 800-288

Printed correspondence lessons are dispatched to the students regularly. These also include response sheets which students are required to complete and return for evaluation. Contact classes are held at various district headquarters for pre-degree and degree courses. For the Master's degree a contact program lasting 10 days each year is required. Overseas students are admitted, subject to equivalence of qualifying courses taken; clearance must also be obtained from the government.

University of California, Irvine   B, M

Graduate School of Management
Irvine, CA 92717
Fields offered: Health care
Year founded: 1965
Ownership: Nonprofit, state

Phone: (714) 824-5374
Fax: (714) 824-5451
E-mail: oars@uci.edu
Website: www.gsm.uci.edu

This part-time M.B.A. with a focus on health care (it's called the Health Care Executive M.B.A.) takes two years to complete. Much of the work is done over the Internet; students meet once a month for three-and-a-half days; the school points out that their campus is only minutes from a major airport, making this a reasonable distance-learning program for someone at an executive level who can afford to make the trips (or have his or her company fund them).

University of Colorado—Boulder   M

Center for Advanced Training in Engineering and Computer Science (CATECS)
Campus Box 435
Boulder, CO 80309
Fields offered: Engineering, computer science, engineering management, telecommunications
Year founded: 1876
Ownership: Nonprofit, state
Phone: (303) 492-6048
Fax: (303) 492-5987
E-mail: micucciv@spot.colorado.edu
Website: www.colorado.edu/CATECS

M.S. and Master of Engineering offered to working adults through distance learning methods, in the following concentrations: aerospace or electrical/computer engineering, engineering management, telecommunications, and computer science. Students take one class per semester, finishing the degree in three-and-a-half to five years. Distance-learning options include videocassettes and television courses. Generally, the only residency required is the defense of thesis or other final project.

University of Colorado—Denver   M

Executive Program in Health Administration
P.O. Box 480006
Denver, CO 80248
Fields offered: Health administration, business administration
Year founded: 1912
Ownership: Nonprofit, state
Phone: (303) 623-1888 • (800) 228-5778
Fax: (303) 623-6228
E-mail: taffe@together.cudenver.edu
Website: www.bus.colorado.edu/extended/home.htm

Master of Science in health administration for working healthcare professionals, through a combination of computer conferencing and on-campus instruction. Students must attend five intensive on-campus sessions in Denver during the two-year program. Instruction is by faculty from 14 accredited health-administration programs that make up the Network for Health Care Management (formerly the Western Network). For information on the

California-based Network, call 510-642-0790. Students in the executive program come from a variety of backgrounds, and include physicians, nurses, pharmacists, group-practice administrators, managed-care administrators, and hospital and long-term care administrators.

University of Delaware   B

Clayton Hall
Newark, DE 19716
Fields offered: Nursing, hotel/restaurant/institutional management
Year founded: 1833
Ownership: Nonprofit, state
Phone: (302) 831-6223 (nursing) or (302) 831-4549 • (800) UD-FOCUS
Fax: (302) 831-3292
E-mail: KATHERINE.WIRTH@mvs.udel.edu
Website: www.udel.edu

Delaware offers two short-residency programs (for their nontraditional resident programs, see the next chapter). These are: a BSN in nursing for R.N.'s; the contact for this program is Madeline Lambrecht at (302) 831-8368. Hospitals can have their staff development office arrange with the FOCUS department at the university to make videotaped courses available to check out. Staff development administers exams; the university grades them and sends students' results. (This course involves 3 weekends on the Delaware Campus.) B.S. in human resources with a major in hotel, restaurant, and institutional management through a program requiring only two 10-day sessions on campus; the contact for this program is Mary Pritchard at (800) UD-FOCUS.

University of Durham   M, D

Business School
Mill Hill Lane
Durham City, DH1 3LB U.K.
Fields offered: Business administration
Year founded: 1832
Ownership: Nonprofit, state
Phone: (44-191) 374-33-87
Fax: (44-191) 374-3389
E-mail: J.F.Ross@durham.ac.uk
Website: www.dur.ac.uk/dubs/mbadl/

In mid 1988 Durham introduced a distance learning M.B.A. (they have offered a traditional M.B.A. since 1967). The program is administered by the University Business School to students in more than 40 countries. The three-to-four-year course of study combines specially written distance-learning materials, annotated texts, audiotapes, and one week per year of intensive residential seminars (first year excluded). A correspondent tells us that they now also offer a non-residential research doctorate, but warns that students must have or acquire excellent research skills.

University of Florida   M

Gainesville, Florida
Fields offered: Construction management

In 1999, our company will be involved in marketing a new distance learning Master's in this field, offered entirely or almost entirely through home study. Details are not available as we go to press, but interested parties will be sent information as soon as it exists. To get on the mailing list, write:

Master's in Construction Management, Financial Times Management, Inc., 6921 Stockton St., El Cerrito, CA 94530 or telephone (888) DEGREE.NET.

University of Hull   M

Asia Pacific Management Centre
10 Anson Road #03-05
Singapore , 079903 Singapore
Fields offered: Business administration
Year founded: 1927
Phone: (65) 225-2825
Fax: (65) 225-3605
E-mail: apmc8@singnet.com.sg
Website: www.apmc.net

The University of Hull offers a distance learning M.B.A. to executives and managers in Singapore, in conjunction with the independent Asia Pacific Management Centre. The program consists of 12 modules and a final project; students complete 2 modules in each three-month "learning cycle." Visiting faculty members from the British Hull conduct seminars and workshop sessions for 8 days every cycle.

University of Illinois   M

Graduate School of Library and Information Science
Champaign, IL 61820
Fields offered: Library and information science
Year founded: 1867
Ownership: Nonprofit, state
Phone: (217) 333-7197 • (800) 982-0914
Fax: (217) 244-302
E-mail: gslis@alexia.lis.uiuc.edu
Website: www.lis.uiuc.edu

An M.S. in library and information sciences tailored to working students. Study begins with a two-week residency, after which students study by distance-learning methods. There is at least one more residential requirement, a three-day weekend. Part-time students are expected to take two to five years to complete this degree. Study takes the form of correspondence, heavy Internet use, a practicum in a local information center, independent study, and courses transferred in.

University of Kentucky   M, D

304 Patterson Office Tower
Lexington, KY 40506
Fields offered: Business, public administration, engineering, family studies, education, mining, pharmacy

Year founded: 1865
Ownership: Nonprofit, state
Phone: (606) 257-4613
Fax: (606) 257-4000
E-mail: admissio@pop.uky.edu
Website: www.rgs.uky.edu

M.B.A. and Master of Public Administration may be earned through a combination of weekend and evening classes. Master of Engineering or Mineral Engineering, M.S. in family studies or special education, Doctor of Pharmacy (for those with a Bachelor of Pharmacy) and Ed.D. in a number of concentrations all available through courses beamed to a large number of remote sites, with a brief residency requirement (usually one or two summer sessions).

Master of Mining Engineering (MMinE) through distance education. The MMinE degree for practicing engineers in mining or related fields through interactive satellite television. It is planned that one mining engineering course per semester will be offered by instructional television. With sufficient enrollment, all appropriate graduate courses will be offered sequentially in this mode. Further information from the Department of Mining Engineering, 230 Mining and Mineral Resources Bldg., Lexington, KY 40506-0107, (606) 257-3818, Fax, (606) 323-1962, e-mail to leonard@engr.uky.edu

University of Mindanao   M

College of Education, Bolton St.
Davao City
Mindanao Island, Philippines
Fields offered: Education
Year founded: 1946
Ownership: Nonprofit, independent

The university's on-the-air project offers a Master's degree in education entirely through radio broadcasts. Students submit term papers, prepare workbooks, and take examinations at the university.

University of Minnesota   B

Program for Individualized Learning
107 Armory
15 Church Street SE
Minneapolis, MN 55455-0137
Fields offered: Many fields
Year founded: 1851
Ownership: Nonprofit, state
Phone: (612) 624-4020
Fax: (612) 624-6369
E-mail: admissions@tc.umn.edu
Website: cored.coled.umn.edu

Nonresident B.A. and B.S. degrees for students who live within commuting distance of the Twin Cities area. The program offers no courses or exams of its own; instead, it assists students in using resources at the university, at other institutions, and in the community. These might include local or correspondence courses, independent study projects, and assessment of prior learning. Attendance

is required at a number of planning sessions; contact the school for further information.

University of Natal   M, D

Private Bag X10
Dalbridge 4014, South Africa
Fields offered: Many fields
Year founded: 1910
Ownership: Nonprofit, state
Phone: (27-31) 260-1111
E-mail: strong@admin.und.ac.za
Website: www.und.ac.za

Natal's Master's and Doctoral degrees are research-based, which means that there is no coursework; the degree candidate does individual, independent research, culminating in a thesis that is submitted for in-person examinations. Requirements for specific degrees may vary; fields include business administration, agriculture, architecture, arts, commerce, economics, education, engineering, languages, medicine, science, and social sciences. The school has two semi-independent campuses, one at Dalbridge/Durban, the other at Pietermaritzburg.

University of New South Wales   M

Australian Graduate School of Business
Sydney 2052, NSW Australia
Fields offered: Business administration
Year founded: 1949
Phone: (61-2) 9931-9410
Fax: (61-2) 9931-9205
E-mail: EMBA@agsm.unsw.edu.au
Website: www.unsw.edu.au/

M.B.A. available through a combination of distance-learning, courses taken at sites around Australia, and four six-day residencies in Sydney.

University of Newcastle   B, M

Open Learning Group
New South Wales, 2308 Australia
Fields offered: Construction management, education
Year founded: 1951
Phone: (61-49) 216-599
Fax: (61-49) 216-932
E-mail: admissions-enquiries@ncl.ac.uk
Website: www.ncl.ac.uk/

Degree programs can be completed largely through distance learning, though one week a year is required in residency. Coursework is delivered by a variety of media, and tutorial support is provided. Offered are a Bachelor of Construction Management and a Bachelor of Education (with concentrations in design & technology, early or primary). Graduate programs are a Master of Early Childhood education, Master of Special Education, Master of Teaching, and Master of Industrial Education. For precise course requirements and residency, contact the school.

University of North Carolina   M

Division of Continuing Education
CB# 1020, The Friday Center
Chapel Hill, NC 27599-1020
Fields offered: Public health, health care administration
Year founded: 1793
Ownership: Nonprofit, state
Phone: (919) 962-1134 • (800) 862-5669
Fax: (919) 962-5549
E-mail: stuserv.ce@mhs.unc.edu
Website: www.unc.edu/depts/fri_cntr/conted.html

The executive Master's programs offer working health professionals the opportunity to earn a Master of Public Health in either management or dental health and a Master of Healthcare Administration over three years, with six on-campus weeks per summer, and two each January. Applicants must have at least three years' experience in their field or a doctoral-level professional degree in an appropriate field.

University of North Dakota   B, M

Grand Forks, ND 58202
Fields offered: Nursing, medical technology, business and public administration, social work, engineering
Year founded: 1883
Ownership: Nonprofit, state
Phone: (701) 777-2711 • (800) 342-8230
Fax: (701) 777-3696
Website: www.und.edu

Degree programs through courses sent to distance sites around the state, by videocassette, interactive television, public and educational network TV, and fax. B.S. in nursing, medical technology, and engineering, Bachelor of Social Work, M.P.A., and M.B.A. On-campus time varies by program; can be as little as two weeks.

Through another department, the school offers the Master of Science in space studies, an in-depth study of the scientific, technical, medical, political, and legal impacts associated with the exploration and development of space. This distance degree program combines videotaped lectures and real-time Internet-based class sessions allowing students worldwide to interact and discuss issues. The "virtual campus" allows all basic function to take place over the Internet—registration, ordering textbooks, downloading course materials, attending classes, and taking exams. Students are expected to spend one week on campus for a "capstone experience" near graduation time. Contact for this program:

Department of Space Studies
P.O. Box 9008
Grand Forks, ND 58202
Phone: (701) 777-2480 • (800) 828-4274
Fax: (701) 777-3650
E-mail: info@space.edu
Website: www.space.edu

University of Notre Dame   M

Executive Programs
126 College of Business Administration
Notre Dame, IN 46556
Fields offered: Business
Year founded: 1842
Ownership: Church
Phone: (219) 631-5285 • (800) 631-3622
Fax: (219) 631-6783
E-mail: CBA.execprog.1@nd.edu
Website: www.nd.edu/~execprog?

The is a video-conference extension of the regular MBA curriculum. Students attend classes on alternating weekends at one of three sites in Indiana, Ohio, or Illinois, for two years.

University of Oklahoma   B, M

College of Liberal Studies
660 Parrington Oval
Norman, OK 73019
Fields offered: Liberal studies
Year founded: 1890
Ownership: Nonprofit, state
Phone: (405) 325-1061 • (800) 522-4389
Fax: (405) 325-7605
E-mail: admrec@ouwww.ucs.
Website: www.uoknor.edu

Bachelor and Master of of Liberal Studies with two or three weeks each year on campus, plus directed independent study. B.L.S. students work in three areas: humanities, natural sciences, and social sciences. Sessions on-campus are required each year, but three of the four years may be waived, based on prior study or passing of an equivalency exam. In the fourth year the student completes an in-depth study and attends a mandatory seminar. There is an upper-division option for applicants with two years of college, which allows them to begin with a five-day residential seminar and complete all three phases in about a year, with the final seminar required, as the four-year B.L.S. There are no majors; students do elective study based on their interests. The M.L.S. is largely for people with specialized Bachelor's degrees who wish a broader education; it begins with a two-week on-campus seminar. See also: National Universities Degree Consortium.

University of Pittsburgh   B

External Studies Program
3808 Forbes Ave.
Pittsburgh, PA 15260
Fields offered: Psychology, economics, history, humanities, social sciences
Year founded: 1787
Ownership: Nonprofit, state
Phone: (412) 624-7210
Fax: (412) 624-7213
E-mail: aabt+@pitt.edu

Website: www.pitt.edu/~ciddeweb
The University of Pittsburgh offers Bachelor of Arts in psychology, economics and history, and area of concentration majors in humanities and societies. In addition, courses required for any degree offered in the College of General Studies (the University of Pittsburgh's evening college) can be fulfilled via distance education. Specially designed self-instructional materials developed by instructors allow students to study independently. Students are expected to attend three three- to four-hour Saturday workshops held for each course at the Pittsburgh campus, in order to interact with the instructor and other students in a classroom setting. Students can take exams at any of eleven off-campus sites, or make arrangements to have them proctored. Courses, faculty, tuition and transcript credits are the same as for Pitt's traditional classroom-based programs.

University of Portsmouth   B, M

Winston Churchill Avenue
Portsmouth, P01 2UP U.K.
Fields offered: Criminal justice studies, policing & police studies
Year founded: 1869
Phone: (44-1705) 876-543
Fax: (44-1705) 843-082
Website: www.port.ac.uk/

The Bachelor of Science in policing and police studies is offered via part-time distance study augmented with the taking of exams; students must be currently serving as police officers. Progress is assessed by combinations of coursework essays and projects and/or by examination. Study schools involving three-day blocks of residency are held in February and July of each year. The M.S. in criminal justice studies is designed for criminal-justice and law-enforcement practitioners, and others interested in crime, criminality, and the criminal justice process. Assessment is by means of coursework assignments (6 essays over the 2-year period of study), and examination (held in February of year one), and a 15,000-word dissertation. Two 2-day residential study periods in the United Kingdom, on Portsmouth's campus, are required each year (these take place in the months of October and February).

University of Sarasota   M, D

5250 17th Street
Sarasota, FL 34235
Fields offered: Business, education, counseling psychology, human services administration
Year founded: 1969
Ownership: Private, independent
Phone: (941) 379-0404 • (800) 331-5995
Fax: (941) 379-9464
E-mail: univsar@compuserve.com
Website: www.sarasota-online.com/university/graduate.html

Master of Arts in Education (M.A.Ed.) with concentrations in educational leadership and curriculum & instruction, M.A. in mental health counseling and human services administration, M.B.A. with several concentrations, Ed.D. in educational leadership, curriculum & instruction, counseling psychology, and human services administration, and D.B.A. with concentrations in information systems, international business, management, and marketing. For all of these programs, a minimum of eight weeks' residence is required; this requirement is split up over traditional winter, summer, and spring break periods. The university's programs consist of seminars, supervised individual research, and writing, combined with the residential sessions. Master's candidates either write a thesis or complete a directed independent-study project. Doctoral students must write a dissertation. Many of the students are teachers and school administrators. The D.B.A. program offers major areas of study in management, marketing, and information systems. (Originally known as Laurence University, the predecessor of the Laurence University that opened in California and is now the University of Santa Barbara.) An Ed.D. in pastoral counseling is supposed to be beginning very soon.

University of South Carolina   M

Columbia, SC 29208-001
Fields offered: Library and information science, engineering, business administration
Year founded: 1801
Ownership: Nonprofit, state
Phone: (803) 777-7000 • (800)-922-9755
Fax: (803) 777-0101
E-mail: gradschool@sc.edu
Website: www.csd.sc.edu

The University of South Carolina beams courses to distance-learning sites by satellite; other learning takes place through e-mail, and audio- and videocassette. They offer a Master's in library and information science (M.L.I.S.) through centers in South Carolina, West Virginia, and Georgia; and M.S. or M.E. in a variety of engineering fields (chemical, civil, mechanical, electrical, and computer), through a program for working engineers, and an M.B.A. through a program that requires 15 Saturday sessions on-campus per year. See also: National Universities Degree Consortium

University of South Florida   B

4202 E. Fowler Ave.
HM5 443
Tampa , FL 33620
Fields offered: Independent studies
Year founded: 1956
Ownership: Nonprofit, state
Phone: (813) 974-4058 • (800) 635-1484
Fax: (813) 974-5101
E-mail: bis@luna.cas.usf.edu
Website: www.cas.usf.edu/bis/index2.html

The Bachelor of Independent Studies program requires from four to six weeks on campus, spread out over three summers. All students must have knowledge across broad areas of study: social sciences, natural sciences, and humanities. Each area has an extensive program of guided independent study and a two-week on-campus seminar for research, writing, peer interaction, and, when relevant, laboratory experience. For four-area students, up to two areas can be waived for those who have sufficient work background, provided they pass an equivalency exam. All four-area students must write a thesis and defend it orally in a one-day examination on campus. The average student takes about five years to complete the degree. Applicants with an A.A. degree—or an A.S. in certain health-related fields—qualify for a two-area curriculum, with no thesis required.

University of Stirling   M

Stirling, FK9 4LA UK
Fields offered: Retailing & wholesaling, public relations, entrepreneurial studies
Year founded: 1967
Phone: (44-1786) 473-171
Fax: (44-1786) 450-201
Website: www.stir.ac.uk

Stirling offers several largely distance-learning Master's degrees, geared to working professionals. The M.S. in entrepreneurial studies is designed for students in the U.K. and abroad; applicants who lack an undergraduate degree but have significant experience in the small-business sector may be admitted if they can prove ability to take on postgraduate-level study. Similarly, the M.S. in public relations may be open to professionals with significant PR experience even if they lack the normal academic qualifications. The M.B.A. in retailing & wholesaling is for persons with high levels of experience; the average student has at least 10 years' work experience in the distributive trades. Students in all three programs are provided with specially designed materials, core textbooks, and audiocassettes. Face-to-face tutorials are expected in some programs.

University of Teesside   M, D

Research Office
Middlesbrough, Cleveland, TS1 3BA United Kingdom
Fields offered: Many fields
Year founded: 1929
Ownership: State
Phone: (44-1642) 384-220
Fax: (44-1642) 384-201
E-mail: K.Ludlow@tees.ac.uk
Website: www.tees.ac.uk/post97/research.htm

Offers the M.Phil. and Ph.D. in many fields through a research model, which means that it is possible for students to register with the university but work largely outside the UK if the facilities available are satisfactory and if the arrangements for supervision will provide frequent and substantial contact between the student and the UK-based supervisor. Required number of visits with supervisor vary by program. A minimum of 6 weeks per year in the UK is required.

University of Tennessee   M

Knoxville, TN 37996
Fields offered: Engineering
Year founded: 1794
Ownership: Nonprofit, state
Phone: (423) 974-1000
Fax: (423) 974-3536
E-mail: gsinfo@utk.edu
Website: cwis.utk.edu

The Master of Science is offered in a wide number of engineering fields (including aerospace, chemical, electrical and computer, science and mechanics, industrial, mechanical, management, etc.) available nationally by videocassette. There is also a corporate M.S. program though courses at a distance center in Kingsport, or at local businessplaces, and a similar program geared to government employees and contractors (but open to locals as well) offered in Oak Ridge. For information on this program, contact:

Joan Howell
Division of Continuing Education
Oak Ridge Graduate Program
P.O. Box 117, 246 Laboratory Road
Oak Ridge, TN 37831-0117
(423) 576-3429 fax (423) 576-9383

In addition, the Department. of Psychoeducational Studies is establishing a doctoral program which allows for nonresident candidates and for collaborative doctorates. Professor John Peters is the person to contact for information on this program.

University of Wales   M, D

University Registry, Cathays Park
Cardiff, CF1 3NS Wales
Fields offered: Many fields
Ownership: Nonprofit, state
Phone: (44-1222) 382-656
Fax: (44-1222) 396-040
E-mail: studentrecruitment@unsw.edu.au (residents of New Zealand and Australia)
internationaloffice@unsw.edu.au (international students)
Website: www.unsw.edu.au/

External Ph.D.'s may be pursued at any of the campuses of the university. Each candidate works with a supervisor, who is a present or former full-time member of the academic staff. An applicant must have an approved Bachelor's degree, demonstrate that there are adequate facilities at the "home base" for pursuing research (library, laboratory, archives, etc.), and be able to pay regular visits to the university (typically three visits a year to meet with the director of studies, or one month a year in continuous work). Initial inquiries to the department head of the relevant department, or the registrar of the institution chosen.

They are: University of Wales, Aberystwyth, Ceredigion SY23 2AX (Fax: 44-1970-611-446); University of Wales, Bangor, Gwynedd LL57 2DG (Fax: 44-1248-370-451); University of Wales Cardiff, Cathays Park, Cardiff CF1 3XA; University of Wales, Swansea, Singleton Park, Swansea SA2 8PP; University of Wales, Lampeter, Ceredigion SA48 7ED; University of Wales, College of Medicine, Heath Park, Cardiff CF4 4XN.

University of Wales, Aberystwyth   B, M, D

Old College
King Street
Aberystwyth
Ceredigion, Wales, SY23 4AT UK
Fields offered: Many fields
Year founded: 1872
Phone: (44-1970) 622-089
Fax: (44-1970) 622-921
E-mail: jdm@aber.ac.uk
Website: www.aber.ac.uk

The Aberystwyth campus of the University of Wales system offers a number of programs though distance learning. Some do require brief residency; contact the school for details. The distance-learning programs are: a B.S. in economics, with a specialization in library and information studies, M.S. in economics with a specialization in the management of library and information systems or in health information management, and M.S.'s in environmental impact assessment, environmental auditing, environmental management, and protected landscape management. In addition, there are M.Phil and Ph.D. degrees that can be studied on a part-time basis, with students traveling to Wales for a couple of weeks a year, or handled full-time through a place of employment. This option is available in the following departments: accounting & finance, art, biological sciences, computer science, economics, education, English, European languages, geography & earth studies, history & Welsh history, information & library sciences, international politics, law, mathematics, physics, rural agriculture, and theater, film, & television studies, and Welsh (Celtic) studies.

University of Wales, Bangor   M

Institute for Financial Management
Bangor, Gwynedd, LL57 2DG Wales, U.K.
Fields offered: Business administration
Ownership: Nonprofit, state
Phone: (44-1248) 371-408
Fax: (44-1248) 370-769
E-mail: R.Henry@bangor.ac.uk
Website: www.bangor.ac.uk/ab/ifm/home.htm

This M.B.A. program (with a concentration in financial management and financial services) is designed specifically for financial managers and "finance sector professionals." Managers from some 50 countries worldwide are currently enrolled. The module-based program culmi-

nates in a final work-related project. Two yearly 3-day residential sessions provide peer-group support and networking, as well as face-to-face faculty contact. Individual students are permitted to vary their program schedules to meet the demands of their specific professional and personal needs.

University of Wales, Lampeter   M

Department of Theology and Religious Studies
Lampeter, Dyfed, SA48 7ED Wales, U.K.
Fields offered: Celtic Christianity
Ownership: Nonprofit, state
Phone: (44-1570) 424-708
Fax: (44-1570) 423-641
E-mail: J.Foster@lamp.ac.uk
Website: www.lamp.ac.uk

An M.A. in Celtic Christianity is offered through full-time, part-time, and nonresidential study. This unique interdisciplinary degree examines all aspects of Celtic Christian civilization, from both the historical and contemporary perspectives.

University of Warwick   M

Distance Learning M.B.A. Office
Warwick Business School
Coventry, CV4 7AL United Kingdom
Fields offered: Business administration
Year founded: 1965
Ownership: Nonprofit, state
Phone: (44-1203) 524-100
Fax: (44-1203) 524-411
E-mail: dlmbainf@wbs.warwick.ac.uk
Website: www.warwick.ac.uk

Warwick offers the M.B.A. through a largely distance-learning format, although three "induction days" are required at the beginning of each of the program's three parts, plus one compulsory eight-day residential seminar. The school offers telephone and e-mail tutorial support, and comprehensive correspondence study materials.

University of Western Sydney, Hawkesbury   B

Bourke Street
Richmond, NSW 2753 Australia
Fields offered: Environmental health, land economy
Year founded: 1989
Phone: (61-45) 701333
Fax: (61-45) 783979
E-mail: p.mckinlay@usw.edu.au
Website: www.hawkesbury.uws.edu.au

Primarily for NSW residents, the programs require approximately a week of residential workshops per semester. Three degree programs are offered via distance learning: a Bachelor of Applied Science in environmental health, a Bachelor of Business in land economy, and a Bachelor of Applied Health. The land economy degree requires a bit more residency than the others, with weekend workshops, local area visits, and study centers.

University of Westminster — M

309 Regent Street
London, W1R 8AL United Kingdom
Fields offered: Management fields
Year founded: 1838
Phone: (44-171) 911-5000
Fax: (44-171) 911 5175
E-mail: international-office@wmin.ac.uk
Website: www.wmin.ac.uk

Westminster offers an M.B.A. with a concentration in design management and a Master of Arts in international business & management, both by distance learning. The M.B.A. is module-based, with a 4-day workshop at the end of each course of study; the M.A. has no required residency, although an optional residential week in July is offered.

University of Wisconsin—Green Bay — B

Extended Degrees Program Office
Green Bay, WI 54301
Fields offered: General studies
Year founded: 1978
Ownership: Nonprofit, state
Phone: (920) 465-2423 • (800) 621-2313
Fax: (920) 465-2032
E-mail: uwgb@uwgb.edu
Website: www.uwgb.edu

Nontraditional program is available only to Wisconsin residents; B.A. in general studies requires at least two seminars held on-campus on Saturdays. Program includes independent study, research projects, internships, radio and television courses, and other learning methods.

University of Wisconsin—Madison — M

Engineering Outreach
1415 Johnson Dr., Rm. 2713
Madison, WI 53706-1691
Fields offered: Engineering
Year founded: 1849
Ownership: Nonprofit, state
Phone: (608) 262-5516
Fax: (608) 262-6400
E-mail: gradadmiss@mail.bascom.wisc.edu
Website: www.wisc.edu

M.S. in nuclear engineering, power electronics, or engineering controls, primarily through satellite television and videocassette. Three weeks on campus required for a summer intersession laboratory course. The Master of Engineering in professional practice can be earned through distance methods (largely teleconferencing and the Internet), with two week-long on-campus sessions

University of Wisconsin—River Falls — B

Extended Degree Program
College of Agriculture
River Falls, WI 54022
Fields offered: Agriculture
Year founded: 1874
Ownership: Nonprofit, state
Phone: (715) 425-3239 • (800) 228-5421
Fax: (715) 425-3304
E-mail: admit@uwrf.edu
Website: www.uwrf.edu

B.S. in agriculture for residents of Wisconsin and Minnesota only. Most of the coursework can be completed through home study, with occasional visits to the River Falls campus (actual number of visits will depend on the courses taken). Credit for agricultural life experience through portfolio assessment, and for departmental and CLEP exams. Financial aid is available. This program may not be unavailable after 1998.

University of Wolverhampton

See: Holborn College

University of Wyoming — B, M

Off-Campus Degree Programs
Laramie, WY 82071
Fields offered: Public administration, social science, administration of justice, adult education, speech pathology
Year founded: 1886
Ownership: Nonprofit, state
Phone: (307) 766-3152 • (800) 448-7801, ext. 5
Fax: (307) 766-3445
E-mail: dragonn@uwyo.edu
Website: uwyo.edu

B.A. in social science or administration of justice, M.A. in adult education, M.S. in speech pathology, and Master of Public Administration through distance-learning courses, including videotaped lectures and an innovative audio teleconferencing technique. The social science program is upper division only; it is assumed that students will transfer in 60 credits of lower-division coursework from another institution. The M.S. requires at least two summers on campus.

Utah State University — M

Vocational Rehabilitation Counselor Training
2865 University Boulevard
Logan, UT 84322-2865
Fields offered: Rehabilitation
Year founded: 1888
Ownership: Nonprofit, state
Phone: (435) 797-0449
Fax: (435) 797-3572
E-mail: info@vrct.usu.edu
Website: vrct.ed.usu.edu

A Master's degree in vocational rehabilitation, geared to training rehabilitation counselors, is offered almost entirely through distance learning. Originally developed to serve rural Utah residents, this program now has students across the U.S. and Canada, and some overseas as well.

Coursework is accomplished via telephone conferencing, viewing of videotaped lectures and other instructional visuals, and Internet support. Approximately 3 one-week summer workshops are required on campus over the course of the degree, and students must complete a supervised internship.

Vermont Institute of Community Involvement

See: Burlington College

Virginia Polytechnic Institute and State University   M

College of Engineering, 333 Norris Hall
Blacksburg, VA 24061
Fields offered: Engineering, political science
Year founded: 1872
Ownership: Nonprofit, state
Phone: (540) 231-5458
Fax: (540) 231-7248
E-mail: laberge@vt.edu
Website: www.vt.edu

M.S. or M.E. in various engineering fields (electrical, mechanical, system, civil, and industrial), though satellite courses available nationwide, and audioconferencing. The On-Line M.A. in Political Science, identical in course content, requirement, and workload to the residential M.A/ degree program offered since 1969. Students can live anywhere in the world and do the necessary work over the Internet. The Department of Political Science phone is (540)-231-6571, email: twluke@vt.edu, www.cyber.vt.edu/psci/olma/olma.html.

Walden University   M, D

415 First Avenue North
Minneapolis, MN 55401
Fields offered: Applied management & decision sciences, education, human services, health services, psychology
Year founded: 1970
Ownership: Nonprofit, independent
Phone: (612) 338-7224 • (800) WALDENU
Fax: (612) 338-5092
E-mail: help@waldenu.edu
Website: www.waldenu.edu

Walden offers graduate education geared to experienced professionals. It offers Ph.D.s in applied management and decision sciences, education, health services, human services, and psychology. The programs consist of self-guided curricula delivered through learning modules, known as knowledge area modules, or KAMs, plus a dissertation. Each KAM is broadly conceptualized, allowing students to tailor a written demonstration of knowledge to their unique areas of professional interest. Fulfillment of 32 residency units is required and can be completed through a variety of options, including intensive four-day weekend sessions held at locations throughout the country, and two- or three-week sessions on the campus of Indiana University.

Master's programs are offered in education and psychology. Courses are delivered through electronic classrooms over the school's website. Students must have access to a personal computer, word-processing software, the Internet, and the World Wide Web.

Weber State University   B

Office of College of Health Professions Outreach Program
Ogden, UT 84408-4011
Fields offered: Allied health sciences
Year founded: 1889
Ownership: State
Phone: (801) 626-7164 • (800) 848-7770, ext.7164
Fax: (801) 626-7922
E-mail: Admissions@weber.edu
Website: www.weber.edu

B.S. in allied health sciences, with concentrations in health administrative services, advanced radiological sciences, respiratory therapy, and advanced dental hygiene. Up to 46 credit hours for CLEP exams, and up to 15 for two full years' military service. At least 45 credit hours must be taken through WSU, through intensive workshops and independent study. Correspondence courses include textbooks, study guides, modules, video- and audiotapes, and other learning aides prepared by the instructor. Student is assigned an instructor for each course, and keeps contact by phone and mail. Student has up to six months to complete each course. Workshops are four three- to four-day sessions per year at various sites, including Billings, MT and Seattle, WA, or two six day "super sessions" at WSU. Exact number required depends on student's precise field of study.

Webster University   M

470 E. Lockwood Avenue
St. Louis , MO 63119
Fields offered: Business, computers, health
Year founded: 1915
Ownership: Nonprofit, independent
Phone: (314) 968-6900
Fax: (314) 968-7112
E-mail: request@websteruniv.edu
Website: www.websteruniv.edu

Now, here's the problem. Their innovative Master's programs, offered in dozens of locations around the U.S., used to be described in glowing terms in this book. We received more than 20 letters from people who enrolled as a result of our report and were happy. Then the coordinator of Experiential and Individual Learning wrote and demanded that we stop providing information on their programs. So we left them out for one edition and, needless to say, got a bunch of letters from people saying, in effect, "How come you didn't put anything in about Webster?" And as we were working on this edition, Charles E. Beech, Director of University Admissions, wrote to ask that the school be deleted, although he didn't explain why. To find out, you'll have to write to him at the address above.

West Virginia Board of Regents B.A. Program   B

203 Student Services Bldg.
West Virginia University
Morgantown, WV 26506
Fields offered: Many fields
Year founded: 1867
Ownership: Nonprofit, state
Phone: (304) 293-5441 • 1-800-344-wvu1
Fax: (304) 293-7490
E-mail: tcarrico@wvu.edu
Website: www.wvu.edu

This B.A. program requires a minimum of 15 semester hours in residence at any of the member schools in the state, and states that "as long as the student can provide evidence that he/she possesses college equivalent knowledge or skills, his/her achievements will be credited and recognized as applicable toward this degree program." The evaluation of life experience costs a modest $50, regardless of the amount of credit granted. The member schools are: Bluefield State College, West Virginia State College, Concord College, West Virginia Tech, Fairmont State College, West Virginia University, Shepherd College, West Liberty State College, Marshall University, and Glenville State College.

West Virginia Institute of Technology   B

Regents B.A. Degree Program
Montgomery, WV 25136
Fields offered: Engineering, engineering technology, business management, accounting, health sciences administration, nursing, dental hygiene, printing, history of government
Year founded: 1895
Ownership: Nonprofit, state
Phone: (304) 442-3071 • (888) 554-8324
Fax: (304) 442-3059

E-mail: wvutech@wvit.wvnet.edu
Website: wvnet.edu

B.A. largely through credit for life-experience and academic learning, equivalency exams, independent study, correspondence courses, supervised fieldwork, and televised classes. Fifteen credit hours must be earned on-campus.

Westminster College (Pennsylvania)   B

New Wilmington, PA 16172
Fields offered: Many fields
Year founded: 1852
Ownership: Nonprofit, church
Phone: (412) 946-7120
Fax: (412) 946-7171
E-mail: admis@westminster.edu
Website: www.westminster.edu

Jesse Thomas Mann, Associate Dean of the College, has written asking us not to describe their innovative Bachelor's degree program. For further information, then, you will need to contact the school directly, or see separate listing in this book under East Central College Consortium.

William Woods University   B, M

College of Graduate and Adult Studies
200 West 12th Street
Fulton, MI 65251
Fields offered: Business administration, management, marketing, education
Year founded: 1870
Ownership: church
Phone: (573) 592-1149 • (800) 995-3199
Fax: (573) 592-1164
E-mail: cgas@iris.wmwoods.edu
Website: www.wmwoods.edu/

Classes meet once a week at various sites throughout Missouri. Program is available only in Missouri.

Wolverhampton Polytechnic

See: Holborn College

SO WHERE DID YOUR REGENTS DEGREE TAKE YOU?
MINE TOOK ME TO ALCATRAZ!

BY MARTIN SPILLANE

Having received my Regents College B.S. in liberal studies, I embarked on the study of continuing education and one day I found myself on a wet and windy voyage to the bleak island prison of Alcatraz, which in its time has housed some of America's most violent criminals. It is not a place normally associated with education or vocational training, yet it was there that I met a self-taught scholar and medical man called Jim Quillen, otherwise known as Federal Prisoner AZ 586. He was a bulky, broad-shouldered man with gray hair, a craggy face and the aura of a heavyweight boxer. He was sitting on the edge of a seemingly inadequate steel chair in a small, cold, harshly lit room, where the wind howled and the rain whipped between the steel bars of the square hole that served as a window. He had a pen in his hand and spectacles perched crookedly on his misshapen nose, and he was peering at the books on the table before him.

Jim Quillen had originally been sentenced to 15 years in a California state prison for robbery, but had escaped and committed other robberies whilst on the run. When cornered by the police he and another escapee had kidnapped two hostages at gunpoint and escaped in a stolen car. For this he had been sentenced to 45 years in a federal prison, with the original 15 years to be served later in the California state penitentiary. He was sent to Alcatraz, where he became embroiled in a major riot and lost all remission. Facing a lifetime in jail, he had declined all contact with his family and had become an institutionalized recluse, hidden in the steel and concrete jungle of the American penal system.

As a child he had endured an unhappy home-life, an alcoholic mother, an openly hostile stepmother, separation from his sister, and life in a series of foster homes. His schooling had been limited by truancy and as a result of petty crime he had been sent to reform school. At 20 he had joined the Marine Corps and completed his six months basic training, only to be discharged when his criminal record came to light. His father, a former soldier, had then disowned him. However, eight years into his 60-year sentence, he had been fortunate in meeting a Roman Catholic chaplain who helped him to find a new faith and to realize that there was another way of life. Thus fortified, he was able to risk the derision of his fellow inmates and he became the prison altar-boy. The chaplain also arranged visits by his family, from whom he was to learn of the death of his mother. The effect of this news was profound, causing him to take stock of his personal attributes and situation, and he began to feel a need for knowledge.

Opportunities for education in legitimate skills were limited in Alcatraz and so he enrolled in the University of California correspondence courses to gain a high school diploma, studying at night by the light from the cellblock corridor. The authorities, recognizing his efforts, permitted him to take extra courses and rewarded his success with the gradual restoration of remission and privileges, and he achieved his high school diploma and then much more. When illness took him into the prison hospital, he gained a new interest and, having recovered, he volunteered to work there as an orderly. Through hard work and medical study, he acquired new skills and a measure of self-respect.

When I met Jim Quillen, that wet and windy day on Alcatraz, my greeting was short and to the point, "I'll bet that 50 years ago, you never thought you would be sitting here today, doing this!" In reply, he smiled broadly, shook my hand warmly, and savored the joke. For Jim Quillen, Convict AZ 586, was back in Alcatraz as a volunteer, autographing copies of his memoirs, published some years earlier by the Golden Gate National Park Association, who now operate the former jail as a national monument. His release on parole in 1960 had facilitated further study and he had gone on to gain membership by examination of the American Society of Radiological Technologists. This had given him a profession and in 11 years he rose to be Chief Technologist and Radiological Supervisor at a California hospital, a job he had held for 15 years. He married, had children and, when he retired, both the president of the United States and the governor of California had acknowledged his rehabilitation by awarding him federal and state pardons for crimes which had originally warranted 60 years in jail.

Should I ever doubt the value of continuing education, I will only have to think back to that grim island prison, and to my meeting with the man for whom such education had provided the means of escape, to a lawful and productive life.

20

Accredited Schools with Nontraditional Residential Programs

I find the three major administrative problems on a campus are sex for the students, athletics for the alumni, and parking for the faculty.

CLARK KERR (WHEN PRESIDENT OF THE UNIVERSITY OF CALIFORNIA)

Any school can claim that it is accredited; the use of that word is not regulated in any way. This chapter includes only those schools that are accepted as "Accredited" under GAAP, Generally Accepted Accreditation Principles. In the U.S., there is near-unanimous agreement on GAAP (although not everyone calls it this, the concept is widely accepted) by the relevant key decision-makers: university registrars and admissions officers, corporate human resource officers, and government agencies.

Note that in some countries, the word "accredited" is not used, although the evaluation process in that country (e.g., the British Royal Charter), is accepted as "accredited" under GAAP.

Note, too, that schools that do not meet the standards of GAAP are not necessarily bad, illegal, or fake. They simply would not be generally accepted as accredited.

All schools in this chapter meet the standards of GAAP, which means that they meet any one of the following six criteria:

GAAP CRITERIA

◆ Accredited by an agency recognized by the Council on Higher Education Accreditation in Washington.

◆ Accredited by an agency recognized by the U.S. Department of Education.

◆ Listed in the International Handbook of Universities (a UNESCO publication).

◆ Listed in the Commonwealth Universities Yearbook.

◆ Listed in the World Education Series, published by PIER (Projects in International Education Research), a joint venture of AACRAO (the American Association of Collegiate Registrars and Admissions Officers) and NAFSA (the Association of International Educators) with the participation of the College Board.

◆ Listed in the Countries Series, published by NOOSR, the National Office for Overseas Skills Recognition, in Australia.

The basic format of each listing is as follows:

Name of School   **A**ssociate's, **B**achelor's, **M**aster's, **D**octorate, **Law, D**iploma
Address
City, State Postal Code Country, if not U.S.
Fields of study offered
Year founded
Ownership (nonprofit or proprietary, state, private, or church-run)
Phone • Toll-free phone
Fax
E-mail address
Website URL

Note: We have in the past given cost information, but this changes so quickly and is so subjective that we have decided to discontinue the practice. If a program is extremely inexpensive, or disproportionately expensive, we've mentioned this in the listing. In most cases, the best way to find out about the cost of any particular program is to contact the school directly.

Aalborg University Centre   B, M, D
Langagervej 2
P.O. Box 159
DK-9100, Aalborg, Denmark
Fields offered: Economics, engineering, business, social work, humanities
Year founded: 1974
Ownership: Nonprofit, state

Phone: (45) 9815-8522
Fax: (45) 9815-1522
Website: www.auc.dk

Students at this experimental Danish university spend one year in residential study, then work on independent-study projects in small groups. All degrees are based on passing examinations.

Acadia University   B

Wolfville, NS BOP 1X0 Canada
Fields offered: Many fields
Year founded: 1838
Ownership: Nonprofit, state
Phone: (902) 542-2201, ext. 141
Fax: (902) 585-1072
E-mail: admissions@acadiau.ca
Website: www.acadiau.ca

Although many courses are offered through correspondence and by teleconference, and a limited number of courses may be transferred from elsewhere, the school wants prospective students to be aware that it is not possible to complete all degree requirements nonresidentially. Many courses offered on audio- or videotape.

Adams State College   M

Department of Teacher Education
Alamosa, CO 81102
Fields offered: Education
Year founded: 1921
Ownership: Nonprofit, state
Phone: (719) 589-7121 • (800) 548-6679
Fax: (719) 589-7522
E-mail: ascadmit@adams.edu
Website: www.adams.edu

Field-based M.A. in elementary or secondary education for working, accredited teachers. Sixteen of the required thirty credit-hours must be taken in residency; the rest can be earned through assessment of prior learning, correspondence and television courses, audio- and videocassettes, and supervised fieldwork. Academic assistance, tutoring, job-placement, and financial aid available.

Adelphi University   B, M, D

University College ABLE Program
Garden City, NY 11530
Fields offered: Many fields
Year founded: 1896
Ownership: Nonprofit, independent
Phone: (516) 877-3400
Fax: (516) 977-3296
E-mail: admissions@adelphi.edu
Website: www.adelphi.edu

B.A. and B.S. available through the ABLE (Adult Baccalaureate Learning Experience) Program, which offers evening and weekend classes during the fall, spring, and summer. The program, which is based on a four-credit system, provides flexible scheduling of classes, including regular courses that meet once weekly. Some courses meet seven times; others meet five times. Credit for prior learning and by examination is possible.

Alabama State University   B

Continuing Education
915 S. Jackson St.
Montgomery, AL 36195
Fields offered: Many fields
Year founded: 1874
Ownership: Nonprofit, state
Phone: (334) 229-4200
Fax: (334) 834-6861
E-mail: admissions@asunet.alasu.edu
Website: www.alasu.edu

Bachelor's degree can be earned through weekend, evening, and summer programs. Credit for independent study, nonacademic prior learning, and by examination.

Alaska Pacific University   B, M

4101 University Dr.
Anchorage, AK 99508
Fields offered: Many fields
Year founded: 1957
Ownership: Nonprofit, church
Phone: (907) 561-1266
Fax: (907) 562-4276
E-mail: apu@corecom.net
Website: www.alaska.net/~apu

Credit for independent study, nonacademic prior learning, and by examination. Thirty-six credits in residency required. Only private university in Alaska. Programs in liberal arts, elementary education, human resources, communications, natural resources, values and service, and management.

Albertus Magnus College   B

Accelerated Degree Program
700 Prospect Street
New Haven, CT 06511
Fields offered: Many fields
Year founded: 1925
Ownership: Nonprofit, independent
Phone: (203) 773-8550 • (800) 394-9982
Fax: (203) 773-3117
E-mail: admissions@albertus.edu
Website: www.albertus.edu

Up to 21 credits towards a B.A. or B.F.A. may be awarded for prior learning, including a wide range of exams. Additional credit may be earned through independent study and/or supervised fieldwork.

Albright College   B

Evening Program
P.O. Box 15234
Reading, PA 19612
Fields offered: Business, computer science
Year founded: 1856

Ownership: Nonprofit, church
Phone: (610) 921-2381
Fax: (610) 921-7530
E-mail: albright@joe.alb.edu
Website: www.alb.edu

B.S. in accounting, business administration, or computer science through evening courses. Up to half the required credits can come from transfer coursework, exams, and/or portfolio assessment.

Alvernia College   B

Reading, PA 19607
Fields offered: Many fields
Year founded: 1958
Ownership: Nonprofit, independent
Phone: (610) 796-8200 • (888) ALVERNIA
Fax: (610) 777-6632
Website: www.alvernia.edu

Abby L. Pfaffman, the Assistant Director of Admissions, has written asking us not to describe the school's weekend, evening, and summer programs. For more information, contact Ms. Pfaffman directly.

Alverno College   B

Weekend College, 3401 S. 39th St.
P.O. Box 343922
Milwaukee, WI 53234-3922
Fields offered: Nursing, professional communication, business, management
Year founded: 1887
Ownership: Nonprofit, independent
Phone: (414) 382-6100 • (800) 933-3401
Fax: (414) 382-6354
E-mail: admissions@alverno.edu
Website: www.alverno.edu

Classes involve intensive study, close working relationships with faculty, and maximum opportunity for self-directed study. The weekend program is a complete college experience with over 1,100 women attending. Previous college credit is not required. B.S.N. Nursing completion for R.N.'s.

Amber University   B, M

1700 Eastgate Drive
Garland, TX 75041
Year founded: 1971
Ownership: Nonprofit, independent
Phone: (972) 279-6511
Fax: (972) 279-9773
E-mail: webmail@ambernet.amberu.edu
Website: www.amberu.edu

Amber is an upper-level and graduate university, offering the B.A., B.S., B.B.A., M.S., M.A., and M.B.A. to adult students (applicants must be over 21 years old; undergraduates must have completed 30 credits of coursework elsewhere). Credit awarded for CLEP exams, military experience, and by portfolio review. Courses meet once a week in the evening or on weekends, with four 10-week sessions each year.

American Health Science University   M

1010 South Joliet Street, #107
Aurora, CO 80012
Fields offered: Business, human services
Year founded: 1980
Phone: (303) 340-2054 • (800) 530-8079
Fax: (303) 367-2577
E-mail: inuted@aol.com
Website: www.nines.com

Accredited certificate programs in nutrition, wholly through distance-learning methods. The program consists of 6 courses, each broken down into a number of modules. The average employed adult, studying one hour a day, will take about 5 months per class, but motivated individuals can progress much more quickly. Support is available by phone and fax, and exams can be taken at a local library or other approved site. A Master's degree is planned for the near future. Formerly known as the National Institute of Nutritional Education.

American International College   B

1000 State St.
Springfield, MA 01109
Fields offered: Business, human services
Year founded: 1885
Ownership: Nonprofit, independent
Phone: (413) 747-6525
Fax: (413) 737-2803
E-mail: inquiry@www.aic.edu
Website: www.aic.edu

The degree is available through evening and weekend study through the College of Continuing and Graduate Studies. A REACH program offers special support for older students who have never attended college.

American Schools of Professional Psychology   M, D

220 S. State St.
Chicago, IL 60604
Fields offered: Clinical psychology
Phone: (312) 899-9900 • (800) 626-4123
Fax: (312) 201-1907
E-mail: aspp@interaccess.com
Website: www.aspp.edu

The American Schools of Professional Psychology (ASPP), which includes the Illinois School of Professional Psychology (ISPP), the Minnesota School of Professional Psychology (MSPP), and the Georgia School of Professional Psychology (GSPP), was established to provide extensive practical training in the area of professional psychology. The M.A., offered at ISPP and GSPP, and the Psy.D. (Doctor of Psychology), offered at all three locations, emphasize the "practitioner" focus in the field of clinical psychology, and all of ASPP's curriculum and field training prepares students to obtain diverse careers in the mental health field. The Psy.D. degree at ISPP is accredited by the American Psychological Association (APA).

American University (DC)   B, M, D

4400 Massachusetts Ave., N.W.
Washington, DC 20016
Fields offered: Many fields
Year founded: 1893
Ownership: Nonprofit, church
Phone: (202) 885-6000
Fax: (202) 885-6014
E-mail: afa@american.edu
Website: www.american.edu

Degrees in a variety of fields can be earned through evening classes, credit for life and job experience, examinations, study abroad, and community-operated programs. The university hosts a "Washington Semester" program. In the innovative Bachelor of Liberal Studies program, a total of 75 credits (of the 120 required for a B.A. in liberal studies) can be transferred from other four-year institutions, and 30 more can come from portfolio evaluation. Forty-five units, however, must be earned in residency. The degree program is designed by the student and can focus on the humanities, social sciences, or natural sciences.

American University of Paris   B

31 Ave. Bosquet
Paris, 75007 France
Fields offered: Many fields
Year founded: 1962
Ownership: Nonprofit, independent
Phone: (33) 45559173 or (212) 983-1414 (USA)
Fax: (33) 47053432 or (212) 983-0444 (USA)
E-mail: admissions@aup.fr or aup@interport.net (USA)
Website: www.aup.fr/

Bachelor's degrees in international business administration, international affairs, art history, French studies, European cultural studies, computer science, international economics, and comparative literature are offered through year-round study in Paris. Summer sessions are also offered. All instruction is in English. The student body is about half American and half from 60 other countries. New York office is at 80 E. 11th St., Suite 434, New York, NY 10003, (212) 677-4870. Formerly American College in Paris.

Anna Maria College   M

Paxton, MA 01612
Fields offered: Business
Year founded: 1946
Ownership: Nonprofit, church
Phone: (508) 849-3300 • (800) 344-4586
Fax: (508) 849-3339
E-mail: csoverow@anna-maria.edu
Website: www.anna-maria.edu

The M.B.A. can be earned in from 12 to 18 months of intensive weekend study at centers in either Paxton or Boston.

Aquinas College   B, M

Continuing Education Program
1607 Robinson Road, SE
Grand Rapids, MI 49506
Fields offered: Education, business, Christian ministry
Year founded: 1922
Ownership: Nonprofit, church
Phone: (616) 459-8281
Fax: (616) 732-4485
E-mail: admissions@aquinas.edu
Website: www.aquinas.edu

Aquinas's mission is to provide a career-oriented liberal arts education, in a Catholic Christian context, to persons beyond conventional college age. Credit is given for life-experience learning, independent study, and some supervised fieldwork. Degrees awarded include the B.A. in general education, B.S. in business administration, M.A. in teaching and Master of Management.

Armstrong Atlantic State College   B, M

11935 Abercorn St.
Savannah, GA 31406
Fields offered: Business, education
Year founded: 1935
Ownership: Nonprofit, state
Phone: (912) 927-5275 • (800) 633-2349
Fax: (912) 927-5387
E-mail: Adrienne_Dillard@mailgate.armstrong.edu
Website: www.armstrong.edu

Bachelor of Arts, Bachelor of Science, Bachelor of Business Administration, Master of Educational Administration, and M.B.A. are offered entirely through evening study.

Armstrong University   B, M

1608 Webster St.
Oakland, CA 94612
Fields offered: Business
Year founded: 1918
Ownership: Proprietary
Phone: (510) 848-2500
Fax: (510) 848-9438
Website: www.armstrong-u.edu

Bachelor's and M.B.A. are offered through day or evening study. Formerly accredited by the regional Western Association, now by ACICS, the accreditation is from the Association of Independent Colleges and Schools.

Audrey Cohen College   B, M

345 Hudson St.
New York, NY 10014-4598
Fields offered: Human service, business, administration
Year founded: 1964
Ownership: Nonprofit, independent
Phone: (212) 343-1234
Fax: (212) 343-7399
Website: www.audrey-cohen.edu

Bachelor of Professional Studies in human service or business; Master of Science in administration. Largely adult population; three full semesters a year give students the option of completing the four-year undergraduate preparation in under three years, and the graduate degree in one year. Each semester focuses on a broad area of activity critical to professional work in the global economy (such as "working effectively in groups," or "acting as an effective supervisor"). Students complete five classes each semester, culminating in a "constructive action" at their worksite or volunteer placement which demonstrates an understanding of the semester's theme. Cohen's Field Development and Job Placement Office helps students identify employment or internship sites, as needed.

Audubon Expedition Institute   B, M
P.O. Box 365
Belfast, ME 04915
Fields offered: Environmental studies, environmental education
Year founded: 1969
Ownership: Nonprofit, independent
Phone: (207) 338-5859 • (888) 287-2234
Fax: (207) 338-1037
E-mail: mwest.aei@usa.net
Website: www.audubon.org/audubon/aei.html
Bachelor or Master of Science in cooperation with the National Audubon Society and Lesley College (of Cambridge, Massachusetts), involving community-based experiential education. Students travel, camp, and in other ways study one bioregion of the U.S. or Canada each semester. About a quarter of each semester is spent in the region's back country—backpacking, hiking, canoeing, skiing, and/or bicycling. Students gain practical knowledge of ecological issues, as well as community-building, cultural traditions, geology, etc. Earning the M.S. involves a year and a half of such expeditions and a one-semester internship. The B.S. involves two years of expeditions, one year of university courses (at a school that has agreed to work with the Institute), and one year of internships. Advanced-placement high-school students and undergraduates from other schools can spend one to four semesters in the expedition setting. See also: Lesley College

Augsburg College   B, M
2211 Riverside Avenue
Minneapolis, MN 55454
Fields offered: Many fields
Year founded: 1869
Ownership: Nonprofit, church
Phone: (612) 330-1743 • (800) 788-5678
Fax: (612) 330-1784
E-mail: wecinfo@augsburg.edu
Website: www.augsburg.edu
Augsburg weekend college offers Bachelor's degrees in accounting, business administration, communications, computer science, economics, education, English, management

information systems, nursing (BSN completion program), psychology, religion, social work, and studio art. Master's degrees are available in social work and "arts in leadership." This weekend college program was designed to allow adults who work or have other week-day commitments to attain a college education. Each course involves periods of concentrated on-campus study, interspersed with independent study. In practice, this usually means that courses meet on alternate weekends, for three-and-a-half hours each.

Augustana College   B, M
29th and Summit
Sioux Falls, SD 57197
Fields offered: Many fields
Year founded: 1860
Ownership: Nonprofit, church
Phone: (605) 336-5516 • (800) 727-2844
Fax: (605) 336-5299
E-mail: info@inst.augie.edu
Website: www.augie.edu
The Twilight Degree Program offers a Bachelor of Arts through courses given in the evening, at the noon hour, or on weekends. Credit for independent study, nonacademic prior learning, and by examination. See also: Quad Cities Graduate Center

Aurora University   B, M
347 S. Gladstone
Aurora, IL 60506-4892
Fields offered: Many fields
Year founded: 1893
Ownership: Nonprofit, independent
Phone: (630) 844-6517
Fax: (630) 844-5463
E-mail: admissions@admin.aurora.edu
Website: www.aurora.edu
Undergraduate degrees in almost all fields can be earned through evening study. Degree offerings include many career areas (accounting, business administration, management, marketing, economics, communication, criminal justice, recreation administration, social work, nursing), as well as liberal arts. Credit for life, vocational, and military experience, etc., assessed through Life Experience/Education Assessment Program. Self-designed degree programs in many areas. Master's degrees programs in career/professional areas (education, nursing, social work, business, information science, recreation administration). All Master's coursework offered in evenings, on campus or at various off-campus sites.

Averett College   B, M
Adult and Continuing Education
420 West Main Street
Danville, VA 24541
Fields offered: Business administration
Year founded: 1859

Ownership: Nonprofit, church
Phone: (804) 791-5600 • (800) 849-9223
Fax: (804) 791-5637
E-mail: ssfisher@uop.oramail@apollogrp.edu
Website: www.averett.edu

Eighty-one of the 123 hours required for a Bachelor of Business Administration, or 30 of the 36 for an M.B.A., can come from life-experience learning, credit for exams, and correspondence courses. Averett stresses that this is a highly structured, rigidly paced program for adult students who want to get their degree as quickly as possible, without interruption.

Avila College   B

Weekend College
11901 Wornall Road
Kansas City, MO 64145
Fields offered: Many fields
Year founded: 1916
Ownership: Nonprofit, church
Phone: (816) 942-8400
Fax: (816) 942-3362
E-mail: admissions@mail.avila.edu
Website: www.avila.edu

Ninety-eight of the required 128 credits for a Bachelor of General Studies from Avila can come from transfer credit, portfolio assessment, CLEP exams, and school-administered exams. The additional 30 credits are earned through weekend courses designed for students of all ages, but particularly those with family or career responsibilities.

Baker University   B, M

School for Professional & Graduate Studies
6800 College Blvd.
Suite 500
Overland Park, KS 66211
Fields offered: Business, management, liberal arts
Year founded: 1858
Ownership: Nonprofit, church
Phone: (913) 594-6451 • (800) 873-4282
Fax: (913) 594-6721
E-mail: adm_scheib@george.bakeru.edu
Website: www.bakeru.edu

B.B.A., M.B.A., Master of Science in management, and Master of Liberal Arts tailored to adult learners. Bachelor's applicants must have completed 60 credits and been employed in their field for at least three years (the school recommends that undergraduate applicants should be at least 23 years old, graduate students at least 25). At the undergraduate level, some credit can be awarded for military experience, exams, and by portfolio assessment. Forty-four (of 124) credits for the B.B.A. must be earned from Baker. Distance-learning options include correspondence and televised courses and independent study.

Baldwin-Wallace College   B, M

275 Eastland Rd.
Berea, OH 44017
Linda L. Young, Registrar
Fields offered: Many fields
Year founded: 1845
Ownership: Nonprofit, church
Phone: (216) 826-2222
Fax: (216) 826-2329
E-mail: ccowie@bw.edu
Website: www.baldwinw.edu

Bachelor of Arts, Bachelor of Science, Bachelor of Science in education, Bachelor of Music, Bachelor of Music Education. Some programs available through evening study or the weekend college, which meets on alternate weekends. Credit accepted for prior learning and CLEP Examinations. Credit also considered for military experience and programs in training per recommendations from the American Council on Education. Master of Business Administration available through evening and Saturday programs. Master of Business Administration Executive program meets on alternate weekends. Master of Arts in Education available evenings during the regular academic year and days during the summer.

Ball State University   M

Muncie, IN 47306
Fields offered: Education, business administration
Year founded: 1918
Ownership: Nonprofit, state
Phone: (765) 289-1241 • (800) 872-0369
Fax: (765) 285-1461
E-mail: D000grad@bsuvc.bsu.edu
Website: www.bsu.edu/UP/cover.html

Master of Education program, including a special program in psychometrics, can be completed entirely through evening study. M.B.A. can be completed through satellite TV courses in cooperating workplaces. The phone number for the M.B.A. program is (317) 285-1931; the contact person is Tamara Estep.

Barat College   B

Lake Forest, IL 60045
Fields offered: Many fields
Year founded: 1858
Ownership: Nonprofit, independent
Phone: (847) 604-6270
Fax: (847) 604-6260
E-mail: bsjb@barat.edu
Website: www.academics.barat.edu

Bachelor of Arts through a combination of coursework and credit for prior learning experiences. Evening students may complete majors in management and business, human resource emphasis, computing and information systems, and communication arts. Barat also offers a degree completion program for nurses, awarding up to 60 credit-hours for their professional training, plus additional credit for CLEP scores and work achievements.

Barry University   B, M, D
11300 NE 2nd Ave.
Miami, FL 33161
Fields offered: Many fields
Year founded: 1940
Ownership: Nonprofit, church
Phone: (305) 899-3000 • (800) 695-2279
Fax: (305) 899-3104
E-mail: dpoole@pcsa01.barry.edu (undergraduate)
mcallahan@pcsa01.barry.edu (graduate)
Website: www.barry.edu

Degrees are offered in accounting, management, marketing, computer science, economics, finance, philosophy, and psychology. Credit for prior professional and work experience. Classes held in various location throughout southern Florida.

Bartlesville Wesleyan College   B
2201 Silver Lake Road
Bartlesville, OK 74006-6299
Year founded: 1910
Ownership: Nonprofit, church
Phone: (918) 333-6151 • (800) 375-4647
Fax: (918) 335-6210
E-mail: gotobwc@aol.com
Website: www.bwc.edu

Offers a number of evening and weekend programs.

Baruch College   B, M
17 Lexington Ave.
New York, NY 10010
Fields offered: Business and public administration
Year founded: 1919
Ownership: Nonprofit, state
Phone: (212) 802-2300
Fax: (212) 802-2310
E-mail: udgbb@cunyvm.cuny.edu (undergraduate) or
Graduate_Admissions@newton.baruch.cuny.edu
Website: www.baruch.cuny.edu

The college of the City University of New York offers the Bachelor of Business Administration, M.B.A., and Master of Public Administration, entirely through evening study.

Bellarmine College   B, M
Newburg Rd.
Louisville, KY 40205
Fields offered: Business, nursing
Year founded: 1950
Ownership: Nonprofit, independent
Phone: (502) 452-8211 • (800) 274-4723
Fax: (502) 452-8033
E-mail: admissions@bellarmine.edu
Website: www.bellarmine.edu/public/index.asp

Bachelor's and Master's degrees in business and nursing can be completed through the FLEX (Flexible Learning, Education eXcellence) plan. Classes generally meet once a week at any of the seven Louisville locations or six outreach locations around the state. Select courses are also offered in an accelerated seven-week format. Credit is given for prior learning and by examination.

Bellevue University   B, M
Galvin Road at Harvell Drive
Bellevue, NE 68005-3098
Fields offered: Many fields
Year founded: 1965
Ownership: Nonprofit, independent
Phone: (402) 293-3766 • (800) 756-7920
Fax: (402) 293-2020
E-mail: astesting@scholars.bellevue.edu
Website: www.bellevue.edu/Online/intro.htm

Bellevue offers evening and weekend classes and summer sessions leading to B.A. and B.S. degrees in many fields. They also offer a Bachelor of Technical Studies (BTS) program in management, business administration, information management, or commercial art designed for graduates of community colleges, and a Bachelor of Professional Studies in business administration of technical services, criminal justice administration, health care management, management, management of human resources, or sales and marketing. (This is an accelerated program designed for working adults to complete their degree in about a year. Applicants for the B.P.S. must have an Associate's degree or 60 credits, be employed, and have "relevant work experience.") A Master of Arts in management is also offered, in a concentrated 16-month program.

Bentley College   B
175 Forest Street
Morrison Hall, Room 200
Waltham, MA 02154
Fields offered: Professional studies
Year founded: 1917
Ownership: Nonprofit, independent
Phone: (781) 891-2000 • (800) 523-2354
Fax: (781) 891-2569
E-mail: moreinfo@bentley.edu
Website: www.bentley.edu

The B.S. in professional studies may be completed in one of the following concentrations: government, applied ethics, behavioral science, communication, or legal studies. Independent study and supervised fieldwork possible. Up to 75 of 120 required credits can come from transfer credit, portfolio assessment, and a number of exams. The average part-time student takes seven to eight years to complete this degree.

Bethany College
See: East Central College Consortium

Bethel College   B

McKenzie, TN 38201
Fields offered: Many fields
Year founded: 1842
Ownership: Nonprofit, church
Phone: (901) 352-4000 • (800) 441-4940
Fax: (901) 352-4069
E-mail: mangemw@bethel/college.edu
Website: www.bethel/college.edu

Credit is given for life experience learning and for internships, and some evening courses are available. Bethel offers 19 basic majors, and it is also possible for students to initiate their own.

Bethune-Cookman College   B

Continuing Education Program
640 2nd Ave.
Daytona Beach, FL 32114
Fields offered: Many fields
Year founded: 1904
Ownership: Nonprofit, church
Phone: (904) 255-1401 • (800) 448-0228
Fax: (904) 257-7027
E-mail: byrdw@cookman.edu
Website: www.bethune.cookman.edu

B.A. and B.S. awarded in fields specifically directed towards "occupational and professional development, personal enrichment, community problems, and critical issues." Credit for ACT and CLEP exams, and for supervised fieldwork.

Birmingham Southern College   B, M

Adult Studies Program
Box A-52, Arkadelphia Rd.
Birmingham, AL 35254
Fields offered: Business, management, education, economics
Year founded: 1856
Ownership: Nonprofit, church
Phone: (205) 226-4600 • (800) 523-5793
Fax: (205) 226-4627
E-mail: dbruns@bsc.edu
Website: www.bsc.edu

Self-paced B.A. and B.S. in accounting, business administration, economics, education, and human resources management, as well as individualized interdisciplinary majors, and an M.A. in public and private management, through evening and weekend classes, independent study, and supervised fieldwork.. Undergraduate applicants must have a full-time job, preferably in their field. Up to 72 semester hours awarded for transfer credit, CLEP and departmental exams, and portfolio assessment.

Bloomsburg University

School of Extended Programs and Graduate Study
Bloomsburg, PA 17815

Fields offered: Many fields
Year founded: 1839
Ownership: Nonprofit, state
Phone: (717) 389-4004
Fax: (717) 389-4741
E-mail: lmichaels@bloomu.edu
Website: www.bloomu.edu

A maximum of 60 credits towards the Bachelor's degree (of the 128 credits required) can be earned through assessment of prior and experiential learning, alone or in combination with equivalency exams and departmental challenge exams prepared by the university. Bloomsburg also offers evening classes and television courses; 32 of the last 64 credits applied towards the degree must be earned in residency.

Boston Architectural Center   B

320 Newbury Street
Boston, MA 02115
Fields offered: Architecture, interior design
Year founded: 1889
Ownership: Nonprofit, independent
Phone: (617) 536-3170
Fax: (617) 536-5829
E-mail: admissions@the-bac.edu
Website: ww.the-bac.edu

This school has an unusual program that allows students to earn a Bachelor of Architecture through a "concurrent work curriculum program." Once enrolled, they can earn credit for working in their field (architecture or interior design) by day, while taking relevant classes at night. Limited credit available by transfer and portfolio assessment.

Boston College   B

Chestnut Hill, MA 02167
Fields offered: Many fields
Year founded: 1863
Ownership: Nonprofit, church
Phone: (617) 552-8000 • (800) 360-2522
Fax: (617) 552-8828
E-mail: ugadmis@bc.edu
Website: www.bc.edu

All of the courses required for the Bachelor of Arts degree in American studies, business, economics, English, history, political science, psychology, and sociology can be earned entirely through evening study. Most courses are taught for two-and-a-half hours, meeting one evening per week.

Boston University   B, M

Metropolitan College
755 Commonwealth Ave.
Boston, MA 02215
Fields offered: Many fields
Year founded: 1839
Ownership: Nonprofit, independent
Phone: (617) 353-3000
Fax: (617) 353—2053

E-mail: admissions@bu.edu (US students)
intadmis@bu.edu (international students)
Website: web.bu.edu

Bachelor of Liberal Studies, Bachelor of Science, Master of Criminal Justice, Master of Liberal Arts, Master of Science in computer information systems, Master of Urban Affairs, and Master of City Planning may be earned through evening or weekend study with the university's Metropolitan College. The Overseas Program, primarily for military and Department of Defense employees, offers Master of Science in business administration, Master of Science in management, Master of Science in computer information systems, Master of Education, Master of Arts in international relations, and Master of Science in mechanical engineering. Locations include Belgium and Germany. Credit for prior learning, independent study, and by examination.

Bowling Green State University   B, M

Office of Continuing Education
300 McFall Center
Bowling Green, OH 43403
Fields offered: Many fields
Year founded: 1910
Ownership: Nonprofit, state
Phone: (419) 372-8181
Fax: (419) 372-8446
E-mail: admissions@bgnet.bgsu.edu (undergraduate)
graduate-admissions@mailserver.bgsu.edu (graduate)
Website: www.bgsu.edu

B.A. degrees in arts and science, business administration, health and human services, and technology, available through evening study. Master's degree program in organizational development, through a degree plan involving a combination of on-campus and independent study. Other evening Master's programs, including an M.B.A. Credit for prior learning, by exam, and portfolio assessment. The school wants us to emphasize that every degree has a nonnegotiable residency requirement.

Bradley University   B, M

1501 W. Bradey Avenue
Peoria, IL 61625
Fields offered: Many fields
Year founded: 1897
Ownership: Nonprofit, independent
Phone: (309) 677-1000 • (800) 447-6460
Fax: (309) 677-2797
E-mail: admissions@bradley.edu
Website: www.bradley.edu

Bachelor's and Master's degrees may be earned through evening, weekend, and summer programs, as well as courses offered on-site at business and industrial locations. Special programs in nursing, engineering, education, computer science, business, manufacturing, international studies, radio and television, and international business. See also: Quad Cities Graduate Center

Brandon University   B, M

270 18th St.
Brandon, MB R7A 6A9 Canada
Fields offered: Education, general studies, arts, science, music, nursing, mental health
Year founded: 1880
Ownership: Nonprofit, independent
Phone: (204) 727-9635 • (800) 644-7644 in MB, Sask, and N. Ont only
Fax: (204) 725-2143
E-mail: bower@brandonu.ca
Website: www.brandonu.ca/

Brandon offers the Bachelor of Education and General Studies, B.A., B.S., Bachelor of Music, Master of Education, and Master of Music through evening, spring, and summer programs. Its Northern Teacher Education Programme is offered in seven remote communities. Distance education courses in education, music, and psychiatric nursing are available. Many of Brandon's students are of native ancestry.

Brenau University   B, M

One Centennial Circle
Gainesville, GA 30501
Fields offered: Business and public administration, management, education, nursing, interior design
Year founded: 1878
Ownership: Nonprofit, independent
Phone: (770) 534-6207 • (800) 252-5119
Fax: (770) 538-4306
E-mail: upchurch@lib.brenau.edu
Website: www.brenau.edu

B.A. and B.S. in business administration, human resource management, public administration, and education (middle grades and elementary); B.S. in nursing; B.F.A.; M.B.A., and M.Ed. in early childhood or middle grades through some combination of evening, weekend, on-line computer classes, independent study, and supervised fieldwork, and courses offered off-campus. Up to 27 of the 120 credits for a Bachelor's (or 6 of the 30–36 for the Master's) may come from transfer credit, military experience, portfolio assessment, and CLEP, DANTES, and departmental exams. There are seven campuses throughout the state of Georgia.

Briar Cliff College   B

3303 Rebecca St.
P.O. Box 2100
Sioux City, IA 51104-2100
Fields offered: Many fields
Year founded: 1930
Ownership: Nonprofit, church
Phone: (712) 279-5460 • (800) 662-3303
Fax: (712) 279-5410
E-mail: admissions@briar-cliff.edu
Website: www.briar-cliff.edu

Briar Cliff offers evening and weekend courses in nursing, human resource management, business administration, accounting, mass communications, theology, and psychology, and an extensive internship program. There is also a weekend B.S.N.-completion program for registered nurses. "Project Assess" provides credit for life experience.

Bridgeport Engineering Institute   B

108 N. Benson Rd.
Fairfield, CT 06430
Fields offered: Engineering
Year founded: 1924
Ownership: Nonprofit, independent
Phone: (203) 254-4147
Fax: (203) 259-9372
E-mail: bei@fair1.fairfield.edu
Website: www.fairfield.edu

Now part of Fairfield University, BEI offers a B.S. in the following engineering fields: electrical, mechanical, information systems, and manufacturing, through part-time evening study. Up to 103 of the 139 credits required my come from transfer credit, CLEP and departmental exams, and portfolio assessment.

Bryant College   B, M

Evening Division
Smithfield, RI 02917
Fields offered: Business administration, criminal justice
Year founded: 1863
Ownership: Nonprofit, independent
Phone: (401) 232-6000 • (800) 622-7001
Fax: (401) 232-6319
E-mail: admissions@bryant.edu
Website: www.bryant.edu

Bachelor of Science in business administration or criminal justice and M.B.A. all offered entirely through evening and weekend study.

California School of Professional Psychology   M, D

2749 Hyde St.
San Francisco, CA 94109
Fields offered: Psychology, organizational behavior
Year founded: 1969
Ownership: Nonprofit, independent
Phone: (415) 346-4500 • (800) 457-1273
Fax: (415) 931-8322
E-mail: admissions@mail.cspp.edu
Website: www.cspp.edu

Ph.D. and Psy.D. programs in clinical psychology, Ph.D. programs in industrial and organizational psychology, and a part-time M.S. program in organizational behavior, offered at campuses in Berkeley, Fresno, Los Angeles, and San Diego. Some evening and weekend courses are scheduled. Clinical Ph.D. programs at all campuses and Clinical Psy.D. program at Los Angeles are accredited by the American Psychological Association.

California State University, Sacramento   B, M

6000 J St.
Sacramento, CA 95819
Fields offered: Many fields
Year founded: 1947
Ownership: Nonprofit, state
Phone: (916) 278-6111
Fax: (916) 278-5722
E-mail: outrch_one@skynet3.csus.edu (undergraduate)
gradctr@csus.edu (graduate)
Website: www.csus.edu

While the following degree programs have at least some nontraditional elements, including independent study and internships: Bachelor of Arts, Bachelor of Science, Bachelor of Music, Master of Arts, Master of Science, and Master of Social Work, the school has asked us to make it VERY VERY clear that they do NOT offer nonresidential or external degrees of any sort. Please don't write to them in the hopes that they might!

Cambridge College   M

Institute of Open Education
15 Mifflin Place
Cambridge, MA 02138
Fields offered: Management, education
Year founded: 1970
Ownership: Nonprofit, independent
Phone: (617) 868-1000 • (800) 877-GRAD
Fax: (617) 349-3545
E-mail: admit@idea.cambridge.edu
Website: www.cambridge.edu/cambridge.html

Graduate programs in education and management through evening and weekend classes designed specifically for the working professional with a Bachelor's degree and five years' work experience in their field. Students who have not earned a Bachelor's but have ten years' experience may first be admitted to the school's two-to-three semester Graduate Studies Preparation Program, which prepares them for grad work. Most students can finish the Master of Education in one year, the Master of Management in less than two.

Campbell University   B, M

P.O. Box 546
Buies Creek, NC 27506
Fields offered: Many fields
Year founded: 1887
Ownership: Nonprofit, church
Phone: (910) 893-1290 • (800) 334-4111
Fax: (910) 893-1288
E-mail: adm@mailcenter.campbell.edu
Website: www.campbell.edu

The Bachelor's and Master's can be earned entirely though evening and weekend study, and are open to active military personnel, veterans, and civilians.

Campbellsville University B

Organizational Administration Major
200 W. College St.
Campbellsville, KY 42718
Fields offered: Organizational administration
Year founded: 1906
Ownership: Nonprofit, church
Phone: (502) 789-5220 • (800) 264-6014 ext. 5220
Fax: (502) 789-5020
E-mail: admissions@campbellsvil.edu.
Website: www.campbellsvil.edu

Bachelor of Science in organizational administration tailored for adult nontraditional students (applicants must be at least 23 years old and have completed 60 credits elsewhere), to prepare them for a career in administrative leadership. A Southern Baptist school, Campbellsville presents all material "from a Christian perspective." Credit available for various exams, and life and military experience by portfolio review. Thirty of the required 128 credits must be earned after enrolling, but distance-learning options include correspondence courses, independent study, and supervised fieldwork.

Canisius College B, M

2001 Main St.
Buffalo, NY 14208
Fields offered: Technical and liberal studies
Year founded: 1870
Ownership: Nonprofit, independent
Phone: (716) 888-2200 • (800) 843-1517
Fax: (716) 888-2525
E-mail: lips@wehle
Website: gort.canisius.edu

Bachelor of Science in technical and liberal studies may be earned through evening and summer programs. Credit for independent study, nonacademic prior learning, and by examination. Up to 50 percent of the credit can come from work done at other approved institutions.

Cardinal Stritch College B, M

Office of Adult Education
6801 N. Yates Rd.
Milwaukee, WI 53217
Fields offered: Many fields
Year founded: 1937
Ownership: Nonprofit, church
Phone: (414) 352-5400 • (800) 347-8822 ext.4040
Fax: (414) 410-4239
E-mail: admitu@acs.stritch.edu
Website: acs.stritch.edu

Bachelor's degrees are offered in many fields. Credit for experiential learning. The business/economics degree can be earned entirely through evening study. Programs that meet one evening a week lead to Bachelor's and Master's degrees in business and management (computer-enhanced) and a Master's in health services administration. In addition,

a certificate in sales productivity and management and a certificate in international business are offered through Programs in Management for Adults.

Carroll College B, M

Part-Time Studies Program
100 N. East Avenue
Waukesha, WI 53186
Fields offered: Business, accounting, communications, computer science, education, nursing, psychology
Year founded: 1846
Ownership: Nonprofit, church
Phone: (414) 547-1211 • (800) 227-7655
Fax: (414) 524-7139
E-mail: ccinfo@ccadmin.cc.edu
Website: www.cc.edu

B.S., B.A. (majors in business, accounting, communications, computer science, education, nursing, and psychology), and Master of Education available entirely through night classes. Credit for military experience, command of a foreign language, and applicable work experience, as well as CLEP (up to 48 credits), AP, and departmental exams. Very flexible schedule; correspondence courses, independent study, and supervised fieldwork available.

Carson-Newman College B, M

Extension Division
Russell Ave.
Jefferson City, TN 37760
Fields offered: Many fields
Year founded: 1851
Ownership: Nonprofit, church
Phone: (423) 471-3223 • (800) 678-9061
Fax: (423) 471-3502
E-mail: sgray@cncadmnt.cn.edu
Website: www.cn.edu

Bachelor of Arts and Bachelor of Science in many fields, available entirely through evening study. Credit by examination, independent study, and for military experience. Self-designed majors are available. Master's degree offered in education.

Castleton State College B, M

Castleton, VT 05735
Fields offered: Teacher and nursing education, business, liberal arts
Year founded: 1787
Ownership: Nonprofit, state
Phone: (802) 468-5611 • (800) 639-8521
Fax: (802) 468-1476
E-mail: tenczap@sparrow.csc.vsc.edu
Website: www.csc.vsc.edu

Bachelor's and Master's can be earned through weekend, summer, and evening classes. Special programs in nursing education. Credit for independent study, nonacademic prior learning, and by examination.

Cedar Crest College B

Allentown, PA 18104
Fields offered: Many fields
Year founded: 1867
Ownership: Nonprofit, church
Phone: (610) 437-4471 • (800) 360-1222
Fax: (610) 437-5955
E-mail: cccadmis@cedarcrest.edu
Website: www.cedarcrest.edu

Bachelor's degree in any of 30 majors may be earned through weekend, evening, and summer classes (minimum of 30 credits must be earned after enrolling). Special programs include nursing, accounting, legal assistant, nuclear medical technology, and genetic engineering technology. Credit for life experience and by proficiency exam.

Centenary College (Louisiana) B

P.O. Box 41188
Shreveport, LA 71134-1188
Fields offered: Many fields
Year founded: 1825
Ownership: Nonprofit, church
Phone: (318) 869-5131 • (800) 234-4448
Fax: (318) 869-5026
Website: www.centenary.edu

Bachelor of Arts, Bachelor of Science, and Bachelor of Music can be earned entirely through evening study.

Centenary College (New Jersey) B

400 Jefferson St.
Hackettstown, NJ 07840
Fields offered: Many fields
Year founded: 1867
Ownership: Nonprofit, independent
Phone: (908) 852-1400, ext. 215 • (800) 236-8679
Fax: (908) 850-9508
E-mail: rankis@centenarycollege.edu
Website: www.centenarycollege.edu

Bachelor's may be earned in fields including equine studies, fashion, interior design, art and design, communication, education, business, liberal arts, psychology, history, math, and English, through weekend, evening, and summer programs. Credit for independent study, nonacademic prior learning, and by examination.

Central Washington University B, M

Ellensburg, WA 98926
Fields offered: Business fields, electronic engineering, law and justice, education
Year founded: 1890
Ownership: Nonprofit, state
Phone: (509) 963-1111
Fax: (509) 963-1241
E-mail: cwuadmis@cwu.edu
Website: www.cwu.edu

B.S. in accounting, business administration, or electronic engineering technology; B.A. in law and justice or education (majors in early childhood or special ed); Master of Education in reading or education administration, through off-campus courses "at convenient times and places" for working adults. Credit for military experience and some exams, independent study, and supervised fieldwork.

Chaminade University B

3140 Waialae Ave.
Honolulu, HI 96816-1578
Fields offered: Many fields
Year founded: 1955
Ownership: Nonprofit, independent
Phone: (808) 735-4711 • (800) 735-3733
Fax: (808) 735-4870
E-mail: cuhadm@lava.net
Website: www.chaminade.edu

Bachelor of Arts, Science, Business Administration, and Fine Arts offered through accelerated evening programs on military bases, as well as the main Honolulu campus. Weekend and summer programs are also available. Credit for military training, independent study, and examinations.

Chapman University B, M

333 N. Glassell St.
Orange, CA 92666
Fields offered: Many fields
Year founded: 1861
Ownership: Nonprofit, independent
Phone: (714) 997-6611
Fax: (714) 997-6713
E-mail: admit@chapman.edu (undergraduate)
delfin@chapman.edu (graduate)
Website: www.chapman.edu

Regional education centers are located at over 50 military installations and civilian locations nationwide. Six-, eight-, nine-, and 10-week terms are available. Some instruction uses T.A.P.E., a telecommunication-assisted program of education.

Cincinnati Bible College and Seminary B, M

2700 Glenway Ave., P.O. Box 04320
Cincinnati, OH 45204-3200
Fields offered: Religious fields
Year founded: 1824
Ownership: Nonprofit, church
Phone: (513) 244-8100 • (800) 949-4CBC
Fax: (513) 244-8140
E-mail: admissions@cincybible.edu
Website: www.cincybible.edu

The Bachelor of Arts, Science, or Music is offered in many fields, ranging from Christian education to Christian ministry to ministry to the deaf. There are also emphases offered in a number of areas such as journalism, psychology, and teacher education. A total of 13 fields of study are available. The Master of Arts can be earned by taking courses in module form. Master's degrees are offered in eleven areas of concentration. Accredited by the North Central Association and the American Association of Bible Colleges.

City University of New York   B
Baccalaureate Program, Graduate Center North
25 W. 43rd Street, #300
New York, NY 10036
Fields offered: Many fields
Year founded: 1961
Ownership: Nonprofit, state
Phone: (212) 642-1600
Fax: (212) 642-2642
E-mail: lig@aquila.gc.cuny.edu
Website: www.gsuc.cuny.edu/ACADEMICPROGRAMS/bacc.htm

Bachelor of Arts and Bachelor of Science for self-motivated students who want to design their own individualized programs (with faculty guidance). Students are encouraged to take advantage of the wide range of resources available through CUNY's seventeen undergraduate colleges, as well as its graduate school. Applicants must have completed at least 15 and no more than 90 credits towards the 120-credit degree. Limited credit awarded for nonclassroom learning, ACT, CLEP, DANTES, and departmental exams, and military experience. The school's material states that, "because students enter the program with from 15 to 90 earned credits, it is not uncommon for a full-time student to graduate within eighteen months; a part-time student after two to three years."

Fields include engineering, architecture, medicine, liberal arts, science, and performing arts. Up to 30 credits may be earned through the Center for Work Education's life experience thesis program, which is designed primarily for working adult members of labor unions. It offers flexible scheduling, weekend classes, and life experience credit. This program's phone number is (212) 650-5301. The Center for Vocational Teacher Education's program—(212) 650-8358—leads to state certification and a B.S. in vocational education.

Clark University   B, M
College of Professional and Continuing Education
950 Main St.
Worcester, MA 01610
Fields offered: Many fields
Year founded: 1953
Ownership: Nonprofit, independent

Phone: (508) 793-7217
Fax: (508) 793-7780
E-mail: admissions@admissions.clarku.edu
Website: www.clarku.edu

Bachelor of Arts in liberal arts, Master of Public Administration, and Master of Arts in liberal arts offered entirely by evening study or summer programs.

Cleveland State University   B, M
E. 24th and Euclid
Cleveland, OH 44115
Fields offered: Many fields
Year founded: 1964
Ownership: Nonprofit, state
Phone: (216) 687-2000 • (888) CSU-OHIO
Fax: (216) 687-9366
E-mail: admissions@csuohio.edu
Website: www.csuohio.edu

Bachelor of Arts, Science, Business Administration, Education, and Engineering; and the M.A., M.S., Master of Urban Affairs, and M.B.A. through evening study and/or Saturday classes.

Coker College   B
Evening and Summer School
Hartsville, SC 29550
Fields offered: Business administration, education, sociology
Year founded: 1908
Ownership: Nonprofit, independent
Phone: (803) 383-8010 • (800) 950-1908
Fax: (803) 383-8197
E-mail: admissions@coker.edu
Website: www.coker.edu

The Bachelor of Science in business administration (concentrations in accounting, finance, operations management, or marketing) and Bachelor of Arts in sociology (concentrations in criminology or social work) can be completed entirely through night classes; the B.A. in education through night classes plus an internship in a local school and a semester of student teaching. Credit for exams and military experience, by portfolio review.

College Misericordia   B
Lake St.
Dallas, PA 18612
Fields offered: Many fields
Year founded: 1924
Ownership: Nonprofit, church
Phone: (717) 675-2181 • (800) 852-7675

Fax: (717) 675-2441
E-mail: admiss@miseri.edu
Website: miseri.edu

Bachelor of Arts in many fields through weekend study; Bachelor of Science in nursing, B.A. in business, and Bachelor of Music through evening study. Master's degrees in nursing, occupational therapy, education, and human services administration. Evening and weekend courses. A Bachelor's degree can be earned in four years of evening study.

College of Mount Saint Joseph   B

Division of Continuing Education
Cincinnati, OH 45233
Fields offered: Many fields
Year founded: 1920
Ownership: Nonprofit, church
Phone: (513) 244-4805 • (800) 654-9314
Fax: (513) 244-4222
E-mail: admissions@saintjoe.edu
Website: www.saintjoe.edu

The P.M. College offers Bachelor's degree programs in accounting, business administration, computer information, graphic and interior design, paralegal studies, liberal arts, nursing, social work, management communication, and religious and pastoral ministry in classes that meet one evening a week. The Weekend College offers the Bachelor in business administration, communication arts, human services, gerontological studies, accounting, liberal arts, or management of nursing services. Weekend classes meet five weekends out of each 13-week term. Each class is three-and-a-half hours long; three can be taken between Friday and Sunday evening. Credit is available for experiential learning.

College of Mount Saint Vincent   B

263rd and Riverdale Ave.
Riverdale, NY 10471
Fields offered: Many fields
Year founded: 1847
Ownership: Nonprofit, independent
Phone: (718) 405-3200 • (800) 665-CMSV
Fax: (718) 601-6392
E-mail: admissns@cmsv.edu
Website: www.cmsv.edu

B.A. and B.S. programs in more than 30 fields through evening, summer, and weekend programs (every other weekend), both on- and off-campus. Also special B.S. for R.N.'s. Up to 30 credits may be granted for experiential learning; credit by examination also possible. More than 250 established internships are available for students. There is also a College Emeritus, with substantially reduced tuition, for students over the age of 55 who have not studied since high school, or have limited college experience.

College of New Rochelle   B

School of New Resources
New Rochelle, NY 10801
Fields offered: Liberal studies, liberal arts
Year founded: 1972
Ownership: Nonprofit, independent
Phone: (914) 632-5300 • (800) 211-7077
Fax: (914) 654-5290
E-mail: admission@cnr.edu
Website: www.cnr.edu

The School of New Resources has six campus sites in the greater New York area—one in New Rochelle and one in each of the five boroughs. Degrees can be earned through evening and weekend study. Credit is given for life experience learning.

College of Notre Dame of Maryland   B

4701 N. Charles St.
Baltimore, MD 21210
Fields offered: Many fields
Year founded: 1873
Ownership: Nonprofit, church
Phone: (410) 435-0100 • (800) 435-0300
Fax: (410) 435-5937
E-mail: admiss@ndm.edu
Website: www.ndm.edu

Bachelor of Arts in 22 majors through weekend, summer, and January programs. Credit for nonacademic prior learning, independent study, and by examination. The literature reminds us, several times, that this Notre Dame is neither in Paris nor in South Bend, but in Baltimore.

College of Saint Catherine   B

2004 Randolph Ave.
St. Paul, MN 55105
Fields offered: Many fields
Year founded: 1905
Ownership: Nonprofit, church
Phone: (612) 690-6505 • (800) 945-4599
Fax: (612) 690-6024
E-mail: admissions@stkate.edu or international@stkate.edu (international students)
Website: www.stkate.edu

Bachelor of Arts programs for adult women in business administration, philosophy, applied ethics, economics, communication, information management, nursing, occupational therapy, social work, and elementary education through weekend college and some evening classes. Credit for CLEP exams, and through CARL, Credit for Academic Relevant Learning.

College of Saint Francis   B, M

500 Wilcox St.
Joliet, IL 60435
Fields offered: Health arts
Year founded: 1920

Ownership: Nonprofit, church
Phone: (815) 740-3360 • (800) 735-7500
Fax: (815) 740-4285
E-mail: Admissions@stfrancis.edu
Website: www.stfrancis.edu

This school has recently changed its name to University of Saint Francis. Bachelor of Science program with a major in health arts for registered nurses and other health professionals. Students are required to complete at least eight courses and may do so at any of the 100 locations in seventeen states, from New Mexico to Pennsylvania. New locations are added regularly. Classes meet one evening a week. Full-time students may complete the degree in less than a year, while those taking one course at a time will normally take two and a half years. One hundred and twenty-eight semester units are required for the degree, of which 32 must be earned after enrollment. Health professionals can receive up to three years worth of credit for previous education and experience through the Prior Learning Assessment Program. A Master's degree program in health services administration is also available off-campus at forty locations in fourteen states.

College of Saint Mary   B

1901 S. 72nd St.
Omaha, NE 68124
Fields offered: Many fields
Year founded: 1923
Ownership: Nonprofit, church
Phone: (402) 399-2400 • (800) 926-5534
Fax: (402) 293-2020
E-mail: enroll@csm.edu
Website: www.csm.edu

Saint Mary's weekend college offers a Bachelor of Science degree in business administration, computer information management, marketing, management, human resources management, and human services. Summer and evening study programs are also available; B.S.N. programs for nurses. Credit by examination and portfolio assessment.

College of Saint Rose   B

432 Western Ave.
Albany, NY 12203
Fields offered: Many fields
Year founded: 1920
Ownership: Nonprofit, independent
Phone: (518) 454-5150 • (800) 637-8556
Fax: (518) 454-2013
E-mail: admit@rosnet.strose.edu
Website: www.strose.edu

Bachelor of Arts or Bachelor of Science of which up to 75 percent of the required credits may be earned through an assessment of prior learning experiences. The assessment can take three months or more. Only students matriculated at the College of Saint Rose are considered for assessment.

College of Saint Scholastica   B, M

1200 Kenwood Ave.
Duluth, MN 55811 USA
Fields offered: Nursing, physical therapy, medical technology
Year founded: 1912
Ownership: Nonprofit, church
Phone: (218) 723-6000 • (800) 447-5444
Fax: (218) 723-6290
E-mail: admissions@css.edu
Website: www.css.edu

Bachelor's and some Master's degrees may be earned through summer and evening classes. Credit for independent study and nonacademic prior learning, and by examination.

College of Santa Fe   B, M

Graduate and External Programs
1600 St. Michael's Drive
Santa Fe, NM 87501-5634
Fields offered: Business administration, education, psychology, humanities
Year founded: 1947
Phone: (505) 473-6177 • (800) 456-2673
Fax: (505) 473-6127
E-mail: admissions@csf.edu
Website: www.csf.edu

Bachelor's degrees in business administration, education, humanities, organizational psychology, psychology, and public administration, M.A. in education, and M.B.A. offered on an accelerated (five terms per year) evening and weekend schedule. Credit towards a degree may be accepted from CLEP exams, nonacademic learning, course challenges, and life experience, by portfolio review. An "assessment course" provides the opportunity for any student to assemble a prior learning portfolio of up to 48 units, under close academic supervision. Classes are offered in Santa Fe, Albuquerque, Los Alamos, and at other selected sites throughout the state all year.

College of Staten Island   B

130 Stuyvesant Place
Staten Island, NY 10301
Fields offered: Many fields
Year founded: 1955
Ownership: Nonprofit, state
Phone: (718) 982-2000 • (800) 982-2010
Fax: (718) 982-2500
E-mail: burton@postbox.csi.cuny.edu
teasley@postbox.csi.cuny.edu
Website: www.csi.cuny.edu

The college is part of the City University of New York and offers Bachelor's degrees in many fields. Qualified students may enter the CUNY Baccalaureate Program, a university-wide program offering individualized courses of study. Credit is earned for classes held on-campus; limited credit may be earned for classes held off-campus and at work sites, independent study projects, work experience, and prior learning experience. Credit by examination, departmental challenge exams, and internships. Noncredit courses available to prepare adult students returning to college.

Colorado Christian University　　B

School of Graduate and Professional Studies
180 S. Garrison St.
Lakewood, CO 80226 USA
Fields offered: Several fields
Year founded: 1914
Ownership: Nonprofit, church
Phone: (303) 202-0100 • (800) 443-2484
Fax: (303) 274-7560
E-mail: questions@ccu.edu
Website: www.ccu.edu

The B.S. in management of human resources, computer information systems management, Christian leadership, or elementary education can be earned in 12 months (18 months for CISM) through evening or weekend programs, if the participant has an A.A. or 56 hours of transferable credit, is at least 25 years old, and prepares a life experience portfolio (which can be worth up to 34 units). Centers in Lakewood, Denver, Colorado Springs and Grand Junction, Colorado. Formerly Rockmont College. No connection whatever with a defunct diploma mill called Colorado Christian University.

Columbia College　　B

1001 Rogers St. (10th and Rogers)
Columbia, MO 65216-0001
Fields offered: Business administration, criminal justice administration, education, history & government, individual studies, psychology, computer information systems
Year founded: 1851
Ownership: Nonprofit, church
Phone: (573) 875-8700 • (800) 325-2986
Fax: (573) 875-7209
E-mail: admissions@email.ccis.edu
Website: www.ccis.edu

This school offers degree completion programs at its Missouri campus, as well as more limited offerings (business administration only) at a Salt Lake City location, and military bases and other branch institutions around the country. Contact the school for current locations. Up to 96 credit hours can be transferred in from course taken at other accredited colleges, as well as CLEP and PEP exams, DANTES, military training, challenge exams, and a variety of verifiable life-experience learning. No more than 60 of the 96 hours can come from nontraditional sources (i.e., nonclassroom learning). Many courses are held nights and weekends to meet the needs of working adults. For information on the Salt Lake City courses, call (801) 355-4449, or (800) 339-7618.

Columbia College of Nursing　　B

2121 E. Newport
Milwaukee, WI 53271
Fields offered: Nursing
Year founded: 1901
Ownership: Nonprofit, independent
Phone: (414) 961-3530 • (800) CARROLL
Fax: (414) 961-4121
E-mail: heinzen@facstaff.wisc.edu
Website: www.cc.edu

Bachelor of Science in nursing through a joint program with Carroll College. Credit for CLEP and departmental exams; nontraditional course options include correspondence classes, independent study, and supervised fieldwork. At least 32 of the required 128 credit-hours must be completed after enrollment.

Concordia University　　B, M

12800 North Lake Shore Drive
Mequon, WI 53097
Fields offered: Management & communications, liberal arts, health care administration, nursing, criminal justice operations
Year founded: 1881
Ownership: Nonprofit, church
Phone: (414) 243-4442 • (800) 665-6564
Fax: (414) 243-4459
E-mail: jholter@bach.cuw.edu
Website: www.cuw.edu

Concordia offers Bachelor's degrees in an accelerated modular format, for full-time working adults. Additional credits can be earned through portfolio assessment, telecourses, correspondence courses, challenge exams, and independent study. School accepts PONSI and ACE recommendations as well as CLEP and DANTE scores. Centers are in Mequon, Green Bay, Madison, and Kenosha, Wisconsin; Fort Wayne and Indianapolis, Indiana; St. Louis, Missouri; and New Orleans, Louisiana. Master's programs in any one of 20 subject areas including computer science, requiring only one week of residence; all communications and correspondence occur through the Internet.

Converse College　　B

Converse II Program
580 E. Main Street
Spartanburg, SC 29302
Fields offered: Many fields
Year founded: 1889
Ownership: Nonprofit, independent
Phone: (864) 596-9000 • (800) 766-1125
Fax: (864) 596-9158
E-mail: info@converse.edu
Website: www.converse.edu

The Converse II program is designed to encourage adult women (24 years old and up) to return to school for a B.A., B.F.A., or Bachelor of Music. Some credit for CLEP exams and by portfolio review; students with theater or music performance experience may exempt some classes; independent study and supervised fieldwork options. CII features simplified application procedure, reduced fees, special financial aid, flexible scheduling, and individualized counseling to women who meet the stated criteria.

Covenant College   B

Quest Program
Lookout Mountain, GA 30750
Fields offered: Organizational management
Year founded: 1955
Ownership: Nonprofit, church
Phone: (706) 820-1560 • (800) 960-5020
Fax: (706) 820-2165
E-mail: vos@covenant.edu
Website: www.covenant.edu

The Bachelor of Arts in organizational management through an innovative program in which groups of twelve to twenty students meet one evening a week for 52 weeks. Nine courses are offered during this period, for one to five weeks each. All students complete a major research project, applying management and organizational behavior studies to a problem or need in their fields or workplaces. All work is done in "a biblical framework"; Covenant is affiliated with the Presbyterian Church of America. A degree program can begin whenever and wherever twelve to twenty students are ready. Applicants must have 60 semester units of credit and five years of work experience to qualify. CLEP and military credit are accepted. Students earn up to 31 units towards graduation (not admission) from life experience. The program is offered in Chattanooga, Tennessee, and four satellite locations within a 30-mile radius.

Creighton University   B, M

California St. at 24th
Omaha, NE 68178
Fields offered: Nursing
Year founded: 1878
Ownership: Nonprofit, independent
Phone: (402) 280-2703 • (800) 544-5071, ext. 2043
Fax: (402) 280-2685
E-mail: admissions@creighton.edu
Website: www.creighton.edu

The Accelerated Nursing Curriculum program offers persons with a B.A. or B.S. in another field the opportunity to earn a professional degree (B.S.N.) in nursing in one year. There is also a three-year Bachelor's/Master's option. Financial aid is available.

Dallas Baptist University   B

3000 Mountain Creek Parkway
Dallas, TX 75211
Fields offered: Many fields
Year founded: 1898
Ownership: Nonprofit, church

Phone: (214) 333-7100 • (800) 460-1DBU.
Fax: (214) 333-5115
E-mail: info@dbu.edu
Website: www.dbu.edu

Most courses are offered evenings and weekends. The Bachelor of Applied Studies program awards up to 30 hours of credits for prior learning experiences in marketing, management, business administration, management information systems, criminal justice, accounting, psychology, public administration, pastoral ministries, social services, and other areas. Credit is generously but realistically awarded for government, military, and other career training. The program has been in existence since 1974 and collaborates with many companies to bring education to the off-campus student.

Dartmouth College   M

M.A.L.S. Admissions
6092 Wentworth Hall
Hanover, NH 03775-3526
Fields offered: Liberal studies
Year founded: 1769
Ownership: Nonprofit, independent
Phone: (603) 646-3592
Fax: (603) 646-3590
E-mail: mals.program@dartmouth.edu
Website: www.dartmouth.edu

Dartmouth College's Master of Arts in liberal studies program is designed to let adults continue a liberal-arts education (each student plans his or her own course of study; there are no core courses and no majors). Students typically attend for three summers, or five consecutive terms. (About 40 percent of the 200 currently active students are from out of the area). The program combines classes, a weekly colloquium, student-led seminars, independent study, and a thesis. Meals and housing are available on the Dartmouth campus, if desired. Seventy-five percent of M.A.L.S. students receive some form of financial assistance.

De La Salle University   B

College of Saint Benilde
2544 Taft Avenue
Manila, Philippines
Fields offered: Business, accounting, management, industrial design
Year founded: 1911
Ownership: Nonprofit, church
Phone: (63) 57-28-15
Fax: (63) 57-27-73
E-mail: admmvr@dlsu.edu.ph
Website: www.dlsu.edu.ph

This Philippine university offers a B.A. in management interdisciplinary studies and a B.S. in business administration, industrial design, business management, or accountancy; all programs designed for working students employed in public services, education, commerce and industry, or other private agencies.

De Paul University · B, M

25 E. Jackson Blvd.
Chicago, IL 60604
Fields offered: Many fields
Year founded: 1898
Ownership: Nonprofit, state
Phone: (312) 362-6709 • (800) 4DE-PAUL
Fax: (312) 362-5322
E-mail: mmeltzer@wppost.depaul.edu
Website: www.depaul.edu

De Paul University's School for New Learning offers alternative B.A. and M.A. programs at three campus locations through weekend and evening programs. Each degree is individually designed, with credit given for learning from life and work experience. The Master of Arts in liberal studies offers adult students the opportunity to design a multidisciplinary liberal arts curriculum, emphasizing team-taught courses and colloquia. All classes meet one evening per week. Students take four core courses, two colloquia, and six elective courses, and finish by completing an "integrating project."

Defiance College · B

701 N. Clinton St.
Defiance, OH 43512
Fields offered: Many fields
Year founded: 1850
Ownership: Nonprofit, church
Phone: (419) 784-4010 • (800)-520-GO-DC ext 4632
Fax: (419) 784—0426
E-mail: ARoth@tdc.edu
Website: www.defiance.edu

Bachelor of Art and Bachelor of Science in a wide variety of fields, through weekend, evening, and summer programs. Credit for prior learning, independent study, and by examination. A two-semester interdisciplinary core course is required of all students. In addition to many traditional majors, unusual majors include municipal and industrial recreation, natural systems, therapeutic recreation, environmental science, and restoration ecology.

Delaware Valley College · B

Doylestown, PA 18901
Fields offered: Business, biology, computer systems, management
Year founded: 1896
Ownership: Nonprofit, independent
Phone: (215) 345-1500 • (800) 2DEL-VAL
Fax: (215) 345-5277
E-mail: admitme@devalcol.edu
Website: www.devalcol.edu

The Bachelor of Science in business, biology, computer systems, and management is available entirely through evening study.

Dixon University Center · B, M

2986 N. 2nd St.
Harrisburg, PA 17110
Fields offered: Many fields
Year founded: 1958
Ownership: Nonprofit, independent
Phone: (717) 720-4000
Fax: (717) 720-4211
E-mail: msix@mailgate.sshechan.edu
Website: www.sshechan.edu

An educational consortium involving the fourteen state institutions of the state system of higher education and Elizabethtown college which offers various degree programs, primarily through evening and weekend study.

Dominican College of Blauvelt · B

Weekend and Accelerated Evening Programs
10 Western Highway
Orangeburg, NY 10962
Fields offered: Many fields
Year founded: 1952
Ownership: Nonprofit, independent
Phone: (914) 359-7800
Fax: (914) 359-2313
Website: www.dc.edu

B.S. in nursing (for R.N.s only), occupational therapy, business, accounting, management, computer information systems, or business administration and B.A. in humanities entirely through weekend and accelerated evening classes. Credit for military and other life experience learning through portfolio assessment, and for a range of exams. Optional independent study and supervised fieldwork for credit.

Drake University · B, M, Law

2507 University Ave.
Des Moines, IA 50311
Fields offered: Many fields
Year founded: 1881
Ownership: Nonprofit, independent
Phone: (515) 271-3181 • (800) 44-DRAKE
Fax: (515) 271-2831
E-mail: admitinfo@acad.drake.edu
Website: www.drake.edu

B.A. and B.S. available entirely through evening and weekend classes in the following majors: accounting, computer information systems, economics, finance, general business, insurance, international business, management, marketing, nursing completion, psychology, and sociology. Study may also design individualized majors. Master's degrees through evening and weekend study in adult education/training and development, education, business administration, counselor education, general studies, mass communications, nursing, and public administration.

Drexel University
B, M

32nd and Chestnut
Philadelphia, PA 19104
Fields offered: Many fields
Year founded: 1891
Ownership: Nonprofit, independent
Phone: (215) 895-2000
Fax: (215) 895-1414
E-mail: admissions@post.drexel.edu
Website: www.drexel.edu

Bachelor of Science in architecture, business administration, engineering, or general studies; Master's in business administration, home economics, or library science, all available through evening study. The M.L.S. (library science) can be earned through evening and weekend classes in two years or less.

Drury Evening College
B

900 N. Benton Ave.
Springfield, MO 65802
Fields offered: Many fields
Year founded: 1873
Ownership: Nonprofit, independent
Phone: (417) 873-7879 • (800) 922-2274
Fax: (417) 873-7821
E-mail: druryad@lib.drury.edu
Website: www.drury.edu

Bachelor of Science may be earned in many fields entirely through evening and weekend study. Advanced placement possible by CLEP or credit by proficiency examination.

East Central College Consortium
B

Hiram College
Hiram, OH 44234
Fields offered: General studies, sciences, humanities and arts, business administration, health
Year founded: 1850
Ownership: Nonprofit, independent
Phone: (330) 569-5125 • (800) 362-5280
Fax: (330) 569-5494
E-mail: admission@hiram.edu
Website: www.hiram.edu

A consortium of seven liberal arts colleges that cooperate to offer the B.A. in general studies, sciences, humanities and arts, business administration, and allied health. Registration at one of the colleges and fulfillment of some residency requirements are mandatory. The schools are Heidelberg College, Hiram College, Marietta College, Mount Union College and Muskingum College (all in Ohio), Bethany College (West Virginia), and Westminster College (Pennsylvania).

East Tennessee State University
B, M, D

P.O. Box 70,731
Johnson City, TN 37614-0731
Fields offered: Many fields
Year founded: 1911
Ownership: Nonprofit, state
Phone: (423) 439-4213 • (800) 462-3878
Fax: (423) 439-7156
E-mail: gradsch@access.etsu-tn.edu
Website: www.east-tenn-st.edu

The Bachelor of General Studies (B.G.S.) degree program provides a learner-centered alternative to traditional programs in which adult students develop individualized interdisciplinary academic programs specifically tailored to their learning needs.

East-West University
B

816 South Michigan Avenue
Chicago, IL 60605
Fields offered: Many fields
Year founded: 1980
Ownership: Nonprofit, independent
Phone: (312) 939-0111
Fax: (312) 939-0083
E-mail: mettha@eastwest.edu
Website: www.eastwest.edu

East-West offers students a number of nontraditional paths to earning a Bachelor's degree, including proficiency exams, weekend and evening classes, a cooperative education program, and an individualized, competency-based nontraditional program. This portfolio-based program allows a student to work closely with a faculty advisor to achieve the student's specific educational goals. The portfolio the student then assembles to demonstrate achieving those goals may include assessment of prior learning, job-training, and supervised on-campus and extension studies. All programs have a required on-campus component, and require both a final project to demonstrate mastery of the field of study and a final oral examination in which the student defends that project.

Eastern Connecticut State University
B, M

83 Windham St.
Willimantic, CT 06226
Fields offered: Liberal arts and sciences, business, education
Year founded: 1889
Ownership: Nonprofit, state
Phone: (860) 465-5000 • (888) 343-ECSU
Fax: (860) 465-4485
E-mail: Admissions@ecsuc.ctstateu.edu
Website: www.ecsu.ctstateu.edu

Bachelor's may be earned through weekend, evening, and summer programs. Credit by examination and for prior nonacademic and military learning. Up to 60 credits can be earned through CLEP exams. Higher tuition for out-of-state students.

Eastern Michigan University   M

Division of Continuing Education
Ypsilanti, MI 48197
Fields offered: Educational administration
Year founded: 1849
Ownership: Nonprofit, state
Phone: (313) 487-1081 • (800) 777-3521
Fax: (313) 487-2316
E-mail: continuing.education@emich.edu
Website: www.emich.edu

The Master of Liberal Studies offers the opportunity to design an individualized interdisciplinary program with an emphasis on technology, women's studies, or social science. Also a weekend M.B.A. and other part-time options for working adults.

Eastern Washington University   B

EWU MS-150
Cheney, WA 99004-2461
Fields offered: General studies
Year founded: 1882
Ownership: Nonprofit, state
Phone: (509) 359-6015 • (888) 740-1914
Fax: (509) 359-6153
E-mail: admissions@ewu.edu
Website: www.ewu.edu

Bachelor of Arts in general studies, specifically for persons with professional or paraprofessional experience, such as mechanics, computer programmers, police officers, nurses, secretaries, firefighters, draftspeople, and others. Twenty-five percent of degree work must be done after enrollment, which usually translates into about one academic year (nine months). A big advantage here is the school's willingness to give life-experience credit to people in fields that other schools might not agree were creditworthy. We have heard from a few people who enrolled in Eastern Washington long enough to get credit for, say, their secretarial experience, and then transferred this credit to another, faster school.

Eckerd College   B

Program for Experienced Learners
4200 54th Avenue South
St. Petersburg, FL 33711
Fields offered: Many fields
Year founded: 1959
Ownership: Nonprofit, independent
Phone: (813) 864-8226 • (800) 234-4635
Fax: (813) 864-8422
E-mail: admissions@eckerd.edu
Website: www.eckerd.edu

External Bachelor's degrees available to U.S. residents only, through weekend, evening, and summer programs. Credit by examination, and for directed independent study and prior learning. Students must complete at least nine courses through Eckerd College.

Edinboro University of Pennsylvania   B

Edinboro, PA 16444
Fields offered: Many fields
Year founded: 1857
Ownership: Nonprofit, state
Phone: (814) 732-2000 • (800) 626-2203
Fax: (814) 732-2420
E-mail: carlin@vax.edinboro.edu
Website: www.edinboro.edu

Bachelor of General Business, Bachelor of Arts in English, speech communication, geography, or psychology, and Bachelor of Science in education or industrial and trade leadership, through evening, weekend, and summer programs. Credit for nonacademic prior learning, independent study, and by examination. Prior learning assessment is done in Edinboro's Life Experience Center and can take a month or less. For a small fee, they will conduct a brief inspection of one's resume or credentials and advise whether or not they think it is worthwhile to go ahead with the more expensive complete assessment. Edinboro's Opportunity College is designed to help adult students earn credit while continuing employment and family responsibilities.

Elmhurst College   B

Office of Adult and Transfer Admission
Elmhurst, IL 60126
Fields offered: Many fields
Year founded: 1871
Ownership: Nonprofit, independent
Phone: (630) 617-3400 • (800) 697-1871
Fax: (630) 617-3282
E-mail: admit@elmhurst.edu
Website: www.elmhurst.edu

Bachelor's degree through weekend, evening, and summer study. Elmhurst offers a degree completion program for working registered nurses, with courses offered in Chicago-area hospitals, and a special accelerated program in business administration. Credit for independent study, prior learning experience, and by examination.

Elmira College   B

Park Place
Elmira, NY 14901
Fields offered: Many fields
Year founded: 1855
Ownership: Nonprofit, independent
Phone: (607) 735-1724 • (800) 935-6472
Fax: (607) 735-1718
E-mail: admissions@elmira.edu
Website: www.elmira.edu

Bachelor of Science and Master of Science, both in education, available entirely through evening study. Fields of concentration include accounting, business, chemistry, computer information systems, education, general studies, human services, mathematics, nursing, psychology, and social studies.

Elon College **B, M**

Elon College, NC 27244
Fields offered: Business, education
Ownership: Nonprofit, church
Phone: (336) 584-9711 • (800) 334-8448
Fax: (336) 538-3986
E-mail: admissns@numen.elon.edu
Website: www.elon.edu
All Bachelor's degrees, an M.B.A., and a Master of Education are available through evening study.

Emmanuel College **B, M**

Adult Learner Degree Program
400 The Fenway
Boston, MA 02115
Fields offered: Liberal arts, health and business administration, nursing, management, education, ministry, public policy
Year founded: 1919
Ownership: Nonprofit, church
Phone: (617) 277-9340 • (800) 331-3227
Fax: (617) 735-9877
E-mail: enroll@emmanuel.edu
Website: www.emmanuel.edu
Bachelor of Liberal Arts, B.S. in health administration, business administration, and nursing; M.A. in human resource management, education, educational pastoral ministry, clinical pastoral counseling, public policy making; Master in School Administration, and Master in School Special Education Technology, all for adult students (age 23 and older). Courses offered late afternoons, evenings, weekends, and summers; accelerated courses are offered at various off-campus sites. Credit for a variety of exams, and up to 16 credits for appropriate life-work experience, through portfolio assessment.

European University Institute **D**

Via dei Roccettini, 5
San Domenico di Fiesole, 50016 Italy
Fields offered: Many fields
Year founded: 1976
Ownership: Nonprofit, state
Phone: (39) 55-50921
Fax: (39) 55-4685-298
Website: www.iue.it/
The institute was established in 1976 by the then nine members of the European Economic Community, although about 20 percent of students today come from outside of the Common Market countries. Students plan independent-study projects under the guidance of faculty tutors and research supervisors, and the degree of Ph.D. is awarded on completion and publication of a dissertation. Fields of study include economics, history and civilization, law, political science, and social sciences.

Evergreen State College **B, M**

Olympia, WA 98505
Fields offered: Many fields
Year founded: 1967
Ownership: Nonprofit, state
Phone: (360) 866-6000
Fax: (360) 866-6823
E-mail: admissions@elwha.evergreen.edu
Website: www.evergreen.edu
Students have the option of creating independent contracts for individual study or research, which is supervised under a faculty mentor. Groups of two or more students may work under a group contract. Credit is given for prior experiential learning and internship programs involving, for instance, work in local hospitals, clinics, or businesses. Full-time and half-time interdisciplinary programs are available on campus as well. The half-time program is geared to working adults, and offers the same courses taken by the majority of Evergreen students, through evening and weekend instruction. Students involved in independent study are still expected to visit the campus and meet with their faculty mentors at least once a month. All transfer students must earn at least 45 of the last 90 quarter hour credits while enrolled at Evergreen to be eligible for a degree.

Fairfield University **B**

General Studies Program
Fairfield, CT 06430
Fields offered: General studies
Year founded: 1942
Ownership: Nonprofit, independent
Phone: (203) 254-4000
Fax: (203) 254-4060
E-mail: admis@fair1.fairfield.edu
Website: www.fairfield.edu
B.A. or B.S. in general studies for working adult students whose educational needs cannot be met by traditional programs. Applicants must be at least 25 years old, and have at least a three-year "interruption in formal education." Up to 75 credits of the 120 requited may be awarded for life-experience learning; credit also available for various equivalency exams. Some courses taught through audio- and videocassette and television courses, as well as independent study.

Fairhaven College **B**

Western Washington University
Bellingham, WA 98225
Fields offered: Many fields
Year founded: 1893
Ownership: Nonprofit, state
Phone: (360) 650-3680
Fax: (360) 650-3037
E-mail: admit@cc.wwu.edu
Website: rowlf.cc.wwu.edu:8080/~fhc/

Fairhaven offers students a fair amount of latitude in designing their own programs for the B.A., B.S., B.F.A. (fine arts), and Bachelor of Music, including a combined B.A./Bachelor of Education program; all programs can combine regular courses, credit from equivalency exams, independent study, supervised fieldwork, and other practical experiences related to the student's academic goals.

Fairleigh Dickinson University   B, M, D

285 Madison St.
Madison, NJ 07940
Fields offered: Many fields
Year founded: 1958
Ownership: Nonprofit, independent
Phone: (201) 692-2553 • (800) 338-8803
Fax: (201) 692-2560
E-mail: info@admit.fdu.edu
Website: www.fdu.edu

B.A., B.S., M.A., M.S., and Doctor of Education programs, offered through centers at Madison, Rutherford, and Teaneck, primarily through evening study. The Doctorate, in educational leadership, consists of formal courses, seminars, and internships, as well as independent study and research. The school also offers a "success program" for persons over the age of 25 who have never attended (or never finished) college. A number of accelerated programs offer the opportunity for students to complete two degrees together in less time than they would normally take separately, including five-year B.A./M.P.A. (public administration), B.A./M.B.A., B.A./M.A. in psychology, and B.A./M.A. in teaching, as well a rare six-year B.S./M.D. or B.S./D.M.D. in medicine or dentistry. Also offered are degree-completion programs for professional athletes over the age of 22.

Fayetteville State University   B, M

Murchinson Rd.
Fayetteville, AR 28301
Fields offered: Many fields
Year founded: 1867
Ownership: Nonprofit, state
Phone: (910) 486-1111 • (800) 377-UofA
Fax: (910) 486-6024
E-mail: uafadmis@comp.uark.edu
Website: www.fsufay.edu

B.A. and B.S. for military personnel, their dependents, and local residents. All work can be completed through weekend and evening study. Some credit given for prior learning experiences and for equivalency exams. The are 24 majors available at the Bachelor's level, and four Master's programs: business administration, administration and supervision, special education, and elementary education.

Ferris State University   B

Gerholz Institute for Lifelong Learning
Big Rapids, MI 49307
Fields offered: Allied health sciences, arts & sciences, business, education, technology

Year founded: 1884
Ownership: Nonprofit, state
Phone: (616) 592-2340 • (800) 562-9130 (MI, IL IN, OH, WI only)
Fax: (616) 592-3539
E-mail: admissio@titan.ferris.edu
Website: www.ferris.edu

A wide variety of off-campus programs through the colleges of allied health sciences, arts & sciences, business, education, and technology are available at selected sites in Michigan, through weekend and evening courses geared to the needs of working adults.

Florida Institute of Technology   M

Graduate Admissions Office
150 W. University Blvd.
Melbourne, FL 32901
Fields offered: Many business and technical fields
Year founded: 1958
Ownership: Nonprofit, independent
Phone: (407) 768-8000 • (800) 888-4348 (undergraduate)
(800) 944-4348 (graduate)
Fax: (407) 984-8461
E-mail: ksimpson@fit.edu
Website: www.fit.edu

M.B.A. in 10 fields and M.S. in computer science, electrical engineering, management, space technology, and many other fields, offered to military and civilians at 15 locations in Florida, New Jersey, Alabama, New Mexico, Virginia, Louisiana, and Maryland. Has incorporated the programs of the former International Graduate School of Behavioral Psychology. FIT has threatened to sue us for mentioning, in earlier editions, the circumstances under which the chairman of their board of trustees resigned—an event described in detail in at least a half a dozen Florida newspapers but no longer in this publication.

Florida State University   M

4750 Collegiate Drive
Panama City, FL 32405
Fields offered: Engineering
Year founded: 1851
Ownership: Nonprofit, state
Phone: (904) 872-4750
Fax: (904) 872-4199
E-mail: admissions@admin.fsu.edu
Website: www.fsu.edu

Master of Science in electrical or mechanical engineering, with a number of specialties in each field, through compressed-video television courses offered electronically from the Tallahassee campus to sites in Panama City.

Fontbonne College   B, M

Options Program
6800 Wydown Blvd.
St. Louis, MO 63105
Fields offered: Business administration

Year founded: 1917
Ownership: Nonprofit, church
Phone: (314) 862-3456
Fax: (314) 889-1451
E-mail: pmusen@fontbonne.edu
Website: www.fontbonne.edu

Bachelor of Business Administration and M.B.A. through the "Options Program," a flexible course of study geared to students over the age of 25 with at least two years' relevant work experience (three for the Master's) who have completed at least 60 credits elsewhere. Credit available for life-experience learning and equivalency exams. All coursework is based in the real-life workplace, and courses meet one night a week for four hours. Every M.B.A. student is issued a laptop computer for coursework, which they may then keep after graduation.

Fordham University   B

School of General Studies
Bronx, NY 10458
Fields offered: Liberal arts, business, premedical
Year founded: 1841
Ownership: Nonprofit, independent
Phone: (718) 817-1000 • (800) FORDHAM
Fax: (718) 817-4925
E-mail: ad_korevec@lars.fordham.edu
Website: www.fordham.edu

Bachelor of Arts, Bachelor of Science, and Bachelor of Business Administration available entirely through evening study or Saturday classes. Credit is given for life experience learning. There is an Esperanza Center for adult Hispanic students, and a separate adult admissions office.

Fort Wright College

See: Heritage College

Francis Marion University   B

Bachelor of General Studies Program
P.O. Box 100547
Florence, SC 29501
Fields offered: General studies
Year founded: 1970
Ownership: Nonprofit, state
Phone: (803) 661-1362 • (800) 368-755
Fax: (803) 661-1165
E-mail: Admission@fmarion.edu
Website: www.fmarion.edu

The Bachelor of General Studies program is offered for adult students (generally over the age of 25) who have earned a variety of college credits, often at a number of institutions, but have not met specific requirements for any one major. Some credit for equivalency exams; up to 90 of the 120 required hours may be transfer credits. Nontraditional study options include independent study and courses by correspondence, newspaper, and television.

Franklin Pierce College   B

Rindge, NH 03461
Fields offered: Management, marketing, CIS, accounting, general studies
Year founded: 1962
Ownership: Nonprofit, independent
Phone: (603) 889-6146 • (800) 437-0048
Fax: (603) 899-4372
E-mail: admissions@rindge.fpc.edu
Website: www.fpc.edu

Bachelor of Science in accounting, computer information systems, financial management, management, marketing, and general studies through weekend, evening, and summer programs offered at satellite campus location. Credit for nonacademic learning available.

Franklin University   B

201 S. Grant Ave.
Columbus, OH 43215
Fields offered: Many fields
Ownership: Nonprofit, independent
Phone: (614) 341-6237 • (888) 341-6237
Fax: (614) 224-8027
E-mail: register@franklin.edu
Website: www.franklin.edu

Bachelor's degrees offered through evening courses, with credit for experiential learning through proficiency testing and portfolio assessment.

Fresno Pacific University   B

Management of Human Relations Program
1717 S. Chestnut Ave.
Fresno, CA 93702
Fields offered: Management of human relations
Year founded: 1944
Ownership: Nonprofit, church
Phone: (209) 453-2000 • (800) 660-6089
Fax: (209) 453-2007
E-mail: ugadmis@fresno.edu
Website: www.fresno.edu

B.A. in management of human relations through a "compressed-time program" for working adults who have at least seven years' experience in their field. Up to 30 units may be awarded for portfolio assessment, and 70 from transfer credit, but the final 30 credit must be earned from Fresno Pacific. Correspondence courses and independent study are available.

Friends World Program of Long Island University   B

Southampton, NY 11968
Fields offered: Many fields
Year founded: 1965
Ownership: Nonprofit, independent
Phone: (516) 283-4000 • (800) 548-7526
Fax: (516) 287-8463

E-mail: FW@southampton.liunet.edu

Website: www.liunet.edu

Bachelor of Arts is earned by combining academic study with independent field research and internships around the world. Faculty at campuses and program centers in the U.S., Costa Rica, England, Israel, Kenya, India, China, and Japan offer four- to 12-week residential programs for cultural orientation, language immersion, and learning plan design prior to the independent field study, which may be carried out in these and other countries. (Since 1965, F.W.C. students have studied in over 70 different countries.) Students may choose from traditional liberal arts majors, as well as such fields as third world development, peace and conflict resolution, UN studies, holistic and traditional healing, appropriate technology, animal behavior, women's studies, and many interdisciplinary majors.

Gannon University   B

University Square

Erie, PA 16541

Fields offered: Management, administrative studies

Year founded: 1925

Ownership: Nonprofit, church

Phone: (814) 871-7000 • (800) -GANNON-U

Fax: (814) 871-7338

E-mail: admissions@gannon.edu

Website: www.gannon.edu

B.S. in management or administrative studies through evening, weekend, and summer courses, especially for students interested in church, career, and social leadership. Although the school is run by the Roman Catholic church, they stress that "the university's environment is one of inclusiveness and cultural diversity."

Gardner-Webb University   B

GOAL Program

Boiling Springs, NC 28017

Fields offered: Many fields

Year founded: 1905

Ownership: Nonprofit, church

Phone: (704) 434-2361 • (800) 288-GOAL

Fax: (704) 434-6246

E-mail: goal@gardner-webb.edu

Website: www.gardner-webb.edu/GWU/main/adult.html

The GOAL (Greater Opportunity for Adult Learners) program allows students who have already completed 64 units elsewhere to finish a B.A. or B.S. entirely through evening classes. Field offered are: B.S. in business administration, business management, health management, accounting, MIS, nursing, human services, or social science (with a concentration in criminal justice); B.A. in religion. Classes are offered at 11 North Carolina locations; credit also available for military experience, proficiency exams, independent study, and supervised fieldwork.

George Fox University   B

Department of Continuing Studies

Newberg, OR 97137

Fields offered: Human resources management

Year founded: 1891

Ownership: Nonprofit, church

Phone: (503) 538-8383 • (800) 765-4369

Fax: (503) 537-3830

E-mail: admissions@georgefox.edu

Website: www.georgefox.edu

B.A. in human resources management for students with at least two years of prior college. Credit available for life-experience learning through portfolio assessment and proficiency exams; cooperative education and independent study are possible.

George Mason University   B, M

Office of Individualized Studies

4400 University Drive

Fairfax, VA 22030

Fields offered: Individualized studies

Year founded: 1957

Ownership: Nonprofit, state

Phone: (703) 993-2400

Fax: (703) 993-2392

E-mail: admissions@gmu.edu

Website: www.gmu.edu

In the Bachelor of Individualized Studies degree (B.I.S.), units may be earned by alternative means, such as equivalency exams or credit for life-experience learning. Applicants must have at least eight years of post–high-school experience in their field. Students work with an academic advisor to design and complete a program of study. A total of 30 units must be completed at George Mason or certain other northern Virginia schools. A Master of Arts in Individual Studies (M.A.I.S.) is available to adult students with at least two years' work experience in the proposed area of study. At least six hours of graduate-level work must be completed before enrolling. Each M.A.I.S. student works out an individual course of study with a faculty member who will supervise the performance of that work. A special project is required, and evening study is available for residential programs.

George Washington University   M, D

2201 G St.

Washington, DC 20052

Fields offered: Education, humanities, social sciences, criminal justice, forensics, telecommunication operations, administration

Year founded: 1821

Ownership: Nonprofit, independent

Phone: (202) 994-6210

Fax: (202) 994-5870

E-mail: gradinfo@gwis2.circ.gwu.edu

Website: www.gwu.edu

Interesting residential programs in the fields of education, humanities, the social sciences, criminal justice, urban learning, forensics, telecommunication operations, and administration, as well as a number of nonresidential programs, described in chapter 16.

Georgia School of Professional Psychology

See: American Schools of Professional Psychology
Georgia Southern University   B
Landrum Box 8092
Statesboro, GA 30460
Fields offered: General studies
Year founded: 1906
Ownership: Nonprofit, state
Phone: (912) 681-5611
Fax: (912) 681-0196
E-mail: admissions@gasou.edu
Website: www.gasou.edu
Bachelor of General Studies allows nontraditional students to combine up to 145 hours of prior liberal-arts education and/or credit from military experience and proficiency exams with 45 units in residence in the specialization of their choice.

Georgia Southwestern University   B

800 Wheatley St.
Americus, GA 31709
Fields offered: Social science, business administration
Year founded: 1906
Ownership: Nonprofit, state
Phone: (912) 928-1279 • (800) 338-0082
Fax: (912) 931-2059
E-mail: gswapp@canes.gsw.peachnet.edu
Website: gswrs6k1.gsw.peachnet.edu
Bachelor of Arts and Bachelor of Science in social science and business administration, entirely through evening study.

Georgian Court College   B

Evening Division
900 Lakewood Ave.
Lakewood, NJ 08701-2697
Fields offered: Many fields
Year founded: 1908
Ownership: Nonprofit, church
Phone: (732) 364-2200 • (800) 458-8422
Fax: (732) 367-3920
E-mail: admissions-ugrad@georgian.edu
Website: www.georgian.edu
This school offers a Bachelor of Arts in art, art history, chemistry, humanities, mathematics, physics, psychology, sociology, or special education and a Bachelor of Science in accounting, biology, or business administration, entirely though evening study. Some credit is offered for military experience and a wide range of proficiency exams, as well as for cooperative education, independent study, and supervised fieldwork.

Golden Gate University   B, M, D, Law

536 Mission St.
San Francisco, CA 94105
Fields offered: Many fields
Year founded: 1901
Ownership: Nonprofit, independent
Phone: (415) 442-7272 • (800) GGU-4YOU
Fax: (415) 442-7807
E-mail: admissions@ggu.edu
Website: www.ggu.edu
B.A. in many management-related fields; B.S. in accounting, insurance management, and transportation; M.B.A.; M.P.A.; M.S. in accounting and taxation; combined M.B.A. and law degree; and a D.P.A. or D.B.A. all entirely through evening and/or weekend study. An "executive M.B.A." program for experienced managers meets every other weekend for 20 months. Off-campus courses are offered in locations around California (including L.A., Sacramento, and San Diego) and at military bases across the country (Arizona, Florida, Idaho, Nevada, New Hampshire, New Mexico, North and South Carolina, Virginia, and Washington, as well as Guantanamo Bay, Cuba). Two Bear family members happily attended Golden Gate before moving on to schools with broader course offerings.

Guilford College   B

Center for Continuing Education
5800 West Friendly Ave.
Greensboro, NC 27410
Fields offered: Many fields
Year founded: 1837
Ownership: Nonprofit, church
Phone: (910) 316-2000 • (800) 992-7759
Fax: (910) 316-2951
E-mail: admission@rascal.guilford.edu
Website: www.guilford.edu
B.A., B.S., and B.F.A. in a number of fields, entirely through evening courses. Credit for up to 64 units of prior academic education; an additional 16 can come from proficiency exams. Independent study and supervised fieldwork also available.

Hamline University   M,D

1536 Hewitt Avenue
Saint Paul, MN 55104
Fields offered: Public administration, liberal studies
Year founded: 1854
Ownership: Nonprofit, church
Phone: (612) 523-2900 • (800) 888-2182
Fax: (612) 523-2987
E-mail: gradprog@piper.hamline.edu
Website: www.hamline.edu/depts/mapa
Hamline is dedicated to serving the needs of working students, offering classes and entire programs through evening

and weekend courses. Currently, they offer a Master's and a Doctorate in public administration through an evening program for public administrators, corporate managers, and lawyers as well as M.A.'s in education and liberal studies and an M.F.A. in writing. Courses can be personalized with the use of independent study, directed reading (mentored by a faculty member) and internships. The school is also in the planning stages of a new Doctorate in public administration, to be offered entirely through distance learning. For more information, contact John Vinton, Director, Public Administration at (612) 641-2858 or e-mail: jvinton@hamline.edu.

Hampshire College   B

Amherst, MA 01002
Fields offered: Many fields
Year founded: 1970
Ownership: Nonprofit, independent
Phone: (413) 549-4600
Fax: (413) 582-5584
E-mail: admissions@hampshire.edu
Website: www.hampshire.edu

The B.A. is earned by completing three levels of study. In Division I (basic studies), students spend three or four semesters in residence taking courses and pursuing research. In Division II (concentration), they gain mastery of their chosen fields through independent study, foreign study, internships, and/or more courses. In Division III (advanced studies) they complete a major project. Each student designs a course of study in close collaboration with faculty. Interdisciplinary study is available in all major liberal arts disciplines.

Harvard University   B, M

Division of Continuing Education
51 Brattle St.
Cambridge, MA 02138
Fields offered: Many fields
Year founded: 1636
Ownership: Nonprofit, independent
Phone: (617) 495-4024
Fax: (617) 495-0500
E-mail: webmaster@hudce.harvard.edu
Website: www.harvard.edu

Harvard's Extension School offers more than 550 courses in 50 fields of study on an open-enrollment basis. Bachelor of Liberal Arts and Master of Liberal Arts, as well as an A.A. and certificates in special studies in administration and management, applied sciences, public health, museum studies, and publishing & communications. In addition, students wishing to learn English can study at the Institute for English Language Programs. Half the units for the Bachelor's degree must be earned at Harvard (in the Extension School, the Summer School, or Harvard College). All work for the Master's degree work must be completed at Harvard. There is a foreign language requirement, and a thesis must be submitted.

Hawaii Pacific University   B, M

1166 Fort Street Mall, #203
Honolulu, HI 96818
Fields offered: Many fields
Ownership: Nonprofit, independent
Phone: (808) 544-0249 • (800) 669-4724
Fax: (808) 544-0280
E-mail: admissions@hpu.edu
Website: www.hpu.edu

The Honolulu campus offers various Bachelor's degrees and an M.B.A. through Adult Continuing Education, for adults who wish to remain fully employed. Credit is given for work experience, military training, and equivalency exams. The M.B.A. offers concentrations in various specialties, as well as an internship option. The Hawaii Loa campus in Kaneohe offers a Bachelor in Organizational Management though an accelerated program for working adults. Up to 30 of 124 credits required can come from life-experience learning, through portfolio assessment, and another 30 from equivalency exams. Applicants must have already earned 60 credits (through the just-mentioned methods, or prior traditional learning); the program meets one night a week and every other Saturday, for 18 months. The Kaneohe campus is at 45-045 Kamehameha Highway, Kaneohe 96744, phone (808) 233-3100.

Heidelberg College   B

310 E. Market St.
Tiffin, OH 44883
Fields offered: Many fields
Year founded: 1850
Ownership: Nonprofit, church
Phone: (419) 448-2000 • (800) HEIDELBERG
Fax: (419) 448-2124
E-mail: adminfo@mail.heidelberg.edu
Website: www.heidelberg.edu

B.A. and B.S. in accounting, allied health, business administration, health services management, psychology, and public relations. Up to 75 percent of the necessary credits may be earned through an assessment of prior learning experiences, which is done on the basis of a portfolio prepared by the student. The assessment fee is $575. Nontraditional courses are available, based on a learning contract model. There is also a weekend college, which meets from Friday evening through Sunday morning during the fall, spring, and summer terms. See also: East Central College Consortium.

Heritage College   B, M

3240 Fork Road
Toppenish, WA 98948
Fields offered: Many fields
Year founded: 1907
Ownership: Nonprofit, independent
Phone: (509) 865-2244
Fax: (509) 865-4469

E-mail: espindolaunderscoreb@heritage.edu
Website: www.heritage.edu

Master of Education through intensive weekend courses on both Toppenish and Omak campuses. Bachelor's degrees available entirely through evening study, with credit for prior learning experiences and equivalency examinations. Credit for work experience available through on-campus LINK program. Formerly known as Fort Wright College.

Hiram College   B

Hiram, OH 44234
Fields offered: Various fields
Year founded: 1850
Ownership: Nonprofit, independent
Phone: (330) 569-5169 • (800) 362-5281
Fax: (330) 569-5944
E-mail: admission@hiram.edu
Website: www.hiram.edu

Bachelor of Arts offered entirely through weekend study. The weekend college meets from Friday evening through Sunday noon, every other weekend. Programs available in fine arts, humanities, social sciences, communications, business management, and allied health. The degree can be completed in a minimum of two academic years; 90 credit hours must be completed at Hiram College. See also: East Central College Consortium.

Hofstra University   B

New College, 1000 Fulton Ave.
Hempstead, NY 11550
Fields offered: Many fields
Year founded: 1935
Ownership: Nonprofit, independent
Phone: (516) 463-5823 • (800) HOFSTRA
Fax: (516) 463-4848
E-mail: nuchzz@hofstra.edu
Website: www.hofstra.edu

Hofstra's New College is a small interdisciplinary liberal arts college offering the B.A. in humanities, natural sciences, social sciences, creative studies, or interdisciplinary studies, based on a combination of individual study on campus, internship projects off campus, and classroom work. Within New College, there is a University Without Walls program for "able adults who can spend only limited time on campus, but whose life situations provide opportunity for full- or part-time learning." This individualized program awards degrees based on development of abilities and competencies, rather than accumulation of credit-hours. New College students can earn up to 32 credits by examination. Many of Hofstra's traditional courses are offered in the evening as well.

Holy Names College   B

3500 Mountain Blvd.
Oakland, CA 94619
Fields offered: Various fields
Year founded: 1868

Ownership: Nonprofit, independent
Phone: (510) 436-1120 • (800) 430-1321
Fax: (510) 436-1199
E-mail: info@hnc.edu
Website: www.hnc.edu

Holy Names's weekend college offers a Bachelor of Arts in business administration/economics, human services, humanistic studies, and nursing; an M.B.A., and an M.A. in English. Classes meet every other weekend for three trimesters. Academic programs and support services are designed for the adult who works full-time.

Hood College   B, M

Rosemont Ave.
Frederick, MD 21701
Fields offered: Many fields
Year founded: 1893
Ownership: Nonprofit, independent
Phone: (301) 663-3131 • (800) 922-1599
Fax: (301) 696-3819
E-mail: undergraduate: admissions@nimue.hood.edu
graduate: hoodgrad@nimue.hood.edu
Website: www.hood.edu

Bachelor's degrees in many fields, in which units may be earned through an assessment of prior learning experiences, conducted by Hood's Learning Assessment and Resource Center. Master of Arts in human sciences for in-service teachers and others, through late afternoon, evening, and summer study.

Howard Payne University   B

HPU Station
Brownwood, TX 76801
Fields offered: General studies
Year founded: 1889
Ownership: Nonprofit, church
Phone: (915) 646-2502 • (800) 880-4478
Fax: (915) 643-7835
E-mail: enroll@hputx.edu
Website: www.hputx.edu

Degree-completion program for students who have already accumulated 60 credits, and have employment experience in their field. Credit for life-experience learning through portfolio assessment, as well as for a range of equivalency exams. The school does offer correspondence courses.

Hunter College   B, M

695 Park Ave.
New York, NY 10021
Fields offered: Many fields
Year founded: 1870
Ownership: Nonprofit, state
Phone: (212) 772-4490
Fax: (212) 650-3336
E-mail: admissions@tzayid.hunter.cuny.edu
Website: www.hunter.cuny.edu

Bachelor of Arts, Bachelor of Science, and Master's degrees in many fields, available entirely through evening study. There are combined Bachelor's/Master's programs in anthropology, economics, English, history, mathematics, music, physics, and sociology.

Huron University   B, M

3-5 Palace Gate
London, W8 5IS England
Fields offered: Many fields
Year founded: 1883
Phone: (44-071) 584-9696
Fax: (44-071) 589-9406
E-mail: inform@liton.com.hk
liton@compuserve.com
Website: home.i-wave.net.hk/~liton/new/huron.html
This the London program of South Dakota–based Huron offers B.A., B.S., and M.B.A. Fields of study include art, art history, international relations, CIS, management, international business marketing, finance, applied economics, humanities, and European studies, with independent study and international internship options. One year must be spent in residence.

Illinois Benedictine University   B, M

5700 College Rd.
Lisle, IL 60532-0900
Fields offered: Many fields
Year founded: 1887
Ownership: Nonprofit, church
Phone: (630) 829-6000
Fax: (630) 829-6301 (undergraduate)
(603) 829-6226 (graduate)
E-mail: admissions@ben.edu
Website: www.ben.edu
Bachelor's degrees in over 30 fields, including accounting, elementary education, health sciences, philosophy, Spanish, and computer science; M.B.A.; Master of Public Health, and M.S. in management of information systems, counseling psychology, fitness management, and management and organizational behavior, all entirely through evening study. Credit is given for prior work and life-experience learning. Formerly Saint Procopius College.

Illinois School of Professional Psychology

See: American Schools of Professional Psychology

Indiana Central College

See: University of Indianapolis

Indiana Institute of Technology   B

1600 E. Washington Blvd.
Fort Wayne, IN 46803-1297
Fields offered: Business administration
Year founded: 1930
Ownership: Nonprofit, independent
Phone: (219) 422-5561, ext. 251 • (800) 937-2448

Fax: (219) 422-7696
E-mail: filus@indtech.edu
Website: www.indtech.edu
Bachelor of Science in business administration. Credit is given for independent study and nonacademic prior learning, and correspondence courses are available.

Indiana State University   M

Terre Haute, IN 47809
Fields offered: Human resources, occupational safety
Year founded: 1865
Ownership: Nonprofit, state
Phone: (812) 237-2642 • (800) 444-GRAD
Fax: (812) 237-4292
E-mail: admissions@indstate.edu
Website: www-isu.indstate.edu
M.S. in occupational safety management or human resource development for higher education and industry (yes, that's the full name of the degree!) through interactive television, offered at sites statewide. Students may also obtain videocassettes of courses when needed. The contact for occupational safety is Portia Plummer at (812) 237-3071.

Indiana University Northwest   B

3400 Broadway
Gary, IN 6408
Fields offered: General studies
Year founded: 1921
Ownership: Nonprofit, state
Phone: (219) 980-6500 • (800) 437-5409
Fax: (219) 980-6670
E-mail: wlee@iunhaw1.iun.indiana.edu
Website: www.iun.indiana.edu
Bachelor of General Studies program designed for students who cannot attend school on a traditional schedule, or those who have prior credit and/or experience in a wide range of fields. Up to 30 credits (of 120 total required) can come from prior experience, through portfolio review; additional credit for CLEP, DANTES, and other exams. After enrollment, students have access to correspondence courses, supervised fieldwork, and other nontraditional options.

Indiana University of Pennsylvania   D

Indiana, PA 15705
Fields offered: Literature, rhetoric and linguistics
Year founded: 1875
Ownership: Nonprofit, state
Phone: (412) 357-2222
Fax: (412) 357-6213
E-mail: registrars-office@grove.iup.edu
Website: www.iup.edu
Indiana University of Pennsylvania offers two Ph.D. concentrations: one in English and American Literature and the second in Rhetoric and Linguistics. Basic coursework can be completed in two consecutive summers of full-time study, with independent study in between. Programs are

arranged to accommodate secondary, community, and four-year college teachers, allowing graduate students to pursue their studies without interrupting their careers. Students can choose from a number of areas related to the humanistic study of literature, including psychology, history, art, and music. Candidacy, comprehensive exams, and a dissertation are required. A language requirement can be met with coursework, exams, or proficiency in a computer language. This is a rigorous program for serious students who wish to be challenged intellectually.

Indiana Wesleyan University   B, M

LEAP Programs
211 E. 45th Street
Marion, IN 46953
Fields offered: Business administration, management, nursing
Year founded: 1920
Ownership: Nonprofit, independent
Phone: (765) 674-9751 • (800) 234-5327
Fax: (765) 674-8028
E-mail: admissions@indwes.edu
Website: www.indwes.edu

The LEAP (Leadership Education for Adult Professionals) program is designed for working adult students, and offers a B.S. and an M.S., both in management or business administration. (Undergraduate applicants must have at least two years of employment experience and 60 credits completed elsewhere; graduate applicants, three years employment). Up to 40 credits can come from portfolio assessment and equivalency exams. Students are required to meet one night a week in class for four hours, and an additional night out of class, also for four hours. The school stresses that these are very intense "lockstep" programs. Formerly Marion College. There is also an MBA which requires four intensive weekends on campus.

Inter-American University   B

405 Ponce De Leon
Hato Rey, PR 00919
Fields offered: Many fields
Year founded: 1960
Ownership: Nonprofit, independent
Phone: (787) 250-2188
Fax: (787) 250-0782
E-mail: mfont@ns.inter.edu
Website: www.coqui.metro.inter.edu

Bachelor's degrees in many fields can be earned through evening and weekend study, summer school, and through a university without walls program. This last, which requires one visit a week to campus, was originally designed for working law enforcement officers but other types of applicants are accepted.

International Academy of Management and Economics   M, D

1061 Metropolitan Avenue
San Antonio Village, P.O. Box 3415
Makati City, Philippines
Fields offered: Management, economics
Phone: 896-4193
Fax: 896-2351

Courses are offered by television in the Philippines (the televised courses can also be obtained on videocassette), leading to a Master's or Doctorate. We have seen a certificate of government recognition from the Philippine Commission of Higher Education, although the school is not listed in the *International Handbook of Universities*. There is some association with the unaccredited Newport University in California.

International College   B

8695 College Pkwy.
Fort Myers, FL 33919
Fields offered: Business administration, accounting, CIS, management
Phone: (941) 774-4700 • (800) 466-0019
Fax: (941) 774-4593
E-mail: brandon@naples.net
Website: www.internationalcollege.edu

Bachelor of Science in the above fields offered through independent study and/or "parallel enrollment," a nontraditional program that combines on-campus courses with off-campus job experience. Up to 25 percent of credit towards a degree can come from assessment of prior life-experience learning.

International Graduate School of Behavioral Science

See: Florida Institute of Technology

International University (Europe)   B, M

The Avenue
Bushey, Watford, WD2 2LN UK
Fields offered: Business, engineering, human behavior, international relations
Ownership: Nonprofit, independent
Phone: (0923) 49067
Website: www.thebiz.co.uk/stateuni.htm

Bachelor's and Master's degrees are offered in residence on the campus near London, through an association with the accredited United States International University in San Diego.

Iona College   B

715 North Ave.
New Rochelle, NY 10801-1890
Fields offered: Various fields
Year founded: 1940
Ownership: Nonprofit, independent

Phone: (914) 633-2000 • (800) 231-IONA
Fax: (914) 633-2020
E-mail: ICAD@iona.edu
Website: www.iona.edu

Bachelor of Arts and Bachelor of Science can be earned entirely through evening, weekend, and summer programs.

Iowa Wesleyan College   B

Office of Continuing Education
601 N. Main Street
Mount Pleasant, IA 52641
Fields offered: Many fields
Year founded: 1842
Ownership: Nonprofit, church
Phone: (319) 385-8021 • (800) 582-2383 ext. 231
Fax: (319) 385-6296
E-mail: admitrwl@iwc.edu
Website: www.iwc.edu

B.A. in accounting, business administration, elementary education, psychology, sociology, and criminal justice; B.S. in nursing, and Bachelor of General Studies, through some combination of evening, weekend, and summer courses, independent study, supervised fieldwork, and televised courses. Credit for prior military and other experience through portfolio assessment, and equivalency exams.

Jacksonville State University   B

227 Stone Center
Jacksonville, AL 36265
Fields offered: General studies
Year founded: 1883
Ownership: Nonprofit, state
Phone: (205) 782-5781 • (800) 231-5291, ext. 5268
Fax: (205) 782-5291
E-mail: info@jsucc.jsu.edu
Website: www.jsu.edu

Bachelor of General Studies through a program that allows students greater freedom to select an individualized course of study, and gives some credit for military experience and possibly other, by portfolio assessment, equivalency exams, and televised courses.

Jacksonville University   B, M

College of Weekend Studies
2800 University Blvd. N.
Jacksonville, FL 32211
Fields offered: Many fields
Year founded: 1934
Ownership: Nonprofit, independent
Phone: (904) 744-3950 • (800) 225-2027
Fax: (904) 744-0101
E-mail: admreq@junix.ju.edu
Website: www.ju.edu

Bachelor of General Studies, Bachelor of Science, including a specialization in nursing (B.S.N.), Executive M.B.A., and M.A. in teaching, all entirely through weekend and independent study. Undergraduate applicants must have already completed 30 units elsewhere, and both undergrad and graduate applicants must have five years' employment or other related experience. Credit for military and other life-experience learning through portfolio assessment, and for equivalency exams.

James Madison University   B

Harrisburg, VA 22807
Fields offered: General studies
Year founded: 1908
Ownership: Nonprofit, state
Phone: (540) 568-6211
Fax: (540) 568-3332
E-mail: gotojmu@jmu.edu
Website: www.jmu.edu

An individualized Bachelor of General Studies that can be tailored to adult returning students' needs. Applicants must have completed 30 units, and have been out of high school for at least four years. Credit for life-experience and military learning, through portfolio assessment, as well as a range of equivalency exams.

John F. Kennedy University   B, M

12 Altarinda Rd.
Orinda, CA 94563
Fields offered: Many fields
Year founded: 1964
Ownership: Nonprofit, independent
Phone: (510) 254-0200
Fax: (510) 254-6964
E-mail: futterman@jfku.edu
Website: www.jfku.edu

Many innovative Bachelor's and Master's programs, in fields including liberal studies, counseling psychology with specializations in marriage, family, and child counseling and transpersonal psychology, museum studies, business administration, holistic health education, sports psychology, arts and consciousness, interdisciplinary consciousness studies, law, career development, and more. The university sees a major role for itself in helping adults to accomplish mid-career changes (their average student is 37 years old). Many programs are available on a part-time basis and are offered on evenings and weekends.

Johns Hopkins University   B, M, D

School of Continuing Studies
102 Shaffer Hall
3400 N. Charles Street
Baltimore, MD 21218
Fields offered: Business, education, liberal arts
Year founded: 1876
Ownership: Nonprofit, independent
Phone: (410) 516-8490
Fax: (410) 516-7704
E-mail: scsinfo@jhu.edu
Website: www.jhu.edu

Bachelor of Liberal Arts; Bachelor of Science; Master of Arts in teaching; Master of Drama Studies; Master of Liberal Arts; Master of Science in business, counseling, education, information and telecommunication systems for business, interdisciplinary science studies, marketing, organization and human resource development, real estate, and special education, and Doctor of Education all offered through evening and weekend courses. The School of Continuing Studies operates off-campus centers in downtown Baltimore, Columbia, Montgomery County, Maryland, and Washington, D.C.

Johnson State College   B

External Degree Program
Johnson, VT 05656
Fields offered: Many fields
Year founded: 1828
Ownership: Nonprofit, state
Phone: (802) 635-2356 ext. 290 • (800) 635-2356
Fax: (802) 635-1230
E-mail: jscapply@badger.jsc.vsc.edu
Website: www.jsc.vsc.edu

This individually tailored Bachelor's degree is set up to allow native Vermonters to earn a self-designed degree, working with a mentor/advisor. Experiential learning credit is accepted as part of the 60 unit-hours needed for entry, and/or the 122 minimum for graduation. Students must earn 30 credits while enrolled in the program, through independent or correspondence study and on- or off-campus coursework.

Kansas Wesleyan University   B

100 E. Claflin
Salina, KS 67401
Fields offered: Many fields
Year founded: 1886
Ownership: Nonprofit, church
Phone: (913) 827-5541 • (800) 874-1154
Fax: (913) 827-0927
E-mail: admissions@diamond.kwu.edu
Website: www.kwu.edu

B.A. and B.S. available in accounting and finance, arts and communication, business administration and economics, computer science, pre-engineering, pre-law, pre-ministerial, teaching, social services, and many health sciences areas. KWU has recently initiated a Bachelor of Applied Science in business that they feel is particularly well suited to the nontraditional student.

Kean College   B

Morris Ave.
Union, NJ 07083
Fields offered: Many fields
Year founded: 1855
Ownership: Nonprofit, state
Phone: (908) 527-2000
Fax: (908) 355-5143

E-mail: admitme@turbo.kean.edu
Website: www.kean.edu

Some degree requirements can be earned through an assessment of prior learning experiences, based on assessment of a student-prepared portfolio.

Keller Graduate School of Management   M

225 W. Washington
Chicago, IL 60606
Fields offered: Business administration
Year founded: 1973
Ownership: Proprietary
Phone: (630) 571-7700
Fax: (630) 574-1969
E-mail: rfredrick@keller.edu
Website: www.kgsm.com

Keller offers a practitioner-oriented M.B.A. program for working adults entirely through evening or weekend study at five Chicago locations, as well as in Phoenix, Arizona; Kansas City, Missouri; and Milwaukee, Wisconsin. They purchased the DeVry Computer Schools in 1987.

Kingston University   M

Perrhyn Road
Kingston upon Thames
Surrey, KT1 2EE England
Fields offered: Business administration
Year founded: 1899
Ownership: Nonprofit, public
Phone: (44-181) 547-2000
Fax: (44-181) 547-7178
E-mail: 2361 C.Gilchrist@Kingston.ac.uk
Website: www.kingston.ac.uk/

Two-year M.B.A. through a distance-learning program, with one weekend on-campus required per month for intensive group study and individual counseling. Geared to midcareer executives who wish to develop their skills.

Lake Erie College   B

391 W. Washington St.
Painesville, OH 44077
Fields offered: Many fields
Year founded: 1856
Ownership: Nonprofit, independent
Phone: (216) 352-3361 • 800-533-4996
Fax: (216) 352-3533
E-mail: lecadmit@lakeerie.edu
Website: www.lakeerie.edu

Bachelor of Arts, Bachelor of Science, and Bachelor of Fine Arts may be earned through weekend and evening study. Special programs: business administration, equestrian studies. Credit for nonacademic prior learning and by examination.

Lake Superior State University   B, M

844 North Campus Court
Sault Sainte Marie, MI 49783
Fields offered: Accounting, business, criminal justice, engineering management, nursing, public administration
Year founded: 1946
Ownership: Nonprofit, state
Phone: (906) 635-2554
Fax: (906) 635-2762
E-mail: scamp@lakers.lssu.edu
Website: www.lssu.edu

The above-listed fields are at Bachelor's level with the exception of public administration (MPA). There is also an MBA available. All tuition is by text, videotape and video-conference. Students must be able to travel to one of four conference sites to participate.

Lamar University   B, M, D

4400 Pt. Arthur Rd.
Beaumont, TX 77710
Fields offered: Many fields
Year founded: 1923
Ownership: Nonprofit, state
Phone: (409) 735-3780 • (800) 458-7558
Fax: (409) 880-8909
E-mail: Melissa G. Chesser
(chessmg@lub002.lamar.edu)
Website: www.lamar.edu

B.A. and B.S. can be earned entirely through evening and summer programs; some Saturday classes in graduate-level education.

Landsdowne College   B, Law

43 Harrington Gardens
London, SW7 4JU England
Fields offered: Business, fine arts, interior design
Phone: (01) 373-7282

Landsdowne follows the curriculum of the accredited New Hampshire College, of Manchester, New Hampshire, and, upon completion of the coursework in London, the students earn their B.S. from New Hampshire. A comparable program is also offered with Drury College in Missouri. Landsdowne also prepares for London University's degree-examinations for the Bachelor of Laws. Its academic council is composed of five present or former administrators of excellent American nontraditional degree programs or schools. B.A. and B.F.A. programs also available.

Lebanon Valley College   B

Annville, PA 17003
Fields offered: Many fields
Year founded: 1866
Ownership: Nonprofit, church
Phone: (717) 867-6100 • (800) 445-6181
Fax: (717) 867-6124
E-mail: feather@lvc.edu

Website: www.lvc.edu
Bachelor of Arts and Bachelor of Science available through weekend, evening, or summer programs. Evening classes meet once a week during the academic year and twice during the summer. Weekend classes meet Friday nights or Saturdays. There is a special two-week "intensive term" in mid May, during which students can complete one entire course. Degrees are offered in a wide variety of fields, including accounting, administration for health care professionals, computer information systems, management, and social service. Credit for experiential learning, and by examination.

Lewis-Clark State College   B

500 8th Ave.
Lewiston, ID 83501
Fields offered: Business, social work, nursing, general studies
Year founded: 1893
Ownership: Nonprofit, state
Phone: (208) 799-5272 • (800) 933-LCSC ext. 2210
Fax: (208) 799-2831
E-mail: admoff@lcsc.edu
Website: www.lcsc.edu

Although the American Council on Education's book, The Electronic University, reports that Lewis-Clark offers non-resident Bachelor's degrees which can be earned through a combination of audio- and videocassettes, televised and correspondence courses, and guided independent study, the college tells us that the ACE is in error.

Lincoln University (MO)   M

Jefferson City, MO 65101
Fields offered: Various fields
Year founded: 1866
Ownership: Nonprofit, state
Phone: (573) 681-5000 • (800) 521-5052
Fax: (573) 681-5566
E-mail: meyerj@lincolnu.edu
Website: www.lincolnu.edu

Master of Education, Master of Arts, and Master of Business Administration may be earned through evening or summer programs. Credit for independent study and by examination.

Lincoln University (PA)

Lincoln University Urban Center
3020 Market Street, 2nd floor
Philadelphia, PA 19104
Phone: (215) 387-2405 • (800) 790-0191
Fax: (215) 387-3834
E-mail: lu.lincoln.edu
Website: www.lincoln.edu/pages/luuc-mhs

Master of Human Services (MHS) degree that is largely non-traditional, although it requires ongoing residency. Classes are held twice a week, usually at various human service agencies in the suburban Philadelphia area. Program relies heavily on portfolio development (although not on prior learning per se). Does not require a Bachelor's degree for admissions; however, students without a Bachelor's must have at least five years' experience in a human services field and be currently employed in the human services.

Long Island University   B, M

C. W. Post Campus
Brookville, NY 11548
Fields offered: Many fields
Year founded: 1954
Ownership: Nonprofit, independent
Phone: (516) 299-2000 • (800) LIU PLAN
Fax: (516) 299-4020
E-mail: scs@luke.liunet.edu
Website: www.cwpost.liunet.edu

This school's weekend college offers a Master of Professional Studies in criminal justice, Master of Public Administration in health care administration and public administration, and a Master of Science in medical biology, as well as evening classes that can be applied to 174 degree programs at the C. W. Post Campus. The PLUS Program gives special attention to the educational needs of adult students who are preparing for a career change or a move up the ladder. Credit for life experience and by examination awarded toward degree fulfillment. The Office of Adult Services serves as the initial point of contact for many adults by providing free educational and career counseling.

Louisiana State University   B, M, D

Evening School
388 Pleasant Hall
Baton Rouge, LA 70803
Fields offered: General studies coursework
Year founded: 1855
Ownership: Nonprofit, state
Phone: (504) 388-6297/388-1175
Fax: (504) 388-6400
E-mail: mmoore2@lsumvs.sncc.lsu.edu (undergraduate)
grdfern@lsuvm.sncc.lsu.edu (graduate)
Website: www.lsu.edu

Bachelor of Arts in history, English, sociology, and business administration; Bachelor of Science in mathematics, psychology, and computer science; Master of Library Science at New Orleans and Shreveport; Master of Science in petroleum engineering at New Orleans; Master of Arts in education at Eunice and Alexandria; Ph.D. in education at Shreveport, all through evening study.

Lourdes College   B

6832 Convent Blvd.
Sylvania, OH 43560
Fields offered: Individualized studies, religious studies, other fields
Year founded: 1958
Ownership: Nonprofit, church
Phone: (419) 885-5291 • 800-878-3210, ext. 299

Fax: (419) 882-3987
E-mail: btanesky@lourdes.edu
Website: www.lourdes.edu

Bachelor of Individualized Studies through evening, weekend, and summer programs. Credit for prior learning, independent study, and by examination. Evening and weekend courses in many fields of study, including business, gerontology, music, occupational therapy, recreational therapy, psychology, nursing, social work, sociology, and art.

Loyola Marymount University   M

Loyola Boulevard at West 80th Street
Los Angeles, CA 90045-2699
Fields offered: Engineering and production management
Year founded: 1914
Ownership: Church
Phone: (310) 338-2721
Fax: (310) 338-7339
E-mail: mmendels@lmumail.lmu.edu
Website: www.lmu.edu

This multidisciplinary evening program is tailored to the needs of working adults who require an M.S. in engineering and production management (EAPM). The two-year program involves courses typically held once a week; most students take two courses per semester, meaning a commitment of two evenings a week to finish the degree in two years. Team projects and a final project or thesis allow students to try different approaches to learning, and then to apply what they've learned to real-life situations.

Loyola University of Chicago   B

Mundelein College of Loyola
6525 N. Sheridan Road, SKY 204
Chicago, IL 60626-5385
Fields offered: Many fields
Year founded: 1870
Ownership: Nonprofit, church
Phone: (312) 915-6508
Fax: (312) 915-6501
E-mail: admission-web@luc.edu
Website: www.luc.edu

Loyola has recently expanded its part-time undergraduate program through affiliation with the formerly independent Mundelein Weekend College. The new program awards B.A. and B.S. degrees in a wide range of fields, including physical and life sciences, humanities, social work, business administration, and education. Students have a choice of day, evening, weekend, or summer courses and, according to a 1992 note in Loyola's newsletter for part-time students, the school "continues to alter its identity as it adapts to the rhythm of the times while clinging resolutely to its essential mission: offering adult students access to higher education."

Maastricht School of Management M

MBA Department
P.O. Box 1203
Maastricht, 6201 BE Netherlands
Fields offered: Business management
Phone: (31-43) 361-8318
Fax: (31-43) 361-8330
E-mail: staff@msm.nl
Website: www.msm.nl

Maastricht offers an "outreach" MBA, in which the degree program, usually packaged in several modules, is administered through an institution local to the student, allowing students to remain employed, and often to complete the program at their own pace, based on the agreement reached with the partner institution and with Maastricht. Outreach centers are currently located in Asia and the Middle East (Singapore, Jakarta, Kuala Lumpur, Penang, Skopje, Cyprus, Cairo, and Debrecen).

Madonna University B, M

36600 Schoolcraft Rd.
Livonia, MI 48150
Fields offered: Many fields
Year founded: 1947
Ownership: Nonprofit, church
Phone: (313) 591-5000 • (800) 852-4951
Fax: (313) 432-5393
E-mail: muinfo@smtp.munet.edu
Website: www.munet.edu

B.A. and B.S. programs are offered in many fields, often through evening classes. Life-experience credits awarded in many areas, including allied health management, business, computer science, criminal justice, gerontology, home economics, and nursing. Such prior learning needs to be described in detail and documented, and is evaluated by means of portfolio assessment, challenge exam, or national standardized tests (CLEP). Cooperative education for credit can be arranged. Thirty semester units in residency are required for the degree.

Malone College B

515 25th St. NW
Canton, OH 44709
Fields offered: Management
Year founded: 1892
Ownership: Nonprofit, church
Phone: (330) 471-8100
Fax: (330) 454-6977
E-mail: admissions@malone.edu
Website: www.malone.edu

B.A. in management through an accelerated, intensive degree-completion program (applicants must have completed at least 60 credit, and be 25 or older). Credit for prior learning through portfolio assessment, and for equivalency exams, cooperative education, and independent study.

Manchester College M

North Manchester, IN 46962
Fields offered: Accounting
Year founded: 1889
Ownership: Nonprofit, church
Phone: (219) 982-5000 • (800) 852-3648
Fax: (219) 982-5043
E-mail: JERohr%STAFF%MC@Manchester.edu
Website: www.manchester.edu

Master's in accounting can be earned entirely through evening study.

Mankato State University B, M

Alternative Degree Program
South Rd. and Ellis Ave.
Mankato, MN 56002
Fields offered: Many fields
Year founded: 1866
Ownership: Nonprofit, state
Phone: (507) 389-2463 • (800) 722-0544
Fax: (507) 389-1040
E-mail: mary_racek@ms1.mankato.msus.edu
Website: www.mankato.msus.edu

B.S. in open studies and M.S. in continuing studies, for alternative students whose "personal, educational, or career goals require a program not confined to the demands of a specific discipline." Credit awarded for military experience, equivalency exams, television courses, independent study, and supervised fieldwork.

Marian College B, M

45 South National Ave.
Fond du Lac, WI 54935
Fields offered: Education, business administration, nursing, radiology
Year founded: 1936
Ownership: Nonprofit, church
Phone: (920) 923-7650 • (800) 262-7426
Fax: (920) 923-7154
E-mail: admit@mariancoll.edu
Website: www.mariancoll.edu

Degree-completion programs leading to Bachelor of Business Administration or B.S. in nursing, operations management, or radiologic technology, as well as an M.A. in education and an M.S. in quality, values, and leadership. Credit for challenge exams and prior nonacademic learning by portfolio assessment. Courses scheduled to meet the needs of working adults.

Marietta College B, M

215 Fifth Street
Marietta, OH 45750-4005
Fields offered: Economics, management, accounting, psychology, and liberal arts and learning
Year founded: 1835
Ownership: Nonprofit, independent

Phone: (614) 376-4643 • (800) 331-7896
Fax: (614) 376-4896
E-mail: admit@mcnet.marietta.edu
Website: www.marietta.edu
Bachelor of Arts in economics, management, accounting, psychology, and liberal arts; Master of Arts in liberal learning through day, evening, and weekend study. Credit available for life experience. See also: East Central College Consortium.

Marion College
See: Indiana Wesleyan University

Marquette University   B
1212 W. Wisconsin Avenue
Milwaukee, WI 53233
Fields offered: Many fields
Year founded: 1881
Ownership: Nonprofit, church
Phone: (414) 288-7302 • (800) 222-6544
Fax: (414) 288-3300
E-mail: go2marquette@marquette.edu
Website: www.mu.edu
Marquette's part-time studies division offers day, evening, and Saturday courses leading to the Bachelor's degree in engineering, criminology and law, political science, advertising, journalism, public relations, organization and leadership, and interpersonal communications.

Mars Hill College   B
Center for Continuing Education
Mars Hill, NC 28754
Year founded: 1856
Ownership: Nonprofit, church
Phone: (704) 689-1166 • (800) 543-1514
Fax: (704) 689-1290
E-mail: admissions@mhc.edu
Website: www.mhc.edu
Bachelor of Science, Bachelor of Arts, and Bachelor of Social Work available through summer and evening classes. Special programs include allied health, social work, and elementary education. Credit for nonacademic prior learning, independent study, and by examination must be completed as part of a regular program at Mars Hill or one of the two off-campus centers in Asheville or Burnsville.

Marshall University Graduate
College   M, D
100 Angus E. Peyton Drive
South Charleston, WV 25303
Fields offered: Many fields
Year founded: 1972
Phone: (304) 746-1901 • (800) 642-9842
Fax: (304) 746-1092
E-mail: ljavins@mugc.edu
Website: www.wvgc.edu

Uses classrooms of other institutions to offer Master's degrees in education, counseling, humanities, psychology, business, engineering, environmental studies, and information systems. Educational Specialists degrees are offered in school psychology and education. Doctor of Education is offered in cooperation with West Virginia University. Classes are offered in late afternoon and evening in many locations in West Virginia. Intensive short courses and workshops are available throughout the year. Formerly West Virginia Graduate College.

Martin University   B, M
2171 Avondale Place
Indianapolis, IN 46218
Fields offered: Many fields
Year founded: 1977
Ownership: Nonprofit, independent
Phone: (317) 543-3235
Fax: (317) 543-3257
Website: www.martin.edu
Martin University's stated mission is "to the poor, the minority, and the adult learner." The average student is 40 years old. They offer the Bachelor's degree in many fields, including accounting, pre-law, chemistry, biology, business, human services, African-American studies, genetic counseling, substance abuse, social services, and music. Many courses through evening and Saturday study. Master's in community psychology and urban, ministry studies. Assessment of prior learning for life-learning credit.

Mary Washington College   M
1301 College Ave.
Fredericksburg, VA 22401
Fields offered: Business administration, engineering
Ownership: Nonprofit, state
Phone: (540) 654-1000 • (888) 692-4968
Fax: (540) 654-1073
E-mail: admit@mwc.edu
Website: www.mwc.edu
Distance-learning M.B.A. and M.E. (engineering) through satellite television and telephone instruction. The M.B.A. is open to Virginia residents only, the M.E. to students worldwide. Also offers a Bachelor of Liberal Studies through evening and summer programs, with credit for independent study, exams, and nonacademic prior learning (by portfolio assessment).

Marycrest International University   B
1607 West 12th St.
Davenport, IA 52804
Fields offered: Many fields
Year founded: 1939
Ownership: Nonprofit
Phone: (319) 326-9512 • (800) 728-9705
Fax: (319) 326-9250
E-mail: mfarber@acc.mcrest.edu
Website: www.mcrest.edu

Degrees in accounting, business administration, professional communication, computer science, pre-law, social work and special studies. Credit for experiential learning and by examination. See also: Quad Cities Graduate Center.

Marygrove College **B, M**
8425 W. McNichols Rd.
Detroit, MI 48221
Fields offered: Many fields
Year founded: 1910
Ownership: Nonprofit, church
Phone: (313) 927-1200
Fax: (313) 864-6670
Website: www.marygrove.edu

B.A., B.S., B.F.A., Bachelor of Music, Bachelor of Social Work, Bachelor of Business Administration, Master of Arts, and Master of Education, all or largely through evening classes. Credit for life-experience learning through portfolio assessment, for equivalency exams, and for cooperative education, independent study, and television courses.

Marylhurst College for Lifelong Learning **B, M**
Marylhurst, OR 97036
Fields offered: Many fields
Year founded: 1893
Ownership: Nonprofit, independent
Phone: (503) 636-8141 • (800) 634-9982
Fax: (503) 636-9526
E-mail: registrar@marylhurst.edu
Website: www.marylhurst.edu

Bachelor of Arts in communication, humanities, human services, social science, science/ math, arts, crafts, and interdisciplinary studies; Bachelor of Fine Arts; Bachelor of Science in management; Bachelor of Music; Master of Science in management; M.B.A.; and M.A. in art therapy. Baccalaureate graduation requirements include a minimum of 40 quarter hours of credit through Marylhurst (22 percent of the degree). Credit is earned by taking Marylhurst courses, courses at other schools, or by correspondence, and through independent studies. Fifty percent of the graduates utilize the Credit for Prior Learning Experience Program to complete their degrees. The average student is 38 years old and enters with about two years of college.

Marymount College **B**
Tarrytown, NY 10591
Fields offered: Many fields
Year founded: 1907
Ownership: Nonprofit, independent
Phone: (914) 332-8295 • (800) 724-4312
Fax: (914) 332-4956
E-mail: admiss@mmc.marymt.edu
Website: www.marymt.edu

Bachelor of Arts and Bachelor of Science degrees in such fields as psychology, English, history, economics, business,

information systems, and elementary education may be earned by spending every second or third weekend on campus to complete as many as twelve credits per term. Weekend courses run from Friday evening through Sunday afternoon. Credit for prior experiential learning.

Maryville University of Saint Louis **B**
13550 Conway Rd.
St. Louis, MO 63141
Fields offered: Many fields
Year founded: 1872
Ownership: Nonprofit, independent
Phone: (314) 529-9300 • (800) 627-9855
Fax: (314) 542-9085
E-mail: wec@maryville.edu
Website: www.maryvillestl.edu

Bachelor's degree programs in management, information systems, psychology, sociology, nursing, and communications are offered through evening and weekend courses. Credit for experiential learning.

Massachusetts College of Liberal Arts **B**
Office of Continuing Education
North Adams, MA 01247
Fields offered: Business administration, computer science, sociology
Year founded: 1894
Ownership: Nonprofit, state
Phone: (413) 662-5000 • (800) 292-6632, ext. 5410
Fax: (413) 662-5010
E-mail: admissions@nasc.mass.edu
Website: www.nasc.mass.edu

A B.S. in business administration or computer science and B.A. in sociology offered through evening degree programs.

Metropolitan State College of Denver **B**
P.O. Box 173362
Denver, CO 80217-3362
Fields offered: Many fields
Year founded: 1963
Ownership: Nonprofit, state
Phone: (303) 556-8514
Fax: (303) 556-6345
Website: www.mscd.edu

Up to half the units required for the Bachelor's degree can come from assessment of prior learning experiences. The assessment is based on a student-prepared portfolio, and the cost is based on the number of units awarded.

Miami Institute of Psychology **D**
8180 N.W. 36th St., Second Floor
Miami, FL 33166.
Fields offered: Psychology
Year founded: 1966
Ownership: Nonprofit, independent
Phone: (305) 593-1223 • (800) 672-3246

Fax: (305) 593-1854
E-mail: zseguinot@mip.edu
Website: www.ccas.edu

The accreditation is for the main campus, the Caribbean Center for Advanced Studies, in Puerto Rico. Ph.D. and Psy.D. degrees are offered in general clinical psychology, clinical psychology and criminal justice, clinical gerontological psychology, and clinical neuropsychology. Some courses available through evening or weekend study.

Michigan State University · M

Office of Admissions and Scholarships
250 Administration Building
East Lansing, MI 48824
Fields offered: Many fields
Year founded: 1855
Ownership: Nonprofit, state
Phone: (517) 355-8332 • (800) 353-4678
Fax: (517) 355-1647
E-mail: admis@pilot.msu.edu
Website: www.msu.edu

John's alma mater offers the Master of Business Administration through evening study at Troy; M.A. in advertising, journalism, and counseling in Birmingham; M.A. in teacher education in Saginaw, Flint, Grand Rapids, and Kalamazoo; Master of Science in nursing in Benton Harbor; Master of Social Work in Sault Ste. Marie and Traverse City. Also, Michigan State offers the M.A. in education through part-time and independent study centers in Japan, England, Thailand, and the Philippines.

Midway College · B

512 E. Stephens St.
Midway, KY 40347
Fields offered: Business administration
Year founded: 1847
Ownership: Nonprofit, church
Phone: (606) 846-4421 • (800) 755-0031
Fax: (606) 846-5349
E-mail: kdouglas@midway.edu.
Website: www.midway.edu

B.A. in business administration entirely through evening classes. Credit for prior learning experiences, equivalency exams, independent study, and supervised fieldwork.

Millersville University of Pennsylvania · B

Millersville, PA 17551
Fields offered: Many fields
Year founded: 1855
Ownership: Nonprofit, state
Phone: (717) 872-3024 • (800) MU-ADMIT
Fax: (717) 871-2147
E-mail: adm_info@mu3.millersv.edu
Website: www.millersv.edu

Bachelor of Arts in English, business administration, economics, history, mathematics, computer science, political science, psychology, social work, and physics may be earned through evening classes or summer sessions. Special program for registered nurses leads to B.A. in nursing. Millersville offers no degree program that can be earned exclusively through evening or summer classes.

Millsaps College · B

Adult Degree Program
Jackson, MS 39210
Fields offered: Liberal studies
Year founded: 1890
Ownership: Nonprofit, church
Phone: (601) 974-1000 • (800) 352-1050
Fax: (601) 354-2624
E-mail: admissions@okra.millsaps.edu
Website: www.millsaps.edu

The Adult Degree Program is scheduled so as to allow adult students to pursue a Bachelor of Liberal Studies while continuing full-time work. Credit awarded for prior learning experiences through portfolio assessment and for equivalency exams, independent study, and supervised fieldwork.

Milwaukee School of Engineering · B, M

1025 N. Broadway
P. O. Box 644
Milwaukee, WI 53201
Fields offered: Engineering, engineering technology, business, and management
Year founded: 1903
Ownership: Nonprofit, independent
Phone: (414) 277-7300 • (800) 332-MSOE
Fax: (414) 277-7475
E-mail: explore@msoe.edu
Website: www.msoe.edu

Bachelor of Science in engineering technology, business, and management; Master of Science in engineering and engineering management, entirely through evening study. Courses are also offered at corporate facilities, other off-campus locations, and via videotape.

Minnesota School of Professional Psychology

See: American Schools of Professional Psychology

Mississippi State University · B, M, D

Office of Continuing Education
P.O. Drawer 5247
Mississippi State, MS 39762
Fields offered: Political science, public policy administration, business administration, general studies, engineering, counselor education, systems management
Year founded: 1878
Ownership: Nonprofit, state
Phone: (601) 325-2131
Fax: (601) 325-7455
E-mail: admit@admissions.msstate.edu (undergraduate)
grad@grad.msstate.edu (graduate)

Website: www.msstate.edu

Bachelor of General Studies, M.A. in political science or public policy administration, and M.B.A. through nontraditional programs, including short, intensive semesters and weekend classes. Credit for equivalency exams. The M.S. in counselor education and in systems management are available to in-state students only. The engineering degrees require one campus visit for an oral exam at the Master's level and one semester of residency for the Doctorate.

Monterey Institute of
International Studies   M

425 Van Buren Street
Monterey, CA 93940
Fields offered: Business administration
Year founded: 1955
Ownership: Nonprofit, independent
Phone: (408) 647-4123 • (800) 824-7235
Fax: (408) 647-4188
E-mail: admit@miis.edu
Website: www.miis.edu

This accredited school offers an accelerated one-year "advanced entry" M.B.A. for qualified applicants, as well as more traditional M.B.A. programs with an international bent. We have written for more information.

Moorhead State University   B

External Studies Program
Moorhead, MN 56563
Fields offered: Many fields
Year founded: 1885
Ownership: Nonprofit, state
Phone: (218) 236-2161 • (800) 593-7246
Fax: (218) 236-2168
E-mail: dragon@mnscu1.moorhead.msus.edu
Website: www.moorhead.msus.edu

Bachelor's degrees in many fields available to students within a 100- to 150-mile radius of the university. Assessment of prior learning is part of the program and is based on evaluation of student-prepared portfolios and interviews with faculty from appropriate departments. Testing, either through oral interviews or in written form, is required in most areas. The assessment fees, which are quite low, are based on the number of units awarded. This program is not open to students outside of the region. Many classes are offered on weekends.

Moravian College

Division of Continuing Studies
Bethlehem, PA 18018
Phone: (610) 861-1400
Fax: (610) 861-3919
E-mail: dcs@moravian.edu
Website: www.moravian.edu

According to Mr. Bernard J. Story, this school does not wish to appear in this book., although they have programs that may well be of interest to readers. For details, you'll have to contact Mr. Story.

Mount Saint Mary College   B, M

Powell Ave.
Newburgh, NY 12550
Fields offered: Many fields
Year founded: 1954
Ownership: Nonprofit, independent
Phone: (914) 561-0800 • (800) YES-MSMC
Fax: (914) 562-6762
E-mail: jilbert@msmc.edu
Website: www.msmc.edu

Bachelor's degree programs in business management and administration, sociology, social sciences, and interdisciplinary studies; Master's in computer science, nursing, and public relations, through evening and weekend study.

Mount Saint Mary's
College (California)   B

12001 Chalon Road
Los Angeles, CA 90049
Fields offered: Business, psychology
Year founded: 1925
Ownership: Nonprofit, church
Phone: (310) 476-2237 • (800) 999-9893
Fax: (310) 954-4379
E-mail: admmsmc@aol.com
Website: www.msmc.la.edu

Bachelor of Science in business and Bachelor of Arts in psychology, through evening and weekend classes. Credit for prior experience by portfolio assessment, and for equivalency exams, independent study, and supervised fieldwork.

Mount Saint Mary's College   B

Bachelor of General Studies Program
Emmitsburg, MD 21727
Fields offered: General studies
Year founded: 1808
Ownership: Nonprofit, church
Phone: (301) 447-6122 • (800) 448-4347
Fax: (301) 447-5755
E-mail: admiss@msmary.edu
Website: www.admis@msmary.edu

Bachelor of General Studies in a degree-completion program (applicants must have completed 85 of the 120 total credits for the degree elsewhere). Credit awarded for prior life and military experience by portfolio assessment, also for equivalency exams, independent study, and supervised fieldwork.

Mount Union College   B

1972 Clark Ave.
Alliance, OH 44601
Fields offered: Many fields
Year founded: 1954
Ownership: Nonprofit, church

Phone: (330) 821-5320 ext. 2590 • (800) 334-6682
Fax: (330) 821-0424
E-mail: calzadea@muc.edu
Website: www.muc.edu

Bachelor's degrees in many fields, in which up to 75 percent of the required units can come from an assessment of prior learning experiences in a program called CARE (Credit for Academically Relevant Experience). The assessment is based on a portfolio, examinations, and/or faculty interviews. The assessment fee is based on the number of units, and is generally about a third the usual cost of that number of units. Courses are also offered through a weekend college program. See also: East Central College Consortium.

Muskingum College

See: East Central College Consortium

Naropa Institute   B, M

2130 Arapahoe Ave.
Boulder, CO 80302
Fields offered: Many fields
Year founded: 1974
Ownership: Nonprofit, independent
Phone: (303) 444-0202 • call and they will call you back
Fax: (303) 546-3583
E-mail: admissions@naropa.edu
Website: www.naropa.edu

Naropa offers an M.A. and upper-division B.A. degrees, non-degree study, and a summer program. Education at Naropa combines the disciplines of the classroom with those of personal awareness through contemplative practices such as sitting meditation, akido, t'ai chi, and others. The combination is intended to cultivate both academic strength and the desire to contribute to the world with understanding and compassion. B.A. programs in "InterArts Studies" (dance/movement, music, and theater), early childhood education, environmental studies, interdisciplinary studies, psychology, religious studies, and writing and literature. M.A. programs in art therapy, gerontology, counseling, and Psychotherapy; M.F.A. writing and poetics. Study-abroad programs in Bali and Nepal.

National Hispanic University   B

14271 Story Road
San Jose, CA 95127-3823
Fields offered: Business, liberal studies, computer science
Year founded: 1981
Ownership: Nonprofit, independent
Phone: (408) 254-6900
Fax: (408) 254-1369
Website: www.nhu.edu

This school offers a multilingual, multicultural approach to higher education. While their programs are relatively traditional, we list them for their innovative approach to the entire question of student diversity, different cultures, and different learning styles. Credit is available for courses taken at other institutions, as well as for military and other training, and CLEP and challenge exams. The school currently offers a B.A. in business administration, a B.A. in liberal studies with a concentration in early childhood education, cross cultural or bilingual instruction, or translation and interpretation studies, and a B.S. in computer science.

National Institute for Higher Education

See: University of Limerick

National University   B, M

University Park
San Diego, CA 92108
Fields offered: Many fields
Year founded: 1971
Ownership: Nonprofit, independent
Phone: (619) 563-7100 • (800) NAT-UNIV
Fax: (619) 642-8714
E-mail: awilliam@nunic.nu.edu
Website: www.nu.edu

Each course is offered in intensive one-month modules, meeting in the evenings and selected Saturdays. Some daytime classes are offered. More than 600 courses begin each month, 12 times a year. Courses are offered in San Diego, Fresno, Irvine, Los Angeles, Sacramento, San Jose, Stockton, and Vista, California. Students may freely transfer from one center to another. Degrees include a Bachelor of Business Administration, B.A. in behavioral science, B.A. in interdisciplinary studies, B.S. in computer science, M.B.A., "Global M.B.A." offered at sites around the world, M.B.A. in health care administration, M.S. in educational technology (school hopes to offer this degree wholly on-line by 1998), M.A. in business with emphasis in human services management or real estate management, and Master of Public Administration. Many courses in the School of Education are offered in 10-day intensive daytime summer sessions. Is awaiting approval for a new Ed.D. program.

National Institute of Nutritional Education   B, M

See American Health Science University

National-Louis University   B, M

2840 Sheridan Rd.
Evanston, IL 60201
Fields offered: Many fields
Year founded: 1886
Ownership: Nonprofit, independent
Phone: (847) 256-5150 • (800) 443-5522
Fax: (847) 256-1057
E-mail: mheu@mclean1.nl.edu
Website: nlu.nl.edu

Bachelor of Arts in applied sciences, in which up to 75 percent of the required units can come from an assessment of prior learning and college transfer credit. The college uti-

225

lizes what it calls the "field-experience model," in which the student follows an intense program of classes (one four-hour session per week) and individual study, while remaining fully employed. The M.S. in management requires 59 four-hour meetings (once a week for 15 months); M.S. in adult and continuing education, 52 weekly meetings (13 months). National-Louis also has a Bachelor's completion program in management and education, designed for registered, licensed, certified allied health professionals. This program lasts 13 months and requires 49 one-night-a-week class meetings. programs are offered around Illinois and in St. Louis, Missouri; McLean, Virginia; Beloit, Wisconsin; Tampa, Florida; Atlanta, Georgia, and Heidelberg, Germany. Formerly called National College of Education.

Nazareth College   B
Continuing Education Program
Rochester, NY 14610
Fields offered: Liberal arts, education
Year founded: 1924
Ownership: Nonprofit, independent
Phone: (716) 586-2525 • (800) 462-3944
Fax: (716) 586-2452
E-mail: tkdarin@naz.edu
Website: www.naz.edu
Bachelor of Arts in liberal arts and Master's in education, for persons over 21, offered entirely through evening study.

Nebraska Wesleyan University   B
Institute for Lifelong Learning
5000 St. Paul Ave.
Lincoln, NE 68504
Fields offered: Many fields
Year founded: 1887
Ownership: Nonprofit, church
Phone: (402) 466-2371 • (800) 541-3818
Fax: (402) 465-2179
E-mail: admissions@NebrWesleyan.edu
Website: www.NebrWesleyan.edu
Bachelor of Arts and Bachelor of Science in many fields, including nursing, through evening classes, with an open admissions policy. Credit for equivalency exams, independent study, and supervised fieldwork.

Neumann College   B
Liberal Studies Program
Aston, PA 19014
Fields offered: Many fields
Year founded: 1965
Ownership: Nonprofit, church
Phone: (610) 459-0905 • (800) 9-NEUMAN
Fax: (610) 459-1370
E-mail: neumann@smtpgate.neumann.edu
Website: www.neumann.edu
Bachelor of Arts or Science in liberal studies, through programs designed to accommodate the schedules and commitments of adult students. Concentrations in accounting, computer and information management, elementary and early childhood education, humanities, marketing, business administration, health care administration, human resource development, and psychology. Credit awarded for life experience learning, by portfolio assessment, equivalency exams, cooperative education, independent study, and supervised fieldwork.

New College of California   B, M, D, Law
50 Fell St.
San Francisco, CA 94102
Fields offered: Humanities (many fields), psychology, poetics, law
Year founded: 1971
Ownership: Nonprofit, independent
Phone: (415) 863-4111 • (888) 437-3460
Fax: (415) 626-5171
E-mail: admissions@ncgate.newcollege.edu
Website: www.newcollege.edu
New College has offered its Bachelor of Arts, Master of Arts, and J.D. degrees using a variety of different approaches, including evening courses, weekend courses, and the weekend college for working adults (a series of long weekend seminars with independent study sessions in between, on-the-job practica, tutorials, and credit for prior learning experience) In 1989, New College took over the nontraditional programs of Antioch University West. The B.A. is offered in humanities (including art, writing, psychology, politics, Latin American studies, anthropology, and much more). There is an M.A. in psychology and in poetics (a unique program combining the critical study and creative writing of poetry). The Science Institute offers science courses designed for people planning to attend professional schools in the health care field. New College was started by Father Jack Leary, former president of Gonzaga University. Traditional courses are offered, generally in three-hour sessions. (The name "New College" comes from Oxford University where their New College was established in the 13th century.)

New Hampshire College   B, M
2500 North River Rd.
Manchester, NH 03106-1045
Fields offered: Human services, social work
Year founded: 1932
Ownership: Nonprofit, independent
Phone: (603) 668-2211 • (800) NHC-4YOU
Fax: (603) 644-3150
E-mail: leewil@nhc.edu
Website: www.nhc.edu
The undergraduate program in human services (concentrations in counseling, administration, labor studies, and criminal justice) is designed to allow people with prior experience to enter as a freshman, sophomore, or junior, depending on their prior work. The M.S. in human services has concentrations in administration, gerontology, and

community service. There is also a Master of Social Work. A full-time student taking three classes would be at the college for one long weekend (Friday through Sunday) or two adjacent weekends (two Saturdays and a Sunday, or vice versa) each month. This program is also offered in London, through Lansdowne College. The Graduate School of Business offers coursework via the Internet leading to an MBA with a certificate in Manufacturing and Service Management. For more information on these wholly distance-learning courses, e-mail Distance Education director Dr. Lee Williams at leewill@nhc.edu.

New York University   B, M

Gallatin Division
715 Broadway, 6th Floor
New York, NY 10003
Fields offered: Many fields
Year founded: 1831
Ownership: Nonprofit, independent
Phone: (212) 998-7370
Fax: (212) 995-4902
E-mail: admissions@nyu.edu
Website: www.nyu.edu

Created in 1972, the Gallatin Division offers mature, self-directed students the opportunity to plan an individualized program of study in more than 150 majors. The Bachelor of Arts degree allows students to combine coursework taken in most of the schools of NYU with internships, private lessons in the arts, and independent study. Students are expected to be thoroughly conversant with a list of great books as a graduation requirement. (Courses in great books and classic texts are offered as part of the curriculum.) Credit for life experience is also available. An extensive internship program offers the opportunity for internships in education, arts and arts administration, media, business, and public/social service. The Master of Arts in Individualized Study involves coursework, internships, and independent study under the supervision of a faculty advisor. A scholarly, creative, or performance thesis is required. Credit is given for career experience learning.

Niagara University   B, M

Niagara, NY 14109
Fields offered: Many fields
Year founded: 1856
Ownership: Nonprofit, independent
Phone: (716) 286-8700 • (800) 462-2111
Fax: (716) 286-8710
E-mail: admissions@niagara.edu
Website: www.niagara.edu

Credit is given for life experience learning, challenge exams, and equivalency exams such as CLEP. Bachelor's degrees in business, nursing, education, arts, and sciences may be earned through day, evening, and summer programs. Niagara

has six divisions: College of Arts and Sciences, College of Business Administration, College of Nursing, College of Education, Travel, Hotel, and Restaurant Administration, and the Division of General Academic Studies.

Nordenfjord World University   B, M, D

Skyum Bjerge, Snedsted
Thy, DK-7752 Denmark
Fields offered: Many fields
Year founded: 1962
Phone: (45-7) 936-234

This is actually six separate schools, to which students come from all over the world for anything from a semester to an entire degree program. New Experimental College, one of the six, was established with the goal of developing a self-perpetuating community of scholars that would have a worldwide effect on technology, economics, and social planning. Although it's not officially recognized by the Danish government, many students arrange with schools in their home countries (including America, where accredited schools have agreed to recognize Nordenfjord) to award degrees based on work done there. Instruction is largely through teacher-directed independent study, with some classes and seminars. Rules and plans are made in the "ting," a New Age-y group meeting. Students nearing the end of their work may call for a "high ting," a combination exam and celebration in which work is presented and discussed. Other units of Nordenfjord specialize in communications, arts and crafts, language, and philosophy.

North Adams State College

See: Massachusetts College of Liberal Arts

North Carolina State University   B, M, D

P. O. Box 7103
Raleigh, NC 27695
Fields offered: Many fields
Year founded: 1887
Ownership: Nonprofit, state
Phone: (919) 515-2434
Fax: (919) 515-2556
E-mail: undergraduateunderscoreadmissions@ncsu.edu
Website: www.ncsu.edu

Bachelor's degrees in many fields, including design, forest resources, and textiles. Evening study available. No credit for work or life experience, but credit by exam available. Master of Public Affairs and Master of Industrial Engineering programs may be offered through evening study at various centers around the state (Charlotte, Fayetteville, Greensboro, and Raleigh). Some courses are also offered by cable television in the Raleigh area, or by videocassette.

North Carolina Wesleyan College   B

Rocky Mount, NC 27804
Fields offered: Accounting, business administration, computer information systems, justice and public policy
Year founded: 1956
Ownership: Nonprofit, church
Phone: (919) 985-5100 • (800) 488-NCWC or 488-6292
Fax: (919) 985-5295
E-mail: adm@ncwc.edu
Website: ncwc.edu

Bachelor's degree in accounting, business administration, computer information systems, and justice and public policy may be earned through evening and summer programs. For North Carolina residents only.

North Central College   B, M

30 N. Brainard St.
Naperville, IL 60566
Fields offered: Many fields
Year founded: 1861
Ownership: Nonprofit, church
Phone: (630) 637-5100 • (800) 411-1861
Fax: (630) 637-5121
E-mail: ncadm@noctrl.edu
Website: www.noctrl.edu

Bachelor of Arts in accounting, communications, computer science, management, marketing, and management information systems may be earned through weekend or evening programs offered in Naperville and Schaumburg/Rolling Meadows. Bachelor of Science in computer science through evening studies. North Central also has a weekend college that meets Friday evening and Saturday, normally every other weekend; six meetings per term.

North Dakota State University   B, M

College of University Studies
Morrill Hall 112
Fargo, ND 58105
Fields offered: Many fields
Year founded: 1890
Ownership: Nonprofit, state
Phone: (701) 231-7014 • (800) 488-NDSU
Fax: (701) 231-7050
E-mail: dthompso@gwmail.nodak.edu
Website: www.ndsu.noddak.edu

Bachelor of University Studies degrees through individually tailored programs in many fields, some available at remote sites, by two-way video. There is a residency requirement of one year or 30 semester credits. Students may earn credit for prior work, and educational and military experiences. The assessment must be done after enrollment and is part of a degree proposal prepared by the student in consultation with an advisor. There is no fee for the assessment. Students usually have a major emphasis or thrust to their proposed course of study but they do not have a major.

They may combine previous academic credit, credit for life experience and non-traditional education, and courses offered by any department on campus. Also, M.Ed or M.S. in counseling, with a number of specializations, largely through two-way video, beamed to designated sites around the state. Some on-campus residency required. Contact for Master's programs: Robert Nielsen (701) 237-7676

Northeastern University   B, M, D, Law

360 Huntington Ave.
Boston, MA 02115
Fields offered: Many fields
Year founded: 1898
Ownership: Nonprofit, independent
Phone: (617) 373-2000
Fax: (617) 373-8780
Website: www.neu.edu

Northeastern offers what UNESCO calls "the world's leading program in cooperative education." They have asked us to delete their listing from this book, but we have chosen not to do so, since the program is of interest to so many people. Most of Northeastern's more than 50,000 students are employed half-time at companies all over the U.S.—while one half the students are attending classes, the other half are working full-time. Every three to six months, they switch. In many cases, two students work together to hold a full-time job in business or industry. Some evening classes are offered. Degrees at all levels are offered in this manner in a wide variety of subjects, from social science to engineering to pharmacology, nursing, and criminal justice.

Northern Illinois University

See: Quad Cities Graduate Center

Northwest Christian College   B

Degree Completion Program
828 E. 11th Ave.
Eugene, OR 97401
Fields offered: Managerial leadership
Year founded: 1895
Ownership: Nonprofit, church
Phone: (541) 343-1641 • (800) 888-6927
Fax: (541) 343-3727
E-mail: info@eve.nwcc.edu
Website: www.nwcc.edu

Bachelor of Science in managerial leadership, designed for the adult student (applicants must have five years of experience in their field, and have completed 75 credits elsewhere). Maximum of 46 credits awarded through portfolio assessment, credit also available for equivalency exams. All students must complete a 60-credit managerial leadership curriculum, which includes 18 credit-hours of bible study.

Northwestern College   B

3003 Snelling Avenue N.
St. Paul, MN 55113
Fields offered: Organizational administration
Year founded: 1902
Ownership: independent, religious
Phone: (612) 631-5100 • (800) 827-6827
Fax: (612) 631-5269
E-mail: admissions@nwc.edu
Website: www.nwc.edu

Degree-completion program awards the B.S. in organizational administration to adult students (25 or older) who have completed at least 86 credits (of 188 required) elsewhere. Credit awarded for equivalency exams, life and military-experience learning by portfolio assessment, and for licenses such as real estate and financial counselor. Particular emphasis is placed upon integrating Christian values, ethics, and faith into the curriculum.

Northwestern University   B, M

University College
339 E. Chicago Ave.
Chicago, IL 60611
Fields offered: Many fields
Year founded: 1851
Ownership: Nonprofit, independent
Phone: (312) 503-6950
Fax: (312) 503-4942
E-mail: ug-admission@nwu.edu (undergraduate)
gradapp@nwu.edu (graduate)
Website: www.nwu.edu

Bachelor's and Master's may be earned through evening and summer programs. Bachelor's degrees offered in anthropology, art history, communications, computer studies, economics, English, environmental studies, fine and performing arts, history, mathematics, organization behavior, philosophy, political science, psychology, radio/tv/film, and sociology. The Master's degrees are in liberal arts and English.

Nova Southeastern University of the Health Sciences   D

College of Pharmacy
1750 NE 168th Street
North Miami Beach, FL 33162
Fields offered: Pharmacology
Year founded: 1979
Ownership: Nonprofit, independent
Phone: (954) 262-7300 • (800) 541-6682
Fax: (954) 262-5740
Website: www.nova.edu

Rigorous but flexible program allows working pharmacists who possess either a B.S. or an M.S. to earn the Pharm.D while remaining fully employed. Courses are offered in the evenings, and students can vary their pace according to work schedule. Some credit for life experience and departmental exams, as well as supervised fieldwork.

Nyack College   B

Adult Degree Completion Program
Nyack, NY 10960
Fields offered: Organizational management
Year founded: 1882
Ownership: Nonprofit, church
Phone: (914) 358-1710
Fax: (914) 358-1751
Website: www.nyackcollege.edu

Bachelor of Science in organizational management through a degree-completion program for students who have already earned 60 credits (of 120 total) elsewhere. Credit for life-experience learning, by portfolio assessment, equivalency exams, cooperative education, correspondence courses, independent study, phone/mail instruction, and supervised fieldwork. Classes meet once a week, for four hours and, according to the school, are more like business seminars than traditional courses. They involve research, discussion, and group problem-solving exercises with peers.

Ohio State University   B, M

Division of Continuing Education
2400 Oletangy River Rd.
Columbus, OH 43210
Fields offered: Many fields
Year founded: 1870
Ownership: Nonprofit, state
Phone: (614) 292-3980
Fax: (614) 292-4818
E-mail: admissions@osu.edu
Website: www.ohio-state.edu

Evening and weekend courses are offered, leading to the following degrees: B.A. in English or history, B.S. in many fields, Bachelor of Business Administration, and M.A. in education, English, history, or journalism. Credit for life-experience learning. Telephone-assisted language program in eastern European languages. Counseling, trouble-shooting, and workshops are available from Ohio's Department of Continuing Education.

Oregon State University   B, M

Office of Continuing Education
327 Snell Hall
Corvallis, OR 97331
Fields offered: Liberal studies, education
Year founded: 1868
Ownership: Nonprofit, state
Phone: (541) 737-0123
Fax: (541) 737-2400
E-mail: osuadmit@orst.edu
Website: www.orst.edu

The Bachelor of Arts and Bachelor of Science are offered in liberal studies, for adult students who have already earned at least 90 units elsewhere. Credit for equivalency exams and through independent study, supervised fieldwork, and television courses. The Master of Education in training and development is a practical, work-based degree.

Ottawa University   B, M
1001 South Cedar Street
Ottawa, KS 66067-3399
Fields offered: Many fields
Year founded: 1865
Ownership: Nonprofit, church
Phone: see below
Fax: see below
E-mail: admiss@ott.edu
Website: www.ott.edu

Ottawa offers Bachelor's completion programs in business/management, psychology, and education or adults residing in the Kansas City, Phoenix, or Milwaukee metropolitan areas, as well as a Master's in human resources through programs in many fields, and a Master's in human resources at Kansas City and Phoenix. Among the nontraditional elements of the program are frequent class beginnings, evening courses, and credit for life-experience learning through portfolio evaluation. Interested parties should contact the appropriate learning center at the address and number below:

Kansas City: 10865 Grandview, Overland Park, KS 66210. Phone: (913) 451-1431; fax (913) 451-0806
Phoenix: 2340 West Mission Lane, Phoenix, AZ 85021. Phone: (602) 371-1188; Fax: 602) 371-0035
Milwaukee: 300 North Corporate Drive, Suite 110, Brookfield, WI 53045
Phone: (414) 879-0200 • Fax: (414) 879-0096

Our Lady of the Lake College   B
5345 Brittany Drive
Baton Rouge, LA 70808
Fields offered: Nursing
Year founded: 1990
Ownership: Church
Phone: (504) 768-1700
Fax: (504) 768-1726
E-mail: hannison@ololcollege.cc.la.us
Website: www.ololcollege.cc.la.us

Offers a B.S. in nursing through a largely traditional program that does, however, allow for some very limited independent study and some credit for CLEP exams.

Our Lady of the Lake University   B
411 S.W. 24th St.
San Antonio, TX 78285
Fields offered: Computer science, management, health care management, human resources, liberal studies
Year founded: 1911
Ownership: Nonprofit, church
Phone: (210) 434-6711 • (800) 436-6558
Fax: (210) 436-0824
Website: www.ollusa.edu

Bachelor's and Master's in computer information systems, management, human resources and organization, health care management, and liberal studies, through weekend study. All classes are scheduled for four hours every other Saturday or Sunday. Credit may be earned through several testing programs and a portfolio process for evaluation of life/work experience at a cost of one third the usual tuition for credit awarded. A 36-semester-hour M.B.A. can be earned in two years. This program utilizes the Decision Theater, a teaching laboratory using computer simulations and models to present real life business situations, enabling students to apply managerial theories to everyday situations.

Pace University   B
1 Pace Plaza
New York, NY 10038
Fields offered: Liberal studies, general studies
Year founded: 1906
Ownership: Nonprofit, independent
Phone: (212) 346-1200
Fax: (212) 346-1933
E-mail: ugnyc@ny2.pace.edu (undergraduate)
gradnyc@ny2.pace.edu (graduate)
Website: www.pace.edu

Bachelor of Arts in liberal studies and Bachelor of Science in general studies through programs designed to accommodate the adult working professional. Credit awarded for military training and life-experience learning, through portfolio assessment, as well as for a range of departmental and equivalency exams.

Pacific Oaks College   B, M
5 Westmoreland Place
Pasadena, CA 91103
Fields offered: Human development
Year founded: 1945
Ownership: Nonprofit, independent
Phone: (626) 397-1351 • (800) 684-0900
Fax: (626) 685-2529
E-mail: PACOAKS@Earthlink.net
Website: www.pacoaks.org

This school's College Outreach Extension provides in-service training for ECE educators. They offer B.A., M.A., and certificate programs designed for part-time students who are working professionals. Evening and weekend courses are offered in Southern California as well as in the San Francisco area, Portland, San Diego, Phoenix, and Seattle.

Palm Beach Atlantic College   B
901 S. Flager
West Palm Beach, FL 33401
Fields offered: Human resource management
Year founded: 1968
Ownership: Nonprofit, church
Phone: (561) 803-2000
Fax: (561) 803-2186
Website: www.pbac.edu

Bachelor of Human Resource Management through a program tailored to the needs of fully employed adults who have earned at least 40 credits already (up to 30 can come through assessment of life experience portfolio, military training). Program is designed to be full-time, one night a week, for 54 weeks. A student entering with 60 credits can expect to finish in one year.

Park College B, M

Parkville, MO 64152
Fields offered: Many fields
Year founded: 1875
Ownership: Nonprofit, church
Phone: (816) 741-2000 • (800) 745-7275
Fax: (816) 746-6423
E-mail: admissions@mail.park.edu
Website: www.park.edu

Park's portfolio plan is an individualized degree completion program for adults, based on a learning contract which specifies credit for prior experience and new work to be done in classrooms and through independent study. Evening classes are offered in the Kansas City area, and degree completion centers are operated on or near military bases in a dozen states. There is a Master of Public Affairs and graduate study in religion for clergy and lay leaders of the Reorganized Church of Jesus Christ of Latter Day Saints.

Pepperdine University B, M, D

24255 Pacific Coast Hwy.
Malibu, CA 90265
Fields offered: Many fields
Year founded: 1937
Ownership: Nonprofit, independent
Phone: (310) 456-4000
Fax: (310) 456-4357
E-mail: admission-seaver@pepperdine.edu (undergraduate)
Website: www.pepperdine.edu

Bachelor of Science in many fields, Master of Arts in education or general psychology, M.S. in educational computing, educational therapy, school management, or administration, Doctor of Education in institutional management or community college administration, all available through a combination of weekend and evening classes in the Los Angeles area. Also, an M.B.A. program for business leaders.

Philadelphia College of Textiles and Science B, M

Evening Division
School House Lane and Henry Ave.
Philadelphia, PA 19144
Fields offered: Business, computers, design, science, textiles, nursing
Year founded: 1884
Ownership: Nonprofit, independent
Phone: (215) 951-2700
Fax: (215) 951-2615
E-mail: admissions@philacol.edu (undergraduate) gradadm@philacol.edu (graduate)

Website: www.philacol.edu

Most of their Bachelor of Science degrees can be earned entirely through evening study. There is a special B.S. for registered nurses (their R.N. training counts for half the needed credits), and another for other health-care professionals. M.B.A. classes meet one evening a week in Bucks and Montgomery counties. Credit given for prior learning, through examination.

Pittsburg State University M

Division of Continuing Studies
1701 South Broadway
215 Russ Hall
Pittsburg, KS 66762-7526
Fields offered: Many fields
Year founded: 1903
Ownership: Nonprofit, state
Phone: (316) 235-4176 • (800) 854-PITT
Fax: (316) 232-7515
E-mail: psuadmit@pittstate.edu
Website: www.pittstate.edu

Master's degrees in many fields can be earned on off-campus sites around southeastern Kansas. While students can enroll on a part-time basis while remaining fully employed, the school wishes us to stress that this is in no way a distance program, and students from outside this region cannot be served by it.

Plymouth State College M

Plymouth, NH 03264
Fields offered: Education
Year founded: 1871
Ownership: Nonprofit, state
Phone: (603) 535-2437 • (800) 842-6900
Fax: (603) 535-2714
E-mail: pscadmit@psc.plymouth.edu
Website: www.plymouth.edu

Master of Arts for classroom teachers, based on attending two eight-week summer sessions, and completing the rest of the requirements by independent study during the nine months in between.

Polytechnic University M

6 Metrotech Center
Brooklyn, NY 11201
Fields offered: Engineering, science, mathematics, management
Year founded: 1854
Ownership: Nonprofit, independent
Phone: (718) 260-3600 • (800) POLYTEC
Fax: (718) 260-3136
E-mail: admitme@poly.edu
Website: www.poly.edu

Master of Science in mathematics, management, science, and engineering (aerospace/mechanical, electrical, and civil), available entirely through evening study at several New York locations.

Pratt Institute   B

200 Willoughby Ave.
Brooklyn, NY 11205
Fields offered: Many fields
Year founded: 1887
Ownership: Nonprofit, independent
Phone: (718) 636-3669 • (800) 331-0834
Fax: (718) 636-3785
Website: www.pratt.edu

Credit awarded for portfolio/work experience/special examinations evaluation. Applicants intending to seek credits by this route should notify the school, but the evaluation process will begin only after the student is registered. Work experience must be substantiated by resume, letters of certification from the applicant's employer(s), and a portfolio. There is a fee for all such evaluations, and for all credits awarded.

Providence College   B, M

Providence, RI 02918
Fields offered: Many fields
Year founded: 1917
Ownership: Nonprofit, church
Phone: (401) 865-1000 • (800) 721-6444
Fax: (401) 865–2826
E-mail: pcadmiss@providence.edu
Website: www.providence.edu

Bachelor of Arts, Bachelor of Science in business administration or law enforcement, and M.B.A., all available entirely through evening study.

Quad Cities Graduate Center   M

639 38th Ave.
Rock Island, IL 61201
Fields offered: Many fields
Year founded: 1969
Ownership: Nonprofit, independent
Phone: (309) 794-7376
Fax: (309) 794-1905
E-mail: Grad_Office@ccmail.wiu.edu
Website: www.gradcenter.org

The center is sponsored by the University of Illinois, Northern Illinois University, the University of Iowa, Teikyo Marycrest University, Augustana College, Iowa State University, University of Northern Iowa, Western Illinois University, St. Ambrose University, and Bradley University. The degree is issued by one of these ten, depending on the program selected. Degrees offered include Master of Arts, Master of Science, M.S. in education, M.S. in engineering, and Master of Business Administration, all available entirely through evening study.

Queens College   B

Adult Collegiate Education
65-30 Kissena Blvd.
Flushing, NY 11367
Fields offered: Many fields
Year founded: 1937
Ownership: Nonprofit, state
Phone: (718) 997-5000
Fax: (718) 793-8044
E-mail: sreantillo@qc1.qc.edu
Website: www.qc.edu

Bachelor of Arts program offers degrees for persons over 30 years old through this division of the City University of New York. Learning takes place through weekend seminars, tutorials, exemption exams, work credit, and supervised independent study. Classes are scheduled to fit the needs of the student. One year of residency is usually required.

Radford University   B

Continuing Education
P.O. Box 6917
Radford, VA 24142
Fields offered: General studies
Year founded: 1910
Ownership: Nonprofit, state
Phone: (540) 831-5000
Fax: (540) 831-5970
E-mail: ruadmiss@runet.edu
Website: www.runet.edu

Bachelor of General Studies consists of a coursework core of arts and sciences courses (English, math, history, etc.), plus an individualized concentration or major. Liberal credit awarded for prior academic and nonacademic work, by portfolio assessment, as well as equivalency exams, and independent directed study. Applicants must be at least 25 years old and have completed 30 or more units of college-level work.

Ramapo College of New Jersey   B

505 Ramapo Rd.
Mahwah, NJ 07430
Fields offered: Many fields
Year founded: 1969
Ownership: Nonprofit, state
Phone: (201) 529-7500
Fax: (201) 529-7508
E-mail: adm@ramapo.edu
Website: www.ramapo.edu

Through a combination of evening and/or Saturday classes, degree-seeking students may complete all degree requirements in biology, business administration (several concentrations), chemistry, computer science, economics, environmental studies, and psychology. Degree-seeking students who are restricted to Saturday study, and who have met the college's general education requirements, may complete a degree in business administration, with a concentration in accounting, management or marketing. Up to 75 credits can be earned by equivalency tests, and through PLEX, the Prior Learning Experience Program.

Research College of Nursing **B**
Accelerated B.S. Option
2316 East Meyer Blvd.
Kansas City, MO 64132
Fields offered: Nursing
Year founded: 1980
Ownership: Nonprofit, independent
Phone: (816) 276-4700 • (800) 842-6776
Fax: (816) 276-3526
E-mail: admission@vax2.rockhurst.edu
Website: www.rockhurst.edu
Bachelor of Science in nursing through an accelerated program that allows students to earn the degree in as little as two years full time, or four years part-time. Credit awarded for equivalency exams, particularly R.N. work, and by portfolio assessment.

Rhode Island College **B**
600 Mount Pleasant Avenue
Providence, RI 02908
Fields offered: General studies
Year founded: 1854
Ownership: Nonprofit, state
Phone: (401) 456-8000 • (800) 669-5760
Fax: (401) 456-8379
E-mail: admissions@grog.ric.edu
Website: www.ric.edu
Bachelor of General Studies in either human studies or business institutions, through a program designed for adults who have been out of school for at least five years. Both majors are broadly interdisciplinary. Credit for departmental and other equivalency exams, television courses, independent study, and supervised fieldwork.

Richmond College **B, M**
Queens Rd.
Richmond, Surrey, TW10 6PJ England
Fields offered: Many fields
Phone: (081) 940-9762
Fax: (081) 332-1596
Richmond is an accredited American college operating in London, with an international student body. The school offers B.A. degrees in 13 fields and an international M.B.A. Their degree-granting authority comes from the Educational Institution Licensure Commission of the District of Columbia.

Rider College **B**
2083 Lawrenceville Rd.
Lawrenceville, NJ 08648
Fields offered: Business administration, chemistry, office administration, liberal studies
Year founded: 1865
Ownership: Nonprofit, independent
Phone: (609) 896-5042 • (800) 257-9026
Fax: (609) 896-8029
E-mail: admissions@rider.edu
Website: www.rider.edu
B.A. in liberal studies, B.S. in business administration, chemistry, and office administration, all available entirely through evening study.

Robert Morris College **B**
Narrows Run Rd.
Coraopolis, PA 15108
Fields offered: Science
Year founded: 1921
Ownership: Nonprofit, independent
Phone: (412) 262-8200 • (800) 762-0097
Fax: (412) 299-2425
Website: www.robert-morris.edu
Bachelor of Science, in which all coursework can be done in the evening.

Rockford College **B, M**
5050 E. State St.
Rockford, IL 61108
Fields offered: Many fields
Year founded: 1847
Ownership: Nonprofit, independent
Phone: (815) 226-4050 • (800) 892-2984
Fax: (815) 226-4119
E-mail: admission@rockford.edu
Website: www.rockford.edu
B.A. in many fields, B.S. in general education, B.F.A., M.A. in teaching, and M.B.A., all available through evening courses.

Rockhurst College **B, M**
1100 Rockhurst Road
Kansas City, MO 64110
Fields offered: Economics, industrial relations, psychology, sociology, business administration
Year founded: 1910
Ownership: Nonprofit, church
Phone: (816) 501-4000 • (800) 842-6776
Fax: (816) 501-4588
E-mail: admission@vax2.rockhurst.edu
Website: vax1.rockhurst.edu
Bachelor of Science and Bachelor of Arts available through evening study; M.B.A. through evening and weekend classes. Cooperative Education Program allows students to alternate semesters of college with full-time salaried work. Internships and practicums in communication, psychology, and politics.

Rockmount College
See: Colorado Christian University

Rocky Mountain College **B**
Billings, MT 59102
Fields offered: Liberal arts, general studies
Year founded: 1878
Ownership: Nonprofit, church

Phone: (406) 657-1020
Fax: (406) 259-9751
E-mail: gouldc@rocky.edu
Website: www.rocky.edu

Bachelor of Arts in liberal arts/general studies through computer conferencing, videocassette, and telephone instruction. One semester generally required on-campus. Essentially a degree-completion program, it offers upper-division general education courses, and courses in education, business, and Native American culture (through the Tribal College Telecommunications Exchange).

Rollins College   B, M

Hamilton Holt School, Evening Degree Programs
1000 Holt Avenue—2725
Winter Park, FL 32789-4499
Fields offered: Many fields
Year founded: 1885
Ownership: Nonprofit, independent
Phone: (407) 646-2232
Fax: (407) 646-2600
E-mail: admission@rollins.edu
Website: www.rollins.edu

Offers Bachelor of Arts degree through evening and weekend study in anthropology/ sociology, economics, English, environmental studies, humanities, international affairs, organizational behavior, organizational communication, psychology, and urban and public affairs. Also offers Master of Liberal Studies degree, an interdisciplinary program for adults, in the evenings on a part-time basis. Classes meet one evening per week during the 14-week term.

Roosevelt University   B

430 S. Michigan Ave.
Chicago, IL 60605
Fields offered: General studies
Year founded: 1945
Ownership: Nonprofit, independent
Phone: (312) 341-3500
Fax: (312) 341-3655
E-mail: wsmyser@acfsysv.roosevelt.edu
Website: www.roosevelt.edu

Bachelor of General Studies in a variety of programs ranging from hospitality management to computer science (32 concentrations available); prior-learning credit available. The degree is offered through the University College, for persons over 25 of age. Classes are held evening and weekends in Chicago and the suburbs, as well as off-campus. Roosevelt offers the "discovery program," through which individuals with no Bachelor's degree can, through a year or less of testing, enter a Master's degree program directly. A Master's degree in general studies is offered on-campus. No relation to the large diploma mill also called Roosevelt University.

Roskilde University Center   B, M

Postbox 260
Roskilde, DK-4000 Denmark
Fields offered: Many fields
Year founded: 1972
Ownership: Nonprofit, state
Phone: (45) 46-75 77 11
Fax: (45) 46-75-74-01
Website: www.ruc.dk

An experimental university, specializing in interdisciplinary studies. Clusters of approximately 60 students, five teachers, and a secretary work together in a house for two years, during which time subgroups work together on interdisciplinary research and creative projects in humanities, social science, and natural science. Nearly 4,000 students are involved. The two years of basic studies are followed by one-and-one-half to three-and-one-half years of specialized studies, leading to the degree. Subjects include foreign language, international development, socio-technological planning, public relations, and sciences. The school wants to be sure we make it clear that all instruction is in Danish, and that it is difficult, although not impossible, for foreigners to gain access.

Rowan College of New Jersey   B

Office of Admissions
Glassboro, NJ 08028
Fields offered: Many fields
Year founded: 1923
Ownership: Nonprofit, state
Phone: (609) 256-4000
Fax: (609) 256-4345
E-mail: nurkowski@heroes.rowan.edu
Website: www.rowan.edu

Bachelor's degrees in many fields, in which some credit can come through an assessment of prior learning experiences, equivalency exams, and transfer credit. There is no fee for the assessment once one has enrolled. Rowan regards itself as "very traditional," and does not want to hear from applicants looking for a nontraditional program, please.

Rutgers University   B

University College
P. O. Box 93740
Camden, NJ 08102-3740
Fields offered: Various fields
Year founded: 1927
Ownership: Nonprofit, state
Phone: (609) 225-6102 • (800) 466-7561
Fax: (609) 225-6537
Website: camden.www.rutgers/edu

Bachelor of Arts and Bachelor of Science in accounting, computer science, management, physics, microelectronics, English, and psychology available through summer and evening classes in Camden.

Sacred Heart University   B, M

5151 Park Avenue
Fairfield, CT 06432
Fields offered: Many fields
Year founded: 1963
Ownership: Nonprofit, independent
Phone: (203) 371-7999
Fax: (203) 365-7609
E-mail: munsterc@sacredheart.edu
Website: www.sacredheart.edu

B.A., B.S., M.A., M.S., and M.B.A. available through evening study. Cooperative education and credit for life/work experience and equivalency exams are available at the Bachelor's level.

Sage Evening College   B, M

140 New Scotland Ave.
Albany, NY 12208
Fields offered: Many fields
Year founded: 1949
Ownership: Nonprofit, independent
Phone: (518) 445-1717 • (888) VERY SAGE
Fax: (518) 465-5414
E-mail: secadm@sage.edu
Website: www.sage.edu

All degree programs are available entirely through evening study. Fields of study include psychology, health education, business, nursing, computer science, sociology, art, and more. Up to 30 of the required 120 units in the Bachelor's program can come from credit for experiential learning.

Saint Ambrose University   B

518 W. Locust St.
Davenport, IA 52803
Fields offered: Many fields
Year founded: 1882
Ownership: Nonprofit, church
Phone: (319) 333-6000 • (800) 383-2627
Fax: (319) 333-6243
E-mail: admit@saunix.sau.edu
Website: www.sau.edu/sau.html

Bachelor of Arts, Bachelor of Science, and Bachelor of Elected Studies may be earned through weekend, evening, and summer programs. Special degree-completion program for nurses, and credit for nonacademic prior learning and by examination. See also: Quad Cities Graduate Center

Saint Edwards University   B, M

3001 S. Congress
Austin, TX 78704
Fields offered: Many fields
Year founded: 1885
Ownership: Nonprofit, independent
Phone: (512) 448-8700
Fax: (512) 448-8492
E-mail: seu.admit@admin.stedwards.edu
Website: www.stedwards.edu

Bachelor's degree program through New College in business, humanities, and social sciences, in which some of the degree requirements can be met by assessment of prior learning. The assessment is based on analysis of a portfolio prepared by the student in a special research course offered for that purpose. The cost is based on a fee for each credit awarded. Saint Edwards also offers a Bachelor of Arts in behavioral sciences and criminal justice. Bachelor of Business Administration, and Master of Business Administration, and human resources, through evening study.

Saint Francis College   B

180 Remsen St.
Brooklyn, NY 11201
Fields offered: Special studies
Year founded: 1884
Ownership: Nonprofit, independent
Phone: (718) 522-2300
Fax: (718) 522-1274
E-mail: glarkin@stfranciscollege.edu
Website: www.stfranciscollege.edu

Bachelor of Science in special studies designed for nontraditional students seeking a flexible program of study tailored to individual needs and interests. Up to 98 credits accepted from other schools and equivalency exams toward a degree. Credit also given for experiential learning. Up to 10 credits may be awarded to armed forces veterans.

Saint Francis College   M

Loretto, PA 15940
Fields offered: Industrial relations, health science (physician's assistant)
Year founded: 1847
Ownership: Nonprofit, church
Phone: (814) 472-3000 • (800) 342-5732
Fax: (814) 472-3044
E-mail: Admissions@SFCPA.EDU
Website: www.sfcpa.edu

M.A. in industrial relations can be earned entirely through evening study at the college's branches in Harrisburg and Pittsburgh, or at the home campus in Loretto.

Saint Francis College   M

Office of Graduate Studies
2701 Spring Street
Fort Wayne, IN 46808
Fields offered: Nursing
Year founded: 1890
Ownership: Nonprofit, church
Phone: (800) 729-4732
Fax: (219) 434-3194

Courses leading to the MSN are delivered to your workplace via videoconferencing. This program is available to in-state students only.

Saint John's College   M

Graduate Institute
Santa Fe, NM 87501
Fields offered: Liberal studies
Year founded: 1864
Ownership: Nonprofit, independent
Phone: (505) 982-3691 • (800) 727-9238
Fax: (505) 984-6003
E-mail: giadm@mailhost.sjca.edu
Website: www.sjcsf.edu

Saint John's has long been known for its full-time undergraduate programs based entirely on a study of great books of Western civilization. They also offer an innovative Master of Arts in liberal studies, also based on great books, over a period of four eight-week summer sessions in four consecutive years, and/or a fall and spring term program of two evenings a week. The program is offered on both the New Mexico campus and the school's Maryland campus, and students are encouraged to move from one to the other. (Maryland address: Saint John's College, Graduate Institute, Annapolis, MD, 21404 (301) 263-2371).

Saint Joseph's University College   B, M

5600 City Ave.
Philadelphia, PA 19131
Fields offered: Many fields
Year founded: 1851
Ownership: Nonprofit, church
Phone: (610) 660-1000 • (888) BE-A-HAWK
Fax: (610) 473-0001
E-mail: admissions@sju.edu
Website: www.sju.edu

B.A. and B.S. offered in more than 30 majors and Master's in business administration, chemistry, computer science, education, health administration, health education, public safety, criminal justice, gerontological services, and American studies, all through evening study. Nontraditional students may also obtain Bachelor's degrees full- or part-time through the Continuing Education program. Up to 5 credits may be transferred from four-year colleges, and 64 from two-year schools. An R.N. may count for up to 60 credits.

Saint Leo College   B

State Rd. 52
St. Leo, FL 33574
Fields offered: Psychology, business, public administration, criminology
Year founded: 1889
Ownership: Nonprofit, church
Phone: (352) 588-8236 • (800) 247-6559
(800) 334-5532 (FL only)
Fax: (352) 588-8390

E-mail: admissns@saintleo.edu
Website: www.saintleo.edu

Bachelor's in psychology, business, public administration, or criminology available through weekend, evening, or summer programs. Weekend students attend classes every other weekend.

Saint Mary College   B

4100 S. 4th St., Traffic Way
Leavenworth, KS 66048
Fields offered: Many fields
Year founded: 1923
Ownership: Nonprofit, church
Phone: (913) 682-5151 • (800) 752-7043
Fax: (913) 758-6140
E-mail: admiss@hub.smcks.edu
Website: www.smcks.edu

Evening programs in Leavenworth in the following majors: accounting, business administration, computer science, human services (client services or criminal justice), and liberal studies. Saint Mary also offers an evening degree-completion program in Kansas City, Kansas, known as the 2 Plus Two program. There is a facility in Johnson County. Saint Mary also offers classes and weekend workshops for teachers that apply toward certificate renewal, including computer classes through the state approved Teacher Education Program in computer studies.

Saint Mary's College (California)   B, M

Extended Education
P. O. Box 5219
Moraga, CA 94575
Fields offered: Management, health services administration, procurement and contract management
Year founded: 1863
Ownership: Nonprofit, church
Phone: (925) 631-4900 • (800) 800-4SMC
Fax: (925) 376-7193
E-mail: smcadmit@stmarys-ca.edu
Website: www.stmarys-ca.edu

The programs offered are: Bachelor of Arts in management or health services administration, Master of Science in health services administration or procurement and contract management, and a paralegal certificate program. The Bachelor's program is based on a learning contract. All students complete a core curriculum, a fieldwork project, and various other courses comprising an area requirement. To enter the program, applicants must have 60 units of previous academic credit and work experience in the degree area.

Saint Peter's College   B, M

2614 Kennedy Blvd.
Jersey City, NJ 07306
Fields offered: Many fields
Year founded: 1872
Ownership: Nonprofit, church

Phone: (201) 333-4400 • (888) SPC-9933
Fax: (201) 451-0036
E-mail: admissions@spcvxa.spc.edu
Website: www.spc.edu

The degree programs are available through evening, weekend, and summer courses. Credit awarded for life experience learning and equivalency exams. Courses also offered at a branch campus in Englewood Cliffs.

Saint Procopius College

See: Illinois Benedictine University

Sam Houston State University   B, M, D

Huntsville, TX 77431-2087
Fields offered: Many fields
Year founded: 1879
Ownership: Nonprofit, state
Phone: (409) 294-1844
Fax: (409) 294-3758
Website: www.shsu.edu

Many subjects are offered through evening and weekend courses. Two-thirds of the coursework for any degree must be completed on-campus. Correspondence courses are offered at the undergraduate level only and a maximum of six correspondence courses (18 semester credit hours) may be applied to an undergraduate degree. The only Doctorate offered is in criminal justice.

San Francisco State University

Extended Education
1600 Holloway Ave.
San Francisco, CA 94132
Fields offered: Many fields
Year founded: 1899
Ownership: Nonprofit, state
Phone: (415) 338-1377
Fax: (415) 338-2514
E-mail: ugadmit@sfsu.edu (undergraduate)
gadmit@sfsu.edu (graduate)
Website: www.sfsu.edu

Associate Dean Jo Volkert wrote asking us to remove SF State's listing, as disappointed readers have apparently misunderstood the school's offerings in the past. However, that would mean omitting a program that many will still find useful. The problem is that although SF State offers "degree credit courses," the extension program does not itself issue any degrees. No matter how many courses an extension student completes, he or she must still apply to SF State University (the separate, traditional branch) or another school, to complete a degree.

San Jose State University   B, M

Washington Square
San Jose, CA 95192
Fields offered: Health care administration, community health/occupational health education, electrical engineering

Year founded: 1857
Ownership: Nonprofit, state
Phone: (408) 924-1000
Fax: (408) 924-1018
E-mail: Contact@AnRnet.sjsu.edu
Website: www.sjsu.edu

Bachelor of Science in health care administration and in community health/occupational health education. Credit is earned through coursework, examinations, directed independent study, and field internships. There is a Master's in electrical engineering through televised courses available within the broadcast area (contact Betty C. Benson, Director, at (408) 924-2636, or bcbenson@sjsuvml.sjsu.edu).

Sarah Lawrence College   B, M

Center for Continuing Education
Bronxville, NY 10708
Fields offered: Liberal arts, fine arts
Year founded: 1926
Ownership: Nonprofit, independent
Phone: (914) 395-2205 • (800) 888-2858
Fax: (914) 395-2668
E-mail: slcadmit@mail.slc.edu.
Website: www.slc.edu

The Center for Continuing Education offers adults the opportunity to earn the Bachelor of Arts through part-time daytime coursework and independent study. Weekly seminars are combined with regular individual conferences with faculty. An individually designed M.A. is also available through the Office of Graduate Programs.

Schiller International University   B, M

U.S. Admissions Office
453 Edgewater Dr.
Dunedin, FL 34698-4964
Fields offered: Many other fields
Year founded: 1964
Phone: (8=13) 736-5082 • (800) 336-4133 outside FL
Fax: (813) 734 0359
E-mail: SIUadmis@aol.com
Website: www.schiller.edu

Schiller International University is an accredited independent coeducational American university with an international focus offering undergraduate and graduate degree programs and semester, summer, and full-year study abroad programs at 10 campuses in six countries: Dunedin, Florida; Central and Greater London, England; Paris and Strasbourg, France; Heidelberg and Berlin, Germany; Engelberg and Leysin, Switzerland; and Madrid, Spain. Fields of study include international business administration, international relations/diplomacy, international hotel/tourism management, and many more. English is the language of instruction at all campuses, and SIU students can transfer among SIU's campuses without losing any credits.

School for International Training   B, M
Kipling Rd., P.O. Box 676
Brattleboro, VT 05302-0676
Fields offered: International studies, language education
Year founded: 1964
Ownership: Nonprofit, independent
Phone: (802) 257-7751 • (800) 451-4465 outside VT
Fax: (802) 258-3248
E-mail: registrar.sit@worldlearning.org
Website: www.worldlearning.org/sit.html
Bachelor of International Studies, through the World Issues Program, a junior/senior year program that combines intensive on-campus study with an overseas internship of at least 27 weeks. M.A. in teaching foreign languages (or English as a second language) and M.A. in intercultural management, which concentrates on developing skills useful in international and intercultural professions. Both M.A.s include an internship, and may be completed in 12 to 16 months.

Seattle University   B, M, D
Broadway and Madison
Seattle, WA 98122-4460
Fields offered: Many fields
Year founded: 1891
Ownership: Nonprofit, church
Phone: (206) 296-5800
Fax: (206) 296-2163
E-mail: admissions@seattleu.edu
Website: www.seattleu.edu/Home.html
Master of Arts in education, Master of Education, Master of Business Administration, Master of Public Administration, Master of Software Engineering, Master of Religious Education, Master of Ministry, Master of Pastoral Ministry, Master of Psychology, and Doctor of Education in educational leadership, all through evening study, summer school, and with some weekend classes. Bachelor's degrees through evening classes in the following fields: accounting, criminal justice, finance, international business, management, nursing, business economics, general business, liberal studies, marketing, and public administration.

Shaw University   B
CAPE, 118 E. South St.
Raleigh, NC 27611
Fields offered: Many fields
Year founded: 1865
Ownership: Nonprofit, church
Phone: (919) 546-8200 • (800) 214-6683
Fax: (919) 546-8301
E-mail: ksmith@shawu.edu
Website: www.raleighcvb.org/shaw.html
Bachelor of Arts and Bachelor of Science for persons who could not otherwise pursue a degree (due to jobs, family obligations, military status, incarceration, distance from campuses, or other special considerations) through the Centers for Alternative Programs of Education (CAPE), located throughout North Carolina. Credit for life-experience and military learning, by portfolio assessment, as well as a wide range of equivalency exams.

Shimer College   B
438 N. Sheridan Rd., P.O. Box A500
Waukegan, IL 60079
Fields offered: General studies, humanities, natural sciences, social sciences
Year founded: 1853
Ownership: Nonprofit, independent
Phone: (847) 623-8400 • (800) 215-7173
Fax: (847) 249-7171
Website: www.shimer.edu/shimer
Shimer was once affiliated with the University of Chicago and still bases its curriculum on original source material and the Socratic, or shared inquiry, method in classes no larger that twelve. The small community combined with the college's organization encourages intense student involvement in all aspects of the college. Degrees may also be earned through a weekend program meeting once every three weekends.

Siena Heights College   B
1247 Siena Heights Dr.
Adrian, MI 49221
Fields offered: Health, business, general studies, trade and industrial areas
Year founded: 1919
Ownership: Nonprofit, church
Phone: (517) 263-0731 • (800) 521-0009 ext. 7180
Fax: (517) 264-7704
E-mail: admssns@sienahts.edu
Website: www.sienahts.edu
The degree completion program offers the opportunity to earn the Bachelor's degree in many fields. Substantial credit is given for prior life experience. Up to 80 percent of the required 120 semester hours can be earned through the assessment (including courses taken elsewhere). New work is done through a combination of evening and weekend classes. The program is designed for students who have already completed at least two years of college.

Silver Lake College   B, M
Career Directed Programs Office
2406 South Alverno Road
Manitowoc, WI 54220
Fields offered: Management, manufacturing systems engineering, technology, accounting, organizational behavior
Year founded: 1935
Ownership: Nonprofit, church
Phone: (920) 684-5955 • (800) 236-4752
Fax: (920) 684-7082
E-mail: admslc@sl.edu
Website: www.sl.edu

B.S. in management, manufacturing systems engineering, technology, and accounting and M.S. in management and organization behavior offered through classes that meet one or two evenings a week, in centers located in Appleton, Green Bay, Fond du Lac, Neenah, Wausau, and the Lakeshore area. Credit awarded for prior academic and nonacademic learning, internships, equivalency exams, and coursework at other schools.

Simmons College   B

Continuing Education
300 The Fenway
Boston, MA 02115
Fields offered: Many fields
Year founded: 1899
Ownership: Nonprofit, independent
Phone: (617) 521-2000 • 800-345-8468
Fax: (617) 521-3199
E-mail: ugadm@vmsvax.simmons.edu
Website: www.simmons.edu

B.A. and B.S. programs for women aged 23 and older, offered on a flexible schedule, including a weekend and evening program for registered nurses. A fair amount of credit toward the degree can be earned through portfolio assessment and equivalency exams (up to 80 of the total 128 credits for all transfer assessment, and 82 from exams, although 48 credits must be earned after enrollment).

Simpson College   B

Adult and Continuing Education
701 N. C St.
Indianola, IA 50125
Fields offered: Accounting, computer science, communication studies, English, management
Year founded: 1860
Ownership: Nonprofit, church
Phone: (515) 961-6251 • (800) 362-2454
Fax: (515) 961-1498
E-mail: admiss@storm.simpson.edu
Website: www.simpson.edu

Bachelor of Arts in accounting, computer science, communication studies, English, or management offered through day, evening, Saturday, or accelerated programs. Classes are held in Indianola and in West Des Moines. Credit for professional licenses, military, and other life experience, through portfolio review, as well as for a wide range of equivalency exams, cooperative education, independent study, and supervised fieldwork.

Sioux Falls College   B

1501 S. Prairie Ave.
Sioux Falls, SD 57105
Fields offered: Organization and management
Year founded: 1883
Ownership: Nonprofit, church
Phone: (605) 331-5000 • (800) 888-1047
Fax: (605) 331-6615

E-mail: kathy.houseman@thecoo.edu
Website: www.thecoo.edu

Working adults who have already earned two to three years' worth of college credit can earn the B.A. in organizational management in 17 months, attending class one evening per week. Credit for prior life-experience and military learning, through portfolio assessment, as well as equivalency exams. Some courses offered at a distance, through audio- and videocassette.

South Dakota State University   B

College of Arts and Sciences, Adm. 122
Brookings, SD 57007
Fields offered: Many fields
Year founded: 1881
Ownership: Nonprofit, state
Phone: (605) 688-4151
Fax: (605) 688-5822
E-mail: sdsuadms@adm.sdstate.edu
Website: www.sdstate.edu

South Dakota State offers a number of nontraditional ways to earn credits towards a Bachelor of General Studies, B.A., or B.S., including equivalency exams, cooperative education, correspondence courses, newspaper and television courses, independent study, and supervised fieldwork.

Southeastern Massachusetts University

See: University of Massachusetts—Dartmouth

Southeastern University   M

501 Eye St. SW
Washington, DC 20024
Fields offered: Business, public administration, accounting, taxation
Year founded: 1879
Ownership: Nonprofit, independent
Phone: (202) 488-8162
Fax: (202) 488-8093
E-mail: jflinter@admin.seu.edu
Website: www.seu.edu

On Saturdays and Sundays, Southeastern offers an M.B.A., M.S. in accounting or taxation, and Master of Business and Public Administration. Classes last all day, once a week, and the degree requires 36 credit hours for completion. An independent study MBA is offered through the Division of Continuing Education and Summer Sessions (DCESS). It is text-based and involves short on-campus periods.

Southern Arkansas University   B

SAU Box 1240
Magnolia, AR 71753
Fields offered: Business administration, industrial technology
Year founded: 1967
Ownership: Nonprofit, state
Phone: (870) 574-4500 • (800) 332-7286
Fax: (870) 574-4520

E-mail: adsonny@mail.saumag.edu
Website: www.saumag.edu

Degree-completion programs for holders of an Associate's degree, through weekend classes. Two degrees available: B.S. in industrial technology, and Bachelor of Business Administration. Limited credit for work and military experiences, and for equivalency exam and PBS telecourses. Credit for independent study and supervised fieldwork.

Southern Illinois University-Carbondale   M

Carbondale, IL 62901
Fields offered: Many fields
Year founded: 1869
Ownership: Nonprofit, state
Phone: (618) 453-2121
Fax: (618) 453-3000
Website: www.siu.edu/cwis

Master of Science in administration of justice, through coursework, independent study, and work projects. Master of Science in engineering biophysics through coursework plus a field internship. Master of Arts in rehabilitation administration, with five weeks of independent study for each week spent on campus. Weekend program in industrial technology. Programs offered at selected military bases.

Southern Vermont College   B

Monument Road
Bennington, VT 05201
Fields offered: Many fields
Year founded: 1926
Ownership: Nonprofit, independent
Phone: (802) 442-5427 • (800) 378-2782
Fax: (802) 447-4695
E-mail: admis@svc.edu
Website: www.svc.edu

Bachelor's degree program for licensed practical nurses offered through the evening extension program, and many courses through evening, weekend, and summer classes. Bachelor's degrees in accounting, business, English, environmental studies, communications, criminal justice, health services, human services, resort management, private security, and social work. Telecourses can fulfill some degree requirements. Independent study and internships are an important element of degree programs, and students with special interests are encouraged to formulate their own degree programs, with the help of a faculty or staff advisor.

Southern Wesleyan University   B, M

Leadership Education for Adult Professionals
Box 497, CWC
Central, SC 29630
Fields offered: Management, Christian ministries
Year founded: 1906
Ownership: Nonprofit, church
Phone: (864) 639-2453 • (800) 264-5327

Fax: (864) 639-0826
Website: www.swu.edu

B.S. in management of human resources, M.A.'s in organizational management and Christian ministries, all "guided by a Christian worldview." The Leadership Education for Adult Professionals (LEAP) program is designed to allow adult learners with previous college work to finish their degrees while still working. Applicants for the B.S. program must have already completed 60 credits in their field; for the M.A., two years' work experience. Maximum of 68 credits awarded for nontraditional prior learning, by portfolio review. Credit for various exams. Students must enroll full-time, which entails class one night per week and an additional study-group meeting each week. Many courses are held off-campus, and some may be taken through guided independent study.

Southwest State University   B

Marshall, MN 56258
Fields offered: Humanities, social science, education, business, science, technology
Year founded: 1963
Ownership: Nonprofit, state
Phone: (507) 537-6286 • (800) 642-0684, ext. 6286
Fax: (507) 537-7154
E-mail: shearer@collin.southwest.msus.edu
Website: www.southwest.msus.edu

Bachelor's degrees may be earned in the above fields through evening classes.

Southwest Texas State University   B

San Marcos, TX 78666
Fields offered: Many fields
Year founded: 1899
Ownership: Nonprofit, state
Phone: (512) 245-2111 • (800) 782-7653, ext. 336
Fax: (512) 245-2033
E-mail: mk03@swt.edu
Website: www.swt.edu

Bachelor of Applied Arts and Sciences offered through schedules that accommodate the nontraditional learner. Credit for life and work experience learning, through portfolio assessment, equivalency exams, cooperative education, correspondence courses, and supervised fieldwork

Southwestern College   M

P.O. Box 4788
Santa Fe, NM 87502-4788
Fields offered: Counseling, art therapy
Year founded: 1979
Ownership: Nonprofit, independent
Phone: (505) 471-5756
Fax: (505) 471-4071
E-mail: swc.lib@sfol.com
Website: www.swclib@sfol.com

This school offers an M.A. in counseling or art therapy through courses geared to adult learners, and emphasizing "self-empowerment, applied psychology, and spiritual discovery." We have written for more details, particularly whether they offer any nontraditional options.

Southwestern College (Kansas)   B, M

Winfield, KS 67156
Fields offered: Organizational resource management, manufacturing technology, business quality management, nursing
Year founded: 1885
Ownership: Nonprofit, church
Phone: (316) 221-7999 • (800) 846-1543
Fax: (316) 221-0808
E-mail: chuckles@jinx.sckans.edu
Website: www.sckans.edu

Southwestern offers Bachelor's-completion programs in organizational resource management, manufacturing technology, business quality management, and nursing through evening and weekend courses located in two outreach centers, in Winfield and Wichita. Credit is available for life-experience learning and CLEP exams.

Spalding University   B

Weekend College
851 S. Fourth St.
Louisville, KY 40203
Fields offered: Business administration, communication, liberal studies, nursing
Year founded: 1814
Ownership: Nonprofit, independent
Phone: (502) 585-9911 • (800) 896-8941
Fax: (502) 585-7158
E-mail: admissions@spaulding30.win.net
Website: www.spalding.edu

Weekend college offers Bachelor of Arts and Bachelor of Science in business administration, communication, liberal studies, and nursing, through courses that meet about five times per 11- to 12-week session. Credit available for life-experience learning, through portfolio assessment, as well as a number of equivalency and departmental exams, cooperative education, independent study, and supervised fieldwork.

Spring Arbor College   B

Alternative Education
106 Main St.
Spring Arbor, MI 49283
Fields offered: Management, human resources, health fields, family life education
Year founded: 1873
Ownership: Nonprofit, church
Phone: (517) 750-1200, ext. 363 • (800) 968-0011
Fax: (517) 750-6620
E-mail: admissions@admin.arbor.edu
Website: www.arbor.edu

Bachelor of Arts degree can possibly be earned in 12 to 18 months through weekend, evening, and/or summer programs if participant has junior status, is employed full time, is 25 years old or older, and prepares a portfolio of life experience for evaluation. Four majors available: management of human resources, management of health sciences and gerontology, management of health promotion, and family life education.

Springfield College   B, M

263 Alden Street
Springfield, MA 01109-3797
Fields offered: Human services
Year founded: 1885
Ownership: Nonprofit, independent
Phone: (413) 748-3204, TTD (413) 748-3236
(800) 343-1257
Fax: (413) 748-3236
E-mail: admissions@spfldcol.edu
Website: www.spfldcol.edu

This small school offers both a B.S. and an M.S. in human services through weekend courses, geared to the needs of working adults. Classes are offered once a month, on a Friday, Saturday, and Sunday. Credit is available for transfer credits and experiential learning at the Bachelor's level, although 48 of 120 credits must be taken through Springfield. Applicants to the Master's program must have an accredited Bachelor's degree and a minimum of five years' experience in human services. Originally founded to train YMCA professionals, the school is committed to community involvement, diversity, and human service.

State University of New York (Buffalo)   B, M

Millard Fillmore College
3435 Main St.
Buffalo, NY 14214
Fields offered: Many fields
Year founded: 1946
Ownership: Nonprofit, state
Phone: (716) 645-2000
Fax: (716) 878-3039
E-mail: ubadmit@acsu.buffalo.edu
Website: wings.buffalo.edu

More than 350 evening classes each semester, in fields including arts and sciences, management, nursing, engineering, and architecture, with credits applicable to various degree programs.

State University of New York College at Plattsburgh   M

Center for Lifelong Learning
Kehoe 413
Plattsburgh, NY 12901
Fields offered: Liberal studies
Year founded: 1889
Ownership: Nonprofit, state
Phone: (518) 564-2000 • (800) 342-3811
Fax: (518) 564-7827

E-mail: apchelp@@sysadm.suny.edu
Website: www.plattsburgh.edu
Master of Arts in liberal studies offered in five broad fields: administration and leadership, educational studies, English language and literature, historical studies, and natural sciences. Student may enroll at any time. Credit for military experience and independent study. Courses are offered in the evening on the Plattsburgh campus, at the Plattsburgh military base, and at several additional sites in northern New York state.

State University of New York (Old Westbury)   B

College at Old Westbury, P. O. Box 210
Old Westbury, NY 11568
Fields offered: Many fields
Year founded: 1967
Ownership: Nonprofit, state
Phone: (516) 876-3000
Fax: (516) 876-3029
E-mail: dunningo@solbdx.oldwestbury.edu
Website: www.oldwestbury.edu
B.A., B.S., and Bachelor of Professional Studies, in which some units can be earned through a combination of assessment of prior experience, and taking equivalency exams.

Stetson University   B

421 Woodland Boulevard
Deland, FL 32720
Fields offered: Many fields
Year founded: 1883
Ownership: Nonprofit, church
Phone: (904) 822-7100 • (800 688-0101
Fax: (904) 822-7112
E-mail: admissions@stetson.edu
Website: www.stetson.edu
Bachelor of Arts and Bachelor of Science in many fields through evening study. Bachelor of Science in medical technology in conjunction with area hospitals. Credit for equivalency exams.

Suffolk University   B, M

Beacon Hill
Boston, MA 02108
Fields offered: Many fields
Year founded: 1906
Ownership: Nonprofit, independent
Phone: (617) 573-8000 • (800) 6-SUFFOLK
Fax: (617) 573-8353
E-mail: admissions@admin.suffolk.edu
Website: www.suffolk.edu
Bachelor of Arts, Bachelor of Science, Master of Business Administration, and Master of Public Administration, all available entirely through evening study. Cooperative program, where students work in jobs related to their majors and graduate in four and a half years (with summer sessions).

Swinburne University of Technology   B

P. O. Box 218, John St.
Hawthorn, Victoria, 3122 Australia
Fields offered: Applied science, engineering, business, graphic design
Year founded: 1908
Ownership: Nonprofit, independent
Phone: (61-3) 819 8647
Fax: (61-3) 9819 5454
E-mail: sgleeson@swin.edu.au
Website: www.swin.edu.au
Swinburne runs cooperative education programs in applied science, engineering, business and graphic design. Under this program students are placed in 12-month, full-time paid industrial work. During this period each student's progress is monitored by a staff member. Students learn in both academic and work settings. Assistance is given to place overseas students in work-experience settings in their home countries.

Technion Institute   M

Faculty of Industrial Engineering and Management
The Technion
Kiryat Hatechnion, Haifa, 3200 Israel
Fields offered: Industrial management
Ownership: Nonprofit, state
Phone: (972-4) 292-593
Fax: (972-4) 325-537
Website: www.technion.ac.il
Master of Science in industrial management requiring one day a week on the campus in Haifa.

Tennessee Wesleyan College   B

College St.
Athens, TN 37303
Fields offered: Business management, accounting
Year founded: 1857
Ownership: Nonprofit, church
Phone: (423) 745-7504 • (800) PICK-TWC
Fax: (423) 744-9968
E-mail: jhead@cococo.net
Website: www.tnwc.edu
The Bachelor of Applied Science in business management or accounting is designed to meet the needs of adult learners who have two years of business-related college studies. Evening classes are held in Knoxville, Chattanooga, Athens, and Oak Ridge, Tennessee.

Texas A & M University   M

College of Business Administration
Kingsville, TX 78363
Fields offered: Business administration
Year founded: 1968
Ownership: Nonprofit, state
Phone: (512) 593-3801
Fax: (512) 593-3107

E-mail: dbigbee@tamuk.edu
Website: www.tamuk.edu
Offers an M.B.A. through Saturday-only courses.

Texas Christian University   B

Office of Extended Education, P. O. Box 32927
Fort Worth, TX 76129
Fields offered: General studies
Year founded: 1873
Ownership: Nonprofit, church
Phone: (817) 921-7130 • (800) TCU-FROG
Fax: (817) 921-7333
E-mail: d.grebel@tcu.edu
Website: www.tcu.edu

Bachelor of General Studies program, available entirely through evening study. At least 30 of the required 124 semester hours must be earned at T.C.U. Credit is given for prior academic work, and for equivalency exams, including a series of exams developed at the university.

Texas Tech University   D

Lubbock, TX 79409
Fields offered: Education
Year founded: 1923
Ownership: Nonprofit, state
Phone: (806) 742-2011
Fax: (806) 742-1615
E-mail: ethridge@ttdcel.coed.ttu.edu
Website: www.ttu.edu

Although Professor Albert B. Smith, Coordinator of the Higher Education Program, has asked us to remove this listing, we found Texas Tech's programs described in other directories, and so have decided to leave them in here, particularly since they offer the Ed.D. in higher education with the possibility of a much shorter residency than most traditional Doctoral programs. Professor Smith may be willing to tell you about their programs.

Thomas Jefferson University   B

1020 Locust St.
Philadelphia, PA 19107
Fields offered: Nursing
Year founded: 1824
Ownership: Nonprofit, independent
Phone: (215) 955-6000 • (800) 247-6933 (press 0)
Fax: (215) 955-5587
E-mail: thomas.coyne@mail.tju.edu
Website: www.tju.edu

The College of Allied Health Sciences offers a B.S. in nursing through evening classes. Applicants must have two years of prior college experience.

Towson State University   B

College of Continuing Studies
Towson, MD 21204
Fields offered: Many fields
Year founded: 1866

Ownership: Nonprofit, state
Phone: (410) 830-2000 • (800) CALL-TSU
Fax: (410) 830-3488
E-mail: frances@towson.edu
Website: www.towson.edu

Bachelor of Arts and Bachelor of Science in many fields, including business administration, psychology, chemistry, mass communications, accounting, education, liberal arts and sciences, and computer science, can be completed through evening study. Also weekend and summer courses. Credit for independent study, nonacademic prior learning, and by examination.

Trinity College   B, M

PACE, 208 Colchester Ave.
Burlington, VT 05401
Fields offered: Many fields
Year founded: 1925
Ownership: Nonprofit, church
Phone: (802) 658-0337 • (888) APPLY-75
Fax: (802) 658-5446
E-mail: thompson@smvax.smcvt.edu
Website: www.trinityvt.edu

Trinity College offers four programs for adult students to begin or resume their education. The PACE program, with a Monday through Friday schedule, offers 28 majors for a B.S./B.A. degree. The Weekend College has classes every other Saturday and/or Sunday for eight weekends a semester, with five majors. The Evening Degree program, offering only a Bachelor of Business Administration, meets two evenings a week for six eight-week terms. Finally, the Graduate Education program offers an M.Ed. to applicants who have taught for at least one year, and have access to a classroom. A minimum of 30 credits in the B.A./B.S. must be earned at Trinity. Applicants are eligible for advanced placement through transfer credit and credit for approved life/work and military experience.

Tufts University   B

REAL Program, Office of Undergraduate Education
Medford, MA 02155
Fields offered: Many fields
Year founded: 1852
Ownership: Nonprofit, independent
Phone: (617) 628-5000
Fax: (617) 381-3703
E-mail: uadmiss_inquiry@infonet.tufts.edu
Website: www.tufts.edu

B.A. and B.S. in many fields through part-time programs scheduled to meet the needs of working adults (applicants must be over 25 years old and have already taken two college-level courses). Limited credit available for equivalency exams.

Tulane University   B, M

University College
125 Gibson Hall

New Orleans, LA 70118
Fields offered: Paralegal studies, social studies, computer information systems, general studies, applied development/health
Year founded: 1834
Ownership: Nonprofit, independent
Phone: (504) 865-5731 • (800) 873-WAVE
Fax: (504) 862-8715
E-mail: undergrad.admission@tulane.edu
Website: caeph.tulane.edu/

B.A. in paralegal studies or social studies, B.S. in CIS, or Bachelor of General Studies, through classes scheduled to meet the needs of working adults. Credit for CLEP exams, independent study, and supervised fieldwork. New Master's program awards an interdisciplinary applied executive M.A. in applied development/health, as well as a number of certificates in environmental, development, and health areas. Classes will be held evenings and weekends, with option to do at least some of the work by distance learning. Credit is awarded for completion of USAID's development studies program (DSP). Contact for this program only:

Tulane University CDS
1925 N. Lynn St. Suite 400
Arlington, VA 22209
(703) 243-1556
WEB.Bertrand@mailhost.tcs.tulane.edu

Tusculum College   B, M

P. O. Box 5049
Greeneville, TN 37743
Fields offered: Many fields
Year founded: 1794
Ownership: Nonprofit, church
Phone: (423) 636-7300 • (800) 729-0256
Fax: (423) 638-7166
E-mail: admissions@tusculum.edu
Website: www.tusculum.edu

Some degree programs are offered through evening classes, and at off-site locations in Knoxville and Chattanooga. In addition, they offer an accelerated Bachelor's degree through classes that meet once a week, for 15 months. For information on this program, contact:

Tusculum College
Professional Studies Program
2200 Sutherland Avenue, Suite 308B
Knoxville, TN 37919
(800) 729-0116

United States International University-Europe   B, M

The Avenue
Bushey, Herts, WD2 2LN England
Fields offered: Business, engineering, hotel management, international relations, human behavior
Ownership: Nonprofit, independent
Phone: (0923) 249067
Website: www.usiu.edu

Bachelor's and Master's degrees are offered in residence on the campus near London, in association with the accredited United States International University in San Diego.

Universidad Iberoamericano   B

Prolongacion Paseo de la Reforma 880
Av. Lounas de Santa Fe
Mexico, D.F. 01210 Mexico
Fields offered: Sociology, theology
Year founded: 1943
Phone: (52-5) 570-61-98
Fax: (52-5) 723-11-04

The Bachelor's degree in sociology or theology is based largely on individual study, with study guides, required weekly group sessions on the university's campus, and individualized tutorial with the faculty, as requested by the student. The time commitment is one of at least five years.

Universidade da Asia Oriental

See: University of East Asia

Université de Paris VII-Vincennes   B, M, D

Route de la Tourelle
Paris, CEDEX 12, 75571, France
Fields offered: Many fields
Ownership: Nonprofit, state
E-mail: lw@uparis8.univ-paris.fr

The Vincennes campus of the University of Paris is known as the "university of second chance." The more than 30,000 students come from more than 100 countries. Degrees in languages, linguistics, social sciences, fine arts, theater, and cinematography through evening, small-group, and student-directed study.

University of Alabama at Birmingham   M

Executive Health Administration Program
Webb Bldg., Room 560
Birmingham, AL 35294-3361
Fields offered: Health administration
Year founded: 1966
Ownership: Nonprofit, state
Phone: (205) 934-8221 • (800) 421-8743
Fax: (205) 975-7114
E-mail: uabadmit@uabdpo.dpo.uab.edu
Website: www.uab.edu

Intensive 24-month "Executive Program" for experienced health-services providers who want to earn an M.S. in health administration while remaining fully employed. Learning occurs on-campus, weekends and evenings, and by correspondence courses, e-mail, and independent study. Applicants must have at least three years' of midlevel experience in their field.

University of Arkansas   M

Fayetteville, AR 72701
Fields offered: Operations management, education, engineering

Year founded: 1871
Ownership: Nonprofit, state
Phone: (501) 575-4401 • (800) 377-UofA
Fax: (501) 575-7575
E-mail: uafadmis@comp.uark.edu
Website: www.uark.edu

Residence requirements for some graduate degrees may be completed off-campus at Graduate Resident Centers located in Camden, Fort Smith, Little Rock, Monticello, Pine Bluff, and Russellville (in Arkansas); at military bases at Blytheville and Little Rock (in Arkansas), at Millington, Tennessee, and in Bolivia. Not all degrees may be completed at all centers. Degrees offered include an M.B.A., M.Ed., and M.S. in engineering, among others.

University of Baltimore   B, M, D

Charles at Mount Royal
Baltimore, MD 21201
Fields offered: Many fields
Year founded: 1925
Ownership: Nonprofit, state
Phone: (410) 837-4200
Fax: (410) 539-3714
E-mail: admissions@ubmail.ubalt.edu
Website: www.ubalt.edu

Bachelor's, Master's, M.B.A., and J.D. may be earned through evening and summer programs. Fields of study include computer science, criminal justice, corporate communication, law, political science, and others. There is an accelerated Bachelor's/Master's program in which some courses can be applied to the requirements for both degrees simultaneously.

University of California, Berkeley   M

Haas School of Business
M. B. A. Evening Program,
1170 Market St.
San Francisco, CA 94102
Fields offered: Business administration
Year founded: 1868
Ownership: Nonprofit, state
Phone: (510) 642-6468
Fax: (510) 643-6659
E-mail: evmbaadm@haas.berkeley.edu
Website: haas.berkeley.edu

Traditional M.B.A. available entirely through evening classes from the Graduate School of Business.

University of California, Davis   B, M

Davis, CA 95616
Fields offered: Various fields
Year founded: 1905
Ownership: Nonprofit, state
Phone: (916) 752-1011
Fax: (916) 752-6363
E-mail: paguilera@unexmail.ucdavis.edu
Website: www.ucdavis.edu

The Academic Reentry Program provides readmission advising for older students who are reentering an academic program after work and life experience. Admission "in exception" may be possible for persons who do not meet the formal admissions requirements if they present evidence of academic potential (test scores, recent coursework, "late bloomers," etc.). Part-time status may be elected by persons who are employed, retired, have family responsibilities, or health problems. No evening classes are offered.

University of California, Irvine   B, M

Campus Dr.
Irvine, CA 92717
Fields offered: Various fields
Year founded: 1965
Ownership: Nonprofit, state
Phone: (714) 824-5011
Fax: (714) 824-5451
E-mail: ogs.uci.edu
Website: www.uci.edu

M.S. in educational administration and M.A. in social ecology or in teaching of Spanish, all through evening study. There is a five-year combined Bachelor's/Master's in business administration.

University of California, Los Angeles   M

John E. Anderson Graduate School of Management
405 Hilgard Avenue
Los Angeles, CA 90024-4151
Fields offered: Business administration
Year founded: 1919
Ownership: Nonprofit, state
Phone: (310) 825-6121
Fax: (310) 206-4151
E-mail: tlifka@saonet.ucla.edu
Website: www.ucla.edu

Master of Business Administration offered through two nontraditional programs: the Executive MBA, a two-year series of Friday and Saturday courses open to successful executives with at least eight years' experience in business; and the Fully Employed MBA, a three-year evening program.

University of California, Santa Barbara   B, M

Santa Barbara, CA 93106
Year founded: 1944
Ownership: Nonprofit, state
Phone: (805) 893-8000
Fax: (805) 893-4445
E-mail: hadamson@xlrn.ucsb.edu
Website: www.ucsb.edu

Bachelor of Arts in law and society, through evening study in the College of Letters and Science; Master of Science in electrical engineering or computer science through e-mail and videocassette, among other instruction methods. B.A. in liberal arts through a distance center in Ventura that is equipped with academic advisers, a computer lab, and library research programs.

University of Central Florida

P.O. Box 25000
Orlando, FL 32816
Year founded: 1963
Ownership: Nonprofit, state
Phone: (407) 823-2000
Fax: (407) 823-3419
E-mail: smckinno@pegasus.cc.ucf.edu
Website: www.ucf.edu

We've heard that they offer some nontraditional programs, but thus far they have not responded to our requests for more information.

University of Central Texas   M

P.O. Box 1416
1901 S. Clear Creek Road
Killeen, TX 76540
Fields offered: Education, business, computer science, social work, criminal justice, social & behavioral sciences
Year founded: 1973
Ownership: Nonprofit, independent
Phone: (254) 526–8262
Fax: (254) 526–8403
E-mail: uct35@vvm.com
Website: www.wm.com.uct

Substantial credit is given for prior learning and career experience toward Master's degrees in education, business, computer science, social work, criminal justice, social & behavioral sciences. Formerly called American Technological University.

University of Chicago   M

5801 Ellis Ave.
Chicago, IL 60637
Fields offered: Business administration
Year founded: 1891
Ownership: Nonprofit, independent
Phone: (773) 702-1234
Fax: (773) 702-9085
E-mail: org_codm@orgmail.uchicago.edu
Website: www.uchicago.edu

The Master of Business Administration is offered in two nontraditional modes: entirely through evening study at a downtown Chicago location and in an Executive Program requiring one day at the downtown location every week for two years, plus a five-day residency seminar.

University of Cincinnati   B

Cincinnati, OH 45221
Fields offered: Many fields
Year founded: 1819
Ownership: Nonprofit, state
Phone: (513) 556-6000 • (800) 827-8728
Fax: (513) 556-2340

E-mail: melody.clark@uc.edu
Website: www.uc.edu

Bachelor's degree in natural science, social science, engineering, humanities, arts, and business administration, which may be earned entirely through evening study. There is an extensive cooperative education program, a weekend university, and an innovative "learning at large" program. See also: Degrees at a Distance Program.

University of Connecticut   B

Stamford, CT 06903
Fields offered: Many fields
Year founded: 1881
Ownership: Nonprofit, state
Phone: (203) 251-8400
Fax: (203) 251-8498
E-mail: swhite@stamford.uconn.edu
Website: www.uconn.edu

Bachelor of Arts and Bachelor of General Studies through evening classes. Credit for independent study and by examination.

University of Delaware   B, M

Clayton Hall
Newark, DE 19716
Fields offered: Many fields
Year founded: 1833
Ownership: Nonprofit, state
Phone: (302) 831-2000
Fax: (302) 831-3292
E-mail: mary.prtchard@mvs.udel.edu
Website: www.udel.edu

Delaware offers a number of degree programs through evening study (for their short-residency programs, see the preceding chapter). These include a B.A. or B.S. in accounting, chemistry, computer and information systems, criminal justice, human resources, engineering technology, English, history, psychology, sociology, and women's studies. Master's degrees can be earned in business, education, engineering, liberal studies, nutrition and dietetics, physical education, and public administration.

University of Detroit Mercy   B, M

4001 McNichols Rd.
Detroit, MI 48221
Fields offered: Many fields
Year founded: 1877
Ownership: Nonprofit, independent
Phone: (313) 993-1000 • (800) 635-5020
Fax: (313) 993-1011
E-mail: admissions@udmercy.edu
Website: www.udmercy.edu

Evening classes leading to a wide variety of Bachelor's and Master's degrees, including a Bachelor of Business Administration in accounting, economics, finance, management, marketing, and personnel, B.A. in criminal justice, B.S. in engineering, nursing, and human resource development, M.B.A., Master of Computer Science, Master of Engineering, Master of Engineering Management, and Master's in criminal justice, education, health services administration, and health care education, among others. Also offers certification programs in elementary and secondary education.

University of Dubuque M
2000 University Ave.
Dubuque, IA 52001-5050
Fields offered: Business administration
Year founded: 1852
Ownership: Nonprofit, private
Phone: (319) 589-3000 • (800) 722-5583
Fax: (319) 589-3682
E-mail: admssns@univ.dbq.edu
Website: www.dbq.edu

M.B.A. for fully employed students, through evening classes on-campus in Dubuque or at distance-learning centers in Singapore, Hong Kong, and Malaysia. A basic level of business knowledge is required; most students are employed in their fields while working on the degree, which can be completed in less than two years.

University of Evansville B
Center for Continuing Education
1800 Lincoln Ave.
Evansville, IN 47722
Fields offered: Many fields
Year founded: 1854
Ownership: Nonprofit, church
Phone: (812) 479-2768 • (800) 423-8633
Fax: (812) 474-2320
E-mail: admisweb@evansville.
Website: www.evansville.edu

The External Studies Program offers a B.A. or B.S. in virtually any field (although not generally in the technical or professional, such as mathematics, chemistry, engineering, computer science, nursing, and education) through a combination of classroom and correspondence courses, coursework from nontraditional sources, proficiency exams, independent study, and credit for life-experience learning. Students can take up to 10 years to finish their self-paced degree program. Credit available for military and other life-experience learning, by portfolio assessment, and for a range of equivalency exams. Twenty-four semester hours are required on campus.

University of Findlay B, M
1000 N. Main St.
Findlay, OH 45840
Fields offered: Many fields
Year founded: 1882
Ownership: Nonprofit, church
Phone: (419) 422-8313 • (800) 472-9502
Fax: (419) 424-4822
E-mail: admisweb@evansville.

Website: www.findlay.edu

Bachelor of Arts or Bachelor of Science can be earned in 58 majors, including business administration, accounting, computer science, systems analysis, and social work, through summer, weekend, and/or evening study. Unusual majors include equestrian studies, nuclear medicine technology, and hazardous waste studies.

University of Georgia B, M, D
Athens, GA 30602
Fields offered: Business administration, early childhood education, public administration
Year founded: 1785
Ownership: Nonprofit, state
Phone: (706) 542-3000
Fax: (706) 542-1466
E-mail: simpsone@gactr.uga.edu
Website: www.uga.edu

Bachelor's and Doctoral programs offered through evening and independent study, the latter limited to the equivalent of one academic year. Master's in early childhood education and public administration available through evening study.

University of Guam B, M
U. O. G. Station
Mangilao, 96923 Guam
Fields offered: Many fields
Year founded: 1952
Ownership: Nonprofit, state
Phone: (671) 735-2970
Fax: (671) 734-2296
E-mail: clowe@uog.edu
Website: uog.uog.edu

Bachelor's degree may be earned through evening and summer programs. Many majors in the colleges of arts and science, education, agriculture and life sciences, and business and public administration.

University of Hartford
200 Bloomfield Avenue
West Hartford, CT 06117
Year founded: 1877
Ownership: Nonprofit, independent
Phone: (860) 768-4100
Fax: (860) 768-4070
E-mail: admission@uhavax.hartford.edu
Website: www.hartford.edu

They have some innovative programs that we would love to list in this book, but they apparently have all the students they need because Ms. Carole Olland, director of admissions, wants them left out, so we are leaving them out.

University of Hawaii—Manoa B, M, D
2444 Dole St.
Honolulu, HI 96822
Fields offered: Many fields
Year founded: 1907

Ownership: Nonprofit, state
Phone: (808) 956-8111
Fax: (808) 956-5286
E-mail: ccecs@serv1.arthum.hawaii.edu
Website: www.hawaii.edu/uhinfo.html

B.A., B.S., M.A., M.S., M.B.A., Ed.D., and Ph.D. in many, many fields, including history, anthropology, mathematics, sociology, educational administration, biology, botany, dance ethnology, Hawaiian, engineering, health sciences, and physics, all through evening study. Some classes are given at Hickham Air Force Base.

University of Hawaii—West Oahu   B

96-043 Ala Ike
Pearl City, HI 96782
Fields offered: Humanities, social science, professional studies
Year founded: 1976
Ownership: Nonprofit, state
Phone: (808) 453-6565
Fax: (808) 453-6076
E-mail: sharonyo@hawaii.edu
Website: www.uhwo.hawaii.edu

Bachelor's degree programs in humanities (English, history, or philosophy), social services (anthropology, psychology, sociology, political science, or economics), or professional studies (business or public administration) are available through daytime and/or evening classes. All degrees can be earned entirely through evening study. Instead of a major in one of these areas, students may pursue study related to a major theme, such as American studies, Asian studies, justice administration, etc. Courses are also offered on weekends, and at three off-campus locations.

University of Illinois

See: Quad Cities Graduate Center

University of Illinois at Springfield   B, M

Springfield, IL 62708
Fields offered: Many fields
Year founded: 1969
Ownership: Nonprofit, state
Phone: (217) 786-6626 • (800) 722-2534
Fax: (217) 786-7188
E-mail: admissions@uis.edu
Website: www.uis.edu

The former Sangamon State University's INO, or individual option, program is based partially on a university without walls models. A learning proposal is developed, a learning contract negotiated, and the student pursues the Bachelor's degree through selected off-campus study, internships, foreign study, independent study, or exchange with other institutions. Evening and weekend classes are offered. Credit for prior learning.

University of Indianapolis   B, M

1400 E. Hanna Ave.
Indianapolis, IN 46227
Fields offered: Many fields
Year founded: 1902
Ownership: Nonprofit, private
Phone: (317) 788-3368 • 800-232-8634.
Fax: (317) 788-3275
E-mail: weigand@uindy.edu
Website: www.uindy.edu

A variety of Bachelor's and Master's degrees can be earned entirely through evening study. The Executive M.B.A. program meets one Friday and three Saturdays each month. In this program, it is possible to earn the degree in two years (comprising 19 Fridays and 50 Saturdays). Formerly called Indiana Central College.

University of Iowa   B, M, D

Division of Continuing Education
116 International Center
Iowa City, IA 52242-1802
Fields offered: Liberal studies, computer science
Year founded: 1847
Ownership: Nonprofit, state
Phone: (319) 335-2575 • (800) 272-6430
Fax: (319) 335-2740
E-mail: credit-programs@uiowa.edu
Website: www.uiowa.edu/~ccp

Nonresident Bachelor of Liberal Studies can be completed through guided correspondence study from anywhere in America, and through Iowa-based interactive and public television courses. Applicants must have completed 62 undergraduate credits elsewhere. B.S. in nursing, M.S. in computer science, and doctorate in pharmacology are offered through off-campus programs geared mainly to corporate subscribers in the Iowa City area, although other are admitted on a space-available basis. Instruction is through closed-circuit television, and one graduate-level seminar on campus is required. See also: Quad Cities Graduate Center.

University of Kansas   M

102 Bailey Hall
School of Education, Graduate Division
Lawrence, KS 66045
Fields offered: Public administration, education
Year founded: 1864
Ownership: Nonprofit, state
Phone: (785) 864-2700 • (888) MTOREAD (Kansas only)
Fax: (785) 864-7895
E-mail: be.a.jayhawk@st37.eds.ukans.edu
Website: www.ukans.edu

Master of Public Administration through evening study, and Master of Science in Education through evening study and at the Kansas City campus (K.U. Regents Center).

University of La Verne   B, M

S. C. E., 1950 3rd St.
La Verne, CA 91750
Fields offered: Many fields
Year founded: 1891
Ownership: Nonprofit, independent
Phone: (909) 593-3511
Fax: (909) 593-0965
E-mail: heckmanm@ulv.edu
Website: www.ulaverne.edu

Bachelor's or Master's may be earned through evening, weekend, and summer programs. Fields include liberal arts, graduate and professional studies, business, communications, behavioral sciences, education, child development, pre-medicine, and pre-law. Residence centers in California, Alaska, Greece, and Italy.

University of Limerick   B, M, D

National Technological Park
Limerick, Ireland
Fields offered: Many fields
Ownership: Nonprofit
Phone: (353-61) 333644
Fax: (353-61) 330316
E-mail: P.L.Colgan@ul.ie
Website: www.ul.ie/

The University of Limerick was established by the Irish government to meet the special needs brought on by the rapid expansion of the Irish economy and its membership in the European Community, which it accomplishes through its programs as well as through wide interaction with the business, industrial, government and community sectors in the Irish and international spheres. Formerly known as National Institute for Higher Education.

University of Louisville   B, M, D

S. 3rd St.
Louisville, KY 40292
Fields offered: Many fields
Year founded: 1798
Ownership: Nonprofit, state
Phone: (502) 852-5555 • (800) 334-8635
Fax: (502) 852-7013
E-mail: d0edge01@ulkyum.louisville.edu
Website: www.louisville.edu

Eighty degree programs at the Bachelor's, Master's, and Ph.D. level are available through part-time and/or evening studies. Evening and weekend courses are offered on the main campus and at two other sites. University of Louisville offers counseling for adults thinking of entering or returning to college, and evening workshops on topics of relevance. The Adult Commuter Center and Evening Student Services (ACCESS) provides a place for adults to call their own for typing, studying, and conversation, as well as university functions (admissions, bookstore, financial aid, etc.). The school has recently begun offering a 13-month M.B.A.

in Hong Kong, with no GMAT and little or no English required. Contact for this program is:
    Jeff Bracker, Brown & Williamson Professor
      of Entrepreneurship
    Phone: (502) 852-4780
    Fax : (502) 588-7557

University of Maine   B, M

Continuing Education
122 Chadbourne Hall
Orono, ME 04469
Fields offered: Many fields
Year founded: 1865
Ownership: Nonprofit, state
Phone: (207) 581-1110
Fax: (207) 581-1604
E-mail: jtoner@maine.maine.edu
Website: www.ume.maine.edu

Bachelor of University Studies, Bachelor of Science in elementary education, Master of Arts in English or speech, M.B.A., M.S. in education or medical technology, Master of Liberal Studies, and Master of Public Administration, all of which may be earned through evening classes given at Orono, as well as many off-campus extension centers.

University of Mary   B, M

7500 University Dr.
Bismark, ND 58501
Fields offered: Various fields
Year founded: 1957
Ownership: Nonprofit, church
Phone: (701) 255-7500 • (800) 288-6279
Fax: (701) 255-7687
E-mail: steph@umary.edu
Website: www.umary.edu

Business and accounting programs available through evening study. Some weekend classes. Credit for prior learning, equivalency exams, and independent study.

University of Massachusetts at Amherst   B, M

University without Walls
Box 35610
Amherst, MA 01002-5610
Fields offered: Many fields
Year founded: 1863
Ownership: Nonprofit, state
Phone: (413) 545-1378
Fax: (413) 545-2328
E-mail: ebrinkerhoff@uww.umass.edu
Website: www.umass.edu/uww

Amherst's university without walls program helps nontraditional students attain a B.A. or B.S. degree through the University of Massachusetts, while working around the kinds of work and family responsibilities most college freshmen don't have. Each UWW student designs his or her own area of study, aided by a UWW advisor. UWW students satisfy the university's graduation requirements through transfer credits, regular university coursework, and independent projects. UWW also awards credit for life-experience based on an extensive portfolio review. The program cannot be done through correspondence; students must live within commuting distance of Amherst or Springfield, Mass.

University of Massachusetts—Boston B
College of Public and Community Service
Boston, MA 02125
Fields offered: Public, community, legal, and human service, housing and community development
Year founded: 1964
Ownership: Nonprofit, state
Phone: (617) 287-5000
Fax: (617) 265-7173
E-mail: babcock@umbcky.cc.umb.edu
Website: www.umb.edu

Bachelor's degree program in the above fields; many of the required units can come from an assessment of prior learning experiences, but there is still a one-year required residency at the university.

University of Massachusetts—Dartmouth B
Old Westport Rd.
North Dartmouth, MA 02747-2300
Fields offered: Many fields
Year founded: 1895
Ownership: Nonprofit, state
Phone: (508) 999-8000
Fax: (508) 999-8901
E-mail: gstone@umassd.edu
Website: www.umassd.edu

Bachelor's degree in criminal justice, sociology, psychology, English, electrical engineering technology, humanities/social science, management, accounting, junior and senior year of nursing program, and others. Up to 25 percent of the required units can be earned through a for-fee assessment of prior learning experience. The assessment is based on evaluation of a portfolio, which is prepared in a class given for that purpose, through the Division of Continuing Education. Formerly Southeastern Massachusetts University.

University of Miami B, M, D
P. O. Box 248025
Coral Gables, FL 33124
Fields offered: Many fields
Year founded: 1925
Ownership: Nonprofit, independent
Phone: (305) 284-2211
Fax: (305) 284-2507
E-mail: admission@miami.edu (U.S. applicants)
intladmis@admiss.msmail.miam (International)
umgrad@umiami.ir.miami. (graduate)
Website: www.miami.edu

M.B.A. with classes held every weekend, for fully-employed persons sponsored by their employers. Miami offers an intriguing Honors Program in medicine, biomedical engineering, law, and marine and atmospheric science. Well-qualified applicants (high school seniors) are admitted simultaneously to the Bachelor's and the Doctoral programs.

University of Michigan M
200 Hill St.
Ann Arbor, MI 48109
Fields offered: Social work, education, nursing
Year founded: 1817
Ownership: Nonprofit, state
Phone: (313) 764-5300
Fax: (313) 936-7736
E-mail: ao-courses@umich.edu
Website: www.umich.edu

The University of Michigan offers graduate courses in social work, and occasionally nursing, through the off-campus program, sponsored by the respective departments and by the Extension Service. Independent study courses at the graduate level as well as the undergraduate level are available through the Extension Service. It is not, however, possible to earn an entire degree through either the off-campus program or the independent study program. Students anywhere in the world can take independent study courses. The School of Business Administration has an evening M.B.A. program.

University of Missouri at Saint Louis B
8001 Natural Bridge Rd.
St. Louis, MO 63121
Fields offered: General studies
Year founded: 1963
Ownership: Nonprofit, state
Phone: (314) 516-5000 • (800) 225-6075
Fax: (314) 516-5378
E-mail: sllockh@wmslvma.umsl.edu
Website: www.umsl.edu

The Continuing Education division offers extension courses during the day and evening at various locations. There is a Bachelor of General Studies program. Some credit is given for life-experience learning.

University of Nebraska—Omaha B
College of Continuing Studies
Omaha, NE 68182
Fields offered: General studies
Year founded: 1908
Ownership: Nonprofit, state
Phone: (402) 554-2800 • 800-858-8648 (NE and IN)
Fax: (402) 554-3555
E-mail: joadams@unomaha.edu
Website: www.unomaha.edu

Courses from many sources, with credits leading to the student-planned Bachelor of General Studies degree, offered "to established adults only." Credit for life-experience and amnesty for past college failures; 24 credit hours must be earned in residence after enrollment. Nebraska-based students only may enter an MBA program delivered by interactive video at certain Nebraska sites. For information, contact (402) 472-2338 or e-mail to unldde@unl.edu.

University of New Hampshire   B, M

Division of Continuing Education
6 Garrison Ave.
Durham, NH 03824
Fields offered: Various fields
Year founded: 1866
Ownership: Nonprofit, state
Phone: (603) 862-1938
Fax: (603) 862-1113
E-mail: wfm@christa.unh.edu
Website: www.unh.edu

A variety of part-time and/or evening classes leading to a Bachelor's for registered nurses, B.S. in engineering technology for experienced engineers, Master of Public Administration, and Master of Library and Information Studies.

University of New Haven   B

300 Orange Ave.
West Haven, CT 06516
Fields offered: Many fields
Year founded: 1920
Ownership: Nonprofit, independent
Phone: (203) 932-7000 • (800) 342-5864
Fax: (203) 937-0756
E-mail: adminfo@charger.newhaven.edu
Website: www.newhaven.edu

Bachelor's degrees in all fields except applied mathematics, natural sciences, English, and world music can be earned on a part-time basis through the Division of Continuing Education, which has day and evening divisions. More than 50 majors are available. Among the unusual ones are air transportation management, arson investigation, forensic science, dietetics, fire science, music and sound recording, and tourism and travel administration.

University of New Mexico

Division of Continuing Education
1634 University Blvd. N.E.
Albuquerque, NM 87131
Year founded: 1889
Ownership: Nonprofit, state
Phone: (505) 277-0111 • (800) CALL-UNM
Fax: (505) 277-6019
E-mail: unmlobos@unm.edu
Website: www.unm.edu

We've heard that they offer some nontraditional programs, but thus far they have not responded to our requests for more information.

University of New Orleans

See: National Universities Degree Consortium

University of Pennsylvania   B, M

Credit Programs, College of General Studies
3440 Market St., #100
Philadelphia, PA 19104-3335
Fields offered: Liberal arts & sciences
Year founded: 1740
Ownership: Nonprofit, independent
Phone: (215) 898-5000 • (800) 434-5689
Fax: (215) 898-5756
E-mail: info@admissions.ugao.upenn.edu (undergraduate)
Website: www.upenn.edu:80

Bachelor of Arts through College of General Studies, a division of Penn's School of Arts and Sciences in which part-time evening students earn the same degree as full-time day students at about one-third the regular tuition. Master of Liberal Arts and Master of Social Gerontology also offered in the evening. Only one Saturday class (biology) is offered, and no credit for life-experience learning.

University of Puerto Rico   B

P. O. Box 5000
Mayaguez, PR 00709
Fields offered: Education
Year founded: 1911
Ownership: Nonprofit, state
Phone: (787) 832-4040
Fax: (787) 834-3031
Website: www._rum.upr.clu.edu

Bachelor's in education for employed teachers, through evening, weekend, and summer classes. Offered through the Division of Academic Extension and Community Services, which was created to provide educational opportunity to the adult working population, disadvantaged groups, and minorities.

University of Quebec   B

Télé-Université
2600 Boulevard Laurier, 7th Étage
Case Postale 10700,
Sainte-Foy, Quebec G1V 4V9 Canada
Fields offered: Many fields
Year founded: 1972
Ownership: Nonprofit, state
Phone: (418) 657-2262
Fax: (418) 657-2094
E-mail: info@teluq.uquebec.ca
Website: www.uquebec.ca

Télé-université is one of the 11 units of the huge University of Quebec. A university without walls program, it offers courses in human and social science, communication, business administration, environmental sciences, computer-assisted education, science and technology, language, distance education, and more. Students use textbooks, special student guides, video- and audiotapes, television, tele-conferencing, and computer networks under the guidance of an assigned tutor/mentor. The primary language of all instruction is French.

University of Redlands   B, M

1200 E. Colton Ave.
Redlands, CA 92374
Fields offered: Liberal arts, business, information systems
Year founded: 1907
Ownership: Nonprofit, independent
Phone: (909) 793-2121 • (800) 455-5064
Fax: (909) 793-2029
E-mail: admissions@uor.
Website: www.uor.edu

Degree programs for working adults throughout Southern California through Redlands' Whitehead Center: B.S. in business and management or information systems, and an M.B.A. Forty units may be earned through portfolio assessment of prior learning. Applicants must have already earned at least 40 units from another institution. The school's Johnson Center offers residential undergraduate programs in which students have almost total academic freedom to create their own majors, or to take advantage of interdisciplinary or custom-designed traditional majors. Johnson students are "graded" by narrative evaluation, mostly live in the same dormitory, and are expected to address issues of community and cross-cultural awareness.

University of Rhode Island   B, M

College of Continuing Education
199 Promenade St.
Providence, RI 02908
Fields offered: General studies, business administration
Year founded: 1892
Ownership: Nonprofit, state
Phone: (401) 277-5160 • (800) 367-1144
Fax: (401) 277-5168
E-mail: joydig@uriacc.uri.edu
Website: www.uri.edu/prov/

Bachelor of Arts, Bachelor of Science, and Bachelor of General Studies degrees. Master of Arts, M.B.A., Master of Public Administration, and Master of Science in Labor and Industrial Relations. Most liberal arts majors offered, plus counseling/human services and manufacturing engineering. Classes meet once a week or on Saturday morning, and evenings. Three major sites for courses, plus at local businesses around the state.

University of Richmond   B

Richmond, VA 23173
Fields offered: Applied studies
Year founded: 1830
Ownership: Nonprofit, state
Phone: (804) 289-8640 • (800) 700-1662
Fax: (804) 287-6003

E-mail: admissions@richmond.edu
Website: www.urich.edu
Bachelor of Applied Studies available only through evening study.

University of San Francisco   B, M

College of Professional Studies
2130 Fulton Street
San Francisco, CA 94117-1080
Fields offered: Many fields
Year founded: 1855
Ownership: Nonprofit, church
Phone: (415) 422-6000
Fax: (415) 422-2303
E-mail: sanfranciscocampus@usfca.edu
Website: www.usfca.edu

The College of Professional Studies administers a variety of undergraduate and graduate programs for working adults, and undergraduates may received credit for experiential learning through USF's Experiential Learning Center. Classes meet one evening a week and/or on Saturdays at a number of California locations. Degrees offered include a Bachelor of Public Administration (with an optional concentration in law enforcement leadership), B.S. programs in organizational behavior, information systems management, and applied economics; Master's programs in environmental management, public administration, human resources and organization development, and nonprofit administration.

University of Scranton   B

Dexter Hanley College
Gallery Building
Scranton, PA 18510-4582
Fields offered: Many fields
Year founded: 1888
Ownership: Nonprofit, church
Phone: (717) 941-7400 • (800) SCRANTON
Fax: (717) 941-6351
E-mail: admissions@uofs.edu
Website: www.uofs.edu

Nineteen evening degree programs leading to Bachelor of Arts or Bachelor of Science, including two designed for R.N.s. Credit for a variety of life experience learning, through portfolio assessment, and for equivalency exams. In addition to evening classes, learning can take place through audio- and videocassettes, independent study, supervised fieldwork, and televised courses.

University of South Alabama   B

Department of Adult Personalized Study
Alpha East 214
Mobile, AL 36688
Fields offered: Many fields
Year founded: 1963
Ownership: Nonprofit, state
Phone: (334) 460-6101 • (800) 872-5247

Fax: (334) 460-7205
E-mail: adms@usamail.usouth.edu
Website: www.usouthal.edu

Bachelor of Arts and Bachelor of Science in many fields, through weekend college and other programs tailored to the needs of adult learners. Credit for life and military experience and for a range of equivalency exams; nontraditional options include audio- and videotaped courses for home study, cooperative education, and independent study.

University of Southern California   B, M, D

University Park
Los Angeles, CA 90089
Fields offered: Many fields
Year founded: 1880
Ownership: Nonprofit, independent
Phone: (213) 740-2311 • (800) 331-0558
Fax: (213) 740-7254
E-mail: gradapp@afs2000a.usc.edu (graduate)
Website: cwis.usc.edu

In the past, USC has offered a wide range of evening and weekend classes, international programs, and other interesting nontraditional options, both on campus and at distant locations. However, when we wrote to ask about any changes for this edition, Mr. Murdoch wrote back to say that because we had made an error in reporting some USC program in the past, he wasn't going to tell us anything now. So you'll have to ask him directly, at the number and address above, what programs still exist.

University of Southern Mississippi   B, M

Interactive Video Network
University of Sourthern Mississippi
Hattiesburg, MS 39406
Fields offered: Education
Year founded: 1910
Ownership: Nonprofit, state
Phone: (601) 266-4356
Fax: (601) 266-4409
E-mail: lharper@whale.st.usm.edu
Website: www.usm.edu

The work for several Bachelor's and Master's degrees in education can be completed by evening and weekend study, or over two summer sessions. In addition, there is an M.A. in the teaching of English and a M.A. in teaching languages, both available through two residential summer sessions with independent study in between. USM also offers between 8 and 16 courses per semester, both grad and undergrad, through distance education technology, specifically compressed video.

University of Tampa   B

School of Continuing Studies
401 W. Kennedy Blvd.
Tampa, FL 33606
Fields offered: Liberal studies, computer information systems, management and marketing

Year founded: 1931
Ownership: Nonprofit, independent
Phone: (813) 253-3333 • (800) 733-4773
Fax: (813) 251-0016
E-mail: Admissions@alpha.utampa.edu
Website: www.utampa.edu

Bachelor of Liberal Studies, B.S. in computer information systems, and Bachelor of Marketing and Management through evening and summer classes, as well as other nontraditional programs. Credit awarded for life-experience learning and for taking equivalency exams, as well as correspondence courses, independent study, and supervised fieldwork.

University of Tennessee at Chattanooga   B, M

615 McCallie Ave.
Chattanooga, TN 37402
Fields offered: Many fields
Year founded: 1886
Ownership: Nonprofit, state
Phone: (423) 755-4662 • (800) 882-6627
Fax: (423) 755-4157
E-mail: pasty_reynolds/admin/ug@hpdesk.utc.edu
Website: www.utc.edu

Bachelor of Arts, Bachelor of Science, Master of Business Administration, Master of Science, and Master of Education, available almost entirely through evening study. Some credit may be given for prior work and volunteer experience through the Individualized Education Program.

University of Tennessee Space Institute   M

B. H. Goethert Parkway
Tullahoma, TN 37388
Fields offered: Industrial engineering, engineering management, aviation systems
Ownership: Nonprofit, state
Phone: (931) 393-7318 • (888) 822-8874 ext.432
Fax: (931) 393-7346
E-mail: kreddy@utsi.edu
Website: www.utsi.edu

M.S. in industrial engineering or engineering management through distance-leaning centers. Also, through a separate distance-learning program (contact: Dr. Ralph Kimberlin, phone (615) 393-7411, fax (615) 455-5912), an M.S. in aviation systems, including flight testing, aircraft design, aviation meteorology, air traffic control, and airport management. Students in this program are required to spend one day on the UTSI campus, defending their thesis.

University of Texas   B, M, D

Arlington, TX 76019
Year founded: 1895
Ownership: Nonprofit, state
Phone: (817) 272-2011 • (800) 687-2882
Fax: (817) 272-5656

253

E-mail: admissions@uta.edu (undergraduate)
graduate.school@uta.edu (graduate)
Website: www.uta.edu
Bachelor of Arts, Master of Arts in many fields, almost entirely through evening study.

University of Toledo   B, M
Adult Liberal Studies
University College
Toledo, OH 43606
Fields offered: Many fields
Year founded: 1872
Ownership: Nonprofit, state
Phone: (419) 530-4242 • (800) 586-5336
Fax: (419) 530-4940
E-mail: rmeinha@utnet.utoledo.edu
Website: www.utoledo.edu

The Adult Liberal Studies program offers people over the age of 25 the opportunity to earn a Bachelor's degree through a combination of independent study, evening classes, regular coursework, and a thesis. All students begin with an introductory planning seminar. Credit is given for CLEP exams. Nine seminars are given in various fields of study, usually one evening a week, for a total of 54 of the required 186 quarter hours. Thirty-five hours of traditional courses must be taken, before writing a thesis in an area of special interest. Toledo also offers 2 + 2 programs that allows Associate's degree holders to complete an accelerated Bachelor's in any of a number of fields.

University of Tulsa   B, M, D
600 S. College Ave.
Tulsa, OK 74104-3189
Fields offered: Business, arts and sciences, engineering, law
Year founded: 1894
Ownership: Nonprofit, independent
Phone: (918) 631-2000 • (800) 331-3050
Fax: (918) 631-2033
E-mail: admission@utulsa.edu (U.S. undergraduate)
inst@utulsa.edu (international undergraduate)
grad@utulsa.edu (graduate)
Website: www.utulsa.edu

All business majors, the M.B.A., and the J.D. are offered through evening study. Student-designed majors are available through the College of Arts and Sciences. Some degree programs can incorporate summer terms, with six- and 12-week sessions.

University of Utah   M
Salt Lake City, UT 84112
Fields offered: Business administration, administration, engineering
Year founded: 1850
Ownership: Nonprofit, state
Phone: (801) 581-7200 • (800) 685-8856
Fax: (801) 581-3007

Website: www.utah.edu
Master of Business Administration may be earned entirely through evening study.

University of Washington   B
UW Extension, GH-21
Seattle, WA 98195
Fields offered: General studies
Year founded: 1861
Ownership: Nonprofit, state
Phone: (206) 543-2100
Fax: (206) 543-9285
E-mail: distance@u.washington.edu
Website: www.washington.edu

The B.A. in general studies is an upper-division degree-completion program that allows students who have completed 75 credits elsewhere to complete a degree part-time Part time students can expect to earn their degree in about three or four years. Some instruction can take place by correspondence courses, but this is essentially a part-time residential program.

University of West Florida   B, M
11000 University Pkwy.
Pensacola, FL 32514
Fields offered: Many fields
Year founded: 1963
Ownership: Nonprofit, state
Phone: (850) 474-2423
Fax: (850) 474-3131
E-mail: adziadon@uwf.edu
Website: www.uwf.edu

B.S. in business administration, M.B.A., Master of Education, and M.A. and M.S. in many fields. Credit available for life-experience learning and equivalency exams, as well as independent study, supervised fieldwork, and, at the Bachelor's level only, cooperative education.

University of West Los Angeles   B
1155 W. Arbor Vitae St.
Inglewood, CA 90301-2902
Fields offered: Paralegal
Year founded: 1966
Ownership: Nonprofit, independent
Phone: (310) 342-5200
Fax: (310) 342-5293
Website: www.unla.edu

Bachelor of Science in paralegal studies for transfer students can be earned through two to three years of evening classes.

University of Wisconsin— Oshkosh   B
800 Algoma Blvd.
Oshkosh, WI 54901
Fields offered: Liberal studies
Year founded: 1871
Ownership: Nonprofit, state

Phone: (920) 424-1234
Fax: (920) 424-7317
E-mail: berens@uwosh.edu
Website: www.uwosh.edu

One hundred twenty-eight credits are required for a Bachelor of Liberal Studies, and it is possible to earn 101 of them through weekend classes. Credits earned through any combination of transfer credits from accredited institutions, evening classes, independent study, accredited television courses, CLEP examinations, and challenge examinations may be applied to this degree. A minimum of 30 credits in residency is required. A prerequisite course that is offered four times a year must be completed to enter the program. Students take one course at a time, meeting three weekends per course. Inexpensive on-campus housing is available for weekend students.

University of Wisconsin— Platteville   B

Extended Degree Program
506 Pioneer Tower
1 University Plaza
Platteville, WI 53818
Fields offered: Business administration
Year founded: 1866
Ownership: Nonprofit, state
Phone: (608) 342-1468 • (800) 362-5460
Fax: (608) 342-1466
E-mail: adams@uwplatt.edu
Website: www.uwplatt.edu

The Extended Degree Program offering the Bachelor's degree in business administration (with optional minor in accounting) was once open to Wisconsin residents only, but now accepts applicants nationwide. Areas of concentration are finance, marketing, management, and human resource management. Credit can be earned through individualized study and evaluation of prior learning achieved through work and life experience. Coursework is increasingly available over the Internet.

University System of New Hampshire   B

School for Lifelong Learning
Dunlap Center
Durham, NH 03824
Fields offered: General studies, professional studies (management, behavioral sciences)
Year founded: 1972
Ownership: Nonprofit, state
Phone: (603) 862-1692
Fax: (603) 862-4975
E-mail: plm@christa.unh.edu
Website: www.unh.edu

Bachelor of General Studies and Bachelor of Professional Studies by independent study, for adults who have already earned at least 60 credit hours elsewhere. Courses are available evenings, weekends, and by videocassette. Learning contracts, credit for life-experience learning, and self-designed degree programs are offered.

Urbana University   B

College Way
Urbana, OH 43078
Fields offered: Business, social sciences, education, natural science, preprofessional
Year founded: 1850
Ownership: Nonprofit, independent
Phone: (937) 484-1301 • (800) 787-2262 (Ohio only)
Fax: (937) 484-1322
E-mail: admiss@urbana.edu
Website: www.urbana.edu

B.S. and B.A. through weekend, evening, and summer programs held at the main campus in Urbana or at branch campuses in Bellefontaine, Dayton, and Columbus. Self-designed majors and credit for independent study are available, but 30 hours of coursework must be completed at Urbana.

Utah State University   B, M

Electronic Distance Education
Logan, UT 84322-3702
Fields offered: Business administration, psychology, social sciences, rehabilitation counseling, education
Year founded: 1888
Ownership: Nonprofit, state
Phone: (801) 797-1134
Fax: (801) 797-4077
E-mail: m.lyon@ce.usu.edu
Website: www.usu.edu

Degree programs offered by telephone and video conferencing at 37 sites in Utah and two in Colorado. Degrees offered: B.S. in business administration or psychology, M.S. in rehabilitation counseling or home economics education, and Master of Social Science in human resource management. See also: National Universities Degree Consortium.

Valley City State University   B

Alternate Learning Program
Valley City, ND 58072
Fields offered: Many fields
Year founded: 1889
Ownership: Nonprofit, state
Phone: (701) 845-7102 • (800) 532-8641
Fax: (701) 845-7245
E-mail: jdrake@prairie.nodak.edu
Website: www.vcsu.nodak.edu

Bachelor of University Studies, B.A., and B.S., including a special B.S. in education, through programs tailored to the needs of adult students. Credit available for life-experience learning and for equivalency exams, as well as cooperative education, independent study, and supervised fieldwork.

Valparaiso University

Valparaiso, IN 46383
Fields offered: Many fields
Year founded: 1859
Ownership: Nonprofit, church
Phone: (219) 464-5000 • (888) GO-VALPO

Fax: (219) 464-5381
E-mail: undergrad_admissions@valpo.edu
Website: www.valpo.edu

Bachelor of Arts in many fields, Master of Music, Master of Education, M.S. in nursing, and M.A. in liberal studies or applied behavioral science, through a variety of nontraditional residential programs, as well as cooperative education, independent study, and supervised fieldwork. Credit awarded for a wide range of equivalency exams.

Vanderbilt University   M

Owen Graduate School of Management
Nashville, TN 37203
Fields offered: Business administration
Year founded: 1873
Ownership: Nonprofit, independent
Phone: (615) 322-2513
Fax: (615) 343-5555
E-mail: owenexec@owen.vanderbilt.edu
Website: www.vanderbilt.edu

Designed for midcareer executives and professionals who want to complete the M.B.A. degree in 22 months of full-time study without giving up their jobs. Classes meet all day Friday and Saturday of alternate weekends.

Villanova University   B

University College
Villanova, PA 19085
Fields offered: Many fields
Year founded: 1842
Ownership: Nonprofit, church
Phone: (610) 519-4500 • (800) 338-7927
Fax: (610) 519-5000
E-mail: admission@email.vill.edu
Website: www.vill.edu

Bachelor's may be earned through weekend, evening, and summer programs. Fields of study include many majors in liberal arts and sciences, accountancy, business administration, engineering, and nursing.

Virginia Commonwealth University   B, M

821 W. Franklin St., Box 2526
Richmond, VA 23284
Fields offered: General studies, interdisciplinary studies
Year founded: 1837
Ownership: Nonprofit, state
Phone: (804) 828-1200 • (800) 828-2269
Fax: (804) 828-1899
E-mail: dclement@hsc.vcu.edu
Website: www.vcu.edu

Bachelor of General Studies for working adults. Individually developed degree requirements in the form of an individualized curriculum plan. Encouragement to utilize CLEP, military, and noncollege health-related education. Some use of courses taught at other institutions of the Capital Consortium for Continuing Higher Education. Program requires a minimum of 30 credits to be completed at VCU

in regular day, evening, or weekend classes. Master of Interdisciplinary Studies Program, serving evening and part-time graduate students, enables students to combine studies in three graduate programs into a coherent, individualized, multidisciplinary program. Program is a joint venture with Virginia State University in Petersburg and requires some study at VSU. Thesis or final project is required.

Virginia State University   B

P.O. Box FF
Petersburg, VA 23803
Fields offered: Individualized studies
Year founded: 1882
Ownership: Nonprofit, state
Phone: (804) 524-5000 • (800) 871-7611
Fax: (804) 524-6506
E-mail: lwinn@vsu.edu
Website: www.vsu.edu

The Bachelor of Individualized Studies program allows "mature students" to create a personalized program that meets their educational goals, in conjunction with an academic advisor. Credit awarded for life/work and military experience and equivalency exams.

Washington University (Missouri)   B, M

University College, One Brookings Drive
St. Louis, MO 63130
Fields offered: Arts and sciences
Year founded: 1853
Ownership: Nonprofit, independent
Phone: (314) 935-5000 • (800) 676-2114
Fax: (314) 935-5799
E-mail: admission@wustl.e
Website: www.wustl.edu

Bachelor of Science, Master of Arts, Master of Liberal Arts, Master of Health Science, and certificates in international affairs and nonprofit management available through evening study in the University College, a division of Arts and Sciences.

Wayland Baptist University   B, M

1900 W. 7th
Plainview, TX 79072
Fields offered: Occupational education, occupational technology, business, religion
Year founded: 1908
Ownership: Nonprofit, church
Phone: (806) 296-5521 • (800) 588-1928
Fax: (806) 296-4580
E-mail: admitu@wbu1.wbu.edu
Website: www.wbu.edu

Bachelor of Science in occupational education, in which over 75% of the necessary units can be earned through an assessment of prior learning experiences. Wayland learning centers are located in Amarillo, Lubbock, Wichita Falls, San Antonio, and Honolulu, as well as on the main campus in Plainview. A degree plan is prepared upon request either prior to or after enrollment, based on documentation submitted by the student. The assessment generally takes less than one month, and there is no cost to the student.

Wayne State University   B

    College of Lifelong Learning
    Interdisciplinary Studies Program
    6001 Cass
    Detroit, MI 48202
    Fields offered: General studies
    Year founded: 1868
    Ownership: Nonprofit, state
    Phone: (313) 577-0832
    Fax: (313) 577-8154
    E-mail: www@cll.wayne.edu
    Website: www.wayne.edu

The Bachelor of Interdisciplinary Studies and the Bachelor of Technical and Interdisciplinary Studies degrees are offered through a combination of television courses, four-hour day or evening workshops, and weekend conferences. Students must complete credit hours in the social sciences, humanities, science and technologies, electives, and interdisciplinary advanced studies. A minimum of 40 semester hours must be completed within the Interdisciplinary Studies Program. Students are welcome to take courses in the other colleges at Wayne State University. Courses are offered at a variety of locations within the Detroit metro area.

Wellesley College   B

    Elizabeth Kaiser Davis Degree Program
    Office of Continuing Education
    Wellesley, MA 02181
    Fields offered: Many fields
    Year founded: 1875
    Ownership: Nonprofit, independent
    Phone: (781) 283-2237
    Fax: (781) 283-3639
    E-mail: admission@wellesley.edu
    Website: www.wellesley.edu

Special program for women over the age of 24 whose education has been interrupted by at least two years. Credit for some equivalency exams.

Wentworth Institute of Technology   B

    550 Huntington Ave.
    Boston, MA 02115
    Fields offered: Technical, design fields
    Year founded: 1904
    Ownership: Nonprofit, independent
    Phone: (617) 442-9010, ext. 264 • (800) 323-9481
    Fax: (617) 989-4399
    E-mail: admissions@wit.edu
    Website: www.wit.edu

Wentworth's weekend college offers Bachelor's degrees in architectural building construction, computer science, construction management, electronics, interior design, and mechanical technical management.

West Virginia University   B, M

    P.O. Box 6009
    Morgantown, WV 26506-6009
    Fields offered: Education, business administration, nursing
    Year founded: 1867
    Ownership: Nonprofit, state
    Phone: (304) 293-0111 • (800) 344-WVU1
    Fax: (304)-293-8991
    E-mail: WVUAdmissions@arc.wvu.edu (undergraduate)
    Website: www.wvu.edu

B.S. and M.S. in nursing through satellite courses, which can be viewed at 16 public sites statewide, and teleconferencing. Some on-campus clinical courses may be required, on a case-by-case basis. Master of Arts in education and M.B.A. available through evening study. "Academic forgiveness" of any less-than-wonderful grades more than five years old. See also: West Virginia Board of Regents B.A. Program.

Western International University   B, M

    10202 N. 19th Ave.
    Phoenix, AZ 85021
    Fields offered: Business, accounting, computers, management, general studies
    Year founded: 1978
    Ownership: Nonprofit, independent
    Phone: (602) 943-2311
    Fax: (602) 371-8637
    E-mail: pkmessel.@apollo.grp.edu
    Website: www.wintu.edu

B.S. in accounting, management, or computer information science, B.A. in general studies, M.B.A., M.S. in accounting or computer information science, offered by evening study on campuses in Arizona and overseas in London. Courses are given in an "accelerated semester" format, in which each course takes one month, meeting two evenings a week. The undergraduate degrees can be completed in 29 months; the Master's in 12. Advanced standing may be awarded to students who prove competent in and can demonstrate knowledge of course content as, for example, through portfolio assessment or challenge examination.

Western Maryland College   M

    Westminster, MD 21157
    Fields offered: Sensory impairment, education of the deaf
    Year founded: 1867
    Ownership: Nonprofit, independent
    Phone: (410) 848-7000 • (800) 638-5005
    Fax: (410) 857-2279
    E-mail: admissio@wmdc.edu
    Website: www.wmdc.edu

M.Ed. and M.S. in sensory impairment, two programs designed to prepare professionals to teach the hearing-impaired and to work with the hearing and visually impaired. Courses are conducted during late afternoon and evening hours, except in the summer. Programs can also be completed in three consecutive nine-week summer sessions, with provision for independent study at home in between.

Western Michigan University B, M, D

Kalamazoo, MI 49008
Fields offered: Many fields
Year founded: 1903
Ownership: Nonprofit, state
Phone: (616) 387-1000
Fax: (616) 387-0958
E-mail: ask-wmu@wmich.edu
Website: www.wmich.edu

B.S. in general university studies available through the Campus III/Weekend College Program; concentrations include applied liberal studies, health studies, technical scientific studies, and applied professional studies. In addition, the following degrees are available entirely through off-campus regional centers: B.S. in general university studies and production technology, Master and Doctor of Public Administration, Master of Public Administration in health care administration, Master of Social Work, M.B.A., Master in Educational Leadership, Master in Early Childhood Education, Master in Elementary Education, Master in Reading, M.S. in vocational education, engineering management, industrial engineering, and mechanical engineering, and Master in Industrial Psychology. Residency requirements can be satisfied through work completed at a WMU Regional Center.

Western Network for Education in Health Administration

See: University of Colorado

Western New England College B, M

School of Continuing Higher Education
Springfield, MA 01119
Year founded: 1919
Ownership: Nonprofit, independent
Phone: (413) 782-1259 • (800) 325-1122
Fax: (413) 782-1746
E-mail: mdobbs@wnec.edu
Website: www.wnec.edu

Bachelor's and Master's degrees in many fields offered through part-time evening study.

Westfield State College B, M

Western Ave.
Westfield, MA 01086
Fields offered: Many fields
Year founded: 1838
Ownership: Nonprofit, state
Phone: (413) 568-3311 • (800) 322-8401
Fax: (413) 562-3613
E-mail: admission@wsc.mass.edu

Website: www.wsc.mass.edu

Weekend, evening, and summer classes leading to a Bachelor of Arts, Bachelor of Science, Master of Arts, Master of Science, Master of Education, and Certificate of Advanced Graduate Study.

Westminster College (Utah) B

Office of Adult and Extended Education
1840 S. 13th East
Salt Lake City, UT 84105
Fields offered: Many fields
Year founded: 1875
Ownership: Nonprofit, independent
Phone: (801) 488-4200 • (800) 748-4753
Fax: (801) 466-6916
E-mail: admispub@wcslc.edu
Website: www.wcslc.edu

Bachelor's degrees in 27 fields. Up to one third of the necessary units may be earned by an assessment of prior learning experiences. Some degrees in business and the social sciences may be earned through evening programs. Assessment is limited to students admitted to a degree program and is done after enrollment, at a cost of $252 for the class and a $350 assessment fee. Also offers a special legal-assistance course through evening classes, which can either be applied towards a Bachelor's degree, or used to obtain specialized positions in the legal field. The program is accredited by the American Bar Association.

Whitworth College B, M

Spokane, WA 99251.
Fields offered: Accounting, business, education, teaching, liberal studies
Year founded: 1890
Ownership: Nonprofit, church
Phone: (509) 777-1000 • (800) 533-4668
Fax: (509) 777-3725
E-mail: tbassen@whitworth.edu
Website: www.whitworth.edu

Bachelor of Arts in accounting, business management, and education, Master of Education, Master in Teaching (MIT), and Bachelor of Liberal Studies through evening and summer programs and independent study. The tuition for degrees earned in the evening and summer is approximately one quarter of that for daytime programs.

Widener University B

Weekend College
Rm. 137, Kapelski
Chester, PA 19013
Fields offered: Nursing, business administration, psychology
Year founded: 1821
Ownership: Nonprofit, independent
Phone: (610) 499-4000
Fax: (610) 876-9751
E-mail: admissions.office@widener.edu

Website: www.widener.edu

B.S. in nursing or business administration and B.A. in psychology entirely through weekend classes, augmented by extensive out-of-class independent study and supervised fieldwork. Credit for life-experience learning and equivalency exams. Some years ago they absorbed the night and weekend programs formerly offered by Pennsylvania Military College.

Wilmington College   B, M, D

320 Dupont Highway
New Castle, DE 19720
Fields offered: Many fields
Year founded: 1967
Ownership: Nonprofit, independent
Phone: (302) 328-9401
Fax: (302) 328-5902
Website: www.wilmcoll.edu

Wilmington offers a number of nontraditional approaches to degree-earning, including accelerated B.S. programs for working R.N.s, and a number of programs that allow credit for life-experience learning and challenge examinations, including Bachelor's degrees in education, behavioral science, criminal justice, accounting, aviation management, banking and finance, communication arts, human resources management, and nursing; M.B.A.; M.S. in human resources management; M.Ed.; and an Ed.D. (for employed teachers or schools administrators only).

Winona State University   B, M

Adult Continuing Education & Extension
Winona, MN 55987
Fields offered: Many fields
Year founded: 1858
Ownership: Nonprofit, state
Phone: (507) 457-5000 • (800) DIAL-WSU ext. 5100
Fax: (507) 457-5586
E-mail: admissions@vax2.winona.msus.edu
Website: www.winona.msus.edu

Bachelor's degrees in arts, sciences, business, education, nursing, and paralegal; M.S. in education, counseling, and educational administration, and an M.B.A. Adult students in undergraduate degrees, except teaching or nursing, may qualify for life-experience credit. Many courses available evenings. Minimum of 48 credits required from WSU.

Wittenberg University   B

School of Continuing Education
P. O. Box 720
Springfield, OH 45501
Fields offered: Many fields
Year founded: 1845
Ownership: Nonprofit, church
Phone: (937) 327-6231 • (800) 677-7558
Fax: (937) 327-6340
E-mail: admission@wittenberg.edu
Website: www.wittenberg.edu

The degrees of B.A. in Liberal Studies and a B.A. degree completion program for registered nurses can be done entirely through evening study. Adults can also enroll in more than 30 day-degree programs. Credit is given for standard equivalency exams, and special exams will be devised in areas not covered by standard tests.

Woodbury University   B, M

7500 Glenoaks
Burbank, CA 91510-7846
Fields offered: Business fields
Year founded: 1884
Ownership: Nonprofit, independent
Phone: (818) 767-0888 • (800) 784-WOOD
Fax: (818) 504-9320
E-mail: admissions@uaxb.woodbury.edu
Website: www.woodbury.edu

This school offers a number of night and weekend programs in business-related fields. The weekend college awards degrees in accounting, business management, finance, human resources development, and marketing. The evening college's degrees are in accounting, business management, and computer information systems. There is also an evening M.B.A. for fully employed professionals.

Xavier University   B, M

Center for Adult and Part-time Students
Cincinnati, OH 45207
Fields offered: Various fields
Year founded: 1831
Ownership: Nonprofit, church
Phone: (513) 745-3355 • (800) 344-4698
Fax: (513) 745-1954
E-mail: xucaps@admin.xu.edu
Website: xavier.xu.edu:8000

Xavier offers a Bachelor of Liberal Arts, a Bachelor of Science in business administration, and other Bachelor's degrees in modern foreign languages, computer science, and communication arts, through weekend and evening study. Extremely low tuition is available for people over 60.

York University   B

4700 Keele Street
Toronto, Ontario M3J 1P3 Canada
Fields offered: Many fields
Year founded: 1959
Ownership: Nonprofit, public
Phone: (416) 736-5825
Fax: (416) 736-5941
E-mail: intlenq@yorku.ca
Website: www.yorku.ca

A full year of the Bachelor of Arts in a wide range of fields or the Bachelor of Administrative studies can be completed via distance learning, using both correspondence study and the Internet. The balance of the degree must be completed on campus.

21

Other Schools with Nonresidential Programs

One could get a first–class education from a shelf of books five feet long.

<small>CHARLES ELIOT, WHEN PRESIDENT OF HARVARD</small>

A ny school can claim that it is accredited; the use of that word is not regulated in any way. This chapter includes only those schools that are not accepted as "Accredited" under GAAP, Generally Accepted Accreditation Principles. In the U.S., there is near-unanimous agreement on GAAP by the relevant key decision-makers: university registrars and admissions officers, corporate human resource officers, and government agencies.

Note that in some countries, the word "accredited" is not used, although the evaluation process in that country (e.g., the British Royal Charter), is accepted as "accredited" under GAAP.

For a school to be considered "accredited," it must meet any one of the following six standards of GAAP. The schools in this chapter do not meet any of the standards. This does not necessarily mean they are bad, illegal, or fake. It simply means they would not be generally accepted as accredited.

GAAP CRITERIA

◆ Accredited by an accrediting agency recognized by the Council on Higher Education Accreditation in Washington.

◆ Accredited by an accrediting agency recognized by the U.S. Department of Education.

◆ Listed in the International Handbook of Universities (a UNESCO publication).

◆ Listed in the Commonwealth Universities Yearbook.

◆ Listed in the World Education Series, published by PIER (Projects in International Education Research), a joint venture of AACRAO (the American Association of Collegiate Registrars and Admissions Officers) and NAFSA (the Association of International Educators) with the participation of the College Board.

◆ Listed in the Countries Series, published by NOOSR, the National Office for Overseas Skills Recognition, in Australia.

To the best of our knowledge, none of the schools in this chapter meet any of the above six criteria.

The basic format of each listing is as follows:

Name of School   **A**ssociate's, **B**achelor's, **M**aster's, **D**octorate, **L**aw, **D**iploma
Address
City, State Postal Code Country, if not U.S.
Fields of study offered
Year founded
Ownership (nonprofit or proprietary, state, private, or church-run)
Phone • Toll-free phone
Fax
E-mail address
Website URL

Note: We have in the past given cost information, but this changes so quickly and is so subjective that we have decided to discontinue the practice. If a program is extremely inexpensive, or disproportionately expensive, we've mentioned this in the listing. In most cases, the best way to find out about the cost of any particular program is to contact the school directly.

Acton University   B, M, D, Law
350 Ward Ave., #106
Honolulu, HI 96814
Fields offered: Many fields
Year founded: 1997
Phone: (808) 263-8500 • (800) 356-6768
Fax: (800) 999-9704

Degrees at all levels in many fields, including law. Originally called Edison University, then Addison University. The address is a mailbox rental store. The catalog we received was postmarked Beaumont, Texas.

Adam Smith University　　B, M, D

1 Main Plaza, #538
2200 Main Street
Wailuku, HI 96793
Fields offered: Many fields
Year founded: 1991
Phone: (808) 242-1819 • (800) 732-3796
Fax: (500) 446-8771

Degrees at all levels in many fields. The address is a mailbox rental store.

Al-Manaf International Islamic University

See: American Coastline University

Alternative Medicines
Research Institute　　B, M, D

Suite 2-4995 James Walk
Vancouver, B.C. V5W 2K3 Canada
Fields offered: Alternative medicine
Phone: (604) 325-7948
Fax: (604) 325-7949

Awards degrees at all levels, as well as diplomas, to practitioners of holistic and alternative medicine, apparently based entirely on work experience and research.

American Coastline Christian University

See: American Coastline University

American Coastline University　　B, M, D

5000 W. Esplanade, #197
Metairie, LA 70006
Fields offered: Many fields
Year founded: 1976
Ownership: Nonprofit, church
E-mail: acuadmiss@aol.com
Website: www.amercoastuniv.edu

Degrees at all levels in many fields. There is also a religious school, American Coastline Christian University, licensed in Florida, and that school in turn has generated Al-Manaf International Islamic University, a department of the school that has no address or phone, but is intended to operate entirely over the Internet. The address is a mailbox rental store. ACU shares office space with Summit University.

American College of Metaphysical
Theology　　B, M, D

8014 Olson Memorial Highway, #210
Golden Valley, MN 55427
Fields offered: Metaphysics, divinity, biblical studies, theocentric business & ethics, comparative religion,

pastoral administration, religious counseling, and religious education
Phone: (612) 504-1391 • (800) 689-5102
Fax: (612) 525-1566
E-mail: jaywise@americancollege.com
Website: www.americancollege.com

Degrees at all levels in the fields listed above. It seems that no work is required, and degrees cost little more than $100.

American Global University　　B, M, D

2800 University Drive # 121
West Des Moines, IA 50266
Fields offered: Many fields
Phone: (515) 279-3958 • (800) 645-0382
Fax: (515) 255-8262
E-mail: Achieve@AmericanGlobalU.edu
Website: www.americanglobalu.edu

Degrees at all levels in many fields.

American Graduate University　　M

733 N. Dodsworth Ave.
Covina, CA 91724
Fields offered: Government contracting, acquisition management
Year founded: 1975
Ownership: Proprietary
Phone: (626) 966–4576
Fax: (626) 915-1709
E-mail: agu@starlink.net
Website: www.agu.edu

Master's degrees in government contracting and acquisition management. Accredited by the National Association of Private Nontraditional Schools and Colleges, a legitimate but unrecognized accreditor.

American Gulf Coast University　　M

758 Kapahulu Avenue, #277
Honolulu, HI 96816
Fields offered: Business administration
E-mail: a28851401@aol.com

M.B.A. through directed independent study. The address is a mailbox rental store.

American Institute for Computer
Sciences　　B, M

2101 Magnolia Ave., #200
Birmingham, AL 35205
Fields offered: Computer science
Year founded: 1989
Phone: (205) 323-6191 • (800) 729-2427
Fax: (205) 328-2229
E-mail: admiss@aics.com
Website: www.aics.edu

B.S. and M.S. in computer science, entirely through distance education. Same ownership as Chadwick University and several health and nutrition schools.

BEARS' GUIDE

American Institute of
Holistic Theology   B, M, D
5600 Market Street, #10
Youngstown, OH 44512-2619 USA
Fields offered: Divinity, metaphysics, naturology, parapsychic science, healtheology
Phone: • (800) 650-HEAL
Fax: (216) 629-2395
E-mail: info@aiht.
Website: www.aiht.edu
Degrees at all levels in the above-listed fields.

American International Open University
See: Clayton University

American International
University (AL)   B, M, D
415 Washington Avenue
Montgomery, AL 36104
Fields offered: Business fields
Phone: • (800) 680-7474
Fax: (404) 845-0098
Website: www.aiu.edu
Business degrees at all levels. Apparently no relationship to the defunct California degree mill or currently operating Hawaii school of the same name.

American International
University (HI)   B, M, D
1188 Bishop Street, #3101
Honolulu, HI 96813
Fields offered: Metaphysics, parapsychology, pastoral hypnotherapy, transpersonal psychology, pastoral counseling, holistic health sciences
Phone: (808) 524-5411/521-8541
Degrees at all levels in the above-listed fields. There is no connection with a diploma mill of this name which operated from California in the 1970s and early 1980s or, apparently, with the unaccredited school currently operating under the same name from Alabama.

American M & N University   B, M, D
112 North Chandler Avenue, #103
Monterey Park, CA 91754
Fields offered: Business, social work, psychology
Phone: (626) 458-4200 • (800) 680-2668
Fax: (626) 570-1554
E-mail: UNISERV@aol.com
Offers degrees at all levels in business, social work, and psychology. Also known as Concord University. The "official" Louisiana address we visited is a mailbox rental store.

American State University   B, M, D
7 Waterfront Plaza, #400
500 Ala Moana Boulevard
Honolulu, HI 96813

Fields offered: Many fields
Year founded: 1995
Phone: • (888) 528-8550
Fax: (888) 922-0927
E-mail: drmarn@amstu.edu
Website: www.amstu.edu
This school offers degrees at all levels in many fields. Also known as Higher Education Research Institute. The address is a mail forwarding service. Sued by the State of Hawaii in 1997, for violation of the laws requiring disclosure of unaccredited status. In August 1998, the *New York Times* reported that they were closing down.

American University in London   B, M, D
97-101 Seven Sisters Road
London, N7 7QP England
Fields offered: Liberal arts, business, engineering
Year founded: 1984
Ownership: Nonprofit, independent
Phone: (44-171) 263-2986
Fax: (44-171) 281-2815
E-mail: aul@ukbusiness.com
Originally established as the London College of Science and Technology in 1984. Name changed to "American University of London" in 1986 and to "American University in London" in 1994. Degrees at all levels in a range of fields.

American University of Hawaii   B, M, D
33 North Market Street
Wailuku, HI 96793
Fields offered: Many fields
Year founded: 1994
Phone: (808) 534-0816
Fax: (808) 534-0917
E-mail: info@auh.edu
Website: www.auh.edu
Accredited by the National Association of Private Nontraditional Schools and Colleges (legitimate but unrecognized). Degrees at all levels in a broad range of fields.

American World University   B, M, D
312 E. College St., #205
Iowa City, IA 52240
Fields offered: Many fields
Ownership: Nonprofit
Phone: (319) 356-6620
Fax: (319) 354-6335
Degrees at all levels in many fields. The address is a secretarial service. President Dr. Maxine Asher assures us there is a campus in Iowa City, but declines to reveal its location.

Athena University   M
Virtual Online University
601 W. Nifong Blvd., #5a
Columbia, MO 65203
Fields offered: Many fields
Year founded: 1995

Phone: (573) 874-4107
Fax: (573) 442-0699
E-mail: cipher@vousi.com
Website: www.athena.edu

This school is administered by an organization called Virtual Online University and, through this organization, offers an online M.B.A.

Barrington College

See: Barrington University

Barrington University   B, M, D

Admissions Office, #10
7177 Hickman Road
Des Moines, IA 50322
Fields offered: Business administration, naturopathy
Year founded: 1993
Phone: (515) 253-0490 • (800) 533-3378
Fax: (515) 276-4847
E-mail: barrington@barrington.edu
Website: www.barrington.edu

Originally Barrington College, they offer degrees at all levels in business administration and naturopathy. The address is a secretarial service.

Belize Institute of Technology   B

P.O. Box 741
38 St. Thomas Street
Belize City, Belize
Fields offered: Business, computer science, electronics, engineering, hospitality
Year founded: 1995
Ownership: Nonprofit
Phone: (501) 2-35744
Fax: (501) 2-45768
E-mail: Bit@Btl.Net
Website: www.clarence.com/home/bit/

Independent-study programs leading to certificates, Associate's, and Bachelor's degrees in business, computer science, electronics, engineering, and hospitality.

Bernadean University   D, Law

21757 Devonshire, #16
Chatsworth, CA 91311
Fields offered: Many fields
Ownership: Nonprofit, church
Phone: (818) 718-2447 • (800) 542-3792
E-mail: blvdmaster@venturablvd.com
Website: www.venturablvd.com/woodland_hills/ WHL45396.html

A division of the Church of Universology, they have offered correspondence degrees in everything from theology to astronutrition to law. They used to offer their graduates a certificate absolving them of all their sins.

Bienville University   B, M, D

778 Chevelle Drive
Baton Rouge, LA 70806
Fields offered: Busines administration, health administration, sports management
Year founded: 1998
Phone: (504) 201-0111 • (800) 473-1530
Fax: (504) 201-0222
E-mail: rcscarr@i-55.com
Website: ww.bienville.edu

Degrees at all levels in the above fields.

Brighton University   B, M, D

1164 Bishop St., #124
Honolulu, HI 96813 USA
Fields offered: Many fields
Year founded: 1991
Ownership: Nonprofit, church
Phone: (808) 531-7075

Degrees in many fields by independent study. This address is a mailbox rental store.

California Coast University   B, M, D

700 N. Main St.
Santa Ana , CA 92701
Fields offered: Engineering, education, behavioral science, business, health care administration
Year founded: 1974
Ownership: Proprietary
Phone: (714) 547-9625 • (800) 854-8768
E-mail: ccu@deltanet.com
Website: www.calcoastuniv.edu/ccu

Degrees are offered at all levels in education, behavioral science, and business. California Coast is approved by the state of California. Former name: California Western University.

California Graduate Institute   B, M, D

1100 Glendon Ave., #1119
Los Angeles, CA 90024
Fields offered: Psychology, psychotherapy, marriage & family therapy
Year founded: 1968
Ownership: Nonprofit, independent
Phone: (310) 208-4240
Fax: (310) 208-0684
E-mail: cgi@ix.netcom.com
Website: www.cgi.edu

Degrees at all levels in psychological fields. Graduates are eligible to take California licensing exams.

California Pacific University   B, M, D

10650 Treena St., # 203
San Diego, CA 92131
Fields offered: Business, management, human behavior
Year founded: 1976
Ownership: Proprietary

Phone: (619) 695-3292 • (800) 458-9667
Fax: (619) 695-3712
E-mail: info@cpu.edu
Website: www.cpu.edu

Bachelor's, Master's, and Doctorate in business administration, M.B.A. with a focus in healthcare management, and M.A. in management and healthcare administration. Approved by the state of California.

California Western University

See: California Coast University

Cambridge State University   B, M, D

855 Pierremont
Shreveport, LA 71106
Phone: (318) 219-0207
Fax: (318) 219-0272

The "campus" is a Mailboxes, Etc. mailbox rental store in a strip mall.

Canadian School of Management   B, M

Herbert House
335 Bay Street
#1120
Toronto, ON M5H 2R3 Canada
Fields offered: Business, management
Year founded: 1976
Ownership: Nonprofit, independent
Phone: (416) 360-3805
Fax: (416) 360-6863
E-mail: csm@c-s-m.org
Website: www.c-s-m.org

Offers nonresident programs in business and management fields. Formerly accredited by the Distance Education and Training Council.

Castlebridge University   B, M, D

Information Services
2301 Kuhio Avenue
#223-113
Honolulu, Hawaii, 96815
Fields offered: Many fields
Phone: (888) 213-1883
Website: www.castlebridgeu.org

Degrees at all levels available in a number of fields, basically centered around the humanitites, from psychology to education to Celtic studies.

Century University   B, M, D

6400 Uptown Blvd NE
#398-W
Albuquerque, NM 87110
Fields offered: Many fields
Year founded: 1978
Ownership: Proprietary
Phone: (505) 889-2711 • (800) 240-6757
Fax: (505) 889-2750
E-mail: centuryu@nm.net
Website: www.centuryuniversity.edu

Degrees at all levels in many fields, generally geared to working professional administrators. Formerly located in California.

Chadwick University   B, M

2112 11th Avenue South
#504
Birmingham, AL 35205-2847
Fields offered: Many fields
Year founded: 1989
Ownership: Proprietary
Phone: (205) 252-4483 • (800) 767-2423
Fax: (205) 252-4480
E-mail: inform@chadwick.edu
Website: www.chadwick.edu

Bachelor's and Master's degrees in many fields. Same ownership as American Institute of Computer Science and two health and nutrition schools.

City Business College

See: International University (Missouri)

City University Los Angeles   B, M, D, Law

P.O. Box 4277
Inglewood, CA 90309-4277
Fields offered: Business, education, humanities, nursing, environmental sciences, law
Year founded: 1974
Ownership: Nonprofit, independent
Phone: (310) 671-0783 • (800) 262-8388 (outside CA)
Fax: (310) 671-0572
E-mail: info@cula.edu
Website: www.cula.edu

Degrees at all levels in the above-listed fields. Not California-approved, but operating under what they call the "right of eminent domain."

Clayton College of Natural Health   **B, M, D**

2140 11th Ave. South, #305
Birmingham, AL 35205
Fields offered: Holistic nutrition, alternative health
Year founded: 1980
Ownership: Proprietary
Phone: (205) 323-8242 • (800) 659-8274
Fax: (205) 323-8232
E-mail: inform@ccnh.edu
Website: www.ccnh.edu
Degrees at all levels.

Colgate University

See Columbus University

College of Security, Technology, and Management   **B, M, D**

128000 South 71 Hwy.
Grandview, MO 64030
Fields offered: Law enforcement, criminal justice
Year founded: 1973
Ownership: Nonprofit, church
Phone: (816) 765-5551 • (888) 567-6621
Fax: (816) 765-1777
E-mail: cstm@qni.com
Website: www.marketlynx.com/cstm
Degrees at all levels in the fields of executive security, law enforcement, and criminal justice.

Columbia Pacific University   **B, M, D**

2105 Digital Drive
Novato, CA 94949
Fields offered: Management, health and human services, arts & sciences
Year founded: 1978
Ownership: Proprietary
Phone: (415) 883-1400 • (800) 552-5522
Fax: (205) 323-8232
E-mail: CPUnvr@aol.com
Website: www.itstime.com/cpu/default.htm
For many years, Columbia Pacific operated from its own building in San Rafael, and was approved by the state to offer degrees at all levels. In 1995, CPU's reapproval was denied. They appealed the decision and continued to operate. When the appeal was denied, the state ordered them closed, but they continued to operate. In late 1997, the state sued to shut the school down. At the trial in February 1998, the judge soundly criticized the state's lawyer and dismissed the case. The state has said it will appeal. The president of CPU writes us (March 1998) that CPU "continues to be fully approved in California. Even if the California oversight authorities weren't in total chaos, CPU would be fully legal and approved and all that." The state Bureau of Private Postsecondary and Vocational Education told us (April 1998) that CPU is "most emphatically not approved."

In July 1998, CPU announced that they are now fully accredited by the Paiute-Shoshone Indian Tribe of Fallon, Nevada.

Columbia Southern University   **B, M, D**

P. O. Box 3110
Orange Beach, AL 36561
Fields offered: Occupational safety & health, environmental engineering, business administration, criminal justice, computer science
Year founded: 1993
Phone: (334) 981-3771 • (800) 977-8449
Fax: (334) 981-3815
E-mail: csu@colsouth.edu
Website: www.colsouth.edu
Degrees at all levels in the above fields, as well as certificates of compliance in the area of environmental compliance management. Formerly the University of Environmental Sciences

Columbus University   **B, M, D**

P.O. Box 7278
Molario, LA 70010-7278
Fields offered: Many fields
Year founded: 1997
Phone: (504) 486-2101
Fax: (504) 483-3265
"Colgate University" advertised in the *Chronicle of Higher Education*, looking for adjunct faculty for its distance-learning programs. After the real Colgate in New York squawked, the name was changed to Columbus. Offers degrees at all levels with, apparently, very little study. We have asked the campus' location, but received no reply.

Commonwealth Open University   **B, M, D**

Palm Chambers,
P. O. Box 119
Road Town, Tortola, British Virgin Islands
Fields offered: Many fields
E-mail: commopu@webdb.com
Website: www.commonwealth.org
Degrees at all levels in many fields through self-paced courses of study. The university is operated from Spain.

Concord University

See: American M & N University

Cook's Institute of Electronics Engineering   **B, M**

1351 Cypress Drive
Jackson, MS 39212
Fields offered: Electronics engineering
Year founded: 1945
Ownership: Proprietary
Phone: (601) 371-1351
Fax: (601) 371-2619
Bachelor's and Master's degrees in computer science and electronics as well.

Bachelor's and Master's degrees in computer science and electronics as well.

Cornwall Independent University

15 Seton Gardens, Treswithian
Camborne, Cornwall TR14 7JS UK

Offers a "non-profession honorary degree classical style," in any subject, although there is apparently a particular focus on nonacademic new age-type fields of interest.

Dominion University of Melchizidek   B, M, D

3750A Airport Road
Mobile, AL 36608
Fields offered: Many fields
E-mail: unserv@aol.com
Website:
www.InfoTechservices.com/DOM/Domuniv.htmor

Degrees at all levels in many fields. "Melchizidek" is, according to The Economist and the Washington Post, a nonexistent country that maintains a one-man embassy in Washington.

EarthNet Institute   B, M

Drawer 10
Cotter, AR 72626
Fields offered: Political science, agriculture, environmental science, health & welfare, global economics, education.
Phone: (870) 425-2757
Fax: (870) 425-6257
E-mail: wolford@eni.edu

Bachelor's and Master's degrees in a number of fields from an institution dedicated to making the world a better place.

Eastern Caribbean University   M, D

503 Hudgins
Basseterre, St. Kitts
Fields offered: Business, education
Year founded: 1997
Phone: (512) 237-2042
Fax: (512) 237-2042
E-mail: info@ecaribbeanu.com

Offering Master's degrees and Doctorates in the fields of business and education, with a number of concentrations. The phones are in Smithville, Texas. The quite elaborate website disappeared without explanation in early 1998.

Eastern Nebraska Christian College

See: Saint John's University of Practical Theology

Eastern University   B, M, D

2535 Wyoming NE, Suite B
Albuquerque, NM 87112
Fields offered: Many fields
Year founded: 1993

Ownership: Private, independent
Phone: (505) 294-2772 • (800) 801-5980
Fax: (505) 294-2772
E-mail: eastuniv@usa.net
Website: shell.rmi.net/~imall/

Degrees at all levels in arts & sciences, business administration, education, human resources, and management, as well as a self-designed program in which students can create their own program.

Emerson College of Herbology   M

582 Cummer Ave.
Willowdale, ON M2K 2M4 Canada
Fields offered: Herbology
Phone: (416) 485-4822
Fax: (905) 303-8724

Master of Herbology through correspondence study.

Eurotechnical Research University   B, M, D

P.O. Box 516
Hilo, HI 96721
Fields offered: Science, engineering, karate
Year founded: 1983
Ownership: Proprietary

Degrees at all levels in science, engineering, and karate. The street address provided is a mailbox rental service.

Evangel Christian University of America

909 N. 18th Street, #123
Monroe, LA 71201
Fields offered: Religious fields
Phone: (318) 343-9006 • (800) 346-4014
Fax: (318) 345-0350
E-mail: info@ecua.edu
Website: www.ecua.edu

Apparently offers degrees in religious fields; we have written for more information.

Fairfax University   B, M, D

P. O. Box 400
Peterborough PE2 6GD, England
Fields offered: Many fields
Year founded: 1986
Ownership: Nonprofit, independent
Phone: +44 1733 239923
Fax: (504) 298-1303
Website: www.btinternet.com/~fairfaxuniversity.ees/INDEX.htm

Degrees at all levels in many fields. Degree-granting authority comes from Louisiana, where the address is a secretarial service.

Faith Bible College   B

4501 Shed Road
Bossier City, LA 71111
Fields offered: Bible studies/theology, religious education

Year founded: 1976
Phone: (318) 746-8400
Fax: (318) 747-9634
E-mail: info@ici.edu
B.A. may be earned entirely by independent study. Joint degree offered with ICI University in Dallas, which is accredited by the Distance Education and Training Council. The joint degree is more expensive, but is accredited.

Farelston College
See: Farelston & Nova Colleges

Farelston & Nova Colleges   B, M, D
P. O. Box 67004
Northland Village
Calgary, AB T2L 2L2 Canada
Fields offered: Any field
Year founded: 1977
Ownership: Nonprofit, independent
Phone: No listed phone
Originally Nova College. Degrees at all levels in any field. Not to be confused with the accredited Nova Southeastern University (which actually had a component called Nova College).

Feather River University   B
P.O. Box 1900
Paradise, CA 95969
Fields offered: Martial arts
Year founded: 1984
Ownership: Nonprofit
Phone: (530) 872-4404 • (800) 442-9799
E-mail: info@frcc.cc.ca.us
Website: www.frcc.cc.ca.us/
Feather River's program allows recognized martial arts practitioners to combine their verifiable martial arts training with previously earned college or university credit, toward a conventional university degree.

Foundation for Economic Education   M
30 South Broadway
Irvington-on-Hudson, NY 10533
Fields offered: Economic theory, business
Phone: (914) 591-7230 • (800) 452-3518
Fax: (914) 591-8910
E-mail: freeman@westnet.com
Website: www.fee.org/
The Foundation does not issue its own degrees, but students who complete the coursework for the M.A. economic theory or history or for an M.B.A. receive the degree from American Commonwealth University.

Frederick W. Taylor University   B, M
346 Rheem Blvd., #203
Moraga, CA 94556
Fields offered: Management, business administration
Phone: (510) 376-0900 • (800) 988-4MBA

Fax: (510) 376-0908
E-mail: taylormba@igc.apc.org
or admissions@ftu.edu
Website: www.ftu.edu/
Degrees offered are a B.S. in management, a B.B.A., and an M.B.A. The programs are approved by the state of California.

Freie und Private Universität Sersi   M, D
Degersheimerstrasse 29
Herisau AR, 9102, Switzerland
Fields offered: Industrial sciences
Phone: (41-71) 352-3525
Fax: (41-71) 352-2560
Graduate degrees in the industrial sciences. The school also uses the English (Private and Independent University), French (Université Libre et Privé), and Italian (Universita Libera e Privata) versions of their name.

George Washington University, Inc.   B, M, D
4995 James Walk, #2
Vancouver, BC V5W 2K3 Canada
Year founded: 1998
Phone: (604) 325-7948
Fax: (604) 325-7949
Degrees at all levels with little or no coursework. Operated by the owner of the Alternative Medicine Research Institute. No connection with the accredited George Washington in DC.

Golden State University
See: Honolulu University of Arts, Sciences, and Humanities. No connection to the diploma mill of the same name.

Greenwich University   B, M, D, Law
103 Kapiolani
P.O. Box 1717
Hilo, HI 96720
Fields offered: Many fields
Year founded: 1972
Phone: (808) 935-9934 • (800) FOR-HILO
Fax: (808) 969-7469
E-mail: grnichu@aloha.net
Website: www.aloha.net/~grnichu
Degrees at all levels in many fields, including non-bar-qualifying law. Greenwich evolved from the International Institute for Advanced Studies (established in St. Louis in 1972, and which still exists as a part of Greenwich).

Harmony College of Applied Science
See: Harmony of Life Fellowship, Inc.

Harmony of Life Fellowship, Inc.   B, M, D
1434 Fremont Ave.
Los Altos, CA 94022

Fields offered: Spiritual science, spiritual healing (which includes spiritual healing, magnetic healing, mind healing, and divine healing), philosophy, psychology, natural healing
Year founded: 1976
Phone: (650) 967-1232
Fax: (650) 961-0777

Degrees at all levels in the above fields. Formerly called Harmony College of Applied Science.

Hawthorne University (Utah)

Founder and Chancellor Alfred Munzert (who lists his doctorate as coming from the "Brantwood Forest School," which we have never been able to locate, threatened with vigor to sue us into oblivion if we said anything whatsoever about his school. Good enough.

Heed University   B, M, D, Law

Alumni and Information Center, P.O. Box 311
Hollywood, FL 33022
Fields offered: Psychology, philosophy, education, business administration, law
Year founded: 1970
Ownership: Nonprofit, independent
Phone: (954) 925-1600

B.A., B.S., M.A., M.S., M.B.A., Ph.D., Ed.D., D.B.A., Doctor of Arts, Doctor of Psychology, and Doctor of Juridical Science (S.J.D.) all entirely through correspondence. Heed also operates Thomas Jefferson College of Law in California, which is recognized by the Committee of Bar Examiners, and awards law degrees through correspondence study, including a four-year J.D., graduates of which may take the California bar.

Honolulu University of Arts, Sciences, and Humanities   B, M, D

500 Ala Moana Blvd., #7-400
Honolulu, HI 96813-4920
Fields offered: Many fields
Year founded: 1978
Ownership: Independent
Phone: (808) 955-7333
Fax: (808) 946-3534
E-mail: honouniv@lava.net
Website: honoluluuniversity.com

Degrees at all levels in many fields. Formerly Golden State University, which operated from four cities in California.

Horizons University   M, D

242 Boulevard Voltaire
75011 Paris, France
Fields offered: Many fields
Year founded: 1991
E-mail: roberta@club-internet.fr
Website: www.h-university.com

Graduate degrees in self-designed fields through distance learning, with optional residential seminars.

Institute for Transpersonal Psychology   M

744 San Antonio Road
Palo Alto, CA 94393
Fields offered: Transpersonal psychology
Phone: (650)493- 4430
Fax: (650)493- 6835
E-mail: itpinfo@best.com
Website: www.tmn.com/itp/Global.html

Master of Arts in transpersonal studies or Master of Transpersonal Psychology offered through their Global Program in online format. Global Master's degree programs are not designed to meet any state licensing requirements for counselors, although the school is approved to operate in the state of California.

Institute of Professional Financial Managers   M, D

16/22 Great Russell St.
London WC1B 3TD, UK
Fields offered: Business adminstration
Year founded: 1992
Phone: (44-171) 580-9407
Fax: (44-171) 323-1766

A self-paced MBA and doctoral program. Claims an association with the Irish Business School in Dublin (we could find no evidence of such a school in Ireland). Jeff Wooller College operates from the same two-room office.

Intercultural Open University   B, M, D

Yn'e Bosk House
De Hoarnen 5
9218 XC Opeinde, Netherlands
Fields offered: Many fields
Phone: (31-512) 372-297
Fax: (31-512) 372-703
E-mail: iouedu@noord.bart.nl
Website: www.noord.bart.nl/~iouedu/IOU.html

Degrees are offered in a wide range of fields, and offices or affiliated schools are listed for many countries.

International College of Higher Education   M

28 Saint James Street
South Petherton
Somerset, TA13 5BW U.K.
Fields offered: Business management
Phone: (011-44) 1460-242-756
Fax: (011-44) 1460-242-757
E-mail: email.intcol@ukonline.co.uk

Apparently operated by the same folks as Somerset University, this school offers an M.B.A.

International Institute for Advanced Studies

See: Greenwich University

International Institute of Theology

See: Westbrook University

International University (Missouri)　　　　B, M, D

1301 S. Noland Rd.
Independence, MO 64055
Fields offered: Many fields
Year founded: 1973
Ownership: Nonprofit, independent
Phone: (816) 461-3633

Degrees at all levels offered through correspondence study. There has in the past been some affiliation with the Sussex College of Technology, which has been identified as a degree mill by major British newspapers and educational authorities. Apparently also some affiliation with the American University in London and with the London Institute of Technology and Research.

International University for Nutrition Education　　　　B, M, D

1161 A Bay Blvd.
Chula Vista, CA 92011
Fields offered: Holistic nutrition
Year founded: 1978
Ownership: Nonprofit, independent
Phone: (619) 424-7590
Fax: (619) 424-7593

Degrees at all levels. The university is was once authorized to grant degrees by the state of California, but is not currently on the list of state approved schools. Formerly Donsbach University, of Huntington Beach and Concord, California.

International University of Professional Studies　　　　B, M, D

P.O. Box 236
Makawao, Maui, HI 96768
Fields offered: Psychology, health, education, expressive arts therapy, transformational psychology, health & wellness services, consciousness studies, transformational education, human resources development
Year founded: 1988
Phone: (808) 877-7722 • (800) 806-0317
Fax: (800) 806-0317 (press *51 and start)
E-mail: iups@healthy.net
Website: www.healthy.net

Degrees at all levels in the above-mentioned fields. Original name: Pacific University of Hawaii.

Irish Business School

See: Institute of Professional Financial Managers

Jeff Wooller College

See: Institute of Professional Financial Managers

Kennedy Western University　　　　B, M, D

200 West 17th Street
Cheyenne, WY 82001-4412
Fields offered: Business administration and management, criminal justice, education, engineering, MIS, psychology, environmental safety, and computer science
Year founded: 1984
Ownership: Proprietary
Phone: (307) 635-6709 • (800) 635-2900
Fax: (307) 635-7363
E-mail: admissions@kw.edu
Website: www.kw.edu

Degrees at all levels in the above-listed fields. Run from California. People living in California cannot enroll. There was an address in Honolulu and Boise, and now Wyoming (from which the degree-granting authority derives).

Kensington International University　　　　B, M, D

25 Kanehoe Bay Drive, 106-239
Kailua, HI 96734
Fields offered: Administration of justice, business administration, education, computer science, engineering (civil, electrical, mechanical), environmental studies, professional studies (psychology, sociology, political science)
Year founded: 1990
Ownership: Proprietary
Phone: (808) 245-5589 • (800) 423-2495
Fax: (818) 240-1707
E-mail: Kensington@earthlink.net
Website: www.kensington.edu

Kensington University had been a California-approved school, but their reapproval was denied in 1995, leading to the establishment of this institution, using a business service address in Hawaii; the school is still run from southern California, offering degrees at all levels by independent study.

Kensington University

See Kensington International University

Kent College

See: La Salle University

Knightsbridge University　　　　B, M, D

1 Palk Street
Torquay, Devon TQ2 5EL England
Fields offered: Almost any field
Phone: (44-803) 201-830
Fax: (44-803) 201-831
Website: www.knightsbridge-university.co.uk

Degrees at all levels in virtually any field through a range of distance learning methods.

Koh-I-Noor University

See: University of Santa Monica

Lael University
B, M, D

3721 St. Bridget
St. Louis, MO 63074
Fields offered: Behavioral studies, social services, ministry
Year founded: 1979
Phone: (314) 426-7000 • (800) 321-LAEL

Evangelical Christian school offers nonresident (residential study is also available) degrees at all levels in the above fields; the 1997 catalog states "LAEL teaches that psychology knows all the problems, Jesus Christ knows all the answers."

La Salle University
B, M, D

(1997 onward)
P.O. Box 4000
Mandeville, LA 70470-4000
Fields offered: Many fields
Year founded: 1997
Ownership: Nonprofit
Phone: (504) 626-3500 • (800) 323-9266
Website: www.distance.edu

Note: for La Salle University prior to mid-1997, see the listing in chapter 27. The following listing pertains to La Salle University from mid-1997 onwards.

La Salle University has been operated since mid 1997 by the La Salle Education Corporation, a new Louisiana corporation run by a five-member Board of Trustees, all of them prominent and politically active Louisiana citizens. It is a non-profit educational foundation. The President of La Salle, professional educator, Dr. John M. Scarpitti, was formerly vice president and treasurer of the regionally-accredited University of Findlay in Ohio. La Salle offers Bachelor's, Master's, and Doctorate degrees entirely by distance learning, in a wide variety of subjects. John Bear was invited to visit the new La Salle in November 1997, for some open and cordial meetings, and a tour of the four large buildings from which the university operates. La Salle is going through the accreditation process of a legitimate but unrecognized accrediting agency.

Lincoln University of the U.S.A.
M

7177 Hickman Road, #10
Des Moines, IA 50322
Fields offered: Business administration
Year founded: 1997
Phone: • (800) 604-6805
Fax: (800) 748-0709 or (512) 270-2192
E-mail: LincolnMBA@aol.com
Website: www.lincolnmba.com

The address is a secretarial service, the same as Barrington University, but there is apparently no connection; offers an M.B.A.

LMII Institution
B, M, D

Wisma Benhill
3rd Floor, #303
406 Jalan Sudirman Kav. 36
Jakarta, 10210 Indonesia
Ownership: Nonprofit, independent
Phone: (001-6221) 570-4278
Fax: (001-6222) 438-254
Website: www.indo.net.id/lmii/htdocs/mba.html

Operates in a partnership with the unaccredited Kennedy-Western University; diplomas are apparently issued from Kennedy-Western rather than LMII.

Los Angeles University
M, D

6862 Vanscoy Ave.
North Hollywood, CA 91605
Year founded: 1964
Ownership: Nonprofit, independent

Director Brimm has asked that we say nothing about his university. Since we know nothing about, other than that it is unaccredited and the address is an unmarked home in a residential neighborhood, there is nothing we can say.

Louisiana Capital University

1923 Roosevelt Ave.
Kenner, LA 70062

Has not responded to several requests for information about their nontraditional programs.

Magellan University
B

6303 E. Tanque Verde, #300
Tucson, AZ 85715
Fields offered: Liberal arts
Year founded: 1996
Phone: (520) 299-3811 • (800) 4wwwedu
Fax: (520) 299-3912
E-mail: response@magellan.edu
Website: www.magellan.edu

Planning Bachelor's degrees in business, management and communication, and history and culture, and Master's degrees in management and quality control.

Maimonides University
B, M, D

16666 NE 19th Avenue, #102
North Miami Beach, FL 33162
Fields offered: Pychology, theology, counseling
Year founded: 1989
Phone: (305) 949-1103
Fax: (954) 725-8414
E-mail: info@maimonidesuniversity.com
Website: maimonidesuniversity.com

Degrees at all levels in the above fields.

Marlborough University
B, M, D

23/1 Caro Mio
GY9 0SE Guernsey, Channel Islands U.K.

Fields offered: Many fields
Phone: (44-1481) 832-515
Fax: (44-1481) 832-515
Degrees at all levels in many fields.

MBA University
See: Rushmore University

Mellen University   B, M, D
Box 450
Lewiston, NY 14092
Year founded: 1993
Ownership: Proprietary
Phone: • (800) 635-5368

Degrees at all levels in a number of fields; for more information on this school's background, you may wish to read what Lingua Franca magazine had to say about them (available for $6 from Lingua Franca, 22 West 38th Street, 4th floor, New York, NY 10018, 212 / 302-0336, ext. 223, subscriptions@linguafranca). Mellen sued Lingua Franca over this article, and lost.

Mesmer Institute
See: University of God's Logos System

Miami Christian University   B
9775 S.W. 87th Avenue
Miami, FL 33176-2900
Fields offered: Theological field
Phone: (305) 595-5315
Fax: (305) 596-4564
E-mail: greene@mcu.edu
Website: mcu.edu

M.C.U, operated by the Jesus Fellowship of Miami, offers courses and degrees in theological fields over the Internet, through a program of mentored study.

Midwestern University
See: Saint John's University of Practical Theology

Mirus University   M
7405 Alban Station Court, #A106
Springfield, VA 22150-2318
Fields offered: Liberal studies
Year founded: 1995
Phone: (703) 912-6404 • (800) 562-4835
Fax: (703) 912-7756
E-mail: cosgb@erols.com

Mirus is a division of an organization called The Teaching Company, which produces a series of audio- and videotapes billed as "Greatest Lectures by America's SuperStar Teachers." Additional written courseware is developed by "contact faculty" who interact with students via phone, e-mail, and post. The program consists of three required core modules of three courses each, in literature, western civilization, and philosophy. Students then select a concentration in one of these three areas, or in religion, music,

or fine arts, and take three electives, to complete the 36-credit-hour, non-thesis program. Every course requires a proctored essay-type final exam. Students can transfer in 9 elective credits, 3 of which may be from life-experience learning. Mirus is in the process of accreditation with DETC.

Monticello University   B, M, D, Law
8600 West 110th Street, #205
Overland Park, KS 66210
Fields offered: Business, law, liberal arts
Year founded: 1997
Phone: (913) 661-0094 • (800) 405-7935
Fax: (913) 661-9414
E-mail: admin@monticello.edu
Website: www.monticello.edu/

Degrees at all levels in business, law, and liberal arts. Formerly known as Thomas Jefferson University. The Kansas address is an insurance agency; the Canadian address is a post office.

Nasson University
1201 Mont Limar Drive #500
Mobile, AL 36609
Year founded: 1997
Phone: (500) 346-6500
Fax: (500) 445-3500
E-mail: dean@nassonu.edu
Website: www.nassonu.edu

The address is that of the A-Plus Communications Center. Mattar purchased some of the assets of the defunct Nasson College once located in Maine, and is now offering degrees at all levels in many fields. Mail we have received is postmarked Rhode Island.

National College of Complimentary Medicine and Sciences   B, M, D
1025 Connecticut Avenue NW, #1012
Washington, DC 20036
Fields offered: Medical and scientific fields
Year founded: 1990
Phone: (202) 857-9727
Fax: (202) 635-7554
E-mail: nccmedsci@aol.com
Website: members.aol.com/nccmedsci/

Degrees in seven "interdisciplinary mission fields of study": nursing, medical/scientific letters, ND vitalogic occupations, intrinsic naturopathy, medical & scientific stewardship, social & community health, and mission services.

Newport University   B, M, D, Law
20101 S.W. Birch Street, #120
Newport Beach, CA 92660-1749
Fields offered: Business, education, psychology, human behavior, law, engineering, religion
Year founded: 1976

Ownership: Proprietary
Phone: (949) 631-1155 • (800) 345-3272
Fax: (949) 631-0555
E-mail: info@newport.edu
Website: www.newport.edu

Degrees at all levels in many fields. Originally known as Newport International University. In 1997 some assets of Newport were sold, and renamed as Westport University, operating from Utah (apparently now in association with the unaccredited Hawthorne University), while other aspects continue to operate as Newport.

North American University   B, M, D

13402 N. Scottsdale Road, B-150
Scottsdale, AZ 85254-4056
Fields offered: Religious and health-related fields
Year founded: 1992
Phone: (602) 948-5100 • (800) 398-8484
Fax: (602) 948-8150

N.A.U. offers degrees at all levels in health and religious fields. Credit for life experience and equivalency exams. Its College of Wellness Science has absorbed some of the programs offered by the now defunct American College of Nutripathy. Apparently no connection with a diploma mill of the same name which operated from Arizona and Florida in the 1980s, or another diploma mills of this name which operated from Utah and Hawaii in the 1990s.

North Central University

See: Southern California University for Professional Studies

Northland Open University   B, M

204 Lambert St., Financial Plaza, #200
Whitehorse, Yukon Y1A 3T2 Canada
Fields offered: Arts, commerce, business administration
Year founded: 1976
Ownership: Nonprofit, independent
Phone: • (800) 263-1619

There has been an affiliation with the Canadian School of Management. Despite the address, the school is apparently run from Toronto.

Nova College

See: Farelston & Nova Colleges

Occidental University of Saint Louis

See: Greenwich University

Open University (Florida)   M

255 S. Orange Avenue
P.O. Box 4916
Orlando, FL 32802
Fields offered: Entrepreneurship
Year founded: 1987
Phone: (407) 649-8488 • (800) 874-0388
Fax: (407) 649-1903

E-mail: info@openu.edu
Website: www.openu.com

A Master's degree in entrepreneurship.

Open University of America   B, M, D

3916 Commander Dr.
Hyattsville, MD 20782
Fields offered: Many fields
Year founded: 1968
Ownership: Nonprofit, independent
Phone: (301) 779-0220

Grants degrees entirely on the basis of prior achievements. When we visited, we found the university in the basement of Chancellor Rodgers' home.

Oxford Open MBA Office

66 Banbury Road
Oxford, OX2 6PR UK

All we know about this school is that it exists and, assumedly, offers open-learning M.B.A.'s. It is not listed in the *Inter-national Handbook of Universities,* and we have written for more information.

Pacific Southern University   B, M, D

9581 W. Pico Blvd.
Los Angeles, CA 90035-1248
Fields offered: Business, management science, social science, engineering, education
Year founded: 1978
Ownership: Proprietary
Phone: (310) 551-0304
Fax: (310) 277-5280

Degrees at all levels by directed nonresident independent study in business, management science, social science, engineering, and education. Approved to grant degrees by the state of California.

Pacific University of Hawaii

Original name of the International University of Professional Studies

Pacific Western University (California)   B, M, D

600 North Sepulveda Boulevard
Los Angeles, CA 90049
Fields offered: Business administration, public administration, management
Year founded: 1977
Ownership: Proprietary
Phone: (310) 471-0306 • (800) 423-3244
Fax: (310) 471-0306
E-mail: Admissions@pwu.com
Website: www.pwu-ca.edu

B.S. in business administration or public administration, an M.B.A., an M.S. in management, and a Ph.D. in business administration. Coursework can be completed through mail, e-mail, or Internet. Same ownership as Pacific Western University (Hawaii), which is run from the same building.

Pacific Western University (Hawaii)   **B, M, D**
1210 Auahi Street
Honolulu, HI 96814-4922
Fields offered: Business, management, science, engineering, social science, education, and the helping professions
Year founded: 1977
Ownership: Proprietary
Phone: (808) 597-1909 • (800) 423-3244
Fax: (310) 587-8603
E-mail: Admissions@pwu.com
Website: www.pwu.com

The school's literature states that "all degree programs are primarily based on what the student has already learned. If the student is worthy, competent, and eminently qualified, the University will confer the appropriate degree."

Permaculture Academy   **Dip, B**
P.O. Box 1
Tyalgum, N.S.W. 2484 Australia
Fields offered: Education, media, community services, finance & business, technical & resource development, architecture & building, research, site design & development.

Courses can be convened anywhere a teacher (approved by the Academy) and a group of 15 or more students can be assembled. The programs are all based on the concept of permaculture, a human-centered ecological philosophy that seeks sustainable farming methods, community building, conservation, and other worthwhile things. Some Americans are currently trying to develop a similar institution here, perhaps in New Mexico. Stay tuned.

Pickering University   **B, M, D**
1155 Fort St. Mall
Honolulu, HI 96813
Fields offered: Many fields
Year founded: 1994
Ownership: Nonprofit, church
Phone: (808) 523-3338 • (888) 871-5181
Fax: (808) 531-1270
E-mail: pickering@pickering.edu
Website: www.pickering.edu

This school offers degrees at all levels by a combination of correspondence, video, software, and Internet courses. Fields of study include theological studies, liberal arts, business management, computer science, engineering, and more.

Preston University
10-B, Street 64, F-8/4
Islamabad, Pakistan
Year founded: 1984

Phone: (92-51) 852-626
Fax: (92-51) 255-817
On-campus and distance learning programs in many fields of study.

Preston University   **B, M, D**
1204 Airport Parkway
Cheyenne, WY 82001
Fields offered: Business administration, computer science
Year founded: 1976
Ownership: Proprietary
Phone: (307) 634-1440
Fax: (307) 634-3091
E-mail: preston@wyoming.com
Website: www.wyoming.com/~preston

Offers degrees at all levels in business administration and computer science.

Private and Independent University
See: Freie und Private Universität Sersi

Robert Kennedy University   **B, M, D, Law**
Leutschenbachstrasse 95
Zurich, 8050 Switzerland
Phone: + 41 - 1 - 308.39.08
Fax: +41 - 1 -308.35.00
E-mail: KennedyUniversity@yahoo.com
Website: www.webspawner.com/users/kennedyuniversity/

The literature states that they are "the First Reality in Switzerland that give you the possibility to continue your study's totally at home or in office, in your own peace." Degrees at all levels.

Rockwell College of Arts and Sciences
See: Eurotechnical Research University

Rushmore University   **M**
370 Anchor Drive, #250
Dakota Dunes, SD 57049
Fields offered: Business administration
Year founded: 1995
Phone: • (888) NO-BS-MBA
Fax: (800) 269-1977
E-mail: pcmba@mbauniversity.com
Website: www.mbauniversity.com

A small, entrepreneurial university run from Georgia (the South Dakota address is a mailbox service), dedicated to business education. Formerly MBA University.

Saint John's University of Practical Theology   **B, M, D**
31916 University Circle
Springfield, LA 70462-8243
Many fields
Year founded: 1969

Ownership: Not-for-profit, church
Phone: (504) 294-2129
Fax: (504) 294-2157
E-mail: st.johns@i-55.com
Website: www.i-55.com/~stjohn

Degreees at all levels in a wide range of fields. Former names: Eastern Nebraska Christian College, Midwestern University. No relation to another unaccredited St. John's University that operated from Louisiana in the 1980s.

Senior University   B, M, D

2900 Simpson Road
#200
Richmond, BC V6X 2P9
Fields offered: Many fields
Year founded: 1993
Ownership: Proprietary
Phone: (604) 244-7754 • (800) 939-7822
Fax: (604) 244-9952
E-mail: registrar@senioru.bc.ca
Website: www.senioru.edu

Licensed through the state of Wyoming. Established and partly owned by Dr. Les Carr, owner of Columbia Pacific University.

Soka University of America   M

26800 W. Mulholland Highway
Calabasas, CA 91302
Fields offered: Education
Year founded: 1987
Ownership: Nonprofit, independent
Phone: (818) 880-6400
Website: www.t.soka.ac.jp:80/Education/SUA/

Soka currently offers an M.A. in second and foreign language education. Approved to operate in the state of California, the school is affiliated with the accredited independent Soka University based in Tokyo.

Somerset University   B, M, D

The Admissions Office
Illminster, Somerset, UK TA19 0YA
Fields offered: Arts, science, business, law, music, theology
Year founded: 1982
Ownership: Proprietary

Degrees at all levels are earned through correspondence study. Founder Raymond Young previously operated Harley University from his beauty salon and St. Giles College. There has been an affiliation with Villarreal University of Peru. See also: International College of Higher Education.

South Pacific University

See: Honolulu University of Arts, Sciences, and Humanities

Southern California University for Professional Studies   B, M, D

1840 East 17 St., #240
Santa Ana, CA 92701-2918
Fields offered: Business, management, marketing, health care administration, international relations, law
Year founded: 1978
Ownership: Private
Phone: (714) 480-0800 • (800) 477-2254
Fax: (714) 480-0834
E-mail: enroll@scups.edu
Website: www.scups.edu/

Approved to operate in the state of California. Degrees at all levels in business administration, Master's and Doctoral degrees in technology. The law school has a paralegal program, and two legal programs. The same people opened North Central University in Arizona in 1997.

Southwest Graduate School

See: Southwest University

Southwest University   B, M, D

2200 Veterans Blvd.
Kenner, LA 70062
Fields offered: Various fields
Year founded: 1982
Ownership: Proprietary
Phone: (504) 468-2900 • (800) 433-5923
Fax: (504) 468-3213
E-mail: southwst@southwest.edu
Website: www.southwest.edu/

Degrees at all levels in business administration, education, counseling and psychology, hospital and public administration, holistic health sciences, engineering, criminal justice, and entrepreneurship. Doctoral programs offered through the Southwest Graduate School, at the same address.

St. Clements University   B, D

P.O. Box 107, Oceanic House
Duke Street
Grand Turk, Turk & Caicos
Fields offered: Professional studies
Year founded: 1995
Phone: (61-8) 8342-0088
Fax: (61-8) 8269-4931
E-mail: admin@stclements.edu
Website: stclements.edu

The B.A. in professional studies and Doctor of Letters (D.Litt) programs.

St. George University   B, M, D

Distance Education Centre
Kokuwajima maehama 111-702
Muya-cho, Naruto-shi, 772 Japan
Fields offered: Many fields
Year founded: 1997

Phone: (81-886) 84-0870
Fax: (81-886) 84-0870
E-mail: japan@stgeorgeuniversity.edu
Website: www.stgeorgeuniversity.edu/worldwide.htm
Degrees offered at all levels in a broad range of subjects from a school established to provide handicapped people with distance education; non-disabled people can enroll as well.

Summit University　　　B, M, D
7508 Hayne Blvd.
New Orleans, LA 70126
Fields offered: Many fields
Year founded: 1988
Ownership: Nonprofit, religious
Phone: (504) 241-0227
Fax: (504) 243-1243
E-mail: sulno9@aol.com
SummtHQ@aol.com
Website: www.summitunivofla.edu

A religious institution, operating an an "assessment university," with the stated mission of "critically assessing a person's lifelong learning" and awarding degrees. Degrees at all levels (including combined Bachelor's/Master's and Master's/Ph.D. programs).

Thomas Jefferson University
See: Monticello University

Trinity College and Seminary　　B, M, D
4233 Medwel Drive, Box 717
Newburgh, IN 47629-0717
Fields offered: Human resource management development, theology, biblical studies, philosophy, history, women's studies, distance education, conflict management, counseling
Year founded: 1969
Ownership: Nonprofit, church
Phone: (812) 858-6595 • (800) 457-5510
Fax: (812) 858-6403
E-mail: 74777,245@CompuServe.com
Website: www.trinitysem.edu

While strongly religious, Trinity does offer some more secular degrees, such as Bachelor's and Master's degrees in human relations management development and women's studies. (Doctorates are all in theological fields, and beyond the scope of this book.) Degrees have been accepted by Britain's traditional and legitimate University of Liverpool, which states they have "accredited" Trinity.

Universitas Sancti Martin
902 Arlington Center, #137
Ada, OK 74820
We have some questions about this school, apparently based in Reynosa, Mexico. All correspondence goes through

Oklahoma, and directory assistance in Reynosa has no listing for such a university. At presstime, Dr. James had not responded to a detailed letter requesting clarification of these and other issues.

Université Libre et Privée
See: Freie und Private Universität

University of Asia　　　B, M, D
P.O Box 148
Campbelltown
South Australia, 5074 Australia
Fields offered: Business
Year founded: 1998
Phone: None
Fax: None
Website: www.uniasia.edu

This institution appeared on the internet in March, 1998. No street address or telephone is provided. The claim is that it is run by "highly qualified acedemics" (sic). Doctorates require two years, 75% by thesis. No names of faculty or administration are provided, but research shows that the Internet site is registered to Bilal Nasrulla and Vicki Noto in Campbelltown.

University of Berkley　　　B, M, D
19785 Twelve Mile Road West, #24
Southfield, MI 48076
Year founded: 1993
Ownership: Nonprofit
Phone: (814) 825-6604
Fax: (814) 825-1104
E-mail: collegeunderscoredegree@uofb.com
Website: www.berkley-u.edu/

Degrees in virtually any subject, from parapsychology to dance, computer engineering to hypnosis. The address is a mail forwarding service in a shopping mall. The FBI told us the university is operated from a small building in Erie, Pennsylvania. No connection, needless to say, with the University of California at Berkeley.

University of God's Logos System　　　B, M, D
11265 Redbird Lane
Baptist, LA 70401
Fields offered: Many fields
Year founded: 1986

The materials received from this school make it appear eccentric, to say the least. They have no phone or fax and the letter, typed in all capitals, included the intriguing sentence "I'm sure you have some grasp And with a name like "Bear" and the Soviet Union state insignia: I thought this birthmark on my meron/front-leg [sic] (like the one on my mother Marilyn William's glutes) was bad, you have my "empathy." Dr. Durand claims to have "the only court-proven non-fraudulent curricula in the nation." The letter was on stationery for the Mesmer Institute, but the connection is unclear.

University of Kings College
See: Canadian School of Management

University of Metaphysics — B, M, D
11684 Ventura Blvd.
Studio City, CA 91604
Fields offered: Metaphysics, metaphysical counseling, new thought ministry
Phone: (818) 763-9343 • (888) 866-4685
Fax: (818) 763-5415
E-mail: oksum@aol.com
Website: www.metaphysics.com
This school is operated by the International Metaphysical Ministry, offering Bachelor's, Master's, and Doctorates in metaphysics, metaphysical counseling, and new thought ministry.

University of Orlando — D, Law
6441 E. Colonial Drive
Orlando, FL 32807
Fields offered: Law, education, business
Year founded: 1995
Phone: (407) 275-2000
Fax: (407) 275-2010
E-mail: lawinfo@uo.edu
Website: www.uo.edu
Offers law degrees, as well as Doctorates in education and business.

University of the Rockies — B, M, D
3525 S. Tamarac Dr., #270
Denver, CO 80237
Fields offered: Education, ministry
Year founded: 1981
Phone: • (800) 292-0555
E-mail: rockies@compuserve.com
Founded in 1981 as the Christian Learning Institute of Denver. The present name was adopted in 1987. All coursework is completed through supervised independent study, leading to degrees at all levels in the above fields.

University of the United States — B, M, D
1201 Mont Limar Drive, #500
Mobile, AL 36609
Fields offered: Many fields
Year founded: 1993
Phone: (500) 675-9500
Fax: (500) 445-3500
E-mail: dean@uus.edu
Website: www.uus.edu
Operates from the same secretarial service address as Nasson University. Like Nasson, it offers degrees at all

levels in a wide range of fields. Mail we received was postmarked Rhode Island.

Virtual Online University — M
Fields offered: Many fields
Year founded: 1994
E-mail: C581646@mizzou1.missouri.edu
or cipher@vousi.com
Website: www.athena.edu
The first-ever wholly online university, existing only in cyberspace, Virtual Online University (which also offers programs through Athena University), began offering classes in 1996. While still very much a work in process, the school's stated mission is to become an accredited school offering low-cost, high-quality education and training. Currently, between Virtual and Athena, they offer some 350 classes, and an M.B.A. program.

Warnborough College
See: Warnborough University

Warnborough International
See: Warnborough University

Warnborough University
London, SE1 8HB U.K.
Fields offered: Many fields
Year founded: 1973
Phone: (44) 171 922 1200
Fax: (44) 171 922 1201
E-mail: admin@warnborough.edu
Website: www.warnborough.edu
Degrees at all levels. Degree-granting authority claimed through their registration in Ireland. We could find no evidence of an actual school in Ireland.

Washington School of Law — M
Washington Institute for Graduate Studies
2268 E. Newcastle Dr.
Sandy, UT 84093
Fields offered: Taxation
Year founded: 1986
Ownership: Nonprofit, independent
Phone: (801) 943-2440
Fax: (801) 944-8586
Graduate programs in psychology, leading to the following degrees: an M.S. in psychology or in professional counseling (the latter of which allows graduates to sit for licensure as a licensed professional counselor), the Ph.D. in clinical psychology, and the Psy.D. in clinical psychology (the latter allows graduates to sit for licensure as a licensed psychologist). Lawyers and CPAs may earn a Master's in taxation (LL.M. Tax for lawyers, M.S. Tax for CPAs) after 360 hours of study, in residence or by videocassette

Washington University
See Washington International University

Washington International University   B, M, D

2752 Woodlawn Drive #5–215
Honolulu, HI 96822
Fields offered: Business, engineering, health care management, computer systems management & information technology, liberal arts
Ownership: Proprietary
Phone: (808) 988-8137
Fax: (808) 988-8105
E-mail: washuniv@op.net
Website: www.wash.edu

Degrees at all levels in the above fields. Formerly Washington University. In a letter dated November 17, 1997, Mr. Yil Karademir of Washington University wrote to Mariah, "Regarding your father's comments to our present or prospective students is [sic] UNPROFESSIONAL at best, and EVIL at worst! Lets [sic] don't [sic] forget that he is a man who also tryed [sic] his luck with a Hawaii University [sic] but failed. . . . I do not wish to take legal action against your father based on a his [sic] e-mail communication with (name of recipient) but if he continues to make negative remarks against Washington University instead of just stating the facts-and we catch again [sic], I shall have no choice to proceed! [sic]"

Fair enough. From now on, facts only. The following are true as of November 24, 1997.

Fact One: The "Non-Student Administrative Center" in Hawaii is, in fact, a secretarial and mail forwarding service called Independent Resource Alternatives, where the manager, Ms. Corinne Uehara, told us they receive and forward mail and phone calls for Washington University.

Fact Two: The Student Communication and Registration Center in Wayne, Pennsylvania is, in fact, a secretarial, telephone answering, and mail forwarding service called Executive Commons, where the manager, Kathleen McNally told us they receive and forward messages for Washington University.

Fact Three: In an application for use of a fictitious business name in Pennsylvania, Kari Lill Karademir of Washington University stated that the "principal place of business" of Washington University is 175 Strafford Avenue, Building 4, Office, in Wayne, Pennsylvania. This is the above-named mail secretarial service.

Fact Four: The questionnaire we sent Washington University was filled out by "Gil Carr, Admissions Coordinator." The threatening letter quoted above came from Mr. Yil Karademir, Financial Director. When we telephoned the Student Communication and Academic Center in Bryn Mawr, Pennsylvania, the phone was answered by Mr. Carr. When we telephoned person-to-person for Yil Karademir a few minutes later, the same person accepted the call.

Fact Five: The Student Communication and Academic Center consists of one small (about 12 by 14 foot) room in a small commercial building. The name "Washington University" does not appear on the building directory.

Fact Six: The lovely photograph on page one of the catalog is of the building in Wayne, Pennsylvania in which the telephone answering service has an office. The address is a secretarial service.

Weimar College   B

20601 W. Paoli Lane.
Weimar, CA 95736
Fields offered: Education
Year founded: 1978
Ownership: Nonprofit, independent
Phone: (916) 637-4111 • (800) 525-9192
Fax: (530) 637-4722
Website: www.weimar.org/ccontact.htm

An extremely conservative school run by the Seventh-Day Adventists, apparently too conservative to even respond to our requests for information. We hear from other sources that they offer a Bachelor's in elementary education at low tuition, and that they don't want to seek accreditation, viewing it as too worldly.

Westbrook University   B, M, D

112 S. Church Street
Aztec, NM 87410
Fields offered: Psychology, natural health, world philosophies
Year founded: 1988
Phone: (505) 334-1115 • (800) 447-6496
Fax: (505) 334-7583
E-mail: admissions@cyberport.com
Website: www.westbrooku.edu

Programs at all levels in the above three concentrations, with a wide range of specializations. Formerly the International Institute of Theology.

Western States University   B, M, D

P. O. Box 430
Doniphan, MO 63935
Fields offered: Many fields
Phone: (573) 996-7388

This school's attorneys have demanded that we not say anything about the school. Fair enough. But about the founder: his claimed doctorate is from a diploma mill whose founders were imprisoned for selling degrees for $600, no questions asked.

Westport University   B, M, D

180 South 300 West, #260
Salt Lake City, UT 84101
Fields offered: Business, education, psychology, law, Christian studies
Phone: (801) 530-0299 • (800) 639-1775
Fax: (801) 530-3169
E-mail: registrar@westport.edu
Website: www.westport.edu

According to the founder of Newport University, he sold some assets, of Newport, but not the name, so the new owner is calling it Westport, and operating it from Utah. Degrees at all levels are offered through their schools of business, education, psychology, religion, and law.

William Carey International University   B, M, D

1539 E. Howard Street
Pasadena, CA 91104
Fields offered: International development
Ownership: Nonprofit, independent
Phone: (626) 398-2152/398-2153
Fax: (626) 398-2111
E-mail: admissions@wciu.edu
Website: www.wciu.edu

Degrees offered at all levels in the field of international development. geared to those interested in missions and missionaries.

William Howard Taft University   M, D, Law

201 East Sandpointe Avenue, #330
Santa Ana, CA 92707
Fields offered: Business, law, education
Year founded: 1976
Ownership: Proprietary
Phone: (714) 850-4800 • (800) 882-4555

Fax: (714) 708-2082
E-mail: admissions@taft.edu
Website: www.taft.edu

Nonresident bar-qualified law program, an Ed.D. designed for educators, M.B.A. programs in entrepreneurship and healthcare administration, and an M.S. in taxation, designed for accountants.

World University

P. O. Box 2470
Benson ,AZ 85602
Fields offered: Spiritual science
Year founded: 1967
Phone: (520) 586-2985
Fax: (520) 586-4764
E-mail: desertsanctuary@theriver.com
Website: www.worlduniversity.org

World University tells us that they are an association of "schools and colleges throughout the world, with a regional campus near Benson, Arizona." No degrees are presently offered from its world headquarters, but its parent institution, incorporated in Arizona and California as the World University Roundtable, awards a "cultural doctorate as a professional honor for career excellence with an acceptable biodata."

Having joined the baseball club at his correspondence school, Darryl Brock has been waiting quite a long time for the first pitch to arrive.

22

Other Schools with
Short Residency Programs

*A log in the woods, with Mark Hopkins at one end and me at the other—
that is a good enough university for me.*

PRESIDENT JAMES GARFIELD

Any school can claim that it is accredited; the use of that word is not regulated in any way. This chapter includes only those schools that are not accepted as "Accredited" under GAAP, Generally Accepted Accreditation Principles. In the U.S., there is near-unanimous agreement on GAAP by the relevant key decision-makers: university registrars and admissions officers, corporate human resource officers, and government agencies.

Note that in some countries, the word "accredited" is not used, although the evaluation process in that country (e.g., the British Royal Charter), is accepted as "accredited" under GAAP.

For a school to be considered "accredited," it must meet any one of the following six standards of GAAP. The schools in this chapter do not meet any of the standards. This does not necessarily mean they are bad, illegal, or fake. It simply means they would not be generally accepted as accredited.

GAAP CRITERIA

◆ Accredited by an accrediting agency recognized by the Council on Higher Education Accreditation in Washington.

◆ Accredited by an accrediting agency recognized by the U.S. Department of Education.

◆ Listed in the International Handbook of Universities (a UNESCO publication).

◆ Listed in the Commonwealth Universities Yearbook.

◆ Listed in the World Education Series, published by PIER (Projects in International Education Research), a joint venture of AACRAO (the American Association of Collegiate Registrars and Admissions Officers) and NAFSA (the Association of International Educators) with the participation of the College Board.

◆ Listed in the Countries Series, published by NOOSR, the National Office for Overseas Skills Recognition, in Australia.

To the best of our knowledge, none of the schools in this chapter meet any of the above six criteria.

The basic format of each listing is as follows:

Name of School	**A**ssociate's, **B**achelor's, **M**aster's, **D**octorate, **L**aw, **D**iploma

Address
City, State Postal Code Country, if not U.S.
Fields of study offered
Year founded
Ownership (nonprofit or proprietary, state, private, or church-run)
Phone • Toll-free phone
Fax
E-mail address
Website URL

Note: We have in the past given cost information, but this changes so quickly and is so subjective that we have decided to discontinue the practice. If a program is extremely inexpensive, or disproportionately expensive, we've mentioned this in the listing. In most cases, the best way to find out about the cost of any particular program is to contact the school directly.

Adizes Graduate School   M, D

820 Moraga Drive
Los Angeles, CA 90049
Fields offered: Organizational transformation
Year founded: 1973
Ownership: Proprietary

Phone: (310) 471-9677
Fax: (310) 471-1227
E-mail: adizes@adizes.com
Website: www.adizes.com
Graduate degrees in organizational transformation require 10 days on campus every 4 months.

American College of Oxford
See: Warnborough International

American Commonwealth University
See: Huron International University

Asia Pacific International University   B, M, D
155 Cyril Magnin Street
San Francisco, CA 94102-2129
Fields offered: Business fields
Year founded: 1991
Phone: (415) 834-2748 • (800) 661-8788
Fax: (415) 834-2758
E-mail: info@APIU.edu
Website: www.APIU.edu
Degrees at all levels in a number of business and finance-related fields.

Berne University   D
P.O. Box 1080
Wolfeboro Falls, NH 03896
Fields offered: Many fields
Year founded: 1993
Phone: (603) 569-8648
Fax: (603) 569-4052
E-mail: berne@berne.edu
Website: www.berne.edu
Master's and doctoral degrees in many fields; one-month residency required in St. Kitts in the Caribbean.

Bob Jones University   B
Office of Extended Education
1700 Wade Hampton Blvd.
Greenville, SC 29614
Fields offered: General studies, arts and sciences, religious fields, education
Year founded: 1927
Ownership: Church
Phone: (864) 242-5100 • (888) BJ-EXT-ED
Fax: (800) 2-FAX-BJU
E-mail: extended@bju.edu
Website: www.bju.edu
Bachelor's degrees in the above fields; up to 30 credits can come from correspondence. A strongly religious school.

Greenleaf University   D
161 Weldon Parkway, #203
Maryland Heights, MO 63043-3107

Fields offered: Leadership, administration, business, education, health & human services
Year founded: 1989
Ownership: Nonprofit, independent
Phone: (314) 567-4477
Fax: (314) 567-4478
E-mail: admin@Ggreenleaf.edu
Website: www.greenleaf.edu
Doctoral degrees in business and professional fields; annual 10-day residency.
Formerly the Institute for Professional Studies.

Human Relations Institute
See: Pacifica Graduate Institute

Huron International University   B, M, D
2801 Camino del Rio South, #201
San Diego, CA 92108-2630
Fields offered: Business, psychology, humanities
Year founded: 1979
Ownership: Proprietary
Phone: (619) 298-9040 • (800) 962-7097
Fax: (619) 298-9056
E-mail: tsereno@hiusd.edu
Website: www.americancomu.edu
Degrees at all levels through a learning contract. Originally known as William Lyon University, then as American Commonwealth University. They had been accredited by ACICS (Accrediting Council for Independent Schools and Colleges), a recognized accreditor, but not as of early 1998; they are apparently appealing this loss of accreditation.

Institute for Advanced Study of Human Sexuality   M, D
1523 Franklin St.
San Francisco, CA 94109.
Fields offered: Human sexuality
Year founded: 1976
Ownership: Proprietary
Phone: (415) 928-1133
E-mail: iashs@iashs.edu
Website: www.iashs.edu
Graduate degrees in the field of human sexuality; 9 weeks residency for the Master's, 15 for the doctorate, more is encouraged. Approved by the state of California.

Institute for Educational Studies   M
P.O. Box 411
Brookfield, VT 05036
Fields offered: Integrative Education
Year founded: 1996
Phone: (802) 276-3717 • (800) 386-7725
Fax: (802) 276-3708
E-mail: ties@tmn.com
Website: www.tmn.com/ties/ties.html
M.A. in integrative education through a combination of Internet courses and two brief summer sessions.

Institute for Professional Studies
See: Greenleaf University

Institute of Imaginal Studies   M, D
47 Sixth St.
Petaluma, CA 94952
Fields offered: Psychology
Phone: (707) 765-1836
Fax: (707) 765-2351

Weekend Master's and doctoral programs in psychology that qualify graduates to sit for the MFCC and Psychology License exams

Institute of Transpersonal Psychology   M
744 San Antonio Road
Palo Alto, CA 94303
Fields offered: Transpersonal psychology
Year founded: 1975
Ownership: Nonprofit
Phone: (650) 493-4430
Fax: (650) 493-6835
E-mail: itpinfo@netcom.com
Website: www.tmn.com/itp/index.html/

Masters degrees in transpersonal psychology and studies. Courses are delivered by text, e-mail and Internet, but students must attend a brief seminar on campus.

Newport Asia Pacific University   M
5000 Birch Street, Suite 4000
Newport Beach, CA 92660
Fields offered: International business, TESOL, intercultural relations
Year founded: 1996
Ownership: Proprietary
Phone: (949) 260-2004
Fax: (949) 260-2099
E-mail: edcenter@japan.cp.jp
Website: www.AsiaPacificU.edu

Master's degrees in the above fields largely through distance learning, with some required short-term residency.

Oxford Graduate School   M, D
American Centre for Religion/Society Studies
505 Oxford Drive
Dayton, TN 37321-6736
Hollis L. Green, Chancellor
Fields offered: Sociological integration of religion and society
Year founded: 1982
Ownership: Nonprofit, church
Phone: (423) 775-6597 • (800) 933-6188
Fax: (423) 775-6599
E-mail: oxnet@oxnet.com
Website: www.oxnet.com

This school (no relation to the other, better known Oxford), offers interdisciplinary programs leading to Master's degrees or Ph.D's in sociological integration of religion and society. Residency is required but flexible.

Pacifica Graduate Institute   M, D
249 Lambert Road
Carpinteria, CA 93013
Fields offered: Psychology, mythology
Year founded: 1974
Ownership: Proprietary, independent
Phone: (805) 969-3626
Fax: (805) 565-1932
E-mail: diane_huerta@pacifica.edu
Website: www.pacifica.edu

M.A. and Ph.D. students attend on-campus courses once a month, in the form of a three-day learning retreat. In most of the degree programs, there is also a one-week summer session. Currently a candidate for accreditation from the Western Associate of Schools and Colleges. Formerly the Human Relations Institute.

School of Natural Healing   M
P.O. Box 412
Springville, UT 84663
Fields offered: Herbology
Year founded: 1953
Phone: (801) 489-4254 • (800) 372-8255
Fax: (801) 489-8341
E-mail: snh@qi3.com
Website: www.schoolofnaturalhealing.com

A program offering the Master of Herbology degree, largely through home study courses, with seven- to nine-day seminars by the school's founder, Dr. John R. Christopher.

University of Santa Barbara   M, D
4050 Calle Real, #200
Santa Barbara, CA 93110
Fields offered: Education, business
Year founded: 1973
Ownership: Nonprofit, independent
Phone: (805) 569-1024
Fax: (805) 967-6289
E-mail: usb.139@juno.com

M.A., Ed.D., and Ph.D. in education, M.B.A., M.S., and Ph.D. in business; all require 3 weeks residency. Originally established in Florida as Laurence University.

University of the Seven Rays   B, M, D
128 Manhattan Ave.
Jersey City Heights, NJ 07307
Fields offered: Esoteric psychology, religion, philosophy, political science, magnetic healing, spiritual economics, transformational politics, cosmology, culture and the creative arts, etc.
Phone: (201) 798-7777
Fax: (201) 659-3263
E-mail: univ7rays@sevenray.com

Website: www.sevenray.com

Bachelor's, Master's, and the Ph.D. in various esoteric sciences, "designed to strengthen the spiritual will, the spiritual love, and the practical spiritual intelligence of its students...." Academic curricula derive "from the teachings of the Christ, the Buddha...and other members of the Spiritual Hierarchy of the Planet." While most of the work is done at a distance, there are necessary meetings of cohort groups several times a year, at almost any pre-arranged location worldwide.

Western Institute for Social Research   B, M, D

3220 Sacramento St.
Berkeley, CA 94702
Fields offered: Psychology, education, social sciences, human services/community development

Year founded: 1975
Ownership: Nonprofit, independent
Phone: (510) 655-2830
Fax: (510) 655-2831
E-mail: wisruniv@aol.com

Degrees at all levels, primarily for people concerned with educational innovation and/or community and social change, through a combination of residential and independent study. Formerly Western Regional Learning Center.

Western Regional Learning Center

See: Western Institute for Social Research

William Lyon University

See: Huron International University

23

Other Schools with
Nontraditional Residential Programs

"Whom are you?" he asked, for he had been to night school.

GEORGE ADE

Any school can claim that it is accredited; the use of that word is not regulated in any way. This chapter includes only those schools that are not accepted as "Accredited" under GAAP, Generally Accepted Accreditation Principles. In the U.S., there is near-unanimous agreement on GAAP by the relevant key decision-makers: university registrars and admissions officers, corporate human resource officers, and government agencies.

Note that in some countries, the word "accredited" is not used, although the evaluation process in that country (e.g., the British Royal Charter), is accepted as "accredited" under GAAP.

For a school to be considered "accredited," it must meet any one of the following six standards of GAAP. The schools in this chapter do not meet any of the standards. This does not necessarily mean they are bad, illegal, or fake. It simply means they would not be generally accepted as accredited.

GAAP CRITERIA

◆ Accredited by an accrediting agency recognized by the Council on Higher Education Accreditation in Washington.

◆ Accredited by an accrediting agency recognized by the U.S. Department of Education.

◆ Listed in the International Handbook of Universities (a UNESCO publication).

◆ Listed in the Commonwealth Universities Yearbook.

◆ Listed in the World Education Series, published by PIER (Projects in International Education Research), a joint venture of AACRAO (the American Association of Collegiate Registrars and Admissions Officers) and NAFSA (the Association of International Educators) with the participation of the College Board.

◆ Listed in the Countries Series, published by NOOSR, the National Office for Overseas Skills Recognition, in Australia.

To the best of our knowledge, none of the schools in this chapter meet any of the above six criteria.

The basic format of each listing is as follows:

Name of School   **A**ssociate's, **B**achelor's, **M**aster's, **D**octorate, **Law, D**iploma
Address
City, State Postal Code Country, if not U.S.
Fields of study offered
Year founded
Ownership (nonprofit or proprietary, state, private, or church-run)
Phone • Toll-free phone
Fax
E-mail address
Website URL

Note: We have in the past given cost information, but this changes so quickly and is so subjective that we have decided to discontinue the practice. If a program is extremely inexpensive, or disproportionately expensive, we've mentioned this in the listing. In most cases, the best way to find out about the cost of any particular program is to contact the school directly.

American Institute of Vedic Studies   **M**
1701 Santa Fe River Road
Santa Fe, NM 87501
Fields offered: Ayurveda
Phone: (505) 983-9385
Fax: (505) 982-5807

E-mail: Vedicinst@aol.
Website: www.consciousnet.com/vedic/
Offers a Master's degree in ayurveda, a traditional Indian approach to health.

American University of Asturias   B
Principado 8
Principado de Asturias
33007 Oviedo, Spain
Fields offered: Many fields
Phone: (34) 579-4634
Fax: (34) 598-5535
E-mail: aua@asturnet.es
Website: www1.asturnet.es/auna/welcome.htm
Bachelor's degrees in a number of fields.

California Graduate School of Marital and Family Therapy
See: California Graduate School of Psychology

California Graduate School of Psychology   M, D
50 El Camino Drive
Corte Madera, CA 94925
Fields offered: Counseling, clinical psychology
Year founded: 1976
Ownership: Nonprofit, independent
Phone: (415) 927-2477
Fax: (415) 927-2490
E-mail: cgsp@cgsp.edu
Website: www.cgsp.edu
Master's degrees and doctorates in psychological fields. Counseling programs qualify graduates for licensure in California. Formerly the California Graduate School of Marital and Family Therapy.

California Institute for Human Science   M, D
701 Garden View Court
Encinitas, CA 92024
Fields offered: Human science, psychology
Year founded: 1992
Ownership: Private
Phone: (760) 634-1771
Fax: (760) 634-1772
E-mail: cihs@adnc.com
Website: www.cihs.edu
This state-approved graduate school offers a number of Master's degrees and Doctorates.

California International University   B, M
2706 Wilshire Blvd.
Los Angeles, CA 90057
Fields offered: Business fields
Year founded: 1973
Ownership: Nonprofit, independent
Phone: (213) 381-3719
Fax: (213) 381-6990

E-mail: jdmcinty@earthlink.net
Evening classes lead to degrees in business management and international business for international students.

California Yuin University   B, M, D
2007 East Compton Blvd.
Compton, CA 90221
Fields offered: Acupuncture, Oriental medicine, Christian theology, business
Ownership: Proprietary
Phone: (310) 609-2705
Fax: (310) 609-1415
E-mail: cyu@yuin.edu
Website: www.yuin.edu
Offers degrees in the above fields through evening, weekend, and off-campus study.

Center for Psychological Studies   D
1398 Solano Ave.
Albany, CA 94706
Fields offered: Clinical, developmental, and organizational psychology
Year founded: 1979
Ownership: Nonprofit, independent
Phone: (510) 524-0291
Fax: (510) 524-4696
Website: www.radioguide.com/cps/cps.htm
Ph.D. in psychological fields for Master's-degree holders. Degrees are approved by the California Council for Private Post-Secondary Education and meet educational requirements for the psychology license. Formerly the Graduate School of Human Behavior.

Chicago National College of Naprapathy   D
3330 N. Milwaukee Avenue
Chicago, IL 60641
Fields offered: Naprapathy
Year founded: 1907
Phone: (773) 282-2686
Fax: (773) 282-2688
E-mail: naprapath@aol.com
Website: pma-online.org/list/558.html
This unaccredited residential school offers an evening program leading to the Doctor of Naprapathy (a discipline concerned with evaluation and treatment of connective tissue disorders). Originally Oakley Smith School of Naprapathy; later changed to the Chicago College of Naprapathy. In 1971 this school merged with the National College of Naprapathy to form the present school.

Dharma Realm Buddhist University   B, M
2001 Talmage Road
Talmage, CA 95481
Fields offered: Buddhist fields, Chinese studies
Year founded: 1976
Phone: (707) 462-0939
Fax: (707) 462-0949

E-mail: drbabtts@jps.net
Website: www.drba.org/drbu.htm
Bachelor's and Master's degrees in Buddhist studies & practice and translation of Buddhist texts, a Bachelor's in Chinese studies, and a Master's in Buddhist education.

European University   B

Amerikalei 131
B-2000 Antwerp, Belgium
Fields offered: Many fields
Phone: (32-3) 216-9896
Fax: (32-3) 216-5868
E-mail: admission.office.antwerp@euruni.be
Website: www.euruni.be/
Bachelor's degrees in many fields; courses held at locations throughout Europe.

Evergreen University   B, M

1506 West 51st Place
Los Angeles, CA 90062
Fields offered: Human services
B.S. and M.S. in human services.

Graduate School of Human Behavior

See: Center for Psychological Studies

Hsi Lai University   B, M

1409 Walnut Grove Ave.
Rosemead, CA 91770
Phone: (626) 571-8811
Fax: (626) 571-1413
E-mail: info@hlu.edu
Website: www.hlu.edu
Courses in Chinese literature and culture, comparative religious studies, Buddhist studies, ESL, and other fields. Approved to operate by the state of California.

Institut P-2000   B, M

P. O. Box 5211
Zurich, 8022 Switzerland
Phone: (41-1) 241-4183
Fax: (41-1) 241-3033
Bachelor's and Master's degrees in psychological fields.

International School of Management   M, D

World Trade Center
1250 6th Ave., 8th floor
San Diego, CA 92101
Fields offered: International management, business administration
Year founded: 1994
Ownership: Private
Phone: (619) 702-9400
Fax: (619) 702-9476
E-mail: ism@inetworld.net
Website: www.ism.edu
M.B.A. and D.B.A. for U.S. nationals only.

International Technological University   B, M, D

1650 Warburton Avenue
Santa Clara, CA 95050
Fields offered: Technological fields, business
Phone: (408) 556-9010
Fax: (408) 556-9012
E-mail: registrar@itu.edu
Website: www.itu.edu
Degrees at all levels in technological fields, plus an M.B.A.

Irvine University College of Law   B, Law

8231 Westminster Boulevard
Westminster, CA 92683
Fields offered: Law
Phone: (714) 373-6949
Fax: (714) 373-0450
Bachelor of Science in laws, which is non–Bar qualifying, and a Juris Doctor, which is.

Ivy University   M

100 S. Fremont Ave.
Building A12
Alhambra, CA 91803
Fields offered: Business
Phone: (626) 282-1096
Fax: (626) 282-8362
E-mail: ivyuniv@earthlink.net
Website: www.ivyuniv.edu/
This state-approved school offers an M.B.A. and an M.A. in management. All instruction is offered in English and Chinese.

Keimyung Baylo University

See South Baylo University

Louisiana Pacific University   B, M

Honolulu, HI
Fields offered: Business and computer-related
Year founded: 1989
Ownership: Proprietary
Residential Bachelor's and Master's degrees in business and computer fields entirely through residential study in Spain at one of several business colleges affiliated with Louisiana Pacific. Originally established as a Louisiana school, then Iowa, and finally Hawaii. No courses are offered directly by Louisiana Pacific.

Northern California Graduate University   D

1710 S. Amphlett Blvd., #124
San Mateo, CA 94402
Fields offered: Psychology, education
Year founded: 1989
Ownership: Nonprofit, independent
Phone: (650) 341-6690
Fax: (650) 655-7665

E-mail: admin@ncgu.edu
Website: www.ncgu.edu
Ph.D.'s in counseling psychology and higher education, as well as Psy.D. and Ed.D. Approved by the state of California.

Northwestern Polytechnic University   B
117 Fourier Ave.
Fremont, CA 94539
Fields offered: Electrical engineering, computer systems engineering
Year founded: 1984
Ownership: Nonprofit, independent
Phone: (510) 657-5911
Fax: (510) 657-8975
E-mail: npuadm@npu2.npu.edu
Website: www.npu.edu/
Offers an evening-study Bachelor's degree–completion program in electrical or computer systems engineering.

Nyingma Institute   Certificate
1815 Highland Place
Berkeley, CA 94709
Fields offered: Human development based on Tibetan Buddhism
Year founded: 1972
Ownership: Nonprofit, independent
Phone: (510) 843-6812
Fax: (510) 486-1679
E-mail: nyingma-institute@nyingma.org
Website: www.nyingma.org
Certificate programs in philosophy, psychology, language study, meditation practice, history, culture, and comparative studies.

Ola Grimsby Institute   M
4420 Hotel Circle Court, Suite 103
San Diego, CA 92108
Fields offered: Orthopedic manual therapy
Year founded: 1990
Ownership: Proprietary
Phone: (619) 298-4116 • (800) 646-6128
Fax: (619) 298-4225
E-mail: janogi@aol.com
Website: www.halcyon.com/rivard/OGI/
Offers a Master's degree in orthopedic manual therapy through courses held one day a week for two years; residential clinic work may be accomplished at centers in Alabama, Alaska, Arizona, California, Florida, Illinois, Kansas, Louisiana, Michigan, Tennessee, Texas, Utah, and Washington, as well as Belgium and Switzerland.

One Institute of Homophile Studies
See: One Institute of Human Relations

One Institute of Human Relations   M, D
3340 Country Club Dr.
Los Angeles, CA 90019

Fields offered: Homophile studies
Year founded: 1956
Ownership: Nonprofit, independent
Phone: (213) 735-5252
Master's and doctoral degrees in homophile sudies; authorized to grant degree by the state of California. Formerly known as One Institute of Homophile Studies.

Open University (Florida)   M
255 S. Orange Avenue
P.O. Box 4916
Orlando, FL 32802
Fields offered: Entrepreneurship
Year founded: 1987
Ownership:
Phone: (407) 649-8488 • (800) 874-0388
Fax: (407) 649-1903
E-mail: info@openu.edu
Website: www.openu.com
A Master's degree in entrepreneurship.

Reykjavik Institute of Education   B, M, D
E-mail: admin@rvik.com
Website: www.rvik.com/edu
Offers degrees at all levels in management, computer science, and information systems, and is apparently registered but not accredited in Iceland. May only exist on the Internet.

Rosebridge Graduate School of Integrative Psychology   M, D
1040 Oak Grove Road, #103
Concord, CA 94518
Anna S. Yabusaki, Ph.D., Dean
Fields offered: Psychology
Year founded: 1978
Phone: (510) 689-0560
Fax: (510) 689-4456
E-mail: rosebrg@wco.com
Website:
The Master's and Psy.D. programs meet California state educational requirements for licensure as a Marriage, Family, and Child Counselor, or, in the case of the Psy.D., licensure as a psychologist in California.

Rudolf Steiner College   B, M
9200 Fair Oaks Blvd.
Fair Oaks, CA 95628
Fields offered: Education and arts
Year founded: 1976
Ownership: Nonprofit, independent
Phone: (916) 961-8727
Fax: (916) 961-8731
E-mail: rsc@steinercollege.org
Website: steinercollege.org
Bacherlor's and Master's degrees in Waldorf-related education and arts. Approved by the state of California.

Ryokan College   B, M, D
11965 Venice Blvd.
Los Angeles, CA 90066
Fields offered: Human behavior, counseling psychology, clinical psychology
Year founded: 1979
Ownership: Nonprofit, independent
Phone: (310) 390-7560
Fax: (310) 391-7956
Website: www.ryokan.edu
Degrees at all levels in psychological fields.

S.A. College of Natural Medicine   Dip
Bergzicht Building
36 De Villiers Street
Fields offered: Natural medicine, herbalism
Year founded: 1987
Phone: (27-21) 853-1596
Fax: (27-21) 853-1596
Website: www.natmed.cp.za
Diplomas in natural or herbal medicine, through distance learning. Coursework is delivered mainly via written assignments and readings, with close faculty contact maintained by telephone and/or audiotape. Affiliated with the British School of Phytotherapy.

Saint George's University (Grenada)   B
U.S. Agent: Medical School Services, Ltd.
One East Main Street
Bay Shore, NY 11706-8399
Fields offered: Many fields
Year founded: 1996
Phone: (516) 665-8500 • (800) 899-6337
Fax: (516) 665-5590
E-mail: sgu_info@sgu.edu
Website: www.stgeorgesuniv.edu/univ/
Bachelor's degrees in social sciences, business, accounting, allied health sciences, and liberal arts

Samra University of Oriental Medicine   M
2828 Beverly Blvd.
Los Angeles, CA 90057
Fields offered: Oriental medicine, acupuncture, herbology
Year founded: 1965
Ownership: Nonprofit, independent
Phone: (310) 202-6444
Fax: (310) 202-6007
E-mail: Info@samra.edu
Website: www.samra.edu/
Classes are taught day, evening, and Saturday, in English, Chinese, and Korean. Minimum time required to earn a degree is 36 months; all students must complete 60 semester credits of general/technical education (some of this requirement can be met with military training.)

San Francisco School of Psychology   M, D
1375 Sutter Street, #218
San Francisco, CA 94109
Fields offered: Psychology
Year founded: 1979
Phone: (415) 563-1779
Fax: (415) 563-9267
E-mail: admin@sfsp.edu
Website: www.sfsp.edu
M.A. and a Psy.D. in psychology; completion of the program qualifies the student for California state licensure.

South Baylo University   B, M, D
1126 N. Brookhurst St.
Anaheim, CA 92801
Fields offered: Oriental medicine, acupuncture
Year founded: 1978
Phone: (714) 533-1495
Nontraditional residential programs in Oriental medicine and acupuncture. Has also gone by the name Keimyung Baylo University.

Southeast Asia Interdisciplinary Development Institute   M, D
Taktak Dr., Atipolo Rizal
AC - P.O. Box 267
Quezon City, Philippines
Fields offered: Organizational development and planning, instruction development and technology
Year founded:
Ownership: Nonprofit
Phone: (63-2) 665-4791
M.A., M.A./Ph.D., and Ph.D. in organizational development and planning.

Southern California Psychoanalytic Institute   D
9024 Olympic Blvd.
Beverly Hills, CA 90211
Fields offered: Psychoanalysis
Year founded: 1950
Ownership: Nonprofit, independent
Phone: (310) 276-2455
Ph.D. in psychoanalysis for psychiatrists, clinical psychologists, and psychiatric social workers; approved to operate by the state of California.

Tien Tao Chong Hua University   B, M, D
5440 Pomona Blvd.
Los Angeles, CA 90022
Fields offered: Tien tao
Year founded: 1990
Ownership: Nonprofit, independent
Phone: (213) 722-6693
Fax: (213) 722-6178

Degrees at all levels in tien tao–oriented studies, which materials on the school describe as a Confucian pursuit of truth and knowledge.

Trinity Graduate School   M
1661 North Raymond, Suite 140
Anaheim, CA 92801
Fields offered: Ethics, philosophy, culture, philosophy
Year founded: 1897
Phone: (714) 639-3962 • (888) 3-TRINITY
Fax: (714) 992-9165
E-mail: sgu@sgsl.edu
Website: www.sgsl.edu
Graduate programs in ethics, philosophy, culture, and philosophy.

University of Creation Spirituality   M
2141 Broadway
Oakland, CA 94612
Fields offered: Humanities
Year founded: 1966
Phone: (510) 835-4827
Fax: (510) 835-0564
E-mail: csmag@hooked.net
Website: www.netser.com/ucs
This unaccredited school has been offering New Age and spiritual workshops and programs for 20 years, including one-week intensives in such subjects as Native American ritual, yoga, creation spirituality, and the like. Now, through an association with New College of California, they are offering an accredited Master's degree in Creation Spirituality in two formats—a nine-month full-time program or a two-year weekend plan. A doctoral program is planned and has temporary state approval, but is not as of presstime accredited.

University for Humanistic Studies   B, M, D
380 Stevens Avenue
Admissions, #210
Solana Beach, CA 92075
Fields offered: Psychology
Year founded: 1977
Ownership: Nonprofit
Phone: (619) 259-9733
Fax: (619) 259-9755
E-mail: uhs@humanistic.e
Website: www.humanistic.edu
Bachelor of Arts in humanistic studies; Master of Arts in psychology, leadership development, sports counseling, and marriage, family, and child counseling; Ph.D. in psychology, and Psy.D.

University of Northern California   B, M, D
101 S. San Antonio Road
Petaluma, CA 94952
Fields offered: Biomedical engineering, languages, applied linguistics

Year founded: 1993
Phone: (707) 765-6400
Fax: (707) 769-8600
E-mail: admits@uncm.ed
Website: www.uncm.edu
B.A. in engineering, applied linguistics, and languages, B.E., M.S., and Ph.D. degrees in biomedical engineering. Approved to operate in the state of California.

University of Santa Monica   M
Center for the Study & Practice of Spiritual Psychology
2107 Wilshire Blvd.
Santa Monica, CA 90403
Fields offered: Applied psychology, counseling psychology
Year founded: 1976
Phone: (310) 829-7402
Website: www.videotex.com/usm/
Master's degrees in applied and counseling psychology. The M.A. in counseling psychology provides the appropriate professional training meeting the educational qualifications for licensing as a Marriage, Family, and Child Counselor in California. Formerly called Koh-I-Noor University.

Western Graduate School of Psychology   M, D
1725 Estudillo
San Leandro, CA 94577
Fields offered: Clinical psychology
Year founded: 1978
Ownership: Nonprofit, independent
Phone: (650) 964-6720
Residential Ph.D. in clinical psychology, approved by the state of California, thus graduates can take the state licensing exams without further qualification. Also an address in Palo Alto. Formerly Palo Alto School of Professional Psychology.

World University of America   B, M, D
107 N. Ventura St.
Ojai, CA 93023
Fields offered: Many fields
Year founded: 1974
Ownership: Nonprofit, independent
Phone: (805) 646-1444
Fax: (805) 646-1217
E-mail: worlduojai@aol.com
Website: www.worldu.edu
Degrees at all levels in many fields, including counseling psychology (graduates are qualified to test for the Marriage, Family, and Child Counseling license), global studies, yoga, spiritual ministry, and hypnotherapy. Not affiliated with the formerly accredited World University of Puerto Rico.

Yuin University
See: California Yuin University

24

High School Diplomas

Education is what remains when you have
forgotten everything you learned in school.

ALBERT EINSTEIN
(ALSO ATTRIBUTED TO B. F. SKINNER)

The first thing to say is that, even if you have not completed high school, you probably will not need to do so in order to enroll in a nontraditional college degree program.

The high school diploma is the usual "ticket of admission" to a traditional university. However, many universities, both traditional and nontraditional, believe that anywhere from two to seven years of life or job experience is at least the equivalent of a high school diploma. So if you are over the age of 25, you should have no trouble finding schools that do not require a high school diploma. If you are between 18 and 25, you may have to shop around a little, or may find it necessary to complete high school (or its equivalent) first.

Here are six ways to complete high school (or its equivalent) and get a high school diploma by nontraditional means:

1. The High School Division of a University

While many of the universities with correspondence programs listed in chapter 13 offer high-school-level correspondence study as well as college-level, only two major universities actually award high school diplomas entirely through correspondence study. These diplomas are the exact equivalent of a traditional high school diploma, and are accepted everywhere.

Texas Tech University High School
P.O. Box 41002
Lubbock, TX 79409
Phone: (806) 742-2352 • (800) MY COURSE
Fax: 806-742-2318
Website: www.dce.ttu.edu/dl/highschl/index.htm

Established in 1993, Texas Tech University High School is a public high school accredited by the Texas Education Agency to provide a State of Texas accredited curriculum to self-motivated traditional and nontraditional students completely at a distance.

University of Nebraska at Lincoln
Independent Study High School
269 Nebraska Center for Continuing Education
33rd and Holdredge Streets,
Lincoln, NE 68583
Phone: (402) 472-1926
Website: www.unl.edu/conted/disted/ishs.html

Founded in 1929 to help small rural schools, and now serving 14,000 students from all 50 states and 135 countries. Accredited by the North Central Association and the Nebraska Department of Education and authorized to grant an accredited high school diploma.

2. State and Local Departments of Education

The state of North Dakota and several local school districts offer people throughout the United States, Canada, and worldwide the opportunity to earn a high school diploma by studying correspondence courses.

North Dakota Department of Public Instruction Division of Independent Study
P. O. Box 5036
State University Station, Fargo, ND 58105
Phone: (701) 239-7282

Bloomington Public Schools
Coordinator of Adult Learning
8900 Portland Ave.
Bloomington, MN 55420
Phone: (612) 885-8511
E-mail: shape4@primenet.com
Website: informns.k12.mn.us:80/~0271eis/mindquest/
Billed as "the world's first public high school diploma completely on the Internet." Courses leading to a high school diploma through a program called Mindquest. The entire program is free for eligible Minnesota residents. Students anywhere in the world may enroll, and there may be tuition agreements that would reduce the costs for out-of-state students.

Vance-Granville Community College
P. O. Box 917
Henderson, NC 27536
Phone: (252) 492-2061
Fax: (252) 430-0460
E-mail: info@vgcc.cc.nc.us
Website: www.vgcc.cc.nc.us
The Adult High School Diploma is available to anyone over the age of 18. Applicants take a diagnostic reading inventory to determine reading proficiency. They must have a high school reading proficiency before beginning other coursework.

Electronic High School
Grand County School District
264 South 400 East
Moab, UT 84532
Fax: (435) 259-6212.
E-mail: morris@tech.grand.k12.ut.us
Website: www.grand.k12.ut.us/ehs/home.shtml
The GCSD Electronic High School is accredited by the Northwest Association. It offers a complete high school curriculum on the Internet leading to high school graduation. The curriculum is the same as used in their adult education classes and alternative high school. Some classes, by nature, are more like correspondence courses because of the amount of work which must be corrected by hand. Some courses are entirely Internet-based.

Virtual High School
Goderich District Collegiate Institute 260
South Street
Goderich, Ontario, Canada N7A 3M5
Phone: (519) 524-7353
Fax: (519) 524-1703
Website: www.virtualhighschool.com
Accredited coursework delivered via the Internet for earning the Ontario Secondary School Diploma. No textbooks to buy and no classes to attend. Electronic or e-text have been designed and developed for each course. A part of the Cyberschool initiatives of the Avon Maitland District School Board, for students throughout Canada and the world.

3. Accredited Private High Schools

Here are some. DETC, the Distance Education and Training Council, is a recognized accreditor, specializing in home study programs, including high school diploma programs.

Cambridge Academy
3855 SE Lake Weir Avenue
Ocala, FL 34480
Phone: (352) 401-3688, (800) 252-3777
Fax: (352) 401-9013
E-mail: CamAcad@aol.com
Website: www. camacademy.com
Founded 1978, and accredited by DETC.

Citizens' High School
188 College Drive
Orange Park, FL 32067
Phone: (904) 276-1700
Fax: (904) 272-6702
E-mail: citzen school@schoolmail.com)
Founded 1981 and accredited by DETC.

Home Study International
P. O. Box 4437
12501 Old Columbia Pike
Silver Spring, MD 20914
Phone: (301) 680-6570 • (800) 394-GROW
E-mail: 74617.74@ compuserve.com
Website: www.hsi.edu
Founded 1909 and accredited by DETC.

ICS-Newport/Pacific High School
925 Oak Street
Scranton, PA 18515
Phone: 717-342-770 • (800) 233-4191
E-mail: stuser@icslearn.com
Website: www.icslearn.com).
Founded 1972. Accredited by DETC. A division of ICS Learning Systems-Harcourt Brace.

Keystone High School
Learning and Evaluation Center
420 West 5th Street
P.O. Box 616
Bloomsburg, PA 17815
Phone: (717) 784-5220 • (800) 255-4937
Fax: (717) 784-2129
E-mail: info@keystonehighschool. com
Website: www.keystonehighschool. com
Founded 1972. A division of NLKK, Inc. Accredited by DETC.

James Madison High School
Professional Career Development Institute
430 Technology Parkway, Norcross, GA 30092
Phone: (770) 729-8400 • (800) 362-7070
Website: www.pcdi.com).
Founded 1987, and accredited by DETC.

Phoenix Academies
3132 West Clarendon Ave.
Phoenix, Arizona 85017
Phone: (800) 426-4952
Fax: (602) 265-7179
E-mail: email@phoenixacademies.org
Website: www.phoenixacademies.org
Accredited by the North Central Association. Founded in 1926 as a correspondence school. Serves over 10,000 school-aged youth and adults throughout the world

Richard M. Millburn High School
14416 Jefferson Davis Highway, Suite 12
Woodbridge, VA 22191
Phone: (703) 494-0147
Accredited by DETC.

Center for Distance Education
14416 Jefferson Davis Highway, Suite 8
Woodbridge, VA 22191
Phone: (703) 494-0147
Fax: (703) 494-6093
E-mail: info@rmhs. edu
Website: www.rmhs.edu)
Founded 1975 and accredited by DETC.

4. Unaccredited distance high schools

As with degrees, the unaccredited schools offer some interesting options, but one must be very, very certain that the diploma will meet one's needs, before undertaking such a program. Here are three options:

CAL Campus
P.O. Box 734
East Rochester, New York 14445
Fax: (716) 381-6648
E-mail: director@calcampus.com
Website: www.calcampus.com
Ray Chasse, who is also involved in the operation of several unaccredited universities in Louisiana and Alabama, has a high school division, run from New York, registered with the state of California, with records storage in Louisiana. The diploma is issued by the American Academy of the American Coastline Professional Development Institute of Studio City, California, affiliated with Chasse's American Coastline University in Louisiana.

Covenant Home Curriculum
17800 West Capitol Drive
Brookfield, WI 53045
Phone: (414) 781-2171
Fax: (414) 781-0589
E-mail: educate@covenanthome.com
Website: covenanthome.com
The school's literature says "A New Kind of Revival is in the Land," and that they offer a "full, eclectic, classical approach" to K-12 education.

Dennison Academy
P.O. Box 2978
Los Angeles, CA 90029
Phone: (323) 662-3226
They state that accreditation is "no guarantee of quality as evidenced by the current state of education in America. Dennison elects not to be accredited." Registered with the Los Angeles County Office of Education and the California State Board of Education. Offers their high school diploma by regular correspondence, or in one day by exam, with an added option, in case of failure, which they call "Cram and retest immediately."

5. Home Schooling

There is a large and growing movement toward educating children at home. It isn't easy, but it can be richly rewarding. There are now quite a few local, regional, and national support organizations, both religious and secular. Here are two national organizations:

Holt Associates Book and Music Store
2269 Massachusetts Ave.
Cambridge, MA 02140.
Phone: (617) 864-3100
E-mail: HoltGWS@aol.com
Website: www.holtgws.com
John Holt is the author of How Children Fail and other books on educational reform, and founded a magazine called Growing Without Schooling. His organization has a nice catalog of educational materials for the home schooler.

Home Schooling Legal Defense Fund
P.O. Box 3000
Purcellville, VA 20134
Phone: (540) 338-7600
Fax: (540) 338-7600
Website: www.hslda
This organization offers advice and information for parents interested in—and/or having legal problems with—home schooling. They also sell a high-school diploma, so that people who home-school their children can still award those children an attractive certificate. This document may not be accepted in some situations, and the Fund's literature makes it clear that, "by sale of this diploma, Home School Legal Defense Fund does not certify completion of any course of study."

6. State Equivalency Examinations

Each of the 50 states offers a high school equivalency examination, sometimes called the G.E.D., which is the equivalent of a high school diploma for virtually all purposes, including admission to college. Although each state's procedures differ, in general the examination takes from 3 to 5 hours, and covers the full range of high school subjects: mathematics, science, language, history, social studies, etc.

It must be taken in person, not by mail. For the details in any given state, contact that state's Department of Education in the state capitol.

(Two members of our family have taken the equivalency exam when they were 15, partway through the 10th grade. As soon as they learned they had passed, they left high school forever. One immediately enrolled in college; the other worked for three years, and then entered a university. Neither had any problem with college admission as a result of their equivalency diploma. And both ended up as straight-A students, despite the lack of whatever they might have learned in three years of high school.)

Our Second Cartoon Caption Contest

Provide a caption and/or the text for the sheet of paper being held (it should have something to do with distance education). The one we like the best wins the one and only prize: publication in the 14th edition, a free copy of the 14th edition, and lunch with the authors, if we ever happen to be in the same place at the same time. Decision of the judges is final.

Send entries to John & Mariah Bear, P.O. Box 7070, Berkeley, CA 94707 USA. Thank you.

25

Law Schools

*Laws are like spider's webs which, if anything small falls into them,
they ensnare it, but large things break through and escape.*

SOLON (7TH CENTURY B.C.E.)

This chapter was revised with the assistance of Roger Agajanian, J.D.

The law is a curiosity of the academic world. On one hand, it is possible to graduate from a world-famous law school and not be able to practice law. And on the other hand, it is possible to practice law without ever having seen the inside of a law school.

What makes this unusual set of circumstances possible is, of course, the Bar exam. In all 50 states of the United States, the way most people are "admitted to the Bar" is by taking and passing this exam. Each state administers its own exam, and there is the Multi-State Bar exam, which is accepted by most states for some or all Bar exam credit.

Until the 20th century, most lawyers learned the law the way Abraham Lincoln, Andrew Jackson, and several other U.S. presidents did—either by apprenticing themselves to a lawyer or a judge or by studying on their own and, when they had learned enough, taking the Bar. A small handful of states still permit this practice, although it is little used. The majority of people who wish to study law nontraditionally deal in one way or another with the state of California, where the study of law is, in many aspects, different from the rest of the U.S. This is why California is considered separately in this chapter.

In a few states, if one graduates from a law school in that state, it is not necessary to take that state's Bar exam in order to practice law. In a few states, graduates of unaccredited law schools may be permitted to take the Bar exam. There are two problems we have in reporting these facts: one is that the situation keeps changing—states seem regularly to revise or reinterpret their regulations—and the other is that rules and regulations seem often to be rather flexible or at least inconsistent in the way they are interpreted (see chapter 29, Bending the Rules).

THE BAR EXAM

The Bar exam has come under increasing criticism in recent years, on a number of grounds.

For one thing, there often seems to be little correlation between performance on the Bar and performance as a lawyer. Most Bar exams, for instance, do not test ability to do legal research, conduct interviews, or argue in court.

In addition, a test score that will pass in one state will fail in another. Consider the score required to pass, in several states, in one recent year:

California:	145	Pennsylvania:	129
New York:	135	Texas:	128
Florida:	130	Wisconsin:	125

One critic has pointed out that if California test takers had gone en masse to New York, their pass rate would have been 74% instead of California's rather dismal 42% that year.

In recent years, the Bar exam has undergone frequent and major changes. Gordon Schaber, former chairman of the ABA's section on legal education, points out that the California exam underwent "10 serious structural changes" over a ten-year period, during which time the pass rate dropped 12%. Following significant changes after that ten-year period, the pass rate dropped another 9%. The failure rate might have been higher, but nearly half the minority graduates at UCLA (which has the largest minority law student population in the state) chose not to take the California Bar exam. The pass rate for some minorities has been significantly lower than for other groups, although the majority of those who failed in California would have passed the New York or Pennsylvania exam with the same scores.

Although the quality of law education is generally felt to continue to improve, the percentage of people passing the Bar has steadily declined in recent years. As one example, Schaber cites an entering Stanford class of which had the highest LSAT (Law School Admissions Test) scores ever, and a grade point average of 3.79 on a scale of 4. Yet when this class graduated four years later and took the Bar exam, only 75% passed—down 17% from a few years earlier.

Can it be, people are asking more and more, that there may be too many lawyers in the world, and the already-established ones are trying to limit the new competition? In recent years, the number of lawyers has increased at more than double the rate of the population as a whole. There are more lawyers in Chicago than in all of Japan; more in New York than in all of England.

THE LAW DEGREE

Until the early 1960s, the law degree earned in America was the LL.B., or Bachelor of Laws. An LL.D., or Doctor of Laws, was available at some schools as an advanced law degree, earned after several years of study beyond the LL.B. Many lawyers didn't like the idea that lots of other professionals (optometrists, podiatrists, civil engineers, etc.) put in three years of study after college and got a Doctorate, while lawyers put in the same time and got just another Bachelor's. Law schools took heed, and almost universally converted the title of the law degree to a J.D., which can stand for Doctor of Jurisprudence or Juris Doctor. Most schools offered their alumni the opportunity to convert their old LL.B.'s into nice shiny J.D.'s. One survey reported that a large percentage accepted, but another report suggests that very few of these actually use the J.D. professionally, still listing the LL.B. in legal directories. In either event, very few lawyers refer to themselves as "Doctor" although those with the J.D. certainly have that option.

Unaccredited Residential Law Schools

Six states and the District of Columbia permit the operation of law schools not accredited by the American Bar Association, but only in California can law study by correspondence also qualify one to take the Bar. The residential schools, located in Alabama, California, Georgia, Massachusetts, Tennessee, Virginia, and D.C., are not nontraditional, in the sense that one must attend classes, and then take the Bar. (California has more than 20 such non-ABA-accredited residential schools, Alabama has two, and the other states mentioned have one each.)

In many situations, graduates of these schools can only take the Bar in the state where the school is located, or in a state in which one has permanent residence. Taking the Bar in a second state typically requires a certain number of years of practice in the first state (3 to 10).

Correspondence Study

California is the only state that regularly permits graduates of correspondence law schools to take the state Bar. One must be a graduate of a school located in California, despite the claims made by certain correspondence law schools in Kansas, Louisiana, and elsewhere. (We say "reg-

ularly" because, as indicated earlier, there are apparently special case exceptions in other states, from time to time.)

There used to be no requirement that the correspondence schools be located in California, but as of 1990, only graduates of California schools are permitted to take the Bar.

The California procedure works like this: after completing one year of law study, which must include a documented 864 hours of study (about 17 hours a week), the student must take the First Year Law Students' Qualifying Exam, known as the "Baby Bar." This is a consumer protection measure, to help students studying law nontraditionally determine whether or not they are making progress. The Baby Bar typically last for eight hours, and includes questions on contracts, torts, and criminal law.

Baby Bar pass rates have averaged less than 20% in recent years. The factors that come into play are:

◆ the quality of the school's course materials and methods (since pass rates have ranged from under 10% to more than 50%);

◆ the first-year law students not giving this examination the respect it deserves; and

◆ the notion that it is law graduates from ABA schools grading non-ABA law students.

Once the Baby Bar is passed, the student then continues for three additional years of study, 864 hours a year. When at least four years have passed and at least 3,456 hours have been logged, the regular Bar exam may be taken.

Copies of recent years' versions of the Baby Bar, with answers, may be purchased from the State Bar of California, P.O. Box 7908, San Francisco, CA 94129.

The Baby Bar is required of all students studying either with correspondence law schools or with unaccredited residential law schools. In the last three years, students from 15 correspondence schools and 26 residential unaccredited schools have taken the regular Bar exam.

Until 1996, law students who took the Baby Bar were "on hold" until the results came in three or four months later; they could not continue their formal studies. A new and very sensible law allows courses completed within a year after the Baby Bar to count for credit

California Exam Performance

One could spend days studying and analyzing the huge amounts of data made available by the State Bar of California, giving pass rates by school, by date, by kind of school, by ethnic background, by number of previous exam attempts, and so forth.

Rather than fill this chapter with endless charts and tables, we have elected to present only the following data:

◆ Complete summary of statistics for a recent Bar exam.

◆ For unaccredited residential schools, first time exam takers' pass rates, cumulative for six consecutive Bar exams (three years).

◆ For correspondence law schools, just the last results.

Please bear in mind that these statistics will vary considerably from year to year and school to school. Also of significance are the statistics on the "parlay" from the Baby Bar to the main Bar. If, for instance, only ten percent of a school's students pass the Baby Bar, and if only 10% of those pass the main Bar, then only one percent of the students (10% of 10%) will actually become lawyers.

Critics of the nontraditional approach argue that the lower pass rates "prove" that the approach cannot work. They point out that one of the largest schools had about a 10% pass rate on the Baby Bar, and then about 25% on the main Bar, suggesting that out of every 100 students who start this program, only two or three will become lawyers.

Supporters point out that truly dedicated and highly motivated students do pass, and that many of these people would never have been able to pursue the degree by traditional means. They also suggest that some people take the Bar exams as a matter of curiosity, with little expectation of passing.

It is clearly the case that for the would-be lawyer who cannot afford either the time or the money for traditional law study, or who cannot gain admission to an accredited law school, California approaches offer the best hope.

In addition to qualifying students for the California Bar, completion of unaccredited law programs may also qualify graduates to take the exams required for practice before U.S. tax and patent courts, workers compensation boards, the Interstate Commerce Commission, and various other federal courts and agencies. As with any degree program, potential students should satisfy themselves in advance that the degree will meet their personal needs.

BECOMING A LAWYER BY APPRENTICESHIP

There are still a few states left where it is possible to qualify for the Bar exam by studying law privately under the supervision of either a lawyer or a judge. A typical law is that of California, which states that to take the Bar without having gone to law school, one must have "studied law diligently and in good faith for at least four years...in a law office in this state and under the personal supervision of a member of the State Bar of California [or] in the chambers and under the personal supervision of a judge of a court of record of this state."

It is not easy to set up an apprenticeship program on ones own, although it can be, and has been done. An interesting alternative is the Law Apprentice Program offers an interesting approach to becoming a lawyer, for people who live in one of thirteen states or the District of Columbia. Two approaches are available:

OVERALL CALIFORNIA BAR DATA

MOST RECENT SESSION, FEBRUARY 1998

	Took	Passed	%
All takers, all schools	**3,895**	**1,558**	**40%**
First-time	1,522	871	57%
Second time	1,190	470	40%
Third or more	1,183	217	18%
ABA-approved schools	**1,329**	**657**	**49%**
First-time takers	537	337	63%
Repeaters	792	320	40%
California-Bar accredited but not ABA-approved	**982**	**270**	**27%**
First timers	275	111	40%
Repeaters	707	159	23%
Not ABA-approved and not California Bar accredited	**209**	**20**	**9%**
First timers	27	1	14%
Repeaters	182	19	10%
Correspondence schools	**72**	**13**	**18%**
First timers	19	5	26%
Repeaters	53	8	15%
Private study with lawyer or judge	**4**	**0**	**0%**
First timers	0	0	0%
Repeaters	4	0	0%
First time takers, demographics			
Males	790	440	56%
Females	637	393	62%
Caucasians	1,041	659	58%
African-Americans	99	21	21%
Hispanics	108	57	53%
Asians	130	77	59%

CORRESPONDENCE LAW SCHOOLS, BABY BAR

TOTAL OF BOTH 1996 EXAMS, MOST RECENT AVAILABLE

	Took	Passed	%
Bernadean University*	2	0	0%
British-American University**	–	–	–
City U. Los Angeles*	2	0	0%
Kensington University*	17	2	12%
LaSalle University (Louisiana)*	16	0	0%
Newport University	20	3	15%
Northwestern California U.	65	15	23%
Oak Brook College of Law	75	44	59%
Saratoga University**	–	–	–
University of Central California	1	0	0%
University of San Gabriel Valley*	1	0	0%
University of Honolulu	1	0	0%
William H. Taft University	73	10	14%

*No longer qualifies students for California Bar
**Too new to have students take exams

MORE CALIFORNIA BAR DATA

The California Bar reports results for first-time takers of the exams, and for all takers, including first timers. Here are recent results, as found on the California Bar's internet website (www.calbar.org/shared/2admndx.htm).

CORRESPONDENCE LAW SCHOOLS, REGULAR BAR

MOST RECENT THREE SESSIONS, THROUGH 1998
FIRST-TIME TAKERS ONLY

	Took	Passed	%
Bernadean University	0	0	0%
City University Los Angeles	0	0	0%
Kensington University	4	0	0%
LaSalle Extension U. (Illinois)	0	0	0%
LaSalle University (Louisiana)	0	0	0%
Newport University	1	0	0%
North American College	0	0	0%
Northwestern California U.	15	5	33%
Ocean University	0	0	0%
Southland University	0	0	0%
Thomas Jefferson College	0	0	0%
University of Central California	0	0	0%
University of San Gabriel Valley	1	0	0%
University of Honolulu	0	0	0%
William H. Taft University	32	8	25%

CORRESPONDENCE LAW SCHOOLS, REGULAR BAR

MOST RECENT THREE SESSIONS, THROUGH 1998
ALL TAKERS

	Took	Passed	%
Bernadean University	0	0	0%
City University Los Angeles	10	0	0%
Kensington University	31	2	6%
LaSalle University (Louisiana)	4	0	0%
Newport University	17	3	18%
North American College	20	2	10%
Northwestern California U.	3	1	33%
Ocean University	3	0	0%
Southland University	2	0	0%
Thomas Jefferson College	8	1	13%
University of Central California	0	0	0%
University of San Gabriel Valley	1	0	0%
William H. Taft University	73	16	22%

1. Training (by videotape plus telephone consulting) to improve the chances of passing the Bar in California or the five states plus D.C. where a person with a non-A.B.A.-approved law degree can take the bar. Students must also enroll in one of the California correspondence law schools.

2. Apprentice training (videotape, telephone, plus local internship with a lawyer) for those nine states where one can take the Bar without having a law degree, after an appropriate apprenticeship (which can be as long as four years).

L.A.P. provides the same law books used in most major law schools, plus hundreds of audio- and videotaped lectures, weekend workshops each month at several locations around the U.S., casebooks, hornbooks, and on-line access to law faculty. Regular classes are also offered every Saturday in the Denver, Colorado area.

Law Apprentice Program
2561 I Road, Grand Junction, CO 81505
(303) 245-6750 or (800) 529-9383
info@lawprogram.com
Website: www.lawprogram.com

CORRESPONDENCE LAW SCHOOLS IN OTHER COUNTRIES

It is theoretically possible to study law either in person or by correspondence study from a country other than the United States, and then qualify for the bar exam, or, in the case of five states, to petition for admission to the bar without taking the exam.. While the situation is different in every state, the common requirement is that the non-US law school must be one in which the principles of English law are taught, and that the training come from an English-speaking common-law nation. (The lone US exception is Louisiana, whose law is based on the Napoleonic code).

The qualifying countries are pretty much limited to Australia, Canada, China (Hong Kong only), England, Ireland, Scotland, and Wales.

But in practice, the only school that offers appropriate correspondence courses leading to the law degree (the Bachelor of Law, or LL.B.) is the University of London.

THE J.D. to LL.M. to BAR EXAM "PARLAY" STRATEGY

There is an intriguing strategy that has been devised for Americans who wish to study law by correspondence, and who do not live in one of the states that will accept or consider either an unaccredited California law degree or the degree of the University of London. The strategy is based on the fact that the Master of Law degree (LL.M.) is in fact a more advanced degree than the Doctor of Jurisprudence (J.D.).

It is theoretically possible for the holder of an unaccredited J.D. to gain admission to an A.B.A.-accredited LL.M. program, and on completion of that LL.M., to sit for the Bar exam in most states. Again, each state has its own rules and interpretations, and some (list follows) offer a more straightforward path than others.

There are three issues at work here:

1. Finding an LL.M.-offering A.B.A.-accredited law school that is willing to accept students with an unaccredited J.D. degree.

2. Making the necessary arrangement with a state, to be confident that one will be able to take the Bar exam under such circumstances.

3. Hoping that the American Bar Association doesn't change the rules, in order to prevent this strategy from working.

With regard to the first, there are at least two California correspondence schools that state they have made arrangements for its J.D. graduates to be admitted to an A.B.A.-accredited LL.M. program. But both British-American University and Saratoga University have been unwilling to tell us which schools, stating that this is proprietary information which they do not wish to reveal to their competition. They say they will convey this information to already-enrolled students. We have not yet asked the approximately-seventy LL.M.-offering schools whether they will do this or not.

With regard to the second, before undertaking five years of study (four for the J.D., one more for the LL.M.), one should be as certain as one can be that one will be permitted to sit for the Bar. There is no precedent here; no one has yet done this. The notion of getting a written guarantee does come to mind.

With regard to the third, it seems clear that the American Bar Association is not enthusiastic about the study of law other than in schools they have accredited. Many states that used to offer either the apprenticeship approach or allow unaccredited schools succumbed to ABA pressure, and have changed their laws. Lawyers such as John Adams, Thomas Jefferson, John Quincy Adams, Andrew Jackson and Abraham Lincoln would no longer be able to qualify in the way they originally did. There is simply no way of knowing if this J.D. to LL.M. to Bar exam parley will attract the attention, the concern, or even the wrath of the A.B.A. and, if so, what the effect will be on people who have completed, or on the path to completion, of their degrees by this path.

The Nature of LL.M. Study

The Master of Laws is not a wildly popular degree option in the U.S., and as a result, there is rarely a waiting list for admission, except perhaps to the top-tier programs such as Harvard and Yale. It is typically regarded as an opportunity for law school graduates to specialize in a certain aspect of

the law, such as taxation, international business, labor law, ocean and coastal law, etc., although there are a fair number of general programs as well.

While the LL.M. is regarded as a full-time residential program, it can be quite nontraditional, in that it is typically based on a one-to-one mentor-student relationship, without classroom attendance. As a result, there is the possibility of negotiating, as with the British research degrees described in appendix E for a course of study involving occasional meetings, which conceivably could be done at least in part by internet, telephone, or other distance means.

The bottom line here is that "parlay" approach is intriguing, but until it has been tested and proven, must be considered at least a bit risky. We look forward to learning more as the pioneers move along this path.

LISTS OF STATES THAT OFFER VARIOUS LAW OPTIONS

States and jurisdictions where people with a non-ABA law degree may petition to take their bar examination

California	Maine
Connecticut	North Carolina
District of Columbia	South Carolina
Georgia	

States where people who have studied law by apprenticeship with a lawyer or judge may petition to take their bar examination

Alaska	Virginia
California	Washington
Maine	West Virginia
New York	Wyoming
Vermont	

States which allow foreign law graduates to petition to practice law without taking their bar examination

Massachusetts	Virginia
Ohio	Washington
Vermont	

States and other jurisdictions which may allow foreign law graduates to practice law after passing their bar examination

Each state is different. Some require some study in that state or at an A.B.A. school in another state. Some only accept Canadian students. Some require a certain amount of law practice in the other country. Some require apprenticeship. It is, of course, essential to learn the exact situation in your state before pursuing law study. Please don't ask us, but instead contact the bar association or society in your state.

Alaska	Ohio
California	Oregon
Colorado	Pennsylvania

Connecticut	Puerto Rico
District of Columbia	Tennessee
Hawaii	Texas
Idaho	Vermont
Nevada	Virginia
New Hampshire	Washington
North Carolina	West Virginia

States in which a person with an unaccredited J.D. and an ABA-accredited LL.M. may petition to take the bar exam

(theoretically possible in almost all states, but these ten are said to offer the least difficult roads of travel)

Arizona	Montana
California	New York
Connecticut	North Carolina
Kansas	Virginia
Michigan	West Virginia

BAR-EXAM QUALIFYING CORRESPONDENCE LAW SCHOOLS

At the time of writing, graduates of all schools in this section qualified to take the California bar exam. Since the rules change from time to time, it would be appropriate to confirm the status with the California Committee of Bar Examiners before embarking on any program. In the past, even when a school was disqualified, graduates were given a generous time period (typically seven years) in which to pass the bar. But, as any lawyer would caution, that is no guarantee of future behavior. And, as suggested in an earlier section, the University of London may qualify one in various ways in eighteen states plus Puerto Rico and the District of Columbia.

Committee of Bar Examiners
555 Franklin St.
San Francisco, CA 94102
(415) 561-8303
E-mail: info@calbar.org
Website: www.calbar.org

Abraham Lincoln University
3000 S. Robertson Blvd, #420
Los Angeles, CA 90034
(310) 204-0222
Fax: (310) 204-7025
E-mail: info@alulaw.com
Website: www.alulaw.com

It is possible to listen to four sample lectures at the school's website.

British-American University
22996 El Toro Road
Lake Forest, CA 92630

(888) 264-3261
Fax: (714) 850-4621
E-mail: info@british-american.edu
Website: www.british-american.edu

Established in 1998 by Roger Agajanian, who also established the Law Apprentice Program described elsewhere. The law students have access to the more-than-100 video lectures that are also a part of the apprentice program.

Newport University School of Law
20101 S.W. Birch St., #120
Newport Beach, CA 92660
(714) 631-1155
Fax: (714) 631-0555
E-mail: info@newport.edu
Website: www.newport.edu

Northwestern California University
1750 Howe Ave., #535
Sacramento, CA 95825
(916) 922-9303
Fax: (916) 922-0418
E-mail: nculaw@aol.com
Website: www.nwculaw.edu

The university divides its law studies into four parts. Students who complete the first two parts earn a Bachelor of Science in law. Those who complete three parts earn the J.D. degree but do not qualify to take the bar exam. Completion of four parts qualifies students to take the California bar.

Oak Brook College of Law and Government Policy
P. O. Box 26870
Fresno, CA
(209) 261-9714 • (888) 33-LEGAL
Fax: (209) 650-7750
E-mail: OBCL@aol.com
Website: www.obcl.edu

Oak Brook has achieved remarkable results on the "Baby Bar," which bodes well for success on the main bar, for students who are comfortable with their mission, as stated in their literature: "At Oak Brook College we believe that our nation has strayed from its Biblical moorings and that its legal system is need of reform. Oak Brook College is committed to training lawyers who understand the Biblical foundations of our legal institutions and who desire to practice law consistent with the Biblical principles of truth, justice, mercy and reconciliation." While the study is done totally by distance learning, mostly using Internet, all new students must attend a one-week orientation conference, held twice a year in Oklahoma City.

Saratoga University
780 Blairwood Court
San Jose, CA 95120.

(408) 927-6760 • (800) 870-4246
E-mail: MHN1st@aol.com
Website: www.saratogau.edu
This relatively new school offers a B.S. in law as well as a Juris Doctor (J.D.) wholly through correspondence. The programs are approved by the state of California, and qualify graduates to sit for the Bar (there is also a non-Bar program for those seeking professional development, etc.) The University states that it has made arrangements with several ABA-accredited law schools, whereby a student can complete either the 3-year (non-bar) or 4-year (bar qualifying) J.D. at Saratoga, then go on to get a one-year LL.M. (Master of Law) at the other school, and thus qualify to take the bar exam in virtually every state

Southern California University for Professional Studies

1840 E. 17th St., #240
Santa Ana, CA 92705
(714) 480-0800 • (800) 825-0725
Fax: (714) 480-0834
E-mail: enroll@scups.edu
Website: www.scups.edu
Approved to operate in the state of California. The law school has a paralegal program, and two legal programs, a B.S. in law, and a Juris Doctor; the J.D. qualifies graduates to sit for the Bar.

University of Honolulu

1031 McHenry Ave.
Modesto, CA 95350
(209) 523-4064
Fax: (209) 522-3312
This unaccredited school offers training for the California Bar, originally from Hawaii, now located in Modesto

University of London

School of Law
Senate House, Malet Street
London WC1E 7HU, England
(44-171) 636-8000
Fax: (44-171) 436-0938
E-mail: admissions@external.lon.ac.uk
Website: www.lon.ac.uk/external
See full listing for this school in chapter 18.

William Howard Taft University

201 East Sandpointe Ave.
Santa Ana, CA 92707
(714) 850-4800 • (800) 882-4555
Fax: (714) 708-2082
E-mail: admissions@taft.edu
Website: www.taft.edu
See full listing in chapter 21.

NON-BAR-EXAM QUALIFYING CORRESPONDENCE LAW SCHOOLS

California law has changed several times with regard to bar qualification. At one time, graduates of unaccredited law schools located anywhere in the US could take the California bar exam. Now only unaccredited schools located in the state (or with mailing addresses in the state, hence the unexpected University of Honolulu in Modesto, California) can qualify graduates to take the California bar.

Thus there are two categories of non-bar-exam qualifying schools: those that once qualified students but don't any more, and those that never did. Addresses are provided for schools still in operation.

Bernadean University

13615 Victory Blvd., #114
Van Nuys, CA 91440
(818) 255-9650 • (800) LIBER-WAY
At one time, graduates qualified to take the California bar. A part of the Church of Universology, which in the past has offered absolution from all sins to its graduates.

City University Los Angeles

3960 Wilshire Blvd., 5th Floor
Los Angeles, CA 90010
(213) 382-3801 • (800) 262-8388
At one time, graduates qualified to take the California bar. Formerly California-approved, but now operating under what they term the power of 'eminent domain.'

Columbia Pacific University

1415 Third St.,
San Rafael, CA 94901
(415) 459-1650 • (800) 227-0119
Offers a three-year non-Bar-qualifying law degree in international law. Graduates never qualified to take the bar. Columbia Pacific's confusing (to us) legal status is described in chapter 31.

Greenwich University

103 Kapiolani,
Hilo, HI 96720
(800) FOR-HILO
A non-bar-qualifying law degree is offered to physicians and other health practitioners. Courses focus on aspects of law of particular relevance to these students.

Kensington University

124 S. Isabel St.,
Glendale, CA 91209
(818) 240-9166 • (800) 423-2495
See description in chapter 21.

LaSalle Extension University

Large correspondence school, at one time accredited by the Distance Education and Training Council. Their Bachelor of Law program qualified for the California bar exams. Closed by its owners, Macmillan Publishing, following loss of accreditation in the early 1980s. No connection with La Salle University, either in Louisiana or in Pennsylvania.

La Salle University
P.O. Box 4000,
Mandeville, Louisiana 70470
(504) 626-3500 • (800) 323-9266

North American College of Law
Apparently no longer operating in La Mirada, California

Southland University
Closed in California and then in Arizona in the mid 1980s.
La Salle University, Missouri, subsequently opened a school
of the same name, under the same management, and using
many of the same materials. Later moved to Louisiana.

Thomas Jefferson School of Law
A part of Heed University, with its main office in the Virgin
Islands. No connection with Jefferson University.

Washington School of Law
2268 E. Newcastle Dr.,
Salt Lake City, UT 84093
(801) 943-2440
Fax: (801) 944-8586
LL.M. and J.S.D. in taxation for lawyers

UNACCREDITED RESIDENTIAL LAW SCHOOLS

These schools all offer the standard law curriculum. Most
have evening and/or weekend courses. While not accredited, they are approved by the California Bar. The only
schools listed are those that have had at least one graduate take the Bar in the last three years.

American College of Law
1717 South State College Blvd., #100
Anaheim, CA 92806
(800) 820-0080

California Southern Law School
3775 Elizabeth Street
Riverside, CA 92506-2495
(909) 683-6760

Central California College of Law
2140 Merced Street, Suite 105
Fresno, CA 93721
(209) 233-4074

Irvine University College of Law
8231 Westminster Blvd.
Westminster, CA 92683
(714) 373-6949

Justice University School of Law
P.O. Box 910
Roseville, CA 95678-0910
(916) 781-7824

Larry H. Layton School of Law
3807 West Sierra Highway, Suite 206
Acton, CA 93510
(805) 269-5291

Oakland College of Law
125 12th Street, 4th Floor
Oakland, CA 94612-4912
(510) 832-5297

Pacific Coast University College of Law
440 Redondo Avenue #203
Long Beach, CA 90814
(562) 439-7346

Pacific West College of Law
1380 South Sanderson Avenue
Anaheim, CA 92806
(714) 535-5661

Peninsula University College of Law
436 Dell Avenue
Mountain View, CA 94043
(650) 964-5044

People's College of Law
660 South Bonnie Brae Street
Los Angeles, CA 90057
(213) 483-0083

Ridgecrest School of Law
995 North Norma
Ridgecrest, CA 93555
(619) 446-6481

Simon Greenleaf School of Law:
name changed to Trinity Law School

Trinity Law School
3855 East La Palma Avenue
Anaheim, CA 92807
(714) 632-3434

University of Northern California
Lorenzo Patino School of Law
1012 J Street
Sacramento, CA 95814
(916) 447-7223

Western Sierra Law School
8376 Hercules Street
La Mesa, CA 91942
(619) 469-2245

INTERSTATE LEGAL STRATEGIES

Since the rules for becoming a lawyer vary so much from
state to state, the question often arises: what about qualifying to practice law in one state (an "easier" one), and then
moving to another state to practice?

It is possible, but quite impractical. Twenty-seven of the 50 states permit lawyers from another state to take the Bar in their state, but, in all but a few cases, only after they have practiced in their "home" state for a minimum number of years, and only if their degree is from an ABA-approved, accredited school. The minimum waiting time ranges from 3 years in Maine and Wisconsin to 20 years in Connecticut, but is 4 or 5 years in most states. Indiana and Iowa will, under certain conditions, permit lawyers admitted in other states to take their Bar with no waiting period.

STUDYING LAW NIGHTS OR WEEKENDS

In previous editions, we included a list of law schools that offered the law degree entirely through evening and/or weekend study. This practice, once relatively rare, has grown so rapidly that there are now a great many schools doing it. Simply check any standard school directory or the yellow pages of your telephone book for this information.

PARALEGAL DEGREES

Many people who are intrigued by the law, and wish to be involved with the law, are unwilling or unable to pursue a law degree or to be admitted to the Bar. A fairly satisfactory solution for some of these people is to pursue an alternative degree, entirely by correspondence, or with short residency, in a law-related subject.

For instance, many people have earned nonresident Master's or Doctorate degrees in business law, law and society, import-export law, consumer law, and so forth. The titles of such degrees are things like M.A. in legal studies or Ph.D. in corporate law. Of course such degrees do not permit one to practice law. Many schools offering nonresident nontraditional degrees will consider such degree programs.

There are also many people with law degrees (both traditional and nontraditional, residential and correspondence) who have never passed the Bar, but who are still working in the law. They have jobs with law firms, primarily doing research, preparing briefs, etc. They cannot meet with clients or appear in court, but they are most definitely lawyers working in the law.

Some of the schools offering paralegal studies (but not degrees) by correspondence are:

Blackstone School
P. O. Box 871449
Dallas, TX 75287
(214) 418-5141 • (800) 826-9228
For many years, this school did offer law degrees which qualified for bar exams. Now the nephew of the founder is operating it as a paralegal school only.

ICS Learning Systems
925 Oak Street
Scranton, PA 18515
(717) 342-7701

E-mail: stuser@icslear.com;
Website: www.icslearn.com
The former International Correspondence School offers courses in many subjects including paralegal study. Accredited by the Distance Education and Training Council.

National Institute for Paralegal Arts and Sciences
164 West Royal Palm Road
Boca Raton, FL 33432
(561) 368-2522 • (800) 669-2555
Fax: 561-368-6827
E-mail: nipas@nipas.net
Website: www.nipas.net
Paralegal specialized Associate's degree program, Paralegal diploma program, paralegal specialty courses and legal nurse consulting. Accredited by the Distance Education and Training Council.

Paralegal Institute, Inc.
2933 W. Indian School Road, Drawer 11408
Phoenix, AZ 85061-1408
(602) 212-0501 • (800) 354-1254
Fax: (602) 212-0502
Courses in legal assistant/paralegal training, Certified Legal Assistant, and Associate degree in Paralegal Studies. Accredited by the Distance Education and Training Council.

Professional Career Development Institute
430 Technology Parkway
Norcross, GA 30092
(770) 729-8400 • (800) 362-7070
Courses in many fields, including paralegal and legal transcriptionist. Accredited by the Distance Education and Training Council.

School of Paralegal Studies
6065 Roswell Road N.E., #3118
Atlanta, GA 30328
(800) 223-4542
In addition to the professional paralegal program, offers advanced specialty programs for paralegals, in civil litigation, real estate law, will, trusts, estate administration, and corporate law. Graduates of the basic program may take their first advanced class for free.

University College
College Park, MD 20742
(301) 985-7036 • (800) 888-UMEC
Offers paralegal training through independent study, with a short residency requirement.

University of West Los Angeles
1155 W. Arbor Vitae St.
Inglewood, CA 90301
(310) 215-3339
B.S. in paralegal studies for transfer students can be earned through two to three years of evening classes.

26

Medical Schools

*Géronte: It seems to me you are locating them wrongly. The heart is
on the left and the liver is on the right.
Sganarelle: Yes, in the old days that was so, but we have changed
all that, and teach medicine by an entirely new method.*

MOLIÈRE

*Note: In early editions, this chapter was restricted to schools offer-
ing only the M.D. degree. Then, for a number of years, in response
to many letters, we changed it to list "health-related" schools.
Now we are changing back to "medical only," since we note that
the line between "health-related" and general schools is increasingly difficult to draw, as in the case, for instance, of a degree in
"running community health organizations," or "nursing management." Now all schools, except those offering the doctor of
medicine, have been relocated to Chapters 18–23, as relevant,
and are appropriately indexed in the subject index at the back.*

There are, of course, no legitimate correspondence medical schools, but there are some nontraditional approaches
to earning a traditional medical degree.

The traditional approach in the U.S. consists of attending a regular college or university for four or more years
to earn a Bachelor's degree (in any field; it need not be scientific), and then going on to medical school for another
four years, after which the Doctor of Medicine (M.D.) is
awarded. Then one spends anywhere from two to eight
years of internships, residency, and training in clinical spe-
cialities (surgery, psychiatry, etc.)

The problems caused by this huge expenditure of time
and money (tuition of $30,000 a year is not uncommon) are
compounded by the even greater problem of admission to
a traditional medical school. The simple fact is that the great
majority of applicants are not admitted. Many schools have
anywhere from two to 50 applicants for each opening.
Although schools are not allowed, by law, to have quotas
by race or by sex, as they once did, they definitely have quotas based on age. Applicants over the age of 30 have a much
harder time getting in, and those over 40 have almost no
chance at all. The schools argue that their precious facilities should not be taken up by persons who will have
fewer years to practice and to serve humanity.

Is There a Shortage of Doctors?

The reason it is so hard to get into medical school is that
there are not enough openings available. And the reason
there are not enough openings available is the subject of
bitter debate between and among medical and political people.

The American Medical Association and the Association
of American Medical Colleges both said throughout the
1980s that we would have too many doctors by the 1990s.
But in 1988, a major study conducted by the RAND
Corporation and the Tufts University School of Medicine
strongly suggested that while there might be a surplus of
general practitioners in some large and pleasant cities,
there would be serious shortages by the year 2000, and
thereafter, especially in major areas of specialty such as
heart, chest, blood, kidney, gastrointestinal, blood disease,
cancer, and infectious disease.

The A.M.A. suggests that too many doctors, whether
from medical schools or from other countries, may mean
that U.S. doctors' skills could deteriorate because the
physician "may not perform certain procedures frequently
enough to maintain a high level of skill." But the RAND/Tufts
study suggests that in the early years of the new millennium,
many areas may not have anywhere near the specialists they
need.

In this context, Andy Rooney writes that "the A.M.A.
sounds like a bricklayers' union. The bricklayers want to limit
membership in the union so that there will always be
more bricks that need to be laid than there are bricklayers to lay them. Doctors don't want a lot of young doctors
offering their services for less so they can pay back the
money they borrowed to get through medical school."

ACCELERATED MEDICAL PROGRAMS

One slightly nontraditional approach to the M.D. is that of compressing the total elapsed time between high school and receiving the M.D. by two or three years. Many schools now offer a "3–4" program in which you enter medical school after the third year of a four-year Bachelor's program, and receive the Bachelor's degree after the first year of medical school. While most accelerated programs take seven years, some take six (Boston University, Lehigh University, Wilkes College, for instance), and one (Wofford College in South Carolina) takes five. The U.S. is, apparently, moving very slowly toward the British system, in which one enters medical school right after high school, and earns the Bachelor of Medicine in four or five years. (In England, the Doctor of Medicine is a less common advanced degree.)

Advanced placement in a medical school

This, annoyingly, is one of those "bending the rules" matters, where we simply cannot be specific. Several schools used to offer people with a Ph.D. a two-year MD, based on the notion that the first two years of medical school are usually spent learning the relevant academic but nonmedical subjects (anatomy, physiology, biology, etc.) On the assumption that a person who has already earned an accredited Ph.D. in certain scientific fields will have this knowledge, these schools used to offer the shorter M.D. to such people. They no longer do. But we still hear from people who have gained advanced placement in an M.D. program based on comparable scientific credentials. As always, there can be no harm in asking, but please don't ask us for school recommendations, since this seems always be done on a case-by-case basis, if at all.

FOREIGN MEDICAL SCHOOLS

In previous editions of this book, several pages were devoted to a discussion of the history, philosophy, and present practice of dealing with foreign medical schools: those in Mexico that cater to English-speaking students from the U.S. and elsewhere, and those throughout the Caribbean established to provide a medical education for Americans unable to get into an American medical school.

The situation is immensely complex, and almost impossible to evaluate for a nonmedical layman. Luckily, 1995 saw the return to print of what we have always considered to be the best reference in the field, a witty, information-packed, delightfully written, and heavily opinionated book called Foreign Medical Schools for U.S. Citizens by Carlos Pestana, M.D., Ph.D., a professor at the University of Texas medical school. Dr. Pestana self-publishes the book, and for people considering looking outside the U.S. for a medical school, it is worth far, far more than the $20 he charges for it by mail (for ordering information, see the bibliography of this book). In brief, his advice is not to even consider foreign school unless your MCAT exams scores are in the

PASS RATES FOR MORE THAN 30,000 PEOPLE WHO TOOK THE USMLE FOR THE FIRST TIME IN 1994–1995

Country of training	Step One	Step Two
Australia	91%	98%
Israel	86%	88%
Canada	82%	99%
United Kingdom	81%	90%
Germany	73%	73%
India	63%	56%
China	59%	39%
Romania	59%	43%
Nigeria	56%	53%
Syria	54%	42%
Poland	51%	46%
Egypt	45%	31%
Italy	40%	29%
Philippines	35%	31%
Russia/Soviet Union	31%	36%
Mexico	20%	20%
Dominican Republic	12%	13%

USMLE EXAM PASS RATES FOR ABOUT 2,500 U.S. CITIZENS TRAINED IN THE FOLLOWING COUNTRIES

Country	Step One 1st try	Step One All tries	Step Two 1st try	Step Two All tries
Israel	89%	97%	78%	94%
Grenada	72%	83%	56%	88%
Dominica	48%	63%	46%	73%
Montserrat	42%	56%	37%	58%
India	42%	51%	53%	65%
Philippines	32%	39%	28$	41%
Italy	23%	30%	17%	42%
Mexico	14%	20%	18%	34%
Dominican Republic	8%	12%	15%	23%

upper 20s or 30s. According to Dr. Pestana, most U.S. students who study abroad come back unable to pass the necessary examinations (currently the USMLE) to qualify for residency training and eventual licensure in the U.S. If this doesn't worry you, get his book. When we bought a new copy in July 1998, we received it in three days, and it included an update written in June 1998!

Note: A small book, called The Official Guide to Caribbean Medical Schools, was published in 1997 by two graduates of the medical school on Saba. It describes the curriculum of six Caribbean schools in some detail, and offers reflections on the Caribbean lifestyle. It is listed in our bibliography.

Using Exam Pass Rates to Judge Schools

People who attend a medical school outside the U.S. and wish to be licensed in the U.S. must pass a qualifying exam, administered by the Educational Commission for Foreign Medical Graduates (3624 Market St., Philadelphia, PA 19104, phone: (215) 386-5900). This United States Medical Licensure Examination (USMLE) has three parts. The first is basic science (anatomy, biochemistry, microbiology, etc.). The second is clinical sciences (medicine, surgery, obstetrics, gynecology, pediatrics, etc.). The third is a practice exam, given after graduation, during residency training.

The ECFMG used to publish pass rates for graduates of specific non-US schools, and they ranged from nearly 100 percent (Sackler in Israel) to near zero. Now all that is available are pass rates by country where the medical schools are located, but that still provides a lot of useful information. Indeed, Dr. Pestana's very strong advice is seriously to consider only schools in Israel, Australia, the UK, and Grenada. Note that the first table, below, is for everyone trained in a given country, US citizens, locals, and others. The second table is just for US citizens. Note, also, that Step Two is typically a harder exam than Step One, and it may be taken either before or after Step One. These data have been swiped from the October 1997 update to Dr. Pestana's book.

THE MEDICAL SCHOOLS

More than 60 foreign schools welcome students from the U.S. and other countries. Here are the ones most highly recommended by Dr. Pestana.

Sackler School of Medicine

University of Tel Aviv, Tel Aviv, Israel
U.S. office: 17 E. 62nd St., New York, NY 10021
(212) 688-8811
Fax: (212) 223-0368.
In Dr. Pestana's opinion, "this is without question the best foreign medical school that a U.S. citizen may attend."

Tuoro College

Technion University, Israel.
U.S. office: Admissions Office/Biomedical Sciences, Tuoro College, Building #10, 135 Carman Road, Dix Hills, NY 11746
(516) 673-3200
Fax: (516) 673-3432

Ben Gurion University of the Negev

Israel
U.S. office: 630 W. 168th St., New York, NY 10032
(212) 305-9587
Fax: (212) 305-3079
E-mail: BGCU-MD@columbia.edu

Royal College of Surgeons, Dublin

123 St. Stephen's Green, Dublin 2, Ireland. Telephone (353-1) 478-0200, Fax (353-1) 478-2100.

Here are the ones Dr. Pestana identifies at "the big players" in recruiting students from other countries.

St. George's University

Grenada, West Indies
U.S. office: One East Main St., Bay Shore, NY 11706-9990
(516) 665-8500 • (800) 899-6337
Fax: (516) 665-5590

Ross University

Dominica, West Indies.
U.S. office: International Educational Admissions, 460 West 34th Street, 12th Floor, New York, NY 10001
(212) 279-550
Fax: (212) 629-3147

Universidad Autonoma de Guadalajara

Americans already resident in Mexico should contact the Foreign Students Office, Avenida Patria 1201, Lomas del Valle, 3A Seccion (Apartado Postal 1-440), Guadalajara, Jalisco, Mexico.
(523) 641-5051, ext. 32345
U.S. office: 10999 IH-10 West, Suite 355, San Antonio, TX 782301356
(210) 561-9559 • (800) 531-5494
Fax: (210) 561-9562

Other Caribbean-Area Schools

There are other medical schools in the Caribbean that specifically cater to Americans. Dr. Pestana has detailed evaluations of most of them (except for one which he refuses to identify, since their lawyers have threatened him so). This particular section is difficult to keep current, since schools come and go. As many as twenty medical schools that once existed in the Dominican Republic and Puerto Rico are no longer there, for instance.

American University of the Caribbean, St. Maarten

(formerly on Montserrat, which was destroyed by a volcano in 1995-1996, one of the hazards of life in the Caribbean).
Medical Education Information Office, 9091 Ponce de Leon Blvd., #201, Coral Gables, FL 33134
(305) 446-0600

Saba University

School of Medicine, Saba
EIC, Inc., P. O. Box 386, Gardner, MA 01440
(508) 630-5122 • (800) 825-7754

Spartan Health Sciences University, Saint Lucia

Skypark II, 6500 Boeing Dr., #L-201, El Paso, TX 79925
(915) 778-5309

University of Health Sciences, Antigua

School of Medicine, Dowhill Campus, P. O. Box 510, St. John's, Antigua
(268) 460-1391

International University of the Americas

We have read about this new institution, offering podiatrists the opportunity to earn an M.D. with ten months in Costa

Rica and another year of study in the U.S., but have been unable to find an address or telephone.

CONSULTING SERVICES

In earlier editions, we have listed various services that advertise heavily (the Sunday *New York Times* seems the most common place), offering to assist in the process of becoming admitted to medical school, whether in the US, the Caribbean, or elsewhere. These services come and go. Some are connected directly with one school (although not always openly). What we have read and been told suggests that it typically makes more sense to deal directly with the schools.

One possible exception could be the Cambridge Overseas Medical Training Programme (COMTP). We present information on this interesting-sounding service, without comment, in the hope that readers familiar with it, or who make contact with it, will provide us with information we can report in later editions.

COMTP was established in 1996, to offer English-speaking candidates the opportunity to earn a medical degree based on three or four years of study in the city of Cambridge and New York, and a final year at a medical school in another country which awards the degree. The only current location is a medical school in Uganda, but others in Europe (Latvia) and the South Pacific (Tonga) may be added.

The initial study is in the city of Cambridge, England: two years for people with a Bachelor's, three years for others. The literature makes it clear that there is no connection with the university there, although local faculty may serve as adjunct faculty for the university in Uganda. Then a year in New York (other US cities may be added), and a year in Africa.

Cambridge Overseas Medical Programme
181a Huntingdon Road
Cambridge CB3 0DJ, England
Telephone (44-1223) 327282
Fax (44-1223) 327292
Email: rv204@hermes.cam.ac.uk

ILLEGAL MEDICAL DEGREES

Very few fake school operators take the higher risk of offering fake medical degrees, although there are a handful of them sprinkled throughout chapter 27, Degree Mills. Two of the largest operations were closed down in 1984 as a result of the F.B.I. Dip Scam operation: the Johann Keppler School of Medicine (which had operated from various addresses in Canada, Switzerland, the U.S., and Mexico), and the United American Medical College (operating from Louisiana, Florida, and California). In both cases, the perpetrators went to prison. But the fake doctor who had been involved with both returned to the scene ten years later, apparently affiliated with a British school that purported to offer surgical training by correspondence study.

In the mid 1980s, it was discovered that two medical schools in the Dominican Republic, known as CETEC and CIFAS, were involved in selling M.D. credentials at a cost of $5,000 to $50,000. It has never been fully determined how many of the more than 5,000 M.D. degrees awarded by these two schools were genuinely earned and how many were sold to people who never attended the school.

More alarmingly, a major California university acknowledged that someone had tampered with their computer records, and had rigged the system to show that at least one unqualified person had a medical degree. Because the school did not retain any paper records whatsoever, they had no simple way to determine how many other fake medical alumni their computer claimed they had.

One man arrested and jailed as a medical-degree broker earned $1,500,000 in fees from his 165 clients, 44 of whom actually passed the foreign medical students' exam and were practicing medicine in the U.S.

Some of the fake schools listed in the chapter on diploma mills have sold medical degrees, most frighteningly sometimes under the name of legitimate schools. Recently, an Arkansas organization that advertised in USA Today was selling the M.D. of Stanford University, no questions asked, for under $400. And, as described in chapter 27, John has a very realistic diploma showing that he earned a medical degree from Harvard. It cost him $50 from a "lost diploma replacement service."

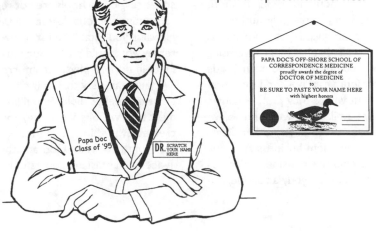

"Trust me. I'm a doctor."

27

Degree Mills

When you deal with a degree mill,
it is like putting a time bomb in your resumé.
It could go off at any time, with dire consequences.

JOHN BEAR

In most earlier editions of this book, the degree mill section began with the following sentence: "Degree mills have been around for hundreds of years, and they are still flourishing all over the world."

Then, for ten or more years, we were able to report that the number of currently operating phony schools significantly diminished as a result of the "DipScam" diploma-mill task force of the FBI, whose work helped secure indictments and, in most cases, convictions of a great many people who were responsible for the operation of scores of phony colleges and universities.

Unfortunately, the trend has reversed and things are getting worse again. With the winding down of DipScam in the early 1990s, and the advent of inexpensive laser printers, color copiers, overnight delivery services, 800, 888, 877 and 500 telephone numbers, faxes, computer bulletin boards, and other accessible technology, most significantly the growth of the Internet, diploma mills have made a real comeback, both in the U.S. and Europe.

There are now dozens of places where one can buy Bachelor's, Master's, Doctorates, even law and medical degrees, with no questions asked, on payment of fees of anywhere from one dollar to several thousand. To demonstrate this, John purchased (for $53) an extremely authentic-looking law degree (Doctor of Jurisprudence) of Harvard University, from an outfit in Florida that has been advertising nationally, complete with an 800 phone number. Their ads have been running for at least four years now, and they even have a little retail establishment where they print diplomas while you wait. Transcripts are available as well. And no, we will not provide the address, or those of any other illegal schools. We have no wish to give them business. And our lawyer has advised us that we could be considered "accessories before the fact" should someone buy a fake degree

and use it to defraud others. (We will, of course, cooperate with law enforcement officers and bona fide investigative reporters.)

One of the main reasons that fake schools continue to exist is that it is so very difficult to define legally exactly what is meant by the term "diploma mill" or "degree mill."

Surely any school that will send you a Ph.D. by return mail on payment of $100, no questions asked, is a fraud. But what about a school that requires a five-page dissertation before awarding the Doctorate? How about 20 pages? 50? 100? 200? Who is to say? One man's degree mill is another man's alternative university. And nobody seems to want the government stepping in to evaluate doctoral dissertations before permitting schools to grant degrees. Would you want [insert the name of your least-favorite politician] grading your thesis?

Another large gray area is the one dealing with religious schools. Because of constitutional safeguards in the U.S. guaranteeing separation of church and state, most states have been reluctant to pass any laws restricting the activities of churches—including their right to grant degrees to all who make an appropriately large donation. In many states, religious schools are not regulated, but are restricted to granting religious degrees. But in some, like Louisiana and Hawaii, if you established your own one-person church yesterday, you could start your university today, and award a Ph.D. in nuclear physics tomorrow.

Many states say that religious schools can only grant religious degrees. A diploma mill in Louisiana took that argument to new limits, when they announced that because God created everything, no matter what you studied, it was the study of the work of God, and therefore a religious degree. Twice, the Louisiana courts upheld this argument!

WHY ARE DEGREE MILLS ALLOWED TO OPERATE?

The answer is that, as just indicated, it is almost impossible to write a law that will discriminate clearly between legitimate schools and mills. Any law that tries to define something that is subjective—obscenity, pornography, threatening behavior, or the quality of a school—is bound to be controversial. There can never be a quantitative means for, in effect, holding a meter up to a school and saying, "This one scores 83; it's legitimate. That one scores 62; it's a degree mill."

Also, degree mills that do not muddy their own local waters, but sell their products only in other states or other countries, are more likely to get away with it longer. A goodly number of degree mills have operated from England, selling their product only to people in other countries (primarily the U.S., Africa, and Asia). Many British authorities seem not to care as long as the only victims are foreigners, and authorities in the U.S. find it virtually impossible to take action against foreign businesses.

After decades of debating these matters (even Prince Charles made a speech about the diploma mill problem), Britain has taken two tiny steps. Step one is to forbid unrecognized schools to call themselves a "University." However, this law had been in effect for about three minutes when one of England's leading diploma mills, the Sussex College of Technology, found the loophole. The law declares that it pertains to everyone enrolling after April 1, 1989. Sussex immediately began offering to backdate applications to March 31, 1989, which appears not to be illegal. They are still getting away with this ploy. Step two is to require that unrecognized schools must say in their literature that they do not operate under a Royal Charter or an Act of Parliament (the two ways schools become legitimately recognized in Britain). This, however, is unlikely even to be noticed by degree-buyers in other lands.

Other states and jurisdictions have tried to craft laws that would permit legitimate nontraditional schools to operate while eliminating degree mills. For instance, for many years California had a law that stated that the main requirement for being authorized by the state to grant degrees was ownership of $50,000 worth of real property. That law was apparently passed to eliminate low-budget fly-by-night degree mills. But $50,000 ain't what it used to be, and from the 1960s through the early 1980s, dozens of shady operators declared that their home or their book collection was worth $50,000 and proceeded to sell degrees with wild abandon.

In 1978, John had the pleasure of advising the *60 Minutes* people from CBS on which California "universities" they might wish to send Mike Wallace in to expose. The proprietor of California Pacifica University was actually arrested while Wallace was interviewing him, and soon after pleaded guilty to multiple counts of mail fraud, and went off to federal prison. Two years later, California Pacifica was still listed in the state's official publication, the *Directory of California Educational Institutions*.

California, thankfully, has tightened things up considerably since then, by eliminating the "authorized" category, and adding requirements that there must be elements of instruction provided by state-*approved* schools. Once again, of course, we have a law trying to define subjective matters.

In 1990, John had the further pleasure of appearing on the nationally syndicated program *Inside Edition* to help expose yet another major degree mill, North American University. Its proprietor, Edward Reddeck, who had previously been to prison for running another fake school, was convicted on multiple counts of mail and wire (telephone) fraud, and sent to federal prison for a few years.

Another reason for the proliferation of degree mills in the past is that the wheels of justice ground very slowly, when they ground at all. Dallas State College was shut down by authorities in Texas in 1975. The same perpetrators almost immediately opened up as Jackson State University in California. When the post office shut off their mail there, they resurfaced with John Quincy Adams University in Oregon. It took 12 more years and a major effort by the FBI before the Dallas State perpetrators were finally brought to justice in a federal courtroom in North Carolina in late 1987, nearly two decades and millions of dollars in revenues after they sold their first Doctorate. And when the FBI, the IRS and the postal inspectors raided a diploma mill in Louisiana in 1995, where they recovered more than $10 million in cash, the page one newspaper account at the time said that these agencies had spent more than five years preparing for their visitation.

It was the entry of the FBI into the diploma mill arena that changed the rules of the game.

DIPSCAM

In the late 1970s, the Federal Bureau of Investigation launched an operation called DipScam (for Diploma Scam), which methodically investigated degree-granting institutions from coast to coast and, abroad, with some cooperation from Scotland Yard and other foreign authorities as well.

John consulted with the FBI on matters of degree mills from 1979 until 1992, when arch diploma mill exposer Special Agent Allen Ezell retired, and DipScam wound down.

The FBI looked into hundreds of unaccredited schools. Some were found to be harmless, innocuous, even good, and no actions were taken. When there was evidence of chicanery, a search warrant was issued, and FBI vans hauled off tons of papers and records. In many cases, but not all, a federal grand jury handed down indictments. And when they did, in many, but not all, cases the indictees pleaded guilty to mail or wire (telephone) fraud, and received fines and sentences in federal prison. When this has happened, it is described in the listing for those schools later in this chapter.

The wording of the federal grand jury indictments is quite wonderful. Here is a sample, from one indictment. (This is just a small excerpt from a thick document.)

SCHEME AND ARTIFICE: Count One: That from some unknown time prior to, on, or about [date] and continuing through some unknown time after [date] within the Western District of North Carolina and elsewhere in the United States, [defendants] did knowingly, intentionally, and unlawfully combine, conspire, confederate and agree with each other and with others to the Grand Jurors both known and unknown, to commit offenses against the United States, that is, having devised and intending to devise a scheme and artifice to defraud and for obtaining money by false and fraudulent pretenses, representations and promises, for the purpose of executing said scheme and artifice to defraud and attempting to do so knowingly and intentionally placing and causing to be placed in a post office and an authorized depository for mail matter, and causing to be delivered by United States mail according to the direction thereon, matters and things to be sent and delivered by the United States Postal Service, in violation of Title 18, United States Code, Sections 1341 and 2, and knowingly and intentionally transmitting and causing to be transmitted by means of wire communication in interstate commerce, certain signs, signals and sounds, to wit, interstate telephone conversations, in violation of Title 18, United States Code, Section 1343.

In other words, they sent fake degrees by mail, and made interstate phone calls to their customers.

In its earlier days, DipScam went after the fake medical schools—the most dangerous degree-sellers of all. They were quickly able to shut down the two worst perpetrators, Johann Keppler School of Medicine and the United American Medical College, and send their respective founders to prison.

DipScam's largest case came to its grand finale in a federal courthouse in Charlotte, North Carolina, in October 1987, with John present as an expert witness and observer. On trial were the seven perpetrators of a long string of degree mills, most recently including Roosevelt University, Loyola University, Cromwell University, University of England at Oxford, Lafayette University, DePaul University, and Southern California University, as well as several fake accrediting agencies.

More than 100 witnesses were called over a two-and-a-half-week period, including many who established the substantial size and scope of bank deposits and investments made by the defendants. Witnesses from Europe testified to the mail forwarding services the defendants used in England, France, Belgium, Germany, Holland, and elsewhere.

The circuslike atmosphere was not helped by the fact that Jim and Tammy Faye Bakker, Jessica Hahn, and company, were appearing in the courtroom right next door, and so the grounds of the courthouse were covered by photographers and reporters, none of whom took much interest in the DipScam trial.

Two of the minor players were dismissed by the judge for lack of definitive evidence, but the five main defendants were found guilty by the jury on all 27 counts of mail fraud, aiding and abetting, and conspiracy. They were sentenced to prison terms ranging from two to seven years.

Even though the DipScam project is no longer active, the FBI, the postal inspectors, and some crusading state agencies are still actively working to keep fake schools from operating and phony degrees from being sold.

WHY DEGREE MILLS PROSPER

The main reason—really the only reason—for the success of degree mills (and drug dealers, and pornographers) is, of course, that people keep on buying their product. They crave the degrees and somehow, despite much evidence to the contrary, they really believe that they are going to get away with it.

Unfortunately, many newspapers and magazines continue to permit the perpetrators to advertise. At this writing, for instance, some of the biggest phony schools advertise in nearly every issue of The Economist, USA Today, Forbes, Psychology Today, Inc., Discover, Investors Business Daily, the International Herald Tribune, regional editions of Time and Newsweek, and dozens of other publications that should know better.

Indeed they do know better. As a public service, we routinely write to such publications to suggest they are doing their readers a disservice by running these ads. With the exception of the Wall Street Journal, which promptly changed its policies, we have failed utterly. In 1997, USA Today told us they were going to change their policies, but they apparently changed their minds. The Economist even wrote to us to say that their readers were smart enough to make up their own minds. Then, when we tried to run a "Diploma Mill Alert" in The Economist, it was rejected, because "We don't run ads critical of our advertisers."

There have been occasions in the past when a class action suit filed on behalf of fraud victims also named the advertising medium where the fraud advertised. We can only hope that such a suit will attract the attention of the lawyers for other such publications.

AN EMPHATIC WARNING

We must warn you, as emphatically as we can, that it is taking a very big risk to buy a fake degree, or to claim to have a degree that you have not earned. It is like putting a time bomb in your resumé. It could go off at any time, with dire consequences. The people who sell fake degrees will probably never suffer at all, but the people who buy them often suffer mightily.

In part as a result of all the publicity the FBI activities have gotten, credentials are being checked out now as never before. Time magazine, in an article on fake degrees (February 5, 1979), said that "with the rate at which job candidates are now fibbing on resumes and faking sheepskins, graduate schools and companies face detective work almost every time they see an application.... Checking up on about 12,000 inquiries a year, U.C.L.A. finds two or three frauds a week. For its part, Yale has accumulated a file of 7,000 or so bogus Old Blues."

Often people get caught when something unexpectedly good happens in their lives, and they become the focus of the news media, which love stories involving fake degrees.

DEGREE MILLS IN THE NEWS

Here is just a small sampling of the stories from our over-flowing file on people who have gotten in trouble over degrees and credentials in recent years.

◆ The Chairman of the Board of a major Florida university resigned, after it became known that he had bought his degrees from an Oklahoma diploma mill. And when we put the name of the school in an earlier edition, the school's lawyers threatened to sue for "revealing" what had been page one news in the papers. Talk about killing the messenger if you don't like the message!

◆ Two American presidential candidates had problems over credentials claims. Joseph Biden's campaign literature "misstated" the nature of his graduate degrees, and Pat Robertson's official biography had to be changed from saying that he did "graduate study, University of London" to "studied briefly at the University of London" after the revelation he had taken only a short undergraduate seminar on art for Americans.

◆ The Superintendent of Schools for California's second largest school district lost his job and faced serious legal consequences when the Stanford Ph.D. he had claimed for years turned out to be a phony one.

◆ A popular columnist for *Forbes* magazine, Srully Blotnick, was dropped from the magazine when his Ph.D. credentials (as well as his research methodology) came under close scrutiny.

◆ Arizona's Teacher of the Year (a major honor in that state) was found to be using a Doctorate he had never earned. A $10,000 prize had to be returned.

◆ The biggest business scandal in Sweden in half a century, the Fermenta affair, was triggered when a former employee of a major industrialist, believed to be the richest man in Sweden, charged (correctly) that the industrialist had lied about possessing two Doctorates. According to *The Economist* magazine, "Fermenta's share price halved as this charge about bogus qualifications spread." A billion-dollar deal with Volvo was canceled in the wake of the scandal.

◆ During the New York City parking meter scandals, one of the government's star witnesses, according to the *Daily News,* "admitted he has a bogus Doctorate from Philathea College...."

◆ In 1985, Congressman Claude Pepper convened a congressional panel, which asserted that more than

500,000 Americans have obtained false credentials or diplomas. (Pepper's staff got him a Ph.D. from Union University. All "Dr. Pepper" allegedly had to do was submit four book reports, which his staff wrote for him.)

◆ As a result of accumulating over 7,000 "client" names from its diploma mill raids, the FBI identified more than 200 federal employees, including 75 in the Defense Department, with bogus degrees.

◆ Congressman Ron Wyden of Oregon said that as many as 40,000 physicians who failed their qualifying exams may nonetheless be practicing medicine.

◆ According to *Sports Illustrated,* the owner of the Indianapolis Colts made the "frequent boast that he played Big Ten football at the University of Illinois, while getting a degree in electrical engineering." The magazine says he neither played football nor earned a degree.

◆ A fake degree scandal rocked Indonesia, with the revelation that a war hero turned businessman was bilked of huge sums of money by an executive of his shipping line, who had been hired because of his Doctorate in economics from a U.S. degree mill, Thomas Edison College of Florida and Arkansas (not the legitimate one in New Jersey).

◆ And even in Russia ... one Alexander Shavlokhov was arrested for selling at least 56 fake degrees of the Gorky Agricultural Institute, at 1,000 rubles each, to industrialists around the country. (Note: Russia once refused to allow us to advertise this book in that country, saying there is no need for it.)

TWO OTHER INSIDIOUS ACADEMIC FRAUDS

In addition to those who sell fake degrees, there are two other "services" that undermine the academic establishment.

One is the so-called "lost diploma replacement service." If you tell them you had a legitimate degree but lost it, they will replace it for a modest fee. That's why John has a Harvard "Doctor of Neurosurgery" diploma hanging on his wall (next to his real Michigan State one). The Harvard phony sold for $49.95. When the FBI raided one such service, in Oregon (they had been advertising in national publications), they found thousands of blank diplomas from hundreds of schools—and records showing an alarmingly large number of clients.

The Oregon service no longer advertises, but others crop up from time to time, such as the one from which John bought his Harvard law degree. Since the services require their clients to sign a disclaimer saying they really had the original degree, and since the diplomas come with a "Novelty Item" sticker (easy to peel off), the services may well be operating legally. On one occasion, at least, the Justice Department was unable to get an indictment from a federal grand jury for these reasons.

The other is term paper and dissertation writing services. Several of them put out catalogues listing over a thousand already written term papers they will sell, and if they don't have what you want, they will write anything from a short paper to a major dissertation for you, for $7 to $10 a page.

HOW THIS CHAPTER HAS CHANGED

Earlier editions used to include all those schools that John regarded as diploma mills, religious and otherwise. The problem with this approach was that many of the schools were, in fact, operating legally, either because they were church-run, or because they were in locations with few or no laws regulating schools. Until 1985, for instance, Arizona had no laws whatsoever regulating universities and degrees, and so a good many degree mills operated from that state. Now, every state but Hawaii has some form of law regulating or registering or approving or accrediting colleges and universities. Some states are very thorough in their licensing process; others have little or no evaluative process, but simply register any school that applies for registration.

Twenty years ago, this chapter also used to give the addresses of the degree mills. We've become convinced that this served no legitimate or useful purpose, so the detailed addresses have been deleted, and we will not supply them if you write to us.

Finally, there are a handful of schools that we firmly believe are diploma mills, but we do not have sufficient proof to say so in print, and we do not enjoy being sued. These schools have been listed among the "Other" schools, generally with descriptions that are less than wonderful, but factual. (At one time, John thought about leaving behind a posthumous edition of this book, so that all the things he knew but dared not say, would finally be aired. But now that John's daughter Mariah has joined the team, you may have to wait another half century for this special edition!)

Some of the borderline institutions were written about in a major series of articles that appeared in the Arizona *Republic* quite a few years ago. The *Republic* received many threats from lawyers and aggrieved school operators, but was never sued over their series. The articles have been reprinted in a booklet called *Diploma Mills: The Paper Merchants*. The booklet is out of print. If you can't find it in a library, we can make you a photocopy for $10 (includes first class postage). Write to John and Mariah Bear, P. O. Box 7070, Berkeley, CA 94707. But don't buy this expecting to get the addresses of the mills; they aren't there either.

THE DIPLOMA MILLS

Here, then, are the many schools that have been publicly identified as diploma mills. From time to time, people have supplied us with information that has persuaded us that a certain school should not have been included here, and we have moved it to the "Miscellaneous Schools" chapter, Chapter 31, or at least provided additional information here.

Please note that more than a few diploma mills take names that are similar to, or identical to, legitimate schools.

"E&T" stands for *Education & Training*, a British magazine that used to report regularly on European and other degree mills. "COE" stands for the Council of Europe, an intergovernmental agency based in Strasbourg, France, which keeps track of what they believe are degree mills in Europe and elsewhere. In addition to the findings from our own research, we report here those institutions which these two European entities have publicly called degree mills.

Academy College of Holy Studies Sheffield, England. Identified as a degree mill by E&T.

Academy of the Science of Man See: Sussex College of Technology

Accademia di Studi Superiori Minerva Milan, Italy. Identified as a degree mill by COE. However, the courts decided otherwise. In District Court of Fiorenzuola d'Arda in 1958, one Amorosa d'Aragona Francesco was brought to trial for using a degree from this school. The court apparently ruled that the school may not be great but it is legal. It moved from Bari to Milan a few years later, and then went out of business.

Accademia di Studi Superiori Phoenix Bari, Italy. Identified as a degree mill by COE. Very likely the same as the school listed above.

Accademia Universale de Governo Cosmo-Astrosofica-Libero de Psico-Biofisica Trieste, Yugoslavia. Identified as a degree mill by COE. Can you imagine what their school cheers sound like?

Accademia Universitaria Internazionale Rome, Italy. Identified as a degree mill by E&T.

Adams Institute of Technology See: National Certificate Company

Addison State University Ottawa, Canada. Bachelor's, Master's, and Doctorates in almost any field but medical or dental are sold for about $30.

Alabama Christian College See: R/G Enterprises. No connection with a legitimate school of this name in Montgomery, Alabama.

Albany Educational Services Northampton, England. Offers to act as an agent to obtain American Bachelor's, Master's, and Doctorates for a fee of $150 to $250. Letters to the director, L. W. Carroll, asking which schools he represents, have not been answered.

Albert Einstein Institut Zurich, Switzerland. Sells the phony degrees of Oxford Collegiate Institute (of the International University). One of the many fake degree operations of Karl Xavier Bleisch.

American College in Switzerland Berne, Switzerland. Totally phony Doctorates are offered by yet another of "Professor Doctor" Karl Xavier Bleisch's degree mills. Affiliations with Georgetown University and with the University of Florida are falsely claimed in this school's literature.

American Extension College of Law Probably related to American Extension School of Law, below.

American Extension School of Law Chicago, Illinois. Identified as a degree mill by COE.

American Institute of Science Indianapolis, Indiana. Identified as a degree mill by COE.

American Institute of Technology See: Bureau for Degree Promotions

American International Academy New York and Washington. Identified as a degree mill by COE.

American International University (CA) Established in California in the 1970s by Edward Reddeck (who was convicted of mail fraud for a previous diploma mill operation, and later went to prison for his University of North America using Missouri, Utah and Hawaii addresses). His employee, Clarence Franklin, left to establish American National University, and was later indicted by a federal grand jury. Degrees of all kinds were sold for $1,600 to $2,500, whether or not the required eight-page dissertation was written. No longer in operation. American International resurfaced briefly in 1987, using a Kansas City, Missouri, address which was a mail forwarding service.

American Legion University U.S. location unknown. Identified as a degree mill by E&T.

American Management Institute See: International Universities Consortium

American Martial Art University Small magazine ads in the mid 1990s offered a "Doctor of Martial Art Philosophy" from this nonexistent school, with the tagline "looks authentic and genuine," for $34.50. Bachelor's and Master's degrees, the small print read, were available at the same price, presumably for fakes with lower self-esteem.

American Medical College (Burma) Rangoon, Burma. Identified as a degree mill by COE.

American Medical College (ID) Nampa, Idaho. Doctor of Medicine degrees have been awarded by this apparently nonexistent school. A student there (with a diploma mill undergraduate degree) provided what appears to be a letter from the Idaho superintendent of public instruction confirming that the school is appropriately registered with his office. There is no listed telephone for them in Nampa.

American National Educational Institute Phony awarder of fake degrees sold by International Awards Committee.

American National University (AZ) Phoenix, Arizona. The university was established by Clarence Franklin, a California chiropractor formerly associated with American International University who was subsequently indicted by a federal grand jury for operating this school. Degrees were offered on payment of fees in the vicinity of $2,000. Accreditation was claimed from the National Accreditation Association, which had been established by Franklin and a colleague in Maryland. Apparently stopped operations in 1983 or 1984. Franklin was convicted of violation of federal law a few years later. A new and unrelated American National University was authorized in California in 1987.

American School of Metaphysics Location unknown. Identified as a degree mill by COE.

American University (CA) San Diego, California. Degrees of all kinds were offered on payment of a fee of $1,500 to $2,500. The claim was made that all degrees were "registered with the government" in Mexico, where the school was allegedly located. No longer in business.

American West University See: California Pacifica University. One of the many fake schools created and run by Ernest Sinclair.

American Western University Operated from a mail drop in Tulsa, Oklahoma, in the early 1980s by Anthony Geruntino of Columbus, Ohio, who later went to federal prison for this school and his next venture, Southwestern University. American Western's mail delivery was stopped in late 1981 by the U.S. Postal Service, at which time a new address was utilized. Affiliated schools included the National College of Arts and Sciences, Northwestern College of Allied Science, Regency College, and Saint Paul's Seminary.

Amritsar University Amritsar, India. Identified as a degree mill by COE.

Anglo-American College of Medicine See: National College

Anglo-American Institute of Drugless Medicine See: National College

Anglo-American University This school's homegrown-looking catalog leads with what most students really care about—"Our diploma . . is printed on superior parchment paper with the University seal embossed in gold. This is a diploma you can be proud to display in your home or office as the proof of your achievement and competence." Their discussion of accreditation is a bit disingenuous as well, although they are very up front about their lack thereof, and like many unaccredited school, they misquote the famous Sosdian & Sharp study on acceptance of nontraditional degrees. Degrees are offered in many fields at all levels, with very generous awards for life-experience learning—indeed, the catalog states in large type "you may have already fulfilled your degree requirements." Almost certainly the product of Edward Reddeck, who has been to jail three times for degree fraud, however, given Hawaii state laws at this time, an operation such as this is not illegal.

Aquinas University of Scholastic Philosophy New York. Identified as a degree mill by E&T.

Argus University Fairplay, Colorado. A fictitious university formed apparently just for fun in 1977. Its stated purpose is selling doctorates to dogs and their humans. The founder writes that Argus "will confer a degree to any dog whose owner sends a check for $5 to Argus University." Same fee for humans, apparently.

Arya University Srinigar, India. Identified as a degree mill by COE.

Aspen Christian College Colorado. Following a local television feature on Denver station KUSA, in which a pet dog was awarded a degree, the attorney general's office took action to close this school, and it is no longer operating.

Aspen University Colorado. This school, as well as Darwin University, run by the same prankster, offers "honorary doctorates" that are clearly intended to be humorous (Doctor of Universal Confusion from "UCLA—the Ulcer Club of Los Angeles)." We list them only on the principle that however innocent the seller's intentions, one never knows what the purchasers might try to pull.

Atlanta Southern University Atlanta, Georgia. See: California Pacifica University. Another of Ernest Sinclair's degree mills. The president of a large respectable university used to tell people his degree was from Atlanta Southern; he doesn't any more.

Atlantic Northeastern University Their address in New York was a mail forwarding service. They offered all degrees, using well-designed and printed promotional materials, almost identical to those used by Pacific Northwestern and Atlantic Southern universities. Fake (but realistic-looking) transcripts were available for an additional fee. Apparently no longer in business.

Atlantic Southern University Operated briefly from addresses in Atlanta, Georgia, and Seattle, Washington. The materials look identical to those of Pacific Northwestern University. Newspaper publicity in 1980 apparently caused them to cease operations.

Australian Institute See: Bureau for Degree Promotions

Avatar Episcopal University London, England. Identified as a degree mill by E&T.

Avatar International University London, England. Identified as a degree mill by E&T.

Benchley State University See: LTD Documents

Benson University Same management as Laurence University of Hawaii.

Bettis Christian University Arkansas. In the mid 1980s, Ph.D.s were sold for $800 by two inmates of the Arkansas State Prison. Another instance of a "university behind walls."

Beulah College Nigeria and Texas. In 1990, offered to award an honorary Doctor of Humanities to anyone sending them $500.

Bible University Ambuhr, North Arcot, India. Identified as a degree mill by COE.

Bonavista University Douglas, Wyoming. All degrees were sold for fees of $500 to $700. Other Bonavista literature had been mailed from Sandy, Utah, and Wilmington, Delaware. No longer in business, at least at those locations.

Bosdon Academy of Music See: ORB

Boston City College See: Regency Enterprises

Boswell Active Promotions This organization has been very active on the Web, offering "fully accredited" "honorary" degrees from "a respected Swiss institution." The degrees are, of course, none of those things and, refreshingly, the man behind them agrees, saying "I make no pretense that these degrees are worth the paper they are printed on. To a true academic, especially one who worked hard for his degree, they are nonsense. To a person from the third world who needs a ticket to a better job, they are interesting." To the person who hires him and then discovers he has a phony degree, they may also be interesting.

Bradford University Same management as Laurence University of Hawaii. No connection with the chartered University of Bradford in England.

Brandenburg University This is a rather disturbing new mill in that it offers fake medical degrees (medical, dental, optometry, osteopathy, and chiropractic, to be exact), as well as any other degree at any level. They have been advertising over the Internet, soliciting people who post to distance learning newsgroups.

Brantridge Forest School See: Sussex College of Technology

Brantridge University For a while, the operator of diploma mills called Sussex College of Technology and Brantridge Forest School in England registered his nonexistent school in Louisiana, but it no longer exists there. It may have taken a convenience address in Hawaii.

Bretton Woods University New Hampshire. Diplomas of this alleged institution have been sold for $15 by a "collector of elite unit militaria" who says they were "obtained through various unknown third parties ... Some are original unawarded certificates, while others could be reproductions."

British College of Soma-Therapy England. Identified as a degree mill by E&T.

British Collegiate Institute London, England. They used to sell degrees of all kinds for a fee of $100 to $300, through the London address, and an agent in Inman, Kansas. The provost was listed as Sir Bernard Waley, O.B.E., M.A., D.Litt. See also: College of Applied Science, London.

Broadhurst University See: West London College of Technology

Brownell University Degrees of this "university that does not now exist" were sold for $10, both by Associated Enterprises of Jacksonville, Florida, and Universal Data Systems of Tustin, California. An extra $5 bought a "professional lettering kit" so you could add any name and date you wish. School rings, decals, and stationery were sold as well. Since the sellers in Tustin (apparently two schoolteachers) slammed the door on a 60 Minutes crew some years ago, the degrees have apparently not been sold.

Brundage Forms Georgia. Brundage sells blank forms for all purposes. His college-degree form, which you can fill in yourself, costs less than a dollar. His motto is "No advice, just forms." Our motto is: "You can get in just as much trouble with a phony 50¢ Doctorate as with a phony $3,000 Doctorate."

Buckner University Texas. All degrees, including some in medicine, were sold for $45 each. They claim there is a real Buckner in Texas. There isn't. The literature says, "We believe this modestly-priced yet extremely impressive document will give you great enjoyment, prestige, and potential profitability." It is also likely to give you the opportunity to meet some nice people from your district attorney's office. The degrees were sold by University Press of Houston, and by Universal Data Systems of Tustin, California (which also sold Brownell and other fake diplomas).

Bureau for Degree Promotions Holland. Sells the fake degrees of Addison State University, Atlantic Southeastern University, the Australian Institute, American Institute of Technology, and International University of India for $50 to $100, and knighthoods at $500.

Calgary College of Technology Calgary, Canada. One of Canada's most ambitious degree mills offered the Bachelor's, Master's, and Doctorate for fees up to $275. The literature included a lengthy profile of the dean, Colonel R. Alan Munro, "Canada's premier Aeronaut." A recent book of heraldry lists "Colonel the Chevalier Raymond Allen Zebulon Leigh Munro, C.M., G.C.L.J., C.L., K.M.L.J., S.M.L.J., A.D.C., C.O.I., C.O.F., M.O.P., B.S.W., M.H.F., LL.B., M.A., LL.D., D.Sc.A., C.D.A.S., F.R.S.A., F.S.A. Scot, A.F.C.A.S.I., C.R.Ae.S., A.F.A.I.A.A., M.A.H.S., M.C.I.M., M.C.I.M.E." Could this be the same person? The Calgary catalog even included a telephone number. That phone was answered, "Spiro's Pizza Parlor." Truly. Could "Ph.D." stand for "Pizza, Home Delivery"?

California Central University A newspaper ad for this school touted "College Degrees! No Studies!" from a post office box in southern California, for the extremely reasonable price of $19.95.

California Christian College See: R/G Enterprises

California Institute of Behavior Sciences California. Humorous but well-designed Doctorates were awarded, at least in the 1960s, with the title of Doctor of Image Dynamics, citing "mastery of Machiavellian Manipulations ... discovery of the failsafe Success Mechanism, and the fail un-safe Failure Mechanism ...."

California Institute of Higher Learning See: London Institute for Applied Research

California Pacifica University Hollywood, California. Widely advertised degree mill operated by Ernest Sinclair. Degrees from California Pacifica or almost any other school one wanted were sold for $3,500. The slick catalog showed photos of faculty and staff, all fictitious. Sinclair was the main subject of a CBS 60 Minutes exposé in April 1978. He pleaded guilty to three of the 36 counts on which he was arrested. While his trial was on, he opened yet another fake school, Hollywood Southern University. Sinclair's advertising was regularly accepted by the New York Times and other major publications. Two years after he was arrested, California Pacifica was still listed in the official California directory of authorized schools! Sinclair once sued John for $4 million for calling his degree mill a degree mill, but he went to prison before we went to trial. One report had it that he continued to sell degrees while in federal prison—if true, the first known instance of a "university behind walls" program.

Canadian Temple College of Life of the International Academy Burnaby, British Columbia, Canada. Identified as a degree mill by COE.

Capital College See: National Certificate Company

Cardinal Publishing Company Florida. They publish a variety of fake diploma forms and blanks.

Carlton University Same management as Laurence University (Hawaii).

Carnegie Institute of Engineering See: Regency Enterprises

Carolina Institute of Human Relations Sumter, South Carolina. Identified as a degree mill by COE.

Carroll Studios Illinois. Since 1988, they have been selling "College Diploma" forms for $2 each, in which the buyer must letter not only his or her own name but the name of the school and degree earned. Two dollars also buys you a marriage certificate, a birth certificate, a divorce certificate, and, if devastated by all of the above, a last will and testament.

Central Board of Higher Education India. Identified as a degree mill by COE.

Central States Research Center Ontario, Canada. They sold well-printed fake diplomas "in memory of famous names." The samples they sent out included Christian College, the Ohio Psychological Association, and Sussex College of Technology. Another address in Columbus, Ohio.

Central University See: National Certificate Company

Charitable University of Delaware Identified as a degree mill by E&T.

Chartered University of Huron Identified as a degree mill by COE.

Chicago Medical College Florida. Their literature says that "Your beautiful 11 x 15 graudate [sic] diploma is printed on the finest sturdy parchtone .... It will add prestige and beauty to your office." Or cell. The price of their medical degree is a mere $450.

Chillicothe Business College Ohio. Identified as a degree mill by E&T.

Chirological College of California Identified as a degree mill by COE.

Christian College See: Central States Research Center

Christian Fellowship Foundation See: Lawford State University

Church of Universal Confusion Nevada. This "school" offers an honorary doctorate in Universal Confusion for a very reasonable $15. It's clearly all in fun (the head of the school is listed as the Grand Poobaa, etc.), but still, we don't recommend listing it on your resume.

City Medical Correspondence College London, England. Identified as a degree mill by E&T.

Clayton Theological Institute California (the address appears to be a private home). Their Doctorate was awarded on completion of a dissertation of at least 25 words and a fee of $3. When this was done (John's dissertation was 27 words; he worked extra hard), he got a nice letter saying that he had indeed been awarded their Doctorate, but if he wanted the actual diploma, it would cost $50 more. Recent letters to the institute have been returned as undeliverable.

Clemson College See: R/G Enterprises

Clinton University Livonia, Michigan. For years, they sold fake degrees of all kinds for $25 and up, offering "a masterpiece so perfect, it absolutely defies detection." Mail to their address is now returned as undeliverable.

Coast University Another name for Gold Coast University; see them later in this chapter.

Colgate College See: R/G Enterprises

College of Applied Science London London, England. The college exists on paper only, but, like Brigadoon, it was real (well, almost real) for one day. As reported by a German magazine, a wealthy German industrialist bought a fake Doctorate from this place, and insisted that it be presented in person. The president, "Commander Sir" Sidney Lawrence enlisted the aid of his friend, "Archbishop" Charles Brearly, who runs several fake universities in Sheffield. They rented a fancy girls' school for the day, installed carpets and candelabra, and rented costumes for their friends, who dressed up as "counts hung around with medals, an abbess in a trailing robe . . . and the knights of the Holy Grail." The German arrived in a Rolls Royce, and received his degree in an impressive ceremony, which only cost him $15,000. Sir Sidney, incidentally, appends a rubber stamp to his letters saying, "Hon. Attorney General U.S.A."

College of Divine Metaphysics England. Identified as a diploma mill by E&T.

College of Franklin and Marshall See: Regency Enterprises

College of Hard Knocks See: USSI

College of Hilton Head See: University of East Georgia

College of Homeopathy Missouri. Identified as a diploma mill by E&T.

College of Journalism West Virginia. Identified as a diploma mill by E&T.

College of Life Florida. Honorary Doctorates were sold for $2, but the school has since gone away.

College of Natural Therapeutics See: International University

College of Naturatrics Missouri. Identified as a diploma mill by E&T.

College of Nonsense Nevada. "You can fool your friends and tell them you have a Doctorate degree. If they don't believe you, you can show your friends your Doctor degree." John bought a Doctor of Politics for $2. A Doctor of Martyrism, Cheerleading, or Nose Blowing would have been 50¢ extra. Silly stuff, but a better-printed diploma than many legitimate schools provide.

College of Spiritual Sciences England. Identified as a diploma mill by E&T.

College of Universal Truth Chicago, Illinois. Identified as a diploma mill by E&T.

Collegii Romanii See: International Honorary Awards Committee

Collegium Technoologicum Sussexensis Britannia See: Sussex College of Technology

Colorado Christian University Subject of a landmark court case in which the state of New York successfully sued to prevent them from selling their degrees to New Yorkers, or to advertise in publications distributed from New York. No connection whatever with the accredited Rockmont College, which changed its name in 1989 to Colorado Christian University.

Columbia School Unknown U.S. location. Identified as a diploma mill by COE.

Columbia State University Quite possibly the biggest and most insidious diploma mill the world has ever known was finally in the process of being closed down as we went to press. On July 6, 1998, these three things happened: the FBI and the Justice Department raided the secret California warehouse where diplomas were being cranked out to the tune of $2 million a month; the Louisiana Attorney General got an injunction to stop the Louisiana mailing service being used; and the Attorneys General of Illinois and Louisiana brought suits for consumer fraud against Columbia State's owner, Ronald Pellar, his wife, and his cousin. An attorney general's press release on this matter can be found at: http://www.laag.com/presshow.cfm?rowid=11&p=/br/laag/

Pellar's ads, which run regularly in major magazines, offer the Bachelor's, Master's, or Ph.D. in 27 days, "fully accredited" (by two non-existent agencies). Enough people fall for this that Columbia State was able to deposit more than $16 million into its bank account number 749-4023968 at California Federal, 570 Camino De Estrella, San Clemente. In late 1997, Pellar was convicted on 11 criminal counts for one of his earlier degree mills (Los Angeles Central District Federal Court, 90.cv.945, Judge Audrey Holmes presiding). He escaped just before the sentencing, and at this writing is a federal fugitive, living in Mexico. The Columbia State catalogue has a photograph of Lyndhurst, a stately home in upstate New York, on its cover, and lists as president Austen Henry Leyard, a well-known archaeologist who died over 100 years ago. Pellar, using the name Herald Crenshaw, has published a book that looks very much like an earlier edition of this one, and indeed is largely copied from ours, but which identifies Columbia State as the best university in the United States (and, for good measure, identifies the quite legitimate Greenwich University, with which John was once associated, as the worst university in the United States).

In 1994, Pellar managed, by a clever ruse, to steal the mailing list of recent buyers of this book. Those people were sent a newsletter from "U.S. Official Publications," in which Pellar, now using the alias Edward Connelly, spent eight pages attacking this book (which he called a "brochure") and John Bear. Needless to say there is no such organization as U.S. Official Publications. Pellar used to be known as Doctor Dante, who was a well-known television and stage hypnotist in the '60s, briefly married Lana Turner, and served a seven-year prison term for attempted murder. While he is on the run, the fake school is run by his wife, Elizabeth Dante and his cousin, Lauri Gerald.

John is often asked why he does not sue Pellar. Even though two lawyers advised that this was the clearest case of libel they'd ever seen, the cost of mounting a proper suit could easily reach six figures, and the probability of collecting a dime from this probably-75-year-old scoundrel following a courtroom victory is small. We can only hope the authorities eventually catch up with him and bring him to justice.

Commercial University Delhi, India. Listed as a degree mill by COE. The Ministry of Education writes that it is a "coaching institution" whose degrees are "not recognised for any purpose." However, a reader in Malaysia maintains that their B.Com. degree exam is comparable to those of University of London, and that at least one graduate has had his degree accepted by the Malaysian government.

Commonwealth School of Law Washington. Identified as a diploma mill by COE.

Commonwealth University California. Degrees of this nonexistent school were sold by mail for $40. Also sold by the same firm: Eastern State University.

Constantina University In 1989, a mailing went out to Italian businessmen, offering them the opportunity to earn a doctorate from this apparently nonexistent school, in association with the accredited Johnson & Wales University (which denied any knowledge of the scheme). For $3,000, they would spend a week in New York, see Niagara Falls, and go home with a Doctorate. According to one source in Italy, more than 100 people signed up.

Continental University In 1990, a reader in Japan sent us a copy of a diploma (dated 1989) from the nonexistent school, allegedly in Los Angeles.

Conway College A correspondent writes that this "school" operates from a post-office box in Conway, New Hampshire, but fraudulently claims to be a division of the University of New Hampshire.

Cosmopolitan University In 1998, this institution arose on the Internet, with a mostly German-language website, but claiming to be in Missouri. In addition to selling degrees of all kinds, they sell honorary consular documents, and honorary doctorates, no questions asked. The website seems to suggest that they are actually operating from Chile. Alleged degree-holders range from German Chancellor Kohl to a minister in Dallas, a journalist in the Netherlands, an attorney in Miami Beach, and the chairman of Daimler Benz.

Cranmer Hall Theological College Identified as a diploma mill by E&T.

Creative University of Southeast London London, England. Identified as a diploma mill by E&T.

Cromwell University London, England. This diploma mill was one of many run for years by the Fowler family of Chicago, five of whom were sentenced to prison in late 1987 for these activities. Cromwell sold degrees of all kinds for $730, through a mail forwarding service. Accreditation was claimed from the nonexistent Western European Accrediting Society of Liederbach, West Germany.

Dallas State College Dallas, Texas. One of the first heavily advertised diploma mills, Dallas State flourished in the early 1970s under the guidance of at least one of the Fowler family of Chicago. In 1975, the attorney general of Texas permanently enjoined Dallas State from operating in that state.

Darthmouth College See: Regency Enterprises

Darwin University See: Aspen University

Delaware Law School Identified as a diploma mill by E&T and we're sorry the people at the genuine Delaware Law School of Widener University are upset that we mention this, but don't blame us when diploma mill operators choose to use the same name as a legitimate school.

DePaul University Paris, France. A diploma mill operated for years by the Fowler family, from a mail forwarding service in Paris. Operations ceased following five Fowlers' sentencing to prison in 1987. Degrees of all kinds were sold for $550, and accreditation was claimed from the Worldwide Accrediting Commission, allegedly of Cannes, France. Other addresses used in Clemson, South Carolina, and Santa Monica, California.

Diplomatic State University See: R/G Enterprises

Diplomatic University See: National Certificate Company

Earl James National University Toronto, Canada. Identified as a diploma mill by COE.

Eastern Missouri Business College The nonexistent school established by the attorney general of Missouri, in a sting operation. During its one day of existence, the head of the International Accrediting Commission for Schools, Colleges and Theological Seminaries visited the one-room office in St. Louis, overlooked the fact that the school had officers named Peelsburi Doobuoy and Wonarrmed Mann, overlooked the fact that the marine biology text was The Little Golden Book of Fishes, did not overlook the accreditation "fee" he was handed, and duly accredited the school, which disappeared forever the next day.

Eastern Orthodox University India. Identified as a diploma mill by COE.

Eastern State University See: Commonwealth University

Eastern University See: National Certificate Company

Ecclesiastical University of Sheffield See: University of Sheffield

Education Certificate Replacement Service According to a notice on the Internet, this service offers "replacement" copies of any degree you might wish. Apparently, this is not illegal, as the proprietor clearly states that these certificates are not original degrees.

Elysion College They used to offer degrees from various addresses in California, although the proprietor was in Mexico. Several book reports or essays and $500 were required to earn the degree. When the proprietor died, his daughter continued the operation from her home in San Francisco. She told authorities she was not operating the school, but an FBI analysis of her garbage revealed that she was, and after her indictment by a federal grand jury, and her guilty plea, Elysion College faded away.

Emerson University California. Identified as a diploma mill by COE.

Empire College of Ophthalmology Canada. Identified as a diploma mill by COE.

Episcopal University of London London, England. Identified as a diploma mill by E&T.

Episcopal University of Saint Peter Port Frankfurt, Germany. Identified as a diploma mill by E&T.

Études universitaires internationales Leichtenstein, Luxembourg. Identified as a diploma mill by COE.

Eugenia Institute of Metaphysics See: ORB

European College of Science and Man Sheffield, England. Identified as a diploma mill by E&T.

Evaluation and Management International Inglewood, California. These folks have sent out a three-page, unsigned letter saying that on receipt of $2,100 they will arrange for the degree of your choice to be issued to you. They require 50 percent down before they reveal the name of the school that is to be your alma mater. Can anyone ever have fallen for this?

Evergreen University In 1989, large ads appeared in civil service and other newspapers, offering the degrees of this school, allegedly in Los Angeles. By the time we learned of it, just a month after the ads ran, the three phone numbers had all been disconnected, and mail was returned as undeliverable.

Faraday College England. Identified as a diploma mill by E&T.

Felix Adler Memorial University Charlotte, North Carolina. Identified as a diploma mill by E&T.

Florida State Christian College Fort Lauderdale, Florida. They used to advertise nationally the availability of Bachelor's, Master's, Doctorates, and honorary Doctorates, until both the postal service and the state of Florida acted to shut them down. They also operated Alpha Psi Omega, a professional society for psychological counselors.

Forest Park University Chicago, Illinois. Identified as a diploma mill by COE.

Four States Cooperative University Texas. Identified as a diploma mill by COE.

Franklin University Same management as Laurence University (Hawaii).

General Delivery University A rather charming and silly Internet endeavor, purporting to be "America's only Genuine Diploma Mill," and offering net surfers the opportunity to download diplomas from such worthy institutions as the Ponzi School of Business and the College of Rock Music, for an eminently reasonable $3.95. It's all quite funny and well done.

Geo-Metaphysical Institute New York. "Here's a great way to get instant status," said their national advertising, offering an ornate personalized and totally phony honorary Doctorate in geo-metaphysics for $5.

Georgia Christian University Georgia. The first pyramid scheme diploma mill. When you "graduate" (buy a degree), you become a professor and can sell degrees to others. When your students buy degrees and become professors, you become a dean and share in their profits, and so on, up the academic ladder.

German-American Dental College Chicago, Illinois. Identified as a diploma mill by COE.

Global Money Consultants This Greek-based organization, operating largely over the Internet, offers much more than no-questions-asked degrees—their services include similarly easy-to-obtain passports, driver's licenses, diplomatic appointments (!), and more. Ranging from $1,500 for a Bachelor's degree to $2,000 for a doctorate, the degrees are awarded from either of two Panamanian universities, the University of the Americas, or Trinity College. The copy regarding the first

university says, "The University does not have a campus or buildings, but is to compare more to a scientific entity." Of course.

Gold Coast University Hawaii. Opened by Edward Reddeck, previously imprisoned for operating other diploma mills. Later changed to Coast University. Although Hawaii authorities showed no interest, federal authorities closed the "school" in 1992 after Reddeck was indicted on many counts of mail fraud and conspiracy. He was convicted on all 22 counts in early 1993, and returned to prison.

Golden State University Operated from California and Colorado in the 1950s and 1960s. Exposed as a degree mill on Paul Coates's television program in 1958. No connection with the legitimate school of the same name that opened in 1979.

Gordon Arlen College England. Identified as a diploma mill by E&T.

Gottbourg University of Switzerland See: ORB

Graduate University See: National Certificate Company

Great Lakes University Michigan. One of several degree mills operated by W. (for Wiley!) Gordon Bennett. Degrees were sold for $200. Also used addresses in Dearborn and Berkeley, Michigan, and Chicago.

Gulf Southern University Louisiana. The literature is identical to that used by several other mills, such as Pacific Northwestern and Atlantic Northeastern. Degrees were sold for $45 to anyone but Louisiana residents.

Hamilton University In mid 1998, we responded to an advertisement offering to find us the perfect school. We submitted a short fictitious resume, and were informed by return mail (the letterhead said Kentucky, but the postmark was Rock Springs, Wyoming) that we had already qualified for a degree from Hamilton University.

Hamilton State University Louisiana. The literature is identical to that used by several other mills, such as Pacific Northwestern and Atlantic Northeastern. Degrees were sold for $45 to anyone but Louisiana residents.

Hancock University Tennessee. Arose briefly in 1995, with ads in USA Today, selling honorary degrees of all kinds, but after a month or so, subsided for a while. Now, they appear to be active again.

Harley University London, England. John found the university in a tiny corner of the London College of Beauty Therapy. The salon receptionist was the university registrar. Ph.D. degrees were awarded on completion of a dissertation of less than 20 pages. The co-proprietor of Harley U. (who refused to tell us the source of his own Ph.D.) wrote that "the details in your booklet are totally untrue in every respect." The detailed questions then put to him in our reply to that letter were never answered. Harley University apparently is no more. Its proprietor later established Saint Giles University College and Somerset University.

Hartford Technical Institute See: Regency Enterprises

Hirshfeld College See: USSI

His Majesty's University of Polytechnics Sacramento, California. Used to sell honorary Doctorates in all subjects (but "no profanities or obscenities") for all of $5. But the "university" closed down many years ago, so please stop trying to write to them, so the former proprietor won't have to write us any more annoyed letters.

Hollywood College California. Identified as a diploma mill by E&T.

Hollywood Southern University See: California Pacifica University

Holy Toledo University American Educational Publishers has invented the delightful and humorous Doctorates of Holy Toledo U., offering the Doctor of Philosophy in Adorableness, Defrosting, Worrying, and other fields. They are nicely designed (the gold seal says, in small type, "My goodness how impressive!") and sold for $12 a dozen.

Honoré College See: ORB

Humberman University College Identified as a diploma mill by E&T.

Idaho College of Commerce See: International Universities Consortium

Illinois State University See: Regency Enterprises

Imperial Philo-Byzantine University Madrid, Spain. Identified as a diploma mill by COE.

Independence University Missouri. Flourished in the late 1970s, offering degrees by correspondence, until exposés in the Chronicle of Higher Education and a Chicago newspaper helped close them down. The Chicago Tribune reported that the headmaster of a prestigious Chicago private school resigned "after disclosures that he was using the office there as a center of activity for the diploma mill." A community college president in Chicago subsequently lost his job for using an Independence Doctorate. There apparently is also a humorous and unrelated Independence University, offering realistic-looking diplomas from its School of Hard Knocks, and signed by "A. Harry World."

Independent Study Programs, Inc. Missouri. Degrees of all kinds sold in the late 1970s. No longer there.

Independent University Academy See: Independent University of Australia

Indiana State University See: Regency Enterprises

Institut Inter-Européen Switzerland. Apparently still operating, offering degrees at all levels in a number of business-related fields.

Institut Patriarcal Saint Irenée Beziers, France. Granted honorary Doctorates to the founder's American colleagues and perhaps others. See also: Inter-State College

Institute of Excellence Florida. All degrees, including medical and dental, at $10 each. The fake diplomas are very poorly printed, and say, in small type, "for novelty purposes only."

Inter-American University Rome, Italy. Identified as a diploma mill by COE.

Inter-State College England, France. Established by Karl Josef Werres, granting honorary Doctorates from England. One of the recipients claims that the college is "legally chartered" to do this, but all that means is that in their corporate charter, they give themselves the right. See also: Institut Patriarcal Saint Irenée.

Intercollegiate University Incorporated in Kansas before World War II. As the American Mercury reported, "Intercollegiate specialized in hanging its M.A. on some of England's minor men of God—for $50; and for a few dollars more, it was willing to bestow a dazzling D.C.L. Before the war this had grown into a roaring and profitable trade, but when wartime law prohibited sending money out of England, the Intercollegiate professors were obliged to suspend their work of international enlightenment."

Internation University U.S. Identified as a diploma mill by E&T.

International Academy for Planetary Planning See: International Honorary Awards Committee

International American University Rome, Italy. Identified as a diploma mill by COE.

International Awards Committee Washington, D.C. For $225, this organization will award an honorary doctorate based on a request for consideration, a copy of your resume, and an outline of your professional, academic, and public service accomplishments.

International College of Associates in Medicine Texas. Used to offer a Ph.D. and a Doctor of Medical Letters on payment of modest fees.

International Honorary Awards Committee California. They sold a wide range of Doctorates and other awards, mostly for $100 or less. The well-designed doctoral diplomas come from Collegii Romanii, the International Academy for Planetary Planning, Two Dragon University, and the Siberian Institute. One can also buy diplomatic regalia including the Grand Cross of the Imperial Order of Constantine and the Sovereign

Order of Leichtenstein, complete with rosettes, medals, and sashes. The late Francis X. Gordon, founder of all these establishments, had a delightful sense of humor about his work. His widow apparently carried it on.

International Open University In 1997 and 1998, John received numerous e-mails from people in the Ukraine, who claimed to be operating branches of this alleged California university. When we explained to them there was no such place, they insisted that it was "fully registrated" by the State of California, and provided a corporate number and an address. That address turned out to be a private home. Presumably someone has formed a corporation with this name, and has sold franchises throughout the Ukraine, Russia, and Moldova. The people there may in fact be providing some educational services, but they are in complete denial regarding the nonexistence of the California "anchor."

International Protestant Birkbest College England. Identified as a diploma mill by E&T.

International Universities Consortium Missouri. In 1989, help-wanted ads appeared in the academic press, soliciting faculty for a consortium of nontraditional schools. Being the suspicious sort, John fabricated a resume of the most outrageous sort, under an assumed name, and submitted it. Shortly thereafter, his nom de plume was appointed to the faculty of what was alleged to be a group of eight "universities"—one a long-established diploma mill (London School for Social Research), one a school we have been suspicious about for years (Northern Utah University), and six new ones, characterized by the common theme that they do not appear to exist (no listed phones). They are: Southwestern University (allegedly in New Mexico), St. Andrews University (allegedly in Baha [sic] California, Mexico), Northwestern Graduate Institute (allegedly Montana), University of the West (allegedly Wyoming), Idaho College of Commerce (allegedly Idaho), and American Management Institute (no location given). Northern Utah actually issued a catalog, complete with the "faculty" names of all those boobs who answered the ad and signed up to be on the staff, no questions asked. But the address and phone numbers in the catalog are not working. Consortium president Warren H. Green writes that the whole scheme, which he defends as completely legitimate, has been canceled.

International University (Greece) Athens, Greece. The literature claims that the Doctorates are nonacademic, but nonetheless fully recognized as educational and professional degrees by the republic of Greece. The embassy of Greece has written to us that this is not a correct statement. The president is listed as a "Right Reverend Bishop Doctor," who later established a "university" in Louisiana. There apparently was, at least at one time, an affiliation with International University of Missouri.

International University (India) Degrees of this institution are sold for $50 to $100 each by the Bureau for Degree Promotion in Holland.

International University (Louisiana) Louisiana. Opened in the early 1980s, offering degrees of all kinds. Accreditation was claimed from the North American Regional Accrediting Commission, which we have never been able to locate. Following a stern letter from the Louisiana Proprietary School Commission, International University apparently faded away. It was incorporated by relatives of a man who later opened La Salle University in Louisiana.

International University (Switzerland) Zurich, Switzerland. One of the many diploma mill operations of Karl Xavier Bleisch, this one selling Bachelor's, Master's, and Doctorates for $500 to $1,000. The literature has a photocopy of a San Jose State College diploma awarded to Celia Ann Bleisch in 1967. What can this mean?

Jackson State University Los Angeles, Nashville, Reno, Chicago. Sold degrees of all kinds for $200. The postal service issued "false representation orders" and stopped their mail years ago, and the perpetrators finally were sentenced to federal prison in 1987. No connection whatsoever with the legitimate school of this name in Mississippi.

Janta Engineering College Karnal, India. Identified as a diploma mill by COE.

Japan Christian College Tokyo, Japan. Identified as a diploma mill by COE.

Jerusalem University Tel Aviv, Israel. Degrees of all kinds are sold for $10 to $40 from this nonexistent university. Buyers must sign a statement that they will not use the degrees for any phony purpose.

Johann Keppler School of Medicine There are very few people daring or stupid enough to start a fake medical school. This was one of the most ambitious, complete with catalog, and an alleged faculty in Switzerland, Canada, and Mexico. The claim was made that the degrees were recognized in many countries. When John asked their representative (who telephoned to make sure he would put them in this book) which countries, he thought a while and then said, "Well, Mauritius for one." All addresses used were mail forwarding services. Accreditation was claimed from the American Coordinated Medical Society, a fake organization started by L. Mitchell Weinberg, who has been to prison several times for fake medical school operations, and who was involved with Keppler as well. Operations ceased in the wake of the FBI DipScam operation in 1983. Weinberg was indicted and sentenced to prison again.

John Hancock University See: Hancock University

319

John Quincy Adams College Portland, Oregon. A totally phony school, selling any degree for $250. Later used addresses in Illinois and Nevada. Operated by the Fowler family, five of whom were sentenced to prison in 1987.

Kennedy Honorary University A relatively new Colorado-based degree mill, offering phony degrees at all levels in a wide range of fields.

Kentucky Christian University Ashland, Kentucky. They offered degrees in everything from chemical engineering to law at all levels for a $300 fee. Same auspices as Ohio Christian and Florida State Christian, all now defunct.

Kentucky Military Institute See: Bretton Woods University

Kenwood Associates Long Green, Maryland. For $15 each or three for $30, they will sell Bachelor's, Master's, or Doctorates in the name of any school, with any degree and any date. Then you can buy, for $12, a Jiu Jitsu Master Instructor certificate to flash when the authorities come to take you away.

Kingsley University See: Bradford University

Lafayette University Amsterdam, Netherlands, through a mail forwarding service. One of many fake schools operated by the Fowler family, five of whom were sentenced to prison for operating diploma mills, in late 1987. Degrees of any sort, with any date, were sold for $725. Accreditation was claimed from an equally fake accrediting agency, the West European Accrediting Society of Liederbach, West Germany.

Lamp Beacon University See: California Pacifica University

LaSalle University (1986 to mid 1997) For a description of the legitimate La Salle University in Louisiana, see the listing in chapter 21. LaSalle University was established by James Kirk (also known as Thomas McPherson and Thomas Kirk), who had earlier operated Southland University and International University (Louisiana). Following ten years of operation in Missouri and Louisiana, in July 1996, the school was raided by a joint task force of the FBI, the Postal Inspection Service, and the Internal Revenue Service, after a five-year investigation. Kirk and several colleagues were subsequently indicted on 18 counts of mail fraud, tax fraud, money laundering, and other charges, and more than $10 million in cash was confiscated. The indictments claimed among other things that more than 15,000 students were being handled by fewer than five faculty, none of them with traditional academic credentials; that the university was run by a church Kirk had established for the purpose of tax evasion; and that the accreditation was from a non-existent agency established by La Salle. Kirk pleaded guilty, in a plea bargain, and was

sentenced to five years in federal prison. He was ordered never to operate a school again. (Kirk married for the fifth or sixth time while in prison, and his new wife's name appears on the literature of Acton (originally Edison) University, which operates from a secretarial service in Hawaii, using literature almost identical to La Salle's). LaSalle students and graduates prior to mid-1997 were given the option of a full refund, but only if they turned in their diplomas, an option accepted by a relatively small number of alumni (Internet users can find a a 16-page report on La Salle from the New Orleans FBI Agent in charge at: www.tamnet.com/news/wcc/affidavit.html).

Laurence University (HI) Hawaii. All degrees in all fields except medicine and law, for a fee of $45. The literature says, "We are confident you will find the benefits you can obtain with a degree from Laurence University are very valuable indeed." The main benefit we can think of is a period of room and board at government expense. The same seller, Associated Enterprises, also issues the fake degrees of Benson University, Carlton University, Kingsley University, Buckner University, Franklin University, and Bradford University. There is, of course, no connection with the legitimate school formerly called Laurence University (now University of Santa Barbara) in California.

Lawford State University Maryland. They used to sell degrees of all kinds for $6.99 from a post office box in Baltimore, now closed. The other school names were Université de Commerce de (sic) Canada and the Christian Fellowship Foundation. The hard-to-decipher signatures on the quite-realistic-looking certificates were "Thoroughly Fake, Ph.D." and "Too Much Fun, Jr."

Leiland College of Arts and Sciences Arose in 1992, offering degrees to martial artists for under $100. Diploma identical to that of Eurotechnical Research University whose president originally opened the post office box used but later turned it over to a colleague, and denied any knowledge of Leiland.

Libera Universita di Psico-Biofisica Trieste, Yugoslavia. (That's what their literature says, even though Trieste is now in Italy and Yugoslavia, of course, no longer exists.) Identified as a diploma mill by E&T.

Life Science College California and Oklahoma. The proprietors were arrested in 1981 for an array of charges, including selling Doctor of Divinity degrees, and income tax evasion through the operation of the college and the associated Life Science Church.

Lincoln-Jefferson University See: California Pacifica University

London College of Physiology England. Identified as a diploma mill by E&T.

London College of Theology England. Identified as a diploma mill by E&T.

London Educational College England. Identified as a diploma mill by E&T.

London Institute for Applied Research England. All right, he did it (as he's been saying in this book for 20 years now). In 1972, while living in England, John was involved in fund-raising for a legitimate school. He figured that since major universities were "selling" their honorary degrees for millions, why not use the same approach on a small scale? He and his associates created L.I.A.R. and ran ads in the U.S. reading "Phony honorary doctorates for sale, $25." Several hundred were sold, but the whole thing seemed to have upset half the world's educational establishment. (The other half thought it was a good gag.) So L.I.A.R. was retired. Then an offer came from a Dutchman who lived in Ethiopia (you must believe us on this—who would make up such a story?) who wanted to trade 100 pounds of Ethiopian ear-pickers and Coptic crosses for the remaining L.I.A.R. certificates. Now he's selling them from Holland without the humorous disclaimer, and has added a bunch more fake school names. And if anyone would like some Ethiopian trinkets, have we got a deal for you!

London School for Social Research London, England. The well-prepared literature offers degrees of all kinds for fees of up to $2,000. The address is in a dingy little building off Leicester Square, where John climbed five flights of stairs so narrow that he had to go up sideways, and at the top found the little one-room office of Archangel Services, a mail-forwarding service that told him they forward the London School mail to Miami. Some literature has also been mailed from Phoenix. See also: International Universities Consortium

London Tottenham International Christian University England. Identified as a diploma mill by E&T.

Loyola State University Illinois. A new venture from a colleague of our old friend Dr. Dante, described in the write-up for Columbia State University in this chapter. The requirements of this latest "school" appear no more rigorous—the catalog states that "all we see, touch, or do becomes a learning experience. Earth becomes our campus and life our instructor." The Illinois attorney general closed them down in short order.

Loyola University Paris, France. Through a mail-forwarding service, degrees of all kinds were sold for a payment of up to $650. The brochure claimed that "Many of our successful graduates have used their transcripts to transfer to other colleges and universities in the U.S.A." If this really did happen, it would have been only because of name confusion with the four legitimate Loyolas in the U.S. The perpetrators of this Loyola were sentenced to federal prison in 1987.

LTD Documents New York. Extremely well-done, and thus especially dangerous, fake diplomas with the name of any school and any degree printed on them for $69.50. Also, preprinted degrees from the nonexistent San Miguel College and Benchley State University for $49.50. They even explain how to "age" a certificate to make it look older.

Lyne College England. Identified as a diploma mill by E&T.

Madison State University See: R/G Enterprises

Marcus Tullius Cicero University San Francisco, California. A Swiss company advertised in the International Herald Tribune that they could provide the "registered legal degree" of the so-called university for a mere $3,000. The diploma indicates that the university is "officially registered" with the secretary of state which, if true, simply means it is a California corporation. Checks are made payable to The Knights of Humanity. There is, of course, no such university in California or, presumably, anywhere else.

Marlowe University New Jersey and Florida. Active during the 1960s and 1970s, selling all kinds of degrees for $150 or less.

Marmaduke University California. Degrees of all kinds were sold for $1,000 and up. The literature reports that "usually the student qualifies for more advanced study than he initialy [sic] expected." Mention was made of a 30-day resident course in the use of lie detectors, but the voice on the phone (answering simply, "Hello") said it had been canceled "because of the building program." Marmaduke was actually once authorized by the state of California, back in the days (late 1970s) when such things were vastly easier.

Martin College Florida. They used to sell degrees of all kinds for $200. Graduates were required to pass some tough exams, as evidenced by this example given in the school's literature: "True or false—the Declaration of Independence was signed on the 4th of July by British Royalty."

Maxsell Corporation Florida. A "diploma replacement service," offering to "recreate any lost or stolen document to your specifications." They go on to assure that "documents are for the exclusive personal use and enjoyment of our clients, and any misuse is their sole responsibility." Glad we got that cleared up.

May Kong College Hong Kong. Also called itself May Kong Evening College of Business and Technology or May Kong Institute. A credentials evaluator from World Education Services forwards a sheaf of documentation on his investigation of this school, which he concludes is a diploma mill. There appears to have been some association with Sussex College of Technology, a notorious British degree mill.

Meta Collegiate Extension Nevada. Chartered in Nevada before World War II, they sold Ph.D.'s for $50, with a 20 percent discount for cash.

Metropolitan Collegiate They sell all degrees, including medical and dental, for $100 or less. The address is a mail-forwarding service which told us that they forward the mail to Yorkshire, England. It is hard to imagine that such things can be tolerated, but this place has been going for years. (We have this little fantasy in which the prime minister becomes gravely ill on a trip abroad, and the doctor who is summoned to treat him "earned" his M.D. from Metropolitan Collegiate.)

Millard Fillmore Institute In 1966, the year John earned his real Doctorate (from Michigan State University), Bob Hope received one of his first honorary Doctorates after making a large gift to Southern Methodist University. Aware that Millard Fillmore, our great 13th president, was the only president who routinely turned down offers of honorary Doctorates (including one from Oxford), John was inspired to create the fictitious Institute, to poke fun at the way universities trade honorary degrees for money. The ornate diploma read, "By virtue of powers which we have invented . . . the honorary and meretricious" title was awarded, "magna cum grano salis" (with a big grain of salt). Many were given away, and some were sold, complete with a cheap plastic frame, for five bucks. Most people thought it was amusing, but a few saw it as a threat to civilization as we know it, and so, after a few years, the fictitious gates of the institute were closed, perhaps forever.

Miller University Philadelphia, Pennsylvania. Identified as a diploma mill by E&T.

Milton University Maryland and New York. Identified as a diploma mill by E&T.

Mindspring Enterprises New Hampshire. This organization offered "real-looking degrees and certificates" in any field but medical, via an ad on America Online, "for novelty purposes only."

Ministerial Training College Sheffield, England. Identified as a diploma mill by COE.

Montserrat University California. Degrees of all kinds were sold for $10 or $20 from a post office box in San Francisco in this name and those of the equally fake Stanton University and Rochfort College. Apparently now defunct.

Morston-Colwyn University England and Canada. Identified as a diploma mill by E&T.

Mount Sinai University USA. Identified as a diploma mill by E&T.

Nassau State Teachers College See: Regency Enterprises

National Certificate Company New York. These people sold the degrees of eight nonexistent universities at $20 to $30 each, and also sold a "make your own" kit consisting of a blank diploma and press-on letters. The eight fake schools are Diplomatic University, Central University, Capital College, Adams Institute of Technology, Eastern University, Western College, Graduate University, and the Southern Institute of Technology. Buyers must sign a statement saying they will not use them for any educational purpose. Suuuuure.

National College Kansas and Oklahoma. Doctorates of all kinds, including medical, were sold by "Dr." Charles E. Downs. Accreditation claimed from a bogus accrediting association established by "Dr." Weinberg, founder of several fake medical schools himself. See also: East Coast University

National College of Arts and Sciences Once a very active mill, finally closed down by authorities in Oklahoma in 1982. Same ownership as American Western, Northwestern College of Allied Science, and other fake schools. A quite wonderful event in the annals of degree mills occurred when a state official in New York innocently wrote to National College to verify a Master's degree claimed by a job applicant. National College misinterpreted the letter, and sent a Master's degree to the state official, in his own name, complete with a transcript listing all the courses taken and grades received!

National Ecclesiastical University Sheffield, England. Identified as a diploma mill by E&T.

National Stevens University California. Identified as a diploma mill by E&T.

National University (Canada) Toronto, Canada. Identified as a diploma mill by COE.

National University (India) Nagpur, India. Identified as a diploma mill by COE.

National University of Colorado Denver, Colorado. Identified as a diploma mill by COE.

National University of Dakota South Dakota. Identified as a diploma mill by E&T.

National University of Sheffield Sheffield, England. Identified as a diploma mill by COE and E&T. No connection, of course, with the legitimate University of Sheffield.

Nebraska College of Physical Medicine England. Degrees in chiropractic and osteopathy are sold to people who, according to newspaper articles, are said to use them to practice medicine.

New Christian Institute of New England See: ORB

New York State College See: R/G Enterprises

Newcastle University England. Not to be confused with the legitimate University of Newcastle. Identified as a diploma mill by E&T.

NIC Inc., Law Enforcement Supply Louisiana. This service has been offering about 100 phony degrees and certificates via the Internet.

North American College of the Artsy With the purchase of the Complete Conductor Kit, the Portable Maestro of St. Paul, Minnesota, awards a Master's degree from the North American College of the Artsy and Somewhat Musically Inclined.

North American University Utah, Hawaii, Missouri. Formerly University of North America. Degree mill, run by Edward Reddeck, who has twice gone to prison for educational frauds. A great many people were defrauded by this "school," largely because national publications like USA Today kept accepting his advertising. Enjoined from operating by Utah in 1989, but the order was ignored. Reddeck was indicted by a federal grand jury in 1992 for mail fraud and conspiracy, convicted in 1993, and imprisoned.

Northern Utah University (or Management Institute) They have been around for years, but now are apparently a part of the International Universities Consortium, described earlier in this chapter. The phone listed in Salt Lake City is not in service, and mail was returned as undeliverable in 1990.

Northwest London College of Applied Science London, England. Same location as the College of Applied Science, London. Also known as Northwest London University. Links with several medical degree mills, including Keppler and the Chicago Medical School. The signature of Karl Josef Werres, founder of Inter-State College and Institut Patriarcal Saint Irenée, and past officer of two large American nontraditional schools, appears on their diploma. Professor Werres wishes people to know that he has nothing to do with this school, and that his name has been forged. Done.

Northwest London University See: Northwest London College of Applied Science

Northwestern College of Allied Sciences Oklahoma City, Oklahoma. Authorities in Oklahoma closed this mill down in 1982. It had been under the same management as American Western, National College, and several other fake schools operated under the cloak of the Disciples of Truth by James Caffey of Springfield, Missouri. Caffey was indicted by a federal grand jury in 1985, pleaded guilty, and was sentenced to prison.

Northwestern Graduate School Allegedly in Montana. See also: International Universities Consortium.

Novastate University We have a photocopy of a degree, issued in 1977, from this apparently nonexistent university. And that's all we know.

Obura University London, England. Identified as a diploma mill by E&T.

Ohio Central College See: Regency Enterprises

Ohio Christian College One of the more active degree mills in the 1960s and 1970s, they sold degrees of all kinds for fees of $200 and up. Literature identical to that of Florida State Christian University, which was closed by authorities in that state. They claimed to be a part of Calvary Grace Christian Churches of Faith, Inc.

Ohio Saint Mathew University Columbus, Ohio. Identified as a diploma mill by E&T.

Open University (Switzerland) Zurich, Switzerland. One of the many diploma mills operated by Karl Xavier Bleisch.

ORB Virginia. A supermarket of phony degrees that offered diplomas from eight nonexistent institutions at fees of $5 to $65 each. The more authentic-sounding ones were more expensive. The schools were: Bosdon Academy of Music, Eugenia Institute of Metaphysics, Gottbourg University of Switzerland, Honoré College of France, New Christian Institute of New England, Royal Academy of Science and Art, Taylor College of England, and Weinberg University of Germany. ORB (other literature reveals that it stands for Occult Research Bureau) has been operated by Raymond Buckland, author and former curator of the Buckland Museum of Magick.

Oriental University Washington, D.C. Identified as a diploma mill by COE.

Oxford College of Applied Science Oxford, England. A diploma mill selling degrees of all kinds. Apparently operated from Switzerland by Karl Xavier Bleisch, who has been involved with many other degree mills.

Oxford College of Arts and Sciences Canada. Identified as a diploma mill by E&T.

Oxford Collegiate Institute Apparently another Oxford-based mill, but we have no details.

Oxford Institute for Applied Research London, England. Fake honorary Doctorates sold for $250.

Pacific College Sold everything from high school diplomas to Doctorates for $75 because they believed that "everyone has the right to live and experience life according to his or her own convictions." This presumably includes convictions for fraud.

Pacific Northwest University In 1996, we received a resume from a prison inmate, listing a B.S. from the phony Jackson State University and an M.B.A. from this school, allegedly in Monterey, California (rather far south to qualify as the Pacific Northwest, and too elusive to qualify as legitimate).

Pacific Southern University New Jersey and California. No connection whatsoever with a the state-approved school of the same name in Los Angeles. This Pacific Southern operates from various post office boxes and offers "degrees you can be pround [sic] of" at $250 each.

Pacific States College Degrees from this nonexistent school have recently been sold for $5 if blank; $15 if professionally lettered. The literature describes them as "some of the finest, most authentic looking college degrees on the market. It is almost impossible to distinguish them from the real thing."

Palm Beach Psychotherapy Training Centre See: Thomas A. Edison College of Florida

Pensacola Trade School See: Regency Enterprises

People's National University USA. Identified as a diploma mill by E&T.

People's National University Identified as a diploma mill by E&T.

Philo-Byzantine University Madrid, Spain. Identified as a diploma mill by E&T.

Phoenix University (Italy) See: Accademia di Studi Superiori Phoenix

Pigeon Hill University An excellent reference site on the Internet, with links to many other sites that can benefit the distance learner, and the tongue-in-cheek (we certainly hope) option of printing out a diploma stating that one has completed a "Master Degree in Educational Surfing" of PHU.

Progressive California. Offered free Ph.D.'s through an ad in Popular Mechanics in the 1990s. Probably related to the Progressive Universal Life Church.

R/G Enterprises Florida. They sold degrees from ten schools with almost-real names at prices up to $37.50. The schools were: Alabama Christian College, California Christian College, Clemson College, Colgate College, Diplomatic State University, Hamilton Institute of Technology, Hamilton State University, Madison State University, New York State College, and Tulsa College. The literature says, "This offer not valid in states where prohibited by law," which doubtless encompasses all 50 of them.

Raighlings University See: USSI

Regency College See: American Western University

Regency Enterprises Missouri. They used to sell degrees with the names of real schools, often slightly changed, such as Stamford (not Stanford) University, or Texas University (not the University of Texas). Others included Cormell University, Indiana State University, Boston City College, the University of Pittsburgh, Illinois State University, Rockford Community College, Hartford Technical Institute, Carnegie Institute of Engineering, Stetson College, Nassau State Teachers College, Darthmouth College, Ohio Central College, College of Franklin & Marshall, and Pensacola Trade School. A blank diploma with a lettering kit was sold for $20. Buyers were asked to sign a statement that they would not use these phony diplomas for any fraudulent purposes, although it's hard to imagine any other use to which they could be put. Don L. Piccolo of Anaheim, California was indicted by a federal grand jury in 1985 for running Regency, and entered a guilty plea.

Rhode Island School of Law Identified as a diploma mill by E&T, which believed it to be in Wyoming.

Rochfort College See: Montserrat University

Rockford Community College See: Regency Enterprises

Roosevelt University Belgium. Degrees of any kind were sold for a "tuition" of $400 to $600. Also used an address in Zurich, Switzerland. Five of the proprietors were sentenced to federal prison in late 1987.

Royal Academy of Science and Art See: ORB

Royal College of Science Identified as a diploma mill by E&T. Apparently affiliated with, or the same as, Empire College of Opthalmology.

Saint Andrews Correspondence College Identified as a diploma mill by E&T.

Saint Andrews Ecumenical Foundation University Identified as a diploma mill by E&T.

Saint Andrews University Allegedly in Mexico. See also: International Universities Consortium

Saint John Chrysostom College London, England. Identified as a diploma mill by E&T.

Saint John's University (India) India. Identified as a diploma mill by COE.

Saint Joseph University New York. They offered Bachelor's, Master's, Doctorates, and law degrees. Some of the literature was well-done, some of it was ludicrous—the name "Saint Joseph," for instance, was often inserted in gaps where clearly some other school's name had once appeared. The location was variously given as New York, Louisiana, and Colorado, even in the same catalog. Degrees cost from $2,000 to $3,000.

Saint Stephen's Educational Bible College Los Angeles, California. The president of this institution, a Baptist minister, pleaded guilty to forgery and grand theft for issuing illegal credentials. He is no longer associated with the school, and they are now operating as a legal, state-approved institution.

San Francisco College of Music and Theater Arts In 1987, a San Francisco man began advertising this apparently nonexistent school in Chinese and African papers. Somehow, it was certified as legitimate by the Immigration and Naturalization Service. The San Francisco Chronicle reports that three Chinese dancers came to San Francisco to train at the school and ended up being forced to work as servants for its founder.

San Miguel College See: LTD Documents

Sands University Yuma, Arizona. Sold degrees of all kinds in the mid 1980s. Proprietor, Wiley Gordon Bennett, who operated from Tennessee, was convicted and sent to prison thanks to the FBI's DipScam operation.

School of Applied Sciences London and New York. Identified as a diploma mill by E&T.

School of Health Science See: Trinity College and University

School of Psychology and Psychotherapy England. Identified as a diploma mill by E&T.

Seattle College Apparently a diploma mill, but that's all the information we have at the moment.

Self-Culture University India. Identified as a diploma mill by COE.

Shield College See: USSI

Siberian Institute See: International Honorary Awards Committee

Sir Edward Heyzer's Free Technical College Hong Kong. Associated with the National University of Canada, identified as a diploma mill by COE.

South China University Hong Kong and Macau. Identified as a diploma mill by E&T.

South Eastern Extension College Essex, England. All degrees but medicine or law, at £20 for one or £45 for three. "Our degrees are indistinguishable from degrees issued by other colleges in the traditional way," the sales letter says. Same ownership as Whitby Hall College.

Southern California University California. One of the many fake school names used by the Fowler family, five of whom were sentenced to prison in 1987 for their part in running diploma mills worldwide. Degrees of all kinds were sold for $200 and up.

Southern Institute of Technbology See: National Certificate Company

Southwestern University Tucson, Arizona and St. George, Utah. The university had its own impressive building in Tucson, with many of the trappings of a real school. But after they sold degrees to an FBI agent during the DipScam operation, several administrators were indicted by a federal grand jury. President Geruntino pleaded guilty, and served a term in federal prison. The names of more than a thousand Southwestern "alumni" were made public, and many jobs were lost as a result, including some in NASA and the Pentagon. Many students had enrolled following a glowing recommendation for the school from an educational guidance service in Columbus, Ohio that was also run by Geruntino.

Southwestern University (NM) Allegedly in Albuquerque, New Mexico. See also: International Universities Consortium

Specialty Document Company California. In 1988, they were selling fake diplomas for a Doctor of Medicine, Doctor of Veterinary Medicine, Bachelor's, and Ph.D. certificates (no school specified) for $1 each, or 100 for $15. Imagine that! A medical degree for 15¢!

Spicer Memorial College India. Identified as a diploma mill by COE.

Stamford Private University Portugal. This school, claiming to be a U.S. institution, has offered degrees at all levels in any field (with the exception of medicine or dentistry) to Portuguese residents, based entirely on life experience. We have written for more information.

Stanton University See: Montserrat University

Staton University In the early 1980s, music teachers in North America received an invitation to join the American Guild of Teachers of Singing, upon which they would be awarded an honorary Doctorate from this nonexistent school, which was supposed to be in Ohio.

Stetson College See: Regency Enterprises

Sussex College of Technology Sussex, England. Perhaps the oldest of Britain's degree mills, Sussex is run by "Dr." Bruce Copen from his home, south of London. At the same address, but with different catalogs, are the Brantridge Forest School and the University of the Science of Man. Each offer "earned" degrees for which a few correspondence courses are required, and "extension awards" which are the same degrees and diplomas for no work at all. Honorary Doctorates are offered free, but there is a $100 engraving charge. "Professor Emeritas" [sic] status costs another $100. One flyer admits Sussex is not "accreditated" [sic] but goes on to say that "No student who has taken our courses and awards have to date had problems." This statement would not be accepted by, among many others, a former high-level state official in Colorado who lost his job when the source of his Doctorate was discovered. Sussex continues to advertise extensively in newspapers and magazines in the U.S. and worldwide. In 1988, a new British law came into effect, forbidding such "schools" to accept students who enrolled after May 1st. Sussex's solution to this minor annoyance was to offer to back-date all applications to April 30th, 1988—a creative response that British law apparently hasn't caught up with yet.

Taurus International University California. The claim is that the Taurus International Society was established in 1764 by James Boswell. The Ph.D. is sold for all of $2, and the Doctor of Whimsey for $1.

Taylor College of England See: ORB

Taylor University of Bio-Psycho-Dynamic Sciences This school was established in Chattanooga, Tennessee, in the early 1920s by some of that city's "most respected citizens, including a philanthropic capitalist, merchant prince, a dentist . . . and a woman of high intelligence." The Doctorate sold for $115, or $103.50 cash in advance.

Temple Bar College Identified as a diploma mill by E&T.

Tennessee Christian University Tennessee. Affiliated with Ohio and Florida State Christian in the sale of fake degrees.

Texas Theological University Texas. Identified as a diploma mill by E&T.

Texas University See: Regency Enterprises

Thomas A. Edison College Florida and Arkansas. Totally fake school run by the Rt. Rev. Dr. George C. Lyon, M.D., Ph.D., LL.D., D.D. After twice being fined heavily and sentenced to prison for running fake schools in Florida, he moved to Arkansas, arriving with an entourage in a red Mercedes and a green Rolls Royce, and bought a vacant church for cash. But the FBI's DipScam operation caught up with him again, and Lyon, now in his 80s, went off to federal prison once again. Thomas A. Edison College managed to fool an awful lot of people over the years, and not just because it sounds like the legitimate nontraditional Edison in New Jersey. This Edison was listed in many otherwise reputable college guides (like Lovejoy's) as a real school for years. Lyon's other nefarious enterprises have included the Palm Beach Psychotherapy Training Center, the Florida Analytic Institute, and an involvement with two phony medical schools, United American Medical College and the Keppler School of Medicine.

Thomas Jefferson University (MO) Missouri. In the early 1980s, catalogs were mailed from this school, allegedly in St. Louis (the address was a private home), but there was never a listed phone, and the postmark was Denver. Degrees at all levels were offered for $1,500 on up. The catalog was almost identical to that used by a legitimate California school. Letters were never answered. With the catalog came a Servicemen's Allotment Account form, for military people to have the "university" paid directly each month from their paycheck, into a bank account in New York.

Thomas University Pennsylvania. They used to sell fake degrees for up to $1,000. They claimed accreditation from the fake Middle States Accrediting Board.

Tremonte University See: USSI

Trinity College See: Global Money Consultants

Trinity College and University This nonexistent school certainly has a cosmopolitan presentation—they have a British address, claim to operate from Spain with licensing from Delaware, and "we will consider awarding degrees in any subject" bsed solely on payment of a fee. They also maintain an equally nonexistent accrediting association, the Correspondence Accreditation Association, which will certify that the degree was in fact purchased.

Trinity Collegiate Institute University England and Switzerland. The London mail service forwards the mail to Karl Bleisch, an operator of many diploma mills in Switzerland. According to an expose in the Times of London, Bleisch told the forwarding service that Trinity was a language school only, with "no question of awarding degrees." Within two months, he was handing out degrees in subjects from beer marketing to scientific massage. (One alumnus went on to start Inter-State College and Institut Patriarcal Saint Irenée.)

Tuit University Georgia. The Doctorates, sold for $10, are amusing when you read the small print, which says, for instance, that the recipient "has not had the time to do the necessary work leading to the degree of Doctor of Philosophy . . . ."

Tulsa College See: R/G Enterprises

Two Dragon University See: International Honorary Awards Committee

United American Medical College A medical degree mill, operated from the apartment of its founder in Louisiana, and from a mail-forwarding service in Canada. The approach was almost identical to that of the Johann Keppler School of Medicine, described earlier. When owner L. Mitchell Weinberg was first arrested (1977) for violating Louisiana school laws, he maintained the school was fully accredited by the American Coordinated Medical Society in California. Indeed, said society wrote that "we of the accreditation committee feel that U.A.M.C. has the highest admission requirements of any medical college in the world . . . due to the great leadership of it's [sic] President, L. Mitchell Weinberg." The founder and proprietor of the American Coordinated

Medical Society is L. Mitchell Weinberg. In 1982, Weinberg pleaded guilty to charges of selling medical degrees and was sentenced to three years in federal prison.

United Free University of England Identified as a diploma mill by E&T.

United States University of America Washington, Florida. The 11-page typewritten catalog actually listed names of some legitimate faculty who had been duped into doing some work for "Dr." Frank Pany and the school he ran from his Florida home, using a Washington, DC mail-forwarding service. One of the faculty, the "Chairman of the Marriage Counseling Department," whose Doctorate was from U.S.U.A. was more candid. "You're in California," he said on the phone. "Why not deal with a degree service closer to home?" In the wake of an FBI visit, and a grand jury indictment in February 1986, "Dr." Pany departed suddenly for Italy.

Universal Bible Institute Birmingham, Alabama. The state declared it was a diploma mill, and ordered it closed, because doctoral degrees could be acquired in less than two months on payment of appropriate fees, and the school was not affiliated with any religious organization. According to Alabama authorities, the institute's president moved to Florida, taking all the records with him, as the Alabama investigation began.

Universal Ecclesiastical University Their Doctorates were offered in any field but law or medicine for a 10-page dissertation, and honorary Doctorates to anyone with "good moral character" plus $200 to spend. Our last letter to Professor Gilbert at the university's address in Manchester, England, was returned with the word "Demolished" written in big blue crayon letters across the front. Let us hope they were referring to the building, not the professor.

Universal Light Church London. Doctor of Divinity, Metaphysics, or Philosophy offered for a hundred dollars or so; for another hundred bucks one can add priest's credentials, or for a big $500, become a bishop.

Universidad Brasileira Rio de Janeiro, Brazil. Identified as a diploma mill by COE.

Universidad Indigenista Moctezuma Andorra's only diploma mill—identified as such by COE.

Universidad Latino-Americana de la Habana Havana, Cuba. Identified as a diploma mill by COE.

Universidad Sintetica Latina y Americana El Salvador. Identified as a diploma mill by COE.

Universidad Tecnológica Nacional Havana, Cuba. Identified as a diploma mill by COE.

Universitaires Internationales Liechtenstein, India, Sudan, Morocco, Japan, etc., etc. Identified as a diploma mill by E&T.

Universitas Iltiensis England, Switzerland. Identified as a diploma mill by E&T.

Universitas Internationalis Studiorum Superiorium Pro Deo In 1989, they began offering "honoris causa" Doctorates from an address in New York, under the imprimatur of the Titular Archbishop of Ephesus.

Universitas Mons Calpe In 1998, they began offering Master's and Doctorates for $1,500 to $2,000. They claim their campus is in Lugano, Switzerland. They claim their accreditation from an unrecognized Wyoming accrediting agency that has no listed telephone.

Universitates Sheffieldensis See: University of Sheffield

Université de Commerce de Canada See: Lawford State University

Université des Science de l'Homme France. Same as University of the Science of Man. See also: Sussex College of Technology

Université Internationale de Paris Paris, France. Identified as a diploma mill by COE.

Université Nouvelle de Paris Paris, France. Identified as a diploma mill by COE.

Université Philotechnique Brussels, Belgium, and Paris, France. Identified as a diploma mill by COE.

Université Voltaire de France Marseilles, France. Identified as a diploma mill by COE.

University College of Nottingham See: Whitby Hall College

University del Puerto Monico Panama. Degrees from this nonexistent institution were sold by Neil Gibson & Company in England, who also represented University de la Romande. They say that "the degree certificates are excellently presented and make a superb and unusual wall decoration. They are for self-esteem only but remain very popular indeed." The same management later opened, but no longer operates, Knightsbridge University.

University in London Same as Obura University. Identified as a diploma mill by E&T.

University of Cape Cod An iffy-sounding school of this name was promoted in eastern Massachusetts in the early 1980s.

University of Corpus Christi Reno, Nevada. Affiliated with the Society of Academic Recognition. Identified as a diploma mill by E&T. No connection with the legitimate school formerly known as University of Corpus Christi but now a part of Texas A & I University.

University of Coventry England. Identified as a diploma mill by E&T. There is a legitimate university with the same name.

University of East Carolina See: University of East Georgia

University of East Georgia Georgia. Degrees in all fields, including medicine, psychiatry, surgery, and neurology sold for $500 and completion of a thesis on "a subject and length of your own choosing." Embarrassingly enough, John was duped by the first literature he received from proprietor John Blazer in 1975, but the game soon became clear. Blazer also operated the University of the Bahama Islands, the College of Hilton Head, the University of East Carolina, and the University of Middle Tennessee. In 1984, he was indicted by a federal grand jury as a result of the FBI's DipScam operation. He pleaded guilty to the charge of mail fraud and was sentenced to prison.

University of Eastern Florida Chicago, Illinois. Degrees of all kinds except medicine and law were sold for $40 each. The school claimed to be a "state chartered university" in Florida (not true).

University of England London, England. Degrees of any kind were sold for about $200 by a school using both this name and the name University of England at Oxford. In 1987, the American proprietors were indicted by a federal grand jury. Five of them were found guilty and sentenced to prison. The founder of Western States University claims a degree from this institution (the school, not the prison).

University of England at Oxford See: University of England

University of Independence A realistic-looking diploma was given or sold as a promotional piece to independent businesspeople. The Ph.D. came from the School of Hard Knocks. A reader sent us a photo of a well-known author and lecturer, from a national magazine, showing the diploma prominently displayed on his wall. Only the school name, the man's name, and "Doctor of Philosophy" are readable. This is one way that even "gag" fake diplomas can be misused.

University of Man's Best Friend A lovely $2 Ph.D. in Love and Loyalty, with paw prints as signatures.

University of Middle Tennessee See: University of East Georgia

University of North America Diploma mill operated by Edward Reddeck from a mail-forwarding service in Missouri in the late 1980s. After he was fined $2,500,000 for this operation, he fled to Utah, changing the name of the school slightly, to North American University (see

separate listing). He was indicted for mail fraud and conspiracy in the spring of 1992, found guilty on all 22 counts in 1993, and sent back to prison.

University of Pittsburg See: Regency Enterprises

University of Rarotonga Fictitious school whose paraphernalia is sold on this South Seas island.

University of Saint Bartholomew After John gave a talk on diploma mills on Australian radio, a number of people called or wrote to mention a school by this name in Oodnadatta, Australia that merrily sold its fake product to Europeans.

University of San Moritz In 1998, this nonexistent "school" began advertising saying "Are you tired of being underpaid for your hard work? Do you want the admiration of your friends, relatives, and loved ones? If your answer is 'yes' you need a diploma from a higher university." They seem to operate only by telephone (from an Ohio area code). When I left a message, the man who called back offered me a diploma by return mail for $125 to $250, plus, for added fees, a transcript (grades of my choice).

University of Sealand Identified as a diploma mill by E&T.

University of Sheffield Sheffield, England. Also called Universitates Sheffieldensis, Ecclesiastical University of Sheffield. There is a legitimate, traditional University of Sheffield, and then there is this fake one, run (according to an article in the Times of London) by Charles Brearly, an auto mechanic who styles himself Ignatius Carelus, successor to Cardinal Barberini of Rheims. He is a sometime associate of "Sir" Sidney Lawrence, proprietor of the College of Applied Science, London. We have received a stern letter from the academic registrar of the real University of Sheffield, suggesting that "in order that our academic standing not be endangered, I would ask that your publication make it quite clear in the future that the college mentioned has no connection whatsoever with this institution." Done, and thanks for thinking that our little book could endanger your large, old, well-established university.

University of Sulgrave England. Identified as a diploma mill by E&T.

University of the Americas An organization called Global Money Consultants has been offering extremely low-priced degrees over the Internet; you send them a CV, a photocopy of your passport, three color photos, and between $1,500 and $2,000 and, within 30 days, they either send you the degree of your choice or your money back. Many fields, including law, but no medical or dentistry. We have been told, we think reliably, that the university is operated by the vice president of an unaccredited California-based Hawaii-registered school.

University of the Bahama Islands See: University of East Georgia

University of the Eastern United States Identified as a diploma mill by E&T.

University of the New World Arizona and Europe. Identified as a diploma mill by E&T.

University of the Old Catholic Church Sheffield, England. Identified as a diploma mill by E&T. Presumably the same management as the fake University of Sheffield.

University of the President Utah. They have sold honorary Doctorates in iridology, psionics, macrobiotics, endogenous endocrinotherapy, and dozens more, in exchange for a $25 "donation."

University of the Republic A fictitious school started by Arizona Republic newspaper reporters Jerry Seper and Rich Robertson as part of a series on degree mills, to show how easy it was to do such things in Arizona at the time. Public outrage led to a tough new school-regulating law being passed.

University of the Science of Man See: Sussex College of Technology

University of the West See: International Universities Consortium

University of Walla Walla California. Advertising in a national women's magazine offered a Doctor of anything ending in "ologist" for $18.90.

University of Winchester London, England. Same address as the London School of Social Research. The $15 diplomas have been widely advertised as "completely spurious, nonetheless as impressive as genuine."

University of Wyoming Of course there is a real one in Laramie, but there is also a fake one. A man named Cunning, using an address in London, England and literature printed in German, has been selling Ph.D.'s, law degrees, and alarmingly, M.D.'s of the University of Wyoming for about $500. We wrote to the general counsel of the real University of Wyoming, thinking they might be interested, but there's been no reply. (Since there's a purveyor of fake degrees named Wiley Bennett, one can't help wondering if they might some day get together, to form a Wiley and Cunning partnership.)

USSI Florida. In late 1994, they began selling a range of documents ranging from the obviously silly (such as Super Mom or Total Airhead) to the highly deceptive. "Diplomas" are offered from Hirshfeld University, Shield College (UK), Tremonte University, Wellingsburg University, Raighlings University, or the College of Hard Knocks. Degrees include Bachelor's, Master's, Doctorates, and law degrees, in a wide range of fields, for prices ranging form $59.50 to $101.50. A warning on the order form states "These novelty items (Certificates) are very realistic in appearance. In view, they may be mistaken as authentic certificates. USSI, it's [sic] staff and any hired agency or service are not liable for any representation by the purchaser of our products." More alarmingly, USSI also offers to produce diplomas from any university and for any degree. To test this, John ordered a medical degree from Harvard. Someone from USSI telephoned him and suggested that they would be willing to make a Harvard law degree instead, and that is what they did.

Vocational University India. Identified as a diploma mill by COE.

Washington International Academy New York. Identified as a diploma mill by E&T.

Webster University Georgia. Identified as a diploma mill by E&T. (There is an accredited school of the same name in Missouri. No connection, of course.)

Weinberg University of West Germany See: ORB

Wellingsburg University See: USSI

Wellington University New Jersey. Offered some correspondents the opportunity to earn a Sri Lankan M.D. upon payment of $1,000. Because of that, this "university" has been moved from the chapter on medical schools to this one.

West London College of Technology London, England. Advertisements appearing in African magazines offered a 12-month correspondence program leading to various qualifications, including the M.B.A., "in association with Broadhurst University." The address given is a mail receiving and forwarding service in London, and there is no telephone. We can find no evidence of the existence of either the West London College or of Broadhurst University.

Western Cascade University California. Degrees of all sorts at $45 each. The address is a mail forwarding service. In an apparent effort to avoid prosecution, they will not sell their product to California residents.

Western College See: National Certificate Company

Western Orthodox University Glastonbury, England. Identified as a diploma mill by E&T.

Western Reserve Educational Services For years, they sold diplomas that they claimed to have "salvaged" from "genuine schools that have gone out of business" from an Ohio post office box. The proprietor, Robert Kim Walton, claimed to have been commended by the Sacred Congregation in Rome—not, one dares hope, for selling fake degrees.

Western University California. One of the early American degree mills, operating from southern California (San Diego and Jacumba) in the 1940s and 1950s. A Western University with addresses in Georgia,

Montana, Colorado, and Delaware has been identified as a diploma mill by E&T; one in India has been identified as a diploma mill by COE.

Whitby Hall College Essex, England. M. Palmer offers degrees of almost any kind for about $100, earned for your resumé and a poem, a story, or a two-page book review. His other school names are the University College of Nottingham, and South Eastern University.

Williams College Idaho. When the late Lane Williams left New Mexico to move his "college" to Mexico, he changed its name from Williams to Elysion. But Williams was apparently left in other hands, and continued to operate, selling Bachelor's and law degrees for about $300 each. See also: Elysion College

Wordsworth Memorial University England and India. Identified as a diploma mill by E&T and by COE.

28

Honorary Doctorates

Why anybody can have a brain. That's a very mediocre commodity.
Back where I come from we have universities—seats of great learning—where men go to become great
thinkers. And when they come out they think deep thoughts, and with no more brains than you have. But
they have one thing you haven't got: a diploma! Therefore by virtue of the authority vested in me by the
Universitatis Committitatum E Pluribus Unum, I hereby confer upon you the Honorary Degree of Th.D.
That's, uh, er, ah, Doctor of Thinkology.

L. FRANK BAUM, THE WIZARD OF OZ

The probable origin of the honorary Doctorate was discussed in chapter 3. The persistence of this "degree"—indeed, its usage has grown tremendously, with more than 50,000 being awarded by major universities in the last decade—is one of the mysteries of the academic world, for there is nothing whatever educational about the honorary Doctorate. It is, purely and simply, a title that some institutions have chosen for a variety of reasons to bestow upon certain people (and a few animals).

That the title given is "Doctor"—the same word used for academic degrees—is what has caused all the confusion, not to mention most of the desirability of the honorary Doctorate. It is exactly as if the government were to honor people by giving them the title of "Senator" or "Judge." Whatever the reason, honorary Doctorates have become highly valuable, even negotiable, commodities.

Not everyone takes them seriously, however. When a German university handed its Doctor of Music diploma to the composer Handel, he rolled it into a dunce cap, placed it on the head of his servant, and said, "There! Now you're a Doctor, too."

Poet Robert Frost expressed particular delight at the announcement of his 40th honorary Doctorate (from Oxford), because he confessed that he had been having the decorative hoods given with each award made into a patchwork quilt, and now it would all come out even. He revealed this en route to England "to collect some more yardage."

When artist Thomas Hart Benton accepted an honorary degree from Rockhurst College, he gestured to the graduating class and said, "I know how those boys behind me feel. They're thinking 'I worked four years for this, and that bum gets it free.'"

One of the curiosities of the honorary Doctorate is that the title given rarely has much relevance to the recipient's qualifications. Hence we have actor Fess Parker getting a Doctor of Letters (from Tennessee, after portraying Davey Crockett), Robert Redford a Doctor of Humane Letters (from Colorado; he said it is "as important to me as my Oscar"), Times Square restaurant owner Dario Toffenetti a Doctor of Laws (from Idaho, for promoting the baked potato), and the late industrialist Clarence Mackay a Doctor of Music (but there was a logical reason for this: his daughter had married Irving Berlin).

Perhaps Mark Twain said it best:

It pleased me beyond measure when Yale made me a Master of Arts, because I didn't know anything about art. I had another convulsion of pleasure when Harvard made me a Doctor of Literature, because I was not competent to doctor anybody's literature but my own. ...I rejoiced again when Missouri University made me a Doctor of Laws because it was all clear profit, I not knowing anything about laws except how to evade them and not get caught. And now at Oxford I am to be made a Doctor of Letters—all clear profit, because what I don't know about letters would make me a millionaire if I could turn it into cash.

Not all titles have been inappropriate, of course. In 1987, Mister Rogers received a Doctor of Humanities (Bowling Green), and led the audience in singing "Won't you be my neighbor." Admiral Byrd received a Doctor of Faith and Fortitude. Charlie McCarthy, the impertinent ventriloquist's dummy, received a Master of Innuendo from Northwestern. Antioch University gave a Master of Communication to a campus switchboard operator, and Brooklyn College, which averages only one honorary degree every four years, gave a Doctor of Delectables to a longtime campus hot dog vendor. A heroic seeing-eye dog named Bonzo received a Doctor of Canine Fidelity from Newark University. A mule named Elwood Blues got a doctorate from Yale. When Southampton College awarded a Doctor of Amphibious Letters to Kermit the Frog, many students expressed displeasure. A marine biology major named Samantha Chie said, "After five years of hard work, now we have a sock talking at our commencement. It's kind of upsetting." And so it goes.

WHY HONORARY DOCTORATES ARE GIVEN

1. To Attract Celebrities to Campus

These humorous (or, some say, ludicrous) examples illuminate one of the four major reasons that honorary Doctorates are given: to bring publicity to the graduation ceremonies of the school. If a small college can lure a baseball star, a movie or television personality, or even the wife of a famous politician to the campus, the commencement is more likely to make the evening news and the next morning's papers, which may help student or faculty recruiting, fundraising, or membership in the alumni association. It may even increase the chances that a top high school quarterback will come to the school next year. Indeed, when John Carroll University awarded an honorary Doctorate to Miami Dolphins coach Don Shula, it almost certainly was not for his academic achievements.

And that is why we have Dr. Marlon Brando, Dr. Henry Fonda, Dr. Michael Bolton, Dr. Arnold Schwarzenegger, Dr. Bruce Willis, Dr. Robert DeNiro, Dr. Jane Fonda, Dr. Bob Hope (more than 40 times over), Dr. Captain Kangaroo, Dr. Michael Jackson, and thousands of others.

High tech came to the world of honorary degrees when Liverpool University awarded its honorary Doctorate to Arthur C. Clarke via a satellite link to Sri Lanka.

Sometimes the publicity is not the kind the school had in mind. St. Joseph's College, a Catholic school, offered its honorary Doctorate to columnist Ann Landers, then created a big flap by withdrawing it after Landers wrote a pro-abortion column. And as Louisiana Tech was presenting its honorary Doctorate to former football quarterback Terry Bradshaw, outraged alumni flew over the ceremony and dropped a cascade of leaflets protesting the award.

There is nothing new going on here. During the Revolutionary War, Harvard gave an honorary degree to Lafayette. When he heard this, Baron von Steuben urged his troops, then approaching Cambridge, to ride through town "like the devil, for if they catch you, they make a doctor of you."

2. To Honor Distinguished Faculty and Administrators

Honorary degrees are often given to honor distinguished faculty at the donating school, or other schools. This is perhaps the most academically defensible reason. In American society, there is nothing equivalent to the national honors given in many European countries (e.g., the Queen's Honours List in Britain, at which hundreds of people each year become knights, ladies, Members of the British Empire, etc.) The honorary Doctorate remains one of the few honors we have to bestow. And so, each June, from 40% to 60% of all honorary degrees go to unknown academics, often, it is said, in the hope that their school will honor someone from our school next year.

This practice has resulted in a new world record. In 1982, then-president of Notre Dame Father Theodore Hesburgh collected his 90th honorary title, eclipsing Herbert Hoover's record of 89. The good Father is now in a head-to-head sheepskin-to-sheepskin battle with the King of Thailand. In early 1998, the King vaulted into first place with honorary doctorate number 137, but Hesburgh surged into the lead in June with two honoraries, moving him up to 138.

3. For Political Reasons

American presidents, British prime ministers, and other statesmen are regularly so honored, and often take the opportunity to make major speeches. Winston Churchill used the occasion of receiving an honorary degree in Missouri to deliver his famous "iron curtain" speech, and General George Marshall announced the Marshall Plan while receiving an honorary Doctorate.

Although every American president has collected some honorary Doctorates (George Washington had seven), none caused quite the furor of Harvard's award of an honorary Doctor of Laws to President Andrew Jackson. The Sons of Harvard erupted in anger. John Quincy Adams wrote about how his alma mater had degraded herself, "conferring her highest literary honors on a barbarian who could not write a sentence of grammar and could hardly spell his own name." Harvard president Josiah Quincy responded, "As the people have twice decided that this man knows enough law to be their ruler, it is not for Harvard College to maintain they are mistaken."

The ceremony itself must have been quite extraordinary. After Jackson had been given the sheepskin and expressed his thanks in a few short remarks, an aide reminded him that he was expected to make a speech in Latin. Thereupon, according to biographer Robert Rayback, he bellowed out, in tones of thunder, all the Latin he knew: "E pluribus unum, sine qua non, multum in parvo, quid pro quo, ne plus ultra." So much for Dr. Jackson.

Haverford College made a rather dramatic political statement when they awarded honorary Doctor of Laws degrees to the 3,000 inhabitants of a French village that helped save the lives of 2,500 Jews during World War II.

Withholding of honorary Doctorates has also been used to make political statements. In 1987, the governing body of Oxford University voted 738 to 319 to withhold an honorary Doctorate from Prime Minister Thatcher because of her role in cutting university research funds. And the proposed awarding of degrees to Richard Nixon has caused controversies in more than a few places—including his alma mater, Duke University, which ultimately turned him down. Indeed, one report had it that during the final days of Watergate, someone in the Nixon administration had the idea that an honorary Doctorate would give Nixon some favorable publicity for a change. The only school they could find that would agree to do it was General Beadle State College, and that is why Air Force One descended into South Dakota one day in the spring of 1974. (General Beadle subsequently changed its name to Dakota State, but denies there was any connection with the Nixon visitation.)

In 1988, it was revealed that the faculty of Dan Quayle's alma mater voted overwhelmingly to deny him an honorary Doctorate, largely because of his poor academic record, but they were overruled by the administration. The same thing happened when predominantly black South Carolina State College offered an honorary degree to Strom Thurmond. "No South Carolinian has done more over the past 40 years to impede the advancement of black people," said a petition signed by most faculty and students. They were overruled by president Albert Smith, hence we have Dr. Senator Thurmond.

The decision of a Jesuit school, Fairfield University in Connecticut, to award an honorary degree to Billy Joel produced some major objections from people who contended that Joel's song *Only the Good Die Young* was insulting to Catholics. He got his degree.

But former Secretary of Transportation Drew Lewis stunned a commencement audience at his alma mater, Haverford College, when he removed his purple doctoral hood after the honorary degree had been bestowed on him. He said that Quakers are supposed to act by consensus, but he had learned that a third of the faculty opposed his award because of his role in breaking the air traffic controllers' strike. The audience gave him a standing ovation.

Not everyone who is offered an honorary degree accepts. While the noble 13th president of the United States, Millard Fillmore, was the only president with a firm policy of rejecting all honoraries (he said that he had not learned to read until he was nearly 20, and just didn't feel comfortable with academic awards), more than a few celebrities have taken the occasion of the offer to make a point or two. Pablo Neruda very publicly rejected an honorary degree from Harvard, because of America's involvement in Vietnam. And when George Bernard Shaw was asked if he would accept a Harvard Doctor of Letters, he replied,

> I cannot pretend that it would be fair for me to accept university degrees when every public reference of mine to our educational system, and especially to the influence of unviersities on it, is fiercely hostile. If Harvard would celebrate its 300th anniversary by burning itself to the ground and sowing its site with salt, the ceremony would give me the greatest satisfaction as an example to all the other famous old corrupters of youth, including Yale, Oxford, Cambridge, the Sorbonne, etc., etc., etc. Under the circumstances, I should let you down very heavily if you undertook to sponsor me.

4. For Money

Although schools sanctimoniously deny there is any connection whatsoever, they have regularly awarded Doctorates to academically undistinguished folks who just happened to donate a bundle of money. How long has this been going on? Well, in *A Distant Mirror*, Barbara Tuchman writes that in the 14th century, the University of Paris "had taken to selling degrees in theology to candidates unwilling to undertake its long and difficult studies."

A few centuries later, George Baker gave Harvard millions for a new business school. Harvard gave George Baker a Doctor of Laws along with their hearty thanks. John Archbold contributed a new football field to Syracuse University. Soon after, he was doctored by Syracuse University. William Randolph Hearst "traded" $100,000 and 400 acres of land to Oglethorpe University for an honorary Doctorate.

A few years ago, a British dry-goods merchant named Isaac Wolfson gave about £10 million to Cambridge University, and they not only gave him an honorary Doctorate, they named a college of the university for him. Then he made the same gift to Oxford, and they too both doctored him and named a college for him. Thus, as one London paper wrote in a caustic editorial, only two men in all history have had a college named for them at both Oxford and Cambridge: Jesus Christ and Isaac Wolfson. (The price seems to be going up. The Kellogg people invested more than £12 million before Oxford renamed another college in favor of the inventor of corn flakes.)

The Shah of Iran made a $1 million gift to the University of Southern California, whose president then hand-carried an honorary Doctorate to Iran. Around the same time, the University of Wisconsin exchanged an honorary Doctorate for a $2.5 million gift from oil millionaire C. George Weeks.

John Hope Franklin of the National Humanities Center worries, as do many others, about "the delicate matter of honorary degrees. One cannot help wondering in how many ways some institutions sell their souls in conferring them.... Better that a university cease to exist altogether than sell its soul."

One solution to this matter is to award the honorary degree first, in the hopes that the recipient will give the school his thanks in the form of a check or other favors. This approach made headlines a while back when the *Washington Post* uncovered the "Koreagate" scandal, in which 11 U.S. congressmen had accepted, among other favors, honorary Doctorates from South Korean universities, complete with all-expense luxury trips to Korea to collect them, in an apparent effort to win congressional approval of the Korean regime.

To their credit, three congressmen rejected the honorary Doctorates. But it is rare indeed for an honorary Doctorate to be turned down. Oxford University used to have a policy, before Richard Nixon came along, of offering an honorary Doctorate to every outgoing U.S. president. Of all those to whom it was offered, only good old Millard Fillmore turned it down, saying that he felt he had done nothing to merit it, and besides, the diploma was in Latin and he never accepted anything he couldn't read.

HOW TO GET AN HONORARY DOCTORATE

How, then, does the ordinary person, who is not a movie star, an athlete, or a millionaire, acquire an honorary Doctorate? There is no simple way, other than buying one from a less-than-respectable institution, or having one printed to order at the neighborhood print shop. Nonetheless, here are five possibilities:

1. **Donate money.** The question naturally arises, how little money does it take to buy an honorary Doctorate from a major accredited university? If the school is in financial trouble, as little as $10,000 has been said to turn the trick. The cheapest case we personally know about is $50,000 from an Arab businessman to an accredited California university whose building fund was in trouble.

   A Los Angeles businessman once ran a small ad in *The New Republic* magazine, offering to donate $10,000 to any accredited school that would give him an honorary degree. When we contacted him, he told John he had gotten the degree, but refused to name the school.

2. **Perform a valuable service.** Honorary Doctorates have gone to heads of fundraising committees, who never gave a dime themselves, to real estate brokers who put together a big deal to acquire more land or refinance a mortgage for the school, to friends of friends of celebrities who managed to get the Senator or the Star or the Second Baseman to speak at the commencement, to a nurseryman who wangled the donation of hundreds of trees and supervised their planting on campus; to a golf pro who donated his time to the college team; and so on.

   Lawyers are sometimes rewarded too. When Cecil Rhodes died in 1902 he left money for scholarships for "white American boys from all 13 states." The lawyer who got this legal mess untangled, and persuaded Parliament to come up with funds for "white American boys" from all the other states, got a Doctor of Civil Law from Oxford for his efforts.

   Perhaps the most valuable service one can perform is finding a cash donor. Remember that $50,000 honorary Doctorate for an Arab businessman, just described? Well, the man who found that donor for the university in question also got an honorary Doctorate, as a finder's fee.

3. **Capitalize on trends.** Honorary Doctorates seem to be rather trendy things, and those trends seem to run for three to five years. For instance, in the late 1950s, space science was in vogue, and people ranging from Wernher von Braun to the founder of a local

rocketry society were being honored. In the 1960s, it was the Peace Corps. Sargent Shriver, its first director, set a record that stood for thirty years by accepting seven Doctorates in one month (June, 1964), and a lot of other Peace Corps people and other youth workers were in demand on commencement platforms. (Nelson Mandela holds the current record, with nine in one day, all from British universities, in some sort of joint ceremony.)

The 1980s seemed heavy on jazz and classical musicians, medical researchers, people who work with the handicapped, the very elderly (several people over 100 got them for no apparent reason other than survival), Vietnam veterans, economists, and public interest lawyers.

In the 1990s, more than a few kudos have gone to authors of children's books, radio talk show hosts, AIDS researchers or counselors, investigative reporters, coaches of non-major sports (lacrosse, rugby, field hockey, volleyball), and schoolteachers. Who knows what the 2000s will bring?

Some people have reported success by directly or, more often, indirectly contacting a school that has given a certain honorary degree this year, suggesting they may wish to consider a similar one next year.

4. **Buy one.** If all you really want is a fancy but meaningless document to hang on the wall (actually, all honorary Doctorates fit that description, but some may be perceived as more meaningless than others), some of the unaccredited but legal schools are likely to oblige. A few years ago, *Spy* magazine had a reporter shop around to buy a degree, honorary or otherwise, and just about every unaccredited school they approached was willing to make the sale. (This caper was reported in their February 1995 edition.)

   Of course any of the diploma mills would be more than pleased to dispense an honorary Doctorate on payment of a fee that can range from 50¢ to over $1,000, but you're on your own for locating those; we don't give out addresses. Another common source of honoraries are the Bible schools, some of which reward donors with honorary degrees. See Appendix E for more information on these.

   But you'll do just as well at the local print shop, where you can have the type set for the diploma of your choice. Just don't get carried away and have a whole batch printed for sale to the public.

5. **Wait.** A few years ago, we wrote that "We think it is inevitable that one or more well-known, respectable, fully-accredited colleges, faced by the cash crunch that is upon so many worthy institutions, will face reality and openly put their honorary Doctorates up for sale." A few years later, it happened. A small, accredited college took out a national ad, suggesting a donation of $25,000. The accrediting agency got

quite upset at this, and the offer was withdrawn. But later, the well-respected Embry-Riddle Aeronautical University bought a Wall Street Journal ad offering a Trusteeship of the University in exchange for a $1 million donation (from an otherwise qualified donor). That, too, caused a furor.

So maybe we are still a bit premature in saying, "Wait." It may be that the deals will continue to go on just below the surface for a while longer.

THE ETIQUETTE OF SOLICITING DEGREES

Here's one that Emily Post never had to deal with. How straightforward should one be in letting it be known that one would like an honorary Doctorate? There is no way to know. Our feeling is that in the majority of situations, the direct approach is inappropriate. One must work through intermediaries—friends of school officials or trustees, who drop hints. But there are some schools and awards committees who seem to find the blunt approach refreshingly candid. These are people who realize and admit that what they are really doing is selling honorary degrees, so why not be up front? The president of a small eastern college told John that he was once approached by a second-rate actor who really wanted an honorary Doctorate, "just like Marlon Brando and Henry Fonda." They negotiated terms, and the degree was awarded the following June—presumably after the check cleared the bank.

On the other hand, a high U.S. Air Force official in Europe got a lot of unfavorable publicity when *Stars and Stripes* revealed that he had solicited honorary Doctorates for himself and some associates from universities that were doing contractual work for the air force. Two of the universities (Southern California and Maryland) turned him down. "It wasn't appropriate to ask for it, and it wasn't appropriate to give it," one school official said. But the third university gave it to him.

The army's counterpart in Europe, when asked if he would solicit honorary Doctorates, replied, "You've got to be out of your tree."

One of the more awkward solicitations came from actor George Wendt, better known as the beer-guzzling Norm on the popular sit-com *Cheers*. Here is how the Miami *Herald* reported the event:

> Notre Dame Coach Lou Holtz looked toward a big Fighting Irish fan—a really big Fighting Irish fan—to motivate his team Friday night. George Wendt...burst into a frenzied pep rally unannounced as the 10,000-plus students chanted 'Norm!'
>
> Wendt proclaimed that the Fighting Irish had some unfinished business to attend to Saturday. As far as motivation speeches go, though, this wasn't much of one. Other than the unfinished-business line, Wendt did little more than yell unintelligibly at the top of his lungs until he was dragged away.
>
> Wendt, who failed out of Notre Dame after three years, asked for an honorary degree, but Holtz gave him an autographed football instead....

IS THERE A DOCTOR IN THE HOUSE?

Here are some of the people who have been 'doctored' by major universities in recent years:

Doctor Ella Fitzgerald	Doctor J. Edgar Hoover	Doctor Gavin McLeod	Doctor Duke Ellington
Doctor Bonnie Raitt	Doctor Dan Rather	Doctor Jane Pauley	Doctor Walter Cronkite
Doctor Roger Maris	Doctor Charles Addams	Doctor Ted Williams	Doctor James Earl Jones
Doctor Isaac Stern	Doctor Candace Bergen	Doctor John Wayne	Doctor Kirk Douglas
Doctor Mister Rogers	Doctor Captain Kangaroo	Doctor Ozzie Nelson	Doctor Marcel Marceau
Doctor Billy Joel	Doctor Pinchas Zuckerman	Doctor Idi Amin	Doctor Sammy Davis Jr.
Doctor B. B. King	Doctor Robert Redford	Doctor Arthur Ashe	Doctor Mrs. Anwar Sadat
Doctor Dolores Hope	Doctor Marvin Hamlisch	Doctor Don King	Doctor Whoopi Goldberg
Doctor Stevie Wonder	Doctor Margot Fonteyn	Doctor Kermit the Frog	Doctor Steven Spielberg
Doctor Doctor Seuss	Doctor Dave Winfield	Doctor Phil Rizzuto	Doctor Sidney Poitier
Doctor Bing Crosby	Doctor Norman Mailer	Doctor Barbra Streisand	Doctor Maurice Sendak
Doctor Helen Hayes	Doctor Aretha Franklin		
Doctor Max Factor	Doctor Leontyne Price	and at least 50,000 more	
Doctor Celia Cruz	Doctor Terry Bradshaw		

THE WONDERFUL WACKY WORLD OF HONORARY DEGREES

Here are just a few of the recipients we learned about in recent years.

Recipient	School	What, why, etc.
Dr. Robin Williams	Juilliard	After lampooning Jesse Helms and Dan Quayle ("President Quayle, raise your right hand. No, your other right hand."), he said "I would like to do something from Hamlet. I just need a moment to prepare." As the crowd roared, he continued, "To be or ... wait! I know this!"
Dr. Patrick Ewing	Shaw University	For his athletic abilities and his work with youth.
Dr. Sonny Bono	National Disaster Conference	The degree in disaster medicine was awarded after he helped carry stretchers following a bus accident in Palm Springs.
Dr. Bill Cosby	University of Maryland	"There are no courses in valet parking, waitressing and grinding coffee. You people are not prepared. You are well-educated and you look cute, but that's not going to do it."
Dr. Mother Teresa	University of Scranton	The degree is in social sciences; as soon as it was awarded, she had a police escort back to the Wilkes-Barre airport.
Dr. Sun Myung Moon	Shaw Divinity School	Dr. Moon was in prison for tax evasion at the time.
Dr. Oprah Winfrey	Morehouse College	Doctor of Humane Letters. She gave $1 million for a scholarship fund at the all-male school.
Dr. Goober	U. of North Alabama	George Lindsey, Goober on the Andy Griffith Show, was a sterling fund raiser for his alma mater.
Dr. Frank Sinatra	Stevens Institute	A third of the graduating class signed a petition objecting, not to Sinatra but to the fact the degree was in engineering. Sinatra was born in Hoboken, site of the school.
Dr. Bryant Gumbel	Bates College	"I was not the hardworking 4.0 student.... Life doesn't end when you graduate with less than a 3.0."
Dr. Elwood Blues	Yale University	This mule received a Doctor of Portage Equus for carrying rocks for the Yale geology team. "We don't consider this a joke," said a National Park Service spokesman. "It's not likely an honorary doctorate has ever been given to a mule before from an Ivy League school."
Dr. Mike Tyson	Central State University	After the ceremony, he told a reporter, "I'm successful, I'm young, I'm single, I'm rich, I have God in my life ... and may I be permitted to say, you are such an incredible-looking woman."
Dr. Victor Borge	University of Denver	"Now that I'm a doctor," he said, "I think I have to get some malpractice insurance."
Dr. Jim Evans	Central Missouri State	He invented Cheerios.
Dr. Cinderella	Miami-Dade College	For her efforts at literacy, as part of a book fair.
Dr. Chevy Chase	Bard College	Speaking to his alma mater, he said, "Never tell the truth. Embellish, patronize, pander, use hyperbole, braggadocio, mollify, but never actually tell the truth. Your job is to act. Keep the dream alive. Also, never call me.
Dr. Alexander Solzhenitsyn	Dartmouth College	Doctor of Letters. He speaks almost no English, refused to be interviewed, and did not speak to the graduating class.
Dr. Dolly Parton	Carson-Newman College	Doctor of Letters for "her personal commitment to the educational and economic vitality of East Tennessee ..."
Dr. Prince Charles	Harvard University	Ronald Reagan was to deliver the keynote address, but declined when Harvard refused him an honorary degree because of the controversy over his academic deficiencies. The Prince of Wales accepted. His eagerly-awaited first words on arrival at Logan Airport: "Hello, how are you?"

Recipient	School	What, why, etc.
Dr. Soupy Sales	Marshall University	The newspaper story was headlined "Degree better than pie in face," when his alma mater presented the award.
Dr. Paul McCartney	University of Sussex	"Just call me Dr. Rock," he said. Since he didn't do too well at school, "it was great to get this degree without having to revise [study] for it."
Dr. Oliver North	Liberty University	Chancellor Jerry Falwell called him an American hero and compared his legal predicament to the suffering of Jesus.
Dr. Magic Johnson	Rust College	He said, "This is the greatest and biggest day of my life. This tops any championship, any MVP I've won. . . ."
Dr. Bob Hope	University of San Diego	On receiving his 44th honorary doctorate, he said, "I love commencement. I love the happy, ecstatic, joyous faces. But enough about the teachers."
Dr. Joe DiMaggio	Columbia University	When he was spotted in the procession, "applause grew and several people chanted 'Joe D., Joe D, Joe D.' He waved."
Dr. Steve Wozniak	University of Colorado	The Apple founder was expelled for tampering with the school's computer system. 25 years later, they gave him a Doctorate.
Dr. Scott Hamilton	Bowling Green State Univ.	The gold medalist never attended the school, but he did learn to skate on the university's ice arena.
Dr. Jerry Lewis	South Central Tech College	He stuck a glass all the way into his mouth, hid behind a giant flower arrangement, then said, "I never know what's going to happen until I get to the podium. I'm guided by instinct."
Dr. Joseph Haydn	Oxford University	He wrote Symphony #92 to thank Oxford for awarding him the degree, but it wasn't done in time, so #91 was played at the ceremony.
Dr. Doctor J	University of Massachusetts	Julius Erving received the honorary doctorate at the same time as his earned Bachelor's in leadership and management.
Dr. Prince Philip	Asian Institute of Technology	For his work in saving the environment and wildlife.
Dr. Milt Hinton	Skidmore College	The Judge, patriarch of jazz bass players, played two songs on his stand-up bass in lieu of making a speech.
Dr. Tony Bennett	Art Institute of Boston	He said, "When I get into the art zone, I forget about any pains that I have." He said he paints and sings every day.
Dr. Ed McMahon	Catholic University	Watch for a diploma in your mailbox.
Dr. Michael Jackson	Fisk University	For his support of the United Negro College Fund.
Dr. Alex Haley	Coast Guard Academy	The author of *Roots* received the academy's first honorary degree. While at sea during World War II, he wrote letters to their girlfriends for shipmates at one dollar each.
Dr. Dustin Hoffman	Santa Monica College	He enrolled there to study music, but took an acting class and never looked back (and never graduated).
Dr. Stan Musial	Washington University	Stan the Man never went to college, but as the newspaper account said, "most college graduates can't hit a curve ball."
Dr. George Bush	University of Kuwait	For his "distinguished leadership, lofty stance, and honorable endeavors in . . . the triumphant restoration of Kuwait's independence and sovereignty."
Dr. George Wallace	Tuskeegee Institute	He said, "Very few people have one. You wouldn't have thought I'd have had that, would you? If I was a bad man, I wouldn't have gotten that. No way."
Dr. Nelson Mandela	Carabobo State University	He was offered hundreds; this one was from Venezuela.

29

Bending the Rules

Any fool can make a rule, and every fool will mind it.

HENRY DAVID THOREAU

One of the most common complaints or admonishments we get from readers goes something like, "You said thus-and-so, but when I inquired of the school, they told me such-and-such." Often, a school claims that a program we have written about does not exist. Sometimes a student achieves something (such as completing a certain degree entirely by correspondence) that we had been told by a high official of the school was impossible.

One of the open secrets in the world of higher education is that the rules are constantly being bent. But, as with the Emperor's new clothes, no one dares point and say what is really going on, especially in print.

The purpose of this brief essay is to acknowledge that this sort of thing happens all the time. If you know that it happens regularly, then at least you are in the same boat with people who are already benefiting from those bent rules.

Unfortunately, we cannot provide many specific examples of bent rules, naming names and all. This is for two good reasons:

1. Many situations where students profit from bent rules would disappear in an instant if anyone dared mention the situation publicly. There is, for instance, a major state university that is forbidden by its charter to grant degrees by correspondence study. But they regularly work out special arrangements whereby students are carried on the books as residential, even though all their work is done by mail. Indeed, some graduates of this school have never set foot on its campus. If this ever got out, the Board of Trustees, the accrediting agency, and all the other universities in that state would probably have conniptions, and the practice would be suspended at once.

2. These kinds of things can change so rapidly, with new personnel or new policies, that a listing of anomalies and curious practices would probably be obsolete before the ink dried.

Consider a few examples of the sort of thing that is going on in higher education every day, whether or not anyone will admit it, except perhaps behind closed doors or after several drinks:

◆ A friend of John's, at a major university, was unable to complete one required course for her Doctorate before she had to leave for another state. This university does not offer correspondence courses, but she was able to convince a professor to enroll her in a regular course, which she would just happen never to visit in person.

◆ A man in graduate school needed to be enrolled in nine units of coursework each semester to keep his employer's tuition assistance plan going. But his job was too demanding one year, and he was unable to do so. The school enrolled him in nine units of "independent study" for which no work was asked or required, and for which a "pass" grade was given.

◆ A woman at a large school needed to complete a certain number of units before an inflexible deadline. When it became clear that she wasn't going to make it, a kindly professor turned in grades for her, and told her she could do the actual coursework later on.

◆ A major state university offers nonresident degrees for people living in that state only. When a reader wrote to say that he, living a thousand miles from that state, was able to complete his degree entirely by correspondence, John asked a contact at that school what was going on. "We will take students from anywhere in our correspondence degree program." she told him, "But for God's sake, don't print that in your book, or we'll be deluged with applicants."

338

◆ If we are to believe a book by a member of Dr. Bill Cosby's dissertation committee at the University of Massachusetts (*Education's Smoking Gun,* by Reginald Damerell), the only class attendance on Cosby's transcript was one weekend seminar, and the only dissertation committee meeting was a dinner party, with spouses, at Cosby's house.

◆ Partway through John's supposedly definitive final doctoral oral exam, a key member of his committee had to leave for an emergency. He scrawled a note, and passed it to the dean who read it, then crumpled it up and threw it away. The grueling exam continued for several hours more. After it was over and the committee had congratulated John and departed, he retrieved the note from the wastebasket. It read, "Please give John my apologies for having to leave, and my congratulations for having passed."

◆ A man applied to a well-known school that has a rigid requirement that all graduate work (thesis or dissertation) must be begun after enrollment. He started to tell an admissions officer about a major piece of independent research he had completed for his employer. "Stop," he was told, "Don't tell me about that. Then you'll be able to use it for your Master's thesis."

◆ We've heard from more than a few people who benefited from the bending of various tuition, scholarship, and financing rules. Working on the theory that an empty seat in a classroom is like an empty seat on an airplane—it can never be filled retroactively—some schools with declining tuition have been unusually generous and/or creative in finding ways to offer those seats to people who could not easily qualify for traditional scholarships, loans, or grants. There is never any harm in asking.

◆ Mariah was initially denied admission to the University of California at Berkeley because of some "irregularities" on her high school transcript. (It was a nontraditional high school.) The high school's records had been destroyed in a fire. The former principal checked with the University and discovered that the admissions people would be glad to admit her, once the computer said it was OK. He typed up a new transcript saying what the computer wanted said. The computer said OK, and three years later, she graduated Phi Beta Kappa. But how many other applicants accepted the initial "No," not knowing that rules can often be bent?

◆ The Heriot-Watt University MBA by distance learning, with which John is involved, had a written policy stating that if a student failed an exam in a compulsory course twice, they could not continue in the program. Some students who had passed several courses, but then failed a course twice, were quietly offered another opportunity. Now, to its credit, the university has made this an official policy, and that particular rule no longer needs to be bent.

Please use this information prudently. It will do no good to pound on a table and say, "What do you mean I can't do this? John Bear says that rules don't mean anything, anyway."

But when faced with a problem, it surely can do no harm to remember that in many, many situations the rules have turned out to be far less rigid than a school's official literature would lead one to believe.

Noted rule bender.

30

Advice for People in Prison

*In the midst of winter I discovered
there was in me an invincible summer.*

ALBERT CAMUS

NOTE: More than a few readers and users of this book are institutionalized. We have invited a man who has completed his accredited Bachelor's, Master's, and Doctorate while in prison, and who consults often with inmates and others around the country, to offer his thoughts and recommendations. There is some very useful advice for noninstitutionalized persons as well. (The above quotation has been on Dr. Dean's bulletin board since he began his baccalaureate.)

ARRANGING ACADEMIC RESOURCES FOR THE INSTITUTIONALIZED

by Douglas G. Dean, Ph.D.

One obstacle for any institutionalized person interested in pursuing a degree is limited resources: availability of community faculty, library facilities, phone access, and financial aid. To overcome these, it helps to streamline the matriculation process. Time spent in preparation prior to admission can help avoid wasted effort and time when in a program, thereby reducing operating expenses and cutting down the number of tuition periods.

A second obstacle is finding ways to ensure that a quality education can be documented. Because courses are generally not prepackaged, it is the student's responsibility to identify varied learning settings, use a range of learning methods, find and recruit community-based faculty, provide objective means to appraise what has been learned, and indeed design the study plan itself.

Finding a Flexible Degree Program

Most well-established degree programs grant credit for a variety of learning experiences. In terms of cost and arrangements required, equivalency examinations and independent study projects are the most expedient. Credit for life-experience learning is another option sometimes offered. If a degree program does not offer at least two of these options, it is unlikely that the program as a whole will be able to accommodate the needs of the institutionalized student.

Writing a Competency-Based Study Plan

The traditional method of acquiring credits is to take narrowly focused courses of two to four credits each. Since the nontraditional student must enlist his or her own instructors, find varied learning methods, and quantify the whole experience, the single-course approach creates much needless duplication of effort.

A better approach is to envision a subject area which is to be studied for 9 to 12 credits (e.g., statistics). As an independent-study project, the student identifies what topics are germane to the area (e.g., probability theory, descriptive statistics, inferential statistics); at what level of comprehension (e.g., introductory through intermediate or advanced); how the topic is to be studied (e.g., directed reading, programmed textbooks), and how the competencies acquired are to be demonstrated (e.g., oral examination, proctored examination including problem solving). This way, a single independent-study project can take the place of a series of successive courses in a given area (e.g., Statistics 101, 201, 301).

Designing the Curriculum

Every accredited degree program has graduation requirements. These requirements broadly define the breadth of subject areas that comprise a liberal arts education and the depth to which they are to be studied. It is the responsibility of the external student not only to identify a curriculum fulfilling these requirements but, in most cases, to design the course content that will comprise each study module.

But how does a student know what an area of study consists of before he or she has studied it? The answer lies in meticulous preparation.

Well in advance of formally applying for an off-campus degree program, the prospective student should obtain course catalogs from several colleges and universities. Look at what these schools consider the core curriculum and what is necessary to fulfill the graduation requirements. With this broad outline in mind, the student can begin to form clusters of courses fulfilling each criterion. This approach helps shape the study plan academically rather than touch it up later as an afterthought.

Next, decide which subjects are of interest within each criterion area. Compare topical areas within each subject as described in the course listings and commonalities will emerge. From there, it is simply a matter of writing to the various instructors for a copy of their course syllabi. These course outlines will provide more detailed information about the subject matter and identify the textbooks currently used at that level of study.

Means of Study

Having decided what is to be studied, the student must then propose various ways to study it.

Equivalency exams (such as CLEP) enable the student to acquire credits instantly, often in core or required areas of study. This helps reduce overall program costs by eliminating the need for textbooks and tuition fees. More importantly, it helps reduce the number of special learning arrangements that must otherwise be made.

"Testing out" of correspondence courses (taking only the examinations, without doing the homework assignments) is another excellent way to acquire credits quickly. This can, however, be an expensive method since full course fees are still assessed. Nonetheless, if a student studies on his or her own in advance according to the course syllabus, and if the instructor can then be convinced to waive prerequisite assignments, it can be an efficient and cost-effective method to use.

Independent-study projects should form the balance of any study plan. With the topical areas, learning objectives, and learning materials identified, an independent study project allows the student to remain with the same instructor(s) from an introductory through an intermediate or advanced level of study. This eliminates the need for new arrangements to be made every two to four credits. An independent study project can take the form of simple directed reading, tutorial instruction, practicum work, or a combination of these methods, culminating in the final product.

Direct tutorial arrangements, similar to the European don system, commit a student to learn under a single instructor until he or she is convinced that the student has mastered a given subject at a predetermined level of competency. The tutoring itself may take the form of directed reading from both primary and secondary sources, writing and orally defending assigned topical papers, monitored practica, and supervised research projects. The caveat is that the tutor determines when a student has satisfied all study requirements, so the study plan should meticulously spell out the breadth and depth of what is to be studied.

One may also be able to use existing classroom courses as a setting in which to evaluate a student's mastery of a given subject. Some institutions periodically offer an on-site college or vocational course (e.g., communications skills). Instead of taking such a course for the standard 2 to 3 credits, the student could arrange for specific communication skills (composition, rhetoric) to be evaluated at a given level of mastery (beginning to advanced). In this single step, a student may be able to earn advanced credit and fulfill all the communication skills core requirements for graduation.

Various professions require practitioners to earn continuing education credits, usually through seminars and/or home study courses. These courses represent the latest knowledge in a given field, come prepackaged with an evaluation test, and are an excellent source of study material. The breadth and depth of specialization offered in such courses is especially useful to students with graduate or postgraduate aspirations.

Independent-study projects require the aid of qualified persons to act as community faculty, and to oversee personally the progress of the work. Therefore, it is highly advantageous to line up faculty in advance of entering the degree program. It is equally important to have alternates available in the event an instructor is unable, for any reason, to fulfill his or her commitment. It is better to anticipate these needs at the preparatory stage than to be scrambling for a replacement while the tuition clock is running.

Multiple Treatments of Subject Matter

The external student is often without benefit of lecture halls, interactions with other students, or readily available academic counseling services. For the institutionalized student, picking up the phone or stopping in to see a faculty member for help with a study problem are not options. This is why alternate methods of study are so valuable.

One approach is to use several textbooks covering the same subject matter. If something does not make sense, there is a different treatment of the subject to turn to.

Programmed textbooks make especially good substitute tutors. A programmed text breaks the subject matter into small segments requiring a response from the reader with periodic tests to check progress. Such texts are now available in many subject areas, but are particularly useful for the sciences. Titles can be obtained from the *Books in Print* subject guide, or by writing directly to textbook publishers.

Audio-visual (A-V) materials can, to some extent, make up for college life without the typical lectures and classes. Writing to A-V departments at large universities often yields a catalog of materials available for rental. These materials frequently take the form of a comprehensive tape series, and may address even the most advanced subject matter. When using such materials, it is best to work through the school or social service department of the student's institution of residence.

Some large campuses have lecture note services, which employ advanced students to attend class lectures and take copious lecture notes, which are then sold to students. Aside from gaining insights into good note-taking, these published notes are an additional treatment of course content, and can indicate what topical areas are given special emphasis. Such notes are especially recommended for new students.

Documenting Study

The administrators of a degree program must be convinced that there are acceptable ways to document what has been learned, and what levels of subject mastery have been achieved, without taking the student's word for it. Community faculty members may be asked to provide written or oral examinations, but it does not hurt to make their jobs easier.

It is highly recommended that each study project be evaluated using a number of means (objective tests, essay exams, oral exams) and documented using a variety of methods (student narrative, faculty narrative, test results, final product, grade equivalent, etc.).

Self-evaluation, not unlike personal logs or journals, provides an excellent primary source from which to glean what a student truly knows, how they came to know it, and what new questions arise from the acquired knowledge. Any future employer or admissions counselor unfamiliar with nontraditional or off-campus degree programs can gain a fuller appreciation of the process through such narratives.

Likewise, a narrative evaluation written by the instructor provides a description of student competencies that ordinary assessment methods are unable to detect or reflect. Nuances of learning style, ability to converse in the field of study, and scholarly integrity are examples of such insights.

Depending on the subject at hand, the final product may take the form of a research monograph, video presentation, musical manuscript, senior thesis, etc.—whatever will best provide proof and record that the student has achieved the target level of competency in that field.

Most professions (accounting, psychology, law, medicine, etc.) have licensing and/or board certification examinations that must be taken. An industry has built up around this need, providing parallel or actual past examinations to help prepare students. By agreeing to take a relevant sample examination under proctored conditions, and negotiating cutoff scores in advance, the community faculty member is relieved of having to design his or her own objective examination for just one student. This approach adds validity to the assessment process, and provides a standardized score that has some universal meaning. This is an optional approach but may be worth the effort.

Recruiting Community Faculty

Just as it is easier for a student to organize a study plan into blocks of subject areas, a competency-based study plan of this sort makes it easier for a prospective instructor to visualize what is being asked of him or her.

A typical independent study project would define for the instructor what specific topics are to be studied, what levels of mastery will be expected of the student, what textbooks or other materials will be used, and what is expected of the instructor.

Many traditional academics are unfamiliar with external degree programs. Consequently, they tend to assume that their role as instructor will require greater effort and time on their part than for the average student, who may expect their services in many roles, from academic advisor to tutor. The more an institutionalized student can do up front to define clearly the role and expected duties of the community faculty member, the more successful a student will be in enlisting instructors for independent study projects.

Instructors may sometimes be found on the staff of the institution where the student resides. They may also be found through a canvassing letter sent to the appropriate department heads at area colleges, universities, and technical schools. The same approach may be used to canvass departments within area businesses, museums, art centers, hospitals, libraries, theaters, zoos, banks, and orchestras, to name but a few. People are often flattered to be asked, providing it is clear to them exactly what they are getting into.

The more a student can operate independently, and rely on community faculty for little more than assessment purposes, the more likely a student will be successful in recruiting help, and thereby broadening the range of study options.

Revealing Your Institutionalized Status

It is generally proper and appropriate to inform potential schools and potential faculty of one's institutionalized status. (Many institutions now have mailing addresses that do not indicate they are, in fact, institutions.) Some schools or individuals may be put off by this, but then you would not want to deal with them anyway. Others may be especially motivated to help.

A recommended approach is to first make a general inquiry about the prospective school or program. With this information in hand, information intended for the general student, one may better tailor inquiries to specific departments or faculty, addressing your specific needs.

Financing the Educational Process

Unfortunately, there are virtually no generalizations to be made here, whatsoever. Each institution seems to have its own policy with regard to the way finances are handled. Some institutionalized persons earn decent wages, and have access to the funds. Others have little or no ability to pay their own way. Some institutions permit financial gifts from relatives or friends; others do not. Some schools make special concessions or have some scholarship funds available for institutionalized persons; many do not. One should contact the financial aid office of the prospective school with any such questions.

342

Again, start with a general inquiry, as would any student, then ask about the applicability of specific programs to your own situation. Often a key element is to find someone on campus, perhaps in the financial aid office or your degree program, who is willing to do the actual legwork, walking your financial aid paperwork to various administrative offices. A financial aid package is of no use to anyone if that package cannot be processed.

America used to embrace the view that funding education for prisoners paid for itself, in a significant reduction in recidivism for better-educated inmates. In 1995, the Omnibus Crime Bill deleted the one-half of one percent of Pell Grants that went to prisoners. In 1998, in the debate over the reauthorization of the Higher Education Act, the party in control of the House and Senate resoundingly defeated attempts to fund educational opportunities for prisoners. This law will not be revisited until the year 2003 or 2004. And, as the icing on this bitter cake, the only foundation that regularly provided tuition money to prisoners, Davis-Putter, made so many grants from its endowment that it ran out of money and went out of business.

Is there any hope? Minimal. Students who are incarcerated in local correctional institutions may be eligible for Pell Grants. Students in state and federal institutions are definitely not eligible for Pell Grants or federal student loans, but they may qualify for Supplemental Educational Opportunity Grants (SEOG) or College Work Study, if the school participates in these so-called "campus-based" programs. Prison education officers should have details on these matters.

In Conclusion

Institutionalized students must be highly self-directed, and honest enough with themselves to recognize if they are not. Because the student lives where he or she works, it takes extra effort to set aside daily study time, not only to put the student in the right frame of mind, but also to accommodate institution schedules. It can mean working with a minimum number of books or tapes to comply with property rules. It can mean study periods that begin at 11 P.M., when the cellhall begins to quiet down. It means long periods of delayed gratification, in an environment where pursuing education is often suspect. And it is the greatest feeling in the world when it all comes together.

"Bon jour. I am here to conduct your final exam for your correspondence course in swordsmanship."

31

Miscellaneous Schools

*There are more things in heaven and earth, Horatio,
than are dreamt of in your philosophy.*

WILLIAM SHAKESPEARE

This chapter replaces the old "Help Wanted" and "Good-bye" indexes; it lists all of the schools that, for whatever reason, are not listed in the other, previous chapters (18 through 27).

There are three main reasons why a school would be listed here rather than there:

1. They have been in earlier editions of this book, and are no longer in business (or findable by us, despite our best efforts);

2. They have been in earlier editions of this book, and, while they are still in business, they no longer offer the nontraditional program(s) earlier described;

3. They are schools which may offer (or have offered) certain degree programs nontraditionally, but about which we have not been able to learn enough information to give them a proper listing.

This represents the most complete compilation of "good-byes" ever—every school that has ever been listed in this book, going back to the first edition in 1974 and what, to the best of our knowledge, has happened to them.

The "best of our knowledge," however, isn't always that complete, and that is the reason for the third group of schools listed in this chapter: those on whom we have fragmentary information, but not enough for a full listing.

We welcome help of (at least!) two kinds:

1. Help in checking out schools: Situations regularly arise in which we'd like to learn more about a certain school. Sometimes we are hindered by distance. One can often learn more from a brief in-person inspection than by hours of research or communi-

cation (such as in the not uncommon case, when a "campus" turns out to be a mail-forwarding service). Sometimes we are hindered by John's notoriety—some schools simply won't communicate with John Bear (or anyone named Bear) at all, or won't answer questions about their programs.

We do have an informal array of pen pals in cities around the world who have been very helpful in checking out schools, either in person or by correspondence—but more are always needed. If you would be willing to do this from time to time, please drop us a card or note to let us know. If you frequently travel to a certain city and could check out schools there, let us know that too. Thank you. (John & Mariah Bear, P.O. Box 7070, Berkeley, CA 94707)

2. Help in learning about specific schools: We are regularly asked for information on certain schools, by law-enforcement officials, personnel officers, reporters, alumni, or other interested members of the public. Often we can help, but many times we cannot. If you know anything about the schools listed below, even if it is only a scrap of information or a bit of hearsay, please let us know. Thank you again. We won't use your name in any way—but if you'd prefer, anonymous letters are acceptable. (If you sent us a letter about any of these schools and see that your information was not incorporated, please don't be dismayed. In the past, updating was a much more haphazard affair. Our new(ish) database has made updating much more reliable although, of course, not perfect. We will keep striving for perfection . . . maybe in the 14th edition . . .)

Abilene Christian University Texas. At one time offered an accredited external M.S. in human relations or management.

Abingdon University Institute United Kingdom. Has not responded to several requests for information about their nontraditional programs.

Academic Credit University Started in Culver City, California by the former president of Southland University and some Ethiopian colleagues; mail is now returned as undeliverable.

Academy of Open Learning They used to offer a Bachelor of Arts in valuation sciences for appraisers, but now mail to their former address in Geneva, Illinois is not answered and there is no listed phone.

Academy of Technical Sciences See: Bedford University

Advanced School of Herbology They were in Sacramento, California, but we cannot locate them now.

Airola College See: North American Colleges of Natural Health Science.

Akademie fur Internationale Kultur This school is apparently located in Muelheim, Germany; a letter from its American agent in Hawaii says that the academy is a consortium of state colleges and universities throughout Europe, offering degrees at all levels. We have written for more information.

Ambassador College The school is still in existence in Big Sandy, Texas (it was formerly located in Pasadena, California), but no longer offers any nontraditional programs.

American College in Paris At one time offered Bachelor's degrees through summer or year-round study in Paris.

American College of Finance Formerly a California authorized school, but mail has been returned as undeliverable and there is no listed telephone in Sunnyvale, California.

American College of Nutripathy Arizona. This alternative healing school ceased operations in 1990; some of its programs (and all student records) are now maintained by North American University of Scottsdale, Arizona.

American Floating University In the 1930s they offered Bachelor and Master of World Affairs degrees to students who studied while traveling on ocean liners. Now they have sunk from view. Constantine Raises of San Francisco was in charge.

American Health Sciences Institute Texas. At one time, offered a diploma in nutritional science and, in an earlier incarnation as the Life Science Institute, awarded doctoral degrees. Now they are apparently gone.

American Institute of Hypnotherapy California. Once offered Bachelor's and Doctorates in hypnotherapy entirely through correspondence study, but a recent letter has been returned marked "forwarding order expired." Any news of their whereabouts would be welcomed.

American Institute of Natural Sciences Saskatoon, Canada. While not claiming to offer degrees, this organization does award a "Master in Mantic Arts" to anyone successfully completing two courses in such fields as crystal healing, palmistry, tea cup reading, and the like. An additional note, not explained, adds that, for "sports industry courses," students obtaining a mark of 70% or greater in the final examination will be awarded a diploma entitling them to "use the letters B.S.Y."

American Institute of Traditional Chinese Medicine This school had been a state-authorized school in San Francisco, but letters to them were returned as undeliverable, and there is no listed telephone number.

American Medical Institute See: Pacific National University

American National University They had been a state-authorized school, but mail to their La Palma, California address was returned as undeliverable and there is no listed telephone. Apparently there was no connection with a diploma mill of this name which operated from California and Arizona in the 1970s and early 1980s.

American Open University This was a well-funded effort by a consortium of traditional universities to establish a nontraditional university in Lincoln, Nebraska. Donald McNeil, a distance-learning visionary who had headed up the similar University of Mid-America, founded AOU. The project ended before any students were enrolled, although some of its programs still exist in limited scope at the New York Institute of Technology (see Chapter 18).

American Pacific University They were formerly a state-authorized school, but mail to the Costa Mesa, California address has been returned as undeliverable, and there is no listed telephone number there. Now we've heard about a school by the same name based in Honolulu, offering degrees at all levels. Stand by for more information.

American Schools California. Never responded to our requests for information about their nontraditional programs, and then one day the request came back marked "forwarding order expired."

American University of Oriental Studies Formerly a state-authorized school. Mail to their Los Angeles address returned as undeliverable, and there is no listed telephone number.

American University of the Caribbean This school, formerly based in Monserrat, in the British West Indies, appears to have vanished.

Americanos College Cyprus. Has not responded to several requests for information about their nontraditional programs.

Americas University Supposedly headquartered in the Bahamas, but they have a secretarial service "campus" in St. Petersburg, Florida. The information provided is quite short on specifics, other than the $11,000 required for a degree. They said that they "will make application to the Crown for appropriate recognition within their purview [and] we anticipate no burden in meeting the required standards." We would anticipate rather substantial burden. In mid-April 1998, the Florida State Board of Independent Colleges and Universities told us they had never heard of Americas University. In response to several questions, we received an e-mail stating that "the website is being deactivated."

Americus University of Natural Health Clearwater, Florida. We've inquired about this school's programs, but in mid 1998, a letter sent to their last known address was returned as undeliverable.

Amwealth University In the early 1990s, they were registered with the Louisiana Board of Regents (then an automatic process), but mail to the New Orleans address was returned as undeliverable, and there is no listed telephone number.

Ana G. Mendez University System Puerto Rico. Has not responded to several requests for information about their nontraditional programs.

Andrew Jackson College Originally established as American Community College, then Andrew Jackson University and Andrew Jackson University College, in Louisiana by Dr. Jean-Maximillien De La Croix de Lafayette. Subsequently used an address that was apparently Dr. De La Croix de Lafayette's home in Maryland, but now apparently no longer in business.

Andrew Jackson University College See: Andrew Jackson College

Anthony University Philadelphia. The predecessor to Susan B. Anthony University, this now-defunct school seemed an honest attempt to create a good alternative university but, according to founder Dr. Albert Schatz, it never got off the ground due to limited funding.

Appalachian State University North Carolina. This accredited school used to offer a B.A. in which over 75% of the credits could come from life-experience learning.

Appraisal College Formerly registered with the Louisiana Board of Regents, then an automatic process. Mail to their Baton Rouge address is returned as undeliverable, and there is no listed telephone number.

Arnould-Taylor Education Ltd. United Kingdom. No longer grants degrees because of changes in British higher education laws. Had offered both a Bachelor's and Master's in Physiatrics entirely through correspondence. Their material emphasized that these were professional—not academic—degrees offered to persons already qualified in the field of physical therapy.

Arthur D. Little Management Education Institute Cambridge, Massachusetts. Offered an accredited M.S. in international management education; asked to be deleted many years ago and we haven't heard from them since.

Asia International Open University Hong Kong. One of two schools (the other is the University of Macau) created when the University of East Asia came under Macau's control, and split its programs between the two new schools. We have written for more information on this school's programs.

Asian American University Formerly authorized to grant degrees by the State of California. Letters to their San Diego address have not been answered, and there is no listed telephone number.

Atlanta Law School Georgia. Unaccredited, and now apparently defunct, law school.

Atlantic Institute of Education An accredited Canadian program offering Master's degrees and Doctorates through distance learning. Closed after they lost their funding.

Atlantic University (NY) New York. As a promotional gimmick once, Atlantic Monthly magazine offered an honorary Doctorate from Atlantic University to new subscribers. A harmless gag, perhaps, but we have now seen two instances in which Atlantic University appeared on a job-application resumé.

August Vollmer University Formerly authorized by the State of California. Mail to their address in Orange, California was returned as undeliverable, and there is no listed telephone number.

Avon University Several bible school administrators have listed degrees from this school, which one said was founded in Boston in 1897, but we have had trouble finding it.

Azusa Pacific College California. At one time offered Master's degrees through evening study.

Babson College Wellesley, Massachusetts. Accredited evening M.B.A. discontinued.

Baden-Powell University of Scouting We learned from an article in a December 1996 publication of the Boy Scouts of America that the Scouts have awarded a

Bachelor's, a Master's, and a Doctorate to scout leaders who attend a one- to three-day training session. The degrees are in the name of Baden-Powell University, named after the founder of the Boy Scouts, Lord Baden-Powell, and alternately referred to as the University of Scouting. Obviously the Scouts are not running a diploma mill, but it could be considered unfortunate that they have chosen academic titles to award to their leaders. When this information was posted on an Internet news group, for instance, there were responses of the following sort: "I know one person with a 'Ph.D' from the Baden-Powell University who always insists that others call him 'Dr.,'" and constantly brags about his 'academic' achievement."

Bay Area Open College California. At one time offered undergraduate degrees through a range of nontraditional methods. Affiliated with the traditional Wright Institute.

Beacon College Established in Boston and later moved to Washington, D.C., Beacon had probably the most flexible, most nontraditional Master's degree ever to achieve traditional accreditation, which was granted in 1981. Accreditation was subsequently lost due to licensing difficulties, and the school went out of business. Former name: Campus-Free College.

Bedford University Operated briefly in Arizona, offering degrees at a time when that state had no laws regulating schools. Closed in 1983. Had offered degrees in conjunction with the Academy of Technical Sciences of Beirut, Lebanon. According to the *Arizona Republic* newspaper, clients of the Educom Counseling Service in California were referred to Bedford as "the school most suited" to their needs. Educom was run by Thomas Lavin, formerly vice president of Kensington University, later Bedford's founder, later still an officer of Clayton University, and his daughter.

Bell Isles College See: College of the Palm Beaches

Ben Franklin Academy and Institute for Advanced Studies Washington, D. C. They offered Bachelor's, Master's, and Doctorates through correspondence study. "Deserving Americans" could request honorary Doctorates, which required a donation. They claimed to be "not just another degree mill, but a fully accredited degree-granting institution." The accreditation was from the American Association of Accredited Colleges and Universities which we could never locate. The former address (P.O. Box 1776) and former phone number (USA-1776) were the best part; at least it shows they had influence somewhere in Washington.

Ben Gurion University of the Negev, Israel. We have read that they may offer some degrees by modem and are trying to get more information.

Bennington College Vermont. A reader informed us they offer an MFA through distance learning, and we have written for more information.

Bentley Institute New Iberiia, Louisiana. At one time, registered with the Louisiana Board of Regents, but apparently never accepted students, and no longer exists.

Berea School of Theology Letters to their address in Linton, Indiana returned as undeliverable.

Berean Christian College A correspondent writes that he sent money to this school at an address in Long Beach, California, but soon after his mail was returned and the phone was disconnected.

Berkeley International University In 1993, advertisements in the *Economist* magazine described a distance-learning M.B.A., but a visit to this school's San Francisco office yielded only the information that their catalog was not yet ready, and some biographical information on members of "The Berkeley Group," many with degrees listed from various Russian universities. Less than a year later, the phones had been disconnected and they were gone.

Beta International University Apparently now out of business (letters to their Chicago address have been returned to sender), Beta was an evangelical Christian school that offered nonreligious degrees of all kinds, including law, by correspondence. Claimed accreditation from "Af Sep," an organization with which we are not familiar. No names were given in their newsprint catalog other than a "Dr. Ellis."

Beverly Law School California. Alternative law school, no longer around.

Biscayne College See: Saint Thomas University

Blake College A reader asked for information on this school, which he said operated in both Mexico and Eugene, Oregon, but have not been able to learn anything.

Board of Governors B.A. Degree Program Springfield, Illinois. This consortium plan offered nonresident B.A.s through a number of Illinois schools; these schools are now offering the plans individually and the consortium apparently no longer exists.

Body Mind College Several letters to the Madisonville, Louisiana address have been returned as undeliverable.

Borinquen University Medical School Mail to their last known address was returned as undeliverable; cannot locate.

Boulder Graduate School This unaccredited school in Boulder, Colorado offered Master's degrees in psychology and counseling and in health and wellness, emphasizing a balance between academic training and experiential learning. Formerly the Colorado Institute of Transpersonal Psychology. Now out of business.

Broadmore University College of Pharmacy Established by some pharmacists, apparently run from Canada, but using an address in Belize, Central America. Most U.S. pharmacy schools have switched from a 5-year Bachelor's to a 6-year Doctor of Pharmacy. This program seems designed for holders of a B.S. in pharmacy who wish the higher degree, earned by home study. The program requires quite a fair amount of continuing education approved by the ACPE which is the accrediting body most state boards of pharmacy recognize. When we attempted to call the only numbers we could find (in an ad in the online edition of *U.S. Pharmacist*), we got an individual's pager service.

California Acupuncture College Letters to their address in Los Angeles were returned as undeliverable. They had campuses in Santa Barbara and San Diego offering a three-year program preparing students to become practitioners of acupuncture and Oriental medicine. Courses were offered in Western sciences, herbology, and homeopathy. They were approved to grant degrees by the state of California.

California American University Formerly authorized by the State of California, but mail sent to their address in Escondido is returned as undeliverable and there is no listed telephone number. Had offered an M.S. in management involving a five-week summer session and tutorials directed by senior professors, all of whom had earned traditional Doctorates.

California Christian College of Los Angeles See: California Christian University

California Christian University Established in Los Angeles (later moved to Adelanto, California) by the Reverend Bishop Doctor Walter G. Rummersfield, B.S., Ms.D., Ps.D., GS-9, D.D., Ph.D.M., Ph.D., Ph.D., D.B.A., S.T.D., J.C.D., J.S.D. Formerly called California Christian College of Los Angeles. Honorary Doctorates were awarded on payment of a donation of "$1,000 or less." Dr. Dr. Dr. Dr. Dr. Dr. Dr. Rummersfield apparently transferred control to new management in the 1980s.

California College of Commerce Letter to their Long Beach address returned marked "forwarding order expired,"

California College of Law Formerly authorized by the State of California, but letters to their Beverly Hills, California address were returned as undeliverable and there is no listed telephone number.

California Institute of Electronics and Materials Science Hemet, Ca. This unaccredited school has not responded to several requests for information about their nontraditional programs.

California Institute of the Arts Valencia, California. Accredited school no longer offers its B.F.A. with up to 75% life-experience learning credit.

California Union University Fullerton, California. All we know about this school right now is that they exist and that their website is in a language other than English. We have asked for, but not received, more information.

California University for Advanced Studies In 1989 they lost their state authorization and closed their offices in Petaluma, California. The school maintained they were harassed out of existence. The state will not comment, other than to say that the school no longer met the requirements for authorization. Many enrolled students were allowed to complete degrees, but many others neither finished nor received refunds, and have been attempting unsuccessfully to locate University owner George Ryan. The "Roberta Bear" who was listed briefly as president is not known to either of us.

California University of Business and Technology Hacienda, California. All we know about this school at the moment is that they are currently approved by the state of California. We have been trying to get more information.

California University of Liberal Physicians A medical degree from this school was claimed by at least one practitioner who claimed to cure paralyzed people by rubbing them with a salve made from freshly-minced bull testicles. His pneumonia cure involved alcohol and red forest snails. We can find no record of this university ever having existed.

Campus-Free College See: Beacon College

Capital City Religious Institute Baton Rouge, Louisiana. Has not responded to several requests for information about their nontraditional programs.

Carthage College Kenosha, Wisconsin. Accredited school no longer offers its Bachelor's with over 75% life-experience learning credit.

Cayman Islands Law School A correspondent asks about this school, which apparently awards law degrees through the University of Liverpool. We are investigating.

Center Graduate College This state-approved school's sole offering was a Master of Arts in education, with a specialization in elementary mathematics. In early 1998, there was no listing for them at their last known location, in Saratoga, California.

Central California College of Law Fresno, California. Apparently this school once offered nontraditional law programs, but a recent letter was returned marked "forwarding order expired."

Central School of Religion This school, operating in England, the U.S., and Australia, was identified as a degree mill by *Education & Training Magazine*. The school's dean, Mark Gretason, has written to express his unhappiness with this. However, we've also heard from the State of Indiana's Commission on Proprietary Education about their questions regarding the school (which has claimed a presence in Indiana). We remain curious about where, exactly, the school gets its degree-granting authority from, and welcome any information from readers that might help to clear this up.

Centro de Estudios Universitarios Xochicalco Cuernavaca, Mexico. There were actually two medical schools by this name: the original, which had recognized programs offered in conjunction with a school in Philadelphia, and the second, apparently an identical program started by a disgruntled faculty member of the first. Neither school is now in business.

Centro Superior De Estudios Empresariales Madrid, Spain. This school at one time offered some nontraditional programs, but a letter sent to their last known address was returned to us, and they are not listed in the *International Handbook of Universities*.

Charles Dederich School of Law This unaccredited law school was operated by the Synanon Foundation. During the short time of their existence in Badger, California, they achieved an impressive success rate in bar exam passes, including 8 out of 9 one year.

Chase University Dr. Elmer P. Chase III sincerely attempted to start a university in various locations, most recently Kenner, Louisiana, but none of them got off the ground, and the effort has apparently been abandoned.

Chicago Conservatory College Offered accredited Bachelor's and Master's of music through evening study.

Chirichua College We heard of this school and asked for a catalog; they wrote back stating they had no printed brochures. The only contact for the school appears to be a P.O. Box. in Magdalena, New Mexico.

Christian Congregation, Inc. They used to issue honorary Doctorates in divinity, in return for a donation. Donors were encouraged to be as generous as circumstances and conscience permitted. Mail to the last address we had, in Monroe, North Carolina, has been returned as undeliverable.

CIFAS School of Medicine Santo Domingo, Dominican Republic. This large Caribbean medical school, which primarily served Americans, was found to be offering a legitimate education through the front door and selling M.D. degrees for up to $27,000 out the back door. Several administrators went to prison for so doing.

Clarksville School of Theology This Clarksville, Tennessee school offered Bachelor's, Master's, and Doctorates in theology under the guidance of Dr. W. Roy Stewart, a popular evangelist. As of 1988, there is no listed telephone number for the school.

Clayton Graduate School See: Clayton University

Clayton Institute of Technology See: Clayton University

Clayton Technical University See: Clayton University

Clayton University The phone is now answered "Clayton University Transcript Service," and the message says that the school is no longer accepting students. However, in 1997 and 1998, readers have reported that Clayton is still operating in Europe, Asia and elsewhere. For many years, they operated as a nonresident institution based in Clayton, Missouri, where they once achieved accreditation candidacy and qualified to receive veterans benefits. Original name: Open University, and later American International Open University. American Coastline University has begun offering its degrees to students "left in the lurch" by Clayton's disappearance. For a few hundred dollars, these people can get either an ACU degree or one from the specially-created-for-this-occasion Clayton Graduate School, with a convenience address in Mobile, Alabama. According to Dr. Ray Chasse, who is orchestrating the "new" Clayton, all board members earned their Ph.D.'s at Clayton (Missouri) and are part of a class action suit filed but not active because they cannot find founder Eugene Stone.

Clinical Hypnosis Center Florida. Apparently once offered an alternative degree in hypnotherapy. Probably the same as the Gracie Institute of Hypnosis.

Clinical Psychotherapy Institute At one time, authorized by the state of California. Letters to their address in San Rafael, California are returned as undeliverable and there is no listed telephone number.

Colby-Sawyer College New London, New Hampshire. No longer offers its accredited evening-study B.S. for women.

Colegio Jacinto Trevino Mercedes, Texas. Offered a bilingual B.A. in interdisciplinary studies to Chicano students through evening programs and community service. Letters returned as undeliverable.

Colgate University See: Columbus University

College for Human Services New York. A one-time unaccredited human services Master's program, primarily for minority students.

College For Lifelong Learning One of four units comprising the University System of New Hampshire, the College offers a non-traditional approach. We have written for more information.

College of Adaptive Education Sciences Inc. At one time registered with the Louisiana Board of Regents. Letters to their address in Baton Rouge were returned as undeliverable, and there is no listed telephone number. A reader informed us of the above address in Hawaii, and that the school may be moving to Pompano, FL.

College of Clinical Hypnosis This Honolulu school used to offer a degree in clinical hypnosis through a $350 correspondence course. The founder and president "earned" his degree from Thomas A. Edison College, a notorious degree mill. In 1988, the phone was disconnected, and there has been no new listing.

College of Oriental Studies This Los Angeles school used to offer Bachelor's, Master's, and Doctorates in philosophy and religion, but they appear to have moved on.

College of Professional Studies This San Francisco, California school took on the international business programs that European University of America had run, but is apparently no longer operating. At least, mail has been returned and there is no listed number in San Francisco.

College of Racine Wisconsin. At one time offered a university without walls program.

College of the Palm Beaches West Palm Beach, Florida. Offered B.A. and M.B.A. through residential study, with a great deal of credit possible for prior experience. Unaccredited but licensed by the state. Declined to provide recent information. Formerly Bell Isles College, then University of Palm Beach.

Colorado Institute of Transpersonal Psychology See: Boulder Graduate School

Colorado Technical College Colorado Springs, Colorado. Used to offer a program through The Source, a computer correspondence system, but it was discontinued.

Columbia University New York. A reader reported Columbia offers a MA in TESOL program in Japan, and we have written for more information.

Columbia West College Los Angeles, California. All we know about this school right now is that it exists and is approved by the state of California to operate. We have asked for, but not received, more information.

Commenius International University A 1981 article in *Monato*, an Esperanto-language magazine, featured an interview with the founder of this school, apparently located in San Diego. Mail addressed to the address given was neither answered nor returned as undeliverable, and there is no listed phone. The claim in the article that the university is "officially approved" by the state of California is not correct.

Commonwealth International University See: International University at Torrey Pines

Concoria Institute La Verne, California. They offered a B.A. in business administration, and claimed an affiliation with Nova College in Canada. The director's Doctorate is from Elysion College, a now-closed California diploma mill.

Cooperating University of America Wilson, North Carolina. A retired professor at one time announced plans to establish a university by this name. The idea was to offer European students the opportunity to study in the U.S., in order "to prevent them from studying in Communist countries." We don't know if it ever happened, but it does not seem to be happening now, perhaps due to the lack of Communist countries to worry about. In October, 1993, a major Swiss newsmagazine, Beobachter, reported that a Swiss psychological school, the E.R. Schwank Institut, was offering the credentials of the C.U.A. of North Carolina.

Creative Development Institute Manila, Philippines. An American reader reports that he was awarded a Ph.D. by this Filipino school, based entirely on his career experience and writings, without having to go to the Philippines. He says many other such degrees have been awarded but we have not been able to locate the school.

Crestmont College At one time registered with the Louisiana Board of Regents, but letters to their address in Baton Rouge have been returned as undeliverable, and there is no listed telephone.

Crown Institute, Inc. New York. An ad in the Economist stated that this institute offers an M.A. in Astrology-Alternative Medicine. We have written for more information.

Cyberam University Also known as Universidad Medico Naturalista Hispano-America. Had offered degrees of all kinds, from psychology to music to astrology, for fees of $150 to $300. Apparently no longer in business.

DeHostos School of Medicine. Puerto Rico. Questionable medical school. Letters returned as undeliverable.

Duarte Costa University Missouri. Questionable school operated by the Servants of the Good Shepherd. Would not give school's address or phone number when their Altoona, PA headquarters was queried.

Dundee Institute of Technology See: Hong Kong Tak Ming College

Earls Croft University A reader asks about this school, located at Redgrove House, 393 Lordship Lane, Dulwie, London, England. According to the university's administrative officer, Dr. R. D. Pendleton, the "university" is registered in Ireland and the school is accredited by the

Life Experience Accreditation Foundation, which we've never heard of. We don't know anything more, except that it's not recognized, and that it's illegal for unrecognized schools to call themselves "university" in England.

East Coast University They offered Master's and Doctorates in many subjects, with literature identical to that of the National Graduate School, National College (see Diploma Mill chapter), Roger Williams College, and National University. Their address was a residential hotel in St. Louis. When John asked for them there, the man at the desk acknowledged they got their mail there, but would say no more. They have used addresses in Mobile, Alabama; Tampa, Brooksville, and Dade City, Florida (also called Roger Williams College there), and Sweet Springs, Missouri. Recent mail to their various addresses has been returned as undeliverable. They claimed accreditation from the International Accrediting Commission for Schools, Colleges, and Theological Seminaries, an unrecognized agency that was enjoined from operating by the state of Missouri.

Ecumenical Institute of Seminary Studies Norwalk, California. This organization once sent John an honorary doctorate, and that's about all we know about them.

Eire International University On the literature of a new international accrediting association, Denis Muhilly, who has been involved with a number of non-wonderful (in our opinion) institutions, is listed as the President of Eire International University, allegedly located in Hawaii. There is no listed telephone number in the state of Hawaii. Dr. Muhilly has written us letters that we regard as extremely insulting.

Emmanuel College Oxford Oxford, England. The claim is made that degrees will be awarded solely on completion of a Master's thesis (about 100 pages) or Doctoral dissertation (about 400 pages) and payment of about $1,800. They have not responded to our inquiries, and we are concerned about the lack of telephone, the absence of names on any of the literature we have seen, and the spelling, several times, of "Ph.D." as P.hD." Somewhat reassuring is their policy of not asking for any money until a proposal has been approved and a faculty advisor assigned, as well as the note, typed onto their flyer, that they are not part of the University of Oxford, and have no Royal Charter.

Escuela de Medicina Benito Juarez–Abraham Lincoln See: Escuela de Medicina Dr. Evaristo Cruz Escobedo

Escuela de Medicina de Saltillo Apparently defunct Mexican medical school.

Escuela de Medicina Dr. Evaristo Cruz Escobedo Saltillo, Mexico. Also known as Universidad Inter-americana and Escuela de Medicina Benito Juarez–Abraham

Lincoln, they were one of the more controversial Mexican medical schools, and, as such, received a lot of bad press. Now, they are gone.

Essenes Research Foundation San Diego, California. They have awarded Ph.D.s through the Graduate School Consortium for the Religious Arts and Sciences. We have never been able to find an address or phone number for them.

Eubanks Conservatory of Music and Arts Los Angeles, California. This state-approved school offered Bachelor's and Master's programs in performance (classical or jazz) theory and composition, accompaniment, church music, and music history. In early 1998, they informed us that they were no longer granting degrees.

Eula Wesley University Arizona, Louisiana. Unaccredited school was originally established in Arizona in founder Samuel Wesley's home, later moved to Louisiana. Wesley told an Arizona Republic reporter that his own Doctorate has been earned from Eula Wesley, "After his thesis ... was reviewed by members of the ... board of directors," whom he identified as two local educators. Both denied ever being on the board, or conferring the degree. "They're lying," Wesley told the reporter. Then, according to the article, "Wesley later admitted ... his degree was an honorary one, and had been awarded by ... James Jenkins, an unemployed janitor, and Eula Wesley, Wesley's mother."

Eureka Foundation In 1996, a correspondent reported that "an open university known as the Eureka Foundation has commenced advertising in Australia." We have not been able to learn more about them.

European University of America They had offered a 10- to 14-month Master's program in San Francisco, California based around a major independent study project centering on international business, but that program is no longer offered, and none of their other offerings are nontraditional.

Extended Learning Program Ohio. A pilot program for external degrees that existed in the 1980s.

Faculté libre de médecine Lille, France. Offered the first two years of medical school through the Catholic University of Lille, after which the student transferred to a school in his or her own country.

Flaming Rainbow University Stilwell, Oklahoma. Flaming Rainbow University, an accredited Oklahoma university, officially closed its doors on February 18, 1992, thereby removing one of the more delightful university names from the arena.

Florida Institute of Remote Sensing Offered correspondence programs and, apparently, a degree in this field, involving interpretation of aerial photos, and other technology. No longer in existence in Marianna, Florida as best we can determine.

Florida State Christian University This school presented an associate with a rather impressive-looking blank diploma as a gift—assumedly so the recipient could fill in the blanks with the title and field of his choice. And that's all we know about them right now.

Franconia College New Hampshire. At one time offered many experimental and innovative programs.

Frank Ross Stewart University System This Centre, Alabama university has offered some courses from time to time, all taught by Mrs. Stewart. Honorary Doctorates have been offered to people who inquired about courses. Mrs. Stewart writes that "we do not find it attractive nor necessary" to be in this book. Well la-de-da.

Franklin and Marshall College Lancaster, Pennsylvania. This accredited school at one time offered an M.S. in physics entirely through evening study.

Free University John once saw a diploma—a huge, spectacular diploma—on a wall. It awarded the "Academic degree of Bachelor of Dentistry" of the Free University for the recipient's exploits on a geographical expedition. We have never been able to locate the university, which was part of the International Federation of Scientific Research Societies. Possibly the same Free U. identified as a diploma mill by E&T magazine.

Freedom College Colorado Springs, Colorado and Santa Ana, California. Established in 1957 by Robert LeFevre, a well-known libertarian author. Later renamed Rampart College. Destroyed by heavy rains (was this a message?) in 1965, reopened in 1968, and closed for good in 1975. Later, LeFevre became president of Southwestern University, an Arizona degree mill that was closed following an FBI investigation.

Freedom University Originally established in Florida, then moved to Albuquerque, New Mexico, this now-defunct school was, according to a correspondent, "put together by the local pagan/artist/martial arts/dancer types quite a number of years ago." No connection with the Freedom College in Colorado.

Freeman University Las Vegas, Nevada. We found them in a Las Vegas phone book, but can't find them in any school directory, nor have our letters to 4440 S. Maryland Parkway been answered.

Fremont College Officers of another university list Doctorates from this school, which they say was or is in Los Angeles, but we can find no evidence of it. According to one correspondent, it may be the same as

a defunct school founded in New Mexico some time in the 1940s, which went out of business following a dust-up with the state department of education.

Galatia University A correspondent saw an advertisement for this school, which he thinks was in Salem, Oregon, and wrote for a catalog. He received a postcard saying they were temporarily out, and would send one soon. Nothing more was heard, and he has lost the address.

Girne American University The former University College of Northern Cyprus is now affiliated with the accredited Southeastern University in Washington, D.C., and indeed advertises itself as the "Girne Campus of Southeastern University," according to a reader in the area. Any further information would be greatly appreciated.

Global Extension University Mulkilteo, Washington. An ad in the *Economist* states GEU offers a unique modular MBA including interactive software with no entry requirements. We have written for more information.

Grace University This Nevis, West Indies medical school is apparently no longer actively recruiting American students. A letter sent to their last known address (a New York–based recruiting office) was returned in 1992, and the phone was disconnected. A reader tells us that he has evidence the school is still operating from Florida, but we have been unable to confirm this.

Gracie Institute of Hypnosis See: Clinical Hypnosis Center

Graduate School for Community Development At one time, authorized by the state of California. Letters to the address in San Diego have been returned as undeliverable, and there is no listed phone.

Graduate School of Patent Resources Washington, D.C. This unaccredited but legitimate school offered advanced study in patent-related matters for lawyers, engineers, and businesspeople, but has no active programs at this time.

Graduate School of the Suggestive Sciences El Cajon, California. They offered Master's degrees and Doctorates in what they called "Hypnoalysis," but letters have been returned as undeliverable.

Great Lakes Bible College No longer offers correspondence courses leading to a degree.

Gulf States University Established in 1977 in South Carolina as Southeastern University. Moved to Louisiana a few years later. Offered doctoral programs requiring several weeks of summer residency in New Orleans. Following financial problems, the university closed in

1987. Many students who had not finished their degrees at the time transferred to the now-accredited University of Sarasota.

Hallmark University All we know about this is that an advertisement once ran in the Los Angeles Times offering a "University for sale."

Hamburger University This is the training school for McDonald's, and they award the Doctor of Hamburgerology to graduates. Now it has been licensed to grant real Associate's degrees.

Hanoi National University Vietnam. A reader informed us they offer an M.A. in English and an M.A. in TESOL both through distance learning programs. We have written for more information.

Hawaii International University Honolulu. Apparently originated in California as American International University, then operated briefly from Hawaii, and administrator Diana Barrymore told us they would be moving to Iuka, Mississippi, but there is no listed telephone number there.

Hawaii University Hawaii. Established by William Onopolis of Ohio to award degrees to clients of his credit evaluation service, this school offered degrees at all levels, in a vast number of fields. A letter to their Hawaii address was returned in mid 1997, with the notation "no forwarding order on file."

Hawthorne University (California) California. Hawthorne opened in the fall of 1982, offering degrees at all levels in general studies, with an emphasis at the Master's level in humanistic computer studies. The school evolved from a formerly state-approved school named Paideia, now apparently alive but dormant in Berkeley. Indeed, seven of Hawthorne's 10 faculty members have their highest degree from Paideia. A letter sent to their last known address in mid 1997 was returned "addressee unknown."

Headlands University Mendocino, California. Had offered highly innovative residential and nonresidential programs which are, alas, now dormant.

Higher Education Research Institute Offered degrees at all levels in nutrition, health sciences, and other fields through home study from a "prestigious, chartered university." That school turned out to be the less-than-wonderful, unaccredited American State University, which offered one applicant a degree by return mail.

Highland University Athens, Tennessee. Once offered a 25-month Ed.D. program involving three four-week summer sessions with independent study in between. Now mail has been returned and there is no listed phone number in Athens. Originally chartered in North Carolina, moved to Sweetwater, Tennessee, then Athens.

Holistic Life University Flourished in San Francisco in the late 1970s and early '80s, but is no longer findable there. They offered coursework that they claimed could be applied to degree programs at Antioch, Redlands, and Sonoma State.

Holy Cross Junior College Merrill, Wisconsin. When the original school of this name went bankrupt, others began offering a Ph.D. program in psychology or education, from the Institute of Learning of Holy Cross Junior College. After a newspaper exposé, holders of the degree (most of them school administrators and psychologists) maintained that they had done substantial work and truly earned their degrees. Critics disagreed, and the school faded away.

Horizon University Established in Shelburne, Ontario, Canada, to offer off-campus degrees based on independent study, with credit for prior learning. Apparently a victim of a 1984 provincial law strictly regulating universities. At least, we cannot locate them now.

Horizon University (Utah) Provo, Utah. Here is a case where a large corporation takes a university name for its training programs, and awards what they call degrees on completion of certain courses. Ameritech is a very large company, and they offer what are undoubtedly useful courses in dealing with their Horizon system for library services. But the degrees are awarded on completion of one or more two-day courses. There is nothing wrong with this, other than the unfortunate nomenclature, since it offers the opportunity for people to say, "I have my degree from Horizon University," which is true but easily misinterpreted.

Houston International University Houston, Texas. They sent a letter saying "Sorry, we are no longer a university." Had specialized in social work and public administration education for Hispanics and other international students for whom English was a second language. Original name was Hispanic International University.

Howard University Washington, D.C. This accredited university no longer offers a university without walls program.

Independence University Missouri. In the mid 1950s, the National Association for Applied Arts and Sciences (an organization we'd never heard of) apparently established a credit bank similar to that of Regents. From this evolved Independence, a degree-granting entity. But it is no more.

Independent University of Australia Morwell, Victoria, Australia. Identified as a diploma mill by E&T. However, we are persuaded by material sent by a person familiar with the school that it was a sincere attempt to establish an alternative university over the constant objections of the educational establishment. It survived from its founding in 1972 until the death of founder Ivan Maddern. Name changed to Independent Universal Academy after the government forbade use of the word "university."

Indiana Northern Graduate School of Professional Management Run from a small dairy farm in Gas City, Indiana, they once offered a management degrees, primarily through independent study, with some class meetings in various northern Indiana cities. Ceased operations in 1985. Originally called Indiana Northern University, but the "university" and the Doctoral programs were dropped by agreement with the state of Indiana, which accredited the school. Run by the Most Reverend Bishop Dr. Gordon Da Costa, Ph.D., Ed.D., D.Sc., D.C., whose only degrees were from Indiana Northern, and who established several accrediting agencies which, in turn, accredited Indiana Northern.

Indiana Northern University See: Indiana Northern Graduate School of Professional Management

Inner City Institute for Performing and Visual Art Los Angeles, California. The Institute is apparently temporarily closed, but they do expect to reopen.

Institute for Information Management At one time, authorized to grant degrees by the state of California. Did not respond to three requests for information, and there is no telephone number in Sunnyvale, California.

Institute for Management Competency San Francisco, California. An unaccredited but state authorized Master's program has been discontinued.

Institute of Global Education Oregon. Offers peace- and spirituality-oriented courses broadcast by short-wave radio, but no degrees. Formerly University of the Air.

Institute of Human-Potential Psychology Palo Alto, California. Offered an external Ph.D. program for a while. Name then changed to Psychological Studies Institute but that, too, seems to have faded away.

Institute of Nutritional Science California. According to a correspondent, this school offered Master's degrees and Doctorates in nutrition through nontraditional programs, but a letter to their last known address came back stamped "attempted, not known."

Institute of Open Education Massachusetts. Once offered a fully accredited M.Ed. through two summer sessions and independent study for working teachers.

Institute of Paranormal Science Fremont, California. Announced the intention of offering a degree program in the early 1980s, but there is no evidence of them now.

Institute of Psychorientology A correspondent writes to ask about this school, which she believes is located somewhere in Texas. He says she's met two people recently who claimed degrees from this institution, which we've never heard of.

Institute of Science and Mathematics Louisiana. Has not responded to several requests for information about their nontraditional programs.

Instituto de Estudios Iberamericanos Saltillo, Mexico. Offered Bachelor's, Master's, and Doctorates, mostly to Americans, with a five-week summer session in Mexico plus independent study. No longer in operation.

International Academy of Philosophy Liechtenstein. Has not responded to several requests for information about their nontraditional programs.

International College Los Angeles, California. Alas, this splendid idea did not survive. They offered Bachelor's, Master's, and Doctorates through private study with tutors worldwide. Apparently many of the well-known tutors (Lawrence Durrell, Yehudi Menuhin, Ravi Shankar, Judy Chicago, etc.) had very few (or no) students. Many of the students transferred to William Lyon University.

International College Hollywood. All we know about this school right now is that it is approved to operate by the state of California. We have written for more information.

International College of Arts and Sciences Athens, Greece. Has not responded to several requests for information about their nontraditional programs.

International College of Natural Health Sciences United Kingdom. A recent letter to this organization, whose legality we'd never been entirely sure of, was returned marked "addressee has gone away."

International Commercial Management Institute A correspondent forwarded a transcript suggesting that this British school offered nonresident business degrees, but a letter to their address in Jersey was returned marked "gone away."

International Free Protestant Episcopal University See: Saint Andrew's Collegiate Seminary

International Graduate School Established in St. Louis in 1980 as the doctoral-level affiliate of the accredited World University (Puerto Rico), offering the Doctorate in business or education. They received candidacy for accreditation with the North Central Association in the remarkably short time of one year. However, the candidacy was withdrawn in late 1987, and in 1988 the school told the state of Missouri that it would be closing down.

International Graduate University They offered Ph.D. degrees in clinical psychology and behavioral science, through an affiliation first with American College of Switzerland and later with Florida Institute of technology, but no longer.

International Institutes of Science and Technology At one time registered with the Louisiana Board of Regents, but letters to them are returned as undeliverable, and there is no listed telephone number in Monroe, Louisiana.

International Japan University At one time, authorized by the state of California, but letters are undeliverable, and there is no listed telephone number in Orange, California.

International Open University Baton Rouge, Louisiana. Has not responded to several requests for information about their nontraditional programs. The "campus" is a mailbox service called The Mailbox Incorporated.

International School of Business and Legal Studies Mail to their London, England address returned as unforwardable. This unaccredited school had awarded degrees entirely on the basis of an applicant's credentials, under somewhat unusual circumstances. They'd solicited agents in other countries, and offered to award degrees on the basis of agents' recommendations. They required that these agents have Doctorates, which they offered to provide for £450, £175 more for wig and gown.

International Studies in Humanistic Psychology In the 1970s they offered a nonresident Ph.D. in their field, from Cotati, California.

International University at Torrey Pines San Diego, California. All we know about this school right now is that it exists, and is approved to operate by the state of California. We have written for more information. There is apparently some association with something called the Commonwealth International University.

International University (California) Pasadena, California. A now-dormant unaccredited school that may or may not have had some ties to Southland University and/or its founder, James (Thomas) Kirk.

International University (Greece) Athens. This apparently unaccredited school (they claimed to be "fully recognized" by the government of Greece; the Greek embassy disagreed) has ceased operations.

International University (New York) Letters are returned as undeliverable, and there is no listed telephone number in New York City. This unaccredited school, formerly incorporated on the West Indies island of St. Kitts, had offered Doctorates in psychoanalysis and psychotherapy. It was apparently a legitimate and useful program, and the faculty had impressive credentials, but the New York connection and the difficulty of getting a catalog (they did not respond to five requests) were a bit odd.

International University "Nicholas Doubrowa" All we know about this school is that it is located in Santiago, Chile, and that it is not listed in the *International Handbook of Universities*. Any information would be appreciated.

International University of America Had offered degrees at all levels in business administration, "designed for managers and executives who seek exposure to state-of-the-art international business theories and practice." Offered programs in Hong Kong and Paris as well. No longer at the San Francisco address or telephone in 1998.

International University of Applied Arts & Sciences At one time registered with the Board of Regents of Louisiana, but letters are returned as undeliverable, and there is no listed telephone in New Orleans.

Internet University Another school from the very busy Ray Chasse of American Coastline University (see their listing in chapter 19). According to him, almost anybody can have free space on the site to promote any educational activity that Chasse views as legitimate.

Iowa Commonwealth College The Iowa State Coordinating Committee for Continuing Education at one time hoped to develop an external degree program by this name.

Irvine College of Business This unaccredited school never responded to requests for information about their nontraditional programs, and in early 1998 a letter sent to their last known address—not surprisingly, in Irvine, California—was returned as undeliverable.

James Tyler Kent College of Homeopathic Medicine Offered a five-year program in homeopathic medicine, from Phoenix, Arizona, but mail was returned and there is no listed phone in Phoenix.

Jamilian University Full-page advertisements in *Omni* magazine (and that ain't cheap) in 1987 and 1988 heralded the arrival of Jamilian University of Reno, Nevada, in which a "much-talked-about but little known group of mystics is offering to share" the "age old secrets for prolonging life and expanding intelligence." We chose not to invest $25 in the admissions package and they chose not to send us a catalog, so you will have to learn the secrets for yourself.

Jean Ray University A reader inquired about this school, allegedly in Namus, Belgium, from which a prominent person in his community had claimed a Doctorate, but we can find out nothing about it.

Jefferson College of Legal Studies At one time registered with the Board of Regents of Louisiana, but letters to their address are returned as undeliverable, and there is no listed telephone in Gretna, Louisiana.

John Marshall Law School Georgia. Unaccredited, and now defunct, law school.

John Rennie University At one time, authorized by the state of California, but letters are returned as undeliverable, and there is no listed telephone in Irvine, California.

Juarez-Lincoln Bilingual University Austin, Texas. Letters returned as undeliverable.

Justice University Justice University was begun by a former professor from Lincoln Law School in Sacramento named S.L. Roullier and had a part time law school. A letter sent to their last known address in Roseville, California was returned in mid 1998.

Kairos College New Mexico. Never responded to several requests for information about their nontraditional programs; the latest letter to their last-known address was returned "attempted, not known."

Keichu Technological Institute Registered with the Louisiana Board of Regents in 1988, but mail to the registered address is returned as undeliverable, and there is no listed phone. President Karl Marx was affiliated with Andrew Jackson University, formerly of Baton Rouge.

Keimyung Baylo University Anaheim, California. Formerly South Baylo University. Nontraditional programs in Oriental medicine and acupuncture. In mid 1997, a letter sent to the last known address was returned as undeliverable.

Keltic University A reader in England inquires about Keltic University, but letters to 3 Vicarage Close, Kirby Muxloe, Leicestershire have not been answered. There is certainly no recognized school by this name in England.

Kensington College Santa Ana, California. All we know about this school right now is that it exists and is approved by the state of California to operate, and is listed on a database of Orange County vocational facilities. We are trying to get more information.

Kripalu Institute Summitt Station, Pennsylvania. They offered a Master's in humanistic studies. There was a connection with an International University in Kayavorahan, India, but the phone is disconnected and mail is returned as undeliverable.

Krisspy University We have been sent a transcript showing a Master's degree from Krisspy University of Bayamon, Puerto Rico, but cannot locate such a school. (Is it possible they merged with Rice University?)

LA International University Louisiana. This school offered unaccredited nonresidential Doctorates in many fields, but a letter sent to their last known address (a secretarial service) was returned marked "forwarding order expired."

La Jolla University California. At one time offered unaccredited student-directed degrees at all levels; a letter to their last known address was returned as "not deliverable."

La Salle Extension University This huge correspondence university discontinued operations in 1982, not long after losing their accreditation from the National Home Study Council (now the Distance Education and Training Council). They had been owned for many years by the Macmillan Publishing Company of New York.

Lafayette University See: Notre Dame de Lafayette University

Lawyer's University In late 1987, a law officer was trying to locate a school of this name, possibly in Florida or Los Altos, California. We could find no trace.

Leadership Institute of Seattle Bellevue, Washington. Offers a B.S. completion program and a Master's in applied behavioral science, apparently through an association with the accredited Bastyr University. We have written for more information.

Leiland College of Arts and Sciences See: Eurotechnical Research University

Leland Stanford University Baton Rouge, Lousiana. Established by friends of a Louisiana state official, who hadn't believed him, when he told them how easy it was to become a legal Louisiana institution. It apparently never accepted students or awarded degrees, but the point was clearly made.

Life Christian University Gardena, California. All we know about this school right now is that it exists and is approved by the state of California to operate. We have written for more information.

Lincoln City University According to a correspondent, this school has sold degrees to students in Hong Kong. We are investigating.

Lincoln University (New Guinea) New Guinea. The degrees were based on writing up to 10 papers in a given field. Established in Arizona when that state had no school laws, it later moved to London England in 1987, where the address was a mail-forwarding service, and then to New Guinea. The university's founder seems to be a sincere scholar and, indeed, Lincoln may have achieved some level of acceptance. Claimed alumni included the head of government for the kingdom of Lesotho, and the former minister for education and culture in Ghana.

Linfield College Oregon. At one time, this accredited school offered Bachelor's programs in which up to 80% of the necessary units could come form a combination of assessment of prior learning and equivalency exams; this option apparently no longer exists.

London Institute of Technology & Research In 1995, this school at least proposed a relationship with Kensington University of California. There were, and as far as we know, still are several odd things about them, such as that London directory assistance has no listing for the school, and that their promotional materials list a Lord Bottemley as a member of the advisory board. Burke's Peerage, however, lists only a Lord Bottomly and we thought it a bit strange to misspell the name of such a prestigious associate. There is also, apparently, some association with the International University based in Missouri. But we don't know anything more at this time.

London International College United Kingdom. Had offered degrees in cooperation with the unaccredited Andrew Jackson University College of Louisiana and, later, Maryland. Apparently out of business.

Lone Mountain College California. At one time offered an external Master's in psychology. The college was absorbed into the University of San Francisco, but the external degree did not survive.

Los Angeles College of Law See: Van Norman University

Los Angeles Institute and Society for Psychoanalytical Studies California. At one time, this unaccredited organization offered graduate degrees in psychoanalytic fields to licensed mental health professionals via resident programs. A letter to their last known address, in mid 1997, was returned stamped "unable to forward."

Los Angeles Psychosocial Center A letter requesting information was returned to sender, but Los Angeles information did have a new listing for them, which yielded a recorded message asking callers to leave a name and phone number for information about psychological services. No one has responded to our messages inquiring about the school's fate.

Louisiana Central University At one time they were registered with the Louisiana Board of Regents, but letters have been returned as undeliverable, and there is no listed telephone in Metairie, Louisiana.

Louisiana Christian University Louisiana. Never responded to our requests for information about their nontraditional programs and, in mid 1997, a letter sent to their last known address was returned stamped "forwarding order expired."

Louisiana International University Inc. At one time they were registered with the Louisiana Board of Regents, but letters have been returned as undeliverable, and there is no listed telephone in New Orleans, Louisiana.

Louisiana University of Medical Sciences Baton Rouge, Louisiana. This unaccredited school never responded to requests for information about their nontraditional programs, and in early 1998 a letter sent to their last known address was returned as undeliverable.

Loyola College Maryland. Once offered a B.S. in nursing for R.N.s with only two days on campus; this program has been discontinued, and while the school exists, they offer only more traditional weekend and evening programs.

Loyola Southwestern University A caller insisted that there is a school by this name in Baton Rouge, Louisiana, but neither we nor the authorities in Louisiana have heard of it or can find it.

Lyle University Operated for a while in the mid 1980s from New Orleans and Metairie, Louisiana, offering Bachelor's, Master's, and Doctorates at $750 for a complete program. Started by a Columbia Pacific University graduate, and quite similar in approach to C.P.U. No longer registered with the Louisiana board of regents, and therefore presumably no longer in business.

Madurai-Kamaraj University India. While we've heard that this school offers a wide range of distance degrees, a letter sent to their last known address was returned as undeliverable. The Internet was not much help, so we would welcome a current address from any reader in the know.

Magna Carta University California. Alternative law school, no longer around.

Manx University In 1987, there was an announcement that a university by this name was to open on the Isle of Man in 1992. A multimillion-pound fundraising appeal was said to have begun, and anyone making a donation, however small, was to become a trustee of the university, at least for a while. The people behind the endeavor chose to remain anonymous, and we can find no evidence that the school ever opened.

Marquis Guiseppe Scicluna International University Foundation In an earlier edition, John wrote that in 1987 the Universal Intelligence Data Bank (of Independence, Missouri) had written to businessmen in Asia offering them an honorary doctorate from this institution, on receipt of a $500 payment. Baron Marcel Dingli-Attard, of the Foundation, has assured us that the offer was only made to a limited number of people, not necessarily in Asia and, in any event, is no longer being made. Our apologies for the incorrect statements made earlier.

Mashdots College This state-approved school had offered undergraduate liberal-arts programs centering on Armenian language and culture. However, a letter sent to their last-known address, in Pasadena, California, in early 1998 came back as undeliverable.

McDonough 35 Prep/Bernadean University At one time registered with the Louisiana Board of Regents, but letters have been returned as undeliverable and there is no listed telephone number in New Orleans. We don't know what the name means, but Bernadean University is described in Chapter 19.

Mellen Research University Apparently a predecessor of Mellen University, it operated from San Francisco, but never granted degrees. Mail to their address is returned as undeliverable, and there is no listed telephone. Mellen is described in Chapter 19.

Mensa University A correspondent reports that Mensa, the international organization for people with high I.Q.s, was at one time associated very briefly with a Maryland university.

Meridian University Lafayette, Louisiana. A private, non-profit religious institution affiliated with the Buddhist Theosophical Society, Meridian at one time offered degrees at all levels, based on prior coursework, credit for "documented personal achievement," examinations, and the school's own upper-division courses. They are apparently out of business, as mail has been returned and the phone has been disconnected.

Metropolitan University Operated in Glendale, California in the 1950s, apparently quite legitimately, offering degrees with substantial life-experience credit. Long gone.

Mid-Valley College of Law Van Nuys, California. Unaccredited, and now defunct, law school.

Midway Baptist College California. The San Diego–based Midway Baptist Church at one time operated an unaccredited college, but no longer does so.

Millikin University This accredited school no longer offers degrees through its Evening Division.

Miskatonic University A fake diploma, purportedly from this nonexistent school, appeared in Masskerade, a humor magazine published in 1983 by the Massey University Students' Association. Once again, though it was clearly a joke, you never know when these things will pop up. Probably the same general geneaology as Myskatonic University.

Missouri Central College Letters are returned and there is no listed telephone number in Clayton, Missouri. This unaccredited school's 10-page catalog had dedicated two pages to a misrepresentation of the Sosdian-Sharp study. No listed faculty or phone.

Mole Ltd. University Louisiana. Created as a joke, and to prove how easy it is to start a university, by entrepreneur C. Denver Mullican, this school granted exactly two degrees (Doctorates, to Mullican's two dogs—whose characters, he claims, were greatly improved by the credentials). Still, he tells us that he received numerous letters from people offering money for the degrees, including $200 from a man in Malaysia who offered to sell the degrees and cut Mullican in for $100 each. He sent the money back. Thus, if you run into anyone claiming a degree from this university, and they're not a dog, something fishy is almost certainly going on.

More University California. Once offered unaccredited degree programs. Now, the descendant of this organization offers "personal enrichment" programs in sensuality, communication, and lifestyle under its original name, Lafayette Morehouse.

Morgan State College At one time offered a nontraditional degree program for urban African Americans, focusing on "black perspective and minority group problems," but no longer does so.

Mount Saint Joseph's College Offered accredited Bachelor's degrees in which over 50% of credit could come from prior learning.

Mundelein College This independent, traditional school, in operation since 1929, had offered a Bachelor's in which up to 75% of credits could be earned through assessment. However, in 1993, their programs were absorbed by Loyola University of Chicago.

Mundi Causa Global University In 1996, we received an e-mail from Eberhard Weber, president of the Mundi Causa Society (no, we're not sure exactly who they are), proclaiming the establishment of a new campus-based university that is intended to differ from traditional universities in that "personal and principled initiative and commitment [will replace] organizational and procedural rigor." We don't have an address for where the campus was to be, but have e-mailed for an update.

Myskatonic University Chaosium Publishing, which comes out with role-playing games based on H.P. Lovecraft's Cthulu mythos stories, has offered Bachelor's, Master's, and Doctoral degrees in medieval metaphysics from Myskatonic University in Arkham, Mass. These are provided as novelties, and have never been suggested as real degrees.

National Christian University There was once one located in Richardson, Texas and another in Dallas. Then some ads appeared for the National Christian

University of Missouri, but one was to write to the dean of theology in Oklahoma City. A National Christian also appears on the Council of Europe's list of degree mills. So far, we remain confused and they remain elusive.

National College for the Natural Healing Arts Birchdale, Minnesota. Offered programs leading to Bachelor's, Master's, and Doctorates in naprapathy, reflexology, iridology, homeopathy, acupuncture, cancer research, and so forth, possibly through nonresidential study. Mail has been returned and there is no listed phone number in Birchdale.

National College of Education Offered accredited Bachelor's degrees in which up to 75% of credit could come from prior learning.

National Graduate School See: East Coast University

National Radio Institute Washington, DC. According to a caller, this school offers degrees in business management and accounting, and is accredited by DETC. We have written for more information.

National University (Missouri) See: East Coast University

New Bridge International College Los Angeles. All we know about this school right now is that it exists, and is approved to grant degrees by the state of California. We have, of course, written for more information.

New World College Louisiana. Once offered unaccredited degrees at all levels; mail to their last known address was returned marked "not for this address." As the school never had a listed phone, we couldn't call to follow up.

Nomad University Seattle, Washington. Presented public classes for groups of 500 or more in cities worldwide, but did not seek accreditation or grant degrees because "education should be for discovery, not for approval." The first three courses were $25 each, and you were not told what they will be; you simply pay and then go. It was all rather charming, but as of early 1998, they seem to have folded up their tents and moved on.

Norfolk State University Virginia. Apparently once offered an external Master's degree in communication.

North American College of Acupuncture Vancouver, British Columbia, Canada. Offered correspondence studies in Chinese medical philosophy and principles of diagnosis. Mail has been returned.

North American College of Law California. Apparently this school once offered nontraditional law programs, but that's all we know, as a letter sent to their last known address was returned as undeliverable.

North American College of Naprapathic Medicine Waldron, AR. A reader tells us of this school, apparently operating out of the founder's home while waiting for state approval. We have written for more information.

North American Colleges of Natural Health Science San Rafael, California. Offered professional career education in holistic natural health sciences. Mail has been returned; no listed telephone. Formerly called Airola College.

North Continental University They have used a P.O. box in Santa Rosa, California, and at one time they put on demonstrations of sacred dance, but they were not state-authorized and our inquiries have never been answered.

Northwest University of Metaphysics Listed as the source of a degree for a faculty member at a traditional school. We have not been able to locate it.

Notre Dame de Lafayette University Offered unaccredited degrees in divinity studies, religious education, pastoral wellness, psychotherapy, theology, counseling, and pastoral psychotherapy. In late 1994, the state of Colorado took action to close the school, although it may have been renamed and relocated to Minnesota. We are investigating this. Initially called just Lafayette University.

Occidental Institute of Chinese Studies A reader asks about this school's degrees; he believes it is located somewhere in Florida, but we haven't found them.

Ocean University At one time they were authorized to grant law and other degrees in California, but no longer. Operated from addresses in Lancaster and Santa Monica.

Oklahoma Baptist University Shawnee, Oklahoma. At one time offered a Bachelor of Arts in Christian studies through a wholly nonresident program, but that has apparently been discontinued.

Open International University In 1996, a continuing education catalog listed this school as the source of one faculty member's Doctorate. We have never seen any other evidence of this school's existence.

Open Learning Agency of Australia Melbourne, Australia. We've been told this school offers distance learning programs, and have written asking for more information.

Open University Singapore. All we know about this school is that it exists, and is apparently government-licensed. We are hoping for a reply to our inquiries, or perhaps enlightenment from one of our readers.

Open University of Complementary Medicine Sri Lanka. The main thing we know about them is that something called Wellington University of New Jersey was offering to sell their M.D. degree for $1,000. We're still waiting for a comment from Sri Lanka.

Orange University of Medical Sciences A major article in the *Los Angeles Times* in 1982 announced the highly controversial impending opening of this investor-owned for-profit medical school. We've often wondered what happened, but haven't been able to find out.

Oregon Institute of Technology Oregon. This accredited school no longer offers any sort of nontraditional program.

Oxford College of Pharmacy Del Mar, California. All we know about this school is that it apparently exists. We have written for more information.

Pacific Baptist University Norwalk, California. All we know about this school right now is that it exists, and is approved to operate in the state of California. We have written for more information on its programs.

Pacific Coast University Registered with the Louisiana Board of Regents at one point, but mail to them is returned as undeliverable, and there is no listed telephone in Baton Rouge. Mark Zeltser was the man behind it.

Pacific College of Oriental Medicine At one time they were authorized by the state of California, but letters have been returned as undeliverable and there is no listed telephone in San Diego.

Pacific Institute for Advanced Studies At one time they were authorized by the state of California, but letters have been returned as undeliverable and there is no listed telephone in Studio City.

Pacific International University At one time, they were authorized to grant degrees by the state of California. They did not respond to three requests for information about their programs. Almost certainly unrelated to the Pacific International University that operated from Hollywood, California, at least through 1964, offering correspondence and residential degrees in science and engineering.

Pacific National University Formerly located in Hollywood, California. Originally called American Medical Institute, this school trained doctors in traditional Chinese medicine, but went dormant after the founder, David Chiu, returned to mainland China. Transcripts can be obtained from University Services in Mobile, Alabama, an organization which exists primarily to provide student services for dormant or defunct institutions.

Pacific School of Nutrition They offered correspondence programs leading to certification as a nutritionist and/or herbologist, through written tutorial. Mail to their last-known address is returned as undeliverable, and there is no listed telephone in Ashland, Oregon.

Pacific States University Los Angeles, California. Offered state-approved degrees in a number of fields, but has discontinued its correspondence program.

Palo Alto School of Professional Psychology See: Western Graduate School of Psychology

Pan Pacific University Alameda, California. Plans are to begin a school by this name on a soon-to-be-defunct naval base.

Pan-African University Washington, D.C. A school created by poet and former schoolteacher Abena Walker, this unaccredited school was the center of a controversy in 1993 when the *Washington Post* ran a series of articles questioning (and, in the case of some columnists, supporting) Walker's credentials, after she came to prominence in developing the D.C. area's first Afro-centric education program for the public schools. She was criticized for holding a self-awarded Master's degree.

Patriot University Colorado. This Baptist-run school apparently offers life-experience credit to members of the ministry, and that's all we know about them right now, except that they claim accreditation from the American Accrediting Association of Theological Institutions.

Pearblossom School We know nothing about this school; a correspondent passed along their web address (www.vc.net/bbd/pps/), but either it no longer exists, or the person who passed it along had the wrong URL. Either way, we'd appreciate help if anyone knows anything.

Pennsylvania Military College Offered B.A. and M.B.A. through evening study; its programs were, according to a correspondent, absorbed by Widener University some years ago.

People's University of the Americas A correspondent has reported that such a university exists, with an address at a post office box in Solna, Sweden, from which no response has been heard. Recently, a second correspondent reports that they are operating from an address in Spain, and managed by the Christian Orthodox Church of Puerto Rico. At presstime, we're not entirely sure it's the same organization or, in fact, what the Spanish school's status is. Stand by.

Permaculture University A Texan named Inger Myhre is in the process of putting together a New Mexico–based school that awards under- and postgraduate degrees in the field of permaculture, based on the work being done by Australia's Permaculture Academy.

Phoenix Medical School Phoenix, Arizona. Incorporated and began recruiting students even though the university existed, as an article in the *Arizona Republic* noted, only "on a few pieces of paper stacked on a rented credenza under a rented scenic picture in a small office [in] Mesa." President Gloria Coates announced an opening date for the university, but apparently it never came to pass.

Phoenix University The president of a bible school lists among his credentials a Ph.D. from the Bari Research Center of Phoenix University for archeological research, bestowed by its president, His Serene Highness Prince Francisco D'Aragona. We are unfamiliar with this institution but see (we suspect) Accademia di Study Superiori Phoenix in Chapter 25, Degree Mills. Certainly not related to the accredited University of Phoenix in Arizona.

Pitzer College California. Once offered an external B.A.

Plantation University A hoax perpetrated by a prankster on an Internet news group, the claim was made that this "venerable" Kentucky institution was accredited by the Southern Commission for Schools and Colleges.

Point Park College Pittsburgh, Pennsylvania. Offered accredited Bachelor's degrees through weekend classes.

Prestige Graduate Degrees All we know is that some school or service advertised in the *Economist* under this heading, offering "Prestige Graduate Degrees by research, residential or distance learning "under the guidance of 'eminent mentors.'"

Professional School for Humanistic Studies Listed as the source of a faculty member at a traditional school's degree. We have not been able to locate the institution.

Professional School of Psychological Studies San Diego, California. At one time, authorized by the state of California. No response to three letters asking for information, and the person who answers the listed telephone says the school no longer exists, and good-bye.

Professional Studies Institute Phoenix, Arizona. Offered unaccredited Bachelor's, Master's, and Doctorates in physical and mental health fields, but can no longer be located.

Prometheus College Tacoma, Washington. Arose in the mid 1970s and rather quickly became a candidate for accreditation. Then suddenly they were gone—perhaps back to Olympus.

Protea Valley University Dr. Bernard Leeman established this school in Toowoomba, Australia in 1991, and registered it in Louisiana, with the intention of providing education for black South African exiles. He gained Archbishop Desmond Tutu's backing for the idea, but abandoned it in the planning stages when it became clear that majority rule was going to become a reality in South Africa.

Psychological Studies Institute See: Institute of Human-Potential Psychology

Quimby College Alamagordo, New Mexico. Offered a B.A. in life arts and an M.A. in spiritual studies and counseling. Locally controversial, perhaps in part because of the focus on aura balancing, and the assertion that the college had its start when the thoughts of Phineas P. Quimby, a New England watchmaker who died in 1866, were transmitted to an Alamagordo woman. No longer findable.

Radvis University A correspondent asks about this school, possibly located in Canada, and we can find no information.

Rampart College See: Freedom College

Rand Graduate Institute Santa Monica, California. At the time they asked to be left out of this book (in the mid '80s) they were offering an accredited apprenticeship-based Ph.D. in policy analysis.

Reid College of Detection of Deception Chicago, Illinois. The college began as a school held in the laboratories of John Reid, a prominent polygraph specialist, then went on to offer a state-authorized M.S. in detection of deception . While Reid's company still exists, it appears that the degree program is no longer.

Rem University A reader has inquired about nontraditional Doctorates in psychology issued by this establishment, possibly in South Euclid, Ohio, but we could find no evidence of it.

Ripon College Wisconsin. Offered accredited Bachelor's degrees in which up to 75% of credit could come from prior learning.

Roanoke College Virginia. Offered a variety of accredited Master's degrees through evening courses.

Rochdale College This legitimate, if unorthodox, institution in Toronto, Canada used to "award" honorary degrees as a fundraising tool for the college to anyone who made a modest donation. The honorary Ph.D. had a watermark; when you held the diploma up to the light, you saw "Caveat Emptor."

Rockwell University Scottsdale, Arizona. They offered degrees of all kinds by correspondence study. The only requirement was the writing of a thesis. A former president of Loyola University in Louisiana was claimed to be one of the five founders. "An education for the 1980s" was their slogan, but they didn't make it through the '80s themselves.

Roger Williams College See: East Coast University. Not to be confused with the fully accredited school by the same name in Rhode Island.

Ross University Dominica, West Indies. This medical school never responded to our requests for information and now our most recent letter, sent to their New York representative (Caribbean Admissions, Inc.) in mid 1997, has been returned as undeliverable.

Royal Orleans University At one time, they were registered with the Board of Regents of Louisiana, but mail is returned as undeliverable and there is no listed telephone number in Lake Charles, Louisiana.

Russell Sage College New York. Offered accredited Bachelor's and Master's degrees in education through evening courses.

Sacred Heart College A program offering a very short residency Bachelor's in management and criminal justice has been canceled, at least for the time being.

Saint Andrew's Collegiate Seminary In the late 1950s, Saint Andrew's was a small and apparently sincere and legitimate seminary in London, England offering Master's and Doctoral work in theology and counseling. Later, to raise funds, the seminary offered honorary Doctorates to clergy and others who made donations. This evolved into awarding nonresidential degrees for life experience in the name of the Saint Andrew's Ecumenical Church Foundation Intercollegiate. This further evolved into a worldwide enterprise, again offering degrees entirely based on resumes, called the International Free Protestant Episcopal University. None of these entities survives today.

Saint Andrew's Ecumenical Church Foundation Intercollegiate See: Saint Andrew's Collegiate Seminary

Saint Bonaventure University Degrees through evening study no longer available.

Saint Charles University DeQuincy, Louisiana. In the spring of 1998, they began advertising in Singapore. We are not familiar with them, and can find no reference to them in standard books or lists of accredited schools. We have telephoned for information, which had not been received at presstime.

Saint Cloud State University Minnesota. Offered accredited Bachelor's degrees in which virtually all credit could come from prior learning experiences.

Saint George Center for Training At one time, they were authorized to grant degrees by the state of California. There was no response to three requests for information on their programs, and there is no listed telephone number in Berkeley.

Saint Giles University College This U.K.-based school offered nonresident Bachelor's, Master's, Doctorates, and certificates in psychology, physiatrics, teacher training, and science. The Doctor of Science program consisted consisted of three lessons: (1) factors influencing children's sweet eating, (2) psychiatry and psychology, and (3) radiation and human health. Raymond Young was the moving force behind Saint Giles, Harley University, and Somerset University.

Saint John's College This London-based school, a division of City Commercial College, did not offer their own degrees, but conducted the coursework leading to a Bachelor's or an M.B.A. from an unspecified-in-their-literature nontraditional school in California. They apparently closed down in the wake of student protests.

Saint John's University A very small school established in Edgard, Louisiana by District Court Judge Thomas Malik, they used to offer nonresident degrees, but that program was discontinued. No connection with the other Saint John's University in Louisiana or the one in New York.

Saint Louis University Missouri. Offered a number of degrees through evening study.

Saint Martin's College and Seminary Wisconsin. This unaccredited school offered nonresidential graduate degrees in business, divinity, and ministry, as well as state-approved programs in alcohol and substance abuse. A letter sent in mid 1997 to their last known address was returned as undeliverable.

Saint Patrick's College, Maynooth See: National Distance Learning Centre

Saint Paul College and Seminary A reader asks about an honorary Doctorate that a co-worker claims from this institution, apparently in Rome, but we have not found it.

Saint Thomas University Miami, Florida. Had offered B.A., B.S. and Mater's degrees through evening, weekend, and summer programs in the School of Continuing and Adult Education. Formerly called Biscayne College.

Samuel Benjamin Thomas University A grand plan by King Theophilus I of the Ashanti Kingdom to establish a distance learning university in Sierra Leone apparently has not yet come to pass.

San Diego State University California. Once offered external Bachelor's and Master's degrees.

San Francisco College of Acupuncture At one time, authorized to grant degrees by the state of California, but letters are returned as undeliverable and there is no listed telephone in San Francisco.

San Francisco Theological Seminary San Anselmo, California. They have discontinued their Doctor of Science in theology once offered through summer sessions, and do not wish us to describe their nonresidential Master of Arts in values program because "we are in the process of curriculum changes and it would be difficult to express the substance and location of the programs at this time."

Santa Barbara University Goleta, California. They appeared in the 1986 directory of schools put out by the state of California, offering Master's and Doctorates in business but by 1988 there was no telephone listing. Presumably not the same as University of Santa Barbara (formerly Laurence University).

Santa Fe College of Natural Medicine Santa Fe, New Mexico. Offered nonresidential Bachelor's, Master's, and Ph.D. programs as well as residential studies. Now there is no response to letters, and the phone has been disconnected.

School of Botany A reader has inquired about an honorary degree a colleague of his was using. Possibly in Spain, but we could not locate it.

Seattle International University Letters to the school have been returned as undeliverable, and there is no listed telephone number in Seattle or Federal Way, Washington. This unaccredited school had offered the B.B.A. and M.B.A. entirely through evening and weekend study.

Sedona College/Sedona University Sedona, Arizona. According to an article in the *Arizona Republic,* an application to operate this school was made in Arizona by two men, one a former employee of Southwestern University (whose owner was imprisoned for selling degrees), the other the police chief of Sedona, whose Doctorate was from De Paul University, a degree mill whose owners were sentenced to prison in 1987. According to a spirited defense of Sedona College in the *Sedona Times* newspaper (September 19, 1984), James H. Smith of California "purchased Sedona College from its founder, Ted Dalton" (president of Newport University). We are uncertain as to whether Sedona ever accepted students, but there is no listed phone for them in Sedona now. We have been told that there were actually two schools—Sedona College and Sedona University—perhaps quite independent of each other.

Sequoia University In 1984 a Los Angeles judge issued a permanent injunction against Sequoia University, which had operated from California and Oklahoma, and its president to cease operation until the school could comply with state education laws. The university had offered degrees in osteopathic medicine, religious studies, hydrotherapy, and physical sciences.

Shelton College This college, founded in Cape May, New Jersey, by fundamentalist radio preacher Carl McIntire, challenged New Jersey's school licensing law, claiming that it should be exempt from licensing under freedom of religion and speech precedents. New Jersey maintained that any exceptions to its right to license would diminish the value and integrity of degrees awarded in the state. We are researching.

Sierra University Orange, California. This school closed in 1994; prior to that, they had offered nonresident state-approved degrees at all levels in business, religion, psychology, health administration, public administration, communications, education, and human behavior.

Sonoma Institute Bodega, California. Offered training for an M.A. in humanistic and transpersonal psychology through a cooperative relationship with the University of Redlands. Apparently no longer in business.

South Atlantic University Established in 1998 in Karachi, Pakistan, to offer nontraditional degrees in business, computer science, engineering, and other fields (but presumably not geography). The telephone/fax number in Karachi is (92-21) 699-4200

Southeastern College of the Assemblies of God Florida. This school at one time offered totally nonresident B.A.'s in religious fields through correspondence courses in combination with a number of other alternative methods, such as supervised fieldwork and independent study. In mid 1996, however, following an investigation by the N.C.A.A. into whether coaches at the school had obtained bogus eligibility for student athletes through these programs, the distance education program was shut down.

Southeastern Graduate School South Carolina. At one time advertised that Doctorates were available in 100 fields, with a one-month residency. Literature made troublesome statements about accreditation eligibility.

Southeastern Institute of Technology Alabama. At one time offered state-approved, though unaccredited, degrees in engineering and management. In mid 1997, a letter sent to their last known address was returned as undeliverable.

Southeastern University See: Gulf States University

Southern California Christian University No longer in business, at least at the address we had for them in Los Angeles.

Southern Eastern University The proprietor, Mr. Grimaldi, assures us that the British newspaper article reporting that he offered to sell thousands of diplomas to an undercover reporter, was in error. He also informs us that the university's plan to move to spacious quarters in London were changed following an IRA bomb attack. When John visited the campus in late 1997, he found the address to be a small unmarked home near the London docks.

Southern International University New Orleans. A letter sent to their last known address was returned as undeliverable. This unaccredited school had offered degrees at all levels in psychology, human behavior, fine arts, and business through wholly nonresident programs. In other matters concerning other schools we've had questions about, founder Dr. Denis Muhilly has been less than pleasant.

Southern Pacific University They began advertising in Asia for degree programs, despite lacking any licensing or approval in their own state of New Mexico. When we questioned their operation, the response was quite hostile. However subsequently, in the spring of 1998, proprietor Anil Verna decided we were not so dreadful, and politely communicated the fact that he was now seeking New Mexico licensing before marching onward.

Southern States University Huntington, California. All we know about this school right now is that it exists, and is approved by the state of California. We have written for more information on their degree programs.

Southland University Southland University operated from Pasadena, California and later from Arizona in the 1980s. Following a visit from the FBI's "DipScam" diploma mill team, which carried off four truckloads of records, Southland closed. No indictments were handed down. La Salle University in St. Louis (later to move to Louisiana) subsequently opened under the same management with similar programs, including some law materials bearing the name Southland. This time the FBI raid bore fruit, and the founder of Southland and La Salle was indicted on 18 counts of mail fraud and related offenses, and sent to federal prison in 1997. La Salle continues under new, legitimate ownership.

Southwest Acupuncture College New Mexico. This unaccredited school offered a three-year program leading to an M.S. in acupuncture or Oriental medicine. In mid 1997, however, a letter to sent to their last known (to us) address was returned as undeliverable.

Southwestern University Law School California. Alternative law school, no longer around.

Spectrum Virtual University In 1995, word on the Internet was of this organization, offering free or virtually free classes in fields ranging from spirituality to Internet issues to creative writing. However, it appears to no longer exist.

State University of Nebraska Used to offer a largely correspondence degree.

Stewart University System See: Frank Ross Stewart University System

Stratton College Navan, Ireland. An external degree program was announced by the college. Then the college was taken over by the Institute of Maintenance Engineering and the degree program was canceled.

Sun Moon University Choongnam, Korea. We've heard from correspondents that this school, apparently associated with the Rev. Moon's Unification Church, offers some nontraditional programs; we have written for more information.

Sunshine University Probably (but we've never been sure) a gag or promotional diploma. The Ph.D. they sent John is quite attractive and appears to be signed by the mayors of three Florida cities and the chairman of the Pinellas County Commission.

Susan B. Anthony University Pennsylvania. Established in the mid 1970s by Dr. Albert Schatz, discoverer of the antibiotic streptomycin, this school offered degrees at all levels in education, environmental studies, naturopathy, and peace and freedom studies. It is no longer operational.

Synthesis Graduate School for the Study of Man San Francisco, California. An ambitious-seeming endeavor that offered the M.A. and Ph.D. in psychology and medical synthesis. Buckminster Fuller and a Nobel laureate in medicine were on the board of advisors. Most faculty were disciples of Roberto Assagioli. But now the school is gone, as best we can determine.

Taiken University Garden Grove, California. All we know about this school right now is that it exists and is approved by the state of California to operate. We have written for more information.

Taiken Wilmington University This school was advertised in USA Today in mid 1997; when John called to request literature, the woman answering the phone said that she didn't know where the university was located, although one correpsondent tells us it's in Taiwan. We never did get literature.

Teachers University A reader asks about this school, which she believes used to exist in Miami, but we can find no evidence of it.

Temple University Philadelphia. Offered accredited degrees at all levels through evening study.

Tennessee Southern University and School of Religion Established in late 1981 for the purpose, according to founder Dr. O. Charles Nix, of "developing students with a special sense of social responsibility, who can organize and apply knowledge for human betterment." Mail to several Tennessee addresses was returned as undeliverable.

Texas Graduate School of International Management Corpus Christi, Texas. This unaccredited school never responded to requests for information about their nontraditional programs, and in early 1998 a letter sent to their last known address was returned as undeliverable.

Theseus International Management Institute France. All we know is that this school exists and offers an MBA. We have written for more information.

Transworld University Santa Clara, California. All we know about this school right now is that it exists and is approved by the state of California to operate. We have written for more information.

Tri-State College and University Several readers have asked about this institution, but letters to Dr. J. Roy Stewart at the Oxon Hill, Maryland address provided were never answered, and there was no listed telephone.

Tyler Kent School of Medicine Arizona. Health-related school, now apparently defunct.

U.S. College of Music Boston, Massachusetts. In the past, the U.S. College of Music has offered degrees in conjunction with Greenwich University. When that affiliation ended, the school briefly offered "decrees" in music and business. Currently, they offer a wide selection of diplomas in music-related fields, but neither degrees nor decrees..

Unification Theological Seminary Offers accredited Master's degrees through residential programs in Barrytown, New York. We had reported on some long-past accreditation problems, but never noted when those problems were favorably resolved. For this oversight, we apologize.

Union College South Africa. Listed in another directory of alternative education as having a correspondence degree program, but inquiries were not answered.

Union University Los Angeles. Unaccredited and somewhat questionable school offered Master's degrees and Doctorates though nonresidential study.

United State Open University Hawaii. This school was once located in Louisiana, then relocated to Hawaii. Now it appears to be defunct.

Universidad Boricua District of Columbia. A university without walls program developed primarily for Puerto Ricans, it no longer appears to exist.

Universidad Interamericana See: Escuela de Medicina Dr. Evaristo Cruz Escobedo

Universidad Medico-Naturalista Hispano-America See: Cyberam University

Universidad Nordestana Dominican Republic. This foreign medical school is apparently no longer accepting American students.

University Associates Graduate School San Diego, California. At one time authorized in California, the school closed in 1987.

University College Academy Christians International In 1987, John was sent a document submitted by a clergyman in Puerto Rico in support of a degree claimed from this entity. The document, purporting to be a certification by the state of New York that "University College" is legitimate and accredited, is clearly a fake. It has a number of misspellings, and is simply not true.

University College of Northern Cyprus See: Girne American University

University de la Romande Pay attention, this is complex. UDLR was established in Sudbury, England, by Neil Gibson & Company. The spokesman for Neil Gibson was John Courage. Then a book was published on nontraditional degrees, by a William Ebbs, calling UDLR the best nontraditional school in the world. John Courage and William Ebbs do not, in fact, exist. They were both pseudonyms for one man, Raymond Seldis, of Neil Gibson & Company. Early advertising identified UDLR as a private and fully accredited Swiss university. The claimed accredited agency turned out not to exist. The university later advertised from a post office box on the Isle of Man, clearly stating that it is not accredited—but the mail went to Sudbury. Degrees were earned by writing a thesis, which can be quite short. Neil Gibson & Company also used to sell degrees that even they admitted were fake, from the University del Puerto Monico, Panama. Now, they are no longer operating (as of February 1998) The same folks started, but no longer run, Knightsbridge University.

University for Metaphysical Studies According to an on-line message a woman named Helen Stewart is planning to create "a virtual metaphysical university and library" under this name, incorporating an international metaphysical library, and that's all we know right now.

University of America Offers nonresident degrees in a wide range of fields. While the school is still operating in Iowa, we do not have current contact information, and a basic Internet search doesn't turn up a website. Any reader help will be greatly appreciated!

University of Applied Studies This school was approved by the state of California to operate, but when we wrote to the Hacienda, California address in early 1998, the letter was returned as undeliverable.

University of Azania The name was registered in England by Dr. Bernard Leeman (see Lincoln University, this chapter), in the hope and expectation of establishing a school that would ultimately be located in a "free South Africa." (Azania is a name that some black South Africans have used for their country.)

University of Beverly Hills The University thrived as an unaccredited school in the 1970s and two of its officers went on to start comparable schools, Century and Kennedy-Western. While UBH ostensibly closed in the mid 1980s, advertising (mostly in Asia), it was incorporated in Iowa by the people who run Louisiana Pacific University. It went on for an additional four or five years, using an address in Council Bluffs. A visitor to the Council Bluffs address found no University of Beverly Hills, but did find an educational service company whose manager became hostile when asked about the University.

University of California, Riverside Their off-campus Master of Administration program has been discontinued.

University of California, San Diego Their nonresidential Bachelor of Arts program has been discontinued.

University of California, Santa Cruz Their B.A. in community studies through evening study has apparently been discontinued.

University of Canterbury Established by two prominent psychologists in Los Angeles, California in the late 1970s. They offered graduate degrees in psychology and other fields with a four-week residency requirement in either California or England, but within a few years they were gone.

University of Central Arizona Tempe, Arizona. Operated in the late 1970s, offering Doctor of Art in education and Doctor of Business Management, based on readings, examinations, and a dissertation. The two founders agreed to a consent judgment and stopped awarding Doctorates.

University of Central California Sacramento, California. Once offered degrees of all kinds by correspondence, typically after a student responded to 100 to 200 multiple-choice, true-or-false, and essay questions to demonstrate competency, followed by independent study, a thesis, and an examination. they were authorized by the state of California, but both the "authorized" status and the university are no more.

University of East Asia See: University of Macau; Asia International Open University (Macau) Ltd.

University of East London Essex, United Kingsom. This school offers flexible undergraduate and graduate programs, but that's about all we know right now. We have written for more information, particularly whether any portion of any degree can be done at a distance.

University of Edinburgh Scotland. We have read this school may offer Doctorates through distance-learning programs, and have written for more information.

University of Generous Knowledge Reston, Virginia. A correspondent forwards some press materials from this decidedly unconventional business school, which claims to use movies instead of books as its primary teaching tools—*Gone with the Wind, Rocky, Top Gun,* and *The Color of Money,* among others. We're not sure whether this is a joke or not, but we'll let you know as soon as the school responds to our inquiries.

University of Guelph Canada. A reader informed us that this school has a distance education program, and we have written for more information.

University of Hong Kong Hong Kong. A reader informed us they offer a Master of Philosophy and a Doctor of Philosophy in English through distance learning programs. We have written for more information.

University of Liverpool See: Cayman Islands Law School

University of Macau Macau. At one time offered wholly nonresident external programs in the English language at Bachelor's at Master's level. A letter sent in mid 1997 was returned marked "gone away." This school was created when the University of East Asia split its programs into two schools; the other is the Asia International Open University.

University of Malaya Kuala Lumpur, Malaysia. A reader informs us they offer MATESOL and an M.Ed. TESOL through distance learning programs. We have written for more information.

University of Mid-America A consortium of 11 midwestern universities, which was to establish the American Open University, spent $14 million from the National Institute of Education in organizing, and then went out of business in 1982 when the NIE shut its purse.

University of Mid-America (Iowa) Council Bluffs, Iowa. In the mid 1980s, when Southwest University agreed with the state of Louisiana to stop granting distance-learning doctorates and to apply for DETC accreditation, the school began an association with some persons who had formerly been involved in the much more serious earlier school by the same name, to serve their current and prospective Doctoral candidates. This lasted for a couple of years, but the school is no longer in existence.

University of Mississippi Offered accredited external Master's degrees and Doctorates.

University of Missouri at Columbia Missouri. Once offered a Bachelor's degree in general agriculture through nontraditional methods. The program has been discontinued, although individuals can still take correspondence courses.

University of Naturopathy A reader inquires about a school of this name that he believed might be operating in East Orange, New Jersey, but there is no listed phone number there.

University of Palm Beach See: College of the Palm Beaches

University of Psychic Sciences Someone sent John a business card for this school, located in National City, California, but we have not been sent any information on what they do. Perhaps they haven't picked up the message we've been beaming them.

University of Puget Sound Offered accredited Bachelor's and Master's degrees through evening study.

University of Rochester Rochester, New York. No longer offers evening study degrees.

University of Saint Lucia School of Medicine This medical school was started on the Caribbean island of Saint Lucia by self-styled "Crazy Eddie" Antar, New York electronics magnate, but closed abruptly a year later, in early 1984, stranding students and faculty. Saint George's University in Grenada agreed to take qualified students, but only 37 of Saint Lucia's 127 were accepted there. No connection with Saint Lucia Health Sciences University.

University of Science and Philosophy This Virginia-based school offers seminars in such fascinating topics as transformational breathwork, transformation through joyful body movement, and searching for God. Their slogan is "Learn how the universe works."

University of Science and Technology Kowloon, Hong Kong. A reader informs us they offer a Master of Philosophy and Doctor of Philosophy in English through distance learning programs. We have written for more information.

University of Sciences in America Louisiana. Did not respond to several requests for information about their nontraditional programs and then, in mid 1997, a letter sent to their last known address, in Baton Rouge, was returned "attempted, not known."

University of Scouting See: Baden-Powell University

University of South Dakota Offered accredited external M.B.A.

University of South Wales No longer offers nontraditional degrees.

University of the Air See: Institute of Global Education

University of the Americas Metairie, Louisiana. At one time, registered with the Board of Regents of Louisiana, but according to Thomas Lavin, who had also been affiliated with Kensington and Bedford Universities, the UOTA never opened for business, and no longer exists.

University of the Pacific Offered accredited Bachelor's degree in which over 80% of credit could come from prior learning.

University of the World A reader says that in 1988 it existed in La Jolla California, but we can't find any trace.

University of Toledo Ohio. Offered accredited Master's and law degrees through evening study.

University of Utopia San Francisco, California. Letter asking for information was returned, and the phone number we'd been given was someone's personal answering machine.

University Without Walls/New Orleans Louisiana. Offered Bachelor's degrees. Now mail is returned, and there is no listed phone.

University Without Walls/Project Success North Hollywood, California. In the mid 1980s their literature described Bachelor's, Master's, and Doctorates in evolutionary systems design, but they are no longer there.

Valley Christian University Fresno, then Clovis, California. Degrees in many fields at all levels by correspondence. Letters neither answered nor returned; no listed telephone.

Van Norman University Los Angeles, California. Unaccredited, and now defunct, law school (degrees were offered through its Los Angeles College of Law).

Video University Jackson, Mississippi. In the early 1980s a major marketing effort was launched for Video U., which intended to offer many training courses. Now the phone has been disconnected.

Villarreal National University In 1988, this large Peruvian university (30,000 residential students) began offering completely nonresident Master's and Doctoral programs, in English at a cost of nearly $10,000 to people living in the U.S. From 1988 to 1991, there may have been certain irregularities, both in the U.S. and in Peru, that could affect the validity of degrees earned during that period. We have been informed that the American Council on Education in Washington, the

U.S. Information Agency in Lima, the Council of Europe in France, and the FBI may all have looked into these matters. At some point, Villarreal entered into an affiliation with Somerset University, an unaccredited British school then using an address in Louisiana, whereby Somerset handled Villarreal matters in the U.S. We have learned nothing more about this mysterious situation.

Washburn University Offered accredited Bachelor's degrees through evening study.

Washington International College Washington, D.C. They offered a B.A. with two weeks' residency, achieved accreditation candidacy status, and then went out of business in 1982.

Wellsgrey College Greeley, Colorado. Advertisements appeared in business publications offering the M.B.A. by computer, but mail was not answered and now there is no phone listing.

West Coast University Los Angeles, California. Offered certificate programs and degrees through evening and weekend study at locations in Southern California. As of early 1998, the phone had been disconnected, and Internet links were no longer active.

West London University United Kingdom. A letter sent to them was returned with the notation "gone away."

Western American University San Diego. All we know about this school right now is that it exists and is approved by the state of California to operate, and that it also has addresses in Irvine and Woodland Hills. We have written for more information.

Western Australia Institute of Technology No longer offers external degrees.

Western Colorado University Grand Junction, Colorado. Offered nonresident degrees in many fields at all levels. Accredited by the unrecognized National Association for Private Nontraditional Schools and Colleges, with whom they shared staff and office space. Financial problems set in, and the doors were closed in the mid 1980s.

Western Governors University In 1995, Governor Mike Leavitt of Utah proposed the development of a multistate program to deliver distance-learning courses and systems, with a special focus on competency-based education. Currently 18 states are involved (Alaska, Arizona, Colorado, Guam, Hawaii, Idaho, Indiana, Montana, Nebraska, Nevada, New Mexico, North Dakota, Oklahoma, Oregon, Texas, Utah, Washington, and Wyoming (with more to join in the near future), and they plan to bring together not only established universities, but also corporate training programs. The

university will be offering Associate's degrees soon, with more programs to follow. Indiana? Has no one taken a geography course?

Western Graduate College Pakistan. The unaccredited school has offered Bachelor's and Master's degrees in business fields, and had an affiliation with American University in London, an unaccredited, Iowa-registered school located in England. A letter sent to their last known address in May of 1997 was returned as undeliverable.

Western Scientific University Opened in southern California in the early 1980s as a "Christian internal, external alternate degree program," offering M.D. (homeopathic) and various Bachelor's, Master's, and Doctorates. Original name: Western University. No longer there.

Western Sierra Law School California. Apparently this school once offered nontraditional law programs, but a letter sent to their last known address, in San Diego, in mid 1997, was returned as undeliverable.

Western States Business University Wilmington, Delaware. At this point, all we know about this school is that it exists, and is not listed in the handbook of regionally accredited universities. We have written for more information.

Western University See: Western Scientific University

Westminster College (Missouri) This old established school for men started a nontraditional campus in Berkeley, California, then closed same in 1977 when it became apparent that the California branch was not upholding the parent school's high academic standards.

Whitman University Michoacan, Mexico. Years ago, John received a "prototype" 1985–1986 bulletin, offering Bachelor's, Master's, and Doctorates through guided independent study. Accreditation was claimed from the International Association of Non-Traditional Schools, England, an association we have not been able to locate. Students were asked to pay tuition in cash ($200 for the Ph.D., $600 for the B.A.), and to send it wrapped in in carbon paper, in a thick envelope. Our letters asking for more information went unanswered, and recently have been returned by the post office.

Wichita State University At one time offered an accredited Bachelor's degree in which over 80% of credits could come from prior learning.

Wild Rose College of Natural Healing Canada. Offered a correspondence program leading to a Wholistic Healing Degree (WHD) or Master Herbalist certificate. In mid 1997, a letter sent to their last known address, in Calgary, was returned as undeliverable.

William Darren University A correspondent asked for information on this school, apparently in or formerly in Phoenix, but we could find no record of them.

Windsor University One of California's first nontraditional schools, Windsor opened in Los Angeles in 1972, soon became a candidate for accreditation, and had an affiliation with Antioch. But things fell apart in the wake of claims of misleading statements and falsified credentials, and Windsor is no more.

Wisconsin International University They are accredited by the unrecognized Accrediting Commission International, but when we telephoned the campus in Wauwautosa, the phone was answered, "Hello," and we never received the literature we asked for. We have been told that the University's main clientele is in the Ukraine. When John attempted to visit the "campus" in August, 1998, he found it to be a private home in a suburban Milwaukee neighborhood.

Woodrow Wilson College of Law Georgia. Unaccredited, and now defunct, law school.

World College West This innovative school in Petaluma, California offered a variety of weekend programs leading to degrees, but ran out of money and closed in 1993.

World Open University South Dakota. Once a part of the Li Institution of Science and Technology (LIST) founded by the late Dr. Shu-Tien Li. Offered Master's and Doctorate degrees through programs guided by their adjunct (part-time) faculty. A letter sent to them in mid 1997 was returned marked "World Open Univ. was closed."

World University Colleges This Canadian school has asked us not to describe their programs and, as we've never received a response to our request for catalogs, we find it easy to comply. Raymond Rodgers, president of this sterling organization, has written to inform us that holding his school to the narrow standards of U.S. accreditation is "arrogant rubbish." Duly noted.

World University (Dominican Republic) Santo Domingo, Dominican Republic. It was a medical school incorporated in Puerto Rico, affiliated with the then-accredited International Institute of the Americas, and recognized by the World Health Organization. But the phone has been disconnected and mail has been returned.

World University (Puerto Rico) There used to be a fully accredited World University with headquarters in Hato Rey, Puerto Rico, and various branches or alliances in places around the U.S., including the International Graduate School in St. Louis and World University of Florida. But the school is no longer accredited if, indeed, they are there at all.

Worldwide/Vancouver University All we know about this school right now is that they exist, don't seem to have a website, and apparently offer Bachelor's and Master's degrees in British Columbia and Washington state. We would appreciate any further information.

Wyoming College of Advanced Studies This school was proposed as a nontraditional program offering nonresidential M.B.A.s, but after some problems with the Board of Education in Wyoming, (primarily having their bond increased from $10,000 to $50,000 as of July 1, 1996) president Richard Crews (also president of Columbia Pacific University) decided, regretfully, that he couldn't afford to invest any more time or money in it.

Yaacov College International We heard that this school offered innovative programs, but when we wrote for information to the address provided (at Y.C.I. World Trade Center in Rotterdam), the letters were returned.

HE STUDIED LAW AT
HOME AND WROTE HIS
LESSONS ON THE BACK
OF A SHOVEL.
NOW HE'S ON THE $5 BILL.
A PUBLIC SERVICE
MESSAGE FROM THE
ACME SHOVEL COMPANY

Appendix A
Glossary of Important Terms

When ideas fail, words come in very handy.

J. W. Goethe

AACRAO: The American Association of Collegiate Registrars and Admissions Officers.

academic year: The period of formal academic instruction, usually from September or October to May or June. Divided into semesters, quarters, or trimesters.

accreditation: Recognition of a school by an independent private organization. Not a governmental function in the U.S. There are more than 100 accrediting agencies, some recognized by the Department of Education and/or CHEA, and some unrecognized, some phony or fraudulent.

ACE: The American Council on Education, an influential non-government association in Washington.

ACT: American College Testing program, administrators of aptitude and achievement tests.

adjunct faculty: Part-time faculty member, often at a nontraditional school, often with a full-time teaching job elsewhere. More and more traditional schools are hiring adjunct faculty, because they don't have to pay them as much or provide health care and other benefits.

advanced placement: Admission to a school at a higher level than one would normally enter, because of getting credit for prior learning experience or passing advanced-placement exams.

alma mater: The school from which one has graduated, as in "My alma mater is Michigan State University."

alternative: Offering an alternate, or different means of pursuing learning or degrees or both. Often used interchangeably with *external* or *nontraditional.*

alumni: Graduates of a school, as in "This school has some distinguished alumni." Technically for males only; females are *alumnae.* The singular is *alumnus* (male) or *alumna* (female), although none of these terms are in common use.

alumni association: A confederation of alumni and alumnae who have joined together to support their alma mater in various ways, generally by donating money.

approved: In California, a level of state recognition of a school generally regarded as one step below *accredited.*

arbitration: A means of settling disputes, as between a student and a school, in which one or more independent arbitrators or judges listen to both sides, and make a decision. A means of avoiding a courtroom trial. Many learning contracts have an arbitration clause. *See binding arbitration; mediation.*

assistantship: A means of assisting students (usually graduate students) financially by offering them part-time academic employment, usually in the form of a teaching assistantship or a research assistantship.

Associate's degree: A degree traditionally awarded by community or junior colleges after two years of residential study, or completion of 60 to 64 semester hours.

asynchronous: not at the same time, as in an asynchronous on-line course, in which the faculty leaves messages for students, who read them later. Opposite of synchronous.

auditing: Sitting in on a class without earning credit for that class.

authorized: Until recently, a form of state recognition of schools in California. This category was phased out beginning in 1990, and now all schools must be approved or accredited to operate. Many formerly authorized schools are now billing themselves as candidates for approval.

Bachelor's degree: Awarded in the U.S. after four years of full-time residential study (two to five years in other countries), or, typically, the earning of 120 to 128 semester units by any means.

binding arbitration: Arbitration in which both parties have agreed in advance that they will abide by the result and take no further legal action.

branch campus: A satellite facility, run by officers of the main campus of a college or university, at another location. Can range from a small office to a full-fledged university center.

campus: The main facility of a college or university, usually comprising buildings, grounds, dormitories, cafeterias and dining halls, sports stadia, etc. The campus of a nontraditional school may consist solely of offices.

CEU: Continuing Education Unit, typically given in training courses at the rate of one for each ten hours of contact time. While standards are maintained by the International Association for Continuing Education and Training, the awarding of CEU's is not regulated, and they are rarely considered as equivalent to academic credit.

Chancellor: Often the highest official of a university. Also a new degree title, proposed by some schools to be a higher degree than the Doctorate, requiring three to five years of additional study.

CHEA: The Council on Higher Education Accreditation, successor to COPA and CORPA as the agency that recognizes accrediting agencies in the US.

CLEP: The College-Level Examination Program, a series of equivalency examinations given nationally each month.

coeducational: Education of men and women on the same campus or in the same program. This is why female students are called coeds.

college: In the U.S., an institution offering programs leading to the Associate's and/or Bachelor's, and sometimes higher degrees. Often used interchangeably with *university,* although traditionally a university is a collection of colleges. In England and elsewhere, *college* may denote part of a university (Kings College, Cambridge) or a private high school (Eton College).

colloquium: A gathering of scholars to discuss a given topic over a period of a few hours to a few days. ("The university is sponsoring a colloquium on marine biology.")

community college: A two-year traditional school, offering programs leading to the Associate's degree and, typically, many noncredit courses in arts, crafts, and vocational fields for community members not interested in a degree. Also called *junior college.*

competency: The philosophy and practice of awarding credit or degrees based on learning skills, rather than time spent in courses.

continuing education credit: *see CEU*

COPA: The Council on Postsecondary Accreditation, a now defunct private nongovernmental organization that recognized accrediting agencies.

CORPA: The Commission on Recognition of Postsecondary Accreditation, a nationwide nonprofit corporation, formed in 1994, that took over the role of *COPA* (see above) in evaluating accrediting agencies and awarding recognition to those found worthy, and then reliquished it to CHEA a couple of years later.

correspondence course: A course offered by mail and completed entirely by home study, often with one or two proctored, or supervised, examinations.

course: A specific unit of instruction, such as a course in microeconomics, or a course in abnormal psychology. Residential courses last for one or more semesters or quarters; correspondence courses often have no rigid time requirements.

cramming: Intensive preparation for an examination. Most testing agencies now admit that cramming can improve scores on exams.

credit: A unit used to record courses taken. Each credit typically represents the number of hours spent in class each week. Hence a 3-credit or 3-unit course would commonly be a class that met three hours each week for one semester or quarter.

curriculum: A program of courses to be taken in pursuit of a degree or other objective.

DANTES: The Defense Activity for Non-Traditional Education Support, which regulates financial aid programs for active military, and administers equivalency exams for military and civilians.

degree: A title conferred by a school to show that a certain course of study has been completed.

Department of Education: In the US, the federal agency concerned with all educational matters in the U.S. that are not handled by the departments of education in the 50 states. In other countries, similar functions are commonly the province of a ministry of education.

DETC: The Distance Education and Training Council (formerly the National Home Study Council) is the recognized accreditor for schools offering degrees and diplomas largely or entirely by distance learning.

diploma: The certificate that shows that a certain course of study has been completed. Diplomas are awarded for completing a degree or other, shorter course of study.

dissertation: The major research project normally required as part of the work for a Doctorate. Dissertations are expected to make a new and creative contribution to the field of study, or to demonstrate one's excellence in the field. See also thesis.

Doctorate: The highest degree one can earn (but see *Chancellor*). Includes Doctor of Philosophy (Ph.D.), Education (Ed.D.), and many other titles.

dormitory: Student living quarters on residential campuses. May include dining halls and classrooms.

early decision: Making a decision on whether to admit a student sooner than decisions are usually made. Offered by some schools primarily as a service either to students applying to several schools, or those who are especially anxious to know the outcome of their application.

ECFMG: The Education Commission for Foreign Medical Graduates, which administers an examination to physicians who have gone to medical school outside the U.S. and wish to practice in the U.S.

electives: Courses one does not have to take, but may elect to take as part of a degree program.

essay test: An examination in which the student writes narrative sentences as answers to questions, instead of the short answers required by a multiple-choice test. Also called a *subjective* test.

equivalency examination: An examination designed to demonstrate knowledge in a subject where the learning was acquired outside a traditional classroom. A person who learned nursing skills while working in a hospital, for instance, could take an equivalency exam to earn credit in, say, obstetrical nursing.

external: Away from the main campus or offices. An external degree may be earned by home study or at locations other than on the school's campus.

FAQ: frequently asked questions. Increasingly, on Internet and in print, information sources provide a list of FAQ's to assist "newbies" (newcomers) in learning more without having to bother people.

fees: Money paid to a school for purposes other than academic tuition. Fees might pay for parking, library services, use of the gymnasium, binding of dissertations, etc.

fellowship: A study grant, usually awarded to a graduate student, and usually requiring no work other than usual academic assignments (as contrasted with an *assistantship*).

financial aid: A catch-all term, including scholarships, loans, fellowships, assistantships, tuition reductions, etc. Many schools have a financial aid officer, whose job it is to deal with all funding questions and problems.

fraternities: Men's fraternal and social organizations, often identified by Greek letters, such as Zeta Beta Tau. There are also professional and scholastic fraternities open to men and women, such as Beta Alpha Psi, the national fraternity for students of accounting.

freshman: The name for the class in its first of four years of traditional study for a Bachelor's degree, and its individual members. ("She is a freshman, and thus is a member of the freshman class.")

grade-point average: The average score a student has made in all his or her classes, weighted by the number of credits or units for each class. Also called G.P.A.

grades: Evaluative scores provided for each course, and often for individual examinations or papers written for that course. There are letter grades (usually A, B, C, D, F) and number grades (usually percentages from 0% to 100%), or on a scale of 0 to 3, 0 to 4, or 0 to 5. Some schools use a pass/fail system with no grades.

graduate: One who has earned a degree from a school. Also, in the US, the programs offered beyond the Bachelor's level. ("He is a graduate of Yale University, and is now doing graduate work at Princeton.") In the UK and elsewhere, the word is *postgraduate*.

graduate school: A school or a division of a university offering work at the Master's or doctoral degree level.

graduate student: One attending graduate school.

GRE: The Graduate Record Examination, which many traditional schools and a few nontraditional ones require for admission to graduate programs, and which can earn credit in some Bachelor's programs.

honor societies: Organizations for persons with a high grade point average or other evidence of outstanding performance. There are local societies on some campuses, and several national organizations, the most prestigious of which is called Phi Beta Kappa.

honor system: A system in which students are trusted not to cheat on examinations, and to obey other rules, without proctors or others monitoring their behavior.

honorary doctorate: A nonacademic award, given regularly by more than 1,000 colleges and universities to honor distinguished scholars, celebrities, and donors of large sums of money. Holders of this award may, and often do, call themselves "Doctor."

junior: The name for the class in its third year of a traditional four-year U.S. Bachelor's degree program, or any member of that class. ("She is a junior this year.")

junior college: See *community college.*

language laboratory: A special room in which students can listen to foreign-language tapes over headphones, allowing many students to be learning different languages at different skill levels at the same time.

learning contract: A formal agreement between a student and a school, specifying independent work to be done by the student, and the amount of credit the school will award on successful completion of the work.

lecture class: A course in which a faculty member lectures to anywhere from a few dozen to many hundreds of students. Often lecture classes are followed by small group discussion sessions led by student assistants or junior faculty.

liberal arts: A term with many complex meanings, but generally referring to the nonscientific curriculum of a university: humanities, arts, social sciences, history, and so forth.

liberal education: Commonly taken to be the opposite of a specialized education; one in which students are required to take courses in a wide range of fields, as well as courses in their major.

licensed: Holding a permit to operate. This can range from a difficult-to-obtain state school license to a simple local business license.

life-experience portfolio: A comprehensive presentation listing and describing all learning experiences in a person's life, with appropriate documentation. The basic document used in assigning academic credit for life-experience learning.

LSAT: The Law School Admission Test, required by most U.S. law schools of all applicants.

maintenance costs: The expenses incurred while attending school, other than tuition and fees. Includes room and board (food), clothing, laundry, postage, travel, etc.

major: The subject or academic department in which a student takes concentrated coursework, leading to a specialty. ("His major is in English literature; she is majoring in chemistry.")

mentor: Faculty member assigned to supervise independent study work at a nontraditional school; comparable to *adjunct* faculty.

minor: The secondary subject or academic department in which a student takes concentrated coursework. ("She has a major in art and a minor in biology.") Optional at most schools.

modem: the device that lets you send and receive messages over a computer and a telephone line.

MCAT: The Medical College Admission Test, required by most U.S. medical schools of all applicants.

multiple-choice test: An examination in which the student chooses the best of several alternative answers provided for each question; also called an *objective test.* ("The capital city of England is (a) Zurich, (b) Ostrogotz-Plakatz, (c) Tokyo, (d) none of the above.")

multiversity: A university system with two or more separate campuses, each a major university in its own right, such as the University of California or the University of Wisconsin.

narrative transcript: A transcript issued by a nontraditional school in which, instead of simply listing the courses completed and grades received, there is a narrative description of the work done and the school's rationale for awarding credit for that work.

nontraditional: Something done in other than the usual or traditional way. In education, refers to learning and degrees completed by methods other than spending many hours in classrooms and lecture halls.

nonresident: (1) A means of instruction in which the student does not need to visit the school; all work is done by correspondence, telephone, or exchange of audiotapes or videotapes; (2) A person who does not meet residency requirements of a given school and, as a result, often has to pay a higher tuition or fees.

objective test: An examination in which questions requiring a very short answer are posed. It can be multiple choice, true-false, fill-in-the-blank, etc. The questions are related to facts (thus objective) rather than to opinions (or subjective).

on line: Connected, via computer, to another party, whether the Internet, a school, or an individual.

on the job: In the U.S., experience or training gained through employment, which may be converted to academic credit. In England, slang for having sex, which either confuses or amuses English people who read about "credit for on-the-job experience."

open admissions: An admissions policy in which everyone who applies is admitted, on the theory that the ones who are unable to do university work will drop out before long.

out-of-state student: One from a state other than that in which the school is located. Because most state colleges and universities have much higher tuition rates for out-of-state students, many people attempt to establish legal residence in the same state as their school.

parallel instruction: A method in which nonresident students do exactly the same work as residential students, during the same general time period, except they do it at home.

pass/fail option: Instead of getting a letter or number grade in a course, the student may elect, at the start of the course, a pass/fail option in which the only grades are either "pass" or "fail." Some schools permit students to elect this option on one or two of their courses each semester.

PEP: Proficiency Examination Program, a series of equivalency exams given nationally every few months.

Phi Beta Kappa: A national honors society that recognizes students with outstanding grades.

plan of study: A detailed description of the program an applicant to a school plans to pursue. Many traditional schools ask for this as part of the admissions procedure. The plan of study should be designed to meet the objectives of the *statement of purpose.*

PONSI: The Program on Non-Collegiate Instruction; they evaluate educational training programs.

portfolio: See *life-experience portfolio.*

postgraduate: The British word for a person or a program more advanced than the Bachelor's level. "She is working on a postgraduate certificate." Equivalent to "graduate" in the US.

prerequisites: Courses that must be taken before certain other courses may be taken. For instance, a course in algebra is often a prerequisite for a course in geometry.

private school: A school that is privately owned, rather than operated by a governmental department.

proctor: A person who supervises the taking of an examination to be certain there is no cheating, and that other rules are followed. Many nontraditional schools permit unproctored examinations.

professional school: School in which one studies for the various professions, including medicine, dentistry, law, nursing, veterinary, optometry, ministry, etc.

PSAT: Preliminary Scholastic Aptitude Test, given annually to high school juniors.

public school: In the U.S., a school operated by the government of a city, county, district, state, or the federal government. In England, a privately owned or run school.

quarter: An academic term at a school on the "quarter system," in which the calendar year is divided into four equal quarters. New courses begin each quarter.

quarter hour: An amount of credit earned for each classroom hour spent in a given course during a given quarter. A course that meets four hours each week for a quarter would probably be worth four quarter hours, or quarter units.

recognized: A term used by some schools to indicate approval from some other organization or governmental body. The term usually does not have a precise meaning, so it may mean different things in different places.

registrar: The official at most colleges and universities who is responsible for maintaining student records and, in many cases, for verifying and validating applications for admission.

rolling admissions: A year-round admissions procedure. Many schools only admit students once or twice a year. A school with rolling admissions considers each application at the time it is received. Many nontraditional schools, especially ones with nonresident programs, have rolling admissions.

SAT: Scholastic Aptitude Test, one of the standard tests given to qualify for admission to colleges and universities.

scholarship: A study grant, either in cash or in the form of tuition or fee reduction.

score: Numerical rating of performance on a test. ("His score on the Graduate Record Exam was not so good.")

semester: A school term, generally four to five months. Schools on the semester system usually have two semesters a year, with a shorter summer session.

semester hour: An amount of credit earned in a course representing one classroom hour per week for a semester. A class that meets three days a week for one hour, or one day a week for three hours, would be worth three semester hours, or semester units.

seminar: A form of instruction combining independent research with meetings of small groups of students and a faculty member, generally to report on reading or research the students have done.

senior: The fourth year of study of a four-year U.S. Bachelor's degree program, or a member of that class. ("Linnea is a senior this year, and is president of the senior class.")

sophomore: The second year of study in a four-year U.S. Bachelor's degree program, or a member of that class.

sorority: A women's social organization, often with its own living quarters on or near a campus, and usually identified with two or three Greek letters, such as Sigma Chi.

special education: Education of the physically or mentally handicapped, or, often, of the gifted.

special student: A student who is not studying for a degree either because he or she is ineligible or does not wish the degree.

statement of purpose: A detailed description of the career the applicant intends to pursue after graduation. A statement of purpose is often requested as part of the admissions procedure at a university.

subject: An area of study or learning covering a single topic, such as the subject of chemistry, or economics, or French literature.

subjective test: An examination in which the answers are in the form of narrative sentences or long or short essays, often expressing opinions rather than reporting facts.

syllabus: A detailed description of a course of study, often including the books to be read, papers to be written, and examinations to be given.

synchronous: at the same time. In a synchronous on-line or satellite course, the faculty and students can interact with one another. Opposite of *asynchronous*.

thesis: The major piece of research that is completed by many Master's degree candidates. A thesis is expected to show a detailed knowledge of one's field and ability to do research and integrate knowledge of the field.

TOEFL: Test of English as a Foreign Language, required by many schools of persons for whom English is not the native language.

traditional education: Education at a residential school in which the Bachelor's degree is completed through four years of classroom study, the Master's in one or two years, and the Doctorate in three to five years.

transcript: A certified copy of the student's academic record, showing courses taken, examinations passed, credits awarded, and grades or scores received.

transfer student: A student who has earned credit in one school, and then transfers to another school.

trimester: A term consisting of one third of an academic year. A school on the trimester system has three equal trimesters each year.

tuition: In the U.S., the money charged for formal instruction. In some schools, tuition is the only expense other than postage. In other schools, there may be fees as well as tuition. In England, tuition refers to the instruction or teaching at a school, such as the tuition offered in history.

tuition waiver: A form of financial assistance in which the school charges little or no tuition.

tutor: See *mentor*. A tutor can also be a hired assistant who helps a student prepare for a given class or examination.

undergraduate: Pertaining to the period of study from the end of high school to the earning of a Bachelor's degree; also to a person in such a course of study. ("Alexis is an undergraduate at Reed College, one of the leading undergraduate schools.")

university: An institution that usually comprises one or more undergraduate colleges, one or more graduate schools, and, often, one or more professional schools

USMLE: The U.S. Medical Licensing Exam, required of everyone who graduates from a non-U.S. medical school and wishes to be licensed in the U.S.

"For my final exam at the Monaco Correspondence Veterinary Institute, they mailed me these two sick animals. I have one week to cure them and mail them back."

Appendix B
Bibliography

*"What! Another of those damned, fat, square, thick books!
Always scribble, scribble, scribble, eh, Mr. Gibbon?"*

THE DUKE OF GLOUCESTER, GIBBON'S PATRON, ON BEING PRESENTED
WITH VOL. III OF HIS DECLINE AND FALL OF THE ROMAN EMPIRE

Most of these books are available in bookstores and libraries, on the Internet through services like www.amazon.com, and from a large service that specializes in providing books to distance education students: Specialty Books, 5833 Industrial Drive, Athens, Ohio 45701, phone (740) 594-2274, fax (740) 593-3045, www.specialty-books.com. Some, however, are sold only or primarily by mail. In those cases we have given ordering information. In addition, some highly recommended books are now out of print. If you feel from the description that they would be useful in your situation, try your local library or a good second-hand bookstore. Where we have prices and other information, we've given it, though of course these things are always subject to change.

GENERAL REFERENCE BOOKS
The Ones We Use Every Day

Commonwealth Universities Yearbook (Association of Commonwealth Universities, London; distributed in US by Stockton Press, New York) This standard reference work covers what they refer to as all schools "in good standing" in 36 countries or areas. Many admissions departments use this book in making admissions or acceptance decisions. More than 600 institutions are described in great detail. About 2,000 pages, $250.

The H.E.P. Higher Education Directory (Higher Education Publications, 6400 Arlington Blvd., Suite 648, Falls Church, VA 22042; (703) 532-2300) We list this first because it is the one we use the most. Until 1983, the U.S. Department of Education published a comprehensive directory of information on colleges and universities. When President Reagan announced his intention to shut down the Department of Education, their publication was discontinued and H.E.P. began publishing an almost identical directory. It emerges toward the end of each year and gives detailed factual information (no opinions or ratings) on all accredited schools. They used to list California-approved schools as well, but stopped in 1988. More than 600 pages, $55.

The Independent Study Catalog (Peterson's Guides). In effect, a master catalog listing all 13,000+ courses offered by more than 140 U.S. and Canadian institutions offering correspondence study. Only the course titles are given, so it is still necessary to write to the individual schools for detailed information. Updated periodically, the latest edition is the 7th, for 1998.

International Handbook of Universities (Groves Dictionaries) 1,506 pages and an amazing $250 price tag. Gives detailed information on virtually every college, university, technical institute, and training school in the world. This is the book that is most used by collegiate registrars and admissions officers to evaluate schools.

The Others

Accredited Institutions of Postsecondary Education (Oryx Press). Issued around the middle of each year, this book lists every accredited institution and candidate for accreditation. This is the book many people use to determine conclusively whether or not a given American school is accredited. 735 pages, $55.

Barron's Profiles of American Colleges (Barron's Education Series). A massive 1,300-page volume that describes every accredited college and university in America, with lists of majors offered by each school.

Best's External Degree Directory by Thomas J. Lavin. More detail than this book but includes many fewer schools, and now quite out of date. At $50 for under 300 typewritten pages, a bit pricey.

Campus-Free College Degrees (8th edition) by Marcie K. Thorson (Thorson Guides). This well-done book covers much of the same territory as ours, but accredited schools only, with considerably longer descriptions of each. Marcie does not include schools outside the US, even when they have U.S. accreditation.

College Degrees by Mail and Modem 1999 by John Bear and Mariah Bear (Ten Speed Press). The publisher asked for a smaller and less comprehensive book on the topic, and this is it. Each year, we select 100 accredited schools with distance degree programs, and write them up in more detail than Bears' Guide. Roughly ⅓ the size of this book for about half the price.

Degrees by Post by Cornelius A. Gillick (Moderne, Manchester, England) A 72-page, $28 book that lumps together completely fraudulent schools, major universities, and a bunch in between. Mr. Gillick seems sincere, but even when published in 1990, many of his listings were extremely out-of-date. (His reference to this book lists an address we left in 1979.)

Directory of External Graduate Programs by Mary C. Kahl (Regents College, Cultural Education Center, Albany NY 12230). Twenty-six typewritten pages; a page on each of 20 programs, with a bit more information on each than in this book.

Distance Degrees by Mark Wilson (Umpqua Education Research Alliance). Accredited schools only. A considerable improvement over the first edition, called *Campus Free Degrees,* and quite reminiscent of Marcie Thorson's book of similar title. While the geographical index lists only US schools, the book also covers a few Canadian and British institutions.

Earn a College Degree at Home by Dennis L. Vinson (Crow Moon Books). Vinson does a decent job in this book that is somewhat reminiscent of ours as of seven or eight years ago. Quite a few of the listings were a bit dated even when the book came out in 1995. Still, it is written in a jolly style, has a lot of inspirational passages, and clearly separates the properly accredited schools from the others.

External Degrees in the Information Age: Legitimate Choices by Eugene Sullivan, David Stewart and Henry Spille (Onyx Press). Now why would they arrange a book on external degrees geographically, not alphabetically. A decent book, but many fewer listings than Thorson, Peterson, Wilson, or us. Nearly 10% of the text is devoted to one school. A very helpful chart comparing school-licensing laws in all the states.

How to Earn a College Degree Without Going to College by James P. Duffy (John Wiley & Sons). Much along the lines of our guide, but describes only Bachelor's programs at accredited schools (fewer than 100 of them) and only wholly nonresident programs. Apparently not updated since 1994.

How to Earn an Advanced Degree Without Going to Graduate School by James P. Duffy (John Wiley & Sons). The graduate-school version of the above book lists 140 accredited nonresidential Master's and doctoral programs. Apparently not updated since 1994.

The Internet University by Dan Corrigan (Cape Software, Box 800, Harwich, MA 02645). A comprehensive guide both to the entire practice of on-line education and courses, and to more than 2,700 actual courses available. Much of the information is also available free on-line at www.caso.com.

Lovejoy's College Guide by Charles T. Straughn & Barbarasue Straughn (Macmillan). Briefer descriptions than other guides, but still a huge book: 1,600 pages, $50. In the past, the usefulness of Lovejoy's has been marred by the listing of some real clinkers, particularly totally phony diploma mills that somehow managed to get past the editors.

Options: a guide to selected opportunities in non-traditional education by David Jones-Delcorde. Our former colleague has published his own book, the first two-thirds are reminiscent of ours; the final third has helpful information on various professional designations, and advice for distance learning students.

Oryx Guide to Distance Learning (Oryx Press). 528 pages for a whopping $116.50. Lists more than 100 accredited U.S. institutions, focusing on audio, video, and on-line instruction.

Peterson's Guide to Distance Learning Programs (Peterson's Guides). Probably the main competitor to our book, this is quite a comprehensive collection of information, although the main focus is on individual courses rather than on complete degree programs. Degree programs can be found in the index. Does not cover unaccredited schools or schools outside North America (except for two of the many British schools). Our real annoyance with this book is that more than one quarter of it, 150 pages, is taken up with paid advertising for schools, which is not identified as paid advertising, but simply as "in depth descriptions."

Peterson's Guide to Graduate and Professional Programs (Peterson's Guides). Five large books, each describing in detail opportunities for residential graduate study in the U.S. Volumes cover social science and humanities, biological and agricultural sciences, physical sciences, and engineering. There is also a summary volume. The series is updated annually.

Peterson's Guide to Four-Year Colleges (Peterson's Guides). Another massive annual directory (some 2,800 pages), covering traditional accredited schools only.

Worldwide Educational Directory by Mohammad S. Mirza (International Educational Services, P.O. Box 10503, Saddar, Karachi 3, Pakistan). Nearly 400 typewritten pages (in English) listing degree and non-degree-granting schools. Most of the data are accurate, but some less-than-wonderful schools are included, without warning, along with the good ones. Lack of index or alphabetized listings makes it very difficult to use.

World-Wide Inventory of Non-Traditional Degree Programs (UNESCO, c/o Unipub, 4611-F Assembly Drive, Lanham, MD 20706-4391). A generally useful United Nations report on what many of the world's nations are doing in the way of nontraditional education. Some helpful school descriptions, and lots of detailed descriptions of evening courses offered by workers' cooperatives in Bulgaria and suchlike.

World Guide to Higher Education (Bowker Publishing Co.). A comprehensive survey, by the United

Nations, of educational systems, degrees, and qualifications, from Afghanistan to Zambia.

CREDIT FOR LIFE-EXPERIENCE LEARNING

Earn College Credit for What You Know by Lois Lamdin (Council for Adult and Experiential Learning, 223 W. Jackson Blvd., #510, Chicago, IL 60606, (312) 922-5909.). How to put together a life experience portfolio: how to gather the necessary information, document it, and assemble it, $25.

Guide to Educational Credit for Training Programs (Oryx Press). Many nontraditional programs use this large volume, based on American Council on Education recommendations, to assign credit for more than 5,000 business, trade union, association, and government agency training programs. 1,200 pages, $85.

Guide to the Evaluation of Educational Experiences in the Armed Forces (Oryx Press). Many schools use this 2,000-page 3-volume set (one for each service) to assess credit for non-school learning. Describes and makes credit recommendations for more than 8,000 military training programs. $35 per volume.

Portfolio Development and Adult Learning: Purposes and Strategies by Alan Mandell and Elana Michelson (Council for Adult and Experiential Learning) Explores the eight approaches to portfolio development courses most typically used at colleges and universities, providing examples of each through a closer examination of prior learning assessment programs offered at 11 institutions of higher learning, $21.50.

Prior Learning Assessment: the portfolio by Marthe Sansregret (Hurtubise HMH, 7360 Newman Blvd., LaSalle, Quebec H8N 1X2 Canada). A well-respected head of assessment for a major university told us that this is the book he asks his students to use, to create their portfolios. It comes with software (Mac or DOS) to make the process more efficient. 166 pages, about $25 including software.

Self-Assessment and Planning Manual by Linda Headley-Walker, *et al* (Regents College, 7 Columbia Circle, Albany, NY 12203). While prepared primarily for potential Regents College students, this inexpensive and splendid 72-page manual could benefit anyone uncertain whether to pursue a nontraditional degree, and, if so, how to go about it. Guided exercises help the reader determine if he or she really needs a degree, how to assess prior educational experience, how to plan financially, and so forth.

Using Licenses and Certificates as Evidence of College-Level Learning by Harriet Cabell (CAEL; see above). A five-page summary of Dr. Cabell's doctoral research, examining the practices of schools that award credit based on applicants' licenses and certificates, $3.

The Value of Personal Learning Outside College by Peter Smith (Acropolis Books). Dr. Smith, the founder of Vermont Community College and later the lieutenant governor of Vermont, has written a charming and very useful book on matters related to earning credit for non-school learning (which, he points out, accounts for 90% of what an adult knows). Many inspiring case histories of adults who pursued this path, plus appendices that help one identify and describe out-of-school learning. (Formerly titled *Your Hidden Credentials*)

MEDICAL SCHOOLS

Foreign Medical Schools for U.S. Citizens by Carlos Pestana, M.D., Ph.D. (P.O. Box 790617, San Antonio, TX 78279-0617). This wonderful book is now back in print in an updated 1995 edition. It gives anecdotal, well-written, and very informative write-ups on the good and less-good best foreign schools for American medical school applicants, as well as application tips and other survival advice. Well worth the $20 (includes shipping by two-day priority mail.)

The Medical School Applicant: advice for pre-medical students by Carlos Pestana, M.D., Ph.D. (see immediately above). Another wonderful book by Dr. Pestana, bringing his unique perspective to all the usual matters that books on medical schools have, and a great deal more, including a remarkable chapter on "Special angles: the dirty tricks department—a frank analysis of unconventional pathways to a medical education," $13.

The Official Guide to Caribbean Medical Schools by S. K. Sarin and R. K. Yalamanchi (CaribMed, Inc., Chicago, IL, www.caribmed.com). Well it's not "official" but it is a helpful little guide (104 pages), describing what it is like to do a Caribbean M.D. (both the authors did so), with detailed descriptions of the six major Caribbean medical schools.

RELIGIOUS SCHOOLS

Name It and Frame It: new opportunities in adult education, and how to avoid being ripped off by 'Christian' degree mills by Steve Levicoff (Institute on Religion and Law). A funny, informative, helpful, abrasive, and in some some respects, quite outrageous book, which invites the dozens of schools called 'degree mills' to sue the author if they don't like their listing. According to the author, none ever has. After publishing four editions, Dr. Levicoff stopped selling his book, and now gives it away free on the Internet (training.loyola.edu/cdld/nifi01.html). A bit out of date now; there may be a new edition in 1999 or 2000.

Walston's Guide to Earning Religious Degrees Nontraditionally by Rick Walston (Persuasion Press, Box 847, Longview, WA 98632). "Josh" Walston and John Bear once collaborated on what they called *Walston & Bear's Guide to Earning Religious Degrees Nontraditionally*. As they had planned, by the 3rd edition, John bowed out, leaving the book entirely in Dr. Walston's hands. Walston is much more accepting than Levicoff of legal unaccredited schools, but takes a strong stand ("Shame," he says) against the many that improperly claim accreditation.

FINANCIAL AID

Finding Money for College by John Bear and Mariah Bear (Ten Speed Press). We collected all the information we could find about the nontraditional and unorthodox approaches to getting a share in the billions of dollars that go unclaimed each year, including barter, real estate and tax gambits, negotiation, creative payment plans, obscure scholarships, foundations that make grants to individuals, etc. Any bookstore can supply or order this book, or you can buy the 1998-1999 edition by mail from us directly (6921 Stockton Ave., El Cerrito, CA 94530 USA, phone (800) 622-9661, www.degree.net)

The Scholarship Book by Daniel Cassidy (Prentice-Hall), **Dan Cassidy's Worldwide College Scholarship Directory** and **Dan Cassidy's Worldwide Graduate Scholarship Directory** (Career Press). These three books are, in effect, a complete printout of the data banks of information used by Cassidy's National Scholarship Research Service, described in chapter 10. Tens of thousands of sources are listed for undergraduate and graduate students, for study in the U.S. and overseas.

The A's and B's of Academic Scholarships by Anna and Robert Leider (Octameron Associates, P.O. Box 248, Alexandria, VA 22301). Lists more than 100,000 scholarships plus advice on earning them.

Don't Miss Out: the ambitious student's guide to financial aid by Anna and Robert Leiter (Octameron). A complement to our *Finding Money* book, this one gives excellent advice (in 144 pages for $8) in pursuing the traditional route to financial aid.

MISCELLANY

Killing the Spirit: Higher Education in America by Page Smith (Viking Penguin). In 1990, one of John's writer-heroes issued this extraordinary book about everything that is wrong in higher education. From page 1: "The major themes might be characterized as the impoverishment of the spirit by 'academic fundamentalism,' the flight from teaching, the meretriciousness of most academic research, the disintegration of the disciplines, the alliance of the universities with the Department of Defense ... etc., and last but not least, the corruptions incident to 'big time' collegiate sports." Read this wonderful book. Or listen to it: Page Smith reads it, on 8 cassettes available from audio book sources.

College on Your Own by Gene R. Hawes and Gail Parker (Bantam Books). This remarkable book, now out of print, serves as a syllabus for a great many fields, for people who want to do college-level work at home, with or without the guidance of a college. A brief overview of each field (anthropology, biology, chemistry, history, etc.) and a detailed reading list for learning more about the field. Quite valuable in preparing learning contracts. Why doesn't some shrewd publisher put this fine volume back in print?

The External Degree as a Credential: Graduates' Experiences in Employment and Further Study by Carol Sosdian and Laure Sharp (National Institute of Education). This 1978 report is probably the most often misquoted and misinterpreted educational survey ever published. Many schools (some good, some not) cite the findings (a high satisfaction level of external students and a high acceptance level of external degrees) without mentioning it related only to fully accredited undergraduate degrees, and has little or no relevance to unaccredited undergraduate or graduate degrees.

External Degrees in the Information Age by Eugene Sullivan, David W. Stewart, and Henry A. Spille (Oryx Press, 1997). In a sense, this is a successor to Stewart and Spille's *Diploma Mills*. It discusses principles of good practice in this field, along with guidelines for identifying bad schools. (We wish the authors didn't write such unkind things about John and about our book elsewhere.)

Getting a College Degree Fast by Joanne Aber (Prometheus Books, 1996). A decent enough book, focusing primarily on following the same path the author did: taking examinations to earn credit. Excellent information is provided on this topic, but not so useful for school and accreditation information (more than a few errors here).

Getting What You Came For: the smart student's guide to earning a Master's or Ph.D. by Robert L. Peters, Ph.D. (Noonday Press, 1997). Another wonderful and extremely helpful book. Quoting from chapter one [*This Book Can Help (and you probably need it)*], "Graduate students run into problems because they do not understand how graduate school works, nor do most undergraduate counselors and graduate departments provide enough realistic guidance. . . . This book tells you what graduate school is really like. . . . I tell you how to create a comprehensive strategy that blends politics, psychology, and planning to ensure that your hard work pays off with a degree and a job." And he does, eloquently, $14.

Hunter's Guide to the College Guides by Bruce Hunter (P. O. Box 9647, Naples, FL 33941). A high school counselor has created this useful evaluation (from "Not helpful" to "Most helpful") of scores of college guidebooks, both general (Lovejoy's, Barrons, etc.) and specific (guides for athletes, religious students, handicapped students, African-American students, and so on). Books are described in considerable detail and no, *Bears' Guide* is not included. Dismissed as falling outside the scope. Such is life.

The Ph.D. Trap by Wilfred Cude (Medicine Label Press, RR2, West Bay, Nova Scotia B0E 3K0 Canada). The author was treated very badly in his own graduate program, which turned him into a reformer. Farley Mowat writes that he is "the kind of reformer this world needs. Humane, literate, reasonable, and utterly implacable, he has just unmasked the gruesome goings on in the academic morgue that deals in doctoral degrees. Any student contemplating the pursuit of a doctorate had better read The Ph.D. Trap as a matter of basic self-preservation. . . ."

Proving You're Qualified: strategies for competent people without college degrees by Charles D. Hayes (Autodidactic Press, Box 872749, Wasilla, Alaska 99687). The author makes a strong case for competence being more important than credentials in life—but, since many gatekeepers disagree, Hayes goes on to show how to, well, how to do what the title says. Ronald Gross, who writes splendid books on education himself, says that "this is the wisest and most useful book I have ever read on this subject."

This Way Out: A guide to alternatives to traditional college education in the U.S. by John Coyne and Tom Hebert (E. P. Dutton). A delightful, if out-of-date book, now out of print, that describes a small number of alternatives in detail, with inspirational interviews with participants. Includes an intriguing essay on self-education by hiring tutors, and sections as diverse as how to study, how to hitchhike successfully, what to do when revolution breaks out in the country in which you are studying, and how to deal with large universities worldwide.

Virtual College by Pam Dixon (Peterson's, 1996) A charming and very helpful little book (and she says nice things about ours, too), focusing on many of the issues the distance learner may face, including transfer of credits, employer acceptance, listing distance degrees on a resume, choosing technology, what it is like to be a distance student, and so on, $10.

Winning the Ph.D. Game by Dr. Richard W. Moore (Dodd, Mead & Co.) Now out of print, this is a lighthearted, extremely useful guidebook for current and prospective doctoral students. Covers the entire process, from selecting schools to career planning. Moore's aim is to "describe the folk wisdom passed from one generation of graduate students to the next (in order to) make the whole process less traumatic." He succeeds admirably. We hope to publish a revised version in 1999 or 2000.

DIPLOMA MILLS

Diploma Mills: Degrees of Fraud by David W. Stewart and Henry A. Spille (Oryx). Originally this book was to provide details on specific operating diploma mills, but sadly, the authors either lost courage or were dissuaded by their attorneys, and it turned out to be only a moderately interesting survey of the history of the problem, with a once useful but now quite dated summary and evaluation of the current school laws in all 50 states.

Diploma Mills: The Paper Merchants by Jerry Seper and Richard Robinson. Reprint of a lengthy series of articles that ran in the Arizona *Republic* newspaper in 1983, describing many institutions they chose to call diploma mills, then operating in Arizona. Many subsequently relocated to other states. The newspaper stopped distributing the booklet; but you can get a photocopy from us for $10 (including first class postage). This is for historical reference only. Please don't buy this booklet expecting to get the addresses of currently operating diploma mills; they aren't in here. John & Mariah Bear, P. O. Box 7070, Berkeley, CA 94707.

ELECTRONIC BULLETIN BOARDS AND INFORMATION SOURCES

There are several 'rest stops' along the information superhighway where people gather electronically to discuss issues relating to distance learning and nontraditional higher education. If you have a computer, a modem, and access to the Internet, you are welcome to join in the discussion, or just "lurk" and read the communications without ever identifying yourself.

The only problem with the Internet is the sheer volume of available information. Just these few locations, representing the tiniest fraction of one percent of what is out there, nonetheless account for thousands of pages of information, and hundreds of new messages every week.

www.degree.net This is our own site, which is used to provide updates to this book, information on the degree programs with which we are involved, diploma mill alerts, and news and gossip from the world of distance education. One new feature is an interactive distance education forum, at www.degree.net/forum.

alt.education.distance Perhaps the most active news group on the Internet discussing nontraditional or alternative education and distance learning is alt.education.distance. It is the one place John checks into regularly to answer questions, make comments, suffer abuse, and gain information.

Peterson's distance education forum was a very popular public forum, but it was badly abused by diploma mill operators and others posting libelous and misleading messages. At this writing, Peterson's has closed the forum down, but it may be revived later at www.Petersons.com.

Distance Ed for Dummies A helpful and amusing site maintained by Emir Mohammed, a young Trinidadian living in Canada. Useful information, good links, off-the-wall humor ("How many diploma mill operators does it take to change a light bulb?") www.angelfire.com/mo/EmirMohammed/index.html

DEOS, the Distance Education Online Service, is a service offered by the Center for Distance Learning at Pennsylvania State University. The on-line access is listserv@psuvm.bitnet.psu.edu Leave a message reading: subscribe deos (your name)

AEDNET (Adult Education Network) is a comparable service offered by Nova Southeastern University. To learn more about them on-line, log in to listserv@alpha. acast.nova.edu and leave a message reading: subscribe aednet (your name)

The International Centre for Distance Learning at Britain's Open University, has an immense amount of information on schools, programs, and publications worldwide. It can be searched free on the Internet at www.icdl.open.ac.uk/icdl/index.htm, or by purchasing a CD from the university.

JOURNALS

The academic journals typically address research aspects of the field (e.g., *The Effectiveness of Synchronous vs. Asynchronous Lectures on Exam Performance*). The main one in the US is the **American Journal of Distance Education,** 403 S. Allen St., #206, Pennsylvania State University, University Park, PA 16801.

The main one in Canada is the **Journal of Distance Education,** published by the Canadian Association for Distance Education, 205-1 Stewart Street, Ottawa, ON K1N 6H7 Canada, and searchable on Internet at ultratext.hil.unb.ca/Texts/JDE/homepgENG.html

The Online Chronicle of Distance Education and Communication is published by Nova Southeastern University, and is available free on the Internet: http://www.fcae.nova.edu/disted/

In Australia, the journal is **Distance Education,** published at the University of Southern Queensland, Distance Education Centre, Toowoomba Queensland 4350, Australia. It is searchable on the Internet at: www.usq.edu.au/dec/decjourn/demain.htm

SELF-SERVING BOOKS

Every so often, the owners of less-than-wonderful schools have published entire books solely to be able to give themselves a splendid write-up in the midst of many other reasonably accurate school listings, and, occasionally, to "get even" on us for daring to criticize their "schools."

Directory of United States Traditional and Alternative Colleges and Universities by Dr. Jean-Maximillien De La Croix de Lafayette. This large $30 volume contains much useful information on schools. Universities are rated by number of stars. Among the small number of top-rated schools in the U.S. is Andrew Jackson University, established by Dr. De La Croix de Lafayette (no connection with the currently operating school of this name in Mississippi).

Guide to Alternative Education by Educational Research Associates. This $35 waste of time claims to be "continuously updated," but the so-called 1996 version we bought not only had hundreds of errors, but it listed schools that went out of business ten or more years ago. We learned about this book when a fictitious name we used in a communication with Century University received a solicitation to buy it. Not surprisingly, the longest and most favorable listing in the entire book is the one for Century University.

Guide to Education Abroad by I. B. Chaudhary. Published from a now-closed P.O. Box in Bombay, this is an illegal pirated copy of our book. If anyone ever sees an ad for this dreadful product, please let us know, so we can commence proper legal action. Thank you.

How to Earn a University Degree Without Ever Leaving Home by William Ebbs. A 54-page book selling for $20, with an astonishing number of errors of fact. Identifies the University de la Romande as the most outstanding nontraditional school in the world. William Ebbs is the pseudonym of Raymond Seldis, administrator, at the time, of the University de la Romande. What an amazing coincidence! The now-defunct California University for Advanced Studies is identified as the second best school in the world.

How to Obtain a College Degree by Mail by Edward P. Reddeck. Reddeck has been imprisoned at least twice for running phony schools, and once published this entire large book solely to be able to include a section extolling his phony American International University as one of the world's best.

Legal University Degrees by Mail (also called **University Degrees by Mail** and **Accredited College Degrees by Correspondence**) by "Jacques Canburry" or, in another printing, "Herald Crenshaw." Written and published by Ronald Pellar, the man who runs the diploma mill called Columbia State University from a mail forwarding service in Louisiana. Not surprisingly, the book chooses the fake Columbia State as the best university in America and refers to our book as a "phony guide," and a "brochure." Despite a cover price of $49.95, the book has been sent free to those who request it. For goodness sake, don't waste any money buying it, but if Pellar will send you a free one, and you enjoy what some have called "educational pornography," then why not. Just don't believe a word it says. He has used many mail forwarding services. The most recent one we know about is Official University Directory, 15568 Brookhurst, #139, Westminster, CA 92683.

The Web Guide to Non-Traditional and Distance Learning University Degree Programs by The Commission on Distance Education. The book is sold by the unrecognized accrediting agency called World Association of Universities and Colleges, and, amazingly, of the forty-eight schools briefly described, half are accredited only by the World Association. All of the introductory essays are written by people associated with the World Association. School descriptions total about 24 pages of text in this slender and expensive volume.

• • •

Finally, a word or two about this book, *Bears' Guide,* from John: "Over the years, some critics have accused me of writing a self-serving book, because kind words were said about schools with which I had some connection or affiliation. This sort of criticism is, I believe, quite unwarranted. Of course I have said positive things about those schools with which I have had some connection over the past 23 years; I wouldn't have become involved with them if I didn't think they were good. But in this book, I have been careful to make clear my connection (as, currently, with the MBA of Heriot-Watt University, and the MS of Leicester University), and I have always treated hundreds of other schools, some of them fierce competitors, very favorably."

Appendix C
About the Personal Counseling Services

If you would like personal advice and recommendations, based on your own specific situation, a personal counseling service is available, by mail. John started this service in 1977, at the request of many readers. While John remains a consultant, since 1981, the actual personal evaluations and consulting are done by two colleagues of his, who are leading experts in the field of nontraditional education.

For a modest fee, these things are done:

1. You will get a long personal letter evaluating your academic needs, recommending the best distance learning degree programs for you, and discussing how these programs work.

2. You will get answers to any questions you may have, and guidance in choosing a degree program and getting started on your studies.

3. You will get detailed, up-to-the-minute information on institutions and programs (also catalogue excerpts) and discussion (as needed) of portfolio assessment, equivalency exams, correspondence courses, online courses, sources of financial aid, and more.

4. You will be entitled to the service for a full year of extended personal advice, and updates on new programs and changes in your distance learning options.

If you are interested in personal counseling, please contact the service with your mailing address and you will be sent descriptive literature and a counseling questionnaire, without cost or obligation.

Once you have these materials, if you wish counseling, simply fill out the questionnaire and return it, with a letter and resumé if you like, along with the fee, and your personal reply and counseling materials will be prepared and airmailed to you.

For free information about this service, write, telephone, fax, or e-mail:

Degree Consulting Services
P. O. Box 3533
Santa Rosa, California 95402
Phone (707) 539-6466, Fax (707) 538-3577
E-mail degrees@sonic.net
Web site: http://www.sonic.net/~degrees

NOTE: Use the above address (etc.) only for matters related to the counseling service. For all other matters, write to us at P.O. Box 7070, Berkeley, CA 94707 or e-mail john.bear@degree.net or mariah@degree.net.

Thank you.

—John and Mariah Bear

Appendix D
Why Religious Schools Are No Longer Listed, and Where to Find Out About Them

From a survey of our readers, it became clear that our chapter on Bible and other religious schools was of interest to a tiny percentage, yet it accounted for a third of our mail and two thirds of our complaint letters. Whatever we said seemed to annoy or anger someone. Also, the majority of the hundreds of nonresident degree programs in religious fields are offered by small "Bible" schools specifically to members of their church or congregation. Many of these require little or no work, other than some Bible lessons, and thus cannot be compared to an academic programs. We acknowledge that there is need for information on these schools. At the moment, it is available from two Christian authors who disagree with each other vigorously on the merit of many schools. The publications of Drs. Josh Walston and Steve Levicoff are described in the Bibliography section. We have tentative plans to revisit this arena with our own book on religious schools and degrees, perhaps in a year or two. Meanwhile, here is a small sampling of available opportunities, bearing in mind that it is also possible to do degrees in religious subjects at many of the schools described in earlier chapters, ranging from Southeastern College of the Assemblies of God to the Union Institute.

ACCREDITED SCHOOLS

Greenwich School of Theology   B, M, D
29 Howbeck Lane, Clarborough, Nr. Retford
Notts. DN22 9LW, U.K.
The Rev. Dr. Byron Evans, Dean of Studies
Religion, theology, related areas
Nonprofit, independent
(44-1777) 703-058, Fax (44-1777) 703-526
Potchefstroom University web site: www.puk.ac.za

There used to be an affiliation with the unaccredited Greenwich University in Hawaii, hence the name. But in 1997, they became an affiliated college of a large, traditional, old South African university, Potchefstroom University (established 1869). Greenwich School of Theology does the training, and Potchefstroom awards the degrees. As a result of this arrangement, Greenwich School of Theology (which has no connection whatsoever now with Greenwich University in Hawaii) became accredited by the Open and Distance Learning Quality Council in London, thus offering an unusual opportunity to earn an accredited nonresident Ph.D. Many students are members of the clergy in the U.K., but lay students and those living elsewhere in the world are welcome. Meetings are occasionally held at various U.K. locations, but all work may be done through correspondence study. In thanks for his help, John was made honorary president of the school, a purely honorary and totally non-participatory post.

ICI University   B
6300 North Belt Line Road
Irving, TX 75063
Dr. George M. Flattery, President
Bible, religious education
1967
Nonprofit, church
(800) 444-0424

ICI offers a Bachelor of Arts entirely nonresidentially through regional and national offices in some 120 or more countries worldwide. Accredited by the Distance Education and Training Council, a recognized accreditor.

Moody Bible Institute   B, M

820 North LaSalle Drive
Chicago, IL 60610
Philip Van Wynen, Dean of Enrollment Management
Religion, music, liberal arts
Nonprofit, independent $$
(312) 329-4000, (800) 955-1123

Some of Moody's Bachelor's and Master's degrees can be earned through courses taken in module form over standard school breaks (Christmas, spring, summer), with independent study in between. Moody also offers 24 correspondence courses, including Greek and Hebrew.

Columbia Theological Seminary   B, M, D

P.O. Box 847
Longview, WA 98632-7521
Dr. Rick Walston, President
Apologetics, Bible, ministry, philosophy, theology
Nonprofit
(360) 577-8039 (phone/fax)

In the school Dr. Walston established, each student, rather than following a preset curriculum, chooses a mentor (from Faraston's faculty, or approved others) who works with the student to develop and fulfill a course of study.

UNACCREDITED SCHOOLS

Bethany Bible College and
Seminary   B, M, D

2311 Hodgesville Road, Box 1944
Dothan, AL 36302
Dr. H. D. Shuemake, Chancellor
Religious studies
Nonprofit $$
(205) 793-3189

Offers residential and nonresidential degrees at all levels in religious fields. Credit awarded for full-time ministry experience.

*"Ever since I bought this outfit at a yard sale,
I've been hoping I could earn a degree to go with it.
This book might be just the ticket."*

Appendix E
Research Doctorates

"Make your friends your teachers and mingle the pleasures of conversation with the advantages of instruction."

BALTASAR GRACIAN, THE ART OF WORLDLY WISDOM

We appreciate the assistance of Dick Adams in preparing this section.

The research doctorate offers an interesting opportunity to earn the degree from a major Royal Chartered British university or an Australian university, with the possibility of little, or even no residency, and at relatively modest cost. Unfortunately, there is no single simple and straightforward procedure to follow, even within departments at the same university, and even from one day to the next. Things are decided very much on a case-by-case basis.

This situation has proven difficult or annoying for Americans who are used to cookbook procedures for dealing with universities.

The research doctorate is typically available to people who already have a Master's. There is no coursework involved, only the designing and executing of a research project, and then writing it up as a dissertation.

At the doctoral level, in Britain and Australia, as elsewhere, admissions rules and decisions are typically made, both formally and informally, in a school's individual departments, rather than by the university admissions or registrar's office. Different departments within a university may well have quite different programs, rules, and procedures.

It is the existence of these "informal" situations that makes things complicated and nonuniform. As far as we know, all doctoral programs ostensibly have some residential requirement, however there are situations in which a department (or even a specific professor within the department) will agree that the residency can be done by telephone, fax, or e-mail, or even by having the professor visit the student at the student's location and expense. Experience suggests that initial contact by old-fashioned mail is the most effective way to begin such a process.

The real problem here is that it is often not possible to determine the residency requirements until after the admissions process is complete, and sometimes not until the occasion of an actual face-to-face meeting. The feedback we have gotten is extremely mixed. Some people are actually doing 100 percent nonresident degrees, and are very happy. But when we make contact with the university, and ask questions, we inevitably are told, "Oh that was a special circumstance." Other people went through the whole admissions process, went to a first meeting in Britain or Australia, and were told, "Now we expect you to return every month" (or every quarter), and were, as a result, quite unhappy.

The only way in which clear advance information has been available, it seems, is when the potential student establishes a relationship (by mail, e-mail, fax, or phone, or even in person) with a specific faculty member within the department, who then becomes, so to speak, his or her sponsor or advocate (the term "promoter" is sometimes used), and helps persuade the school's decision-makers that this particular student should be allowed to do the degree nonresidentially (or with minimal residency).

Clearly a lot of research is required by the student, both in choosing the university (or universities) to apply to, and, if appropriate, learning about the faculty within the department, and establishing communication with them. Here are a few guidelines:

1. Determine if the university has a department offering the topic(s) you wish. Almost all of the British and Australian universities are available on Internet. The best source we've found for electronic addresses is the education section of www.yahoo. If this is not possible, then library research is called for. Some foreign universities' catalogs (or calendars, as they are often called) are available on microfiche cards, along with those of U.S. universities.

2. Determine whether research doctorates are possible in that topic. This will almost certainly mean reading the catalogs—some will be available on the

Internet, others you may need to have sent to you. Some universities have combined catalogs with all departments listed; others issue a separate catalog, or prospectus, for each separate department or school.

3. Open communication with the department, or perhaps with a specific faculty member within the department. Some people have said that the approach that worked for them was to learn the names of the faculty, do some research to see what they had written (articles, books) or otherwise learn their special interests (sometimes catalogs give this information); then begin an academic correspondence, asking questions or commenting on their work. Only then, after exchange of a few communications, did they bring up the notion of doing a research doctorate under the supervision of that person.

A helpful reader named Dick Adams suggests sending a request for information to the Office of Post-Graduate Studies at every University you can identify as having a department in your field. Then identify the research areas of the faculty. Read some of their published research. Formulate some research questions. Eliminate the parochial research questions. Prepare two or three research proposals and send them to the Office of Post-Graduate studies. Then wait for the responses.

A search in British and Australian bookstores yielded two books that offer some guidance, although neither is quite as simple and straightforward as we might have wished. They are:

How to Get a Ph.D. by Estelle M. Phillips and D. S. Pugh. Open University Press (Buckingham and Philadelphia), 1996. It is identified as "a handbook and survival manual for Ph.D. students, providing a practical, realistic understanding of the processes of doing research for a doctorate." It specifically addresses the particular problems of overseas students.

Working for a Doctorate: a guide for the humanities and social sciences by Norman Graves and Ved Varmna. Routledge (London and New York), 1997. Addresses the problems of the research process, finance, and time management. It is identified as "a vital guide and companion to anyone studying for, supervising or contemplating a doctoral degree in the humanities or social sciences."

SOME OF THE SCHOOLS

Here are the names and locations of *some* universities where readers have told us they are doing nonresident or very short residency research doctorates. But please remember, it may do no good simply to write or call and say, "I want to do a research doctorate." It might work, or it might cause annoyance and frustration on both ends.

Pursuit of a doctorate is a major investment of time, energy, and money. We strongly suggest treating it seriously by doing your own research and due diligence first. And do let us know what you learn, perhaps to help smooth the path a bit for those who follow you.

The United Kingdom

Aberdeen University, Aberdeen AB9 1FX Scotland, www.abdn.ac.uk

Aston University, Aston Triangle, Birmingham B4 7ET, www.aston.ac.uk/home.html

Coventry University, Priory St., Coventry CV1 5FB, England, www.coventry.ac.uk

DeMontfort University, The Gateway, Leicester LE1 9BH, England, www.dmu.ac.uk/Leicester/index.html

Heriot-Watt University, Riccarton, Edinburgh EH14 4AS, Scotland, www.hw.ac.uk

Manchester Metropolitan University, All Saints, Manchester M15 6BH, www.mmu.ac.uk

Oxford Brookes University, Gipsy Lane, Headington, Oxford OX3 0BP, www.brookes.ac.uk

South Bank University, 103 Borough Road, London SE1 0AA, England, www.southbank-university.ac.uk

Thames Valley University, St. Mary's Road, Ealing, London W5 5RF, www.tvu.ac.uk

University of Bradford, Bradford, West Yorks BD7 1DP, www.brad.ac.uk

University of Brighton, Mithras House, Brighton BN2 4AT, www.bton.ac.uk

University of Dundee, Dundee DD1 4HN, Scotland, www.dundee.ac.uk

University of Durham, Old Shire Hall, Durham DH1 3HP, www.dur.ac.uk

University of Edinburgh, South Bridge, Edinburgh EH8 9YL, Scotland, www.ed.ac.uk

University of Glasgow, Glasgow G12 8QQ, Scotland, www.gla.ac.uk

University of Kent, Canterbury, Kent CT2 7NZ, www.ukc.ac.uk

University of Luton, Park Square, Luton LU1 3JU, www.luton.ac.uk

University of Manchester, Oxford Road, Manchester, M13 9PL www.man.ac.uk

University of Newcastle, Newcastle upon Tyne NE1 7RU, www.ncl.ac.uk

University of Northumbria, Ellison Place, Newcastle upon Tyne NE1 8ST, www.unn.ac.uk

University of Stirling, Stirling FK9 4LA, Scotland, www.stir.ac.uk

University of Strathclyde, Glasgow G1 1Xq, Scotland, www.strath.ac.uk

University of Wales, University Registry, Cathays Park, Cardiff CF1 3NS, www.cf.ac.uk

University of Warwick, Coventry CV4 7AL, England, www.warwick.ac.uk

University of the West of England, Coldharbour Lane, Frenchay, Bristol BS16 12QY, England, www.uwe.ac.uk

University of Westminster, 309 Regent St., London W1R 8AL, England, www.westminster.ac.uk

Australia

Charles Sturt University, The Grange, Panorama Ave., Bathurst, NSW, www.csu.edu.au

Deakin University, Geelong, Victoria, www.deakin.edu.au

Edith Cowan University, Pearson St., Churchlands, Western Australia 6018, www.cowan.edu.au

James Cook University, Townsville, Queensland 4811, www.jcu.edu.au

Monash University, Wellington Road, Clayton, Victoria 3168, www.monash.edu.au

Southern Cross University, PO Box 157, Lismore, NSW 2480, www.scu.edu.au

University of Southern Queensland, Toowoomba, Queensland 4350, www.usq.edu.au

Subject Index

For years, our readers have been telling us how nice it would be if *Bears' Guide* had, in addition to a complex index to schools, a complete index to the *subjects* said schools offer. We agree that it would be extremely helpful if a reader interested in, say an M.S. in financial planning could easily discern all the schools offering that degree, rather than having to skim through the entire book. Improvements have been made with each edition, and the following list *is* the most complete ever. Unfortunately, it's still not as comprehensive as we'd like, for a few reasons: (1) Many schools don't give us full information in the first place, either through oversight or, more likely, because knowing that courses and faculty are subject to change, they use a noncommittal statement like "many arts and science degrees are offered" to avoid error. (2) Some schools (mainly the big state colleges and universities, as well as some ambitious nontraditional institutions) offer so many subjects that it would be ridiculous to list them all. That's why, in the school listings, you'll often see the notation "many fields" instead of specific subjects.

Therefore, it will be necessary for you to review the school listings, looking for those that say "many fields." This single matter is the cause of most of the *unjustified* complaints we get: "I was looking for a degree in forestry, and I didn't find it in your book." If you write to us thus, we will respond saying. "See the text on page 388." It is also the case that many unaccredited schools offer independent study in almost any field a student may wish. See chapters 21–23 for those unaccredited schools with a wide range of fields; only accredited programs are indexed here.

Finally, bear in mind that many subject areas are so broad ("general studies") or all-inclusive ("social science") that a wide range of things can be done in them. Further, there are "side door" approaches to various fields. If a school offers only "history" and a student wishes to study "technology," it may be possible to do a degree in the history of technology. "Education" is another commonly used side door.

A

Accounting
College of Great Falls (B, NR), 100
Hong Kong Tak Ming College (B, NR), 110
Marywood University (B, SR), 161
Universidad Interamericana de Educacion a Distancia de Panama (B-M, NR), 131
Upper Iowa University (B, NR), 147–148

Acoustics
Pennsylvania State University (M, SR), 165

Addiction studies
Graceland College (B, SR), 158–159

Administration
Central Michigan University (B-M, NR), 97–98
Nova Southeastern University (M-D, SR), 164
Universidad de San Jose (M-D, SR), 174
Universidad Estatal a Distancia (B-M, NR), 131
Universidad Interamericana de Educacion a Distancia de Panama (B-M, NR), 131
Walden University (M-D, SR), 148, 184

Aeronautics
Embry-Riddle Aeronautical University (B-M, NR), 104

Agriculture
Kansas State University (B, NR), 113
Korea National Open University (B, SR), 160
Oklahoma State University (M, NR), 122
Universidad del Tolima (B, NR), 131
Universidad Nacional Autonoma de Honduras (B, NR), 131–132
University of Wisconsin–River Falls (B, SR), 183

Animal sciences
Kansas State University (B, NR), 113

Anthropology
University of Southern Colorado (B, NR), 143

Art
Maine College of Art (M, SR), 160–161
Norwich University (M, SR), 164
Rochester Institute of Technology (B-M, SR), 167

Art therapy
Norwich University (M, SR), 164

Aviation safety
Central Missouri State University (M, NR), 98

B

Business (general; not MBA)
Anadolu Universitesi (B, NR), 92
Andrew Jackson University (B-M, NR), 92
Baker College On-Line (B, NR), 93–94
Bellevue University (B-M, NR), 94
Boricua College (B, SR), 153–154
California National University for Advanced Studies (B-M, NR), 96
City University (Bellevue, WA) (B, NR), 99–100
Clarkson College (B, NR), 100
College of Great Falls (B, NR), 100
College of West Virginia (B, NR), 100–101
Columbia Union College (A-B, NR), 101
David N. Myers College (B, NR), 102
Eastern New Mexico University (B-M, SR), 157
Empire State College (B-M, NR), 104–105
Emporia State University (B, NR), 105
Fort Hayes State University (B, NR), 106
Hampton University (B, NR), 108
Holborn College (B, NR), 109
Hong Kong Tak Ming College (B, NR), 110
Institute of Public Administration (B, NR), 111
International Correspondence Schools (A, NR), 111–112

B=Bachelor's • M=Master's • D=Doctorate • NR=Nonresident • SR=Short Residency

Maharishi University of Management (M, NR), 116
Nova Southeastern University (M-D, SR), 164
Oklahoma State University (M, NR), 122
Rensselaer Polytechnic Institute (M, NR), 127
Rice University (M, SR), 166
Southern Polytechnic State University (M, SR), 171
Stanford University (M, NR), 128–129
University of Colorado–Boulder (M, SR), 176
University of Idaho (M, NR), 136
University of Iowa (M, NR), 137
University of Nebraska–Lincoln (M, NR), 139–140
University of Phoenix Online (M, NR), 142
University of Sunderland (M, NR), 144
Webster University (Missouri) (M, SR), 184–185

Construction management
University of Brighton (M, SR), 175–176
University of Florida (M, SR), 177
University of Hong Kong (M, NR), 136
University of Newcastle (B, SR), 178

Counseling. See Psychology and counseling

Criminal justice
Andrew Jackson University (B-M, NR), 92
Bellevue University (B, NR), 94
Bemidji State University (B, NR), 94
Central Missouri State University (M, NR), 98
College of Great Falls (B, NR), 100
College of West Virginia (B, NR), 100–101
Friends University (B-M, SR), 158
University of Portsmouth (B-M, SR), 180

Criminology
Simon Fraser University (B, NR), 127
Southern Oregon University (B, SR), 170–171

D

Design
Rochester Institute of Technology (B-M, SR), 167

E

Economics
Anadolu Universitesi (B, NR), 92
Hosei University (B, NR), 110
Institute of Public Administration (M, NR), 111
Instituto Politecnico Nacional (B, NR), 111
Ramkhamhaeng University (B-M, NR), 126

Universitas Terbuka (B, NR), 132–133
University of Hong Kong (M, NR), 136
University of Pittsburgh (B, SR), 179–180
University of Southern Colorado (B, NR), 143

Education
Andrews University (D, SR), 152
Antioch University Seattle (B-M, SR), 152
Australian Catholic University (B, NR), 93
Ball State University (M, NR), 94
Bangladesh Open University (B, NR), 94
Boricua College (B, SR), 153–154
Brock University (B, NR), 95
Brunel University (B-M, NR), 95
California State University, Northridge (B-M, NR), 97
Chadron State College (M, NR), 98
City University (Bellevue, WA) (M, NR), 99–100
Columbia University (M-D, SR), 156
East Carolina University (M, SR), 157
Emporia State University (M, NR), 105
Fielding Institute (M-D, SR), 157–158
Fitchburg State College (M, NR), 106
Flinders University of South Australia (B-M-D, NR), 106
Florida Atlantic University (M, SR), 158
Fort Hayes State University (B, NR), 106
Graduate School of America (M-D, SR), 159
Grand Canyon University (M, NR), 107
Griffith University (B-M, NR), 108
Indiana University System (M, NR), 111
James Cook University (B-M-D, NR), 112
Keele University (M, NR), 113
Korea National Open University (B, SR), 160
Montana State University (M, SR), 162
New Mexico State University (M, SR), 120, 163
Northeastern Illinois University (B-M, SR), 163
Northern Arizona University (M, SR), 163
Northern Territory University (B-M, NR), 121
Nova Southeastern University (M-D, SR), 164
Oxford Brookes University (M, SR), 165
Pennsylvania State University (M, SR), 165
Prescott College (B, SR), 165–166
Purdue University (M, SR), 166
Queensland University of Technology (B-M, NR), 125
Ramkhamhaeng University (B-M, NR), 126
Saint Francis Xavier University (M, SR), 167–168
Saint Mary's College (Minnesota) (M, SR), 168
Southern Oregon University (M, SR), 170–171

Southwestern Assemblies of God University (B, SR), 171
Texas Wesleyan University (M, NR), 129–130
Universidad de Monterrey (M, SR), 173–174
Universidad de San Jose (M-D, SR), 174
Universidad del Tolima (B, NR), 131
Universidad Estatal a Distancia (B-M, NR), 131
Universidad Interamericana de Educacion a Distancia de Panama (B-M, NR), 131
Universidad Nacional Autonoma de Honduras (B, NR), 131–132
Universidad Pedagogica Nacional (B, NR), 132
Universitas Terbuka (B, NR), 132–133
University of Adelaide (B-M, NR), 133
University of Alaska (B-M, NR), 133
University of Birmingham (B-M, NR), 133–134
University of Calgary (M, SR), 176
University of Idaho (M, NR), 136
University of Kentucky (M, SR), 177–178
University of Manchester (M, NR), 138
University of Mindanao (M, SR), 178
University of Nairobi (B, NR), 139
University of Nebraska–Lincoln (M-D, NR), 139–140
University of Newcastle (B-M, SR), 178
University of Northern Colorado (M, NR), 140
University of Sarasota (M-D, SR), 180
University of Sunderland (B, NR), 144
University of Surrey (M, NR), 144–145
University of the Philippines Open University (D, NR), 145
University of Wyoming (M, SR), 183
Walden University (M-D, SR), 148, 184
Western Washington University (M, SR), 185
William Woods University (B-M, SR), 185

Education administration
California State University, Fresno (M, NR), 96–97

Educational technology
George Washington University (M, NR), 106

Educational training systems design
University of Twente (M, NR), 145

Emergency medical services
Allegheny University of the Health Sciences (B, NR), 92
American College of Prehospital Medicine (A-B, NR), 92

B=Bachelor's • M=Master's • D=Doctorate • NR=Nonresident • SR=Short Residency

Engineering

Arizona State University (M, NR), 93
Auburn University (M, SR), 153
California National University for Advanced Studies (B-M, NR), 96
California State University, Fullerton (M, NR), 97
California State University, Northridge (B-M, NR), 97
Capitol College (B, NR), 97
Colorado State University (B-M-D, NR), 101
Engineering Education Australia (B-M, NR), 105
Florida Atlantic University (M, SR), 158
Georgia Institute of Technology (M, NR), 106-107
GMI Engineering and Management Institute (M, NR), 107
Grantham College of Engineering (A-B, NR), 107-108
Illinois Institute of Technology (M, SR), 110, 159
Kansas State University (M, NR), 113
Kettering University (M, NR), 114
Lehigh University (M, NR), 114
Mary Washington College (M, NR), 116-117
Massachusetts Institute of Technology (M, SR), 161
Michigan Technological University (B-D, SR), 162
New Mexico State University (M, SR), 120, 163
Oklahoma State University (M, NR), 122
Old Dominion University (B-M, NR), 122
Open University of Sri Lanka (B-M-D, SR), 165
Purdue University (M, SR), 166
Rensselaer Polytechnic Institute (M, NR), 127
Rice University (M, SR), 166
Stanford University (M, NR), 128-129
Universidad NUR (B, NR), 132
University of Colorado–Boulder (M, SR), 176
University of Idaho (M, NR), 136
University of Illinois at Urbana-Champaign (M, NR), 136-137
University of Kentucky (M, SR), 177-178
University of Manchester (M, NR), 138
University of Massachusetts–Amherst (M, NR), 139
University of Missouri–Rolla (M, NR), 139
University of Nebraska–Lincoln (M, NR), 139-140
University of South Carolina (M, SR), 180
University of Sunderland (B, NR), 144
University of Tennessee, Knoxville (M, SR), 181

University of Virginia (M, NR), 145-146
University of Wisconsin–Madison (M, SR), 146-147, 183
Virginia Polytechnic Institute and State University (M, SR), 184
Western Washington University (B, SR), 185
World College (B, NR), 149

English

Aston University (M, NR), 93
Nova Southeastern University (M-D, SR), 164
University of Surrey (M, NR), 144-145

Entrepreneurial studies

University of Stirling (M, SR), 181

Environmental studies

Andrew Jackson University (M, NR), 92
University of Denver (M, NR), 135
University of Waterloo (B, NR), 146
University of Westminster (B, SR), 183

Estate management

College of Estate Management (B, NR), 100

F

Family studies

University of Kentucky (M, SR), 177-178
University of Nebraska–Lincoln (M, NR), 139-140

Fashion

Manchester Metropolitan University (B, NR), 116
Western Washington University (B, SR), 185

Film

Burlington College (B, SR), 154

Finance and banking

Universidad del Tolima (B, NR), 131
Universidad Estatal a Distancia (B-M, NR), 131
Universidad Mexicana del Noreste (B, NR), 131
Universidad Nacional de la Patagonia San Juan Bosco (B, NR), 132
University of Hong Kong (M, NR), 136

Financial planning and services

American College (M, SR), 151-152
College for Financial Planning (M, NR), 100

Fire protection

California State University, Los Angeles (B, NR), 97
FEMA National Fire Academy (B, NR), 105
Worcester Polytechnic Institute (M, NR), 149

Forestry

Buckinghampshire College (M, NR), 95
Lakehead University (M, NR), 114

G

General studies

Indiana University (B-M, NR), 110
Indiana University Southeast (B, NR), 110
Indiana University System (B, NR), 111
Lakehead University (B, NR), 114
Louisiana College (B, NR), 115
Manhattan College (B, NR), 116
Oakland University (B, NR), 121
Rhodec International (B, NR), 127
Simon Fraser University (B, NR), 127
University of Nevada–Reno (B, NR), 140
University of Wisconsin–Green Bay (B, SR), 183

Genetics

Universidad Nacional de la Patagonia San Juan Bosco (B, NR), 132

Geographic information systems

Manchester Metropolitan University (B, NR), 116
University of Huddersfield (M, NR), 136

Geography

Universidad Nacional de Educacion "Enrique Guzman Y Valle" (B, SR), 174
Wilfrid Laurier University (B, NR), 149

German

Queens University (B, NR), 125

Government administration

Christopher Newport University (B, NR), 99

Graphic arts

Rochester Institute of Technology (B-M, SR), 167

Greek

Potchefstroom University for Christian Higher Education (B-M-D, NR), 125

H

Health administration

California National University for Advanced Studies (B-M, NR), 96
College of West Virginia (B, NR), 100-101
Institute of Public Administration (M, NR), 111
Saint Joseph's College (B-M, SR), 168
Trinity University (M, SR), 173
Tulane University (M, NR), 130
University of Bradford (M, NR), 134
University of Colorado–Denver (M, SR), 176-177
University of Dallas (M, NR), 134-135
University of Derby (M, NR), 135

B=Bachelor's • M=Master's • D=Doctorate • NR=Nonresident • SR=Short Residency

B=Bachelor's • M=Master's • D=Doctorate • NR=Nonresident • SR=Short Residency

B=Bachelor's • M=Master's • D=Doctorate • NR=Nonresident • SR=Short Residency

B=Bachelor's • M=Master's • D=Doctorate • NR=Nonresident • SR=Short Residency

School and Organization Index

This is an index to all the schools in chapters 18 through 27 and chapter 31. Schools mentioned incidently in other chapters are not indexed.

A FEW OF THE THOUSANDS OF UNSOLICITED TESTIMONIALS RECEIVED

What a masterpiece of real information. I was very hesitant to purchase your book since my experience has been that "shortcut help" books tend to be so general or so filled with wishful untried theories that they are worthless. Yours was neither. The guide took me right where I wanted to be, a process that would have taken me so long by myself it would never be completed.
—*Phillip Wilson*

I am a proud graduate of the University of the State of New York at Albany who will tell you that John Bear's book is **worth ten times whatever you paid for it.** —*Richard D. Adams, CPA*

John Bear . . . has probably influenced more people than any other one single individual as regards issues such as academic institutional validity, etc. Countless tens of thousands have consulted him yea these decades. . . and his word has been as good as gospel! I, for one, chose three of the four graduate institutions I have attended after reading about them in Bear's Guide. **The book is directly responsible for two of my master's degrees and my doctorate.**
—*Dr. Steve Williams, Harding University*

I have been reading Bear's guides since 1980. **They are the best; nothing else comes close.** Buy it, read it, then read it again. —*Richard Douglas*

In my humble opinion, this is **simply the best book available on distance education.** I bought my first copy in 1979 and read it cover to cover. Thanks to the book, I was able to earn my BS in Business. Now I have the latest edition and am researching Ph.D. programs. —*Alan Flaten*

Bear's Guide is **worth its weight in gold, and it is pretty heavy!** It is invaluable for sorting through the hype and mystery. —*Patrick McKee*

Just wanted you to know I appreciate your efforts in this area of work. **We regularly use your publication.**
—*Perry Robinson*, Higher Education Department, American Federation of Teachers

I have found your books on non-traditional learning and college degrees **the most useful of any I have found,** and I recommend them to anyone who will stand still long enough to hear my comments.
—*Ken Collier*, Director, Centre for Learning Accreditation, Athabasca University

I find the guide to be **invaluable,** for myself and others at my University whom I counsel. Keep up the excellent work! —*Avis Quinn*

Thank you for being **a valuable resource for those of us who need reality-based information.**
—*Mary Baker*

If you are interested in distance or alternative education, this is the book to have. **It has enriched my life.** —*Richard Best*

I bought your famous book here in Germany and I was **deeply impressed with your competence,** and the wonderful information.   *—Jürgen Buchner*

I'm currently in the distance degree program of Ohio University, which I located by reading one of your books. Thank you and **keep up the great work.**   *—Beverly Parks*

Thank you for your book. I just got into an accredited distance MA TESOL program. **I couldn't have done it without you.**   *—Douglas Evans*

I am the tuition assistance program coordinator for a U.S. based, automotive manufacturer. I consider Bear's Guide **a must as a professional resource** for administration of the tuition assistance program at my company, and for my future educational goals.   *—Dennis Gale*

May God continue to bless you and your family. **You were instrumental in changing my life** in a wonderfully positive way!   *—Brenda Vance Rollins, Ed.D.*

Living and working in China is not exactly the easiest venue from which to contemplate continuing my education, especially at the doctoral level, but **thanks to you it's working.**
—Martin Fox

Your books are *great*. **You probably have done more for distance learning than any individual.**
—Sheila Danzig

Your guide continues to be **the preeminent work of its kind.**   *—Paul Steer*

Your advice is **objective, to the point, and shows you have an unbiased method** of evaluating schools and others claiming to be such. From Bear's Guide, I found the University of Sarasota, and their short-residency Doctor of Education.   *—Steve Lorenze*

When I was working in Learning Assessment at Marylhurst College, your book was **the most valuable advising resource on my shelf.**   *—Jeff R. Sweeney*

Bear's Guide is the "bible" for such information. It is, in my experience, very fairly and objectively edited, which means it sometimes comes in for the ire of both non-traditional programs which don't receive good reviews *and* traditional educators, who are uncomfortable with *any* non-traditional program getting good reviews. As department chair in the adult degree program of a traditional Catholic college, I think the reviews are to be taken seriously.
—Kathleen Taylor, Saint Mary's College

I found it **informative, inspiring, and entertaining to boot.**   *—Barry Wong*

I received a nice salary increase after finishing the Ph.D. program I learned about in your book.
—Tom Woodle, Dean of Continuing Education

Your book is worth its weight in gold!   *—Carl Reek*

Thank you so much for saving me $1700 which I was just about to send to a fake school.
—Victor Araujo

BEREAN UNIVERSITY
of the Assemblies of God

"Anointed Learning Where You Are!"

- A.A., B.A., and M.A. degrees
- Nondegree studies
- Ministerial preparation
- Studies for enrichment
- Choice of majors
- Credit for prior learning
- Study center arrangements for group study in churches
- Accredited by the Distance Education and Training Council

For more information:
1445 Boonville Ave.
Springfield, MO 65802
1-800-443-1083
Berean@ag.org
http://www.berean.edu
fax: 417-862-5318

---

orthwood University offers accelerated programs designed to put a **bachelor of business administration degree** in qualifying students' hands in just 15 to 24 months. Attend classes nights or weekends at one of more than 30 locations across the country. Choose from a variety of coursework options, including nights, weekends, seminars, independent studies, and one-week courses. Learn practical applications for the real world. Credit is granted for competencies gained from work and life experience.

At Northwood University, it's our belief that learning should be a lifelong pursuit. Getting your degree shouldn't!

If you agree, call us at 1-800-445-5873 or 1-517-837-4411 today!

WE BRING THE BEST IN LIFELONG LEARNING TO YOU

INDIANA UNIVERSITY

Earn an IU degree through distance learning, on campus, or through a combination of distance learning and on-campus courses.

INDIANA UNIVERSITY
- Founded in 1820
- Fully accredited by the North Central Assoc.
- One of the world's top research universities
- Most wired public university and one of the top 20 cyberspace universities in the U.S.
- Winner of more awards for distance learning courses than any other university in the U.S.

WE OFFER
- 300 distance learning courses
- a two-year associate degree and four-year bachelor's degree
- a master's degree in adult education
- certificates in labor studies and in healthcare accounting and financial management

YOU CAN EARN CREDIT
- for courses completed at other regionally accredited colleges and universities
- on the basis of CLEP or DANTES subject examinations
- for self-acquired competency (life experience)
- for military service education and training
- for ACE/PONSI approved noncollegiate-sponsored instruction and training

Phone: **1-800-334-1011 (U.S.)**
Phone: (+1) 812-855-2292 (outside U.S.)
E-mail: bulletin@indiana.edu
WWW: www.indiana.edu/~iudisted/
Postal mail: Indiana University, Owen Hall 001, Bloomington, IN 47405

Regents College grads are virtually smarter than the rest.

That's because they found a way to get ahead in their careers with the college that makes learning more accessible, more affordable and more accommodating than the rest.

You don't have to drop out of "life" to learn and earn your degree with Regents College...where we believe that *"what you know is more important than how you acquire the knowledge."*

- Awards Baccalaureate and Associate Degrees in BUSINESS, LIBERAL ARTS, NURSING, TECHNOLOGY, and a MASTER OF ARTS degree in LIBERAL STUDIES
- Apply credits you've already earned
- Earn credit through college-level proficiency exams including Regents College Examinations
- Earn credit through distance courses, telecourses, on-line computer and video courses
- Benefit from no residency requirement

America's First Virtual University

REGENTS COLLEGE.

1-888-647-2388 • www.regents.edu • e-mail: jbears@regents.edu

Accredited by the Commission on Higher Education of the Middle States Association of Colleges and Schools: 3642 Market Street, Philadelphia, PA 19104, 215-662-5606. The degree programs in nursing are accredited by the National League for Nursing Accrediting Commission: 61 Broadway, 33rd Floor • New York, NY 10006 • 800-669-9656. Regents College admits students of any race, color and national or ethnic origin.

GRADUATE EDUCATION AT YOUR FINGERTIPS

Walden University offers graduate programs that enable busy adults to pursue an advanced degree without interrupting career and family. Unlike traditional campus-based programs, your classroom is as close as your computer. Through distance delivery, Walden students set their own schedules and work from their own location when it's convenient to them.

Walden University offers graduate programs in:

- Education (M.S./Ph.D.)
- Health Services (Ph.D.)
- Psychology (M.S./Ph.D.)
- Human Services (Ph.D.)
- Management (Ph.D.)

Some master's programs can be completed entirely online in as little as 18 months. Innovative Ph.D. programs combine technology, faculty mentors and flexible residencies.

Global in reach . . . Personal in approach . . . Our student-centered programs have been serving distance learners for 28 years.

E-mail Walden University's Office of Recruitment at **request@waldenu.edu**, visit our Web site at **www.waldenu.edu** or call **1-800-444-6795, ext. 500** for complete information.

Walden University
155 Fifth Avenue South
Minneapolis, MN 55401

Walden University is accredited by the North Central Association of Colleges & Schools
30 North LaSalle, Suite 2400 • Chicago, Illinois 60602-2504 • (312)263-0456

REACH A NEW LEVEL OF EXPERTISE

EARN YOUR MASTER'S DEGREE ENTIRELY BY DISTANCE LEARNING

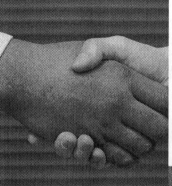

You can earn your Master's degree in Training and Human Resources Management in two years without taking time off work.

THE CAMPUS COMES TO YOU!

- All course materials are provided
- Study wherever you are, no travel or class attendance is required
- Personalized academic support and student contact is available by phone, fax, mail, internet, or email

GAIN A PROFESSIONAL EDGE

- Advance your career by gaining in-depth knowledge of regional and national training and HR issues
- Leicester University is a major British university, fully accredited in the US and the UK, with over 2,000 distance learning students from 30 different countries
- Program offers a global perspective with North America and international case studies

DON'T WAIT! NEW SESSIONS START IN APRIL AND OCTOBER.

Leicester University
MS in Training and HRM
Financial Times Management
6921 Stockton Avenue, Suite 13
El Cerrito, CA 94530

Phone: 888-LEICESTER
        or 510-528-3984
Fax: 510-528-3555
Email: LUinfo@FTManagement.net

IN THE US & CANADA CALL TOLL-FREE 888-LEICESTER

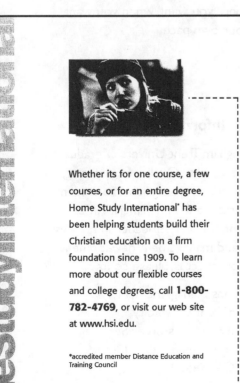

What Differentiates You From the Competition?

Quality.

Nottingham Trent University Graduate Programs in

Total Quality

Quality Engineering

Customer Service Management

The Quality Unit of Nottingham Trent University offers a range of graduate programs to benefit anyone who has a significant role in improving the quality of goods and/or services in a fast-paced, competitive environment.

The Benefits of Quality Degrees

- Understand, monitor & achieve quality
- Understand the customer in business or public service
- Stimulate changes within your organization for competitive advantage
- Develop skills in analysis, problem solving, creativity, synthesis & interpretation
- Sharpen interpersonal & team-working skills

The Benefits of Distance Learning

- Spread the cost over several years
- Comprehensive study guidance
- Study where you want, when you want, and at your own pace

For More Information

The Nottingham Trent University graduate programs in Quality, Quality Engineering, and Customer Service are available to students in North America from Financial Times Management, the market leader in business education and management development. For a free prospectus, please contact:

Financial Times Management, Inc.
Nottingham Trent University
MS in Quality and Customer Service
6921 Stockton Avenue, Suite 13
El Cerrito, CA 94530

Phone: 888-534-2378
Fax: 510-528-3555
Email: NTUinfo@FTManagement.net

The Nottingham Trent University

In the US & Canada call toll-free 888-534-2378 or 510-528-3984

Stand Out in a Crowd.

Attend Leeds Metropolitan University School of Information Management

Master of Science in Information Management by Distance Learning

This advanced degree in Information Management will enable you and your organization to use information management as a competitive tool and will help you stand out from the crowded group of generalist MBAs.

And since you get your degree completely by distance learning, you study when and where you want; there's no need to take time off from work, uproot your family, or travel in order to go back to school.

Whether you work for a multinational company or a small business, the management of information as a strategic business tool is essential for success.

LEEDS METROPOLITAN UNIVERSITY

The Leeds Metropolitan University MS in Information Management will let you:

- Examine current and future information management issues facing businesses
- Use information as a corporate resource in a competitive environment
- Create information strategies that contribute to an organization's business plan
- Review a range of technologies
- Trace the development of globalization and the information society
- Follow the changes in electronic commerce
- Understand the interaction between people and computers
- Manage organizational change

Questions?

The Leeds Metropolitan University MS in Information Management is available to students in North America from Financial Times Management, the market leader in business education and management development. For a free prospectus, please contact:

Financial Times Management, Inc.
Leeds Metropolitan University
MS in Information Management
6921 Stockton Avenue, Suite 13
El Cerrito, CA 94530

Phone: 888-534-2378
Fax: 510-528-3555
E-mail: LMUinfo@FTManagement.net

**In the US & Canada call toll-free
888-534-2378 or 510-528-3984**

SAME SIZE AS OTHER PAPERS
FIVE TIMES
THE INTERNATIONAL COVERAGE

The Financial Times is the only daily newspaper of international business. Published six days a week and trusted by over a million readers worldwide, the Financial Times brings you:

- More international business news than any other publication.

- The most authoritative source of news, analysis and opinion on global business.

- A special focus on emerging markets, finance and economics, international companies, politics and technology.

- Over 200 single-topic reports on industries, countries and regions.

- A U.S. edition specially edited to the international interests of U.S. readers.

Available at your newsstand or call 1-800-628-8088 to subscribe.

FINANCIAL TIMES
The global daily of business